The Cambridge Companion to

WAGNER

....

EDITED BY

Thomas S. Grey

CAMBRIDGE
UNIVERSITY PRESS

CAMBRIDGE UNIVERSITY PRESS
Cambridge, New York, Melbourne, Madrid, Cape Town, Singapore, São Paulo, Delhi

Cambridge University Press
The Edinburgh Building, Cambridge CB2 8RU, UK

Published in the United States of America by Cambridge University Press, New York

www.cambridge.org
Information on this title: www.cambridge.org/9780521644396

© Cambridge University Press 2008

First published 2008

Printed in the United Kingdom at the University Press, Cambridge

A catalogue record for this publication is available from the British Library

ISBN 978-0-521-64299-6 hardback
ISBN 978-0-521-64439-6 paperback

Contents

List of illustrations   *page* vii
Notes on contributors   ix
Preface and acknowledgements   xiii
Chronology   xvii
List of abbreviations   xxxvii

PART I **Biographical and historical contexts**   1

1   Wagner lives: issues in autobiography
    John Deathridge   3
2   *Meister* Richard's apprenticeship: the early operas (1833–1840)
    Thomas S. Grey   18
3   To the Dresden barricades: the genesis of Wagner's
    political ideas
    Mitchell Cohen   47

PART II **Opera, music, drama**   65

4   The "Romantic operas" and the turn to myth
    Stewart Spencer   67
5   *Der Ring des Nibelungen*: conception and interpretation
    Barry Millington   74
6   Leitmotif, temporality, and musical design in the *Ring*
    Thomas S. Grey   85
7   *Tristan und Isolde*: essence and appearance
    John Daverio   115
8   Performing Germany in Wagner's *Die Meistersinger von
    Nürnberg*
    Stephen McClatchie   134
9   *Parsifal*: redemption and *Kunstreligion*
    Glenn Stanley   151

PART III **Ideas and ideology in the *Gesamtkunstwerk***   177

10   The urge to communicate: the prose writings as theory
    and practice
    James Treadwell   179
11   Critique as passion and polemic: Nietzsche and Wagner
    Dieter Borchmeyer   192
12   The Jewish question
    Thomas S. Grey   203

PART IV **After Wagner: influence and interpretation**   219

13 "Wagnerism": responses to Wagner in music and the arts
    Annegret Fauser   221
14 Wagner and the Third Reich: myths and realities
    Pamela M. Potter   235
15 Wagner on stage: aesthetic, dramaturgical, and social
    considerations
    Mike Ashman   246
16 Criticism and analysis: current perspectives
    Arnold Whittall   276

    Notes   290
    Select bibliography   328
    Index   338

Illustrations

15.1. *Götterdämmerung*, Act 3 (conclusion): stage design by Josef Hoffmann for the first Bayreuth festival, 1876. *page* 247

15.2. *Der fliegende Holländer*: design for the Dutchman's ship by Ewald Dülberg for the Kroll Opera, Berlin, 1929. 250

15.3. *Die Walküre*, Act 3: directed and designed by Wolfgang Wagner; Bayreuth festival, 1960. 253

15.4. *Siegfried*, Act 3 (final scene): directed and designed by Wieland Wagner; Bayreuth festival, 1951. 253

15.5. *Tristan und Isolde*, Act 3: directed and designed by Wieland Wagner; Bayreuth festival, 1962. 255

15.6. *Götterdämmerung*, Act 2: directed and designed by Wieland Wagner; Bayreuth festival, 1965. 255

15.7. *Götterdämmerung*, Act 3 (Wotan grieves during the funeral music for the slain Siegfried): directed by Joachim Herz, designed by Rudolf Heinrich; Leipzig, 1975. 257

15.8. *Die Meistersinger*, Act 3 (the festival meadow): directed by Joachim Herz, designed by Rudolf Heinrich; Leipzig, 1960. 258

15.9. *Die Meistersinger*, Act 3 (the festival meadow): directed and designed by Wieland Wagner; Bayreuth festival, 1964. 258

15.10. *Götterdämmerung*, Act 1: Siegfried (Jean Cox) drinks the potion of forgetfulness, watched by Gutrune (Hanna Lisowska) and the reflection of Hagen (Bengt Rundgren); directed by Götz Friedrich, designed by Josef Svoboda; Royal Opera House, Covent Garden, 1976. 260

15.11. *Die Walküre*: Gwyneth Jones as Brünnhilde; directed by Götz Friedrich, designed by Josef Svoboda, costumes by Ingrid Rosell; Royal Opera House, Covent Garden, 1977. 260

15.12. *Siegfried*, Act 1: René Kollo as Siegfried and Heinz Zednik as Mime; directed by Patrice Chéreau, designed by Richard Peduzzi; Bayreuth festival, 1976. 262

15.13. *Siegfried*, Act 1 (forging scene): directed by Patrice Chéreau, designed by Richard Peduzzi; Bayreuth festival, 1976. 262

15.14. *Der fliegende Holländer*, Act 1: directed by Harry Kupfer, designed by Peter Sykora; Bayreuth festival, 1978. 264

15.15. *Parsifal*, Act 1: Kundry (Gail Gilmore) lying with Amfortas
(John Bröcheler), as narrated by Gurnemanz; directed by Ruth
Berghaus, designed by Axel Manthey; Frankfurt, 1982.   266

15.16. *Das Rheingold*, scene 2: directed by Richard Jones, designed
by Nigel Lowery; Royal Opera House, Covent Garden, 1994. 268

15.17. *Siegfried*, Act 3 (final scene): directed by Richard Jones,
designed by Nigel Lowery; Royal Opera House, Covent
Garden, 1996.   268

15.18. *Götterdämmerung*, Act 3: directed by Richard Jones, designed
by Nigel Lowery; Royal Opera House, Covent Garden, 1996. 269

15.19. *Götterdämmerung*, Act 3: directed by David Alden, designed
by Gideon Davey; Munich, Bavarian State Opera, 2003.
Photograph © Wilfried Hoesl   271

Notes on contributors

Mike Ashman is active as both a stage director and a writer on opera performance. He has produced for Opera Zuid and the Royal College of Music Opera School, and has served as staff director of the Welsh National Opera and the Royal Opera House, Covent Garden. His directorial work focuses on nineteenth- and twentieth-century repertories, including a *Ring* cycle for Den Norske Opera and a touring version of *Tristan und Isolde*. He has contributed chapters to *Wagner in Performance* (1992) and *Verdi in Performance* (2001).

Dieter Borchmeyer is Professor Emeritus of Modern German Literature and Theater at the University of Heidelberg and president of the Bavarian Academy of Fine Arts. His work encompasses German literature of the eighteenth through twentieth centuries, including the intersection of theater, music, and opera. Among his numerous publications concerning Richard Wagner are *Das Theater Richard Wagners: Idee – Dichtung – Wirkung* (1982; trans. Stewart Spencer as *Richard Wagner: Theory and Theatre*, 1991), *Die Götter tanzen Cancan: Richard Wagners Liebesrevolten* (1992), *Das Tribschener Idyll: Nietzsche – Cosima – Wagner. Eine Textcollage* (1998), *Drama and the World of Richard Wagner* (2003), and an edition of Wagner's collected writings (1983).

Mitchell Cohen is Professor of Political Theory at Bernard Baruch College and the Graduate School of the City University of New York. He is coeditor of *Dissent*, a journal of social, political, and cultural discussion, and the author of *The Wager of Lucien Goldmann* (1994) and *Zion and State* (1987). He edited *Rebels and Reactionaries: An Anthology of Political Short Stories* (1992) and coedited *Princeton Readings in Political Thought* (1995).

John Daverio (1954–2003) was Professor of Music at Boston University. A specialist in the German Romantics, he authored *Nineteenth-Century Music and the German Romantic Ideology* (1993), the critical biography *Robert Schumann: Herald of a New Poetic Age* (1997), and the collection of essays *Crossing Paths: Schubert, Schumann, and Brahms* (2002).

John Deathridge is King Edward Professor of Music at King's College London. A leading Wagner scholar and critic, he is the author of *Wagner's Rienzi: A Reappraisal Based on a Study of the Sketches and Drafts* (1977) and a coauthor of *The New Grove Wagner* (1984, with Carl Dahlhaus), coeditor of the *Wagner Werk-Verzeichnis: Verzeichnis der musikalischen Werke Richard Wagners und ihrer Quellen* (*WWV*; 1986, with Martin Geck and Egon Voss), and editor/translator of the *Wagner Handbook* (1992). His critical edition of Wagner's *Lohengrin* appeared in 2007 (Eulenberg), and a collection of essays on Wagner and related topics (*Wagner Beyond Good and Evil*) is forthcoming in 2008.

Annegret Fauser is Professor of Music and Adjunct Professor in Women's Studies at the University of North Carolina at Chapel Hill. Her research involves French and American music and culture in the nineteenth and twentieth centuries, women's music, exoticism, cultural transfer, nationalism, opera, and song. Recent publications include *Musical Encounters at the 1889 Paris World's Fair* (2005) and an edition of reviews of the first performance of Jules Massenet's opera *Esclarmonde* (2001). She is coeditor of the correspondence of Nadia Boulanger and Aaron Copland, and of a volume on the institutions of French musical theater (forthcoming).

Thomas S. Grey is Professor of Music at Stanford University. He is the author of *Wagner's Musical Prose: Texts and Contexts* (1995), and the editor and coauthor of *Richard Wagner*: The Flying Dutchman (2000).

Stephen McClatchie currently serves as vice-president, academic and research, at Mount Allison University, Canada. Before that he taught in the music department of the University of Regina, Saskatchewan. He is the author of *Analyzing Wagner's Operas: Alfred Lorenz and German Nationalist Ideology* (1998) as well as numerous articles on Wagner, Mahler, and the musical culture of *fin-de-siècle* Vienna. His edition of the family letters of Gustav Mahler is forthcoming in German and English. A recipient of several grants from the Social Sciences and Humanities Research Council of Canada, Dr. McClatchie was a member of the SSHRC Working Group on the Future of the Humanities (1999–2001).

Barry Millington has served as an editor and contributor to *The New Grove Dictionary of Music and Musicians* and as music critic for the *Musical Times*, the London *Times*, the London *Evening Standard*, and the *BBC Music Magazine*. He is also the founder and artistic director of the Hampstead and Highgate Festival and served as dramaturgical adviser on the new production of *Lohengrin* at the Bayreuth festival. His publications on Wagner include a monograph (1984; 2nd edn. 1993), *The Wagner Compendium* (editor, 1992), *Wagner in Performance* (editor, 1992), a major collection of Wagner's letters in translation (1987), and *Wagner's Ring of the Nibelung: A Companion* (1993), the last three in collaboration with Stewart Spencer. His articles on Wagner topics have appeared in *The Oxford Illustrated History of Opera* (1994), *Opera*, *Cambridge Opera Journal*, *Wagner*, and the *Musical Times*. He is the editor of a new *Wagner Journal* (2007–).

Pamela M. Potter is Professor of Music at the University of Wisconsin-Madison. She has written extensively on music and politics in twentieth-century Germany, especially the history of German musicology (*Most German of the Arts: Musicology and Society from the Weimar Republic to the End of Hitler's Reich* (1998; German edn., 2000) and the cultural role of music in constructing national identity (*Music and German National Identity*, coedited with Celia Applegate, 2002). Current projects include a history of musical life in twentieth-century Berlin and a study of Nazi aesthetics in the visual and performing arts.

Stewart Spencer taught medieval German literature at the University of London and has translated books on Bach, Liszt, Mozart, and Wagner. He has also written widely on Wagner, having served as contributor to and editor of numerous volumes on the composer and his work.

Glenn Stanley, Professor of Music at the University of Connecticut, is reviews editor of *19th-Century Music*. He is the editor of *The Cambridge Companion to Beethoven* and has contributed articles to the *Cambridge Companions* on

Schubert, and Mendelssohn. Recent publications include studies of musical historiography in divided Germany after World War II (in *Deutsche Leitkultur Musik? Zur Musikgeschichte nach dem Holocaust*, ed. Albrecht Riethmüller) and the role of orchestration and independent orchestral music in the Romantic oratorio (Detlef Altenburg, ed., *Eine Namenlose Mittelgattung: Gattungen und Formen des Oratoriums im 19. Jahrhundert*). Several essays are forthcoming in the *Beethoven-Handbuch*, ed. Albrecht Riethmüller and Rainer Cadenbach.

James Treadwell has served as lecturer and junior research fellow at the University of Oxford, and assistant professor of English at McGill University. He authored *Interpreting Wagner* (2003) and *Autobiographical Writing and British Literature, 1783–1834* (2005).

Arnold Whittall is Professor Emeritus of Music Theory and Analysis at King's College London. His chief interest has been nineteenth- and twentieth-century music, with special reference to modern British composers, as well as the music of Wagner. Major publications include *Musical Composition in the Twentieth Century* (1999), first published as *Music Since the First World War* (1977). His work for radio includes thirty-six broadcasts introducing contemporary music for the BBC College Concerts from 1977 to 1983. Dr. Whittall has been a frequent contributor of articles and reviews to the *Musical Times*, among other journals.

Preface and acknowledgements

As long as there are books, it seems, there will be books on Wagner. The claims of this one are relatively modest, geared to the general aims of the *Cambridge Companion* series to provide an accessible portrait of the artist as we see him today, and at the same time to offer information about his life, times, works, and reception. In the case of Wagner, "reception" involves not only critical attitudes toward the music over time, but considerable social, political, and ideological dimensions as well. With his voluminous theoretical writings Wagner himself fueled the debate as to whether his operas and "music dramas" should be considered primarily *musical* artworks, or rather a new kind of artwork of ideas – a "total artwork" (*Gesamtkunstwerk*) integrating music, voice, poetry, and the arts of the theater in a way that finally realized the ambitions opera had harbored, if only fitfully, from the beginning. The designation of the *Ring* cycle and *Parsifal* as "stage-festival plays" (*Bühnenfestspiele*) articulates their author's sense of them as objects of cultic ritual or worship and as texts for hermeneutic exegesis: the foundation of a modern religion of art. Whatever one thinks about such grand claims for the Wagnerian "synthesis," there is no question as to the composer's unusual genius for developing the materials of myth and legend in modern dramatic form rife with symbolic, psychological, and social meaning. As a result, discussions of his work tend, even more than in the case of opera generally, toward interpretations of character and meaning and away from analysis or evaluation of music, aside from specialized professional-academic attention to the latter. Wagner to some extent foresaw and condoned, or at least accepted, this disproportionate division of critical labor. The fact that he thought of such things at all is a sign of his "modernity"; Bach, Mozart, Beethoven, Rossini, or any of their contemporaries showed little evidence of wondering about how their works would be studied and interpreted by future generations, except perhaps within the profession of musical composition as such. The current *Companion* reflects the traditional emphasis on a broader discourse of "ideas" in Wagner's oeuvre (and their influence) over specialized analytical discussion of the musical scores. Nonetheless, the music has not been ignored, and it is always worth repeating the adage that without the scores Wagner's "ideas" would have had little or no impact, unless perhaps he had pursued some altogether different line of creative work.

About half of the chapters in this collection are devoted to the musical-dramatic oeuvre as such, the other half addressing matters of biography (chapter 1), social and political background (chapter 3), issues in Wagner's writings and their intellectual and social context (part III: chapters 10 through 12), and matters of influence, reception, performance history, and scholarship (part IV: chapters 13 through 16). Anyone who reads or skims the volume as a whole will likely be struck by the prominence of debates over Wagner's notorious anti-Semitism, its role in his posthumous influence, and how it might be confronted by scholars, critics, producers, and audiences today. As editor I could have made more effort to suppress what might appear as a certain redundancy on this topic (let alone contributing a whole further chapter to it). On reflection, however, it occurred to me that this possible redundancy serves as a good index of the indisputable prominence of this topic in Wagner studies and public discussion over the past fifteen or twenty years. This repoliticizing of the "Wagner question" (or at least of this particular one) can be seen as a reaction to the long period – about four decades – after the end of World War II during which scholarship and criticism were largely concerned with rehabilitating the figure of Wagner in the wake of his appropriation as a cultural icon by the Nazi regime, not to mention the anti-Romantic and anti-Wagnerian polemics of modernist intellectuals and artists since the beginning of the twentieth century. Since even general introductory "companion" volumes of this kind cannot help recording, in some small way, the cultural trends and preoccupations of their historical moment, it seemed to me just as well to leave these exposed rather than trying to hide them. I trust, too, that beyond this topic of Wagner's anti-Semitism and its possible residue in the musical-dramatic oeuvre the chapters of this *Companion* succeed in registering some concrete, quantifiable "advances" in biographical, musicological, and critical scholarship – that the contents of the volume succeed in being up to date by design, too, and not merely as a passive reflection of the critical *Zeitgeist*.

Wagner's major musical stage-works are few enough that it does not seem necessary to append a catalogue of them to this volume; his prose writings are so many and of such varied and unequal interest that a catalogue of those seems impractical here. The fairly extensive chronology of Wagner's life and career that is included here (xvii–xxxvi) contains information about most of the composer's musical works, both major and minor, and some information on his principal writings. More detailed listings of the works, their genesis and surviving sources, and of the published prose are all readily available in Barry Millington's entries on Wagner in the *New Grove Dictionary of Music and Musicians* as well as *The New Grove Dictionary of Opera*, among other places. Readers desirous of more comprehensive information about the genesis and publication history of the music and libretti can find the sum of modern scholarly knowledge collected in the *Wagner Werk-Verzeichnis*.

The bibliography included at the end of this volume is naturally very selective. To a large – though not entirely comprehensive – extent it serves as a list of works cited within the individual chapters. In addition, it attempts to list significant or at any rate representative writings on Wagner's life and works and their influence, interpretation, and reception – mainly in English and German, and mainly works available in print or reprint. Not included in the bibliography is the important field of periodicals devoted to Wagner and matters Wagnerian. As early as the 1850s such journals as the *Neue Zeitschrift für Musik* and the *Anregungen für Kunst, Leben und Wissenschaft* served as literary organs for the Wagnerian cause, at least *pro tem*, until the high tide of Wagnerism gave birth to a spate of dedicated journals starting with the *Bayreuther Blätter* (1878–1938), followed by the short-lived but culturally significant *Revue wagnérienne* (1885–88), the organ of English Wagnerism *The Meister* (1885–95), and sporadic attempts at founding a Wagner *Jahrbuch* before World War I. The many Wagner Societies established around the world since then have produced a large number of newsletters and serial publications, among which the journal of the British Wagner Society (*Wagner*, 1980–2005) is a rich source of shorter articles, reviews, and documents. More recently the bilingual *WagnerSpectrum* (German and English, 2005–) has entered this field, providing a forum for scholarship and reviews that address the interests of opera audiences as well as academic scholars, and the still newer *Wagner Journal* (2007–) follows suit in these aims.

The chronology owes much to those compiled by Barry Millington (*The Wagner Compendium*, 1992) and Stewart Spencer (*Wagner Remembered*, 2000), as well as the older, extensive chronologies of Otto Strobel (1952) and Martin Gregor-Dellin (1972; 2nd edn. 1983). Stewart Spencer quickly and expertly reviewed the present chronology, helping to correct various oversights and omissions. I would also like to express my thanks to Dieter Borchmeyer for allowing me to include a somewhat abridged, newly translated version of his chapter on Wagner and Nietzsche from *Drama and the World of Richard Wagner* (Princeton, 2003). Ilias Chrissochoidis has provided a keen scholarly eye in matters of editing, bibliography, and fact-checking, as well as in assembling the index. As with several previous projects, I'm very grateful for Bruno Ruviaro's meticulous setting of musical examples (and hereby acknowledge any mistakes to be my own!). Rebecca Jones and Karen Anderson Howes were consistently helpful and just patient enough during production. Above all, of course, I want to thank the whole roster of contributors for their willingness to collaborate, for their contributions, and for their enforced patience with the gradual genesis of the project. The presence of John Daverio's chapter on *Tristan* is evidence of the very extended gestation of the project. Initial plans for the *Companion* go back some ten years and John had already produced an essay by 1999, before a hiatus of some four years on the project and shortly before his own tragic and untimely death. Thus, I also take this opportunity to remember John Daverio as a penetrating, wide-ranging scholar of Romantic music, and as an uncommonly kind and generous person.

Chronology
(Selected biographical events and points of reference)

1813   *22 May* Richard Wagner born, last of nine children to Johanna Rosine and Carl Friedrich Wagner, in Leipzig.
16 August "Wilhelm Richard Wagner" baptized in the Thomaskirche in Leipzig.
26–27 August Napoleon victorious against the Bohemian army at Dresden, but defeated *16–19 October* in the Völkerschlacht or Battle of Nations near Leipzig.
23 November Carl Friedrich Wagner, police actuary in Leipzig and amateur actor, dies of typhoid fever.

1814   *28 August* Johanna Wagner remarries, to the close family friend Ludwig Geyer, a painter and actor. Circumstances suggest that Geyer could have been Richard's biological father, as he himself seems to have (sometimes) believed. The family moves to Dresden before the end of the year.

1815   *September to June* Congress of Vienna.

1817   First schooling, in Dresden, under Royal Saxon Vice-Kantor, Karl Friedrich Schmidt.

1820   Further schooling and earliest musical instruction (piano) under Christian Wetzel, a pastor in Possendorf near Dresden.

1821   *30 September* Ludwig Geyer dies of tuberculosis.

1822   *December* Richard "Geyer" matriculates at the Dresden Kreuzschule.

1826   Interest in the classics, dating back to 1823 (claims later to have translated excerpts from the *Odyssey*), and in writing poetry and drama. *Leubald*, tragedy in five acts, begun (?).
December The family moves to Prague where elder sister Rosalie is engaged at the theater. Richard remains at school in Dresden.

1827   *Spring* Undertakes a walking trip from Dresden to Prague in the company of a school friend, Rudolf Böhme.
Summer Visits Leipzig, including uncle Adolf Wagner (1774–1835), a scholar and writer with significant literary connections.
December Joins family in Leipzig, where most have returned.

1828   *21 January* Now as Richard Wagner, matriculates at the
       Nicolaischule in Leipzig.
       Spring–summer Finishes the tragedy *Leubald* and
       decides to compose his own incidental music. Studies of basic
       harmony and counterpoint, first independently (with J. B.
       Logier's *Method of Thorough-bass*) and then with Christian
       Müller, a member of the Gewandhaus orchestra.

1829   First attempts at composition: piano sonatas in D minor and
       F minor, string quartet in D major, concert aria (?) – none
       preserved. Later claims (in *ML*) to have heard Wilhelmine
       Schröder-Devrient in the role of Leonore (*Fidelio*) in Leipzig in
       this year (April?), although evidence of the performance is
       lacking.
       28 September Sister Rosalie performs the role of Fenella in
       D. F. E. Auber's *La muette de Portici* in Leipzig.

1830   *16 June* Transfers to the Thomasschule in Leipzig.
       Spring Begins a pastoral opera (*Schäferoper*) modeled on
       Goethe's *Die Laune des Verliebten*. During this year composes
       four or five overtures (*WWV* 10–14), including the so-called
       Drumbeat Overture (cf. *ML*) and one to Schiller's *Bride of
       Messina* (all lost, apart from fragments of *WWV* 13).
       6 October Offers publisher Schott a piano arrangement of
       Beethoven's Ninth Symphony (*WWV* 9, completed Easter 1831,
       but not published). Demonstrations in Leipzig (October) in the
       wake of Paris "July revolution."
       25 December Drumbeat Overture (*WWV* 10) performed under
       Heinrich Dorn in a concert at the Leipzig theater.

1831   Composes six Lieder and one *Melodram* ("Ach neige, du
       Schmerzenreiche") from Goethe's *Faust* (voice and piano).
       Another overture (D minor), a piano sonata (B flat), and a
       fantasia (F-sharp minor) composed (*WWV* 20–22).
       23 February Matriculates at the University of Leipzig, though
       without completing any course of study.
       Fall Musical studies with Theodor Weinlig, Thomaskantor in
       Leipzig.

1832   Two overtures performed in Gewandhaus concerts (Leipzig);
       C major symphony (*WWV* 29, composed spring 1832) per-
       formed in Prague in November. Piano sonata in A (*WWV* 26),
       overture and incidental music to Raupach's *König Enzio*
       (*WWV* 24) composed.

November–December Begins work on an opera, *Die Hochzeit*; text and some musical numbers completed, but the project is abandoned the following year.

23, 27 December Schröder-Devrient performs in *Der Freischütz* and *Fidelio* in Leipzig.

1833   *January* Finishes libretto of first completed opera, *Die Feen* (*The Fairies*; after C. Gozzi, *La donna serpente* [*The Serpent Woman*]). (Score completed January 1834.)

17 January Moves to Würzburg to work as chorus director and musical coach for brother Albert.

1834   *21 January* Returns to Leipzig after completing score of *Die Feen*. Influence of Heinrich Laube (first meeting in 1832) and "Young German" movement (1834–35).

March Schröder-Devrient performs in Bellini's *I Capuleti e i Montecchi* in Leipzig, as well as *Fidelio* and Rossini's *Otello*.

10 June First published essay, "On German Opera," appears in Laube's *Zeitung für die elegante Welt*.

Summer Vacation in Bohemia with Theodor Apel; conceives plan for opera after Shakespeare's *Measure for Measure*, as *Das Liebesverbot* (*The Ban on Love*). While engaged as music director of Heinrich Bethmann's theater troupe during summer season in Bad Lauchstädt, meets and becomes intimate with Minna Planer.

August–September A symphony in E major (*WWV* 35) begun; incomplete.

1835   Continues as music director for Bethmann's theater troupe, in Magdeburg.

January Overture and incidental music for five-act drama *Columbus* by Theodor Apel. Begins composition of *Das Liebesverbot* (completed by March 1836).

Summer Travels to southern Germany and Bohemia looking for singers to engage at Magdeburg. While visiting his sister and her husband, Klara and Heinrich Wolfram, in Nuremberg, witnesses a late-night disturbance in the streets later recalled in the scenario of *Die Meistersinger*. Begins the "Red Pocket-Book," notes toward a future autobiography. After Minna Planer takes up an engagement in Berlin, Wagner begins more urgent courtship.

1836   *29 March* With almost no rehearsal, Wagner attempts to stage the recently completed *Das Liebesverbot* in Magdeburg prior to dissolution of the troupe there.

July Settles in Königsberg (following Minna). Remains there, with some employment in the theater, through May 1837. Completes the concert overture "Polonia." Drafts a libretto for a grand opera after the historical novel by Heinrich Koenig, *Die hohe Braut* (*The High-Born Bride*; summer–fall); sends scenario to Eugène Scribe in Paris. (Full libretto drafted in Dresden, August 1842.)

24 November Marries Minna Planer in Tragheim, near Königsberg.

1837 *15 March* Completes another "national" overture, on "Rule Britannia."

June–July Trouble with Minna, who several times leaves Wagner (staying mainly in and around Dresden). Receives contract for post of music director in Riga through Karl Holtei, in Berlin. Reads Bulwer-Lytton's novel *Rienzi, Last of the Roman Tribunes* and sketches scenario for a grand opera on the subject.

September Takes up post in Riga, where Minna joins him again in October.

1838 *Spring* Writes libretto for comic opera, *Männerlist grösser als Frauenlist, oder die glückliche Bärenfamilie*, a modernized version of a story from the *Arabian Nights*, which he intends to compose in a *Singspiel* idiom appropriate for performance in Riga (breaks off composition after three numbers).

August Libretto for *Rienzi* completed (by 6 August) and composition begun immediately. Act 1 completed (orchestral draft) by 6 December.

Between September 1837 and March 1839 conducts twenty-six different works including operas by Mozart (four), Beethoven, Cherubini, Weber, Adam (two), Auber (three), and Meyerbeer (*Robert le diable*), as well as orchestral concerts (Beethoven).

1839 *March* Loses contract with the Riga theater. Continues work on *Rienzi* (orchestral draft of Act 2 completed 9 April).

Spring–summer Plans to flee creditors in Riga and to settle in Paris.

19 July Richard, Minna, and their dog begin voyage (by sea) from Baltic coast to France, via London.

27–29 July Bad storms beset the ship (*Thetis*), which docks temporarily on the southern coast of Norway (Sandvika).

12 August Arrival in London.

20 August Arrival in France (Boulogne-sur-mer), staying through 16 September; first meeting with Giacomo Meyerbeer, in Boulogne.

17 September Arrival in Paris.

November Hears Beethoven's Ninth Symphony at the Société des Concerts (Conservatoire) under François Habeneck, as well as one of the first performances of Berlioz's *Roméo et Juliette*.

December Drafts an orchestral movement after Goethe's *Faust* (completed January 1840; revised 1855 as *Eine Faust-Ouvertüre*, WWV 59).

1840   *Winter* Begins Act 3 of *Rienzi* (whole opera completed 19 November). Composes several songs to French texts.

6 May Sends prose sketch for a short (one-act) opera on the subject of the "Flying Dutchman" to Scribe, afterwards to Meyerbeer.

12 July First of series of articles for *Revue et Gazette Musicale de Paris* published ("De la musique allemande").

Fall Works on operatic arrangements and score proofs (Donizetti, Halévy) for Maurice Schlesinger.

1841   *Winter* Composes some initial sections of *Der fliegende Holländer* (*The Flying Dutchman*), including Senta's Ballad.

18 March Meyerbeer recommends *Rienzi* to Baron von Lüttichau, intendant of the court opera in Dresden. First encounter with Franz Liszt (late March).

29 April Richard and Minna move to Meudon, outside Paris.

18–28 May Libretto of *Der fliegende Holländer* completed.

11 July Begins composition of *Der fliegende Holländer*; draft completed 22 August, full score by end of November.

1842   *Winter* Sketches operatic projects *Die Sarazenin* (historical-mythical opera on the early Hohenstaufen dynasty in Italy) and *Die Bergwerke zu Falun* (after E. T. A. Hoffmann).

7 April Richard and Minna leave Paris for Dresden, arrive 12 April.

22 June–8 July Drafts scenario of *Tannhäuser* (at first titled *Der Venusberg*).

20 October Premiere of *Rienzi* in Dresden, Wagner's first major success.

1843   *2 January* Premiere of *Der fliegende Holländer* in Dresden, a more limited success.

2 February Appointed Royal Saxon Kapellmeister, in conjunction with Karl Gottlieb Reissiger.

6 July Performance of *Das Liebesmahl der Apostel* for men's and boys' chorus and orchestra in the Dresden Frauenkirche (1,200 singers and 100 players).

Summer Reads Jacob Grimm's *Teutonic Mythology* while vacationing in Bohemia (Teplitz). Begins composition of *Tannhäuser* (completed 13 April 1845).

Fall Begins book collection that will include classical Greek drama, medieval German poetry and legendary sources, and assorted modern philosophical and literary texts.

1844   *January* Conducts performances of *Der fliegende Holländer* in Berlin.

November Gasparo Spontini visits Dresden, at Wagner's invitation, to oversee production of *La vestale* featuring Schröder-Devrient and Josef Tichatschek (creators of leading roles in *Rienzi* and *Tannhäuser*), as well as Wagner's young niece, Johanna Wagner.

1845   *Summer* In Marienbad, studies sources of the Lohengrin and Parsifal legends, drafts scenarios for *Lohengrin* and *Die Meistersinger von Nürnberg*.

19 October Premiere of *Tannhäuser* in Dresden.

November Finishes libretto of *Lohengrin*; reads it publicly at Dresden "Engelklub," with Robert Schumann and various artists in attendance (17 December).

1846   *5 April* Conducts Beethoven's Ninth Symphony for Palm Sunday concert (publishes essays in *Dresdner Anzeiger* regarding the work and the performance).

30 July Composition draft of *Lohengrin* completed (orchestral draft completed 29 August 1847, full score 28 April 1848).

August Facing financial difficulties, Wagner takes out a large loan (5,000 thalers) from the theater pension fund. A further loan requested from Meyerbeer is turned down (26 November).

31 October Prose draft to a five-act drama, *Friedrich I* (Barbarossa).

1847   *24 February* Wagner's arrangement and translation of Gluck's *Iphigénie en Aulide* produced at the Dresden court theater.

Summer Readings in Greek drama, Roman history, Hegel.

24 October Conducts *Rienzi* in Berlin; production fails to achieve the hoped-for breakthrough for Wagner in the Prussian capital (in Berlin from 18 September through 6 November).

1848   *9 January* Wagner's mother Johanna dies.

February–March Political insurrections in Paris with immediate repercussions in German states and Austria. Wagner continues series of orchestral concerts in Dresden, in addition to operatic productions.

16 April Conducts orchestral concert (Palm Sunday) featuring Beethoven's Symphony No. 8.

June Delivers speech to the Dresden Vaterlandsverein (a political discussion group), "How Do Republican Aims Relate to the Institution of Monarchy?" (published anonymously in the *Dresdner Anzeiger* 15 June).

4 October Completes prose scenario for a drama on the Nibelung Saga (published version: "The Nibelung Myth"); prose draft for a libretto, *Siegfrieds Tod* (*Siegfried's Death*), 20 October; draft of libretto completed 28 November. An essay entitled "The Wibelungs: World-History from the Saga," written between late 1848 and early 1849, speculates on mythographic connections between Siegfried, Friedrich Barbarossa, the Nibelungen hoard, and the Holy Grail.

1849   *January* Draft of a spoken drama, *Jesus of Nazareth*.

5–8 May Involvement in the political uprising in Dresden, occasioned by Friedrich August II's dissolution of the two Saxon chambers of deputies.

9–28 May Flees Dresden, stopping in Eisenach (the Wartburg) and Weimar (Franz Liszt), before continuing to Zurich on a false passport.

2 June Arrives in Paris, at Liszt's suggestion, to look for career opportunities. Returns to Zurich a month later.

Summer Writes long essay on *Art and Revolution*, followed by *The Artwork of the Future* (finished 4 November); published 1849 and 1850, respectively.

1850   *January, March* Prose drafts of an opera scenario, *Wieland the Smith*.

1 February Returns to Paris, in search of further opportunities.

March–April Involvement with Jessie Laussot (Bordeaux); plans to separate from Minna and travel abroad. After some months of unsettled existence, returns to Zurich and Minna (3 July).

May Visits with Julie Ritter and family (from Dresden) in Villeneuve (Lake Geneva); acquires promise of subsidy from Ritter together with the Laussot family.

August Composition sketches for opening scenes (prologue) of *Siegfried's Death*. Writes essay "Judaism in Music" (published

	3, 6 September in the *Neue Zeitschrift für Musik*). *Lohengrin* premiered under Liszt in Weimar, 28 August.
1851	*January–February* Completes draft of major theoretical treatise, *Opera and Drama* (published 1852); favorite parrot Papo dies 12 February.

May–June Prose scenario followed by full libretto for a "prequel" to *Siegfried's Death* entitled *Young Siegfried* (*Der junge Siegfried*).

August An "artistic" autobiography drafted as *A Communication to My Friends* (published 1852).

15 September–23 November Hydrotherapy cure pursued at Albisbrunn, near Zurich.

November First prose drafts of *Das Rheingold* and *Die Walküre*.

1852 *February* Meets Otto and Mathilde Wesendonck.

25 April–2 May Conducts performances of *Der fliegende Holländer* in Zurich.

1 July Completes libretto of *Die Walküre*.

Summer Travels in the Alps and the Italian lakes.

3 November Completes libretto of *Das Rheingold*.

15 December Completes revisions to *Siegfried's Death* (eventually to become *Götterdämmerung*), following those to *Young Siegfried*. Complete text of *Ring* cycle read aloud at the house of François and Eliza Wille, 18–19 December.

1853 *February* Private printing (fifty copies) of the text of the *Ring* cycle. Larger public reading in Zurich (Hotel Baur au Lac), 16–19 February 1853.

May Concerts of opera excerpts (up through *Lohengrin*) in Zurich.

2–10 July Visit from Liszt, followed by travels in the Alps with Georg Herwegh (14 July–10 August).

24 August–10 September Travels via Turin to the Ligurian coast (Genoa, La Spezia); later account (*ML*) posits the conception of the music for the beginning of *Das Rheingold* during a fevered sleep in La Spezia (early September).

October Journeys via Basel, Paris back to Zurich, partly in the company of Liszt and Carolyn Sayn-Wittgenstein (meets Cosima Liszt in Paris).

November Begins composition of *Das Rheingold*.

1854 *14 January* Composition draft of *Das Rheingold* completed; full score completed 28 May.

28 June Begins composition draft of *Die Walküre*, completed 27 December.

Fall Begins reading Schopenhauer, *The World as Will and Representation*.

1855   *January* Begins orchestration of *Die Walküre*.

26 February Travels via Paris to London. Directs series of concerts in London, March–June 1855.

30 June Returns to Zurich.

December (or earlier) First ideas for a musico-dramatic treatment of the Tristan and Isolde story.

1856   *23 March* Fair copy of *Die Walküre* orchestral score completed.

16 May Prose sketch of drama on Buddhist legend, *Die Sieger* (*The Victors*).

Summer Pursues water cure in Mornex.

September Begins composition draft of *Siegfried*, Act 1. (Definitive titles of *Siegfried* and *Götterdämmerung* established spring 1856.) Orchestral draft begun 11 October and completed 31 March 1857.

13 October–27 November Franz Liszt visits Wagner in Zurich, with Princess Wittgenstein. Auditions of *Walküre*, Act 1 (Liszt at the piano) in Zurich, 22 October. Liszt and Wagner present orchestral concerts in St. Gallen (Symphonic Poems of Liszt, Beethoven's *Eroica* Symphony).

19 December First musical ideas for *Tristan und Isolde* sketched.

1857   *15 February* Finishes "open letter" on Liszt's Symphonic Poems (published in the *Neue Zeitschrift für Musik*).

April Moves with Minna into the guest cottage (Asyl) of Otto and Mathilde Wesendonck, outside Zurich (Enge). First ideas for *Parsifal* libretto sketched.

22 May On his birthday, begins composition draft of *Siegfried*, Act 2.

26–27 June Breaks off simultaneous work on composition and orchestral drafts of *Siegfried*, Act 2 (at "Forest Murmurs" episode), and resumes in mid-summer (completed 30 July, 9 August, respectively).

18 August Cosima Liszt marries Hans von Bülow in Berlin.

20 August–18 September Prose draft and libretto of *Tristan und Isolde*.

1 October Begins composition draft of *Tristan*, Act 1, completed 31 December.

December Sets several poems by Mathilde Wesendonck, using ideas partially reworked afterwards in *Tristan und Isolde*.

1858   *15 January–6 February* Travels to Paris in wake of domestic
tensions regarding his intimacy with Mathilde Wesendonck.
3 April Orchestral score of *Tristan*, Act 1, completed.
7 April Following Richard's return to Zurich, Minna intercepts a
letter to Mathilde Wesendonck; Minna seeks therapy in
Brestenberg (15 April–15 July) for heart ailment; continued
domestic tensions lead to Richard's departure from Zurich
toward the end of the summer.
4 May Begins composition draft of *Tristan*, Act 2, completed
1 July (full score completed 18 March 1859).
30 August Occupies rooms in the Palazzo Giustiniani in Venice,
with Karl Ritter.

1859   *24–28 March* Travels via Milan to Lucerne. Settles in Lucerne
following brief return to Zurich (2–3 April).
9 April Begins composition draft of *Tristan*, Act 3, completed
16 July. Orchestral draft 1 May–19 July, full score completed
6 August.
6–11 September Travels via Zurich to Paris. Minna joins Richard
17 November.

1860   *25 January, 1 and 8 February* Concerts at the Théâtre Italien
attract attention of a broad public including Auguste Gaspérini,
Louvre curator Frédéric Villot, writers Charles Baudelaire and
Champfleury, artist Gustave Doré, musicians Stephen Heller,
Gounod, Saint-Saëns, and others.
24–28 March Concerts in Brussels.
May Auditions of *Tristan*, Act 2, at the house of Pauline
Viardot-Garcia.
Summer Travels with Minna (Bad Soden, Frankfurt, Baden-
Baden).
September Publication of French prose translations of the
Dresden operas (*Quatre poèmes d'opéras*) with prefatory essay
addressed to Frédéric Villot (prefatory essay republished in
German as *"Zukunftsmusik"* [*"Music of the Future"*], 1861).
October–December New "Bacchanale" and revisions to Act 1
of *Tannhäuser* for Paris production (completed 28 January
1861).

1861   *13 March* Premiere of the revised French score of
Tannhäuser at the Paris opera (Rue le Peletier); oppositional
voices led by the Jockey Club create legendary scandal, and
the production is canceled after third performance
(24 March).

May Successful production of *Lohengrin* in Vienna (first time Wagner hears or sees it); Vienna court opera promises to mount the premiere of *Tristan und Isolde*.

July–August Minna returns to Bad Soden, Richard follows (from Paris); visits with Liszt and family in Weimar, stops in Nuremberg, Munich en route to Vienna.

September–October Initial rehearsals of *Tristan* in Vienna gradually falter, in part due to continuing indisposition and incapacity of the tenor Aloys Ander.

November Visit with Otto and Mathilde Wesendonck in Venice. On the train ride back to Vienna, Wagner claims (*ML*) to have conceived the main ideas of the *Meistersinger* Prelude (Act 1). Completes full prose draft for the new opera 18 November, reads aloud to invited public at Schott's in Mainz, 3 December.

1862 *25–31 January* Libretto of *Die Meistersinger* completed.

5 February Reads libretto to invited guests at Schott's again, in Mainz. Settles temporarily in Biebrich, near Mainz (mid-February). Troubles with Minna (visits in Biebrich, 21 February–3 March).

13–20 April Drafts Prelude to Act 1 of *Die Meistersinger* (Prelude to Act 3 drafted 22 May).

July Visits from Hans and Cosima von Bülow, Ludwig and Malvina Schnorr von Carolsfeld (later to create title roles in *Tristan und Isolde*) in Biebrich.

1 November Conducts *Meistersinger* Prelude in Leipzig; visits Minna in Dresden (3 November).

14 November Settles again in Vienna, still with hopes for a Viennese premiere of *Tristan*. Friendship with actress Friederike Meyer (alienating her sister, Luise Dustmann, the intended creator of Isolde). Reads *Meistersinger* libretto at the house of Dr. Josef Standthartner, in Eduard Hanslick's presence (23 November).

26 December Conducts concert of his music at the Theater an der Wien (further concerts January 1863).

1863 *January* Prepares *Ring* librettos for publication. Concerts in Vienna (1, 11 January), resulting only in financial losses.

February Travels via Berlin, Königsberg to St. Petersburg for concerts, also in Moscow, March–April.

May New, expensively appointed lodgings in Penzing (Vienna). Completes in score the opening scene of *Die Meistersinger*, Act 1 (mid-June). Friendship with Peter Cornelius.

July Concerts in Budapest.

4 November New production of *Der fliegende Holländer* in Prague. Further contact with court and theater in Karlsruhe (ongoing since 1861).

28 November Visits with Bülows in Berlin, en route to concerts in Löwenberg and Breslau. Intimacy with Cosima von Bülow begins ("Amid tears and sobs we confessed that henceforth we would only belong to one another," *ML*, suppressed in earlier editions).

1864   *23 March* Fleeing creditors in Vienna, arrives in Munich. Travels in southern Germany and Switzerland, arriving 29 April in Stuttgart.

3 May On the day following the death of Giacomo Meyerbeer in Paris (as Wagner later observed), cabinet secretary Franz von Pfistermeister delivers a summons from King Ludwig II of Bavaria, to whom Wagner is presented in Munich, 4 May. Arrangements for Ludwig's patronage of Wagner begin.

14 May Moves into a villa (Haus Pellet) rented for him by Ludwig on Lake Starnberg in Bavaria. Cosima von Bülow visits there with daughters Daniela and Blandine, 29 June; Hans von Bülow arrives 7 July.

July–August First of various writings produced on behalf of Ludwig ("On State and Religion"), and draft of *Huldigungsmarsch* (*March of Homage*).

September–October Rents lodgings in Munich (Briennerstrasse). Fair copy of orchestral score of *Siegfried*, Act 1, scene 2 (27 September). Contract with Ludwig for completion of the *Ring* project.

20 November Hans and Cosima von Bülow move to Munich.

4 December Der fliegende Holländer produced at Munich court theater. Orchestral draft of *Siegfried*, Act 2, begun (22 December).

1865   *February–March* Anti-Wagner sentiment in Munich begins to surface.

10 April First child of Wagner and Cosima, Isolde, born in Munich (christened von Bülow).

11 May Rehearsals for premiere of *Tristan und Isolde* begin in Munich. Minna Wagner writes her will (Dresden).

10 June Hans von Bülow conducts the premiere of *Tristan und Isolde* in Munich, with Ludwig and Malvina Schnorr von Carolsfeld. Further performances 13, 19 June, 1 July.

17 July Begins dictation to Cosima of autobiography (to 1864), *Mein Leben*.

27–31 August Prose draft of *Parsifal* (here, *Parzival*).

14–27 September Series of journal entries for Ludwig, published 1878 as "What Is German?"

December In the face of increasing political hostility to his presence and activities in Munich, Wagner leaves the city and settles at first near Geneva (Les Artichauts). Continues composition draft of *Die Meistersinger*, Act 1 (January 1866).

1866   *25 January* Minna Wagner dies, in Dresden.

April Rents villa (Haus Tribschen) on Lake Lucerne. Cosima, Daniela, and Blandine von Bülow come to stay.

15 May Begins composition draft of *Die Meistersinger*, Act 2. Ludwig visits at Tribschen for Wagner's birthday (22–24 May).

10 June Leaving his post as court pianist in Munich, Hans von Bülow arrives at Tribschen.

September Hans von Bülow moves to Basel, Cosima remains at Tribschen. Orchestral draft of *Die Meistersinger*, Act 2, completed (23 September).

24 December Gives Ludwig autograph score of *Das Liebesverbot* as Christmas present; fair copies of full scores of *Rheingold* and *Walküre* previously offered as birthday presents (25 August 1865, 1866).

1867   *7 February* Composition draft of *Die Meistersinger*, Act 3, completed; orchestral draft completed 5 March.

17 February Eva, second child of Cosima by Richard, born at Tribschen.

Spring Extended visits to Munich, Starnberg, and contact with Ludwig II. *Lohengrin* produced in Munich in June.

Summer Orchestration of *Die Meistersinger*, completed 24 October.

16 September Cosima and daughters return to Munich and to husband Hans.

24 December Gives Ludwig II autograph full score of *Die Meistersinger*.

1868   *Spring* Brochure *German Art and German Politics*, second edition of *Opera and Drama*, "Recollections of Ludwig Schnorr von Carolsfeld" (died 21 July 1865) prepared for publication.

21 May Wagner arrives in Munich to attend rehearsals of *Die Meistersinger*; premiere 21 June (St. John's Day) at the Munich court opera, under Hans von Bülow.

August Notes for a drama, *Luther's Wedding*.

14 September–6 October Travels with Cosima to northern Italy. Decision to seek her divorce from Hans von Bülow, and to inform Ludwig II of the situation.

8 November Meets Friedrich Nietzsche at the home of Wagner's brother-in-law Hermann Brockhaus, Leipzig.

16 November Cosima returns with daughters Isolde and Eva to Tribschen.

24 December Gives Ludwig II autograph full score of *Rienzi*.

1869   *1 January* Cosima begins diaries of her life with Wagner, continued through the day of his death.

January Writes new "afterword" to "Judaism in Music" essay, republished as a brochure under Wagner's own name in March.

23 February Fair copy of full score of *Siegfried*, Act 2, completed; composition draft of Act 3 begun 1 March.

7 May Elected a member of the Royal Academy of the Arts in Berlin.

17 May Nietzsche, now appointed professor in Basel, makes his first visit to Tribschen.

6 June Wagner's first and only son (the third child by Cosima), Siegfried Helferich, born at Tribschen.

14 June Composition draft of *Siegfried*, Act 3, completed; orchestral draft completed 5 August.

September Attends rehearsals for the Munich production (world premiere) of *Das Rheingold* (22 September), which he opposed but had been unable to prevent, conducted by Franz Wüllner.

October Composition draft of *Götterdämmerung* begun. Writes essay "On Conducting" (October–November).

1870   *11 January* Begins orchestral draft of *Götterdämmerung* (Prologue).

5 March Attention drawn to Bayreuth (Markgräfliches Opernhaus) as possible venue for the complete "festival" performance of the *Ring* cycle.

26 June Die Walküre premiered in Munich; as with *Das Rheingold* (1869), Wüllner conducts.

18 July Divorce of Hans and Cosima von Bülow ratified in Berlin.

19 July War declared between France and Prussia. Visit from Catulle and Judith (Gautier-)Mendès, Villiers de L'Isle-Adam, Henri Duparc, Camille Saint-Saëns leads to personal and political conflicts.

20 July–7 September Drafts musical-philosophical essay *Beethoven* in honor of the 100th anniversary of the composer's birth.

25 August Cosima married to Richard Wagner in the Protestant church at Lucerne.

October–November A comedy "in the manner of Aristophanes" (*Eine Kapitulation*) satirizing the fortunes of France and the Parisians in the conflict with Prussia and allied German states conceived as libretto for a modern political operetta in the style of Offenbach. Hans Richter attempts to compose music.

December Completes orchestral tone-poem on themes from *Siegfried*, the *Siegfried-Idyll*, privately premiered on Christmas day in honor of Cosima's birthday (24 December). Private printing of the first volume of memoirs (*Mein Leben*).

1871 *5 February* Full score of *Siegfried*, Act 3, completed.

February–March Composition of *Kaisermarsch* (Imperial March) in honor of the new German Reich and its emperor, Wilhelm I.

March–April Writings on opera ("On the Destiny of Opera") and the Bayreuth festival scheme.

3–9 April Nietzsche visits at Tribschen and reads draft, *The Origins and Goal of Tragedy*. At Wagner's suggestion, he subsequently revises the book to address the modern music drama in relation to ancient tragedy (as *The Birth of Tragedy from the Spirit of Music*), presented to Wagner in proofs, 2 January 1872.

15–20 April Travels with Cosima to Bayreuth. Considers the eighteenth-century margrave's opera house (Markgräfliches Opernhaus) briefly as a venue for his future festival.

April–May Travels with Cosima to Berlin (received by Bismarck, 3 May), Leipzig, Darmstadt with an eye to preparations for Bayreuth project. Conducts orchestral concert in the Royal Opera House, Berlin, 5 May.

24 June Composition draft of *Götterdämmerung*, Act 2, begun (orchestral draft completed 19 November). *Rienzi* produced in Munich (27 June).

31 October Completes "Recollections of Auber."

1–7 November, 14–15 December Preliminary arrangements with city council of Bayreuth regarding plans for festival and theater.

1872 *4 January* Composition draft of *Götterdämmerung*, Act 3, begun (orchestral draft completed 23 July).

24 January–4 February More travels (Berlin, Weimar, Bayreuth) regarding financing and administration of the Bayreuth festival. Deed to property of the eventual villa Wahnfried acquired, 1 February.

25 April Nietzsche's last (of twenty-three) visits to the Wagner family at Tribschen.

30 April Cosima and rest of household join Richard in Bayreuth.

6–13 May Concert tour to Vienna.

22 May On Wagner's birthday the foundation-laying ceremony of the festival theater is celebrated, including performance of Beethoven's Ninth Symphony.

June–September Wagner family occupies lodgings in the Hotel Fantaisie outside Bayreuth. "On Actors and Singers" completed 14 September. Moves late September to no. 7 Dammallee.

31 July–22 August Completes dictation (to Cosima) of the second section of *Mein Leben* (to 1850), privately printed in December.

10 November–14 December Talent-scouting tour for potential singers for Bayreuth project (Würzburg, Frankfurt, Darmstadt, Mannheim, Stuttgart, Strasbourg, Karlsruhe, Wiesbaden, Cologne, Düsseldorf, Hannover, Madgeburg, Dessau, Leipzig).

1873   *12 January–7 February* Further travels to Dresden (performance of *Rienzi*, meeting with Wesendoncks), Berlin, Hamburg (conducts concerts), Schwerin, and Berlin again (conducts concert 4 February).

March "On the Performance of Beethoven's Ninth Symphony."

Late April Travels to Cologne (conducts concert 24 April), Kassel, Leipzig.

3 May Full score of *Götterdämmerung*, Act 1, begun (full score of Act 2 completed 26 June 1874; full score of Act 3 completed 21 November 1874).

22 May Wagner's sixtieth birthday celebrated with a concert in the Markgräfliches Opernhaus in Bayreuth. With Cosima, attends performance of Liszt's *Christus* in Weimar, 29 May.

24 June Submits to Bismarck essay on "The Festival Theater at Bayreuth" in hopes of gaining state support for the project (not forthcoming).

September Anton Bruckner visits in Bayreuth and presents Wagner with score and dedication of his Symphony No. 3 in D minor.

30 October–2 November Nietzsche visits in Bayreuth.

21 November Discusses with court secretary Lorenz von Düfflipp proposals for subsidy by Ludwig II for the festival theater project. By the following February (1874) Ludwig agrees to extending him a line of credit. Back in Bayreuth (28 November) meets with machinist Karl Brandt of Darmstadt and painter-designer Josef Hoffmann of Vienna regarding production plans for the *Ring* cycle.

1874   *16 January* Drafts proposal (unsuccessful) for imperial subsidy of the Bayreuth festival, for one-third of total costs.

28 April The Wagner family moves into the newly built Villa Wahnfried in Bayreuth (building costs covered by Ludwig II).

20 May Hans Richter arrives in Bayreuth to consult about musical preparation for the *Ring* cycle, and embarks on two-week tour regarding singers. Several arrive later in June (including Emil Scaria, Franz Betz, Georg Unger, and Karl Hill) to work with Wagner. In July Amalie Materna, Marianne Brandt, Albert Niemann, and Carl Schlosser do likewise.

4–15 August Further visit from Nietzsche in Bayreuth; growing tensions.

1 December Visits Coburg to consult with Brückner brothers Max and Gotthold about stage sets. Invites Emil Doepler of Berlin to design costumes (17 December).

1875   *20 February–16 March* Cosima and Richard travel to Vienna for concerts (1 and 14 March) as well as a joint concert with Liszt in Budapest, 10 March.

9–26 April Cosima and Richard travel via Leipzig (hear Schumann's *Genoveva*), Hannover, Braunschweig to Berlin for concerts with Materna and Niemann. Return to Vienna for a third concert (6 May).

July–August Proceeds from spring concerts help pay for rehearsals with singers and orchestra of the *Ring* cycle, now planned for the following summer. Richter conducts.

1 November–17 December Consults on new productions of *Tannhäuser* and *Lohengrin* in Vienna (first performances 22 November, 15 December, under Richter). Hears Richter conduct Verdi's *Requiem*.

1876   *8 February* Contract for composition of a march for centennial festivities commemorating American independence (4 July 1876), commissioned through Theodor Thomas (drafted 15–20 February, orchestration finished 17 March).

4–23 March Trip to Berlin for local premiere of *Tristan und Isolde*.

3 June–9 August Final series of rehearsals for the Bayreuth festival premiere of the *Ring des Nibelungen* cycle. (Ludwig II attends dress rehearsals 6–9 August.)

13, 14, 16, 17 August First Bayreuth festival performances of the *Ring* cycle. Second cycle 20–23 August, third cycle 27–30 August. Many illustrious visitors. Despite subsidies and fund-raising programs, festival concludes with deficit of approximately 148,000 Reichsmark.

Late summer Affair with Judith Gautier (recently divorced from Catulle Mendès).

14 September–20 December Wagner travels with family via Munich to Italy (Verona, Bologna, Sorrento, Naples, Rome, Florence). Final encounter with Nietzsche in Sorrento, late October.

1877 *1 January* Drafts a circular to the Society of Patrons entreating continued support of the Bayreuth festival, and to petition the German Reichstag to that end as well.

February–April Libretto of *Parsifal* developed; completed 19 April.

30 April–4 June Travels with Cosima to London. Eight concerts given (with Hans Richter) in Albert Hall, 7–29 May, to raise money toward festival debts. Reads libretto of *Parsifal* to invited audience at 12 Orme Square, Bayswater, 17 May, following audience at Windsor with Queen Victoria, who asks after Wagner's dog Rus, among other things.

June Richard and Cosima join children in Bad Ems.

5–28 July Visits in Heidelberg, Nuremberg, Weimar, and Switzerland (Lucerne).

Late September Composition and orchestral drafts of *Parsifal*, Act 1, begun (orchestral draft completed 31 January 1878).

7 October Hans von Wolzogen settles in Bayreuth, to serve as editor of the *Bayreuther Blätter* (1878–1938). Wagner's contributions include "Modern," "Public and Popularity," "The Public in Time and Space" (1878); "Shall We Hope?" "On Poetry and Composition," "On Opera Poetry and Composition in Particular," "On the Application of Music to the Drama," "Against Vivisection: Open Letter to Ernst von Weber" (1879), "Religion and Art" (1880), and several "supplements" ("What Avails This Knowledge?" "Know Thyself," "Heroism and Christianity").

1878 *March* Begins composition and orchestral drafts of *Parsifal*, Act 2 (completed 11 October).

Nietzsche (who received *Parsifal* libretto on 3 January, with strongly mixed feelings) sends Wagner *Human, All Too Human*. His attachment to Cosima remains strong, despite his distance from Wagner.

20–31 August Franz Liszt visits in Bayreuth.

30 October Composition draft of *Parsifal*, Act 3, begun; works on composition and orchestral drafts of Act 3 through 26 April 1879.

17–23 November *Ring* cycle performed in Munich.

25 December Prelude to *Parsifal* performed at Wahnfried for Cosima's birthday.

1879 *January* Complete *Ring* cycles produced in Leipzig.

21–31 August Franz Liszt visits in Bayreuth.

23 August Begins full score of *Parsifal* (Act 1 completed 25 April 1881; Act 2 completed 20 October 1881; Act 3 completed 13 January 1882).

20 October Heinrich von Stein (philosopher, poet, and student of liberal socialist Karl Eugen Dühring) settles at Wahnfried as tutor to Siegfried.

31 December Wagner and family travel via Munich to Italy.

1880 *4 January* Family occupies Villa d'Angri in Posillipo, near Naples.

18 January Russian artist Paul von Joukowsky visits the Wagners in Posillipo.

9 March Engelbert Humperdinck visits the Wagners in Posilippo (later assists with copying of *Parsifal* in Bayreuth). Dictation of *Mein Leben* concluded, late March.

22 May Act 1 Grail scene of *Parsifal* performed (with Humperdinck, Joseph Rubinstein, and the Wagner children) for Wagner's birthday.

8 August–30 October Family travels to Tuscany, Venice.

25 August Final privately printed volume of *Mein Leben* presented to Ludwig II.

31 October–17 November Visit in Munich (with painter Franz von Lenbach, conductor Hermann Levi). Performances of *Fliegende Holländer, Tristan, Lohengrin*. Returns to Bayreuth, 17 November.

1881 *5–9 May* Production of *Ring* cycle in Berlin, arranged by Angelo Neumann based on original Bayreuth festival and Leipzig 1879 productions (Wagner attends).

11 May Count Arthur Gobineau visits at Bayreuth for several weeks. (Wagner reads Gobineau's *Essai sur l'inégalité des races humaines* [*Essay on the Inequality of the Human Races*] the previous February.)

26 June Hermann Levi stays at Wahnfried. Preparatory work toward *Parsifal* production (June–July).

22 September–9 October Franz Liszt visits in Bayreuth.

1 November Wagner and family travel via Munich and Verona to Palermo, arriving 5 November. Full score of *Parsifal*, Act 3, begun 8 November; Joseph Rubinstein completes piano-vocal score of the opera (published 1882).

1882 *13 January* Completes orchestration of *Parsifal* (Act 3).
February Moves to Villa Gangi (Palermo) and the following month to the Grand Hôtel des Bains, Acireale, in conjunction with engagement of Blandine von Bülow to Count Biagio Gravina (married 25 August in Bayreuth).
April In view of continuing health trouble and poor weather, Wagner family begins return trip to Bayreuth.
Spring "Royal loggia" ("Königsbau") added to front of festival theater.
5 May Beginning of complete *Ring* cycles at Her Majesty's Theatre, London.
11 May–17 June Count Gobineau visits again in Bayreuth.
2 July Rehearsals for *Parsifal* begin.
15 July–30 August Liszt visits in Bayreuth (with some weeks in Weimar).
26 July Premiere of *Parsifal* at the second Bayreuth festival, conducted by Hermann Levi. Sixteen performances through 29 August. Wagner suffers heart trouble during the run of performances, but conducts the final part of Act 3 in last performance.
14 September Wagner and family leave for Venice, arrive 16 September and occupy (18 September) apartments in the Palazzo Vendramin-Calergi.
19 November Liszt visits in Venice, through 13 January 1883.
24 December Wagner conducts his early C-major symphony in a concert at the Teatro la Fenice in Venice, for Cosima's birthday; Liszt performs as well.

1883 *11–13 February* Works on an essay "On the Feminine Element in the Human."
13 February Richard Wagner dies in Venice, 3:30 p.m.
16 February Wagner's body is returned to Bayreuth, accompanied by his family, Hans Richter, Adolf Gross (subsequently financial adviser to the Wagner family). Wagner buried at Wahnfried, 18 February.

Abbreviations

CWD   *Cosima Wagner's Diaries*, ed. Martin Gregor-Dellin and Dietrich
      Mack, trans. Geoffrey Skelton, 2 vols. (New York and London,
      1978–80).

GS   Richard Wagner, *Gesammelte Schriften und Dichtungen*, 10 vols.
      (Leipzig, 1887–1911).

ML   Richard Wagner, *My Life*, trans. Andrew Gray (Cambridge,
      1983).

PW   *Richard Wagner's Prose Works*, trans. William Ashton Ellis,
      8 vols. (New York, 1966; orig. edn., 1895–1912).

SB   Richard Wagner, *Sämtliche Briefe*, ed. Gertrud Strobel, Werner
      Wolf, et al., 16 vols. to date (Leipzig, 1967–2000; Wiesbaden,
      1999–).

SL   Stewart Spencer and Barry Millington, eds., *Selected Letters of
      Richard Wagner* (London and New York, 1988).

SSD   Richard Wagner, *Sämtliche Schriften und Dichtungen*, 16 vols.
      (Leipzig, 1911–16).

SW   Richard Wagner, *Sämtliche Werke*, ed. Carl Dahlhaus (Mainz,
      1970–).

WWV   *Wagner Werk-Verzeichnis: Verzeichnis der musikalischen Werke
      Richard Wagners und ihrer Quellen*, ed. John Deathridge, Martin
      Geck, and Egon Voss (Mainz and New York, 1986).

Biographical and historical contexts

1 Wagner lives: issues in autobiography

JOHN DEATHRIDGE

Wagner's biography has been researched to within an inch of its life. It has been dissected, drenched with no end of detail, eroticized, vilified, heroicized, and several times filmed.[1] Its foundations are the collected writings, which in the first instance Wagner edited himself in the spirit of an autobiographical enterprise,[2] a separate and lengthy autobiography *Mein Leben* (*My Life*) dictated to his mistress and later second wife Cosima,[3] notebooks and diaries,[4] photographs and portraits,[5] an unusually large number of letters,[6] mounds of anecdotal gossip, and no end of documentation on the way he lived and how his contemporaries saw him.[7] In this sense, he is almost the exact antithesis of Shakespeare, whose life, or at least what is safely known about it in terms of verifiable "facts," can be told in a relatively short space. I have summarized the history of Wagner biography elsewhere.[8] Here I want to look at Wagner's own portrayals of his life, some issues they raise, the philosophical spirit in which I believe they were attempted, and their effect on the generation that came immediately after him.

Biographers of Shakespeare have had to resort to imaginative reconstructions and not infrequently to forged documents that have accorded their subject more lives than a cat.[9] In stark contrast, there appears to be only one life for Wagner, which he did his best to determine in large part himself. It was also a singular life in another sense: maverick, turbulent, exceptionally creative on many levels, never afraid to attempt the impossible, uncannily prescient of modern thinking about media and human psychology, genuinely revolutionary in aspiration, and yet prone to an institutionalism with proto-fascist traits that were largely, but not only, the result of posthumous aggrandizement on the part of his apostles and admirers.[10] In all its colorful detail, the story has been repeated so many times – with its hero's adventures, amours, tribulations, and eventual acceptance among Western music's cultural elite all in their proper place – that at first sight it seems like a never-changing biographical myth.

To speak of Wagner's life in the singular, however, is seriously to underestimate his own sophisticated view of biography and autobiography and the appreciable distance of that view from the standard mapping of famous lives in the nineteenth century. Lytton Strachey rightly spoke in his *Eminent Victorians* of the "air of slow, funereal barbarism" of the (normally) two leather-bound volumes produced by the biographical undertaker of Victorian times, whose bounden duty it was to incarcerate the distinguished personage in an everlasting literary mausoleum.[11] There is no reason to suppose that Wagner would have disagreed with him. Strachey admitted the value of these gloomy reservoirs of information for his speculative approach to biography. And Wagner, too, was not slow to appoint an official biographer, Carl Friedrich Glasenapp, who began with the obligatory two volumes, later expanding them to six after Wagner's death.[12] A schoolteacher from Riga, Glasenapp not only had frequent personal contact with his subject and hence ample opportunity to get acquainted at first hand with his memories and intentions, but also privileged access to many sources zealously protected by Wagner's immediate family circle. These included the diaries of Cosima, which she continued from day to day with a stubborn and almost bureaucratic thoroughness for fourteen years until just before Wagner's death, supremely conscious of the biographical burden that had been placed upon her.[13]

The "life" as a totality

Wagner began dictating *Mein Leben* to Cosima on 17 July 1865 in Munich at the request of King Ludwig II of Bavaria and finally concluded its fourth and last part (covering the years 1861–64) fifteen years later in Naples on 25 July 1880. The first page of the manuscript (entirely in Cosima's hand except for corrections and additions by Wagner) bears their entwined initials "W[agner] R[ichard] C[osima]" (*ML* 741). This signaling of a pact between them was subsequently reinforced by the beginning of Cosima's diaries four years later on 1 January 1869, effectively turning her for good into the historian of her husband-to-be (they were formally married on 25 August 1870), despite her ostensible intention, expressed in the very first entry, to convey to her children "every hour" of *her* life, and not his. There were occasional doubts:

> I want to convey the essence of R. to my children with all possible clarity, and in consequence try to set down every word he speaks, even about myself, forgetting all modesty, so that the picture be kept intact for them – yet I feel the attempt is failing: how can I convey the sound of his voice, the intonations, his movements, and the expression in his eyes? But perhaps it is better than nothing, and so I shall continue with my bungling efforts.   (21 March 1873)

Still, Cosima's awareness that the aging composer would never have the inclination or the energy to complete *Mein Leben* – which ends with the young king calling Richard to Munich in 1864 and so delivering him from a spiral of impecuniousness and anxiety – gave her the increasing certainty that she would be regarded as the authentic biographical conduit of his life's final stage. Not unjustly described by one prominent critic as "the foreign secretary of the Holy Grail,"[14] she soon became, after his death, the longstanding prime minister of everything concerning the perpetual refurbishment of his legacy. Only three days before he died, Richard told her that he still intended "to finish the biography" (*CWD*: 9 February 1883). Even this was only the last remnant of an earlier promise he had made to the king that he would continue *Mein Leben* up to the moment his wife had herself begun "to keep a most exact record of my life and work, so that after my death my whole life up to the last hour will one day be available in every detail [*lückenlos*] to my son."[15]

Wagner's ambition to present his life to his son as a totality, with the aid of Cosima's diaries, raises three complicated issues. First, the concept depends, in terms of its narrative strategy and underlying ideology, to no small extent on the inclusion of his own death. Jean-Jacques Rousseau in his *Confessions*, the first part of which was published in 1782, placed the vanity of his life and its immediacy in the foreground as an entity – unremitting self-knowledge as a bastion against the untruth of the mere biographer's "ingenious fictions"[16] – and precluded death because the present emotion of the subject and the reliving of the subject's history in the act of writing were for him paramount. A certain confessional style and the re-enactment of history subjectively in the moment were crucial for Wagner, too, as we shall see. The creation of the self through writing, however, was conditioned in Wagner's case to a great extent by a score-settling with the outer world, a "history" not just external to himself, but one also in need of "correction" that must end, according to the metaphysics of pessimism that pervade his works and writings, in the welcome escape of the subject in death.

A second issue arises from the fact that anyone wanting to present their life in literary form, especially one like Wagner's that has been lived in the supposed spirit of a Greek tragic hero transposed into the mayhem of the modern world (a common male autobiographical model in the nineteenth century), knows that it will be impossible to narrate the all-important death of the hero in their own words. To put it another way, the search for wholeness in autobiography is plagued by the difficulty that in the real world one cannot tell the tale from a position beyond the grave, unlike countless fictions (e.g., the film *Sunset Boulevard*) that take advantage of a narrator miraculously able to recount their own death and the logical steps of the life that led up to it. There is no doubt that the older Wagner became the more remorselessly he pursued this idea of the single life "up to the last hour" that could be presented to posterity as a unified vision. He did not enter into intimate relations with Cosima solely to ensure the survival of that vision of course. But she was nearly twenty-five years younger (and outlived him for forty-seven), making it clear from the start that she would in all likelihood be in a position to finish the story on his behalf.

The much-discussed issue of gender relations in nineteenth-century biography and autobiography is a third issue,[17] if only because the striking narrative reticence of Cosima's diaries does not always conceal the real sentiments of a strong-willed woman under the severe constraints of (for the time) obligatory self-erasure. On 21 November 1874, the momentous day that saw the completion of *Der Ring des Nibelungen* twenty-six years after it had been started, Cosima experienced some shabby treatment from her husband. Instead of uttering the usual passive words of the admiring wife, she involved her own feelings in the situation with some unusually revealing thoughts. Launching into a bitter description of how she and her children had burst into tears, she asked, not without self-pitying rhetoric, why she was being denied the right to celebrate the completion of the grand project to which she had dedicated her life "in suffering"; "How could I express my gratitude other than through the destruction of all urges toward a personal existence? ... If a genius completes his flight at so lofty a level, what is left for a poor woman to do [except] to suffer in love and rapture?" What follows in the diaries is still more eloquent. There are no entries at all until 3 December 1874: almost two weeks of complete silence.

The redoubtable Mrs. Oliphant, discussing Lucy Hutchinson's *Memoirs of the Life of Colonel Hutchinson* in *Blackwood's Edinburgh Magazine* in 1882, pointed out that this "noble memorial" to Lucy's deceased Roundhead husband was erected without a single "I" in the narrative, followed by Lucy effacing herself, "as if she died with him."[18] Cosima did use the "I," as we have just seen, though for much of the time it was part of a tense conformity to the ideology of female sacrifice in the name of male authority that included recording the life of that authority "up to the last hour." But on 13 February 1883, the day of Wagner's death, Cosima wrote nothing. She took no food for hours, insisted on being alone with his body for the rest of the day and night, cut off her hair and laid it in his coffin, accompanied the body from Venice back to Bayreuth in black robes, and remained hidden from sight for more than a year, receiving nobody and speaking only to her children. Lucy Hutchinson's reticence about her role in her husband's life, Mrs. Oliphant suggested, was the means by which she achieved immortality for herself. Stung by rumors of an imminent decline in the fortunes of the Bayreuth festival theater, Cosima returned from her condition of extreme self-denial to become its renowned guardian for over twenty years – a right she had earned in the shadow of her husband with years of discreet labor and self-effacement, most of them recorded faithfully in the diaries that were to secure her lasting fame.

The rewritten diary and metaphors of experience

In terms of genuine autobiography, Wagner's life remains a fragment to this day. Moreover, the fate of the diary he started when barely in his twenties in correct anticipation of his illustrious career is indicative of an unexpected complexity with respect not only to sources, but also to the nuanced, and indeed modern, view he took of the whole enterprise. The early diary is known as "The Red Pocket-Book" (*Die rote Brieftasche*) because in *Mein Leben* Wagner reports that in August 1835 he began using "a large red pocket-book" to make notes for his "future [auto] biography" (*ML* 108, trans. modified). To King Ludwig he described this document as a means of sketching "vivid tokens of experience, as if for the eye [*plastische Merkmale des Erlebten, gleichsam für das Auge*]" in order to hold on to a quasi-visible memory of his impressions and their "inner feeling [*des innerlich Empfundenen*]."[19] This striking statement transforms the diary at once from an omnium gatherum of facts into tiny snapshots of a life serving to remind their creator of his subjective reactions to the events in it.

A few years later, Wagner's recording of his life became still more interesting. At the point in the dictation of *Mein Leben* when, within its narrative, his health and finances really began to take a turn for the worse (Easter 1846), he sat down – in February 1868 – to create a second diary out of the first. These revised "vivid tokens of experience" are known as the "Annals," which in their complete form run to thirty-six pages of print.[20] Except for its first four pages, which only go as far as Wagner's arrival in Paris on 17 September 1839, the rest of the "Red Pocket-Book" is lost, most commentators assuming, though no proof exists, that Wagner simply destroyed it. According to Otto Strobel, "the further forward he got in the portrayal of his life, the more he felt constrained by the fact that the Pocket-Book naturally contained a great deal that was impossible to dictate [in *Mein Leben*] to his friend and later wife." Given Cosima's forbearance in her diaries toward his past affairs (and whatever else) the observation is not entirely compelling. But Strobel then came up with a less banal reason: "he also wanted to see some things *differently* to when he first made a note of them under the immediate impression of what he was experiencing at the time."[21]

All of a sudden we are in Proustian territory. To support the idea of autobiography as process – never finished, never complacent – Wagner clearly felt the need to confront experiences noted in the past with an immediate response in the present about his recorded memory of them. Or, as Georges Gusdorf put it in a seminal essay on autobiography, "a second reading of experience . . . is truer than the first because it adds to experience itself a consciousness of it."[22] The factual discrepancies between Wagner's earlier and later accounts of himself and their many striking changes of emphasis can therefore be accounted for by his instinct for a double-edged narrative informed by a philosophical awareness of its own process. He regarded his life as a totality – an epitaph configured by the element of death as an end-point that paradoxically attempted to convey his life as he lived it. But he also wished to present his life as a series of lived "moments" that resist the idea of a finite end, a contradiction reflecting both an underlying discomfiture with the image of himself as eternal monument, and a hankering for the status that image enjoyed in the nineteenth century.

Skeptical observers with forensic instincts may wince at this argument, unable to quell suspicions of an elaborate ruse to justify some barefaced lying on Wagner's part. Indeed, the problematic aspect of Gusdorf's argument is the claim that the "literary, artistic function" of autobiography is of greater importance than its "historic and objective function in spite of the claims made by positivist criticism."[23] Gusdorf admits that the historian has a duty to countermand self-biography with cold facts and alternative narratives. But he is not prepared to concede the exposure of the "literary, artistic function" itself as ideology, or to put it more benignly, as an elaboration or distortion of fact in the name of a larger vision with its own subjective "truth" that transforms harsh realities into positive and powerful images. Wagner's claim in *Mein Leben* that he heard Wilhelmine Schröder-Devrient sing Leonore in Beethoven's *Fidelio* in Leipzig in 1829 has no evidence to support it. And the scholarly fuss that ensued after the present writer pointed that out in *The New Grove Wagner* (1984) still failed to produce any.[24] The observation was not meant to discredit Wagner. On the contrary, it was intended to draw attention to a deliberately constructed metaphor of huge psychological importance to him in his later years: the great singer of his youth as redemptive "woman of the future" carrying the spirit of Beethoven and the destiny of true German art in her hands.

And it is not the only alternative story. Take the one about the "impoverished" revolutionary in exile in Switzerland in the 1850s.[25] Contrary to the impression given in *Mein Leben*, Wagner was accorded privileged treatment from the outset and received substantial financial support, including huge sums from Otto Wesendonck, whose patronage in total was second only to that of King Ludwig II.[26] But his royalist sympathies, anti-Semitism, ultra-conservative friends (like Bernhard Spyri), dallying with the archaic, love of ostentatious luxury (Liszt wrote to the Princess of Sayn-Wittgenstein of his "dandified" appearance and penchant for wearing "a hat of slightly pinkish white"), and elitist disdain for democracy gradually alienated most of his fellow émigrés with liberal views, including Georg Herwegh, who came to know a rather different Wagner from the one they were expecting. In *Mein Leben* Wagner needed the myth of the genius among the scrooges and inhibited intellectuals in "this little philistine state" (*ML* 424, trans. modified) to downplay the support he had received from Otto and Mathilde Wesendonck, and for good measure to gloat that Zurich had thus forfeited its chances of becoming his Bayreuth.

The creator of the momentous artwork of the future may have invented a tendentious yarn about how he narrowly escaped the land of the cuckoo clock. Equally, in terms of his literary view of autobiography that has no qualms about the use of fictional strategies, the reasons for its tendentious-ness are not entirely trivial. Wagner tells of exciting and dangerous expeditions up sheer-faced glaciers and precipitous descents from verti-ginous peaks at this memorable moment in *Mein Leben*, all of them tinged with entertaining theatrical exaggeration. But a comment to the effect that a letter from Herwegh dragged him down from his "lofty Alpine impres-sions into the unpleasant everyday world" (*ML* 483) immediately suggests that the exaggeration is actually a way of bringing home to the reader the contrasting "lives" of the artist: the one emphatically identified with subjective freedom and nature, the other marooned in the narrow confines of day-to-day living. Wagner's devout Swiss biographer, Max Fehr, who naïvely claimed that Switzerland for all Wagnerians is "hallowed soil,"[27] reports that in 1855 Wagner seriously considered the village of Brunnen on Lake Lucerne as his festival site for the first production of *Der Ring des Nibelungen*, in full view of the spectacular mountains of Uri and the famous Mythenstein near Rütli, the birthplace of the Swiss confederation. Lake barges fastened together by carpenters in the bay of Brunnen would function as the stage, while the audience would be seated along the shore. Apparently the whole fantastic plan was only abandoned when the reali-zation dawned that the waters in the bay could become disruptive in stormy weather. But whether accurate or not (Fehr gives no source[28]) the very idea of striving for a myth-laden natural setting for the perfor-mance of the *Ring* is manna to the enraptured Wagnerian imagination, immediately setting into relief as incidental the mere "facts" of the real life of the artist, which can be distorted at will to accommodate the larger picture.

This is still more obvious in a fascinating autobiographical essay, *A Communication to My Friends* (1851), written near the beginning of Wagner's stay in Switzerland, in which (in a move familiar to students of early Romanticism) he equates his life not just with one opposed to the mundane world, in which he exists in reality, but with the work of art itself. "I make *life*," he wrote, "the first and foremost condition of the phenomenon of the work of art," later defining this phenomenon as a "development *in time*."[29] As his emphases suggest, arid notions of time-lessness and a "life" not lived to the full do not define the present; only the life of the true artist and the work of art together are its "moving, willing, and fashioning organ."[30] His view is not identical with the anti-chronological aesthetic of some of the new biographers in the 1920s (e.g., the self-styled "psychographer" Gamaliel Bradford[31]) though the striking psychological and philosophical ambition of *A Communication to My Friends* does place it well beyond those nineteenth-century biographies that he regularly read and criticized.[32]

Yet it is not generally realized how obsessed Wagner himself was with chronology, often dating his manuscripts not just to the day, but to the exact time of day.[33] This Goethe-like ambition to determine history as his own philologist, so to speak, looks at first sight like an attempt to create a "timeless" archival monument in keeping with conventional nineteenth-century biographical ethics, contrary to his professed views on the subject. The logic of his narrative, however, suggests that the punctilious dating of manuscripts is merely the converse activity of the genuine artist who, as the dynamic "organ" of presence, is therefore all the more capable of escaping the chronological force of history. The ideal life is never equivalent to the mere dating of musical works, only to its exact opposite: the experience of time in their actual realization. Or, as he put it in the foreword to his collected writings:

> [The reader] will thus inwardly grasp that these are not the collected works
> of a writer, but a record of the life's work of an artist, who in his art, over and
> above the general pattern of things, sought life. This life, however, is
> precisely the *true music*, which I recognize as the only genuine art of the
> present and the future. (*GS* I:vi)

The collected writings as autobiography: the uses and abuses of chronology

Wagner edited ten volumes of his collected writings, the first nine appearing in the early 1870s and a tenth in 1883, the year of his death. In the foreword – in many respects a key text to the understanding of his entire output – he says that he is publishing them in chronological sequence in order to show "how the most diverse of occasions always awoke in me *one* motif that is at the core of my entire project as a writer, even though my writings are so dispersed" (*GS* I:iv). Almost in the same breath, he claims that the ordering of the writings according to when they were written "has the advantage of preventing the impression of a truly scientific system among so much that is disparate" (*ibid.*). Nowhere is the contradiction explained. Wagner almost certainly knew that there could never be a truly unified method of bringing together diverse subjects such as autobiography, history, philosophy, politics, music theory, the texts of the works themselves, and performance practice as an ordered system. If he wanted to present his life as a consequential unfolding of events, he realized that he had to modify the writings and their ordering at significant junctures. Indeed, the occasional manipulation of chronology, discreet addition, self-censorship, minor rewriting, telling omission, and many another modification amounting to a "second" experience of the original texts are why, among other reasons, the ten-volume edition must count as one of the most illuminating parts of his autobiographical legacy.

The early "Autobiographical Sketch" (1843), placed right at the start of the collected writings (out of chronological order), is an early example of how Wagner presented his various "lives." The artist who has to fight for his existence in the real world of politics and poverty is set against the occasional episode when the artist experiences time creatively outside it in a nearly mythic realm, including the famous one about the stormy ship's journey from Riga to London via Norway that inspired him to write *Der fliegende Holländer* (*The Flying Dutchman*). And the essay ends with a suddenly redemptive sentence that hankers after a mythical dimension of time beyond all pedantry and dryly objective chronology: "I left [Paris] in the spring of 1842. For the first time I saw the Rhine: with glistening tears in my eyes I, poor artist, swore eternal fidelity to my German fatherland" (*GS* I:19). Nothing could have better suited the intransigent Francophobe that Wagner had become in the meantime when he set about preparing the publication of his collected writings in 1871.

But the Wagner of the early 1840s was not quite the fanatic nationalist of the early 1870s and the essay had to have its wings clipped. A self-critical sentence in favor of Italian opera to the effect that "Germans who write operas" are incapable of writing an "independent free melody" had to go.[34] And other essays in the first volume – most of them originally written in Paris (1839–42) – had to succumb similarly to discreet make-overs. In the essay *On German Music*, which first appeared in a Parisian journal in 1840, an actual event like the successful international premiere of an opera by Rossini is set against a mythical primal scene of German music. Within the confines of this unsullied *Heimat*, according to the young Wagner, there exists an opportunity for the German genius to arise "out of his limited world . . . to create something universal" (*GS* I:160). And remarkably, Meyerbeer is cited as the prime example of the German composer who can set out, *must* set out, "in alien terrain [*auf fremdem Terrain*]" on the path of a truly universal art with its roots in his native land. For the 58-year-old composer who had long since made Meyerbeer his archenemy and celebrated the defeat of France in the Franco-Prussian War in 1871, this was simply unacceptable. In the version edited for the collected writings, the pro-French sentiments of his younger self are provided with ironic footnotes, and the passages praising Meyerbeer remorselessly cut.[35]

There is much more. The essay *The Wibelungs* in the second volume describes, among other things, a supposed relationship between a historical figure, Friedrich Barbarossa, and a mythical one, Siegfried. In his edition, Wagner placed it just before the libretto of *Siegfrieds Tod* (the first version of *Götterdämmerung*) as an example of a neat transition of the artist from history to myth, opera to music drama, and, above all, the final escape of the artist into exile and subjective freedom from the narrowing constraints of institutionalized culture. What he did not say – and not only because it would have seemed utterly pedantic – was that he continued to work on the essay for some time after the summer of 1848 when this famous peripeteia in his life is supposed to have taken place.[36] Had the essay been placed a year later, where it really belongs, it would have muddied the core of the narrative: the beginning of the flight of the artist *before* the Dresden uprising in May 1849 from the alienating world of Parisian historical opera, toward his creation *after* the revolution of a "true" music that presents a mythic "life" beyond history.

But *Der Ring des Nibelungen* did not escape the dramaturgical methods of the Parisians entirely; its concluding images of volatile nature and collapse alone are unthinkable without Auber's *La muette de Portici* or Meyerbeer's *Le prophète*. And famous readings of it as historical and political allegory like Shaw's *The Perfect Wagnerite* (1898) will always present a convincing, if partial, truth that contradicts its place in the collected writings as the desired removal of the artist from history and politics into myth. Indeed, the possibilities Wagner found in myth, which he claimed enabled a new kind of music of great authenticity and power (as opposed to music still rooted in the real world of facts and appearances), reflect only one side of his life and work at the time, suggesting that his chronology is more part of a vivid theatrical construct than an objective way of reflecting the messier reality of how he actually evolved as an artist. More generally, his method served to underpin the literary enactment of a life as a work of art, a "development *in time*," in which various contradictory strands, embracing both the mundane and the ideal, accordingly converged (and this is the narrative's monumentalizing moment) toward a final and crowning achievement. The tenth and last volume, edited posthumously "in chronological sequence" according "to the express intention of the Master" (*GS* X:iii), ends not with a last-written theoretical essay, open letter, or autobiographical communication, but with an artistic creation, the complete text of *Parsifal* (actually published some years before) and its last line: "Redemption to the Redeemer."

The "life" after Wagner

Wagner's original intention to bequeath a single "life" to posterity – one that would include a description of his final hour by his wife – was thwarted at the last minute by the very same (and very common) subjugation of the female subject that had made a continuous authentic narrative of that life seem possible in the first place. It was a small sign that the concept of his life as a totality was doomed to failure from the beginning. The four-year gap between the end of *Mein Leben* and the start of Cosima's diaries, to cite just one instance, is covered only by the "Annals," the rewritten diary Wagner created in 1868. Consequently, the part of the diary covering the years 1864–68 was published at the end of a modern German edition of *Mein Leben* in 1976 in the belief that, together with the first publication of Cosima's diaries in 1976/77, they would, in the words of the editor, at last enable everyone to survey Wagner's life in its entirety on the basis of an unbroken line of "autobiographical testimony [*Selbstzeugnisse*]."[37] As the English translators of the edition tactfully point out, however, while the "Annals" may be valuable material for the biographer, "they do not constitute autobiography" (*ML* 758). And neither for that matter do Cosima's diaries, which, despite the impression of self-biography by proxy they may give to some, fuse the trivial with the important in almost surreal fashion, as diaries tend to do. What they cannot offer is a coherent narrative of a life. For critical Wagner biographers, often confronted in any case with a tortuous legacy of sex, lies, and invidious hype in the sources they have to deal with,[38] the task of piecing together his life on the basis of "authentic" documents is therefore less straightforward than it seems to be at first sight.

In the case of the autobiographer, Nietzsche's admonition comes to mind that a self-reflective account can be dangerous if it is seen to be "useful and important for one's activity to interpret it *falsely*."[39] It may not be wrong to suppose that this salutary warning has its origin in Nietzsche's experience with the first three volumes of the private edition of *Mein Leben*, the proofs of which he corrected when still on good terms with Wagner in the early 1870s. His involvement with *Mein Leben* even included the invention and supervision of the crest on the title pages of the volumes, which merges an image of the seven-star constellation called the Plough (*der Wagen*) with a vulture (*Geier*) that was duly provided by Nietzsche, on Wagner's recommendation, with a distinctive ruff to distinguish it from an eagle.[40] The crest was meant to symbolize a "double" paternity, the natural father Friedrich Wagner and the stepfather Ludwig Geyer. Given the strikingly contrasted characters of the "fathers" – the one an intellectual bureaucrat, the other an actor and painter – the crest poses an interpretative challenge for any truly alert biographer, as its inventor was the first to realize. Geyer was not Jewish; but his name had sufficient Jewish resonance for an older and more skeptical Nietzsche and his friend Heinrich Köselitz (also known as Peter Gast) to play with the idea that Geyer was the real father, and Wagner hence possibly of Jewish extraction. Köselitz joked that on learning (incorrectly) that the mother, or one of her lovers, was called "Beer" he spent an entire evening referring to Wagner as "Geyerbeer."[41] More importantly – and fatefully – Nietzsche let hints of these malicious speculations spill over into a notorious footnote in the first postscript of his polemical *The Case of Wagner*:

> Was Wagner a German at all? . . . His father was an actor by the name of Geyer. A Geyer [vulture] is practically an Adler [eagle]. – What has hitherto circulated as "Wagner's Life" is *fable convenue* [i.e., a myth that has gained acceptance], if not worse. I confess my mistrust of every point attested to by Wagner himself.[42]

Concerning Wagner's life, this was not Nietzsche's only spectacular volte-face. In 1872 he complained to his friend Erwin Rohde that a newly published pamphlet called *Richard Wagner: A Psychiatric Study* by Theodor Puschmann used tactics that spurned crude rejection for the more subtle approach of "insidious, deeply malicious innuendo" that would "undermine the confidence of the coming generation."[43] Five years after Wagner's death in 1888, he had no hesitation in using such tactics himself, claiming that Wagner is a "neurosis"; "Our physicians and physiologists," he writes, "confront their most interesting case [of degeneration] in Wagner, at least a very complete case."[44] Indeed, Nietzsche proved to be the leader in a more general desire to dent Wagner's posthumous (and massive) cultural authority by using aspects of his life to question his sanity, the stability of his body, his virility and sexual orientation, and even his racial character. In Wagner's case, already symptomatic of an age rapidly becoming disenchanted with masculine "genius," Nietzsche had finally opened up what Norma Clarke has trenchantly called the "dreadful prospect . . . of male failure."[45]

Soon after the appearance of Puschmann's pamphlet came the publication of sixteen letters from Wagner to a Viennese seamstress in the highly respected Viennese daily newspaper *Neue freie Presse*. Containing orders for satin bedspreads, silk ribbons, rose garlands, and countless satin dressing gowns, the letters were prefaced by the editor, Daniel Spitzer, with Hunding's line from *Die Walküre*, "How like the woman he looks," which in its original context has quite a different meaning. The way was open for the adoption of Wagner by the leaders of the movement for homosexual emancipation in the third volume of Magnus Hirschfeld's *Yearbook for Sexual Intermediary Stages with Special Consideration of Homosexuality* (1901) and Hanns Fuchs's book *Richard Wagner and Homosexuality* (1903). And it was open for many other Wagners retrieved in a classic essay by a modern scholar, Isolde Vetter, from notorious publications in the past, where he was described, among other things, as a sadist, an effeminate male running around in bisexually suggestive lace drawers, a criminally insane egotist, an epileptic, a dermatitic fetishist (!), a transvestite and hemorrhoid sufferer, a megalomaniac hysteric, a non-Nordic sensualist, a paranoiac, a graphomaniac, and a just good old plain degenerate.[46]

Even in Wagner's most intimate circle there were tremors of discontent, especially about *Mein Leben*. When Cosima wrote to King Ludwig II of Wagner's worry about the impression the "hopelessly repugnant experiences" in his life would make on the "cherished exalted one," she was herself already sounding apprehensive. "Had I not fervently implored him to say everything, everything, however embarrassing," she told the king, "he would not have taken note of many things."[47] The subjective tone of *Mein Leben* did indeed go beyond the boundaries of what was then acceptable in biography and autobiography. After obtaining a copy in 1892 that had been surreptitiously struck off by the printer of the private edition, Wagner's early biographer Mrs. Burrell, clearly expecting something different, refused to believe that Wagner could be its author and became obsessed with the idea that he was "not responsible"[48] for the book. Its uninhibited subjectivity was probably also the reason why, after his death, Cosima asked the recipients of the edition (limited to fifteen and later eighteen copies) to return the volumes to Bayreuth, where most of them were destroyed. Even the king obliged. One of Wagner's Swiss friends, Jakob Sulzer, who had known the composer well in the years after the Dresden revolution, wrote in a letter to Mathilde Wesendonck in August 1887 that he hoped *Mein Leben* would never come to light "in its authentic shape." Having been briefly privy to the first part of the memoir in its original private printing in 1870, he surmised (as Martin Gregor-Dellin suggests) that, due to the "nature of its psychological origin," the truth might not be well served. "Wagner's was an extremely subjective nature," Sulzer wrote; "his entire knowledge of the world, the entire knowledge that he wanted of the world, was what he got from the arbitrary reflection of it that he carried in his own consciousness."[49]

But that was precisely the point. Sulzer unwittingly put his finger on the reason for the existence of an autobiography that had consciously eschewed attempts to recall the past as accurately as was humanly possible in favor of a radical theodicy of selfhood. Quite apart from Wagner's deliberate attempts in his works and autobiographical writings to go far beyond the dialectical tension between the private and the public that had defined the Romantic sense of self, even the involuntary gap, which Gusdorf sees between the avowed plan of autobiography to retrace the history of a life and "its deepest intentions,"[50] is blithely overridden by Wagner, who practically from the start set out to construct himself as an evolving subjective presence at odds with the "fact" of real chronological time, fully cognizant of the philosophical implications of such a move.

That this strategy came into conflict with Wagner's ambition to bequeath to his son and to posterity the authentic narrative of a life completely formed to the point of including his own death explains the insecurities not far beneath the surface of his autobiographical writings, not to mention those of his biographers. Far too many of them strive to treat the texts as if they are "straight" narratives, only quickly to come up against a blank wall of puzzled incomprehension when the realization dawns that the narrator is not telling the truth in any simple sense of the word. There is an air of repression about it all – the ego seeking involuntarily to evade certain memories and feelings that could endanger its sense of wholeness and existence in the present – and the wounds Nietzsche and others sought to inflict on Wagner's cultural authority were no doubt the result of a shrewd perception of the remarkable psychological radicalism of the texts, including some of his letters, which made him vulnerable to gleeful, hand-rubbing posturing about the propriety of his behavior.

Nor is the problematic status of Wagner's writings about his life confined to their interpretation by his critics. Worries among his closest allies also contributed to the bifurcation of his image into the ogre of doubtful probity and "the *artist* and creator of so many immortal masterpieces, who should not and cannot be impugned,"[51] as (of all people) the editor of the 1906 edition of his "letters to a seamstress" put it, at the same time alluding to supposed sexual abnormalities that made no difference to the genius of the music. It is no accident that *Mein Leben* had to wait for the age of Freud and the "new biography" for its first public printing in 1911. But even those who read it intelligently could not dislodge the already longstanding cliché of a Wagner at once "perverse" and "great" – a grotesque parody of his own division of himself into the artist rooted in a supposedly degenerate world and his heroic Other who sought life in the "*true music*." The candor of his writings about himself and misunderstandings of their *raison d'être*, in other words, helped to create the myth of two apparently irreconcilable Wagners that is still the line of least resistance in any untroubled admiration of his art. The irony is that it was Wagner himself who first set out to challenge the apparent discrepancy. The naïve separation of the "so-called genius" (*GS* II:2) from reality, and also from a direct warts-and-all subjectivism well beyond Romanticism, was one he rejected. It is exactly this insight, however, together with his skeptical view of the role of autobiography in the nine-teenth century, that places Wagner's narratives about himself among the most remarkable and underappreciated of modern autobiographical testimonies.

2 *Meister* Richard's apprenticeship: the early operas (1833–1840)

THOMAS S. GREY

Richard Wagner's early approach to an operatic career was oblique, yet inexorable. As a boy he was raised in a *gesamtkünstlerisch* environment, so to speak – an educated bourgeois milieu that cultivated the arts both domestically and professionally. His stepfather, Ludwig Geyer, was a painter as well as an actor; among his sisters were an accomplished actress (the eldest, Rosalie) and a singer (Klara); his brother Albert was a tenor and sometime opera director; his uncle Adolf Wagner was something of a scholar and critic who had been on friendly terms with Ludwig Tieck and E.T.A. Hoffmann, though he looked less kindly on the performing arts; and the father he never knew and whose paternity remained a large question mark, Carl Friedrich Wagner, had been for his part an amateur actor and devoted theater-goer until his death in 1814. Music, in this environment, existed as the handmaiden to drama and poetry. The commingling of spoken theater and opera in the Wagner family circle was altogether characteristic of German theatrical culture in this period, similar to England and to some extent France in this respect; only the Italian repertory represented what the later Wagner might have called "absolute" opera.

According to his own later testimony, Wagner's early enthusiasms shuttled between Homer and Greek tragedy, the plays of Shakespeare, Goethe, and Schiller, the fantastic tales of Hoffmann, the music of Beethoven, and eventually the operas of Carl Maria von Weber. Indeed, the picture of his artistic development or *Bildung* as an enthusiastic dilettantism ignited by the spark of genius derives above all from Wagner's autobiographical accounts. The completion of a Shakespearean–Gothic farrago entitled *Leubald und Adelaïde*, replete with vengeful spirits and countless murders, spurred the dilatory schoolboy to learn the rudiments of theory and composition from a copy of J. B. Logier's primer on harmony and thorough-bass (accumulating in the process serious overdue fines on the copy borrowed from Friedrich Wieck's musical lending library in Leipzig), with the aim of concocting incidental music along the lines of Beethoven's for *Egmont*, as he claimed.[1] (The "spirit music" he had in mind would have been better served by Weber's *Freischütz* and *Euryanthe*, of which the former had been another youthful passion.) In the meantime the young man's Hoffmannesque musical mysticism fed itself on the Beethoven

symphonies, especially the Fifth, the Seventh, and the Ninth; a piano transcription of the complete Ninth Symphony from around 1829 (*WWV* 9)
as well as a manuscript copy of the full score attest to this infatuation.
But the capstone of Wagner's early aesthetic experiences that would point
him definitively toward opera is a more contested biographical point: a
performance by the singer-actress Wilhelmine Schröder-Devrient allegedly
in the title role of Beethoven's *Fidelio* in Leipzig in 1829. In *My Life* Wagner
puts great emphasis on his first impression of Schröder-Devrient's electri-
fying musical-theatrical persona, dating it to his sixteenth year. "When I
look back across my entire life," he wrote, "I find no event to place beside
this" (*ML* 37). The claim has been obscured by lack of evidence for the
alleged "guest performance," and by the fact that in the earlier 1843 autobiographical sketch he mentions only a later Schröder-Devrient performance
as Romeo in Bellini's *I Capuleti e i Montecchi*, in 1834, described with similar
enthusiasm but with different results. In this version, the aspiring dramatic
composer was thrown into doubts on the efficacy of the "intellectual" German
approach to opera in comparison to the more earthy, sensual, and directly
melodic idiom of the modern *bel canto* genre (*PW* I:9).

Whatever the (elusive) truth behind these two versions of the Schröder-
Devrient "epiphany," the discrepancy remains telling, for Wagner's operatic
coming-of-age coincided with a moment of great stylistic ferment in the
history of nineteenth-century opera in the years around 1830. The 1820s
had witnessed the hopeful blossoming of a new German "Romantic" genre,
starting with Weber's *Freischütz* in 1821 and the through-composed, "grand
Romantic opera" *Euryanthe* in 1823. In between these dates an 1822 revival
of *Fidelio* had, in fact, catapulted the teenaged Wilhelmine Schröder (a year
before her marriage to the actor Karl Devrient) to international celebrity
and finally convinced audiences of the viability of Beethoven's opera. In the
meantime, Louis Spohr's *Jessonda* (1823), Weber's *Oberon* (1826), and
the early works of Heinrich Marschner (*Der Vampyr* [1828], *Der Templer
und die Jüdin* [1829]) contributed to a newly successful profile of German
opera after two fallow decades since Mozart's death. German opera in this
decade was viewed in direct competition with the international successes
of Rossini. Then, by 1830, the landscape was again changing radically:
Bellini's operas from *Il pirata* (1827) to *I Capuleti* (1830), *La sonnambula*,
and *Norma* (both 1831) reasserted the international dominance of
Italian opera. A similar impact was exerted by Parisian opera, starting
with D.-F.-E. Auber's path-breaking *grand opéra* of revolutionary spectacle,
La muette de Portici (1828), followed by Rossini's *Guillaume Tell* (1829)
and Meyerbeer's *Robert le diable* (1831). And simultaneously, a new breed
of French *opéra comique* infused with the energies of Rossinian opera
and French "boulevard" melodrama was making even greater inroads on

German stages, with works such as Auber's *Fra Diavolo* (1830) and Ferdinand Hérold's *Zampa* (1831). These Italian and French works, and many more like them, traveled quickly, so that when Richard Wagner set about fashioning himself as an operatic composer in the early 1830s he was faced with a truly dizzying array of possibilities.[2] Between the alleged 1829 Leipzig *Fidelio* of Schröder-Devrient and her 1834 *Capuleti* the young Wagner found himself at an operatic crossroads.

In between these dates he managed to complete some more serious musical studies, largely under the tutelage of the Leipzig Thomaskantor, Theodor Weinlig;[3] he also attained his first practical experience in the theater as *répétiteur* (rehearsal coach) and general musical assistant to his brother Albert, an operatic tenor and stage manager, with the small but enterprising town theater of Würzburg throughout most of 1833. By the following January (1834) Richard had completed his first operatic score, a "grand Romantic opera" entitled *Die Feen* (*The Fairies*) to a libretto of his own making, based on Carlo Gozzi's "dramatic fairy tale," *La donna serpente* (*The Serpent Woman*). Thus, when Schröder-Devrient's Romeo (among other experiences) pointed out to him the complex crossroads of operatic possibility later that year, we might say that his formal apprenticeship had been concluded, and he was poised to begin his *Wanderjahre* or journeyman years. These would take him far afield, both geographically and stylistically, until he returned to his home state of Saxony in 1842. The premiere of *Der fliegende Holländer* (*The Flying Dutchman*) in Dresden at the beginning of 1843 and his appointment as Royal Saxon Kapellmeister soon thereafter would mark his elevation to the rank of "master" (as his acolytes would fondly address him in later years) in his career as musical dramatist. The remainder of this chapter is concerned with the efforts of the "apprentice" and the "journeyman," and with the early routes taken by the eventual *Meister* of Bayreuth. After outlining the external stages of the early career path across the 1830s I will try to summarize what Wagner attempted and achieved in the first three completed operas (*Die Feen*, *Das Liebesverbot* [*The Ban on Love*], *Rienzi*), and to trace some stylistic, technical, and dramatic or imaginative "leitmotifs" (including the roots of that famous Wagnerian device itself) connecting the youthful oeuvre with the canonic works of the "master."

In the footsteps of Meyerbeer

If we date Wagner's accession to the status of mature master with the premiere of *Der fliegende Holländer* and the appointment as music director in Dresden, then his *Wanderjahre* coincide precisely with the decade of his twenties, between 1833 and 1843. It was a decade rich in experiences, artistic as well as personal, but the basic stations of the emergent career can be enumerated simply enough. Upon completing *Die Feen* toward the end of his year in Würzburg, the young composer had high hopes of a premiere in Leipzig. After brief negotiations and despite the efforts of his sister Rosalie, the leading lady of spoken theater there at the time, it was ultimately declined. Before long Wagner moved on to a new post as music director for a theater troupe based in Magdeburg and to a new operatic project, a "grand Romantic comic opera" based on Shakespeare's *Measure for Measure*, which he entitled *Das Liebesverbot*. The composition of this text reflected a broader musical-aesthetic project of absorbing the lyrical and lively rhythmical impulses of Bellinian *bel canto* and of Auber's recent successes in both *grand* and *comique* genres. The result was meant to be a characteristically German synthesis of these audience-tested ingredients of foreign opera with the conscientious symphonic workmanship of native traditions. Coinciding with this new stylistic experiment was Wagner's impetuous first marriage to the actress Minna Planer and an allegiance to the hedonistic, anti-metaphysical, liberal cultural politics of the current Young German movement. The Magdeburg stint concluded with the young Wagner's second attempt at a premiere, this time of *Das Liebesverbot*. Now, as music director, he was able to engineer this himself, blithely disregarding the vast discrepancy between means and ends. What we know of the result comes from his wry account of the effort in *My Life*, which he had previously excerpted to stand in for the libretto in the original editions of his collected writings (GS I:20–31; PW VII:5–18; and ML 83, 111–19). Despite the virtually unprecedented scope of these two early scores, Wagner was soon willing to put them aside for good and chalk up all this effort to a learning experience.[4] Apart from the compositional practice afforded him by these two projects, by no means negligible, he now clearly understood the necessity of attaining a professional arena commensurate with his artistic ambitions. The model he looked to was Giacomo Meyerbeer, especially in the wake of the phenomenal success in 1836 of his second Parisian grand opera, *Les Huguenots*.

Of course, one year of assistant-conducting in Würzburg and a year and a half directing a threadbare company in Magdeburg, without any credible performance of an opera of his own, scarcely formed a sufficient basis for the great leap forward he had in mind. For several more years he toiled in the provinces, with a temporary engagement as conductor in Königsberg (1837) and a slightly longer one, further east on the Baltic coast in the German-speaking, Russian-controlled Latvian city of Riga (to the beginning of 1839). During most of his time in Riga Wagner was at work on the grand historical opera in five acts, *Rienzi*, which from the outset he regarded as his ticket out of the provinces. "Paris or bust" was now his inner mantra. And, in fact, only a few months into his very first independent appointment, in Magdeburg, he had mapped out for himself a career path modeled on Meyerbeer's that would take him from Germany to Paris by way of Italy, in order to acquire some extra polish in his handling of the operatic voice. The notion of Italy as a training ground for the German opera composer, as in the days of Handel, Gluck, Hasse, and Mozart, was by now nearly obsolete, though Meyerbeer and Otto Nicolai had still followed it. Wagner was serious about learning something from Bellini, but when he wrote in October 1834 to Theodor Apel, his closest intimate since school days, with the proposal that he accompany Richard on this cosmopolitan musical journeyman's itinerary, he was perhaps only half in earnest. He clearly entertained some hopes that his well-off young friend might help subsidize the fantasy, fueled as it was in part by their common "Young German" enthusiasm for the aesthetic-sensual paradise depicted in Heinse's *Ardinghello*, yearned for by Goethe's Mignon, and more recently popularized for German youth in the travel writings of Heinrich Laube and others. The passionate insistence of his proposal to Apel is in any case wholly characteristic. (As he confided to Apel, Minna Planer had yielded to his sexual advances less from love or desire than from a sense of helplessness in the face of his importunity.) Recalling his travels with Apel through the Bohemian countryside the previous summer, when he drafted *Das Liebesverbot*, Wagner invokes the "divine licentious-ness" that beckons beyond the Alps, at the same time merging his poetic fancies with what he sees as a practical route to success:

> Yes, my dearest Theodor, my plan is now firmly and irrevocably made. My Fairies [*Die Feen*] must be performed in 3 or 4 good theaters in order to lay the ground for my Ban on Love [*Das Liebesverbot*], which I am at present in the process of completing. I am bound to make a name for myself with this opera, and acquire both fame and fortune; and if I am lucky enough to achieve both of these, I shall go to Italy, taking them and you with me; this, I should add, will be in the spring of 1836. In Italy I shall write an Italian opera and, depending on how things turn out, maybe more than one; and then when we are tanned and strong, we shall turn to France. I'll write a French opera in Paris, and God only knows where I'll end up then! But at least I know *who* I shall be: no longer a German philistine. This career of mine must be yours as well. (*SL* 23–24, trans. emended; *SB* I:167–68)

In the event, *Das Liebesverbot* had to stand in for Italy and Italian opera (Wagner in fact transposes the setting of Shakespeare's *Measure for Measure* to Sicily), and in a very real stylistic sense it served as a bridge from Italian and lighter French styles to the grand opera already envisioned as the goal of his *Wanderjahre*. Just before taking up the Kapellmeister post in Riga, Wagner wrote directly to Meyerbeer, confirming his goals as they began to take on ever firmer outlines. (He was at the same time following up an earlier, abortive attempt to establish contact with the librettist Eugène Scribe, who he hoped would collaborate with him, as he had with Meyerbeer.) Wagner's letter of self-introduction to Meyerbeer is frank and, at the moment of its writing, undoubtedly sincere. He mentions the passion for Beethoven that first drew him to music as a vocation, but adds that, since the beginning of his fledgling career in opera, "my views on the present state of music, and above all dramatic music, have undergone a significant change, and it would be futile of me to deny that it was your works which suggested this new direction to me" (letter of 4 February 1837; *SL* 42). Nor is it empty flattery when he continues: "in you I behold the perfect embodiment of the task that confronts the German artist, a task you have solved by dint of having mastered the merits of the Italian and French Schools in order to give *universal* validity to the products of that genius. This, then, is what more or less set me upon my present course" (*SL* 42–43).[5]

With this "Parisian" grand opera, *Rienzi*, on his own (for now, German) text about halfway completed, Wagner finally launched himself and his wife Minna on an adventurous sea voyage from East Prussia to Paris in the summer of 1839. *Rienzi* was not fated to see the boards of the Paris opera until 1869, by which time it was a relic of a former life. The two and a half years Wagner spent in Paris were a period of frustration and hardship. To some extent he continued to absorb the lessons of French grand opera, a genre whose ambitious scale, effective dramaturgy, scenic plenitude, and rich stylistic palette he still admired. But for the most part, these lessons had been learned even before Wagner arrived in Paris; the net result of the Parisian sojourn was rather to reorient the composer toward his German Romantic roots, instrumental (Beethoven) as well as operatic (Weber, et al.). The composition of *Der fliegende Holländer* during the end of the Paris stay was the fruit of this reaction, and even *Rienzi* was to achieve its first performance, and establish its composer's fame at last, back in his childhood home of Dresden.[6]

Richard Wagner, the poet and the composer (*Die Feen*)

While Wagner was still an infant the Napoleonic armies waged battles outside Dresden (August 1813) and Leipzig (October 1813). The Battle of Leipzig, also called the Völkerschlacht or Battle of Nations, sealed Napoleon's defeat in central Europe. Only now did Austria and Saxony join in the Prussian resistance to Napoleon, and the Battle of Leipzig became a patriotic rallying point for the rest of the century. E.T.A. Hoffmann, who almost exactly crossed paths with the Wagner family in moving from Dresden to Leipzig at the end of the year, recalled these recent conflicts in framing his famous dialogue between the German poet, Ferdinand, and his musician friend, Ludwig, on the nature of opera and its prospects in German culture of the time, "The Poet and the Composer." Since Richard Wagner developed a vivid awareness of Hoffmann during his early teens (Hoffmann had also befriended Richard's uncle Adolf, whom he addressed familiarly as "Alf"), one can't help but suppose that Hoffmann's dialogic essay on the aesthetics of Romantic opera made a significant impact on the young man, intent on proving himself both as a dramatist and as a musician.

At the center of Hoffmann's vignette is a proposal by Ludwig (the composer) about the suitability of Carlo Gozzi's "dramatic fairy tales" or fables (*fiabe teatrali*, 1760–65) as the basis for Romantic opera libretti, with their fanciful admixture of the comic, the serious, and the fantastic. The dialogue includes a lengthy précis of *The Raven* (*Il corvo*), of which uncle Adolf Wagner himself happens to have made a German translation (as *Der Rabe*). The young Richard Wagner's choice of another Gozzi "tale," *La donna serpente*, as the basis of his first completed opera, *Die Feen*, points almost ineluctably to Hoffmann's influence. Hoffmann's composer Ludwig resists the notion of devising his own libretto, even though he is full of opinions on what should go into one; he is too much the pure musician to be bothered with fussing over rhyme schemes, meter, and the like. Wagner, of course, overleaped such scruples. First, he rechristened the main characters of Gozzi's play, whose names reflect the *Arabian Nights* inspiration of this *fiaba* and others (Farruscad, Cherestanì, Canzade, Rezia, etc.), with Germanic and Ossianic names taken over from his early Gothic horror-play, *Die Hochzeit*, a text he had completed but then discarded upon its meeting with the strong disapproval of his sister Rosalie. The fairy princess becomes Ada, her mortal suitor is called Arindal, his strong and noble sister, Lora, and her beloved warrior, Morald. The *commedia* masks that formed an integral part of Gozzi's plays, in a conscious homage to Venetian traditions, are transformed into a pair of *Singspiel* comedians, Gernot and Drolla. A character of indeterminate status named Gunther mediates between them and the serious roles.

At the core of the story is the Ur-Romantic motif of the supernatural being in love with a human, already the subject of Hoffmann's own opera, *Undine*, after the influential story of the Baron de la Motte Fouqué.[7] (Wagner elaborated the motif again in *Lohengrin* and echoed it throughout his oeuvre in the pairings of the Dutchman and Senta, Venus and Tannhäuser, Brünnhilde and Siegfried, perhaps even Kundry and Parsifal.) Wagner also found in Gozzi the motif of the forbidden question: like Lohengrin, the fairy princess Cherestanì (Wagner's Ada) insists that her mortal partner not ask after her name or her "kind." This stricture has already been broken before the opera begins, however, and two further series of trials of the mortal prince, Arindal, structure the second and third acts of both Gozzi's and Wagner's dramas. First he must promise not to curse her, despite the exhibition of apparently abominable acts of cruelty against his children and his kingdom. His failure of this test, in Act 2, turns Cherestanì into a loathsome serpent (in Gozzi), or into a lifeless statue (in Wagner). In the last set of trials, individual combat against supernatural foes, the prince is aided by the secret counsel of a beneficent wizard (Gozzi) or magical talismans provided by the same (Wagner). But Wagner exchanges Gozzi's Jungian archetype of the beloved female object become life-threatening monster (later alluded to in details of *Siegfried*, Acts 2 and 3) for the more traditional operatic motif of Orpheus. His Arindal reanimates the petrified Ada through song, to the accompaniment of a magic lyre or harp. Instead of winning her over to mortality, however, he joins her in the Romantic fairy realm, leaving his kingdom and all worldly concerns to his sister, Lora, and her husband. From the beginning, Wagner's hero is preoccupied with love and the forms of its expression, as well as with guilt and redemption. Like many of Wagner's future heroes, he is not of this world.[8]

The elements of chivalric romance and magic spectacle in the Gozzi source look back to the knights and sorceresses of Tasso or Ariosto, but Wagner reimagines that world through the stylistic lens of works such as Weber's *Euryanthe* and *Oberon*, Louis Spohr's *Jessonda*, and Marschner's *Hans Heiling* (which shares the Romantic dilemma of a mixed fairy/mortal marriage, though it did not premiere until after he had already begun composing *Die Feen*). The spirit of Mozart's *Zauberflöte* stands somewhere in the background of it all, though only really audible in the comic duet scene for Gernot and Drolla in Act 2. And while *Die Feen* shares nothing of its "realistic" modern melodrama, the musico-dramatic energies of *Fidelio* are a still more important source of inspiration. The measure of the apprentice's achievement can best be read from the solo scenes (arias) of the protagonists, Ada and Arindal, anticipating the extended monologues often at the dramatic heart of the later music dramas, and from the ambitiously scaled ensemble finales.

Arindal's entrance aria ("Wo find ich dich, wo wird mir Trost") lamenting the sudden disappearance of Ada (when he posed the "forbidden question") seems to take its cue from the scene and aria of Lysiart, the jealous and conscience-tormented villain of Weber's *Euryanthe*, which opens the second act.[9] Both are agitated, multisection soliloquies in C minor, enfolding a restful, wistful interlude before they press on to a furious and nihilistic conclusion. Wagner would later mine Lysiart's aria again in the Flying Dutchman's opening monologue, another tormented

C-minor *scena*; all three scenes involve a similar dying-out effect at the end. Still more freely constructed than Lysiart's "Vengeance" aria is Arindal's "mad scene" (the scene and aria, "Halloh! Halloh! Lasst alle Hunde los!") in Act 3 of *Die Feen*. In the introductory F-minor *scena* he relives the first discovery of his fairy wife, Ada, whom he hunted in the shape of a deer. In his fevered recreation of the scene, he imagines that he kills her before learning who/what she is. Again there is an internal cantabile episode, here a vision of immortal transfiguration (in E major, the key associated with the fairy realm throughout the opera). When this vision fades, the number dissolves into arioso fragments in F minor, as Arindal sinks back unconscious. The largest solo number is Ada's in Act 2. Like those of Arindal, the scene begins as an agitated monologue, and moves, in this case, to an extended allegro in D major expressing a heroic resolve in gestures reminiscent of "Ich folg' dem innern Triebe," the final phase of Leonore's great scene and aria in *Fidelio*. In this case, Ada projects the heroic resolve onto Arindal, who will in fact disappoint her in this regard.

Arindal's failure to withstand the tests imposed on him by Ada is the subject of the opera's most ambitious musico-dramatic conception, the finale to Act 2, which follows directly on her big scene and aria. Italian opera since Rossini could furnish models for considerably extended finales, but the dramatic material of Wagner's second act finale is too manifold and discursive to be contained in the orderly progression of those models. The energetic stretta in which the finale issues ("Ertönet, Jubelklänge, zum Himmelhoch empor") celebrates a military victory that also serves to highlight Arindal's personal failure and despair. This music draws on the martial idiom of Spontini's finales and forms an audible bridge between those and the finales of *Rienzi* or Act 1 of *Lohengrin*. The victory is the outcome of an offstage battle that initiates this Act 2 finale. (That Arindal's foes and their motives for attack are left utterly vague is partly the fault of the fairy-tale source; Gozzi simply calls them "Moors," forgetful of the Arabian character of his own hero's milieu.) In between, Arindal is reunited with his children from Ada, only to see them cast into a fiery furnace, then to see his armies hopelessly routed – both illusions created by Ada to test his will power. Believing all is lost, Arindal curses Ada, thereby losing her and discovering (to his further distress) the illusory nature of those catastrophes. Only now does Ada reveal her supernatural origin – not in response to the "forbidden question," which we never hear posed, in fact. We can hardly be surprised if the net effect is somewhat diffuse. Nonetheless, the sequence of Ada's *gran scena* and this finale leaves no doubt of the young composer's natural feeling for musical drama and his ambition to work on an unprecedented scale.

"Ja, glühend wie des Südens Hauch" (*Das Liebesverbot*)

Almost as soon as he had completed *Die Feen*, Wagner began to feel dissatisfied with it or, rather, with what he was beginning to regard as the awkward, pedantic, provincial elements of German opera of the day. The rejection of his score by the Leipzig theater administration and, at about the same time, the experience of Schröder-Devrient as Romeo in Bellini's *Capuleti* conspired to send him in a new direction, one further-more in harmony with the new climate of Young German rebellion against bourgeois values and academic learning.[10] Central to the Young German creed was the denunciation of perceived hypocrisy in modern German society, politics, and culture. The intellectual postures of idealist metaphysics were to be exposed as such, and the physical realities of life and art celebrated instead. It was in this spirit that Wagner adapted Shakespeare's *Measure for Measure* to the libretto of his next opera, *Das Liebesverbot*.

In Shakespeare's famously grim "comedy," the puritanical Angelo has been deputized to serve in place of the Duke of Vienna, who charges Angelo with improving the morals of the city while he, in fact, stays behind to observe in the disguise of a friar. When a generally upstanding young nobleman, Claudio, is caught in the snares of Angelo's draconian new laws suppressing fornication, Claudio's sister Isabella, destined for the convent, is conscripted to plead on his behalf. Angelo's own dormant or suppressed desires are enflamed by Isabella's beauty and chastity; he agrees to suspend her brother's death sentence if she will yield her own person in return. The fiancée whom Angelo had once callously rejected, Mariana, is substituted for Isabella (the "bed trick" popularized by the tales of Boccaccio). After Angelo compounds his guilt by attempting to proceed with Claudio's execution, Isabella denounces him to the Duke, who has witnessed the whole affair while incognito.

Wagner preserves most of the plot and main characters (except the Duke, who is now truly absent); yet he transposes the whole to a distinctly brighter key and register. Shakespeare's play represents sexual desire as troublesome, at best, and potentially degrading, if not inherently sinful. It shares a contemporary assumption, as Katharine E. Maus notes, that morality and sexual conduct "could and should be legislated."[11] Wagner, on the other hand, uses Angelo's sexual repression and hypocrisy to preach free love and to denounce the legislation of morality altogether. He moves the setting to Palermo, probably influenced in part by the picturesque Sicilian and Neapolitan settings of such contemporary favorites as *Robert le diable*, *Zampa*, and *La muette de Portici*. Angelo, however, is turned into a German regent, "Friedrich" (presumably of Hohenstaufen extraction), pointing up the thematic contrast between hypocritical "German" prudishness and Mediterranean naturalness or spontaneity. This contrast relates likewise to the lesson at hand in matters of operatic style. To drive home the point, Wagner has Isabella betrothed in the end not to the virtuous Duke, but to the libertine Lucio (here, Luzio, who is not quite the unregenerate rogue of *Measure for Measure*).[12] Wagner makes further use of his Italian setting to recast the conflict more broadly as one between a "carnivalesque" popular spirit and the agents of authority and oppression: in Palermo, Friedrich's "ban on love" is allied to an edict suppressing the rites of carnival.[13]

Wagner, for his part, had suddenly come to feel himself oppressed or hemmed in by the false authority of German music. He did not question its authority in the instrumental realm, where Beethoven would always reign supreme. But he began to question whether its values were sufficiently well suited to the exigencies of drama and of operatic singing. Schröder-Devrient's performance of Romeo in Bellini's opera (no doubt an atypical and in some sense very "German" interpretation) led him to question, as he afterwards recalled, "the choice of means that could lead to a great success" in the theater:

> While I was far from overestimating Bellini's own achievement, it none the less struck me that the stuff from which his music was made was better calculated to create a warm, living impression than was the fussy, overconscientious approach with which we Germans thought to achieve a dramatic truth that was in reality merely the strained appearance of such "truth." The lazy, characterless quality of our modern Italians, no less than the light frivolity of the new French school, seemed to challenge us serious, conscientious Germans to appropriate the better, more effective aspects of our rivals' music in order to outstrip them decisively in the production of true works of art.   ("Autobiographical Sketch," *GS* I:9–10)

Thus, *Das Liebesverbot* is not an attempt to write an Italian opera according to the "Meyerbeerian" plan Wagner had proposed to Apel, nor to write an *opéra comique* of the sort that had become a staple of the German stage in the works of Boieldieu, Hérold, and Auber. Rather, it seeks to combine Bellinian lyricism, the taught rhythmic energy of post-Rossinian choruses, the supple, discreetly accompanied *parlando* dialogue of Auber's comedies, and the whole stylistic palette of Auber's historical drama *La muette de Portici*, while infusing all of these with Wagner's abiding sense of "solid German workmanship."

The overture is already emblematic in this regard. It begins with deliberate frivolity, quoting Luzio's carnival song from the Act 2 finale; but almost immediately this music becomes involved in acts of dramatic signification in the German manner, when the motive of Friedrich's Ban on Love (Example 2.1) tries to stop the carnival song in its tracks. Luzio's song theme mocks and taunts the motive of authority, until both are swept away by the theme of Friedrich's illicit passion (Wagner's version of a

Ex. 2.1

[Clarinet, Bassoon, Trombone, Ophicleide, Strings]

Rossini crescendo). The loose structure tends toward the potpourri of the *opéra comique* overture, but again Wagner cannot resist episodes of Germanic harmonic development, precipitated by the "signifying" motive of Friedrich's Ban. Luzio's song and Friedrich's "passionate" crescendo have in common a harmonic formula that permeates the score, probably under the influence of Hérold's *Zampa*, which was very much in Wagner's ears in this period: the formula is a simple progression from I to IV by way of a chromatic passing tone (♯5, or ♭6 descending, creating either a passing augmented triad or minor subdominant), usually grounded by a tonic pedal. (See Examples 2.2a, 2.2b, and 2.2c, including a version from the Act 1 finale of *Zampa* used in the overture to that work; Hérold's overture includes a similar "signifying" interruption of a rollicking theme, intimating the vengeance wrought by the statue of the betrayed Alice upon the libertine pirate Zampa.) This harmonic formula is not used as a conscious "motive," like that of Friedrich's Ban – Wagner seems rather to have reacted instinctively to its diastolic quality, a broad swelling or intake and outtake of breath, which musical-expressive gesture he manages to relate to the whole spectrum of passions represented in his comedy.

In solo and duet scenes Wagner applies the current Italian structures in flexible, dramatically canny ways.[14] The duet encompassing Isabella's interview with her imprisoned brother Claudio at the opening of Act 2 (no. 7) moves quickly toward a cabaletta-like section with solo and duo strophes ("Ha welch ein Tod für Lieb' und Ehre") expressing Claudio's proud resolve to lay down his life for Isabella's honor. The tone and form of the cabaletta suggest the matter is settled, when Claudio interrupts his sister with his doubts. He concludes the scene with an energetic attempt to restore the C-major heroics of the cabaletta, recalling its use of that same harmonic formula described above ("O Schwester sieh', O sieh' auf meine Reue!"), though he is unable to repair the breach. Wagner creates a special urgency by ending the scene, as he would later do sometimes in *Rienzi*, with a condensed stretta in place of a whole two-strophe cabaletta. Friedrich's scene and aria (no. 10) intensify through words and music Angelo's speeches in both scene 2 and scene 4 of Act 2 of *Measure for*

Ex. 2.2a

Ex. 2.2b

Ex. 2.2c

Measure reflecting on his unexpected passion. The scene is punctuated with references to the Ban on Love motive, now projecting Friedrich's own tormented conscience. The text of his cantabile, "Ja, glühend wie des Südens Hauch brennt mir die Flamme in der Brust" ("Yes, like the warm breath of the southern breeze, this flame burns in my breast") might be taken as a motto of Wagner's own discovery of the expressive value of the "Southern" idioms he had once contemned, even if this chromatically swelling, rather densely textured music is one of the score's less Italianate moments. A rapturous cabaletta ("O Wonne, himmlisches Entzücken") is precipitated in the classic manner by the delivery of a message: Isabella's feigned consent to his proposal. Tripping "carnival" music taunts his conscience in between the strophes of the cabaletta, and the second strophe is dramatically interrupted by thoughts of Claudio's fate (and relevant musical reminiscences). In a new Wagnerian gesture, Friedrich, quite unlike Shakespeare's Angelo, resolves not only to carry out Claudio's sentence but also to end his own life once he has indulged his forbidden passion. Thoughts of physical desire and annihilation mingle in a delirious frenzy: "Wie trag' ich Qualen und Entzücken, es harret Tod und Wollust mein" ("How can I bear these torments and delights; death and pleasure await me").[15] Leading into this final phase of the aria is a development of a short chromatic figure that anticipates, appropriately enough, moments of *Tristan und Isolde* (Example 2.3).

Das Liebesverbot betrays something of an identity complex – one that reflects that of Wagner himself as a novice opera composer in the 1830s. Despite the Italianisms in the numbers just described, the work is in essence a German *opéra comique* – unrelated, that is, to a *Singspiel* tradition – with scarcely concealed aspirations to grand opera. The few bits of spoken dialogue that remain are entirely out of proportion to the rest, almost like accidental relics of some earlier plan. Certainly the comic portions of the score model themselves on Auber's lighter comic style, though lightness is a quality Wagner attains only with much effort, if at all.[16] The final sequence of numbers in Act 1 is representative of the whole stylistic spectrum of the score, as well as the composer's ambitions in the direction of a new kind of through-composed drama. The Act 1 finale (no. 6) follows a loose concatenation headed "Aria, Duet, Trio and Ensemble" (no. 5) without a break, and together they probably include as many notes as constitute some entire operas in Wagner's early repertory. The first part, involving the comic characters Brighella, Pontio Pilato, and Dorella (the former two roughly equivalent to Shakespeare's Elbow and Pompey), shows Wagner trying to master the kind of fleet, motivically accompanied conversation and bouncy dance song he knew from works like Auber's *Fra Diavolo, Le Maçon,* or *Lestocq,* while the finale emulates the massed choral

Ex. 2.3

scenes of *La muette de Portici*. The element of popular insurrection informing the finales of both Acts 1 and 2 is clearly derived from that model, and has nothing to do with Shakespeare's play.

Isabella's role in the Act 1 finale probably owes more than a little to the impact of Wilhelmine Schröder-Devrient. Her dramatic intervention on behalf of her brother Claudio, fighting her way through an unruly crowd to confront Friedrich, paraphrases Leonore's climactic utterance in *Fidelio*, confronting the tyrannous Pizarro: "Töt erst sein Weib!" ("Erst hört noch mich! Ich bin die Schwester," Example 2.4). In a tripartite aria, embedded in the first finale, Wagner's Isabella begins by pleading the quality of mercy but ends with a veritable paean to erotic love, offering a much franker provocation of Friedrich's desire that anything uttered by Shakespeare's more circumspect heroine. (This modification of the role

Ex. 2.4

again suggests the musical and dramatic ardor for which Schröder-Devrient was so celebrated, and perhaps something of her personal reputation as a passionate, liberated woman which clearly fascinated the young Wagner as well.) He reframes the central confrontation of Isabella and Angelo/Friedrich in grand-operatic terms, within the public arena of massed chorus and ensemble. Her initial plea and his indecent proposal take place aside, but then Isabella invites back the crowd in an attempt to denounce Friedrich. In foiling this ("Who will believe thee, Isabel? My unsoiled name . . . will so your accusation overweigh that you shall stifle in your own report . . . My false o'erweighs your true," as Angelo argues) Friedrich precipitates a broad *adagio concertato* movement, converting to an energetic ensemble and choral stretta of truly delirious proportions when Isabella conceives the plan of substituting the betrayed Mariana for herself as a means of conferring justice upon all.[17]

A diploma in grand opera (*Rienzi*)

However much Wagner revised the tone of *Measure for Measure* toward a spirit of carnivalesque hedonism and rebellion in *Das Liebesverbot*, he still responded to the essential gravity of Shakespeare's play. The frenzied excess of the Act 1 finale is not that of Rossinian buffa; Wagner's compositional eye is already trained on grand opera. By the time he completed *Rienzi* in 1840, and certainly by the time of its premiere in 1842, his artistic preoccupations had moved on, or back, to the question of a specifically German opera, and how to reform and expand the "Romantic" genre he had begun with in *Die Feen*. But in the meantime, during the later 1830s, Wagner was intent on mastering the prestigious genre of the moment: French grand opera. The truly enthusiastic reception of *Rienzi* in Dresden in the final months of 1842 was the breakthrough for which Wagner had been waiting so long and working so hard. This success, sealed by the appointment as Royal Saxon Kapellmeister several months later, was a diploma of sorts recognizing the achievements of the aspiring composer, librettist, and conductor: the *Meisterbrief* or master's certificate that formalized the completion of a strenuous "course" in contemporary operatic genres. (Ironically, the work he himself regarded as true evidence of an original mastery – *Der fliegende Holländer* – received scant initial acclaim and was largely ignored by the public for some decades.)

Rienzi was the second of two projects in the field of grand opera, both derived from recent historical novels. In the summer of 1836 Wagner devised a scenario based on Heinrich König's novel *Die hohe Braut*, concerning love across class lines: Bianca, the "noble bride" of the title, loves a commoner, Giuseppe, who becomes swept up in conspiracy and revolt. Set in Italian-ruled Savoy of the 1790s and capitalizing on the picturesque background of the Alpes Maritimes and the French Riviera, the *Hohe Braut* project continued the emulation of *La muette de Portici* begun in *Das Liebesverbot*; Wagner confidently sent his scenario off to Eugène Scribe in Paris, thinking thus to lay the groundwork for the great Parisian campaign he was beginning to plot in his mind. A year later (summer 1837) Wagner had abandoned this first "Parisian" project and moved on to Bulwer-Lytton's novel of medieval Rome, *Rienzi, Last of the Tribunes*. Bulwer-Lytton's previous success, *The Last Days of Pompeii*, had proven the author's affinity with grand-operatic drama and spectacle, but the moral and political conflicts between the idealistic *Volkstribun* Rienzi, the corrupt nobility, and the plebeian leaders spoke more to Wagner's dramatic instincts.[18]

With *Rienzi* Wagner finally put aside the model of Auber's *La muette* and turned to others better suited to the gravitas of his Roman subject: Spontini's proto-grand operas (*La vestale, Fernand Cortez, Olympie*) and *La Juive* of Scribe and Halévy (1835). In May 1836 Wagner heard Spontini conduct *Fernand Cortez* in Berlin. The music and above all the performance provided a critical impetus. The "exceptionally precise, fiery and superbly organized way the whole work was brought off" was a revelation, he recalls; it gave him a whole new picture of the potential "dignity of major theatrical undertakings, which in all their [constituent] parts could be elevated by alert rhythmic control into a singular and incomparable form of art" (*ML* 124). Appropriate to its themes of inspired leadership and the renewal of ancient Roman pomp and civic virtue, *Rienzi* was conceived in the spirit of a directorial "total artwork" after the example of Spontini.[19]

The drama of Rienzi's struggles with feuding noble clans and with the Vatican's claims to secular power in fourteenth-century Rome (only loosely modeled on the historical figure of Cola di Rienzo), the frequent appeals to the "glory that was Rome," and a post-revolutionary bourgeois skepticism toward the power of the "mob" as well as the old clergy allowed Wagner to draw on the musical-dramatic ambience of both *La vestale* and *La Juive*.[20] The portrait of a fickle crowd – alternately enthusiastic, cowed, and unruly – still benefits from the example of *La muette*, supplemented possibly by impressions of Meyerbeer's *Les Huguenots* (1836).[21] The role of Rienzi, closely identified with the principal tenor of the Dresden royal opera, Josef Tichatschek, is regarded as the starting point of the Wagnerian Heldentenor as vocal *Fach*, however much the melodic idiom differs from roles like Siegfried or Tristan. To avoid a competing heroic tenor role, Wagner casts the young patrician Adriano as a mezzo-soprano trouser role. We might detect shades of the heroic castrato in this casting, but the composer was inspired rather by the Romeo and Fidelio of Schröder-Devrient (she also created the role of Adriano). The soprano role of Rienzi's sister, Irene, remains more in the background. As the portrait of a heroically devoted sister, however, she provides an interesting link between the earlier figures of Lora (Arindal's warrior-sister in *Die Feen*) and Isabella in *Das Liebesverbot* and the future Volsung twin, Sieglinde, in *Die Walküre* – a motif that has been related to Wagner's deep youthful devotion to his actress sister, Rosalie.[22] At the drama's climax Irene sacrifices Adriano's love in order to stand by her brother when – betrayed by the nobles, the church, and the people alike – he faces immolation in the burning Capitol.

The vocal achievements of the Dresden cast, a splendid *mise-en-scène* including as much (or more) ballet and general panoply than anything to be seen in Paris, a score synthesizing the most effective ingredients of modern operatic styles, and an expertly constructed (if sprawling) dramatic libretto all contributed to Wagner's first signal success. That was in October 1842, when he had already completed the score of *Der fliegende Holländer*. That next, more "radical" work would have to ride rather feebly on the coattails of *Rienzi*'s fame. Eventually, the more durable success of the "Dresden" operas, *Tannhäuser* and *Lohengrin*, and of the subsequent music dramas, would consign *Rienzi* to the margins of the repertoire.

The posthumous fame of *Rienzi* is linked in some part to the name of Adolf Hitler. According to a much-cited account by Hitler's youthful associate, August Kubizek, the future Führer experienced something akin to an epiphany on hearing and seeing this work in the early years of the twentieth century: "In that hour it all began."[23] As recorded by Kubizek, the remark leaves much open to interpretation ("it," for example). But even setting aside the nationalistic totem Wagner and his oeuvre had become in the years before World War I, it is not difficult to see how Hitler might have been mesmerized by *Rienzi*'s theatrical embodiment of a charismatic *Führerprinzip*. He leaves the stage after his opening scenes with the messianic words: "The hour approaches, my high calling summons me . . . Soon you will see me again; my mission approaches its completion."[24] Then, toward the beginning of the Act 1 finale, he makes a grand re-entry from the church of the Lateran, "in full armor but with his head bared." Preparing this entry is an a cappella hymn to the "reawakening" of Rome's freedom and glory after a millennium of shame and oppression. The people, and the orchestra, greet him ecstatically, acclaiming him their new king. Rienzi demurs, and accepts instead the ancient republican title of "people's tribune." In every step of Rienzi's career – from this acclamation as leader and savior of the *Volk*, through military struggle, violent suppression of mutinous factions, betrayal, and the final immolation at the hands of a world that has failed to follow his vision – Hitler would doubtless have found sustenance for his fantasies. Whether this sustenance was primarily aesthetic, psychological, or political is another question; what it says about his understanding of Wagner's larger achievement is another question, too.

"Grand opera," Wagner frankly confessed in his 1851 *Communication to My Friends*, "stood before me, with all its scenic-musical display, its effect-laden and massively scaled musical passions." His intent, he adds, was "not simply to imitate it, but to outdo all previous examples through a reckless outlay of means" (*GS* IV:258). As we have seen, a similar impulse informed his operas from the very beginning.[25] With *Rienzi*, however, Wagner was at least able to purge himself of the impulse. Now he had absorbed, synthesized, and "outdone" all the available models and could turn his efforts toward becoming the figure we think of today as Wagner. It is crucial to remember, however, that the Wagnerian "music drama" was not an experiment conducted in the isolation of some kind of Faustian aesthetic laboratory. Without Wagner's immersion in the generic and stylistic achievements of his immediate predecessors throughout his first creative decade, the music drama as we know it would never have succeeded, or even materialized.

Like its models, *Rienzi* is dominated by ensemble numbers, and above all by its extended choral-ensemble finales. Each of the five acts has a substantial finale encompassing some mixture of ceremony, lyric expression, and action – the later finales (Acts 4 and 5) being more compact and the central ones (Acts 2 and 3) the most expansive, after the dramaturgical precepts of Eugène Scribe and his collaborators. The score includes three trio scenes (the later two, in Acts 2 and 4, involving considerable choral participation), two duet scenes (Adriano and Irene in Act 1, Rienzi and Irene in Act 5), and only two very concentrated solo scenes: the aria of the conscience-wracked Adriano in Act 3 and Rienzi's famous prayer beginning Act 5. Adriano's aria is a concise adaptation of the Bellinian model: a rueful cantabile reverie ("In seiner Blüte bleicht mein Leben") is framed by anxious responses to the noises of the plebeian–patrician conflict offstage, and the number concludes with the mere vestige of a cabaletta ("Du Gnadengott ... Mit Kraft und Segen waffne mich!"), reproducing the gesture and function but not the structure of the type. To put this further in proportion: Adriano's aria and Rienzi's prayer account for all of fifteen pages within the nearly six hundred of the Breitkopf and Härtel vocal score. (Such proportions are obviously very far removed from the *opera seria* of a century earlier.) The other end of the spectrum is represented by the Act 2 finale, with its massive pantomime and ballet.[26] At the height of his brief civic glory, Rienzi stages for his new subjects the story of Tarquin's rape of Lucretia, the vanquishing of tyranny led by Brutus, and a series of games and dances illustrating the spiritual communion between the old Rome and the new. The patricians' assassination attempt on the tribune, their sentencing, and Rienzi's ill-advised clemency comprise the various phases of ensemble and chorus that conclude the act. Here and elsewhere, the heavily scored, march-based choral sequences are cast in an updated Spontinian idiom.

It is likely that when Wagner composed the first two acts of *Rienzi*, while still in Germany, he knew no more of Meyerbeer than *Robert le diable*. By the time he completed the later acts in Paris (1840) he had certainly become acquainted with *Les Huguenots*. His admiration of Meyerbeer's "gigantic, almost oppressive expansion of forms" (in a contemporary unpublished essay on *Les Huguenots*) is undoubtedly sincere. It reflects just the kind of thing he was striving for in *Rienzi*, as does his praise for the famous "consecration of the daggers" ensemble in Act 4:

> Just consider how the composer has succeeded in maintaining a continuous intensification of excitement [*fortwährende Steigerung*] throughout this

tremendously extended number, never lapsing for a moment, but arriving, after a furiously impassioned outburst, at the highest fever pitch, the very ideal of fanatical expression!   (*SSD* XII:29–30)

The Trio and Chorus (no. 11) in Wagner's own Act 4 (a nocturnal conspiracy between Adriano and the disaffected Roman magistrates, Cecco and Baroncelli) were surely composed with Meyerbeer's ensemble in mind. Some of his greatest achievements – the recognition scene of Siegmund and Sieglinde in Act 1 of *Die Walküre*, the love scene at the center of *Tristan und Isolde*, or the concluding scene of Act 2 in *Götterdämmerung* – represent the natural evolution of this same ideal. The genealogy is most obvious in the *Götterdämmerung* example, a conspiratorial trio for Hagen, Gunther, and Brünnhilde that makes no attempt to disguise its roots in grand opera, while its motivic and harmonic language integrate it securely in the musico-dramatic world of the *Ring*.

Some leitmotifs

The overture to *Rienzi* begins with a sustained solo trumpet tone, porten-tously swelling and twice repeated. We learn the significance of this sound at the end of the third scene, when it intrudes on the just finished love duet of Irene and Adriano. "What sound is that?" she asks, unnerved ("Was für ein Klang?"). "How dreadful," he replies ("Wie schauerlich!"); "That was the war-call of the Colonnas." *Rienzi* is full of such effects: the alarums and tocsins that were a fixture in the sonic landscape of grand opera, along with hunting calls, chanting monks, and other kinds of playing and sing-ing that mediated between the stage and the implied spaces behind or beyond. At the same time, the frisson felt by Irene and Adriano at this dreadful, disembodied tone recalls the experiences of Wagner as a hyper-sensitive or hyperacute Romantic child responding to "uncanny" musical impressions, such as the tuning of the orchestra in the Grosser Garten in Dresden ("the fifths on the violin struck me as a greeting from another world") or the tones of an unseen violin emanating from a palace in the Ostraallee and strangely mingling with the ornamental garlands of flowers and mute instruments adorning the exterior (*ML* 29–30).[27] From the beginning, that is, he was alert to the power of musical tones to produce strong "intimations," as well as to awaken memories. This, of course, was a power that he would harness in the "leitmotif," the technique so closely identified with the later music dramas.

     In concluding this overview of the early operas, let us consider a few ways in which they prefigure this technique of musical "anticipation and recollection," as well as some other striking anticipations here of mythic or psychological motifs that would be recalled and transformed in the mature oeuvre.

Scholarly-critical consensus views the full-fledged Wagnerian leitmotif technique as a product of the *Ring* cycle. It was in anticipation of the *Ring*, indeed, that the composer theorized the concept in part 3 of *Opera and Drama* (1851).[28] A broader practice of thematic-melodic "reminiscence" or quotation in opera, however, extends back to the late eighteenth century. By the 1830s and 1840s the idea of treating selected melodic ideas as a special class of dramatic "signifier" was not rare; nor, on the other hand, was it especially common. No one before Wagner, certainly, thought to develop it into a dual compositional and semiotic "system." Just as certainly, Wagner was giving serious thought to the possibilities of such "signifying" musical motives in his earliest works.

Rienzi, the last of the three early operas, actually makes the least use of such recurring musical themes, apart from a broad family of signals, fanfares, and martial themes that characterizes the score. If we do not count the citation of themes from the opera within the overture (Rienzi's Prayer and several choral march themes), there are only two recurring motives in the score. Most evident is Rienzi's call to arms, "Santo spirito, cavaliere!" (Example 2.5). More of a motto or a "device," in the heraldic sense, than a motive susceptible to development, it is designed as a simple call-and-response formula. (In the overture and the Act 3 battle sequence it is, however, subject to some mimetic distortions and struggles.) The other theme belongs to the category of the "stage curse" that plays a large role in the genesis of the operatic leitmotif. This is the oath Rienzi previously swore to himself to avenge the slaughter of a younger brother, an innocent bystander to the patricians' reckless feuding: "Woe to him who has shed a kinsman's blood!" (Example 2.6). In character and significance this idea forms a natural obverse of the "Santo spirito" motto; in outlining a portentous half-cadence in the minor mode, it sets a model for a number of later leitmotifs. On the whole, though, the extroverted historical drama of *Rienzi* did not seem to Wagner the appropriate place for experimenting with subtleties of motivic reminiscence.

More is attempted in the way of motivic recall in the very first opera, *Die Feen*, due partly to its ancestry in Weber's operas, no doubt. Despite the turn away from those models in *Das Liebesverbot*, the second opera makes a great deal of at least one particular motive. The "title" theme (so to speak) – signifying the suppression of carnival and carnal love and, more generally, the hypocrisy of the law and its oppression of individual freedoms (see Example 2.1) – is recalled and developed on a number of occasions throughout the score.

Ex. 2.5

San - to spi - ri-to ca - va - lie - re! San - to spi - ri-to ca - va - lie - re!

Ex. 2.6

Weh' dem, der ein ver-wan - dtes Blut zu rä - chen hat!

In *Die Feen*, the treatment of the "fairy march" figure in terms of scoring, key, and dynamics looks forward in appropriate ways to the motivic emblem of the title character in *Lohengrin*. The slow introduction to the overture introduces the "authentic" version, in E major, whose nobility is also something diminutive, delicate, and far away (Example 2.7a). When Ada ponders in her Act 2 aria the option of abandoning her doomed mortal love and returning whence she came, the miniature march is recalled in similar scoring and dynamics, freely developed and ending back in E ("Ich könnte Allem mich entziehn . . . in ew'ger Schöne unsterblich, unverwelklich blühn!"). However, when she is acclaimed queen of her realm in the finale to Act 1 and her higher nature is first revealed to the human characters, the march-theme grows in volume and moves to C major (Example 2.7b shows the orchestral reiteration as she is carried away in a triumphal cart). When in the final scene Ada returns to life from stone, a tentative recollection of the delicate E-major version prefaces the speech of her father, as *deus ex machina*, inviting Arindal to immortality. The final chorus welcomes Arindal to the fairy kingdom with a vigorously accompanied allegro transformation, still in the native "fairy" key of E. (Did Wagner perhaps know Mendelssohn's overture to *A Midsummer Night's Dream* at this time?)

Ballad or *Romanze* melodies were among the earliest candidates for operatic reminiscence, since they tended to be easily recognizable, and also because their original narrative burden or dramatic context was often relevant to later situations. Gernot's *Romanze* about the "evil witch Dilnovaz" in Act 1 of *Die Feen* provides Arindal with an object lesson against courting supernatural species. With its shivering string tremolos and thumping timpani punctuating the verses, it is really a semi-comic number, even if Gernot means it in earnest (Example 2.8a). But at the climax of the Act 2 finale, when Arindal's understanding of Ada's identity

Ex. 2.7a

Ex. 2.7b

is being put to the utmost test, the theme of the *Romanze* is thrice recalled and twice transformed with utterly serious dramatic import – first *pianissimo* and then *fortissimo*, each time over a descending chromatic tetrachord (Example 2.8b, 2.8c). A less felicitous set of recollections and anticipations involve the orchestral theme from the concluding phase of Ada's big aria in Act 2, also serving as the closing theme of the overture's sonata-form (Example 2.9). Wagner would recall this flatfooted and foursquare brand of melody – even the same descending scalar contour with chromatic passing tones – to express similar states of elation in *Der fliegende Holländer* (e.g., the

Ex. 2.8a

Ex. 2.8b

Ex. 2.8c

Senta–Dutchman duet) and *Tannhäuser*. Apparently it was only with some effort he was able to forget it.

Das Liebesverbot contains one very audible anticipation of the later, familiar Wagner: a pre-echo of the theme of "absolution" from Tannhäuser's Rome narration (related in turn to the "Dresden Amen" used in *Parsifal*). Here the theme frames the duet of Isabella and Mariana

Ex. 2.9

in praise of the cloistered life. In the duet with her brother Claudio in Act 2 Isabella quotes the swelling phrases of Friedrich's lust. She does so in a tone of barely suppressed outrage that dislocates it from its original harmonic formula (see Example 2.2b) so that it briefly reels keyless before reaching a half-cadence in C (Example 2.10): "Hear what occurred: at his feet he saw me, and was seized by a criminal passion; at the cost of my dishonor he promised your life and pardon!" The orchestral introduction to the duet ends with a poignant recollection of a phrase, prominent in the opening scene, to which Claudio expressed hope that Isabella might intervene to save him (Example 2.11a). Now oboe and horn recall this "hopeful" theme quietly, over a descending chromatic tenor line and tonic pedal (Example 2.11b). In both cases, the altered recollection makes an expressive point beyond the mere act of citation: the musical image of Friedrich's lust is distorted by Isabella's indignation; the contours of Claudio's earlier hope are inflected with wistful resignation. The latter example, an expressively inflected instrumental memory of an original vocal utterance, precisely fits the "theory" of leitmotif articulated later in *Opera and Drama*.

Still, these remain isolated instances within a score primarily concerned with other, more immediate forms of musical expression. Only the figure of Friedrich's Ban on Love (Example 2.1) is deployed with a frequency and variety that anticipates later practices. Its portentous statements in the overture and the introductory ensemble leave no question as to the motive's significance. Moreover, it resembles later, "true" leitmotifs in being a malleable, memorable fragment rather than a periodically structured tune or phrase. It recurs often enough throughout the score

Ex. 2.10

Ex. 2.11a

Ex. 2.11b

that the listener is never in danger of forgetting it, and these recurrences
are felt to be significant. Above all, as demonstrated in Friedrich's scene
and aria (no. 10), the motive insinuates itself into the musical discourse to
variable psychological effect. At the beginning of the scene it runs through
Friedrich's mind as an uneasy *idée fixe* ("What has become of the system
you set so well in place? . . . The vengeful force of [love] makes you neglect

Ex. 2.12

duty and honor"). A deliberate, unaltered statement accompanies his resolution to sign Claudio's death warrant after all, and to subject himself to the same decree. After Friedrich gives full vent to his tormented passion in the cabaletta, an allegro transformation of the motive (Example 2.12), is sutured on to the "Tristanesque" gestures of that passion (see Example 2.3). The almost grotesque quality of these final measures conveys something of Friedrich's conflicted state, beyond anything articulated in the text.

Although *Der fliegende Holländer* would be Wagner's principal portal into the domain of myth, and hence music drama, we have seen that some psychological, dramatic, or indeed "mythic" tropes of the later works are clearly prefigured in the early ones. These are most striking in *Die Feen*, whose fairy-tale wonders bridge the elements of magic and the marvelous in baroque opera or Mozart's *Zauberflöte* and Weber's *Oberon* with works like *Lohengrin* and *Parsifal*. Ada's proscription against asking after "her name and kind" and her desire to leave behind an enchanted homeland for the sake of human love return as central themes in *Lohengrin*. The thematic linking of the power of song to the power of love in Arindal's reanimation of the petrified Ada prefigures elements of both *Tannhäuser* and *Die Meistersinger*; and Ada herself is transformed from a Venus figure, as her mortal detractors painted her, into a figure of purity and redemption, like Elisabeth.

In Gozzi and Shakespeare Wagner had found noble, devoted sisters for the heroes of *Die Feen* and *Das Liebesverbot*. For *Rienzi* he invented one (Irene) to replace the original hero's wife. In the final act, Rienzi apostrophizes Rome as a "noble bride" whose love seems to have failed him in the end, while Irene renounces Adriano and assumes herself the abandoned mantle of "Rome," Rienzi's bride ("In our faithful union, in this chaste breast Rome still lives"). The progression of these sibling relationships leads in the direction of the mythically glorified incest of Siegmund and Sieglinde. (Shakespeare's Isabella, as Wagner would have known, warns Claudio that yielding up her virginity to save his life would be "a kind of incest"; but, not yet a Wagnerian heroine herself, she disapproves.)[29]

Both Claudio and Friedrich, on different sides of the moral fence, struggle like Tannhäuser with the conflicting claims of body and soul, the profane and the sacred. And while Wagner revises *Measure for Measure* as a celebration of carnivalesque release, *Die Feen* and *Rienzi* both end with a foretaste of classic Wagnerian redemption, the heroes transcending this life for a glorious "beyond." For Arindal it is the immortality of a fairy kingdom, perhaps something akin to the "distant spirit realm" described by Hoffmann's composer – a dream-like place of "flowery paths" and Romantic marvels where speech becomes music.[30] Rienzi's immortality is that conferred by posterity, though better realized through an operatic immolation than in the sordid facts of history. (Cola di Rienzo was murdered by an angry mob and dismembered; his remains – at least in Schiller's account – were handed over to the Jews, who "burned them over a slow fire in revenge on one who had denounced them and their trades.")[31] Between Arindal and Rienzi Wagner outlines a spectrum of redemptive options comprehending the apotheosis of virtually all his subsequent heroes and heroines.

3 To the Dresden barricades: the genesis of Wagner's political ideas

MITCHELL COHEN

Colliding worlds: the revolutionary impulse

On 28 May 1849, a political refugee named Richard Wagner crossed Lake Constance on a steamer to Switzerland. He had spent most of the previous month in flight or hiding because of his role in an uprising in Dresden that had begun on 3 May and was crushed within four days. Before then, for seven years, he served as Kapellmeister in the Saxon capital; he was now a wanted man. His closest comrades in the revolt, including his musical colleague and friend, August Röckel, were captured and soon condemned to death. (The sentences were not carried out, though these others did serve extended prison sentences.) The revolutionary provisional government had quit Dresden before advancing Prussian and Saxon troops. Most of its leaders, aiming to regroup, made their way to Chemnitz, to the west. The Kapellmeister – who had backed but was not a member of the government – went too, but stopped at a different hotel. Consequently, he did not fall into the trap that awaited the other insurrectionists.

Wagner scurried away, arriving eventually in Weimar where Franz Liszt, who was then rehearsing *Tannhäuser*, sheltered him. "I found it difficult to tell my friend that I had not left Dresden as Royal Kapellmeister in an entirely regular way," Wagner recalled. "To tell the truth," he added, "I had an extremely hazy conception of my relationship to the laws of what was, in the narrower sense, my native country. Had I committed a criminal act according to these laws or not? I couldn't come to any real conclusion about it" (*ML* 412).

He was not being truthful. Wagner was a vigorous participant in the uprising and had long had radical sentiments. As a very young man, he had been enthralled by the revolutionary tumult of 1830, stimulated by the overthrow of the French monarch in July of that year. In the ensuing decade he was close to the Young Germans,[1] a loose collection of writers with mostly republican and liberal political sympathies. And consider Wagner's pre-1849 operas. Colliding realms, each with divergent rules (and representing opposing desires), feature in almost all these works:

- In *Die Feen* (*The Fairies*, 1833–34), his first completed opera, a fairy world contrasts to the human world, and a half-fairy princess unites with a human monarch after overcoming a fairy king's decree, aimed at thwarting their passion;

- *Das Liebesverbot* (*The Ban on Love*; 1834–36) pits a rigid, puritanical German regent against spirited Sicilians;
- In an opera scenario that Wagner never put to music, *Die hohe Braut* (*The High-Born Bride*, first sketched in 1836), the protagonists rebel on behalf of love and freedom against aristocratic strictures and values. It is set in the environs of Nice in 1792, and they hope for victory by the approaching French republican army;
- *Rienzi* (1837–40) presents a struggle between popular classes and nobles;
- *Der fliegende Holländer* (*The Flying Dutchman*; 1840–41) opposes the Dutchman's sea-bound wandering to custom-bound, confined life on shore;
- *Tannhäuser* (1842–45) opposes the Venusberg to the Wartburg;
- Lohengrin, in the opera named for him (1845–48), comes from an ideal world of faith to flawed Brabant, and is proclaimed the duchy's new "defender" ("Schützer von Brabant"), in place of an apparently vanished feudal line.

It could be said that Wagner's "colliding-worlds motif" found its way directly into politics in May 1849. In the period before Dresden citizens clashed fiercely with their rulers, Wagner devoted considerable energy to talking politics and more; he associated and identified with radicals and reformers, and participated in their conclaves. He joined the Vaterlands-verein (Fatherland Society), a radical republican organization that emerged in the spring of 1848 as Saxony's leading opposition movement, and he gave a controversial speech to one of its public meetings. All this was during a dramatic period of insurgence across the continent. Wagner later veiled his revolutionary enthusiasms, fearful of their consequences for his artistic goals. But weeks before the outbreak of violence in 1849, he wrote an (unsigned) article with unmistakable sentiments for a radical paper called *Das Volksblatt*, announcing that "The lofty goddess Revolution comes rustling on the wings of storm." She tells the world: "I will break the power of the mighty, of law, of property." Over and again she repeats: "I will destroy the order of things."[2]

When order was restored and Wagner became a refugee, he wrote to his wife Minna, still in Dresden, that he had been "consumed with an inner rage."[3] Why? He was not entirely forthcoming. We know that he was frustrated professionally; his proposals to reform the theater had come to nothing. He finished *Lohengrin* in early 1848 just when the revolutions broke out, and in December his superiors in Dresden canceled plans for its production there. This was undoubtedly due in part to the political sympathies he had expressed in previous months. Now he was embittered, and he no longer cared about his position as Kapellmeister, as he later claimed (*ML* 380). He was resolved that his artistic ambitions could not be fulfilled apart from social and political revolution. Although after the Dresden uprising failed he assured Minna that he was turning his back on revolution,[4] his radicalism effervesced continually in essays and letters from the first period of what turned into a thirteen-year exile. In December 1849, half a year after the Dresden uprising, he still insisted that "works of art cannot be created at present, they can only be prepared for by means of revolutionary activity, by destroying and crushing everything that is worth crushing and destroying. That is our task, and only people totally different from us will be the true creative artists ... Destruction alone is what is now needed."[5]

Humanity and the law

Wagner lived in an era of potent political myths: "The People," "The Nation," "The Individual," "The Revolution," "The Jew." He was an artist, not a political theorist, and insisted that myth rather than history revealed truth. Even when he chose historical subjects for operas – whether *Rienzi* or a never completed *Friedrich Barbarossa* or Hans Sachs in *Die Meistersinger von Nürnberg* – Wagner mythologized them. He believed that "reflective understanding [*der reflektierende Verstand*]" undermines and fragments "the poetic view of the Whole," as he wrote in *Opera and Drama* (1850–51).[6] He wanted to "emotionalize" the intellect, and his poetic quest for wholeness in art – it took form as his idea of a "total work of art" – is homologous to a quest for a totalizing community that abolishes politics in order to free what he called "the purely human." This is why he wrote that "no-one can write poetry without being political," but added that "we must have no more politics" (*PW* II:187). The point of politics was liberation from the state. This would allow art and humanity to be one, which is also what Wagner, like many Romantics, imagined art and community to have been in ancient Athens. Sometimes Wagner uses "the purely human" to indicate a timeless human essence, although sometimes he seems to imply that to be purely human is to be German. The "purely human" was the animating principle of a story he retold in different ways. Once, humanity was whole. Then it fragmented. Redemption would make it whole again.

Three political ideas shaped Wagner's quest for redemption in a post-political totality: anarchism, republican nationalism, and anti-Semitism. These ideas overlapped each other and artistic concerns in Wagner's often overwrought mind. Scholars disagree about how to date his first engagement with each, the extent to which their fluid contents shifted about in his view of the world, and their presence in his artistic works. It seems certain, however, that they all came into overlapping focus for him – critics might call it a blur – in the revolution of 1848–49 and its aftermath.

Something underlies the overlap: an obsession with law. While he is a proponent of equality before the law in the draft of *Die hohe Braut* and in *Rienzi*, elsewhere – indeed, virtually everywhere else in his works – the arbitrary force of law is seen to throttle the "purely human." It represses genuine needs, stifling their authentic expression in love and individuality. Compare, for example, a work written long before 1849 to one written after. *Das Liebesverbot* reworks Shakespeare's *Measure for Measure*, resetting it from Vienna to Palermo. Friedrich, the German regent in Sicily, prohibits carnival – that is, he bars love-making and pleasure – and provokes rebellion among a fun-loving population (the Sicilian *Volk*, one might say). After assorted tussles, including a scene that mocks courts with gusto, and after the revelation at the opera's end that the decree-maker cannot live by his own diktat, Friedrich is chased from power. The hero of *Siegfried*, created almost two decades later, is a being of instinct who wields a self-made sword named "Nothung" (Need) against the law-laden spear of "The Wanderer," who is really Wotan, the king of the gods. After smashing the inscribed, old laws – the old regime – the youth bounds up a mountain to love, to Brünnhilde.

For all their artistic differences, these works share a motif: the opposition of law to love. This motif does change character. The People intervene in *Das Liebesverbot* while Siegfried acts alone. By the time he wrote *Siegfried*, Wagner had experienced a popular upheaval and its failure. In *Das Liebesverbot*, a beloved king returns and ends arbitrary rulership while in *Götterdämmerung*, the conclusion of *The Ring of the Nibelung*, the gods are consumed in burning Valhalla – and we already know (from *Siegfried*) that Wotan stepped aside after his spear shattered.

But that is Wagner's final version. The earliest version of what became *Götterdämmerung* was called *Siegfried's Death*, and Wagner wrote its text in the fall of 1848, when German lands were rife with political turmoil. In fact, the leader of Saxony's Vaterlandsverein, Robert Blum, had just been executed in Vienna, a city Wagner visited the previous summer. *Siegfried's Death* culminates in an image of redemption emerging out of death and destruction. Yet the king of the gods is not undone, and Brünnhilde, in glory, leads Siegfried into the skies. The chorus sings praise of Wotan as well as of that noble pair as they ascend to Valhalla for "bliss without end." The forces of evil are swept into the Rhine's deep, which surely resembles what Wagner wished would happen to the old regimes. But radical sentiments seem to give way to a hankering for an authority figure. The acclaim of Wotan echoes, perhaps not too distantly, the sentiments of Sicilians toward their returning monarch in *Das Liebesverbot*: Brünnhilde and Siegfried are to be "All-Father's free helpmates." A true king and his free people are bound by love, not regulation. Wagner expressed a similar idea in his speech in mid-June 1848 to the Dresden Vaterlandsverein. "What is the relation between Republican Aims and the Monarchy?," Wagner asked some 3,000 people in a public garden (his speech was published the next day). Before he answered, he denounced aristocrats and declared that a free *Volk* should consist of "one great class" embracing everyone "on dear German soil." Man, "the crown of creation," ought to be freed from "bondage" to "sallow metal" (i.e., gold); this would come when a "great war of liberation" does away with "demonic" money, usury, bankers, and "paper juggling."[7] Afterwards, the king can be "most republican of the republicans" and "the first of the *Volk*," for Saxon kingship is based on "the full warm *confidence of love*," not the "cold and calculating State-idea" (*PW* IV:141, 143).

Anarchist influences: Proudhon and Bakunin

Wagner tried to explain to his irritated employers that the Vaterlandsverein represented the party of the future: he was attempting to secure the king's proper place there. Dresden authorities probably found the distance too short between Wagner's enthusiasm for a *Volk* with a republican king, and the idea, cherished by most democratic republicans and nationalists, that the *Volk* should be "sovereign." Wagner's views in the ensuing year could have pacified them little for if, in fall 1848, he could still present Brünnhilde and Siegfried ascending to Wotan's Valhalla, by April 1849 Wagner's "goddess of Revolution" descends to earth proclaiming the downfall (*Untergang*, a favorite Wagnerian term) of the existing order.

Two anarchists, one French and one Russian, particularly influenced Wagner. Both Pierre-Joseph Proudhon and Mikhail Bakunin imagined that individuals could be free only if cooperative, stateless societies supplanted hierarchy and capitalist competition. After 1849, Wagner tried to leave the impression that he had encountered radical ideas only in the lead-up to the Dresden upheaval, and that he was converted to Proudhon's notion of "a new moral order" thanks to his close friend August Röckel. Röckel was Wagner's assistant conductor until radical activities brought about his dismissal by the court in the summer of 1848 (*ML* 373). It is probable, however, that Wagner became familiar with Proudhon's ideas in conversations with fellow German exiles during his earlier stay in Paris (1839–42). The city's atmosphere was then intensely political. There was an outpouring of left-wing literature (including Proudhon's *What Is Property?*). Radical criticisms of the established order undoubtedly appealed to a man who lived as Wagner did, in poverty and mounting frustration as he failed to establish himself in the glittering world of the Paris Opéra.

Proudhon became an advocate of a world of federated "associations," and Wagner too became a proponent of federalism. Even after the older Wagner left "the Revolution" behind, he remained a proponent of federalism for Germany. He dedicated the second edition of *Opera and Drama* in 1868 to Constantin Frantz, a conservative, pan-German federalist (and anti-Semite). While Wagner's nationalism, his fetishized *Volk*-ism, his advocacy of an unmediated relation between a leader (a king) and the People, and his anti-Semitism all anticipate aspects of Nazism, his persistent federalism, rooted partly in anarchist antipathy toward centralization (and probably also in Saxon dislike of Prussia), precludes classifying his politics as totalitarian. And Wagner's federal nationalism was certainly at play when he later chose Bayreuth, a provincial town, for his Festspielhaus.

Wagner apparently met Bakunin through August Röckel and had an "extensive association" with him in secret (Bakunin was then in hiding), dating from around New Year 1848–49.[8] "Everything about him was on a colossal scale," the composer recalled, adding that "he had a strength suggestive of primitive exuberance" (*ML* 985). Bakunin had studied philosophy in Berlin, and stays in Paris, Zurich, and Prague led to personal acquaintances with leading European revolutionary intellectuals. "The passion for destruction is a creative passion," he wrote in 1842 in an article published by the "Young Hegelian" philosopher and activist Arnold Ruge.[9] This theme features prominently in Wagner's work, too, and he reports that in conversation Bakunin extolled "the childishly demonic delight of the Russian people in fire." A worldwide conflagration would be ignited if the Russian peasant, "in whom the natural goodness of the oppressed human nature survived in its most child-like form," was convinced that God wanted him to incinerate the castles of the "masters" – "together with everything in them." Nonetheless, Wagner tells us that after Bakunin, in disguise, heard him rehearse Beethoven's Ninth Symphony in the spring of 1849, he called to the Kapellmeister that "if all music were lost in the coming world conflagration, we should risk our lives to preserve this symphony" (*ML* 384). It is difficult to tell what Wagner thought of his friend's pan-Slavism (German politics was of little interest to Bakunin), but it is easy to imagine that Bakunin's obsession with fire and purification attracted him. Both *Rienzi* and the *Ring* end in flames; Wagner signed some of his early articles "W. Freudenfeuer" ("W. Joyfire").[10]

Wagner, like Bakunin, was taken by the radical humanist philosophy of Ludwig Feuerbach (whose name, ironically, means "brook of fire"). This philosopher argued that "God" is simply a projection of "alienated man." Once this is recognized, the "Absolute" becomes humanity itself. In the current era, Feuerbach maintained, egoism and fragmentation rule; they constitute a "realm" of "detached souls." But *Noth* (need or necessity) impels humans toward their "species-being" – that is, their communal nature – in a "realm" of "embodied living, souls."[11]

Wagner's writings in *Das Volksblatt* are filled with Feuerbachian language. If we combine these with Bakunin's themes and Wagner's own motif of "colliding worlds" (as described earlier), a fairly complete picture of his politics emerges. The composer-anarchist charged that the state and its laws thwart the quest for the "purely human"; his poem "Die Noth," which appeared in *Das Volksblatt* in late March 1849, anticipates the stroke of Siegfried's Nothung against Wotan's spear. *Noth*, Wagner declares, is poised to crack the chains that truss humanity. The world of fakery, greed, and especially paper money will go up in flames. God, he declared in "The Revolution," published in *Das Volksblatt* a week later, will become man in "the embodied revolution" (*PW* VIII:238).

Nationalism and anti-Semitism

Was this also to be a nationalist revolution? Republicanism and nationalism often blurred into each other in nineteenth-century Europe. In the German case, many opponents of the old regimes perceived national unity to be the prerequisite of political progress. In *The Artwork of the Future*, written in October 1849, Wagner defines the *Volk* as all "who feel a common and collective Need [*gemeinschaftliche Noth*]" (*PW* I:75). He dedicated it to Feuerbach although the dedication vanished in later editions. This disappearance was due, undoubtedly, to his subsequent desire for distance from his past revolutionary inspirations. It was also likely due to the metamorphosis of his idea of "collective Need" into something increasingly exclusionary.

But nationalist feelings were expressed much earlier by Wagner. His first article, "On German Opera" (1834), complained that German composers were unable to touch their own people because they used forms (like oratorios) that were inappropriate to the times. He seems about to suggest a nationalist remedy to what appears a nationalist's question when, instead, he strikes a decidedly cosmopolitan note: "We must take the era by the ears and honestly try to cultivate its modern forms; and he will be master who writes neither Italian, nor French – nor even German" (*PW* VIII:55–56, 58). Consider the distance between this formulation and a letter from 1843 to a friend who had shared his Parisian miseries. Wagner expresses "alarm" at the "depths [to which] our national sense of honour has sunk with respect to dramatic music . . . the long period during which our theatres were exclusively open to French and Italian music continues to have repercussions." Now he goes on to say that "opera composers cannot be *European*, – so the question is – either *German* or *French*!"[12]

What accounts for Wagner's shift? Most likely his Paris stay. His writings and letters say little then about politics, but a poor German with great artistic hopes would have been cautious about expressing his leanings. Not long before Wagner's arrival in 1839, Auguste Blanqui led an abortive uprising and its supporters among radical German exiles had to flee France. In the summer of 1840 France and Germany came close to war when Adolphe Thiers's government threatened to invade the Rhineland (as a distraction from a foreign policy failure in what is now called the Middle East). This provoked an outpouring of political poetry and songs in German lands. Nikolas Becker's poem "Der deutsche Rhein" quickly became the chief anthem of the so-called Rhine Song Movement. Contests took place to set it to music, and its opening lines became famous: "They shall not have it, our free German Rhine." Rebuttals in verse came from leading French writers including Alphonse de Lamartine, Edgar Quinet, and Alfred de Musset.

As these competing nationalisms chanted at each other, Wagner was trying to eke out a living in the French capital by writing piano arrangements of works by famous composers as well as articles and stories. In his prose, he celebrated Beethoven and German music, and presented a "fictional" account of a suffering German composer in Paris. Later, in his autobiography, Wagner called these works vengeance "for all my humiliations" (*ML* 190). His frustrations sometimes even echoed Becker and his *Rheinlied*. In an exasperated review of a French version of Weber's *Der Freischütz*, for instance, Wagner declared to his German readers, "They have not been able to kill it – our dear and wonderful *Freischütz*."[13] Wagner left Paris feeling intense hostility toward the French.

One can conjecture with some confidence that Wagner's experience of the "Rhine Crisis" left its traces in the concept of his first composed "music drama," *Das Rheingold*, which begins the epic of a world-mythical struggle with a violation of German nature. When he wrote its prose draft in 1851, Wagner certainly understood how a violation of the Rhine by an alien would resonate within German audiences. In an autobiographical sketch written at the end of 1842, he described melodramatically his own reaction when, on the way from Parisian poverty toward anticipated success in Dresden, he saw the Rhine for the first time: "with hot tears in my eyes, I, poor artist, swore fidelity to my German fatherland" (*PW* I:19). He wrote later that he had perceived "deep significance" in crossing "the legendary German Rhine," and then seeing, also for the first time, the Wartburg Castle – "so rich in history and myth" – in a ray of light in the midst of a storm (*ML* 219).[14]

Tannhäuser was the first opera he wrote after his return to Dresden. It takes place at the Wartburg and is centered around a song contest among medieval *Minnesänger*. In the decades before the 1848–49 revolutions, music and song festivals – together with choral and gymnastic societies – played spirited roles in German nationalism, serving as proxies for opposition politics that had no other outlet. If the Rhine was a natural icon for German nationalism, the Wartburg was a historical one. In the Middle Ages this castle-fortress had been the site of contests among singers of courtly love (the *Minnesänger*), who sang and composed didactic epics. In the sixteenth century, Luther translated the Gospels into German there. The building overlooks Eisenach, where Bach was born. At the beginning of Wagner's own lifetime, in October 1817, the Wartburg hosted a portentous festival of the *Burschenschaften*, pan-German student fraternities that saw themselves as heirs to the German resistance to Napoleon. Dismayed by the conservative, Metternich-inspired postwar settlement, the *Burschenschaft* movement idealized youth and promoted a mélange of democratic radicalism and cultural-ethnic chauvinism. "There was much talk of freedom and equality," as Herbert Marcuse notes, "but it was a freedom that could be the vested privilege of the Teutonic race alone ... Hatred of the French went along with hatred of the Jews, Catholics and 'nobles' ... the state was to be built from 'below' through the sheer enthusiasm of the masses, and the 'natural' unity of the *Volk* was to supersede the stratified order of state and society."[15] They sang chorales for a unified "Vaterland," paraded, did gymnastics, and burned "alien" books. Among the professors who came to encourage them was post-Kantian philosopher Jakob Fries, who had recently published a pamphlet warning of the "menace" to German "character" posed by Jews.

Wagner's politics can be seen, at least in part, as a spiritual offspring of the *Burschenschaften* mix of nationalism, anti-establishment radicalism, and Siegfried-like enthusiasm. Hegel, who was one of their strongest foes and even supported the Metternich-initiated Carlsbad Decrees of 1819 that repressed them, warned that Fries and the *Burschenschaften* served up a dangerous brew of "heart, friendship, and inspiration."[16] History, for Hegel, was a grand story in which humanity's "spirit" became ever more rational; it culminates politically in constitutional states, animated by law. For Wagner, the state filled the historical space in between the Fall and Redemption. The intellect ought to be "emotionalized" through art, and humanity's history would culminate in "the necessary downfall of the state" (*GS* IV:65; *PW* II:191–92). Deified *völkisch* humanity – a community born of common *Noth* – would achieve self-realization, and thus the truly human, again. That Wagner had imbibed that brew of *Burschenschaften* rhetoric – and that it remained in his system – can be detected in an essay he initially sketched in 1865, eventually published under the title "What Is German?" Here he felt compelled to chastise Metternich for the repression of the *Burschenschaften* some four and a half decades after the event. He also suggested that this repression opened the way for "the Jewish speculator" to "infiltrate" and to dominate Germans.[17]

Wagner's anti-Semitism had received its most potent expression a decade and a half earlier in his notorious essay "Judaism in Music," a classic in hate-literature. He published it in September 1850 under the pseudonym "K. Freigedank" ("Free-thought") and again under his own name in 1869, just as Saxony granted citizenship rights to its Jews and the Northern German Confederation separated political rights from confessional (religious) membership.[18] Scholars argue about how Wagner's fierce bigotry evolved, if it is embedded in his works, and what implications ought (or ought not) to be drawn.[19] The term "anti-Semitism" was invented in the 1870s to indicate a transmutation of earlier traditions of religious intolerance into more explicitly cultural and ethnic bias. Racial and national justifications of bigotry increasingly supplemented or reinvented older religious rationales. A concomitant identification of Jewishness with commerce, usury, and rigid legalism lent itself, in turn, to a crude assimilation of Judaism to capitalism among some critics of market societies, and to an identification of Jews with established power. Wagner's attacks on Jews were part of these developments. When he attacked Giacomo Meyerbeer in "Judaism in Music," he portrayed this Berlin Jew – who had become the leading figure of French *grand Opéra*, whose popular opera *Les Huguenots* censured intolerance, and who had tried to help Wagner in Paris – as a rootless composer concerned solely with turning out stage-works to make money. "This perpetually kind and obliging man reminds me of the darkest ... period of my life," Wagner later explained to Franz Liszt: "I cannot exist as an artist ... without sensing in Meyerbeer my total antithesis."[20]

Wagner had numerous Jewish acquaintances (and friends) in that dark period and had been dependent on some of them. It is conceivable that personal resentments translated into generalized venom against the backdrop of his own wretchedness and the nationalist fevers of the Rhine crisis. Wagner referred to Meyerbeer as a "cunning trickster" in early 1842.[21] This was just before he returned to Dresden where there had recently been considerable debate about the status of Jews. A struggle for official recognition of their tiny community there had gained momentum, although nothing points to interest in them on Wagner's part before he was Kapellmeister. A synagogue opened in 1840 near Dresden's opera house. Its architect, Gottfried Semper (who was not Jewish), was to have a terse friendship with Wagner over the years. Three decades later, in one of the odder incidents of Wagner's long history of anomalous relations to Jews, the composer decided that he wanted to place in his home outside Zurich a copy of a consecrated lamp designed by Semper for the synagogue. It is evident, then, that Wagner had been inside this Jewish house of worship. (Perhaps he heard there the "Jewish music" he later demeaned.) He would chastise Meyerbeer for what he claimed was a Jew's inability to connect cause and effect in art, that is, for being unable to fuse music with language and purpose in drama. Jews, Wagner implied, were foreign to the German language and creativity. Curiously, German Jews were experimenting and arguing about the role of language in their liturgy just at the time Wagner returned to Dresden. They debated whether or not reforms of their customs would assist their integration into the surrounding society. Dresden Jewish leaders were prominent in the discussion and Jewish prayer services in Dresden began (with hesitation) to mix some German language sermons, brief prayers, and chorales with the traditional Hebrew.[22]

Did Wagner follow these discussions and then make perverse use of motifs in them? A Royal Kapellmeister held responsibilities for church music and it is conceivable that he heard something of this debate about the relation between German and Jewish culture. In 1846 the Kapellmeister befriended Berthold Auerbach, a German Jew whose tales and plays were then popular and who had written on the plausibility of German–Jewish "synthesis." Wagner described him as "the first Jew with whom I could discuss the whole subject of Judaism with a hearty lack of inhibition" (*ML* 325). A Dresden colleague of Auerbach was the writer Karl Gutzkow. Gutzkow's historical play *Uriel Costa*, which received considerable attention, told the story of a seventeenth-century Marrano in Amsterdam who returned to, clashed with, and was banned by a rigid Jewish community, leading finally to his suicide. Wagner quarreled with Gutzkow about the incidental music for a scene in *Uriel Costa* in which "the eponymous hero recanted his alleged heresy" (*ML* 323). It is certainly curious that within a few years Wagner concluded "Judaism in Music" by telling contemporary Jews they could be redeemed from the "curse" on them only by renouncing Judaism, and by sharing the fate of Ahasuerus, the Wandering Jew of Christian mythology. Redemption would come only with "downfall," he asserted.[23]

Marx, Bauer, and "Judaism in Music"

Anti-Jewish rancor crisscrossed social, political, and intellectual lines. Judaism, Feuerbach determined, was "the religion of the most narrow-hearted egoism."[24] Proudhon and Bakunin railed against Jews, whom they identified with capitalism. Arthur Schopenhauer, whose pessimistic metaphysics were embraced by Wagner after the failure of the 1849 revolution, despised Judaism because he thought it fostered "optimism" and affirmed a this-worldly existence. (Schopenhauer embraced a Platonic "utopia" in which "despotism of . . . genuine nobility" would be "achieved by mating the most magnanimous men with the cleverest and most gifted women.")[25] A debate on the Jewish question took place in the 1840s among the Young "Left" Hegelians, most famously between Bruno Bauer and Karl Marx, after Friedrich Wilhelm IV ascended Prussia's throne and called for a "German-Christian" state. Bauer argued that Christians and Jews would only be "free" by renouncing all religion and particularism. There was no point in supporting Jewish emancipation; "human emancipation" was needed. But Bauer also repeated a cliché of the times: "the Jew" might have no political rights, but he still "rules the fate of Europe" thanks to financial power.[26]

Marx, himself a Jew, argued that "human" and "political" emancipation were distinct. The latter, while allowing for the continuation of bourgeois society, still represented "great progress."[27] A "modern" state separated religion and state, and therefore states "which cannot yet *politically* emancipate the Jews" were "underdeveloped."[28] Human emancipation, however, demanded the transcendence of religion along with bourgeois society and the state.[29] Marx, like Bauer, identified "practical" Judaism with bourgeois society and commerce. Unlike Bauer, Marx asserted that money had become a "world power" both "through" the Jew but "also apart from him." Nonetheless, "money is the jealous god of Israel, beside which no other god may exist." He concluded that "the *social* emancipation of the Jew is *the emancipation of society from Judaism*."[30]

Did Wagner read Bauer and Marx? Both were well known to Wagner's friends, if not to him, and he was also acquainted with the editors who published them, Georg Herwegh, the radical poet, and Arnold Ruge, who was based briefly in Dresden. Mikhail Bakunin not only knew these men personally: he was the sole non-German to write for the journal in which Marx's first writings on the Jewish question appeared, the *Deutsch-Französische Jahrbücher*, which proposed "unity" between French political "praxis" and German philosophy. Wagner was then seeking to divorce anything German from anything French, but it is plausible that the Bauer–Marx exchange inspired his assertion in "Judaism in Music" that "irrelevant liberal battles" were being fought in the "sky of illusion," while Jews had taken control of the "beautiful earth of reality." Jews do not need emancipation, he proposed, but "it is we who require to fight for emancipation from the Jew," for "as the world is constituted today, the Jew is more than emancipated, he is the ruler. And he will continue to rule as long as money remains the power to which all our activities are subjected."

Wagner then quickly links this imagined reality to art. For two thousand "unhappy years" artists tried to create great cultural works, but today "the Jew" turns them into "art-business."[31] He "possesses a God of his own." Great art originates in the *Volk*'s common spirit and "a language, its expression, and evolution are not separate elements, but part of an historical community."[32] Jews, clearly, are not part of Wagner's community:

> We are repelled ... by the purely aural aspect of Jewish speech. Contact with our culture has not, after two thousand years, weaned the Jew away from the peculiarities of semitic pronunciation. The shrill, sibilant buzzing of his voice falls strangely and unpleasantly on our ears ... When we listen to a Jew talking we are unconsciously upset by the complete lack of purely human expression in his speech.[33]

In other words, Jews cannot express "purely human experience" or translate true human passion into music or enunciate feelings in song.[34] In a synagogue you encounter "nonsensical gurgling, yodeling, and cackling." These "rhythms and melismata" unconsciously inform and corrupt any music composed by supposedly "cultured Jews."[35] Mendelssohn may have had talent but this baptized Jew could not have created art that moves people "to the depth" of their "being."[36] Then there is a "widely renowned Jewish composer" – clearly Meyerbeer, though not named here – whom Wagner thinks does to opera what Judaism, more generally, does to art. Finally, he turns on Heinrich Heine, whom he brands an author of "poetic lies." Wagner's rant culminates, like many of his works, with a theme of redemption through downfall or destruction. Judaism must be rejected; only when the Jew becomes a real human being – by denying himself totally – can he be redeemed.

Anarchism, socialism, and humanism had no intrinsic intellectual link to anti-Semitism. Advocates of each have opposed anti-Semitism, which often drew from left-wing, conservative nationalist, and religious motifs, among others. Wagner would be hailed as a precursor by the racially charged anti-Semitic movement that emerged in the late nineteenth century. Some of its foremost foes came, however, from the social democratic left. One Marxist critic, Karl Kautsky, published just before World War I a tract on *Rasse und Judentum* that directly addressed Wagner's views of Jewish "pronunciation." "No doubt a Siegfried speaking with a Jewish accent would be impossible on stage," wrote Kautsky, seeming to concur with the composer. But then he noted that Wagner's "dialect was ... that of Saxony." Apply Wagner's theory to Wagner, Kautsky suggested, and the conclusion would be that "civilization has not succeeded in surmounting the peculiar stubbornness of the Saxon character in the Saxon mode of pronunciation, in spite of their two thousand years of contact with

European nations." A "reasonable" person would then ask if "the influence of the Saxons on music" had not been "disastrous."[37]

Kautsky's jibe implies what is evident: Wagner's humanism had limited humanity. His "free thought" was, at best, that of a "wildly 'emotionalized' intellect." Yet even if we distinguish in principle Wagner's anarchism, anti-Semitism, and artistic visions, they still blur into each other in his projection of a *Noth*-bred, linguistically homogeneous *Volk*. As an anarchist, he wanted the "People's Need" to be freed of the state's shackles as well as from those imposed by aristocrats and competitive, commercial social relations. But when he asserts this, his language comes close to that which he uses when attacking Jewish emancipation, and drifts unmistakably toward an exclusionary nationalism. It is the "egotistical" needs (commerce) of Jews that set them apart naturally from the needs of the *Volk*. The "modern egoist," Wagner wrote, "cannot grasp ... inner need." He lives through "external" wants like money-making, and these are also what motivate a certain type of artist.[38]

Alberich, the lustful, bearded dwarf of *Das Rheingold*, is a being like this, and that is why he cannot unite with the Rhine maidens. He tears the gold from its rightful place – in the "free German Rhine" – where it yields beauty naturally; he curses love so that he can forge a ring that will give him power over the external world. Even if interpreters dispute the presence of Wagner's anti-Semitic sentiments in his art, the composer himself seems to confirm it in *Das Rheingold*. In a late essay, "Know Thyself," he associated the "Nibelung Ring" with sinister Jewish power; it was part of a continuum that runs from "demon" gold through paper money, stock, and credit. This, he proposed, is what throttles humanity in contemporary civilization, a "barbaric–Judaic mixture."[39] Although Jews were not his target when Wagner had mounted Dresden's barricades over two decades before writing this, there seem to be continuities between some of his agitations and motives before and after the uprising – even if they changed shape.

On the barricades: Wagner and the 1849 Dresden uprising

A year of volatile German politics culminated in a final revolutionary surge in the spring of 1849. All the underlying questions surfaced: would Germany unify? Under what political regime? What social regime? At about the same time Wagner wrote "Die Noth" and "The Revolution," the Frankfurt assembly, which had been meeting for over a year in search of a solution to German problems, readied a constitution that aimed to unite German lands (except Austria), and proposed that Prussia's Friedrich

Wilhelm IV become emperor. Both the Saxon Diet (then dominated by democrats and liberals) and the Vaterlandsverein supported this offer. Prussia's ruler rejected it. In March, Saxony's monarch, Friedrich August II, had dismissed the more liberal government he had appointed a year before and then, after some wavering, supported Prussia and dissolved the Saxon Diet. On 30 April, one of its radical members, August Röckel, left for Prague, fearing arrest now that he lacked parliamentary immunity. Richard Wagner briefly replaced him as editor of *Das Volksblatt*. After the Diet's dissolution, throngs milled in Dresden's streets. Troops fired on them, turmoil intensified, and on the night of 3–4 May the king fled down the Elbe to his summer palace. He sent a telegram to Berlin asking for Prussian military help. A revolutionary provisional government composed of republican democrats and liberals formed in Dresden.

When Wagner later sought a pardon for his activities during these days, Dresden's police told their superiors that "sometime Kapellmeister Wagner was intimately acquainted with the ringleaders of the insurrection." Six weeks before it began, he attended secret meetings with a "Dr. Schwartz" (Bakunin, that is) in the home of a "law student Neumann," where authorities suspected explosives were harbored. Wagner was accused of using his own garden for meetings to plan the arming of the populace. Before Easter – so the accusations continue – Wagner and Röckel sought to procure hand grenades.[40] The police reported that Wagner was at the town hall meeting when the provisional government was proclaimed, and that he wrote to Röckel urging quick return to Dresden because "[p]eople are preparing for a decisive conflict." Wagner worried, however, that "the revolution may come *too soon*."[41]

The composer's own account is melodramatic and, like much of his autobiographical writing, has motives other than strict reliability. He had been in a print shop working on *Das Volksblatt* when the turmoil began, he tells us. He went as an "observer" to a Vaterlandsverein meeting, and roamed the streets, which had a yellowish-brown cast that reminded him of a solar eclipse. When the bells of St. Ann's Church chimed to signal revolt, Wagner felt "great, almost extravagant well-being." He made his way to the old market square where Wilhelmine Schröder-Devrient, the famed soprano who inspired Wagner as a younger man and who created the roles of Adriano in *Rienzi*, Senta in *The Flying Dutchman*, and Venus in *Tannhäuser*, urged on demonstrators (*ML* 391). Hans von Bülow reported shortly after the upheaval that a student told him of hearing Wagner himself "speaking to the people from a balcony."[42] In the next days, Wagner, amidst the furor, imagined writing a play about Achilles.

Bakunin had been planning to leave Dresden when the uprising began, but he quickly joined the rebels, even though he thought they could not succeed. Wagner chanced upon him "wandering elegantly in a black dress coat" and smoking a cigar (*ML* 394–95). Finally, the royal attack came, and it turned into one of the bloodiest episodes of 1848–49 in Germany. Wagner climbed up and down the Kreuzkirche tower as an "observer" – he seems in fact to have observed military movements on behalf of the provisional government – and spent a night on its top discussing politics and religion with a teacher posted alongside him. As morning came, the composer (so he professed) heard a nightingale sing along with the Marseillaise sung by local miners marching toward Dresden to help its defenders. At about 11:00 a.m. on 6 May he saw the old opera house, where a month earlier he had conducted Beethoven, in flames. Apparently the fire was set by rebels to stall royal advances. The burning opera house convinced Wagner that "strategic purposes" would "always predominate in the world over aesthetic considerations." (It was an ugly building any-way, he remarked; *ML* 400.) When the military situation became hopeless, Bakunin urged the provisional government to "blow itself up, together with the town hall, for which I had enough gunpowder." Alas, "they did not want to."[43] Its members were more amenable to his alternative suggestion that they flee and regroup. Wagner fled, as well.

Renunciation of the revolutionary will

Accounts of Wagner's post-Dresden development usually stress how his view of the world transformed owing to the failure of the uprising, and later, after 1854, due to his encounter with Arthur Schopenhauer's *The World as Will and Representation*. This treatise, Wagner wrote, "entered my lonely life like a gift from heaven."[44] More precisely, perhaps, Schopenhauer's pessimistic metaphysics resonated within Wagner now that the "goddess of revolution" had descended to earth but failed to implant his ideals there, leaving him facing the chasm between two worlds, that of daily life and that of the "essence" of things, as described by Schopenhauer. The void in Wagner's post-revolutionary life would be filled not just by his creative work but also by a practical endeavor, his project of a festival theater in Bayreuth devoted to his own work.

Wagner's surging *Noth* was displaced, at least in principle, by Schopenhauerian "renunciation of the Will," the hope that egotism and human suffering could dissolve into a Nirvana-like "true peace that is higher than all reason," an "ocean-like calmness of the spirit."[45] It is the peace imagined by Wotan's resignation in the final version of *The Ring*; by the "Liebestod" of *Tristan und Isolde*; by escape from what Hans Sachs calls *Wahn* ("illusion") in *Die Meistersinger von Nürnberg*; and by the bond between self-abnegation and redemption in *Parsifal*. The latter, Wagner's final stage-work and written specifically for his Bayreuth theater, culminates in an image of purified community rapturously at home in itself. Its opposite, the realm of evil Klingsor, has fallen and Kundry, Klingsor's conflicted servant, is lifeless.

Before he crossed Lake Constance to Switzerland and exile, Wagner visited the Wartburg castle. "I had strange thoughts about my own destiny on first entering this building, foreknown to me so intimately, at the very time my days in Germany were numbered," he recounted later in his autobiography (*ML* 414). Wagner may well have been reimagining his sentiments there to enhance his myth of himself, but nationalist symbols of place – the Wartburg, Nuremberg, the Rhine – traverse his life as well as his works from the 1840s on. Undoubtedly, he intended the festival theater at Bayreuth to be one of them. Wagner wrote that his idea of a festival in this small Franconian town was inspired in part by the pre-1848 song and gymnastic festivals which, as we have seen, were surrogate expressions of German nationalism.[46] The post-revolutionary Wagner no longer called for the state's downfall, and accepted gladly Ludwig II's royal patronage. Unfortunately, his nationalism and prejudices, especially against Jews and the French, remained aggressive, and vulgar, and they remained animating "Needs" of the doting community that surrounded him in Bayreuth, imagining itself redeemed through his work.

PART II

Opera, music, drama

4 The "Romantic operas" and the turn to myth

STEWART SPENCER

In describing *Der fliegende Holländer* (*The Flying Dutchman*), *Tannhäuser*, and *Lohengrin* as "Romantic operas,"[1] Wagner fell back on a term that he had first used for *Die Feen* (*The Fairies*) in 1833–34, but the taxonomical similarity conceals an ideological difference that we can best understand only by briefly examining the conceptual background to these works.

As a literary movement, Romanticism had emerged at the end of the eighteenth century as a protest against the utilitarian, skeptical spirit of the Enlightenment. If Kant had lamented the limits of the powers of reason, Fichte now proceeded to glorify the potentialities of the imagination, opening the floodgates of subjectivity and the irrational, often expressed in the language of Catholic mysticism. At first the movement was apolitical, but the sense of inadequacy induced by the dissolution of the Holy Roman Empire and by the Wars of Liberation of 1813–15 led to a desire to escape from the sordid, reactionary present into a past in which Germany had once been united and strong. One of the leading apologists of the Romantic movement, August Wilhelm Schlegel, summed up the aims of his fellow poets with reference to this feeling of nostalgia: "The poetry of the ancients was that of possession, ours is that of longing."[2] *Sehnsucht*, or longing, became a leading motif of Romantic poetry, specifically a longing to re-create the world of the Middle Ages.

Romanticism came naturally to a composer like Wagner who had been brought up in the world of the theater and whose uncle, Adolf Wagner, was a leading Romantic scholar.[3] Many typical Romantic themes are to be found in *Die Feen*: the fairy setting, the inspirational role of women, the escapist triumph of the human spirit over the cramping bonds of mortality, the theme of madness, the Orphic status of the poet, and the redemptive power of love. Indeed, the very idea of adapting Gozzi's *La donna serpente* (*The Serpent Woman*) as the basis of the libretto of *Die Feen* was inspired by that arch-Romantic, E. T. A. Hoffmann. But Hoffmann's seminal text, "The Poet and the Composer," dates from 1813.[4] By the 1830s literary Romanticism was played out in Germany, Wagner's belated interest in its storehouse of ideas distinctly out of fashion. As Heine complained with some justification in *The Romantic School* (1836), "The German Middle Ages have entered into our midst in broad daylight and are sucking the lifeblood from our breast."[5] The vampiric nature of this anemic Romanticism was reviled by the leading writers of a new movement in literary thought, Young Germany, whose programs of political reform, inspired by the radical changes that were taking place in England and France at this time, were aimed at social amelioration.[6] Writers such as Heinrich Laube and Karl Gutzkow spoke out against existing social and political conditions, against philistinism and the mysticization of religion. And both men served terms of imprisonment in consequence. Epicureanism was the watchword of a movement that Wagner himself espoused in the mid-1830s in the wake of *Die Feen*, when he rewrote Shakespeare's *Measure for Measure*, retitling it *Das Liebesverbot* (*The Ban on Love*) and pillorying German puritanism, which he contrasted with Southern hedonism.

Whether or not there is any truth to Wagner's entertaining account of the disastrous first performance of *Das Liebesverbot* in Magdeburg on 29 March 1836 (*ML* 118–19), there seems little doubt that he himself felt the experience to be determinative. This and similar setbacks and humiliations in Königsberg, Riga, and Paris served to promote his sense of isolation as an artist. He felt at odds with his environment and gave expression to his sense of frustration and misunderstanding in the series of operas that followed: in *Rienzi, Der fliegende Holländer, Tannhäuser,* and *Lohengrin* the artist is seen in conflict with society, with Wagner using medieval subject matter – at least in three of these works – to advance unmedieval ideas. The medieval artist had been a part of society, content on the whole to remain anonymous and regarding himself as the mouthpiece of a tradition whose social values he shared. A different view was propounded by the Romantics of the early nineteenth century, for whom the poet was the realization of the highest human potential, an instrument in the transformation of the world into a spiritual, poetic state. To quote Novalis in his fragmentary *Heinrich von Ofterdingen*: "It is precisely in this joy of being able to reveal to the world what lies beyond it and of responding to the primal urge of our existence that the source of poetry lies ... Poets should at one and the same time be prophets and priests, lawgivers and physicians."[7] The biblical imagery is intentional: the poet is a figure of redemption. Wagner's Tannhäuser is Heinrich von Ofterdingen,[8] but there can be no clearer contrast between the early Romantic and the Wagnerian concept of the poet than that which divides Novalis's solipsistic seer from Wagner's tormented, guilt-ridden artist who, far from offering redemption to others, craves it for himself.

For all their dissimilarity on a musical and formal level, *Rienzi* and *Der fliegende Holländer* both deal, at least in part, with the theme of the outsider and the despair caused by his sense of Otherness. The theme of the artist as a tormented pariah cast out from respectable society was not unknown, of course, to a writer like Heinrich Heine, and it is one that readily appealed to Wagner, too.

According to *My Life* (*ML* 45), Wagner was introduced to Heine's works by a Hanoverian student by the name of Schröter in Leipzig in 1831. A passing allusion to "Das Herz ist mir bedrückt" from *Das Buch der Lieder* (1827) in Wagner's letter to Theodor Apel of 8 April 1835 (*SB* I:196) certainly suggests an intimate familiarity with the poet's self-mocking, ironical tone and a sense of affinity with the latter's anti-Romantic attitudinizing that chimes with the Young German ideals that the composer adopted at this time.[9] At what point Wagner went on to read Heine's "Aus den Memoiren des Herren Schnabelewopski" – the source of *Der fliegende Holländer* – is impossible to say for certain, although it was probably during his time in Riga between August 1837 and July 1839.[10] Heine famously interweaves his version of the legend of the mariner doomed to sail the seven seas until redeemed by the love of a woman with an account of a visit to the theater in Amsterdam, where he claims to have seen the beginning and end of a play on the subject of the Flying Dutchman, the intervening acts being occupied by his dalliance with a "Dutch Messalina."[11] The end of the narrative strikes a markedly ironical note that subverts all that has gone before it, suggesting a writer who has seen the illusions of his youth destroyed and who now trivializes all that might undermine his resultant sense of cynicism.[12] By removing the note of irony, Wagner was left with a narrative that draws on many of the themes of German literature from the early Romantics onward: the legend of the Wandering Jew,[13] the feeling of *Weltschmerz*,[14] philistinism, magnetism,[15] redemption through love, and the sort of *Liebestod*, or love-death, that Wagner had exploited in most of his works from *Leubald* (1826–28) onward.[16] But, as before, the superficial similarity should not be allowed to obscure the underlying difference: for a Romantic like Novalis, death was seen as the supreme voluptuous experience,[17] whereas for Wagner it was the quietus that brought an end to all of life's sufferings.

Wagner increasingly denied Heine any credit for *Der fliegende Holländer*.[18] If, in 1843, he had still been keen to depict himself as a literary dandy, happy to claim Heine as a kindred spirit, his thinking was soon to develop along *völkisch* lines, persuading him that not only the Flying Dutchman but his later heroes, too, were a product of the *Volk* whose gene pool emphatically excluded a Jewish writer like Heine.[19]

Heine's name is also linked to Wagner's next completed stage-work, *Tannhäuser*, the tale of a medieval bard redeemed from his erotic impulses by the love of the saintly Elisabeth: the poet's transcription of the "Tannhäuser Ballad" from *Des Knaben Wunderhorn*,[20] together with his own anti-Romantic retelling of it, appeared in the third volume of *Der Salon* in

1837. Wagner's failure to mention Heine as his source may be part of the same strategy of denial and obfuscation described earlier, yet here it is possible to provide the composer with an alibi: in his autobiography, Wagner writes of a *Volksbuch*, or chapbook, whose appeal lay above all in the "fleeting" link that it forged between the "Tannhäuser Ballad" and the Wartburg song contest (*ML* 212). Wagner was almost certainly alluding here to Ludwig Bechstein's anthology of legends about Eisenach and the Wartburg, *Der Sagenschatz und die Sagenkreise des Thüringerlandes*, published in 1835. In his introduction, Bechstein expresses his belief that "legends are a sacred and common possession of the people,"[21] a Romantic conviction that could well have encouraged Wagner to regard the collection as a *Volksbuch*. Bechstein then goes on to rehearse the legends, among others, of the Wartburg song contest,[22] Saint Elisabeth of Hungary, and Tannhäuser and the Venusberg, before reproducing one of the printed versions of *Das Lied von dem Danheüser* that were popular in Germany in the first third of the sixteenth century. Crucially, the version given by Bechstein includes a stanza missing from both *Des Knaben Wunderhorn* and Heine, in which Danheüser appeals to the Virgin Mary to release him from the Venusberg, resulting in Venus's abrupt, but now understandable, volte-face.[23]

That Wagner believed he was dealing with a genuine medieval tradition is clear from his dismissive attitude toward the Romantic writers whom he accused of having falsified it: Tieck, for example, was charged with promoting a "coquettish mysticism and Catholic frivolity" in *Der getreue Eckart und der Tannenhäuser* (*GS* IV:269), while Hoffmann in *Der Kampf der Sänger* was said to have had "a very odd idea of the genuine tradition" (*ML* 212). Seeking "the authentic form of this attractive legend" (*ibid.*), Wagner set about studying the medieval version of the Wartburg song contest. In this he was helped by Lucas's *Ueber den Krieg von Wartburg* (1838), procured for him by one of his friends in Paris, Samuel Lehrs. Lucas forged an even closer bond between the two legends than Bechstein had done by assimilating the figures of Heinrich von Ofterdingen, the central character in the song contest, and the minstrel Tannhäuser.[24] For a copy of the *Wartburgkrieg*, however, Wagner would have had to turn to Friedrich Heinrich von der Hagen's four-volume edition of the *Minnesang* poets,[25] which also provided him with detailed sketches of the singers involved in the contest.[26] Wagner retained the form of the contest, together with a handful of motifs,[27] but replaced its content: the subject is no longer the traditional generosity of medieval princes but "the nature of love." And here we find Wagner drawing on a further tradition of the Middle Ages, that of the love lyric, as mediated by von der Hagen.[28]

For Wagner, as he admitted in *My Life*, the world of medieval German literary scholarship that was opened up to him in Paris was "completely new" (*ML* 213), and he continued to explore it throughout the 1840s, when he acquired and read the writings of many of the leading medieval scholars of their day, from Jacob and Wilhelm Grimm to Friedrich Heinrich von der Hagen, Ludwig Ettmüller, Karl Lachmann, Franz Joseph Mone, and Karl Simrock.[29] But it is a world that he saw filtered through the lens of his own literary and personal experiences of the 1830s and 1840s. The sense of alienation fostered by his years in Paris from 1839 to 1842 filled him, by his own admission, with an intense affinity for all things German, while the Young German movement left its mark on *Tannhäuser* in the form of the hero's sensuality, the role of the *poète maudit*, and the work's anti-Catholic thrust. A similar development may be found in *Lohengrin*, which Wagner began in 1845 and completed in 1848. Lohengrin is the artist – in this case the composer of *Tannhäuser* – who descends to earth in search of self-fulfillment, only to find disillusionment and annihilation. Other familiar themes include German nationalism and the destructive force of the love that prompts Elsa to ask the forbidden question and demand to know more about her rescuer's mysterious origins. Here, too, the principal source could well be termed a *Volksbuch*, in this case the *Deutsche Sagen* of Jacob and Wilhelm Grimm (1816–18), which contains no fewer than seven legends related to the Swan Knight. And once again Wagner supplemented this primary source with a number of scholarly texts: the *Parzival* and *Titurel* of Wolfram von Eschenbach in the editions of San Marte (1841) and Simrock (1842), Ferdinand Gloekle's edition of the late thirteenth-century *Lohengrin*, with Joseph von Görres's speculative introduction (1813), and, to add local color, Jacob Grimm's *Deutsche Rechtsalterthümer* (1828) and Leopold August Warnkönig's three-volume *Flandrische Staats- und Rechtsgeschichte bis zum Jahr 1305* (1835–42). This last-named reading matter was bound up with Wagner's wish to create as accurate a picture as possible of Brabant in the first half of the tenth century,[30] much as *Tannhäuser* had been an evocation of Thuringia in the first decade of the thirteenth century.[31] History, rather than myth, continued to interest Wagner for much of the 1840s, not just in his completed operas, but also in the unfinished *Die Sarazenin* (1841–43) and *Friedrich I* (1846–49), set respectively in the middle of the thirteenth and the twelfth centuries.

Wagner himself does not seem to have drawn any fundamental distinction between legend and myth, but came to see both as outpourings of the popular spirit. While regularly describing the subjects of his Dresden operas as folk legends, he first uses the term "myth" in 1848 to describe a more archaic, all-embracing manifestation of the spirit of the German people. Writing in his *Gespräch über die Poesie* in 1800, Friedrich Schlegel had compared the Germans with the Greeks and lamented the fact that "we have no mythology,"[32] an omission that Jacob Grimm had set out to rectify in his *Deutsche Mythologie* of 1835. Wagner claims to have read Grimm's polyglot compendium of unassimilated quotations during the summer of 1843, later describing the experience as a "complete rebirth" (*ML* 260). If so, it was a much protracted birth, producing no tangible results until the summer of 1848. But in the meantime he had not been intellectually idle. Responding to a series of appeals for an opera on that epitome of nationalist aspirations, the *Nibelungenlied*,[33] he began to accumulate editions of the poem, arguing retrospectively (*GS* IV:312–14) that the attractiveness of a poem set firmly in the early thirteenth century, with all the trappings of medieval chivalry, had inevitably started to wane once he developed anarchic leanings. History could not predict the future. Myth alone could embody the universal struggle between the forces of reaction and a more enlightened regime. It was in order to excavate what he believed was the mythic substratum of the material that Wagner proceeded to delve more deeply into the Scandinavian versions of the legend, versions which, in keeping with the thinking of his age, he regarded as more ancient and therefore as more prototypically German. At the same time, he became engrossed in the scholarly debate over the historical or mythological origins of the Nibelung narrative[34] and even made his own contribution to it in his essay *The Wibelungs* of 1848.[35] It seems to have been his "medieval German studies"[36] of 1848 that alerted him to the mythological interpretation of history: in the writings of Mone, Lachmann, and Grimm,[37] he would have found precisely the sort of blurring of the borders between history and myth that characterizes *The Wibelungs*. In their attempts to reconstruct the prototypical Nibelung myth, all these writers were motivated by their Romantic belief in the essential oneness of the different surviving versions of the narrative. But whereas their interest was antiquarian, Wagner aimed to use myth in a dynamic, didactic way. History per se was now seen as arid and reductive, while containing within it the potential for a tautegorical interpretation – hence Wagner's belief that there was a "mythic identity" between Barbarossa and Siegfried and between the Ghibellines and the Nibelungs (*GS* II:120); hence, too, his impatience with those "scholars" who failed to understand this. In propounding this view, Wagner may have been encouraged by his reading of Hegel[38] and Droysen,[39] for both of whom Greek myth had a political role to play.

This political dimension needs stressing, for far too often Wagner's comment that "the myth is true for all time and its content, densely compressed, inexhaustible for all ages" (*GS* IV:64) has been ripped from its context and quoted by writers anxious to deny any unpalatable aspects of the *Ring* and its performance history. But this sentence comes at the end of a passage in which Wagner places his own political interpretation on the myth of Creon and Antigone: it is *this* myth that is "true for all time," *this* myth which, "densely compressed," is "inexhaustible for all ages." And the gloss that Wagner places on it is quintessentially his own, its explicit antithesis between power politics and the redemptive power of love a direct product of his mid-century reading of the writings of Hegel and Feuerbach. In espousing myth in this way, Wagner was seeking to reverse the historicist trend of his age,[40] a move bound up with his disenchantment with the direction then being taken by his German homeland on an industrial, political, and cultural level. By going further back in time than his Romantic predecessors and by tapping into the *völkisch* thinking of his day,[41] Wagner was able to lay the foundations for all his subsequent works, in which the palimpsest of Romanticism is overwritten by mythicized history and secularized myth.

5 *Der Ring des Nibelungen*: conception and interpretation

BARRY MILLINGTON

The genesis of the *Ring* project

The outline of the drama that was to become *Der Ring des Nibelungen*, namely "Der Nibelungen-Mythus: Als Entwurf zu einem Drama,"[1] dates from October 1848, the same year as the "Plan for the Organization of a German National Theater for the Kingdom of Saxony," Wagner's radical proposal to establish an association of dramatists and composers along with a drama school and expanded court orchestra. That manifesto for theatrical reform naturally reflected Wagner's sociopolitical outlook of the period, hostile as it was to the status quo presided over by the aristocracy. The same preoccupation with nationhood and freedom also informed the contemporary reception of Greek drama, especially as mediated by the leading translator and commentator Johann Gustav Droysen.

The essays of the revolutionary period elaborate the emergent concept of the Wagnerian music drama in greater detail. *Art and Revolution* (1849) celebrates the Greek drama with its integration of all the arts, contrasting it with the vacuous, mercenary theater of the modern age. *The Artwork of the Future* (also 1849) develops this theme, proposing a *Gesamtkunstwerk*, or "total work of art," that would unite dance, music, and poetry in a new kind of theater designed solely according to aesthetic and artistic criteria, no longer for commercial gain or social ostentation. And finally, *Opera and Drama* (1850–51), after offering a critique of the genres of modern opera and analyzing the nature and history of theater, attempts to illuminate the linguistic, dramatic, and musical ingredients of the proposed *Gesamtkunstwerk*.

The influence of Greek drama

Greek drama, in which Wagner had been evincing increasing interest during the 1840s, profoundly influenced the *Ring* tetralogy in several important ways. To begin with, the very notion of a tetralogy is fundamental to Greek drama, the Athenian festivals in the age of Aeschylus and Euripides consisting of a series of three tragedies being succeeded by the lighter entertainment of a satyr-play (a pattern Wagner to some extent reversed, with *Das Rheingold* as a shorter prologue to the principal trilogy). Moreover, the Greeks regarded their drama as essentially a religious ritual, to be celebrated in a special festival, attended by all sections of society, rather than as part of the diurnal round. Wagner, too, wanted people of all classes to set aside time to immerse themselves in drama, rather than attending the theater in a state of exhaustion after a tiring day in paid employment. No less important to Wagner was the fearless, life-enhancing ethos of Greek culture, which he (under the influence of Ludwig Feuerbach) counterposed to the craven, guilt-ridden spirit of Christianity as manifested in the modern age. Further elements of Greek drama appropriated by Wagner were the confrontations of pairs of characters as a dramaturgical principle and the linking of successive episodes with the themes of guilt and a curse. Wagner's development of the leitmotif principle itself may have been influenced by Aeschylus's use of recurrent imagery.[2]

Aborted dramatic projects of the revolutionary years

The five-year period between the completion of the score of *Lohengrin* in April 1848 and the commencement of *Das Rheingold* in November 1853 may have been musically barren, but these years gave rise to some fifty essays and articles, many substantial (such as *Opera and Drama*), others shorter disquisitions on subjects such as theater reform or program notes.[3] No less importantly, these were years in which Wagner initiated a number of dramatic projects, all of which were aborted but whose preoccupations throw revealing light on the *Ring* project shortly to be undertaken. During this period also, the text of the *Ring* itself was drafted and elaborated into near-final form and even published privately by Wagner in 1853.

The first of these projects, *Friedrich I*, was a drama in five acts concerned with the Hohenstaufen emperor Friedrich Barbarossa, and probably intended to be an opera.[4] This text originated in October 1846, while Wagner was at work on *Lohengrin*. A sketch of that date was returned to and extended during the winter of 1848–49, shortly after he had set down the outline for the new project, *Der Nibelungen-Mythus*. Wagner's claim that he abandoned the subject of the Hohenstaufen emperor as soon as he realized that the Nibelung myth had more potential for an opera does not withstand close scrutiny: the later sketch for *Friedrich I* is in Roman script, and Wagner did not abandon the traditional Gothic script until mid-December 1848 – hence the authoritative dating of winter 1848–49. But if this post-*Nibelungen-Mythus* dating proves that Wagner was still brooding on Barbarossa even after discovering the Nibelungs, the more interesting question is why.

In fact, the legend of Barbarossa was a powerful expression of German identity at this time of strong national feeling. According to this legend, the original home of mankind was thought to be in India: there was believed to have been a primordial kingdom – a Golden Age – in the mountains of Asia. The rulership was supposed to have passed down through various dynasties, from the first Asiatic and Indian kings, through Troy and the "Trojan" Franks and Romans, to the Hohenstaufen rulers of the Middle Ages. (The kinship of such a theory to the mythology of an "Aryan" race cultivated by the National Socialists in the following century scarcely needs underlining.) The Hohenstaufen Friedrich Barbarossa (1123–90), originally a Swabian duke and from 1152 the Holy Roman Emperor, was engaged in a lifelong struggle against the power of the Church. He died on the way to the Holy Land in the Third Crusade and, again according to the legend, remained sleeping in the Kyffhäuser mountains, to awake one day when his people had need of him. Thus, the Hohenstaufens would return and restore the Holy Roman Empire of the German nation in all its glory. Wagner's intended opera, or drama, on Friedrich Barbarossa was to tell the story of the struggle between the Ghibellines, headed by Barbarossa, and the Guelfs, headed by the Duke of Saxony, Henry the Lion. It was also to set forth the conflict between temporal and spiritual power, between the Emperor and the Church.

Of particular interest is the way Wagner casts Barbarossa as the liberating ruler who will bring peace and justice to the people. The concept of a progressive, liberating ruler was also propounded in Wagner's public speech of 1848, "How Do Republican Endeavours Stand in Relation to the Monarchy?," and it was to find dramatic form in *Friedrich I*. The legendary monarch was to wake from his slumber, return from the middle of the mountain to the real world and preside over a golden new era of peace and justice, one in which due respect would be accorded to the arts – and no doubt to composers engaged on commercially unviable music dramas.

In this context, it is significant to note the congruity of Wagner's conception with the economic analysis articulated in the *Communist Manifesto* of Marx and Engels, dating from the same year, 1848. Under Barbarossa's rule, opined Wagner, the ideal world of nature had prevailed, but from private wealth and property emerged the rule of the aristocracy and the rise of class society.

In his essay *The Wibelungs* (1848), Wagner elaborated the background to the aborted Barbarossa drama, retelling the legend of the sleeping emperor awaiting the call to save the German race.[5] But he also introduced some further motifs worth noting. First, he discusses the legend of the

Nibelungs, the hero Siegfried – described as the god of light or a sun god – and the hoard which Siegfried wins, and with it immeasurable power. Second, he describes how the legend of a great treasure hoard amassed by the Nibelung clan became transmuted over the centuries into that of the Holy Grail. Third, he associates Friedrich Barbarossa with Siegfried. "When will you return, Friedrich, O glorious Siegfried!" is the essay's final heroic exhortation; "When will you slay the evil, gnawing dragon of humanity?" (*SSD* XII:229).[6] Friedrich/Siegfried is pictured in his mountain lair, surrounded by the hoard of the Nibelungs, at his side the sharp sword that once struck down the grim dragon.

So much for the first aborted dramatic project of the revolutionary period. The second, *Jesus von Nazareth*, dating from January to April 1849, seems also to have been intended as an opera and in five acts (see *WWV*, 337–39, which also reproduces the sole surviving musical sketch). In this detailed prose sketch, and in the commentary appended to it, Jesus is portrayed as a social revolutionary. If the influence of liberal religious critics such as David Friedrich Strauss and Bruno Bauer is evident in the liberation of Jesus from the straitjacket of the Gospels, that of materialist social philosophers Ludwig Feuerbach and Pierre-Joseph Proudhon is clear from the tirades against private property and accumulated wealth and in the elevation of love above marriage and other oppressive legally binding contracts. All these preoccupations were to loom large in the *Ring*.

The third revolutionary project, an Achilles drama, dates from early 1849 to 1850 and was once again probably intended to be an opera, though only a few prose fragments remain (see *WWV*, 340). "Achilles rejects the immortality his mother Thetis offers him," reads one. "His mother acknowledges that Achilles is greater than the elements (the gods)." In other words, Achilles was conceived as a supreme hero, half-human, half-divine. Another fragment reads: "Man is the perfection of God. The eternal Gods are the elements that engender Man. Thus creation finds its completion in Man" (*SSD* XII:283; see *PW* VIII:367–68). Here again Wagner's thinking has been influenced by Feuerbach: humanity as the crowning achievement of God's creation – indeed, ultimately superseding its creator. And Achilles – like Siegfried, Jesus, and Barbarossa – is the noble heroic figure personifying that humanity at its greatest.

The fourth and final project of these years, *Wieland der Schmied* (December 1849 to March 1850), exists only in the form of two prose sketches, but it was certainly intended as an opera, as is clear from the title of the second sketch: "Heldenoper in drei Akten" (heroic opera in three acts; see *WWV*, 341–43). Wieland, a skilled smith, is forced to forge swords for the evil king Neiding. Lamed by his enemy, Wieland succeeds in making wings instead, on which he eventually flies to freedom with his beloved Schwanhilde. Wagner undoubtedly identified himself with Wieland as the artist figure whose fetters symbolize the constraints on the striving Romantic genius. The story was plundered from the Nordic sagas, the same repository of mythological material from which the *Ring* itself was to be drawn. Also in evidence here is a whole range of motifs that were central to Wagner's works both before and after *Wieland*: a forbidden question (already featured in *Lohengrin* and *Die Feen* [*The Fairies*]); an injured swan (to reappear in *Parsifal*); a valkyrie, a clever smith, bellows to stoke a fire, a forged sword, and a ring conferring limitless power, all shortly to be found in *Der Ring des Nibelungen* (*The Ring of the Nibelung*).

In the peroration to the 1849 essay *The Artwork of the Future*, which contains an outline of the Wieland story, Wagner identifies the down-trodden, fettered hero not only with himself but also with the German people, reduced to slavery by princes and other masters. In that peroration Wagner addresses the *Volk* as follows: "O unique and glorious race! You have created this for yourselves, you yourselves are this Wieland! Forge your wings and soar aloft!" (*GS* III:177; see *PW* I:213). Abandoning his original plan of making from this material an opera that could be per-formed in Paris, Wagner left this project unfinished too.[7] But like the other abandoned projects of this period, it focused philosophical and political ideas – even specific motifs such as the clever smith and the forging of a sword and of an all-important ring – that were soon to be incorporated in the *Ring*. Fundamental to all these abandoned projects is the notion of a solar hero, a sun god who will bring redemption to the world. Friedrich Barbarossa, Achilles, Jesus of Nazareth, Wieland the Smith: they are all variations on a theme that was to consolidate in the figure of the fearless dragon-slaying hero, Siegfried.

The *Ring* as a "festival drama" and the Bayreuth project

A letter from Wagner to his friend Ernst Benedikt Kietz postmarked 14 September 1850 adumbrates a scheme to build a theater "here on the spot" (i.e., near Zurich), constructed from wooden planks. Three performances of the work (at this point still styled as *Siegfrieds Tod* [*Siegfried's Death*])[8] would be given, "one after the other in the space of a week" and audi-ences would be invited free of charge. Following the performances, "the theatre would then be demolished and the whole affair would be over and done with" (*SL* 217). The utopian aspect of the project is emphasized in a letter of a week later to Theodor Uhlig (*SB* III:426), in which Wagner adds that after the final performance his score should, for good measure, be burned as well.

Realizing – as Eduard Devrient had pointed out to him – that *Siegfrieds Tod* contained too much back-narration, he wrote the following year (1851) a further drama, called *Der junge Siegfried* (*The Young Siegfried*), to precede it. Although this satisfactorily dealt with the story of the hero's younger days, he decided that yet more of the earlier stages of the story needed to be dramatized. He therefore added *Die Walküre* and *Das Rheingold* (1851–52), but then returned to revise *Der junge Siegfried* and *Siegfrieds Tod*, making Wotan rather than Siegfried the central figure of the cycle as a whole. At some point – the precise date is still a matter of contention – he also altered the ending so that the gods and Valhalla were all destroyed by fire. *Der junge Siegfried* and *Siegfrieds Tod* were eventually renamed *Siegfried* and *Götterdämmerung*. At this stage Wagner was still proposing to "run up a theatre," now on the Rhine, "and send out invitations to a great dramatic festival" (letter to Uhlig, [12 November 1851]: *SL* 234). Moreover, the project was still essentially part of his revolutionary program, but the notion that the world had to change before it could be performed ("A *performance* is something I can conceive of only *after the Revolution*": *ibid.*) had to be abandoned in the light of the failure of that revolution (see chapter 3 in this volume).

The collapse of the revolutionary ideal inevitably undermined the utopian thrust of the *Ring* project. Yet the cycle made progress in the 1850s, before being abandoned, temporarily, in 1857, when the composer paused to carry out the projects of *Tristan und Isolde* and afterwards *Die Meistersinger*. Though sustained work on it was not to be resumed until 1869, Wagner published the poem of the *Ring* in 1863, prefacing it with an exposition of the project.[9] In this preface he posits three performances of the cycle in a provisional theater constructed in "one of the smaller towns of Germany" (*GS* VI:273; *PW* III:274), suitably appointed, where there would be no conflict with existing institutions. The theater was to be made, possibly, out of wood and was to feature an amphitheater-like auditorium and invisible orchestra.[10]

The latter features were incorporated into the plans for a festival theater in Munich, discussed with the architect Gottfried Semper shortly after the accession of Ludwig II in 1864 and the first stage of Ludwig's enthusiastic patronage of the composer. That scheme proved abortive, but the "Festspielhaus" or festival theater that was eventually built in Bayreuth (the roof-raising ceremony took place on 2 August 1873) incorporated all the elements fundamental to Wagner's conception: the wooden construction (the outer walls are lath and plaster), the amphitheater-like auditorium (both more Greek and more democratic than the traditional horseshoe design with balcony and side boxes), the sunken (and covered) orchestra pit, and a double proscenium (with six pairs of parallel proscenia receding to the rear of the stalls). The purpose of those tricks of perspective, and of concealing the orchestral musicians in the pit, was to create a "mystic abyss," with "spectral-sounding music" emanating as if from the womb of the earth; supported by this sounding substrate, the scenic picture on stage with its seemingly larger-than-life figures "becomes the truest simulacrum of life itself" (GS IX:338; see PW V:335).

Interpretive history

Given the ideological shift in the *Ring* from revolutionary utopianism to a Schopenhauerian acceptance of inevitable suffering and loss – a transformation reflecting a drift in the zeitgeist as much as an evolution in Wagner's own philosophy of life – it is unsurprising that the work has been subjected to a bracingly varied, even contradictory, range of interpretations.

The first attempt to interpret the *Ring* in symbolic or allegorical terms was George Bernard Shaw's *The Perfect Wagnerite* (1898). For Shaw the *Ring* was a political allegory exposing the oppression and injustice brought about by rampant capitalism. The plutocrat Alberich enslaves the Nibelungs with the "whip of starvation"; lovelessness and greed, the inevitable result of exploitation for profit, pervert the natural order of things. Siegfried is the naïve anarchist hero who will overturn religion, law, and order to free humanity from its fetters. Such an interpretation, while clearly reflecting Shaw's own socialist outlook, was also consistent with the origins of the work in the revolutionary period of 1848–49.

In Shaw's view the allegory collapses after the second act of *Siegfried*, degenerating formally into grand opera and philosophically from revolutionism toward what he called a "love panacea." Exaggerated as Shaw's identification of grand operatic elements in *Götterdämmerung* is, the explanation of the shift offered in the third edition (1913) is apropos: the Siegfrieds of 1848 had turned out, by the 1870s, to be "hopeless political failures," while the Wotans and Alberichs had flourished. By 1876 the modern-day Alberich had become a pillar of the establishment and was even on his way to becoming a model philanthropic employer.

In Germany, particularly in the decades following his death, Wagner had been appropriated by the political right, notably the nationalists, for whom Bayreuth was to become not just a shrine but a powerhouse for idealism of a reactionary, Aryan supremacist kind. The key figure in the ideological transition from the Wilhelminian era (1888–1918) to Nazism (1933–45) was Houston Stewart Chamberlain, the Englishman who married Wagner's daughter Eva and whose *Grundlagen des 19. Jahrhunderts*

(*Foundations of the Nineteenth Century*) provided an insidious, but hugely influential, Aryan interpretation of German history.[11] Wilhelm II willingly accepted Chamberlain's designation of his role as that of Siegfried the dragon-slayer, whose divine mission it was to restore the former glory of the fatherland.[12] At a performance of *Siegfried* at Bayreuth in 1914, the entire audience, sensing the moment of destiny, reputedly leapt to its feet at Siegfried's cry "Nothung! Nothung! Neidliches Schwert!" ("Nothung! Nothung! Longed-for sword!").[13]

The festival's house journal, the *Bayreuther Blätter* (established by Hans von Wolzogen in 1878), exhibited a tendency in the years leading up to World War I to depoliticize the work – just as both Wagner and his whole oeuvre were depoliticized by Chamberlain, with all references to revolutionary activity airbrushed out – and instead to give it a spiritual/religious, specifically Christian, connotation. After the Great War, it was often interpreted as a parable of the decline of the German Empire: the spirit of Siegfried was required to fulfill the noble destiny of the Germans.[14]

Curiously, the *Ring* was given hardly any exegetical treatment at all in the *Bayreuther Blätter* during the 1920s and 1930s.[15] Adolf Hitler, however, when handed the metaphorical sword of destiny by Chamberlain in an emotionally charged encounter in 1923, did not hesitate to equate the characters and action of the *Ring* with his own scenario for a "redeemed" Germany.[16] Central to his reading was the notion of a global, Manichean struggle fought to the death between the forces of light and dark (the heroic Siegmund and the dragon-slaying Siegfried on the one hand, the subhuman, verminous Nibelungs on the other), a struggle analogous to that of the Aryans against the Jews on which he had systematically embarked.

From a very different perspective, the critics of the Frankfurt School in the 1920s and 1930s also sought to interpret Wagner's work as a parable of social and cultural decline. Walter Benjamin discussed Wagner in terms of "bourgeois false consciousness"[17] that separated art from man's social existence, while T. W. Adorno, in his seminal essay *Versuch über Wagner*,[18] anatomized Wagner as reactionary rather than revolutionary: a terrorist, but a bourgeois one.[19] Adorno experienced the *Ring*, rather like Shaw, as something of a betrayal: the harnessing of "a failed insurrection and nihilistic metaphysics."[20]

In the aftermath of World War II and the Holocaust, further attempts were made to depoliticize Wagner's work. Wieland Wagner's first *Ring* at Bayreuth (1951) consciously eschewed its Teutonic and Nordic associations in favor of more universalized, archetypal forms (Wagner's espousal of Greek drama provided inspiration here). Stripping the dimly lit stage to its bare essentials (increasingly so as the production was revived in subsequent years and in his second and last production of 1965), Wieland dispensed with conventional props (picture-book castles, fairy-tale dragons, naturalistic trees), attempting rather to penetrate to the irreducible core represented by the familiar symbols. In an interview of 1965 he denied that the *Ring* was, as generally believed, a Germanic heroic epic based on the philosophy of Schopenhauer. "For me it is," he said, "firstly, a revival of Greek tragedy; secondly, a return to mythical sources; and thirdly, moralistic drama in the manner both of Schiller and of Brecht. The *Ring* is the mirror which Richard Wagner holds up to humanity."[21]

Of the left-wing intellectuals whom Wieland attracted to Bayreuth – Adorno, Ernst Bloch, and Hans Mayer among them – it was notably Adorno who provided the theoretical basis for his explorations into depth psychology. In other respects, the influence of these Marxist-trained critics was less visible: liberating Wagner's works from their dubious legacy was, of course, in itself a political gesture, though the world was not yet ready for the explicitly political productions of the decades to follow.

More directly analogous to Wieland's conception, inasmuch as it deals in mythic archetypes, was the psychoanalytic, unapologetically apolitical interpretation of Robert Donington, expounded in *Wagner's* Ring *and Its Symbols* (1963).[22] Donington drew his inspiration from Jungian psychology and its notion of a collective unconscious inhabited by archetypes, reading the mythological elements – dragon, bear, heroes, world ash tree – in terms of Jung's archetypal symbols, while the characters and their motivations are seen as externalizations of the composite human psyche: ego, persona, shadow, *anima, animus*. Thus Wotan's actions are the ego's assertion of willful authority, Brünnhilde fulfills the role of *anima* (inner femininity) for both Wotan and Siegfried, and Siegfried's fight with the dragon represents an archetypal confrontation with mother-longing, while the final death and ritual purgation (cremation) undergone by the main characters signify transformation in the psyche.

Donington's analysis has attracted a certain amount of adverse criticism, some of the most stringent from Deryck Cooke in *I Saw the World End*.[23] Attempting his own, somewhat fundamentalist, interpretation – endeavoring to uncover the "manifest" meaning of the *Ring*, asserting Wagner's insistence on the "purely human," and reclaiming love as the paramount social force – Cooke lambasted Donington for his interiorization of human relations that renders the *Ring* an allegory of "everyman's psychological development" instead of the broader parable of social relations Cooke believed it to be.[24] There is some force in such criticisms. Yet the fact remains that Donington's analysis makes sense of many of the tetralogy's notorious conundrums – among them: why does Siegmund have to die? Why can neither Alberich nor Brünnhilde harness the power of the ring in their hour of need? How can we account for the different versions of the night Siegfried spends beside Brünnhilde? Moreover, insights from psychoanalytic approaches such as Donington's (the interplay between the conscious and the unconscious, the notion of the cycle as simulacrum of the human psyche) have informed some of the most richly satisfying interpretations of the *Ring*, both on stage and in the form of commentary.

A more sympathetic confrontation with Donington, launched by a Jungian fellow-traveler, is Jean-Jacques Nattiez's *Wagner Androgyne*.[25] While rejecting what he regards as "the straitjacket of psychoanalytic exegesis, be it Freudian or Jungian" (objecting to the reductionist tendency of analysis by archetypes), Nattiez nevertheless elaborated his own brilliant thesis employing psychoanalytical models of both Freudian and Jungian provenance.[26] Just as Wagner perceived art as the union of feminine and masculine principles (music and poetry respectively), so, Nattiez claimed, the *Ring* should be understood as an androgynous symbolic union in which Brünnhilde and Siegfried, representing respectively music and poetry, merge their individual identities, achieving a primal state of unity through the oblivion of death. The great strength of Nattiez's exegesis is that it is rooted in Wagner's own aesthetic and theoretical oeuvre. Thus, for example, the observation that "the love duet in the third act of *Siegfried* is dominated by the idea of androgyny" is buttressed by a series of textual and musical references relating to the male characteristics given Brünnhilde and the female ones given Siegfried.[27] Quotations from *Opera and Drama* and from letters of Wagner in this context clinch the argument: "the true human being is both man and woman" (25/26 January 1854 to August Röckel: *SL* 303); "My essay on the nature of opera, the final fruits of my deliberations, has assumed greater dimensions than I had first supposed: but if I wish to demonstrate that music (as a woman) must necessarily be impregnated by a poet (as a man), then I must ensure that this glorious woman is not abandoned to the first passing libertine, but that she is made pregnant only by the man who yearns for womankind with true, irresistible love" (25 November 1850 to Liszt: *SL* 220–21).

Meanwhile, the face of Wagner opera production was radically transformed over the final three decades of the twentieth century. This is not the place for a detailed examination of production history;[28] rather, some salient aspects as they relate to the interpretive history of the *Ring* may be noted. Two seminal productions of the 1970s, those of Joachim Herz (Leipzig, 1973–76) and Patrice Chéreau (Bayreuth, 1976), addressed the social and political issues of the *Ring* in a direct, confrontational fashion. Harry Kupfer (Bayreuth, 1988) investigated further the environmental issues: the desecration of nature leading inexorably to global (nuclear) catastrophe.[29]

Less explicitly political, yet no less iconoclastic, was Ruth Berghaus's surreal, image-rich commentary on the Wagnerian legacy (Frankfurt, 1985–87). Her development of a non-naturalistic style, charged with potent references to the Theater of the Absurd, influenced the work of many subsequent directors, not least Richard Jones (Covent Garden, 1994–95) and Peter Konwitschny (*Götterdämmerung*, Stuttgart, 2002). Other important productions of this era include those of Ulrich Melchinger (Kassel, 1970–74), Götz Friedrich (Covent Garden, 1974–76), Nikolaus Lehnhoff (Munich, 1987), Herbert Wernicke (Brussels, 1991), Robert Carsen (Cologne, 2000), David Alden (Munich, 2002–03), and Keith Warner (Covent Garden, 2004–06). What most, if not all, of these productions share is a skepticism with regard to the Wagnerian tradition, toward the ethos of the sublime and the cult of the hero.[30]

The anti-Semitic subtext identified by many commentators in Wagner's characterization of the Nibelungs Alberich and Mime[31] has also been incorporated in certain stage conceptions. Some directors have chosen to emphasize the overtones of racial supremacy in Acts 1 and 2 of *Siegfried* (Mime is cunning and devious, he whines, screeches, shuffles, nods, and blinks, is weak-kneed and hunchbacked, with rheumy eyes and drooping ears; Siegfried, by contrast, is defined with Manichean bluntness as everything Mime is not: radiant, the bringer of light, smiling, strong, heroic, and erect). Others have endeavored to confront the thinly disguised embodiment of Aryan supremacy, depicting Siegfried as an overgrown boy scout, a crass, loutish youth rather than the noble figure of legend. Such stagings are congruent with the widespread distaste in modern times for uncritical representations of the heroic. Wotan too has generally been portrayed unsympathetically, for example by Chéreau, Friedrich, and Kupfer, as a ruthless, power-hungry dictator of overweening ambition.

The deliberate anachronisms of many contemporary, postmodernist productions – settings, costumes, and props refracting the modern world to their audience – are combined in the best of them with a mythic or otherwise universalizing dimension. In this sense, Wagner's aim to set forth, in allegorical form, the potentially catastrophic degradation of values he perceived in contemporary society is accomplished with all the emotional force and immediacy the modern theater can command.

6 Leitmotif, temporality, and musical design in the *Ring*

THOMAS S. GREY

New paths

In the first years of the nineteenth century, Ludwig van Beethoven famously announced to a friend, the violinist Wenzel Krumpholz, that he intended to embark on an entirely "new path." Half a century later, in 1853, Robert Schumann proclaimed the advent of the young Johannes Brahms in the same terms – *Neue Bahnen*, new paths – in a valedictory feature of sorts in the progressive musical journal he himself had founded, the *Neue Zeitschrift für Musik*. This was a deliberate provocation, since the journal's new editor, Franz Brendel, was currently championing the radical theories of Richard Wagner, which provided much better fodder for journalistic debate than did the mostly unpublished works of a quiet twenty-year-old pianist. Beethoven's earlier "new path" gradually became apparent in works like the *Eroica* Symphony, while the novelty of Brahms's voice was much slower to be heard by the larger public. But probably the most emphatic decision made by any composer to chart a whole new course was that made by Wagner, at precisely the time of Schumann's tribute to Brahms. Indeed, Wagner himself later spoke of the "new path," or *neue Bahn*, he entered in *Das Rheingold*.[1]

After completing *Lohengrin* Wagner became swept up in the socialist-revolutionary ferment that seized much of Europe when a popular uprising overturned the reign of Louis-Philippe and threw France into a state of political and social turmoil at the beginning of 1848. It was in 1848, too, that Wagner first formulated the idea for a great national operatic epic based on the medieval *Nibelungenlied*.[2] A year later he found himself exiled from Saxony and the other German states, in a condition of great nervous excitement that would last for some time. (His creative "new path" would also be accompanied by a decade of wanderings, between 1849 and 1859: from Paris and Zurich to Venice and Lucerne, with a side trip to London.) The bulk of his theoretical writing comes from this period of political and mental agitation, and these writings are mostly concerned, explicitly or implicitly, with the gestation of his *magnum opus*, as Wagner clearly conceived it from the beginning. The revolutionary, even anarchistic rhetoric that nourished him in these years contributed something to his sense that his opera about the legendary hero Siegfried would mark the beginning of a whole new era of operatic, musical, indeed cultural history. When the projected opera – at first styled *Siegfrieds Tod* (*Siegfried's Death*) – began to metamorphose into a cycle of two, three, and finally four dramas, the stakes increased accordingly. In the meantime Wagner had been furiously meditating on a whole new kind of musical-dramatic "artwork" that would make the very concept of "opera" obsolete (see chapter 10). When, at long last, he began composing the first installment of *Der Ring des Nibelungen* (*The Ring of the Nibelung*) in the final months of 1853, Wagner was acutely conscious of the radically experimental nature of the enterprise.

The texts for the *Ring* dramas were written essentially in reverse order, as is often pointed out, starting with the prose draft of *Götterdämmerung* (as *Siegfrieds Tod*) in October 1848, and concluding with the verse draft of *Das Rheingold* about four years later (3 November 1852).[3] In turning to the musical composition Wagner did begin at the beginning, with *Das Rheingold*, and several factors allowed him (even encouraged him) to approach this first score in a radically experimental vein. Where the *Götterdämmerung* libretto was still conceived under the impress of "grand historical opera," as were *Tannhäuser* and *Lohengrin*, by the time Wagner got to writing the final texts of the *Ring* he had worked through the theoretical upheavals of the "Zurich" writings (including *Opera and Drama*) and persuaded himself of the need for a radical break with everything hitherto known as "opera." Moreover, since *Das Rheingold* is styled as a "prologue" to the cycle proper – otherwise comprising a trilogy of full-length, three-act dramas – Wagner felt even more at liberty to experiment here with dramatic and musical structure.

Once this prologue is underway and we have emerged from the time-less depths of the river Rhine, what probably strikes most listeners about the style of *Rheingold* is the relentlessly talky "realism," or the absence of lyrical "numbers," as the first audiences would have seen it. Aria- or duet-like scenes play a larger role in all of the subsequent dramas, even if "arias and duets" per se are still banished, of course. The singing of the three Rhine maidens in the first scene does offer just a few glimpses of the old, innocent world of aria and ensemble singing, partly as a means of tempting and teasing Alberich. But when Flosshilde seems to begin a lyrical duet with Alberich ("Seligster Mann!" / "Süßeste Maid!"), the whole manner is shown up as a parody. Characters are allowed brief moments of lyrical reflection when such reflection constitutes a genuine "dramatic action" – for instance, Wotan's dreamy, self-satisfied contemplation of his new fortress, Valhalla, at the beginning of scene 2 and the end of scene 4. When characters are charged with a more formal manner of utterance, the musical setting will reflect this, too, as in the case of Alberich's parting curse, Erda's warning to Wotan, or Donner's conjuring of the rainbow bridge to Valhalla (all in the final scene). Otherwise, Wagner cleaves to a style of motivically supported musical recitation, in monologue or dialogue, rooted in "accompanied" recitative or *scena* styles of earlier opera. (Like those earlier idioms, this one is allowed to blossom into brief passages of arioso.) This new manner is prescribed to some extent by the prose-like effect of the short, non-rhyming alliterative text lines (*Stabreim*), devised in imitation of medieval Germanic poetry. Without the rhyming, stanzaic structures of traditional libretto verse, Wagner is not tempted to lapse into the periodic phraseology of traditional operatic aria. Equally radical is the abandonment of extended units grounded in a single, clearly defined tonality.[4] What could Wagner offer to compensate in the way of compelling musical "discourse," melody, design, or some new conception of operatic singing? This was the great challenge that faced him on his "new path."

Leitmotif: a brief introduction

Perhaps the most important, and certainly the most apparent, single element of Wagner's "new path," his response to the challenge of reinventing opera as a new kind of musical drama, was the leitmotif. This famous Wagnerian bequest to music history was not so named by Wagner himself. The term "leitmotif" became naturalized in the wake of the first Bayreuth festivals, where Hans von Wolzogen's explanatory guides or *Leitfaden* illustrated with the principal motives of the score popularized the concept of these "leading motives" associated with all aspects of the cast, props, symbols, and ideas of the cycle.[5] The designation of Wolzogen's guides (*Leitfäden*, or "guiding threads") could be applied to any manual meant to help the uninitiated navigate a complex, unfamiliar discipline. But even before he began cataloguing the musical-dramatic motives of Wagner's works, the term "leitmotif" (*Leitmotiv*) had started to be applied to these associative, signifying musical themes that had assumed such a prominent role in Wagner's mature works, with the implication that they themselves constituted a "thread" or rather network, at once musical and semantic, unifying and explicating these works.

Wagner himself refrained from naming either the technique or the individual motives within the operas, although he certainly attempted to theorize about them, in the third and last part of the treatise *Opera and Drama*, before starting on the composition of the *Ring*. Like so much in that treatise, the theory of associative or referential motives remained vague, prolix, but suggestive. He did not arrive there at any particular name for the practice. The terms he does use – such as "melodic moments" or "elements" (*melodische Momente*), "orchestral melody," or simply "motives" – are either cumbersome or inconsistent, so the word "leitmotif" fills a terminological need, just as it often proves a practical necessity to attach names to the individual leitmotifs (following Wolzogen and other early commentators), simply in order to begin identifying, interpreting, or analyzing them.[6] Of course, the idea of attributing dramatic import to a specific, recurring musical idea was not new to the *Ring*. *Lohengrin* had made prominent use of such motives (identified, for example, with the title figure, with the command that Elsa never ask his name or, more subtly, with the villainess Ortrud, whose presence evokes a nexus of slithery, sinister, readily shifting figures), and Wagner had experimented with the practice since his very earliest operatic efforts (see chapter 2). Drastically new, however, was the idea of constructing essentially the entire musical fabric of the score from themes or motives of this kind. In this way, so Wagner speculated, the orchestral accompaniment would be at every moment dramatically relevant, no mere harmonic-rhythmic carpet on which singers would strut their melodic finery, as of old. On the other hand, it forced the composer to devise some kind of compromise between a crude indexical underscoring of characters and stage properties, on the one hand, and the need to create effective musical momentum and structure, on the other – a compelling musical rhetoric to supplant the conventional designs of "absolute" operatic melody Wagner had chosen to dismiss.

Der Ring des Nibelungen as a whole contains some sixty or seventy distinct musical motives of this kind, or upwards of a hundred or more if one were to include the many variants and transformations that are generated in the course of the cycle.[7] Which is to say, too, that leitmotifs in the *Ring* do not have an absolutely fixed identity: it is often difficult to name them accurately, and impossible to make an exact tally, since they tend to shift shape, hence also character and meaning. Deryck Cooke, following Wagner's own lead, stressed the idea of "families" of related motives and variants generated by a smaller repertoire of what Wagner referred to as "plastic [i.e., malleable] nature motives."[8] Before considering how Wagner uses motives to compose his scores and how they relate to the musical setting of the text (vocal line), we might consider some types of leitmotif in the *Ring*, if not a systematic typology.

Some of the most distinct, dramatically important motives are ones whose function derives from that of recurring themes in earlier operas, also related to recurring verbal tags or formulas in spoken drama (especially melodrama, where they were doubtless shadowed by appropriate musical gestures). This family of traditional functions would include curses, spells, prophecies, talismans, and oracular riddles: things that, by their very nature, tend to recur in meaningful, portentous ways within a drama or story. (Related to these types or functions would be another of the earliest forms of operatic "reminiscence" material: a ballad that might recount important history or legend with repercussions for present and future events. Senta's ballad in *Der fliegende Holländer* [*The Flying Dutchman*] is a relic of this tradition, and a bridge between it and the leitmotif technique of the music dramas.) Several foundational leitmotifs presented in *Das Rheingold* belong to these categories, such as those associated with Alberich's Curse on Love (scene 1) and later on the ring (scene 4), the Ring itself, the Rhine gold, the Tarnhelm, the hero's Sword ("envisioned" by Wotan near the end), and Erda's warning to Wotan about the ring and the "doom of the gods."

These originary, "primitive" motives overlap or interrelate in terms of dramatic function as well as musical identity. Alberich's original Curse on Love, by means of which he secures the power to forge the ring, begins as a prophecy or warning oracle, uttered by the Rhine maiden Woglinde: "Only he who renounces the power of love, only he who spurns the pleasure of love, only *he* may conjure the magic to forge the ring from the gold" (see Example 6.1, the motive usually called Renunciation of Love). In fact, Alberich's active curse on love only alludes to Woglinde's musical phrase (at "So verfluch' ich die Liebe!" / "Thus do I curse love!") rather than restating it; but this allusion is prefaced by ominous distortions of the Rhine-gold motive and a fragment of the Ring motive, which is itself embedded in the tail of Woglinde's phrase ("zum Reif zu zwingen das Gold"). The Ring motive likewise begins as a prophecy of what might be. Wellgunde informs the curious dwarf, almost casually: "He could inherit the world, who makes from the Rhine-gold this ring, conferring infinite power" (Example 6.2a). When Alberich, a few moments later, mulls over her words, the motive takes on a slightly more determinate, more ominous form, emphasizing the half-diminished seventh chord that will be a characteristic sonority throughout (outlined in contour by mm. 1 and 3 of Example 6.2b), and issuing in a fragment of that other interesting prophecy, "Nur wer der Minne Macht entsagt" ("Only he who forswears the power of love"). When in the last scene of *Rheingold* Alberich curses the ring itself, after Wotan has wrested it from him, his curse takes the form of a full rhetorical-musical "period" of some sixty measures. Embedded within this snarling, unmelodic arioso is a pregnant textual-musical fragment that clearly represents the Curse as such ("As by a curse I obtained it, accursed be this ring!"). Just as the text here also alludes to the preliminary curse – on love – the musical line alludes to the Ring, tracing in reverse

Ex. 6.1

Ex. 6.2a

Ex. 6.2b

Ex. 6.3

the pitches and contour of Alberich's "Der Welt Erbe ..." quoted in Example 6.2b (Example 6.3). The larger musical "period" here, Alberich's angry parting arioso, cites the Ring's descending chain of minor thirds several times, emphasizing the interrelation of Curse and Ring, just as Alberich's text makes it clear how the terms of his curse have largely inhered in the ring from the beginning (through the renunciation of love).

Ex. 6.4a

Ex. 6.4b

Two other important and clearly denotational leitmotifs introduced in *Das Rheingold* are similarly attached to "talismanic" properties like the Ring: the Tarnhelm and the Sword (Nothung). The motive of the Tarnhelm also partakes of the quality of a magic spell, a ritualized formula. It is introduced as a simple but mysterious harmonic progression (Example 6.4a), as Alberich first seizes the Tarnhelm from Mime, who forged it for him. The magic formula is completed by Alberich with the necessary verbal spell: "Night and fog: like to none!" (Example 6.4b). The motive of the hero's Sword is presented instead as an "anticipation," a musical and mental presentiment of an object not yet materially realized. Wotan, "as if seized by a great thought," envisions the race of human heroes he will breed as future guardians of his new stronghold: "Thus I greet the fortress, safe from fear and dread" (Example 6.5). It belongs to the larger family of simple, noble, triadic motives usually associated with natural phenomena (the Rhine, Freia's apples of eternal youth, Donner's thunder, the rainbow bridge to Valhalla). Strictly speaking, the Sword is no natural object; but through its musical motive it is thus allied to the positive qualities of natural things. By contrast, the Tarnhelm motive, though compounded of triads, is characterized by semi-tone voice leading and is prone to chromatic-enharmonic reinterpretation; it belongs to an opposing genus of chromaticized motives associated with evil, trickery, magic, and various kinds of artifice. The explicit denotational role of the

Ex. 6.5

Sword motive is realized only in the course of Act 1 of *Die Walküre*, but then very emphatically so, with Siegmund's discovery of the sword implanted by his father, Wotan, in Hunding's ash tree forming the climax of the whole long recognition scene between the twins Siegmund and Sieglinde. The treatment of the Sword motive thus reflects very accurately the "theory" of musical-dramatic motives provisionally outlined in *Opera and Drama*. It is always an instrumental figure, a bold trumpet fanfare, though subject to unlimited dynamic and timbral variation. The orchestra sounds it at the end of *Rheingold*, as we saw, and throughout Act 1 of *Walküre* in anticipation of the explicit, defining dramatic context, when Siegmund finally draws it from the ash tree and names it Nothung. From that point on, further citations of the motive are to be understood as "reminiscences." Most of those motives illustrated so far could be accommodated to this original theory. (The theory leaves the orchestral anticipation of motives as optional; essential is only the exposition of motive in a definitive dramatic context, supported by vocal utterance or by gesture.)

A last basic category that might be mentioned – also because it touches on some basic pre- or misconceptions about the practice – is that of motives identified with individual characters. The notion of such "personal" leitmotifs as sounding captions, like the placard of vaudeville acts or the inter-title of silent films, is obviously a trivialization (early critics compared them to the texted banners of medieval sacred painting). Even

Ex. 6.6

so, some of the less subtle figures in the cycle – the Giants in *Rheingold* or Hunding in *Die Walküre*, for example – are treated rather like this. Sieglinde opens the door to her hut and there stands Hunding in full battle gear, announced by a consort of tubas playing his dour, lumbering leitmotif (Example 6.6). His entrance has been anticipated, though, by a less blatant version of the motive just a moment earlier, muffled and slightly distorted as if heard through the closed door, and the ears of a nervous Sieglinde. More than a calling card, the motive acts like a kind of nimbus externalizing the character's qualities and the effect of his presence on those around him. Wotan's noble Valhalla theme does the same, even when his "presence" is merely narrative, as in this first act of *Die Walküre*. But Wagner is able to extract pregnant gestures, even purely rhythmic ones, from apparently blunt "indexical" motives like those of Hunding or the Giants. These submotivic gestures or rhythms can serve as the basis of more sophisticated, dramatic musical developments, as happens with the Hunding rhythm later in Act 2 of *Walküre*, for instance. (Having been once formally introduced, in fact, Hunding is never again re-presented in the company of his basic leitmotif, which tends instead to glower in the background in ominously repetitive fragments.) Siegmund and Sieglinde, by contrast, are treated very differently, and aptly so, since their identities are at first only a matter of vague mutual intuition. The motivic ideas that accompany their first appearances, in quick succession, do not represent them as characters as much as they convey gestures or deportment: Siegmund sinking down in exhaustion, Sieglinde leaning over him, tentative and solicitous. These gestures are soon forgotten in favor of a motive shared equally between them, a tender, arching line identified with their sense of instinctive mutual attraction (Example 6.7). Again, this motive does not represent identity but expresses "feelings" (as Wagner would surely have insisted); and in a sense these feelings, as they are motivically elaborated in the course of the act, also identify who these twins "really are." The darkly noble theme of the Volsung clan (Example 6.8) does acquire a more

Ex. 6.7

Ex. 6.8

indexical function. But it begins as an orchestral "anticipation," at the end of Siegmund's narration to Hunding and Sieglinde, evoking the tragic nobility of his family and their fate rather than acting as a simple musical sign of Siegmund as an individual character.

The situation becomes more complex still with the central characters of the *Ring* cycle, Brünnhilde and Siegfried. For one thing, their leitmotifs grow and change with them. Brünnhilde has her characteristic, vibrant war-cry ("Hojotoho!"), and Siegfried his boisterous, youthful horn-call. These begin as sounds produced by the characters themselves, sounds that also happen to communicate something of their original natures. (Siegfried's horn, like those of Roland or Oberon, is another sort of emblematic property, a physical leitmotif.) Siegfried's identity as the epic hero, on the other hand, begins as a prophecy – hence a motive of "anticipation" – when Brünnhilde and Wotan allude to his future role before she is placed into the bonds of her "magic sleep" (Example 6.9). His horn-call changes character with his passage from adolescence to manhood. When he emerges from the nuptial cave in the prologue to *Götterdämmerung*, the motive is broadly and majestically transformed, down a tone from F to E-flat major (Examples 6.10a and 6.10b). Brünnhilde's transformation is greater still, from valkyrie to human woman: she exchanges the musical "riding habit" she shared with all her valkyrie sisters (the theme of their famous ride) for an entirely new figure

Ex. 6.9

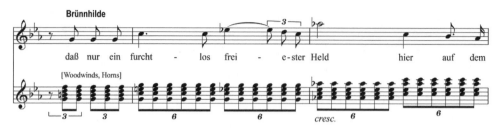

Ex. 6.10a

Ex. 6.10b

(Example 6.11), more vocal in conception, although the instrumental turn-figure that energizes its opening intervallic leap is of the essence. The opening of her new motive demands some counterbalancing continuation; characteristically, this is not fixed within the motive, but left open to different possibilities on virtually every occurrence. Siegfried's and Brünnhilde's new, "mature" motives engage in a kind of musical dialogue throughout this second scene of the *Götterdämmerung* prologue, leaving no doubt as to their identification with hero and heroine. Siegfried's is

Ex. 6.11

essentially lost to him once he imbibes Hagen's draught of forgetfulness, and is recuperated only in the music that commemorates him after his death (the orchestral eulogy and transition to the last scene of the cycle, known as "Siegfried's Funeral Music"). Brünnhilde's remains with her throughout most of the opera. However, it serves less to announce her presence on stage than as a subject of musical discourse wherever she, as vulnerable and betrayed woman, is the subject of the dramatic action.

Leitmotif and dramatic composition

The very notion of compounding a large, complex musical score (let alone a cycle of them) from a network of referential, signifying motives might seem like a case of typically Teutonic theoretical speculation, anticipating attempts of Schoenberg and others to reinvent the basic materials of composition in the following century. Certainly many early critics regarded it in this light, as an overweening, quixotic experiment, especially in light of the similarly overweening pronouncements in Wagner's writings. At the same time, the "system" has exercised from the start an irresistible exegetical fascination. The motivically illustrated guides and commentaries issued by Wolzogen and company, as Wagner had already feared, encouraged the belief that the key to "understanding" the music dramas lay in decoding the leitmotivic network. Earlier instances of motivic reminiscence in opera, including Wagner's early operas, had been limited to marginal glosses, for the most part. They might achieve genuine dramatic-rhetorical prominence, as does the Ban on Love motive in *Das Liebesverbot* (see chapter 2), but the composition as such does not really rely on them. As a way of broaching the many complex issues presented by the music of the *Ring* cycle, it might be fruitful to ask how – in the case of a few representative passages – it is "composed of" leitmotifs, and what else is involved in transmuting this peculiar raw material into musical composition, and a musical form of drama. Without trying to read the finished score in conformity with the tentative theories of *Opera and Drama*, it could nonetheless be instructive to consider three dramatic modes roughly corresponding to the "tenses" of leitmotif Wagner had described there in terms of anticipation, realization, and reminiscence (future, present, and past). In the following sample passages, these three musical-dramatic "tenses" are reflected in dramatic modes we can identify as prophecy (monologic address), action (dialogue), and epic recapitulation (narrative).

Prophecy (monologue)
The prophetic warning uttered by the earth-goddess, Erda, to Wotan in the final scene of *Das Rheingold* was inspired by the famous "Voluspa," the strange sibylline utterances, addressed to Odin, that open the *Poetic Edda* (*Codex Regius*). Erda's words to Wotan are much more to the point than the apocalyptic ravings of her unnamed prototype: she reminds him of Alberich's curse on the ring (the terms of which ought to be fresh enough in his memory) and warns him that retaining possession of it will ultimately threaten the very existence of the gods. Erda's appearance is styled as a scene of prophecy, an oracle: the stage darkens, and amidst a "bluish light" her form rises from a "rocky cleft," heralded by fortissimo octaves in trombones, bass tremolo, and timpani. Her utterance is monologic, though addressed specifically to Wotan, who punctuates it with a question ("Who are you, ominous woman?") and a demand ("Stay, that I might know more!"). A warning such as she issues here ("Let go of the ring, and avoid catastrophe") should presuppose free will and the ability to avert disaster by choosing the right course. But precisely because it is styled as an oracle, rhetorically and musically, the fate she warns against assumes an aspect of inevitable destiny. The Twilight of the Gods is foreordained here, just as it was in the "Voluspa," even if Wotan is nominally treated as a free moral agent in a modern sense.

As a monologic utterance, rhetorically self-contained, Erda's speech suggests an operatic aria. In context, however, it represents what Wagner had theorized as the musical-dramatic alternative to the aria (or the subsections thereof): a "poetic-musical period."[9] As the name implies, this was understood as a unit exhibiting some degree of complementary rhetorical and musical coherence. Such units would be seamlessly integrated within the larger, ongoing dramatic and musical discourse of a scene and, in turn, an entire act. The "period" comprising Erda's single brief appearance in *Das Rheingold* is unusually self-contained with respect to the rest of the score, reflecting the autonomy of Erda as a figure and the isolated nature of her speech. Nonetheless, it illustrates the way leitmotif can be at once textually responsive and still help to structure "periods" or whole scenes in the *Ring* generally.

We can view the whole passage (given as Example 6.12) as being in C-sharp minor, the key appearing – like Erda herself – suddenly, without preparation, and melting away with Erda's disappearance from the stage. (A full musical caesura occurs six measures after the end of Example 6.12, where the scene's principal rising motive is echoed one last time, only now in E-flat minor.) This C-sharp minor tonic is most clearly established at the beginning and end of her central speech, in between Wotan's two interjections (see m. 16 and m. 54 in Example 6.12). Thematically, the period coheres around its principal leitmotif, announced by tubas and bassoons at the beginning of the excerpt. This is a minor-mode transposition of the original arpeggiated triadic Nature or Rhine motive on which the whole Prelude to *Das Rheingold* is based; here it is recoined in a slow, darkened version as Erda's leitmotif. The motive thus characterizes Erda as an emanation of primal, natural forces, at the same time evoking the cloud or threat under which nature and gods alike find themselves as a result of Alberich's ring. The same figure initiates a mid-section to the larger period in m. 27, returned to the major mode (E) and given a flowing string accompaniment that briefly recalls its original, "natural," unclouded form when Erda refers to her daughters, the Norns. Folded into this mid-section is another, more emphatic contrast when she adumbrates the threat at hand: the halting rhythms and diminished harmony that framed Alberich's curse (m. 36, sometimes called the "Nibelung's Hate" or "Envy") preface the distorted, chromaticized version of the Rhine maidens' salutation to the Rhine-gold ("Höre! Höre! Höre!"), a figure associated in scene 3 with Alberich's dominion. Then the orchestra gestures at a return, momentarily recalling Erda's motive in the C-sharp minor tonic (m. 43). Rhetorically, however, this is no *da capo* but a peroration, or at any rate a culmination, as Erda arrives at her point: "All that is must end! A dark day dawns for the gods: I urge you, part with the ring!" The only wholly new motive of the passage is introduced now by means of inverting Erda's darkly prophetic "nature" motive so that it descends over a Neapolitan cadential harmony ($\flat\mathrm{II}^6$ or D^6), generating the leitmotif of the Twilight of the Gods. (While she speaks of a dark day "dawning," the German *Dämmerung* can refer to both dawn and dusk.) Appended to this, the Ring motive (mm. 49–51) hovers for a moment as a sort of leitmotivic "cadenza," while its up-and-down contour echoes and reinforces the up-and-down relationship of Erda's motive and the Twilight of the Gods, just presented. Further echoes of Erda's motive round out the "period," outlining C-sharp minor in the treble while the harmonic foundation gradually erodes.

Ex. 6.12

Ex. 6.12 (cont.)

Ex. 6.12 (cont.)

As a whole, then, Erda's address to Wotan illustrates the transformation of the free-standing aria into a "poetic-musical period," integrated within the larger, continuous musical-dramatic fabric. Her opening lines are purely declamatory, in the manner of recitative, and brief enough not to interrupt the sense of an ongoing motivic discourse. Her own leitmotif is briefly "anticipated" in the orchestra at the very beginning, prior to its textual-vocal "definition" ("Wie alles war, weiß ich"), in keeping with the original theory of motives (though not so different from the way an orchestral ritornello anticipates the main theme of an aria). Elements of tonal and motivic contrast and return are deployed in a relatively traditional manner, too, still allowing for dramatic culmination in place of formal restatement, and for a naturalistic elision with the action that follows. Citation of other leitmotifs is kept to a minimum, but after the declamatory introduction (from m. 16 on) all the material is leitmotivic. Rather than devising a new motive in mentioning the Norns, Wagner merely hints at their kinship with Erda and with the natural universe, at the same time providing a conventional tonal contrast within the relative major, E. Just as Erda merely alludes to Alberich's curse, rather than citing it, the orchestra recalls only its accompanimental frame, allowing Wagner to reserve a more portentous citation of the Curse motive for the subsequent murder of Fasolt by Fafner. The new motive of the Twilight of the Gods inserted after the apparent gesture of musical reprise at m. 43 is, as mentioned, motivically derived by inversion of the passage's principal motive, and can furthermore be heard as part of a reprise-like function or gesture since its Neapolitan (D) harmony was already heard in an analogous position, though over a tonic pedal, in the first phrase of the central "period" (m. 21). Wagner even achieves a felicitous detail of semantic coordination here, as both two-measure fragments of Neapolitan harmony accompany references to the future: "all that will be, I see as well" and "a dark day dawns for the gods." Erda, who adapts the originary motivic contour of the entire cycle, could be read as figuring the leitmotivic discourse of the "omniscient" Wagnerian orchestra altogether.[10] "All that was, I know; all that is, and all that will be, I see as well." (Wagner later likened the "invisible orchestra" at Bayreuth to "the steams rising from Gaia's primeval womb beneath the seat of the Pythia," the Delphic oracle; *GS* IX:338.) Through leitmotif, as mentioned, the orchestra was meant to obtain mastery over dramatic time, to speak freely of what is past, passing, and to come (theoretically, in reverse order). If critics have become skeptical about the orchestra's claims to such dramatic omniscience, the "truth-value" of leitmotivic reference, we can recall that Erda's own omniscience is seriously challenged later in the cycle, when Wotan awakens her in Act 3 of *Siegfried* only to tell her how much the world has changed.[11]

Action (dialogue)

The defining principle of music drama, as a more "evolved" species of opera, could be identified as a dialogic conception of musical form, or formal process. As Wagner well knew, extended duet scenes had become the lifeblood of French grand opera and much Italian opera at the time he began his study of the art. If associative, referential motives, or leitmotifs, were to form the basic material of his new musical drama, coalescing at the first level of musical structure into "poetic-musical periods," the model for concatenating such periods into a developing, evolving series would be dramatic dialogue: a dialectical confrontation leading to some climactic point of crisis, and then its resolution. If musical form were to grow naturally from dramatic form, as argued in *Opera and Drama*, a dialogic principle would be the natural point of reference.

A majority of scenes in *Der Ring des Nibelungen* are indeed conceived dialogically, as arguments or confrontations. (These might involve multiple participants, such as the three Rhine maidens vs. Alberich in *Rheingold*, scene 2, or the Gibichung family and vassals backing Siegfried in his altercation with Brünnhilde in Act 2 of *Götterdämmerung*.) Act 2 of *Die Walküre* offers good examples of classically structured dramatic arguments, realized as musical process: first between Wotan and Fricka, and later between Brünnhilde and Siegmund (the "Annunciation of Death" scene).[12] Even Wotan's great monologue, in between these, is a kind of interior dialogue. In every case, the outcome of the confrontation has some critical bearing on the larger progress of the dramatic cycle. Wagner is usually careful to limit external events accordingly, focusing each scene on one crucial decision or deed. (This is one main reason for the impression that his dramas are all talk and little action.) One of the shorter scenes from the later part of the cycle, the confrontation between Siegfried and the Wanderer at the base of Brünnhilde's rock in Act 3, scene 2, of *Siegfried*, can illustrate some of the compositional features of this basic Wagnerian technique, the musical-dramatic dialogue.

Wotan's attempt to block Siegfried's ascent to the sleeping Brünnhilde is a scene entirely of Wagner's invention.[13] Wotan's action is counterintuitive, on the level of dramatic plot; the scene only makes sense in the psychological, indeed strongly pre-Freudian, sense of an initiatory process culminating in Siegfried's discovery of Brünnhilde.[14] It is in this spirit that Wotan himself seems to have set up the encounter. Following the supernatural counsel of the Woodbird (the counsel of nature itself), Siegfried is intent on scaling the mountain where Brünnhilde lies in the bonds of sleep. Wotan stands in his way and poses a series of questions, a kind of ritual catechism whose only apparent aim is the cultivation of self-knowledge in the hitherto unreflective young hero. As usual with Siegfried,

Wagner's attempt to portray youthful, naïve self-confidence results in something more like aggressive petulance. In any case, the showdown between youth and paternal authority figure allows Siegfried to slay the "father" symbolically, in destroying the symbol of his power (the spear inscribed with the treaties that confer Wotan's divine authority, but which have also hobbled his ability to cope with the dilemma of Alberich's ring). In the preceding scene with Erda we have just heard Wotan proclaim his desire for precisely this end, and predict (at the introduction of the World Inheritance motive) the advent of an era of free human "heroes" following the demise of the treaty-bound, morally compromised gods. The victory of the sword Nothung over Wotan's spear encapsulates this destiny, clearing the path to Siegfried's union with a newly mortal Brünnhilde.

This scene at the center of Act 3 parallels – even parodies, in a sense – the analogously placed scene between Wotan and Mime in Act 1. In both cases Wotan is disguised as the Wanderer, and in both cases the dialogue involves ritualized questions. Mime, the weak and negative figure, fails to pose the one necessary question ("Who will re-forge Nothung?"), nor can he answer it; Siegfried, on the other hand, brushes aside the Wanderer's apparently meddlesome questions, sticking purposefully to *his* one "needful question" ("Where is the path to the sleeping maid, Brünnhilde?"). In between, though, he also reverses the pattern of questioning, asking the Wanderer with a "naïve" candor (bordering on bratty impertinence) about his odd hat and his missing eye. (The reversal of roles in the questioning also mirrors the pattern of exchange in Act 1, scene 2.) The scene begins and ends with explicit "action" music. Siegfried enters in the wake of his Woodbird guide, accompanied by the same propulsive version of the Woodbird/Forest music that concluded Act 2, creating an explicit musical suture between that earlier exit and this entrance. The same music briefly leads him, even in the absence of the Woodbird itself, toward Brünnhilde's fire (from "Strahlend nun offen steht mir die Straße"), and the scene concludes with another forward-directed orchestral transition, a seething leitmotivic fantasia illustrating Siegfried's ascent through the flames that guard the sleeping valkyrie. Framed by these directional transitions, this brief scene as a whole takes on a transitional character, joining the weightier (likewise dialogic) scenes on either side: Wotan and Erda, Siegfried and Brünnhilde.

The propulsive music derived from the end of Act 2 continues from Siegfried's entrance up to the first of Wotan's questions. Here Wagner introduces a short refrain gesture (Example 6.13a) that will recur systematically with each further question, until Siegfried finally deflects the questioning (Example 6.13b). This new motive, like several adopted by Wotan-as-Wanderer in Act 1, scene 2, is a kind of temporary disguise,

Ex. 6.13a

Ex. 6.13b

here reflecting the good-natured, avuncular tone he takes with Siegfried, but at the same time delivering a strong check to the eagerly propulsive music of Siegfried's new quest. Thus, the dialogue is divided, both dramatically and musically, into two phases. The first, more easygoing one is structured around five statements (and two fragmentary developments) of the Wanderer's "questioning" refrain. The second phase takes a more serious, ominous turn, leading as it does to Siegfried's defiance of Wotan and the shattering of Wotan's spear. The continuity of this second phase is effected by reiterations of three motives: a downward coiling figure that is often developed by rising sequences expressive – here, as originally in Act 2 of *Die Walküre* – of Wotan's mounting anger or unrest (Example 6.14a); the related, more emphatically descending gesture of his Spear motive (Example 6.14b); and a Volsung motive quoted from Act 1 of *Die Walküre* (Example 6.14c), representing the familial bond that Wotan feels toward his antagonist, even though he cannot express it overtly. The loosely structural repetition of these motives across the two phases of the dialogue allows Wagner to insert other, more fleeting leitmotivic references into the texture (for example, Fafner, the reforging of Nothung, the Magic Fire and Valkyrie motives, the Sword) without causing it to devolve into a sheer patchwork.

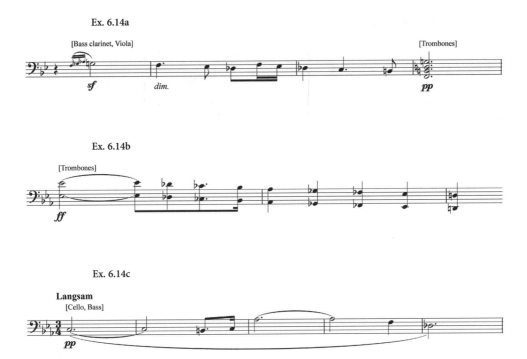

Ex. 6.14a

Ex. 6.14b

Ex. 6.14c

The Wanderer's questioning refrain (Example 6.13a) exhibits expressive and gestural qualities that are dramatically to the purpose – Hans von Wolzogen dubbed it the motive of *Vaterfreude* (paternal joy or pride). It shares a structural characteristic of many leitmotifs in allowing for different continuations: after the first statement, the others continue as in Example 6.13b and lead into one or another leitmotivic reference. It is likely that we are meant to hear this as a lighter variant of the Valhalla/ Wotan motive, which in fact dominates the end of this first phase of dialogue, as Siegfried redirects the questions to the Wanderer. This shift in direction dislodges the motive from its initially stable tonality of E flat (to C), prepared by two fragmentary, developmental references to the refrain. After that, the motive will never be heard again in *Siegfried* or anywhere else. In this it represents a not insignificant category of musical motives in the *Ring* whose function – musical-structural as well as dramatic – is limited to a single scene.

These may share some features of "genuine" leitmotifs (ones that recur throughout the cycle), or even be derived from them (as this one may be from Valhalla). Yet they function like the recurring motivic gestures that unify individual scenes in contemporary non-Wagnerian opera, too. Here, the motive serves above all to scan the structure of the dialogue, up to the point of Siegfried's commandeering and tonal

Ex. 6.15

dislodging of the figure, concluding the first phase of the scene and inaugurating the second.

This second phase begins with Wotan's gentle, resigned admonition: "If you knew me, bold youth, you would spare me this scorn" (the first statement of Example 6.14a). Wotan now dominates the dialogue, and there is no stable tonal center until the large F-major cadence that sends Siegfried on his way up the mountain ("Jetzt lock' ich ein liebes Gesell!"). The energy of the dialogic conflict is displaced, to some extent, into the orchestra, where the motive of Wotan's displeasure (Example 6.14a) is increasingly developed, in both musical and semantic dialogue with the motives of his power (the Spear, Example 6.14b) and of his paternal bond with Siegfried (Example 6.14c). The clash of sword and spear at the scene's climax is an example of leitmotif in its most overtly semiotic function. Even so, these gestures – the aggressive upward stroke of the Sword, the descent and rhythmic disintegration of the Spear (Example 6.15) – convey a meaning beyond the denotative ones invested in them by mechanism of textual-musical alignment. As Wotan disappears from view, never to reappear on stage, we hear the Twilight of the Gods motive in hushed string tremolo, on the appropriate Neapolitan-sixth harmony (here, D flat). Wotan collects the pieces of his shattered spear, while Siegfried gathers up the various leitmotivic properties he will carry with him on his quest.

How successfully Wagner integrates individual referential motivic gestures throughout a scene like this remains a matter of subjective critical judgement. A still closer reading than the one offered here could reveal a pattern of increasing tension and complexity in the individual "periods," leading up to the great crash of Wotan's breaking spear (in place of a conventional tonal or thematic reprise). For its original audience, the style demanded a real leap of musical faith, as Wagner himself freely admitted – indeed, demanded. That such a scene works at all, however, depends on the way he was able to harness the elements of motive, tonality, harmonic rhythm, and overall musical pacing to the larger structure of his dramatic dialogue. Like any skilled librettist, Wagner was careful to devise this structure with the potential of music's contribution in mind.

Epic recapitulation (narrative)

Once *Siegfried's Death* became *Götterdämmerung*, the concluding drama of the *Ring* cycle, it acquired a significant recapitulatory dimension. Enacting the mythic background of this original drama across a "prologue" (*Das Rheingold*) and two further dramas (*Die Walküre, Siegfried*) not only allowed Wagner to integrate mythological and symbolic layers that were wholly absent from the source of *Siegfried's Death* (the *Nibelungenlied*), it also provided the opportunity to introduce and develop a larger network of leitmotifs. The most powerful function of the leitmotif is the evocation of things *past*, its ability to infuse the dramatic present with an epic history, and *Götterdämmerung* is the richest beneficiary of this capacity. The Norns' scene that was retained as a prologue to the (now) final drama becomes something of a treatise on the role of leitmotif in negotiating the temporality of music drama, with each Norn discoursing in turn on the past, the present, and the future. Subsequently, Siegfried and Brünnhilde appear as a bridge from the immediate past (their first courtship) to the immediate future (the drama of Siegfried at the Gibichungs' court). Act 3 of *Götterdämmerung*, concerned with the quasi-sacrificial death of Siegfried out of which the whole cycle evolved, is equally preoccupied with taking stock, dramatically and musically, of all that has been.

The musical saturation of the present by the past is exemplified in the very opening moments of Act 3. Siegfried's horn-call, heard both in the orchestra and offstage, situates us at once in the dramatic present of the hunting scene that is the setting for the hero's murder. This is answered by three musical gestures, all relating to the present (as yet invisible) dramatic setting, but also to the immediate past: the tritone-accompanied half-step motive of Siegfried's Death (which we have just heard plotted in the closing scene of Act 2); Hagen's ominous steer-horn, used to summon his vassals in the preceding act; and another horn-call, answering Siegfried's on the dominant chord (C), which was likewise introduced amidst the wedding festivities just concluded (Example 6.16).[15] Siegfried's horn replies blithely to this ill-omened congeries, and the orchestra then touches back

Ex. 6.16

on the origins of the entire cycle (transposed here to F), preparing the reappearance of the Rhine maidens with recollections of the flowing, canonic nature motive of the river Rhine, the maidens' call to the Rhinegold, and the motive of the Gold itself. A distant utopian past and a recent corrupt and threatening past are thus musically woven into the sounding texture of the present with remarkable economy.

To justify his murder of Siegfried in this act, Hagen needs to restore the hero's memory so that Siegfried, by recalling his own courtship of Brünnhilde, will appear to confirm his (unwittingly) perjured testimony regarding her and the ring in Act 2, and hence the betrayal of his blood-brotherhood oath to Gunther. The business of a forgetfulness potion in Act 1 and its antidote, now secretly administered to Siegfried, has often been seen as one of the most egregious contrivances of the *Ring* plot. Yet as handled in the musical composition of the drama it acquires surprisingly sophisticated psychological nuances, adding to the temporal dimension of leitmotif technique interesting implications for the role of memory in the perception and interpretation of musical processes. The semantic – rather than directly expressive or locally structural – function of leitmotifs depends on our memory of their origins and earlier uses. A motive might tug at our memory, as happens to the drugged Siegfried, without our being able to recall quite accurately where we have heard it before and what it seemed to signify. Quite apart from the magic herb Hagen surreptitiously mixes in Siegfried's wine during this scene, it is the "talking cure" he arranges that seems to be the real means of restoring Siegfried's faculties.

Hagen harps on Siegfried's legendary capacity to interpret the song of birds – a skill akin, we might say, to interpreting the sense of musical melody or motives. In response, the hero agrees to tell the "fairy tale" of his youth. In telling the tale, and through the musical recollections this involves, he is led naturally, inexorably to the recovery of his first memories of Brünnhilde and how the Woodbird's song directed him to her. The narration begins with a summary of his early upbringing in the forest ("Mime hieß ein mürrischer Zwerg"), and once Siegfried taps the flow of memory he overcomes the artificial blockage engineered by Hagen's potion. As soon as he gets to the critical confession ("I loosened the helm of the noble maiden, my kiss boldly awoke her: O! how ardently the beautiful Brünnhilde embraced me!"), Hagen pierces him with his spear. But Siegfried sings on ("Brünnhilde! Heilige Braut!"), reprising the music of Brünnhilde's awakening and her greeting to the sun. Even when he collapses, finally bereft of life and breath, the orchestra continues to reminisce, in the form of a leitmotivic eulogy that recalls motives pertaining to his father, his mother, the heroic sword, the prophecy of his own birth, and his union with Brünnhilde at the beginning of the present drama (all of this in the interlude known as "Siegfried's Funeral" music). Afterwards, Brünnhilde's closing address (the "Immolation" scene) begins as a musical reprise, or dramatic realization, of the third Norn's prophecies in the prologue. This reprise, in turn, is completed by the orchestra accompanying the images of apocalypse and purgation that bring down the final curtain. Just as the original *Siegfried's Death* needed to be supplemented with an extensive dramatic and musical (leitmotivic) exposition, so the eventual *Götterdämmerung*, especially its final act, becomes an extended recapitulation, an attempt to sort through the events of the cycle and to lead us toward some ultimate conclusion. Wagner had difficulty getting started with the *Ring* cycle and with ending it. Significantly, perhaps, the trouble about getting started was musical, while the trouble with the ending was textual, finding the right words (the various revisions to Brünnhilde's closing speech). By the time he got to composing the end, music was available in abundance.

The narrative-recapitulatory thrust of the third act of *Götterdämmerung* begins only after a final scene of prophecy: the Rhine maidens' warning to Siegfried about his fatal ring. In Act 1, Brünnhilde had refused to yield the ring to Waltraute, demanding its return to the Rhine maidens, because of its value to her as a pledge of Siegfried's love. Siegfried has the ring in Act 3 only because he has *forgotten* his love for Brünnhilde, forgetting in some crucial sense who she and he himself really "are." He has no compelling reason to withhold the ring from the Rhine maidens, and he nearly gives it to them. Only his male pride prevents this (he refuses to be cowed by their threats of curses and death). At the same time, there is a sense that he cannot let go of it *until* he remembers its actual significance. Although Hagen restores Siegfried's memory only as a means of justifying his murder, extracting an unwitting confession, the flood of Siegfried's returning memory is essential to the closure of the cycle on all levels.

Hagen's repeated references to Siegfried's preternatural understanding of birdsong are accompanied not only, or even primarily, by the motive of the Woodbird, but by a little motivic tail we may perhaps recall no more clearly than Siegfried himself (Example 6.17a). This tail belongs, in fact, to the motive of the World Inheritance that celebrated his union with Brünnhilde at the end of *Siegfried*, and it was the last thing we heard before he imbibed the potion of forgetfulness proffered him by Gutrune, as he promised never to forget to drink first to her memory ("den ersten Trunk zu treuer Minne, Brünnhilde, bring ich dir!"). Precisely this phrase will form the cadence to his final narrative, culminating in his newly recovered memory of her: "O wie mich brünstig da umschlang / der schönen Brünnhilde Arm!" (Example 6.17b). Within 180 measures Siegfried retraces the entire content of the previous drama, those "tales of his youth" ("Mären aus meinen jungen Tagen"). The emphasis of his narrative is necessarily selective, however. The reforging of Nothung and the slaying of Fafner are each dispatched in a few measures. Altogether the events of the first half of *Siegfried* are pressed into a single "poetic-musical period" moving loosely between G and D minor (From "Mime hieß ein mürrischer Zwerg" to "dort fällt ich Fafner, den Wurm"). Siegfried devotes most of his attention to

Ex. 6.17a

dolce ed espressivo

Ex. 6.17b

his miraculous perception of the Woodbird's voice, thanks to the blood of Fafner. As in the earlier forest scene the music hovers around E major, until Siegfried breaks through to C major just as Hagen interrupts him.[16] It was that episode in the forest Hagen particularly asked about, and which Siegfried seems instinctively to understand he must revisit more closely. Dwelling this way on the E-major music of forest murmurs and bird song confers a cohesive musical center on Siegfried's narration, if one that hovers tentatively rather than insisting on closure.

When Siegfried at last remembers the final chapter of *Siegfried*, the discovery of the sleeping Brünnhilde, the music suddenly lurches toward C major (the World Inheritance motive, including the small figure that first intruded to jog his memory; see Example 6.17a). Here Hagen interrupts him, fatally, and only in his dying moments does Siegfried recall this final chapter *in extenso*, reliving the music of Brünnhilde's awakening as he gradually closes his own eyes forever. There C major opens out to E once again, and is returned to C minor to begin the last, orchestral, phase of Siegfried's musical voyage through the past: the "funeral music" transition to the concluding scene. These tonal links can suggest how loosely articulated "poetic-musical periods" (Siegfried's narration, his "swan song," and his orchestral obsequies) interlock within a broader musical-dramatic progress. Between the second and third such "periods" within Siegfried's

Ex. 6.18

narration – that is, before he quotes the Woodbird's advice to seek out Brünnhilde – Hagen offers the antidote to the potion that had cleansed his mind of her memory, and the orchestra reminds us of the motives involved in that scene of forgetting. But, as Siegfried picks up the thread of his story, it seems to be the process of *musical* narration that restores his memory, one musical gesture leading into another, dragging it up to the light of consciousness from wherever these things lay buried.

Leitmotif, then, is not just the musical labeling of people and things (or the verbal labeling of motives); it is also a matter of musical memory, of recalling things dimly remembered and seeing what sense we can make of them in a new context. The leitmotivically saturated orchestral epilogue to the final scene of *Götterdämmerung*, as the stage-world is engulfed in fire and water, is a feast of musical nostalgia or, better, a pageant: motives from throughout the epic hail us one last time as they float by in the universal deluge. Part of the poignant effect of the motive picked up by Brünnhilde at the end (in addition to its expressive deployment of falling sevenths, rescaled in stepwise ascent) has perhaps to do with the recollection of a musical gesture all but forgotten (Example 6.18). The referential value of this figure, first heard in Act 3 of *Die Walküre* after Brünnhilde announces that Sieglinde will give birth to the hero Siegfried, has been a famous puzzle because it never recurs in the meantime to shore up its identity.[17] Its return at the very end is a beautiful surprise. Leitmotif offered Wagner various challenges and opportunities in bridging his jobs as a dramatist and as a composer. It continues to fascinate as a means, however problematic, of making music speak or signify. But we also like leitmotifs simply for coming back. We might love this last one best of all, as it seems Brünnhilde does, for being one of the most expressive, but also most prodigal, of the whole *Ring* cycle. Nearly forgotten, it returns just in time. It still acquires no determinate meaning, but its effect recalls Stendhal's definition of beauty, "the promise of happiness," gesturing toward some future beyond even *this* magnificent end.

7 *Tristan und Isolde*: essence and appearance

JOHN DAVERIO

When Gerda Buddenbrook presents Edmund Pfühl with piano arrange-ments of selections from Wagner's *Tristan und Isolde*, the bookish but genial music-master in Thomas Mann's novel *Buddenbrooks* shrinks back in horror: "I won't play this, madam. I am your most obedient servant, but I will not play it. That is not music . . . It is pure chaos! It is demagoguery, blasphemy, and madness! It is a fragrant frog with thunderbolts! It is the end of all morality in the arts. I will not play it!" Eventually he gives in to Gerda's persistent requests, but soon breaks off for fear of the adverse effects the music may have on her impressionable son, Hanno: "And think of the child, the child sitting there in his chair. He stole in quietly to hear music – do you wish to poison his mind for good and all?" As it turns out, Pfühl's concerns are not unwarranted. In the next-to-last chapter of the novel Hanno loses himself in an improvisatory reverie at the keyboard, a fantasy whose climactic passage (with its "unyielding surge," "chromatic struggle upward," and "convulsions of desire") clearly hearkens to the closing pages of Wagner's *Tristan* (that is, Isolde's "Transfiguration" or *Liebestod*). The next chapter begins ominously ("Cases of typhoid fever take the following course") and goes on to recount the early demise of young Hanno Buddenbrook. This final scion of a decaying family, Mann suggests (if not without irony), passes away through and in some sense because of his extended Tristanesque daydreaming.[1]

This implied connection between Wagner's *Tristan und Isolde* and both moral and physical decay becomes explicit in Mann's own story "Tristan," where the consumptive heroine/victim contributes to her own demise by rendering the opera's love music at the piano (contrary to doctor's orders). Even more clearly than in *Buddenbrooks*, Wagner's music is portrayed here as a kind of forbidden fruit, an intoxicant that lays bare the proximity of beauty and death, rapture and despair, eroticism and spiritual transcendence.[2]

In short, Wagner's *Tristan* functions in Mann's literary imagination as an emblem of decadence. In this he followed Nietzsche's lead, as he did in regarding the work as at once sublime and dangerous.[3] Little wonder that *Tristan* was embraced by those French, English, and Italian authors of the generation between Nietzsche and Mann, collectively known as the "deca-dents," who devoted themselves (in the words of Frank Kermode) to an exploration of all "the perversities of pleasure and pain."[4] For this group, *Tristan* was a prime symbol of morbid desire, spiritual corruption, and feverish hedonism. In George Moore's *Evelyn Innes*, for instance, the "gnawing, creeping sensuality" of the opera's love music elicits shudders and tremors from the title character. Gabriele d'Annunzio speaks of Isolde's passion inspiring a "homicidal will" in his novel of decadent Wagnerism, *Il trionfo della morte* (*The Triumph of Death*). Bewitched by Wagner's "satanic music," the lovers in Joséphin Péladan's *Victoire du mari* (*The Husband's Victory*) "abandon themselves to erotic excesses."[5] And Wagner's own identification of the opera's characteristic "color" as "mauve, a sort of lilac" (*CWD*: 3 June 1878) aligns it with an equally characteristic representation of the decadent ideal, as embodied in the favored flower symbol of the orchid.

At the same time, Wagner's own acknowledgement of the "decadence" of his *Tristan* is tinged by an irony wholly lacking in the writings of d'Annunzio, Huysmans, and the like. As he approached the end of the composition, he wrote to Mathilde Wesendonck (the opera's famous muse) in a letter of April 1859: "Child! This Tristan is turning into something *terrible*! This final act!!! —— I fear the opera will be banned – unless the whole thing is parodied in a bad performance – : only mediocre performances can save me! Perfectly *good* ones will be bound to drive people mad" (*SL* 452). The exaggerated tone of the comment suggests that it was not to be taken too seriously, and perhaps even that the decadent surface of *Tristan* is a foil for other qualities in the work. And, indeed, there is a strand in the opera's reception that addresses precisely this other side of the coin.

Richard Pohl, for instance, spoke early on about the "simple grandeur" and the "moderate yet compelling power" of the work.[6] And Nietzsche described it in similar terms in the essay "Richard Wagner in Bayreuth" (the fourth and final essay of the collection *Unfashionable Observations*, completed in 1876 just prior to his break with the composer): "It is a drama with the severest austerity of form, overwhelming in its simple grandeur and precisely suited to the mystery of which it speaks, the mystery of death in life, of unity in duality."[7] Even before committing a note of *Tristan* to paper, Wagner himself envisioned a final product undergirded by the most elemental of structures, "the simplest, but most full-blooded musical conception," as he described this initial inspiration to Franz Liszt in a letter of mid-December 1854 (*SL* 324).

All of these descriptions point to an underlying clarity of design that contrasts sharply with the sensual and luxurious surface of the finished score, which so captured the later decadent imagination. Wagner reflected on the fundamental architecture of the score in a remark recorded in Cosima Wagner's diary in early 1871, describing the opera as consisting essentially of "three love scenes" (*CWD*: 16 January 1871). The scenes he had in mind were evidently the long dialogue that closes Act 1, culminating in the drinking of the potion (where much of the music from the Prelude is recalled and transformed), the vast love duet at the center of Act 2, and the final stages of Act 3, beginning with Tristan's vision of Isolde and concluding with Isolde's "Transfiguration" monologue.[8] The architecture of the whole turns on the strategic placement of these scenes and their interrelationship. The Act 2 love scene can be viewed as a continuation of the dialogue at the end of Act 1; the music across the end of Act 3, on the other hand, recalls, transforms, and synthesizes important passages from the Act 1 Prelude and both preceding acts.

Supporting these relationships between the extended love scenes in each act is a tonal plan at once original and simple. The concluding dialogue of Act 1, like the first Prelude, alternates between the tonal centers of A and C. The same pairing governs the first half of the Act 2 love scene (the so-called *Tagesgespräch*, a dialogic rumination on day and night), but eventually gives way to the pair of keys situated a half-step lower, A flat and B. In a telling example of Wagner's ability to intertwine textual and musical material, he reserves the decisive shift toward the lower member of the A flat/B pair for the words "O sink hernieder, Nacht der Liebe" ("O descend upon us, night of love"). Finally, Isolde's Act 3 Transfiguration remains within the orbit of the lower tonal pair, moving from A flat to a radiant close in B major. While the tonal trajectory of the opera thus appears to describe a motion *up* by step (from A to B), there is a sense in which it proceeds at the same time by moving *downwards* by half-step (the transposition of the A/C pair down to A flat/B).[9] This confounding of "up" and "down" makes for a kind of large-scale tonal weightlessness, a musical analogue of Isolde's final, gradual absorption into the ebb and flow of the elements.

If the architecture of *Tristan* is grounded in these three love scenes, two further scenes, based on narrative recollection, further contribute to that "austerity of form" that Nietzsche found characteristic of the work. Isolde's impassioned narration that forms the core of Act 1, scene 3, where she recounts how she once healed the sick hero, Tristan (disguised as Tantris), has its counterpart in the extended passage from Tristan's Act 3 "Delirium" monologue, reflecting on the implications of the "terrible" love potion. The broadly parallel relation of these passages is also placed in relief by the disposition of male and female voices in them: Isolde narrates to Brangäne, Tristan to Kurwenal. Another element of broadly symmetrical planning can be seen in the use of "real" or "phenomenal" offstage music at the opening of each act: the sailor's song of Act 1, the hunting horns of Act 2, and the shepherd's melancholy piping of Act 3.

In sum, the "decadent" exterior of *Tristan* is held in check by a solidly architectural (one is almost tempted to say classical) foundation. In a series of essays written at the beginning of the nineteenth century, the poet Friedrich Hölderlin placed just this sort of opposition at the center of his theory of poetry. For Hölderlin, every poem embodies a dialectic between appearance (*Schein*), the side most clearly displayed to the reader or listener, and essence, which Hölderlin calls the fundamental tone or mood (*Grundton*). In this view, the essence of a poem is only thinkable in conjunction with an appearance to which it is sharply *opposed*. Hence both qualities – one manifest, the other latent – are simultaneously present at every moment in the poem. The particulars of Hölderlin's poetic theory – his linking of the diverse "tones" of heroic, naïve, ideal, and so forth – are of less importance than the insight that the dialectic in an artwork is not merely a matter of contrast, of oppositions unfolding over time, but of the tension between coexistent qualities.[10]

Although nearly all artworks will exhibit a dialectic between essence and appearance to some degree, the tensions between the two are particularly acute in Wagner's *Tristan*, in no small part due to the power of the musical surface or "appearance" (in this view) to exercise such an overwhelming impact on listeners. The persistent dualism of Wagner's approach to outward effect vs. supporting design extends to nearly every parameter of *Tristan*: text–music relationships, literary and philosophical traits, musical language, and generic codes. Considering, too, that the opera itself centrally thematizes the dialectic of "appearances" and "essences" (as symbolized, for example, in night and day), a parsing of these dualities in the music and dramatic conception of the opera is a potentially rewarding critical approach.

Reciprocities of music, words, and "poetic ideas"

To say that in *Tristan und Isolde* music reigns supreme over poetry may seem like a tired cliché. Even so, the cliché is not without documentary support. For one thing, numerous entries in Cosima's diaries suggest that Wagner himself subscribed to this point of view. For instance, reacting to a letter from an admirer received in October 1881 (expressing the wish that, in the event of a global cataclysm, at least *Tristan* would survive!), Wagner remarked that in *Tristan* he had given himself up "entirely to music," while in other works "the drama had imposed a tighter check on the musical flow" (*CWD*: 4 October 1881). Similarly, a few days earlier he noted that in *Tristan* he had felt "the need to push himself to the limit, musically, since in the *Nibelungen* [by contrast] the requirements of the drama frequently forced him to restrict the musical expression" (*CWD*: 1 October 1881).

Ex. 7.1a

Ex. 7.1b

Some aspects of the opera's genesis seem to tell the same story. Wagner's concentrated work on *Tristan* fell within the two-year period between August–September 1857, when he drafted the prose scenario and text, and August 1859, when he finished scoring Act 3, although he already had begun to contemplate a musico-dramatic treatment of the medieval legend by the end of 1854 (the fateful year in which he encountered the writings of Schopenhauer). The earliest surviving musical sketches date from 19 December 1856. At that moment he was still in the throes of composing the second act of *Siegfried* when, as he told the young Princess Marie zu Sayn-Wittgenstein, "*Tristan* got in my way in the form of a melodic thread that kept springing up whenever I wanted to leave it." Moreover, this melodic thread – later elaborated in the tranquil G-flat episode within the Act 2 duet, "Lausch, Geliebter!" following Brangäne's watch-song – first came to Wagner as "music without text"[11] (Examples 7.1a, 7.1b). Likewise a melody that Wagner harmonized in May 1857, without (as he told Mathilde Wesendonck) having the least idea what to do with it, was wholly untexted to start with (Example 7.2a). This was tentatively adapted to lines from the last act of *Siegfried*, otherwise uncomposed as yet (Siegfried to Brünnhilde: "Sangst du mir nicht, dein Wissen sei das Leuchten der Liebe zu mir?"); eventually it found its proper place within the episode known as Brangäne's "Consolation" ("Welcher Wahn, welch' eitles Zürnen"), her response to Isolde's "Narration" in Act 1, scene 3 (Example 7.2b). Around this same time Wagner noted, in his printed copy of the *Ring* poem, music to another line from Act 3 of *Siegfried* ("Süß erbebet mir ihr blühender Mund") which approximates the chromatically ascending motive complex of the *Tristan* Prelude.[12]

Yet, while these examples seem to speak to the primacy of musical over poetic inspiration, either because the music was initially conceived without text or because it migrated at will from one text to another, they in fact do nothing of the kind. The sketches simply indicate that the music

Ex. 7.2a

Ex. 7.2b

was not at first bound up with specific *words*. In each case, however, the music most certainly was bound to a poetic idea. The sketches from December 1856, though conceived as "music without text," survive on a sheet with the heading "Liebesscene [love scene]. Tristan und Isolde." The May 1857 fragments, first earmarked for *Siegfried*, Act 3, but ultimately positioned in the Brangäne's "Consolation" episode, were linked in both cases to texts dealing with the power of love. In the first setting Siegfried asks rhetorically of Brünnhilde: "Didn't you sing to me that your wisdom and the light of your love for me were both one?" In the second instance Brangäne concludes with a specific reference to the power of love ("der Minne Macht"). And similarly, the line from *Siegfried* that had been tentatively provided with music anticipating the core material of the *Tristan* Prelude intimates the first stirrings of Siegfried's desire for Brünnhilde. In *Tristan*, this music serves as a continuing emblem of the lovers' unfulfilled longing.

These examples show that "music without text" (or music straddling a number of texts) may nonetheless be firmly rooted in a poetic idea, feeling, or conceit. At the same time, they lend some credence to attempts by scholars such as Carolyn Abbate to deconstruct the "myth" that *Tristan* contains Wagner's "least text-bound music" and is in that way also his most symphonic or musically "absolute."[13] It is also less true than generally supposed that in this score the music overwhelms the text. There are relatively few passages where this is inevitably the case, among them the central and closing portions of the Act 2 love scene and Isolde's "Transfiguration." Granted, these are among the opera's most important musical passages; but to generalize from them alone is to ignore many passages of equal musical and dramatic significance (Isolde's "Narration" in Act 1, King Marke's monologue-lament in Act 2, much of Tristan's "Delirium" scene in Act 3), and to undercut the significance of the words in *Tristan* generally, a text rich in poetic detail and psychological nuance.

It might therefore be more sensible to argue for a reciprocal relationship between the textual and musical elements of *Tristan*, one element aspiring to the condition of the other.[14] On the one hand, we could interpret the prominence of rhetorical devices such as parallelism, intensified repetition, and antithesis as a sign of the "musical" properties of the *Tristan* poem. Conversely, many of the opera's musical ideas seem every bit as palpable and vivid as poetic images (the opening gesture of the Prelude is the first of many such instances). The title characters themselves allegorize the interplay of poetry and music in the opera. Both Abbate and Jean-Jacques Nattiez view Tristan as an emblem of poetry, and Nattiez further interprets Isolde as an allegorical representation of music.[15] But while they more or less agree on the emblematic quality of the characters, Abbate and Nattiez have differing opinions on who takes the lead. For Abbate, Tristan's is the "authorial" voice, whereas for Nattiez it is Isolde who "dictates to the poet-composer" as the "female spirit of music."[16] Both are right in terms of the passages on which they base their arguments: in Abbate's case, the *Tagesgespräch* from the Act 2 love scene; in Nattiez's case, the "Transfiguration" monologue from the end of the opera.

The fact that plausible arguments can be constructed for such diametrically opposed views suggests a larger truth that was well summed up by Charles Baudelaire, before *Tristan* had even reached the stage. Wagner, he maintained, "found it impossible not to think in a double manner, poetically and musically; not to catch sight of each idea in two simultaneous forms, one of the two arts coming into play where the frontiers of the other were marked out."[17] Though his remark was stimulated by the "Romantic operas" just then becoming widely known (*Der fliegende Holländer* [*The Flying Dutchman*], *Tannhäuser*, *Lohengrin*), it applies equally to *Tristan*. If anything, this "double manner" observed by Baudelaire takes an even more striking form in the mature music drama. To express it in the language of Hölderlin's poetic theory of "tones": while *music* of incredible immediacy and power determines the "appearance" of *Tristan*, its fundamental tone is *poetic* through and through. Neither aspect is conceivable without the other.

Philosophy, desire, and romantic "magic"

In his *Unfashionable Observations*, Nietzsche dubbed *Tristan* "the true *opus metaphysicum* of all art," a brilliant realization of Wagner's attempt to produce "philosophy in sound."[18] These turns of phrase call to mind the crucial influence of Arthur Schopenhauer on the genesis of this drama. In the same letter to Liszt that first announced the inspiration for this "simplest, but most full-blooded musical conception" of the Tristan legend, the composer also reported on his discovery of Schopenhauer, who had recently entered his "lonely life like a gift from heaven" (*SL* 323). Not long before this, in the fall of 1854, Wagner had received a copy of Schopenhauer's principal work, *The World as Will and Representation*, from the writer Georg Herwegh, a fellow émigré in Zurich; by his own testimony he read it no fewer than four times within a short period. Cosima Wagner's diaries bear witness to her husband's enduring attraction to Schopenhauer. Indeed, up to the very end of his life Wagner looked to the philosopher as a "supreme legislator," a thinker worthy of serving as a mentor to the whole German people.

Nonetheless, even during the first flush of enthusiasm for Schopenhauer in the 1850s Wagner did not hesitate to modify some of his ideas – "to expand and ... even to correct his system," as the composer put it to Mathilde Wesendonck in a letter of 1 December 1858 (*SL* 432). Throughout *The World as Will and Representation*, and more explicitly in a chapter on "the metaphysics of sexual love," the philosopher maintained that the Will expresses itself above all in libidinal desire. But whereas Schopenhauer saw the path to redemption in the negation or denial of this blind urge, as of all manifestations of the Will (and hence of the alienating effects of "individuation," our appearance in the world as beings separate from the primal forces that bring us and all things into being), Wagner argued that the Will can and must be assuaged *through* the experience of sexual love. It is no coincidence that he first articulated this thesis (in December 1858) soon after drafting his great paean to sexual love in the second act of *Tristan* (*SL* 432). On reflection, though, this deviation from Schopenhauerian theory is not so great as it might appear. Both philosopher and composer recognized the essentially erotic quality of the Will, and both agreed on the ultimate, necessary goal of its pacification (by one means or other). Thus, in the concluding pages of *Tristan und Isolde* the Will is at once affirmed and negated: affirmed through the unmistakably sensual, desiring quality of the music, and negated as Isolde expires to the transcendent strains of the final cadence.[19]

Wagner's "correction" of Schopenhauer also involved motifs borrowed from the writings of the early German Romantics. As Thomas Mann, among many others, pointed out, there are striking literary antecedents for *Tristan* in Novalis's *Hymnen an die Nacht* (*Hymns to the Night*) and in the novel *Lucinde*, Friedrich Schlegel's "little book of ill repute."[20] While there is no incontrovertible evidence that Wagner read either of these, the parallels in ideological content, rhetorical thrust, and poetic imagery between Novalis's poetry, Schlegel's novel, and Wagner's opera are too numerous to be ascribed to mere coincidence. The contrast Novalis and Schlegel draw between Night and Day – the former a "homeland" and a realm of ultimate truth, the latter a symbol of deception and illusion – resonate no less powerfully with the text of *Tristan* than does the mystical affinity these writers sensed between Night, Love, and Death. Many passages in the long colloquy between Tristan and Isolde in Act 2 (the *Tagesgespräch*) echo the rhetorical structure of "chiasmus," a linking of lines by inverted parallelism, as found in such lines as the following from Schlegel's *Lucinde*:

> Julius. "My love, I found holy peace only in yearning."
> Lucinde. "And I found holy yearning only in peace."[21]

Finally, Wagner seems to have borrowed and/or echoed specific images and metaphors from both writers: the death potion occurs also in Schlegel, the figure of "night-sightedness" in Novalis, and that of a "consecration unto Night" in both of their writings.[22]

Wagner's conflation of Schopenhauer's philosophy with motifs drawn from the early German Romantics accords metaphysical dignity to a quintessentially physical phenomenon: sexual love. This *opus metaphysicum* is also deeply implicated in the arts of magic, whose central emblem is the love potion that Tristan and Isolde consume under the impression that it is a fatal poison. The significance of the love potion is frequently downplayed. Carl Dahlhaus argues, for example, that it "simply brings into the open something which already exists but has not previously been admitted" (that is, the pre-existing emotional bond between the two title characters). Like other commentators before him, Dahlhaus would have us believe that the love potion is without intrinsic power: the lovers confess their true feelings because they believe they are about to die.[23] Both of these claims, however, are open to debate. The qualifying adverb "simply" in the preceding quote encourages us to forget that if the pre-existing "something" referred to here (Tristan and Isolde's pre-existing passion) were not brought into the open, the drama would not unfold as it does – in fact, there would be no drama at all. Likewise, what the lovers happen to *think* as they consume the potion is immaterial compared to what they *feel* under its influence; and, as Wagner's stage directions make eminently clear, the physical effects of the drink are swift and irreversible. Tristan and Isolde "gaze steadily into one another's eyes, their expression of death-defiance soon giving way to passionate ardor." Far from emerging from a process of rational thought, the lovers' latent ardor rises to consciousness as a result of a process over which they have no control – a process at least closely akin to magic.

The tendency to explain away the magical elements in *Tristan und Isolde* may be attributed to a variety of factors. First, critics are probably embarrassed by Wagner's recourse to the kind of theatrical stock-in-trade

Ex. 7.3a

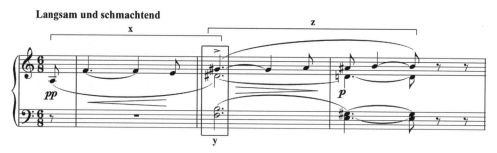

Ex. 7.3b

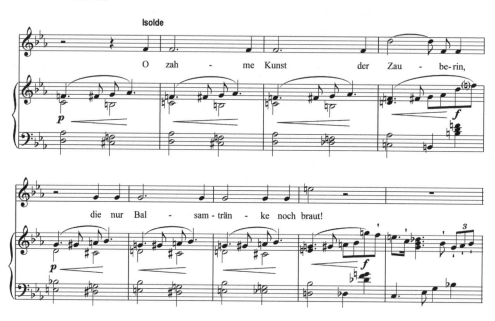

that he decried in his writings. Second, even in an age in which metaphysics is viewed with profound skepticism, it still retains considerably more cachet than old-fashioned magic. All the same, magic *does* assume a commanding presence in *Tristan*, its poetic significance being underscored by Wagner's musical language in general and his use of harmony in particular. The very first harmony we hear in the score, the famous *Tristan* chord, might just as well be called the "Magic" chord in view of its inherent musical properties and the poetic associations it acquires. At the outset of the Act 1 Prelude, the chord (marked "y" in Example 7.3a) serves as the meeting point of the languid opening melodic gestures (x) and the chromatic ascent through a minor third that grows out of it (z) – all three elements forming a motivic complex which Wagner deploys at

Ex. 7.4

critical junctures throughout the work.[24] In a telling stroke, the first bit of text with which the complex is linked brings a reference to magic. As shown in Example 7.3b, a rhythmically transformed and sequentially intensified variant of elements (y) and (z) supports Isolde's allusion to the "feeble art of the sorceress who can only brew balsams." (The passage is thick with irony: by scoffing at the inconsequentiality of this lesser magical craft passed on to her through her mother, Isolde herself seems to echo those critics who denigrate the power of the potion; yet before long Isolde will discover that this potion-brewing art of her mother is not so feeble, after all.) Next, the rhetorical question posed by Brangäne in Act 1, scene 3, and repeated by Isolde in the following scene ("Kennst du der Mutter Künste nicht?" / "Do you not know of your/my mother's magic arts?") calls up elements (y) and (z) of the motive complex at the original pitch level and rhythmic values of the opening of the Prelude. Wagner interweaves the same elements within the orchestral texture at Tristan's passionate apostrophe to the potion and its effects in the Act 2 love scene ("O Heil dem Tranke, heil seinem Saft! Heil seines Zaubers hehrer Kraft!). Finally, Tristan's realization, at the height of his "Delirium" monologue in Act 3, that he himself had in some sense brewed this potion ("Ich selbst, ich hab' ihn gebraut!") is articulated by a massive orchestral outburst incorporating element (y) of the complex – that is, the *Tristan* chord (Example 7.4).

The chord and the motivic complex in which it is embedded are often interpreted as emblems of incessant longing. And, to be sure, they often figure in dramatic situations where the lovers' thwarted desire provides this subtext. Yet given the poetic associations in the passages cited in the preceding paragraph, Wagner is also positing a close link between desire and magic. Taken together, these passages establish the *Tristan* chord as a primary vehicle of *harmonic* magic and mutability. In Isolde's bitter allusion to her mother's "enfeebled" magic, the chord is initially heard as the II^7 of the local tonic, C minor. In the subsequent rhetorical questions regarding the mother's magic arts ("Kennst du der Mutter Künste nicht?"), the chord is presented as an altered form of either a diminished-seventh chord or a "French" augmented-sixth chord. In Tristan's "Delirium" monologue it appears as a minor triad with added sixth degree. Nor is the *Tristan* chord the only agency of harmonic magic in the opera. The continual wavering between keys a half-step apart in the central love scene and elsewhere (see n. 9) is made possible by the enharmonic equivalence of the dominant-seventh and "German" augmented-sixth chords, the latter implying a key a half-step higher than the former. While Wagner was hardly the first composer to exploit this equivalence, he arguably employed it in *Tristan* more systematically, and more persistently, than any of his predecessors – a musical conjuror who reveled in unleashing the magic latent in the tonal harmonic system.

These aspects of the musical-poetic physiognomy of the *Tristan* score might allow us to situate the work within the tradition of the magic opera, a genre whose roots (loosely defined) can be traced back through Weber's *Der Freischütz*, Mozart's *Zauberflöte*, Gluck's *Armide*, Handel's *Orlando furioso* and *Alcina*, back to the beginnings of opera in the early seventeenth century. Such an interpretation will naturally center on Isolde, who is (or becomes), like Schlegel's Lucinde, a "priestess of love," but also a sorceress (*Zauberin*), and in that sense a descendant of the female practitioners of magic in earlier operas. In giving the magical dimension of *Tristan* its due, moreover, we will be better able to recognize a crucial link between the physical and the metaphysical in Wagner's work – between a tangible stage property and its physiological effects, on one hand, and the transcendence of those effects at the end of the opera, on the other.

Rhetorical dialectics and the "art of transition"

Of all his manifold achievements in *Tristan und Isolde*, Wagner was proudest of its embodiment of what he famously identified in a letter to Mathilde Wesendonck as his "most profound and delicate art, the art of transition [*Kunst des Übergangs*]" (29 October 1859: *SL* 474–77). Intended as a means of mediating between sharply contrasting affective states or moods, this "art of transition" constituted, in Wagner's opinion, the "secret" of his musical form. And since for Wagner "form" was synonymous with the total fabric of a composition, this particular "art" bore on every domain of his musical language. As he boasted to Frau Wesendonck, his quest for unity and clarity on the largest scale led him to discover harmonic, melodic, and rhythmic devices the likes of which had never been imagined before.

As the prime example of this new art of dramatically determined musical transition, Wagner singled out the Act 2 love scene of *Tristan*, the draft of which he had completed less than a year before. "The opening of this scene," he writes, "presents a life overflowing with all the most violent emotions, – its ending the most solemn and heartfelt longing for death [*das weihevollste, innigste Todesverlangen*]. These are the pillars: and now you see, child, how I have joined these pillars together, and how the one of them leads over into the other" (*SL* 475). As we have observed, the harmonic design of the love scene turns on the motion from the tonal pairing of A and C to its counterpart a half-step lower, A flat and B. Wagner effects the transition from one pair to the other (thus binding together the tonal pillars of the scene) through a process of infiltration. While the first half of the process is dominated by the A/C pair, allusions to the tonalities of the lower pair prefigure the definitive establishment of A flat in the lyrical episode, "O sink hernieder." Conversely, echoes of the A tonality from the initial pairing resound as the second half of the scene progresses further from A flat back up to B.

These tonal-harmonic elements are in turn coordinated with tempo: quick at the outset, slow for the central episode ("O sink hernieder"), and gradually accelerating toward the B-major goal (from "O ew'ge Nacht"). Likewise these elements are coordinated with motivic and rhythmic details of the larger scene. Extended stretches of the first part of the duet scene derive their melodic substance from the so-called Day motive, in myriad transformations. And just as elements of the A flat/B pairing begin to influence the tonal character of the scene's first half (otherwise oriented to A and C), so too are motives associated with longing and death gradually interwoven with the Day motive and its variants. In mediating between these motivic families, Wagner uncovers their latent affinities. At the climax of Tristan's apostrophe to the love potion and its powers ("O Heil dem Tranke") a variant of the Day motive leads without break into one of the chief musical symbols of longing, a link made possible because the chromatic ascent of the latter can be neatly dovetailed with the melodic shape of the former (see Example 7.5). A bit later in the scene, Wagner moves with ease between motivic families by assimilating the rhythm of the motive Death-Devoted Head ("Todgeweihtes Haupt") to the rhythm of the Day motive (see Example 7.6). These are only a few of the many places in the love scene where Wagner's "art of transition" generates the kind of "endless melody" which he perfected in the score of *Tristan und Isolde*.[25]

Ex. 7.5

Day   Longing

Ex. 7.6

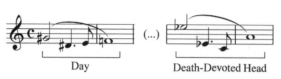

Day   Death-Devoted Head

Not every moment in the scene exemplifies such a "gradual and delicate process" as described in Wagner's letter to Mathilde Wesendonck. In terms of harmony, the first portion of the scene in particular abounds in unsettling effects, including the unexpected outburst of A-flat major within a B-flat context at Tristan's greeting of Isolde; or, somewhat later, the equally startling outburst on the *Tristan* chord as he proclaims himself and Isolde "initiates of the night" (*Nacht-Geweihte*). Similarly, the rapid juxtaposition of tonalities a third apart lends heightened intensity to the lovers' ecstatic reunion at the beginning of the scene and to the opening phase of Tristan's apostrophe to the love potion. While the harmonic progression *within* most phrases is notably seamless, the tonal motion *between* them, or at cadential moments, is often articulated by rather abrupt shifts. Disjunctions of this type frequently involve semi-tonal progressions (both up and down) in the bass, as illustrated in Examples 7.7 and 7.8.

These passages invite interpretation as harmonic analogues of a motivic process that Wagner discussed some years later in the essay "On the Application of Music to the Drama" (1879). Commenting on the differences between dance-based instrumental forms and those available to the musical drama, Wagner identified the former as necessarily lacking all traces of "rhetorical dialectics," a direct confrontation between these of "diametrically opposed character," and hence devoid of the kind of conflict that defines genuine drama (*GS* IX:178; *PW* VI:176). Interestingly, one of the composer's first statements on the dramatic potential of such harmonic confrontation appears in a source known as the *Tristan* sketchbook, dating from around 1856. This fragment (headed "On Modulation") distinguishes between harmonic change in "pure instrumental music" and in music drama: "Swift and free transitions are in the latter often just as necessary as they are unjustified in the former" (*SSD* XII:280). Thus, the notion of

Ex. 7.7

Ex. 7.8

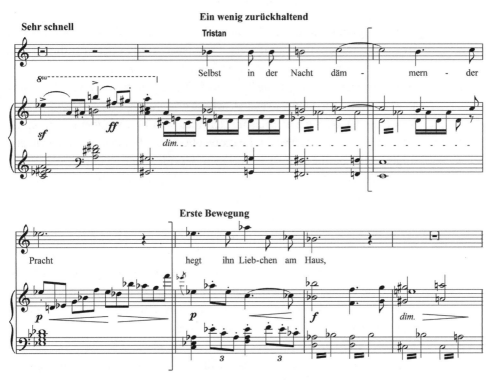

rhetorical dialectics arose in principle – if not in name – within fairly close proximity to Wagner's theorizing on the "art of transition."

Apparently designating quite different phenomena, the "art of transition" and the idea of "rhetorical dialectics" are in fact mutually dependent. Wagner said as much in the 29 October letter to Mathilde Wesendonck, admitting there that everything "abrupt and sudden" was now "repugnant" to him, although such effects were sometimes "unavoidable and necessary" (*SL* 475). In both Example 7.7 and Example 7.8, the rhetorically dialectic progression arises at precisely the point where intimations of the A-flat tonality encroach on one member of the other of the A/C tonal pair. On the one hand, the incursions of A flat in the first part of the scene prepare for the full-scale modulation to that key at "O sink hernieder"; on the other hand, they create striking disturbances in the harmonic flow.[26] The art of transition and rhetorical dialectics thus relate as appearance to essence: while listeners may be initially mesmerized by the seamless transitions between extremes in the love scene, they will discover, on reflection, the degree to which the musical surface is articulated by the idea of rhetorical dialectics.

From the epic past to the musical future: medieval romance as modern *Musikdrama*

The chief poetic source for Wagner's *Tristan und Isolde* was Gottfried von Strassburg's eponymous poem left unfinished at the poet's death in 1210. Gottfried's verse romance of nearly 20,000 lines was based in turn on a French source, the *Roman de Tristan* of Thomas of Brittany. Gottfried was an elegant and mellifluous versifier whose graceful rhymes and fondness for rhetorical devices such as chiasmus left their mark on Wagner's text. At the same time, Wagner subjected the scope of Gottfried's poem to rather drastic surgery, eliminating characters and episodes (including all of those involving Tristan's deceitful wife, the "other" Isolde, called Isolde of the White Hands), and thereby reducing his source to its bare essentials – the "three love scenes" he pointed out to Cosima in 1871.[27]

In this he was merely putting into practice what he had argued for in his discussion of the problematic relation of dramatic and epic genres in *Opera and Drama*. A firm believer in the historical contingency of poetic genres, Wagner felt that the modern dramatist had no choice but to draw on the tradition of the *Roman*, that is, the modern European literary tradition extending from the medieval verse *romance* through the poetic epics of Ariosto and Tasso, to (in Wagner's view) the plays of Shakespeare no less than the modern novels of Walter Scott or Honoré de Balzac. Yet aspiring dramatists were faced with a dilemma insofar as the true nature of the *Roman* or modern epic "does not really correspond with that of drama" (*GS* IV:17; *PW* II:136). And although Wagner tended to identify the "true nature" of the epic genre's formal criteria (e.g., multiplicity of incident as opposed to the dramatic "unities"), he further differentiated epic and drama in terms of content (social-historical content in the *Roman* or novel, subjective thought and feeling in the drama), mode of presentation (narrative or indirect vs. "sensuous" and immediate), and concomitant temporal mode (narrative past tense vs. dramatic presence) (*GS* IV:6–29, 45–50; *PW* II:124–47, 168–73). According to Wagner's theory, these differences could be resolved only in the *musical* drama, which would "redeem" the poetic or prose *Roman* "from its 'sinful' state by its dramatic concentration on the 'purely human.'"[28]

Given this dependence on epic genres, the musical genre becomes an equivocal one, despite its glorification as the one true and necessary synthesis. Nietzsche took a still more equivocal view of Wagner's status as dramatist, claiming (in *The Case of Wagner*) that he was no real dramatist at all, but just a "lover of pretty words," a shrewd rhetorician whose pronouncements on behalf of drama allowed him to feign "superiority over the word 'opera.'"[29] Thomas Mann also found it difficult to regard Wagner as a dramatist in the proper sense; but, rather than branding him as a poseur, as Nietzsche did, he called him a practitioner of "theatrical epic."[30] For Mann, an "undercurrent of epic" ran through Wagner's works – the *Ring* cycle most obviously, but *Tristan und Isolde* as well.

Invoking the meaning of the ancient Doric word from which "drama" derived, Wagner labeled *Tristan und Isolde* an "action" (*Handlung*), even though, as he later confessed, the work contains precious little *visible* action ("On the Name *Musikdrama*": *PW* V:303). Indeed, much of the opera's action occupies an inner, visible realm. Moreover, a fair amount of the work suspends action of any kind while the characters recount events both seen and unseen. Two important such passages of epic retelling already mentioned more than once are Isolde's background "Narration" in Act 1 and large stretches of Tristan's "Delirium" scene in Act 3. But there are numerous others, as well: in Act 1, Kurwenal's ballad of the fate of Morold and Isolde's account to Tristan of her healing of the sick "Tantris"; in Act 2, nearly the entire first half of the love scene and much of King Marke's monologue; in Act 3, Korean's account of how Tristan returned to his homeland Kareol and Brangäne's admission of having divulged the secret of the love potion to King Marke. As in the case of the *Ring*, Wagner may have *intended* to purge his sources of these epic retellings; but, in the end, they nonetheless came to form a constitutive element of his poetic text and, indeed, of his very conception of musical drama (not least as opportunities for leitmotivic recall and, more broadly, for establishing a whole network of leitmotivic discourse relating past, present, and future).[31]

As often as not, the present moment in *Tristan* is merely an occasion for characters to conjure up prehistory, where their thoughts and feelings lie deeply buried. In her Act 1 "Narration," for instance, Isolde discloses the twofold structure of her shame, enmeshed in both personal and political factors: Tristan's affront to the dignity of the Irish kingdom, and his initial rejection of Isolde's love. The roots of Tristan's psychological makeup are even more firmly embedded in the past. Just before partaking of the love potion (supposing it a poison), he speaks of it as the "only solace for eternal grief." What, then, is the origin of this sadness inscribed (*tristesse*) in his very name? He provides a partial answer toward the end of Act 2 in his cryptic response to Marke's speech: "Wohin nun Tristan scheidet" ("Whither Tristan now departs"). Unable to explain his apparently flagrant betrayal of Marke's trust, Tristan turns to Isolde, inviting her to return with him to the "night-realm" ("nächt'ge Land") where he – like she and all others – was born. In proffering this invitation he reveals a crucial detail: that his mother died in giving birth to him. The allusion to the music of "O sink hernieder" at precisely this moment thus establishes an unmistakable connection between Tristan's passion for Isolde and his lifelong guilt over the death of his mother.

Additional layers of prehistory come to light in Tristan's "Delirium" monologue. As Joseph Kerman has shown, the monologue consists of two great emotional cycles, each traversing the same path from "recollection and curse" to "relapse and [renewed] anticipation."[32] In the extended passage of recollection from the second cycle, Tristan reveals a further source of his grief: his father's death almost immediately after conceiving him (and, hence, another lost parent for whose fate he feels his own birth is responsible).[33] Sounding throughout much of this section is the shepherd's "old tune" (*alte Weise*), its doleful quality enhanced by the timbre of the onstage English horn that plays it. This strange tune acts as a catalyst to Tristan's memory, stimulating him to remember the moment from his childhood when he learned of the circumstances surrounding his birth and his parents' deaths. Furthermore, the tune is gradually transformed *within* the process of remembering it: just after Tristan recalls his parents' deaths, the tune wells up in the orchestra, shared by oboe and clarinet, and its diatonic Head motive is replaced by two interlocking chromatic lines (see Examples 7.9a, 7.9b). We hear the shepherd's melody as Tristan does: grief-laden, distorted, filtered through the recesses of memory.

Born under an unlucky star, Tristan is fated to long for death while at the same time that very longing prevents him from attaining the repose he so ardently desires. His dilemma is therefore a temporal one, a truth whose

Ex. 7.9a and 7.9b

frightening implications he fully grasps only in the climactic passage of the "Delirium" scene. The heartrending cry with which he assumes responsibility for having, in effect, brewed the disastrous love potion himself, "from father's need and mother's woe" ("Aus Vaters Not und Mutter-Weh"), is itself a highly charged sounding metaphor for his realization of the way in which his present suffering is intertwined with his own history. The tragedy of this condition resides in his inability to escape from a present weighted down by the past.[34] Wagner emphasizes this point musically through a threefold sequential repetition of the rising chromatic figure from the Act 1 Prelude (the Desire motive), a reprise culminating now in defeat and indecision as the third link in the sequential chain yields inexorably to the first, again.

While Tristan's monologue ends with a musical representation of "eternal recurrence," it is left for Isolde to deliver her beloved from this vicious circle. With the clarity of a sublime vision, her final "Transfiguration" monologue demonstrates that there *is* a way out of the futile struggle between presence and pastness. Wagner sums this up beautifully in the concluding measures of the opera, where one last reference to the opening motive complex of the Prelude melts into a luminous cadence in B major. This ending provides a necessary resolution, of course; but at a deeper level it signifies more. An emblem of futurity, it points the way to redemption from the entanglements of the past.

Of all the dualities in Wagner's *Tristan und Isolde*, perhaps none is as difficult to come to terms with as that between dramatic and epic elements. In outward appearance and design a drama, it is thoroughly suffused with the ruminative, reminiscent tone of epic, romance, and the novel. Yet in the final moments of the opera Isolde tips the temporal balance toward the future, imbuing the end of the work with the teleological character of drama. *Tristan* closes thus on a utopian note, a quality it shares with classical drama in general. Surely it was this quality that led Hölderlin, who had theorized the dialectic of essence and appearance at the beginning of the nineteenth century, to characterize drama as the most "ideal" of literary genres – an opinion Wagner obviously shared.

8 Performing Germany in Wagner's *Die Meistersinger von Nürnberg*

STEPHEN McCLATCHIE

There is a long tradition of identifying Wagner's *Die Meistersinger von Nürnberg* with Germany and Germany with *Die Meistersinger*, regarding the work as more than just an opera (or even music drama), but rather the very emblem of a nation. The connection of nation and art is intertwined throughout the history of *Die Meistersinger*. Three very different examples can serve to illustrate the point. In *Beyond Good and Evil*, Friedrich Nietzsche described the Act 1 Prelude as "a truly genuine token of the German soul ... This kind of music expresses best what I think of the Germans: they belong to the day before yesterday and the day after tomorrow – *as yet they have no today*."[1] A popular turn-of-the-century operatic guide called *Die Meistersinger* "the most beautiful, the most German of all operas."[2] And Nazi propaganda minister, Joseph Goebbels, in a radio address before a 1933 broadcast of the opening Bayreuth festival production of *Meistersinger* commented that: "Of all [Wagner's] music dramas *Die Meistersinger* stands out as the most German. It is simply the incarnation of our national identity."[3] The perennial "German question" ("what is Germany?") underlies this work, as it does most of Wagner's works, not simply by virtue of the proximity of German unification (1871) to its premiere (1868), but also through the resonance of this event in Wagner's contemporary writings, in the genesis of the work, and especially in its reception.

The genesis of *Die Meistersinger* parallels that of Germany itself. Although the poem was first sketched in July 1845 as a type of "satyr play" to be appended to *Tannhäuser*, it was not finished nor the music composed until the 1860s; the work was completed in October 1867 and given its first performance in Munich on 21 June 1868. Throughout this decade, the forces leading toward German unification were advancing: from the appointment of Otto von Bismarck as Prussian chancellor in 1862, the Schleswig-Holstein conflict in 1863–64 (resulting in the region's annexation to Prussia), the defeat of Austria in the Austro-Prussian war in 1866 (resulting in the end of the German Confederation and the annexation of Hanover, Hesse, Nassau, and Frankfurt to Prussia), and, finally, the German victory in the Franco-Prussian war of 1870–71, culminating in the proclamation of the German Empire at Versailles on 18 January 1871. Austrian playwright Hugo von

Hofmannsthal was not the first to make the connection between the two events when he wrote that "the national emotionalism of *Die Meistersinger* is the gift of a nationalistically heightened moment in time (the perceptible *becoming* [*Werden*] of German unification)."[4] In fact, the work is haunted by dreams of nationhood. For Theodor Adorno, *Meistersinger* was "compromised by nationalistic thought,"[5] and, writing in 1963, he noted that "[t]he stormy applause that one may still encounter following a performance of, say, *Die Meistersinger*, the self-affirmation of the public, which it hears from within Wagner's music, still has something about it of the old virulent evil."[6] Thomas Mann was also troubled by the work, writing in 1950 that "*Die Meistersinger* contains the most wonderful music, but it is not *entirely* coincidental that Hitler liked it so much."[7]

Die Meistersinger has been used throughout its history in this fashion to forge collective and cultural memories for and of the German *Volk*, socially and politically instrumentalized, so that it seems fair to say the work itself "performs" the identity of its author's nation. Significantly, the work itself thematizes performance and many of its phenomenal performances (such as the "Wach auf!" chorus in Act 3) contribute, in turn, to the sense of the opera as a "performance" of national identity. In Mann's words, "Wagner is indeed 'German' and 'national' to an exemplary – perhaps all too exemplary – degree. For *as well* as being an eruptive revelation of the German character, this *oeuvre* is also a theatrical representation of it."[8] This performance of nation casts a shadow over the work, of course, given its use during the Third Reich, where its performance furthered the National Socialist understanding of the "performance" or achievement (*Leistung*) of a national culture, a concept defined by Rudy Koshar as referring to the "whole range of practices necessary to create and represent new Germans" with an emotional attachment to the Reich.[9]

As a historical locus, the city of Nuremberg, too, shares this tradition of sociocultural instrumentalization. The nostalgic and indeed anti-modern view of the city that originated with the early Romantic writers Ludwig Tieck and Wilhelm Heinrich Wackenroder carried forward throughout the nineteenth century and was furthered by Wagner himself. Remarkably long-lived, as we will see, it was coopted by the political right in the interwar years and became an important aspect of the Nazi state. The annual Nazi Party rallies (*Reichsparteitage*) were held there between 1933 and 1939 and the notorious racial laws – known as the Nuremberg Laws – were proclaimed at the 1935 rally. After the war, the victorious allies drew on the symbolism of Nuremberg when they chose to hold the war crimes trials in that city. Coming to terms with Wagner's *Die Meistersinger von Nürnberg* thus requires, as well, the confrontation of these various historical and political associations.

Performing Germany

The unification of Germany in 1871 turned the German Question from an idealized or philosophical one into a question of practical political importance: what would Germany be? Pre-unification Germany was what has been termed a *Kulturnation* by Friedrich Meinecke – an entity characterized by a common culture (language, literature, religion, etc.) rather than a common social order, politics, or history.[10] How does a *Kulturnation* become a political nation? (Wagner had his own ideas on the subject, to which we will turn in a moment.)

Older scholarship understood "nation" as an inevitable and organic product of modernity. In this view, Germany was the product of a social and economic transformation from a traditional to a modern industrial state. This commonly accepted interpretation began to shift in the 1980s with the publication of Benedict Anderson's *Imagined Communities: Reflections on the Origin and Spread of Nationalism*.[11] Anderson saw "nation" as a cultural artefact, a result of the creation and manipulation of traditions and memories. Other writers, such as Anthony Smith (*The Ethnic Origins of Nations*, 1986), took Anderson's insight and similarly stressed the cultural roots of nationhood (language, myth of descent, religion, history, etc.) but noted that a collective effort was required at some point to bring all of these elements together in the process of constructing a national identity.[12] But how *do* people imagine a nation? And, once it is imagined, how is it internalized?[13]

More recent work on the idea of "nation" has focused on the role of collective or cultural memory in constructing nation. In John Gillis's words, "memories and identities are not fixed things, but representations or constructions of reality, subjective rather than objective phenomena ... Identities and memories are not things we think *about*, but things we think *with*."[14] In some sense, they are things that must be performed, even if unconsciously and unintentionally. The concept could also be understood as myth (Wagner would have understood it in this fashion). There is a striking temporal (con)fusion involved, since the cultural recall of collective memory is, as Mieke Bal puts it, "an activity occurring in the present, in which the past is continuously modified and re-described even as it continues to shape the future."[15] Or similarly, as Koshar has written: "public memory looks forward as it directs its gaze backward in time."[16] National memory work is thus both retrospective and anticipatory in a way that resonates curiously with Nietzsche's estimation of *Die Meistersinger*, cited above. Or again, in Koshar's words: "Memory serves not only to legitimize the nation historically but to give it a purchase on the future, to ground the nation in a historical narrative whose ending is even more ineffable than the beginning." To engage with history, whether scholarly or creatively, argues Koshar, is to "project the past into the future[,] carry on the ill-defined sense of responsibility to successors, and . . . rob the past of its specificity [to] capture it for future action."[17] It is important to note that this is a continuing and continuous activity and is in no way static. For Gillis, national identities "are, like everything historical, constructed and reconstructed; and it is our responsibility to decode them in order to discover the relationships they create and sustain";[18] moreover, "the making and the reception of memories, personal and collective, are embedded in a specific cultural, social, and political context."[19] Here the idea of agency is crucial: who is doing the construction and reconstruction of national identity? What and whose interests are being served?

The materials that may be marshaled for the creation of collective memory are almost limitless, from ideas of "home" or the preservation of historical structures to the complicated interplay between local and national traditions.[20] But culture and the arts always play a central role.[21] To take one example not entirely unrelated to *Meistersinger*, a number of scholars have recently studied the growing symbolic and political function of public festivals, celebrations, and commemorations (often of cultural figures) in nineteenth- and early twentieth-century Germany to show how they helped first to anticipate and then to buttress German unity.[22] Two important tendencies emerge throughout the nineteenth century. First, there is a double move away from the present toward both the past and the future:

> [Festivals] more and more shifted their function away from the constituting
> of societal reality and the portrayal of social structures toward the
> symbolization of societal self-interpretations and ideological convictions.
> In other words: festivals showed societies less and less how they are and
> more and more how they once were or ought to be in the future.[23]

And, second, there is a shift in focus in these events from the celebration of the enlightened individual toward the "staging of the people" (*Volk*) themselves.[24] There was such a conscious effort by cultural and political elites to create this cultural or collective memory through such events that, in the end, "[n]ineteenth-century commemorations were largely for, but not of, the people."[25]

Wagner's *Die Meistersinger von Nürnberg* helped to construct the German nation along such lines in the 1860s and 1870s. In its attempt to forge collective memory, it thus functioned in a sense like a public festival, as depicted on stage in its own culminating scene. The national identity that it helped to shape continued to be developed through the Nazi era. Adorno understood this process well and used it to explain the seductive nature of the work:

> The expression of sweet nostalgia merges with the allure of the familiar, the promise of security at home, together with the feeling, "When was I here before?," and the archetypes of the bourgeois find themselves invested with the nimbus of what is long since past . . . Each listener has the feeling that it belongs to him alone, that it is a communication from his long-forgotten childhood, and from this shared *déjà vu* the phantasmagoria of the collective is constructed . . . [I]t stirs up, gratifies and even legitimates ideologically an impulse that adult life has only and not wholly successfully managed to master. It relaxes everyone's limbs, not just Sachs's, and, as the demagogue of the feelings, the composer demonstrates the right reactions in which everyone then joins. Nowhere is Wagner more mythological than in the modernity of such pleasures . . . Wagner fraudulently presents the historical German past as its essence. In this way he has invested concepts such as "ancestors" and "the people" with that absoluteness that was subsequently unleashed in an outburst of absolute horror. This manipulated awakening of memory is the exact opposite of enlightenment.[26]

While critics continue to debate the extent to which the national identity constructed in *Die Meistersinger* fed directly into the ideals and ideology of the Third Reich, there can be little doubt that a distinct cultural genealogy links the two. In what follows, I investigate some aspects of troubled cultural legacy of Wagner's opera from his time down to the present.

Performing the Second Reich

Wagner's writings on nation form the background to *Die Meistersinger von Nürnberg*. Of particular interest is the constellation of materials around *Meistersinger* itself: the essays "Was ist Deutsch?" ("What Is German?," 1865), *Deutsche Kunst und deutsche Politik* (*German Art and German Politics*, 1868); *Beethoven* (1871); the republication with an extended postlude of *Das Judentum in der Musik* (*Judaism in Music*, 2nd edn., 1869); and Wagner's correspondence with political historian Constantin Frantz among others. Hannu Salmi has studied Wagner's political activity, both in itself and as expressed in his works, during the crucial years of German unification, 1864–71, and has clearly demonstrated Wagner's participation in the widespread yearning for a united, strong German nation.[27]

Throughout his life, Wagner identified himself with the German nation and constantly linked his own art with the fate of Germany. For example, in a letter to Constantin Frantz written during the composition of *Meistersinger*, Wagner wrote: "my own artistic ideal stands or falls with the salvation of Germany; without Germany's greatness my art was only a dream: if this dream is to find fulfilment, Germany, too, must necessarily attain her preordained greatness."[28] He also identified himself during the

1860s with Hans Sachs, often signing this name to his letters to Ludwig II of Bavaria.[29] During the 1860s, Wagner tried to create an image of Germanness and the German nation in his writings (where the earlier writings were largely concerned with theories of art). *Deutsche Kunst und deutsche Politik* is a particularly clear example of this tendency.

The language in which Wagner casts these thoughts is interesting. Salmi has shown how Wagner uses contrasted oppositions as a rhetorical strategy in his writings. The binary oppositions discussed by Salmi are: German (also "primally" German and "fundamentally German")/non-German; national/cosmopolitan; kingdom/democracy; culture/civilization; idealism/materialism; reproduction/imitation (*Nachbildung/Nachahmung*); originality/epigonism; true/false; noble/debased; and past/present. Jacques Derrida and others have shown how Western thought in general tends to be constructed around such binarisms in which one term (the first, above) carries with it all the value. We thus tend to construct ourselves, our nations, our genders, and so on, on the basis of what we are *not*; the first term could not exist without the second as its shadow, its negative definition. Wagner uses the same linguistic strategy with respect to Germany both in his writings and in *Die Meistersinger* itself.[30]

For the Wagner of the 1860s and later, the category "non-German" elided both the French and the Jews (German or otherwise). For example, *Deutsche Kunst und deutsche Politik* turns on a distinction between French materialist civilization and German *Geist* or *Kultur* (see, for example, GS VIII:34–35). Elsewhere in his writings he contrasts what he saw as the rootless Jews with the German nation. According to Wagner, the past was formulated through myths, which were the building material for national identity. Wagner's myth of Germany strove to rectify Nietzsche's characterization of the nation as "atomistic chaos." Wagner's ideal was that of a nation striving from political disunity toward unity, valorizing a glorious past over a decadent present: "the German of the past was to be the German of the future."[31] Wagner's language creates "Germanness" as an ideal type – brave, universal, solid, true, free, etc. – and juxtaposes this with the Other: international, cosmopolitan, French, Jew, etc.[32]

Unsurprisingly, Wagner's rhetorical oppositions are also reflected through the lens of art. Like his Romantic forebears, Wagner saw the *Volk* as both the impetus and the requirement for art. This view originates with Herder, who wrote of the *Volksgeist* (spirit of the *Volk*) as the primary unifying force of the people and a catalyst for art and human activity in general.[33] Since art promotes social coherence, it is inescapably political. In a series of diary jottings from September 1865 (what later became the essay "Was ist Deutsch?"), Wagner argued that all great art has a political significance and, further, that German politics will be redeemed by

German art. Salmi calls this fusion of art and politics "one of the most central of Wagner's intellectual political ideas."[34]

In the mid-1860s, Wagner hoped that Bavaria under King Ludwig II (who had rescued him from penury in true fairy-tale fashion in May 1864) would become the model German state in its fusion of art and politics. *Die Meistersinger* is dedicated to Ludwig, and many of Wagner's writings from the time, such as the 1865 diary entries just mentioned, took the form of advice to the king. Wagner believed that a state achieved its ideal essence through the personality of its king (as one removed from party politics) and was dismayed that diplomats rather than princes currently controlled the levers of power.[35]

An important component of Wagner's thought was the universal mission of Germany and German culture, which was like a spring around which all people gather for rebirth: "By a most natural instinct the nations turn back to the fount of their renewing; and, strange to say, they there find the German *Reich* itself."[36] This idea derived largely from Constantin Frantz (1817–91) with whom Wagner corresponded extensively in 1866. Frantz, an anti-Semite like Wagner, held up the Germans as the Chosen People of the Christian age in such works as his *Untersuchungen über das europäische Gleichgewicht* (*Inquiry into the European Balance of Power*, 1859) and *Die Wiederherstellung Deutschlands* (*The Rehabilitation of Germany*, 1865). After receiving the *Meistersinger* poem from Wagner, Frantz encouraged him to give musical expression to his thoughts about the German mission, as a "morning greeting to the German nation in order to awaken it from sleep."[37] Frantz's language would later find an eerie echo in Nazi rhetoric.

Die Meistersinger von Nürnberg can be seen as a musical parallel to *Deutsche Kunst und deutsche Politik*, an attempt to construct a nation and a people united by art.[38] Nietzsche understood the connection when he wrote, aphoristically: "*Meistersinger* – anti-civilization; the German against the French."[39] An important ideological influence on Wagner in this regard was Georg Gottfried Gervinus, whose *Geschichte der deutschen Nationalliteratur* (1835–42) argued that the development of German litera-ture to the end of the eighteenth century was the articulation of Germany's national identity, but that this latter could only be transcended or further developed by transforming this cultural energy into political energy.[40]

Meistersinger was also part of the confluence of events that prompted the republication of *Das Judentum in der Musik* under Wagner's own name in 1869. Whereas the original 1850 edition attacked Mendelssohn and Meyerbeer as exemplars of "Jewishness in music," the long afterword appended to the 1869 reissue is directed against an alleged conspiracy of Jewish critics. As Wagner wrote in April 1869 to Carl Tausig, "the unprecedented insolence of the Viennese press on the occasion of the

[Vienna premiere of *Meistersinger*], the continual, brazen lie-mongering about me, and its truly destructive effects have finally persuaded me to take this step [i.e., the republication of *Judentum in der Musik*], regardless of its consequences, more especially after I had been questioned on the matter."[41] In fact, one anonymous reviewer saw the essay as "a literary pendant to the *Prügelszene* in *Die Meistersinger*,"[42] and several protests against early productions of *Die Meistersinger* were tied to the republication of *Das Judentum in der Musik*.[43]

Much recent writing on Wagner has focused on whether his undeniable anti-Semitism was reflected in his music and/or details of characterization in the dramas. The character of the Merker in *Die Meistersinger*, Sixtus Beckmesser, has attracted much of this attention. The argument (which stems largely from Adorno's comment that "all the rejects of Wagner's works are caricatures of Jews"[44]) points to an apparent allusion to the old-German fairy tale of the Jew in the thorn bush (also first pointed out by Adorno) as well as alleged physiological and vocal stereotypes of Jews (e.g., screeching voice, distorted speech or *Mauscheln*, lack of creative talent) in forming the character of Beckmesser as a scapegoat who must be banished from the *Volk* at the end of the work.[45] It is a seductive argument, particularly since it was well known that Beckmesser (originally called "Veit Hanslich") was a thinly disguised caricature of the influential Viennese (and Jewish) music critic, Eduard Hanslick.

A more complex reading has been advanced by Marc Weiner and David Levin, both of whom argue that Wagner's works are self-reflexive, "dramatizing the paradigm upon which they are based."[46] According to Levin, Wagner's

> aspiration to a totalizing representation produces the need for an object that does not belong. In [his] works, the role of the societal bad object is conflated with the role of the aesthetic bad object. That is, the scheming, unappealing character comes to bear aesthetic qualities that the work seeks to disavow.[47]

Although elsewhere he calls this an "aesthetics of anti-Semitism,"[48] Levin's most recent formulation here understands the exclusion of Beckmesser at the end of *Meistersinger* as a political gesture, too, as part of the process of constructing Germany. In this regard, Beckmesser need not be regarded as a Jew for this ideological process to work. (And, as David Dennis has demonstrated, anti-Semitism is not a major factor in the political appropriation of *Die Meistersinger*.)[49]

Die Meistersinger is German in its setting, in its theme, in its characters, and in its history: Wagner drew heavily on Johann Christoph Wagenseil's *Buch von der Meister-Singer holdseligen Kunst Anfang, Fortübung, Nutzbarkeiten,*

und Lehrsätzen (1697, appended to his *De civitate noribergensi commentatio*)
for the names and practices of the Meistersinger and their songs – the bar form
used by the historical Meistersinger is explained by Kothner in Act 1 and
forms the basis for all of the "diegetic" songs performed within the drama as
such.[50] The poem also draws on Lutheran chorale in the opening scene
(which, of course, also alludes to Bach) as well as in the "Wach auf!" chorus,
a setting of Luther's words from his 1523 *Die wittenbergisch Nachtigall*. And,
as mentioned, the final scene on the *Festwiese* draws on the "staging of the
Volk" characteristic of nineteenth-century public festivals.[51]

Hans Sachs's final speech is the primary locus of this activity of nation-
building. Here, in response to Walther's impetuous rejection of the laurel
wreath crowning him a Meistersinger, Sachs lectures him on the importance of respecting the "holy German art" of the Meistersinger, which
will survive even if the Holy Roman Empire should "dissolve in mist" in
the face of the "foreign [*welsche*] mists" and "foreign vanities" of a "false,
foreign rule." Sachs clearly links the art of the Meistersinger with national
culture and, in lecturing Walther, is in fact exhorting the *Volk* (and the
audience) to honor the legacy of holy German art. Here, all in attendance,
on stage and off, become the *Volk*.[52] And where Eva and Walther perform
in opposition to the congregation's chorale in the first scene (their pantomime in between the phrases), in the final scene they sing in unison with
the people and are thus absorbed into the *Volk*.

Die Meistersinger is also both a reflection and a further development
of the myth of Nuremberg – like that of Germany itself, based on a
contrast between an idealized past and an imperfect present. The free,
imperial city of Nuremberg became part of Bavaria only in 1806, with
Napoleon's dissolution of the Holy Roman Empire. The medieval and
Renaissance timber houses in the Altstadt survived almost intact from the
time of Hans Sachs himself – and Wagner drew on the mythology of
Nuremberg in his insistence on having real, three-dimensional houses
for Act 2.[53] To the Romantics, Nuremberg was the mythical heart of Old
Germany, the home of Sachs and Albrecht Dürer, devoted to art. Wagner,
too, wrote of the city in these terms in his letters to Ludwig II; for
example:

> Nuremberg, the old, true seat of German art, German uniqueness and
> splendour, the powerful old free city, well-preserved like a precious jewel,
> reborn through the labours of its serenely happy, solid, enlightened and
> liberal populace under the patronage of the Bavarian throne.[54]

Scholars who have examined the Nuremberg myth have pointed out the
need to read the city on several levels: as a historical city; as an economi-
cally successful free city; as the geographical and spiritual heart of true

Germany; as a romantic, utopian ideal of a pre-industrial social collective (*Gemeinschaft*); and as a bulwark against modernity.[55] Like most similar constructions, the myth does not correspond with reality. While it was true that Nuremberg was one of the first cities to convert to Lutheranism and had banned Jews for centuries, the Protestant status of Nuremberg was not "as absolute and frictionless" as Wagner presents it; instead, historical Nuremberg was "the site of a divided population and of key conflicts and negotiations of the Reformation."[56]

Die Meistersinger von Nürnberg was understood as a national opera from its earliest performances, just as Wagner himself was understood as the embodiment or essence of Germanness.[57] Its initial audiences regarded the ending as an affirmation of the Second Reich – indeed, a 1981 exhibition catalogue characterized the work between 1888 and 1918 as a "Wilhelminian Festival Opera."[58] On the other hand, as Thomas Grey has noted, before World War I Wagnerism and anti-Wagnerism were equally cosmopolitan phenomena. Commentators, both pro- and anti-Wagner, made no distinction between the particularly political, national works, such as *Meistersinger* and *Der Ring des Nibelungen*, and the more apolitical, modern ones (*Tristan und Isolde, Parsifal*).[59] Nationalists elsewhere were not more opposed to *Meistersinger* than to Wagner's other works (although foreign productions did sometimes cut Sachs's final speech) – to them "it was all equally and indelibly German." Contemporary critics, both German and foreign, focused primarily on the universal, aesthetic theme of the opera (the tension between innovation and tradition and the obvious parallel this had with Wagner's *Zukunftsmusik*). For Germans themselves, however, it was natural to see German music as pre-eminent; as Grey points out, Hanslick was just as much a believer in holy German art as Wagner.

Performing the Third Reich

Following the German defeat in World War I, Bayreuth became a locus of right-wing opposition to the Weimar Republic. Siegfried Wagner's wife, Winifred, in particular became an early supporter of Hitler, who was first received in Wahnfried in 1923.[60] Wagner and his *Meistersinger* became potent symbols of a vanished, idealized past. In 1924, when the Bayreuth festival opened again after the war, it was no accident that *Die Meistersinger* was chosen for the first performance. Indeed, this symbolic link with the past was heightened (and embodied) by the presence of the 86-year-old Cosima for the first act. The audience stood silently from Sachs's "Zerging im Dunst" to the end of the opera and then sang all three verses of the German national anthem (the *Deutschlandslied*), much to the consternation of the foreign guests (whose presence – and cash – was crucial to the success of the festival). For subsequent performances, Siegfried distributed printed cards which asked the audience "to refrain from all of the well-meaning singing; 'art is what matters here' (*Hier gilt's der Kunst*)."[61]

In his shift from apolitical conservatism toward initially pained, then fervent support of the Weimar Republic, Thomas Mann was the paradigmatic "progressive" German of the interwar years. His initial views are expressed in his wartime *Reflections of a Nonpolitical Man*, which outlines the dichotomy between native *Kultur* and foreign or cosmopolitan *Zivilisation* that was so characteristic of German thought in the period. Significantly, Mann uses Nietzsche's *Meistersinger* aphorism (quoted above) to frame his argument.[62] While he subsequently refined and revised much of his thinking about Wagner, particularly in the wake of his forced emigration from Nazi Germany, many of his views did not change: it was in these *Reflections* where Mann first commented on Wagner's works as the "theatrical representation" of German national identity.[63] In other words, Mann did not differ greatly from his contemporaries' views of the composer. In the midst of an extended discussion of Pfitzner's *Palestrina* in the chapter "On Virtue," Mann raises the "obvious" comparison with *Meistersinger* and cites approvingly a comment by Pfitzner that "the *Meistersinger* is the apotheosis of the new, a praise of the future and of life; in *Palestrina* everything tends toward the past, it is dominated by *sympathy with death*."[64]

Oddly enough, Mann's view of *Die Meistersinger* was also that of the National Socialists. According to Ernst "Putzi" Hanfstaengl, *Die Meistersinger* was Hitler's favorite opera (he saw it on his first visit to the Bayreuth festival in 1925). Its theme of the metaphorical springtime of life and art resonated with the Nazis' belief that they, too, were responsible for a national awakening, the dawning of a new age;[65] for example, in "Wagner's *Meistersinger* and Our Times," Peter Raabe writes that *Meistersinger* symbolizes "the spirit of youth marching forward over decaying formalism; victory of progressives over those stuck in sterile old ways."[66] The Nazi slogan "Deutschland Erwache!" resonates quite clearly with *Die Meistersinger's* "Wach auf!" and may in fact have been modeled on it. Goebbels certainly saw the connection, writing in his diary on 1 August 1932: "in the evening we went together to *Die Meistersinger*. At the great 'Wach auf!' chorus, shivers ran down one's spine. It will now soon also be the case in Germany. We must now attain power."[67] In a speech before a 1933 radio broadcast of the opening Bayreuth *Meistersinger*, Goebbels expanded on the connection:

> There is certainly no work in all the music literature of the German *Volk* that
> so closely relates to our times and our spiritual condition . . . How often
> in recent years has its rousing mass chorus *Wach auf, es nahet gen den
> Tag* been heard by ardently longing, faithful Germans as a tangible
> symbol of the reawakening of the German *Volk* out of the deep political
> and spiritual narcosis of November 1918? . . . [*Die Meistersinger* is the]
> incarnation of our *Volkstum* [representing] everything that marks and fills
> the German soul.[68]

A performance of the chorus concluded Goebbels's speech on Nazi cultural policy at the opening of the Reichskulturkammer on 15 November
1933.

Die Meistersinger was pressed into service by the Nazis again and again,
beginning even before they came to power in January 1933.[69] To give only
a few examples, the *Meistersinger* prelude was on the program of the
Leipzig memorial celebration of the fiftieth anniversary of Wagner's
death (which Hitler attended on 14 February 1933); an evening performance of *Meistersinger* under Furtwängler followed the opening of
the Nazi-ruled Reichstag on 13 March 1933; and the ceremonial Day of
Potsdam (21 March 1933) concluded with a performance of *Meistersinger*
at the Berlin Staatsoper, again under Furtwängler. After a torchlit parade,
Hitler and his entourage arrived for the third act. At Goebbels's instructions, the audience and those on stage turned to Hitler during the "Wach
auf!" chorus to render their homage.[70]

The opening of the 1933 Bayreuth festival on 6 August with a new production of *Meistersinger* coincided with Hitler's first visit as Reichskanzler.
In an ironic echo of Siegfried Wagner's plea for an "apolitical" Bayreuth,
cards were distributed to the audience requesting them to refrain from
singing the German national anthem or the "Horst Wessel" song (a Nazi
street song) after the performance, adding that "there is no more splendid
expression of the German spirit than the eternal works of the Master
himself."[71] *Meistersinger* was performed again in 1934 and, in a new production by Wieland Wagner, in 1943 and 1944. These last performances
included members of the Hitler Jugend (Hitler Youth), the Bund deutscher
Mädel (League of German Girls), and the SS-Standarte Wiking on stage
for the final scene (since the Bayreuth chorus had been decimated by the
exigencies of the war); the SS guard also played the introductory fanfares
from the balcony. (Frederic Spotts aptly characterizes this as a "moral
nadir" of Bayreuth.)[72]

Two particular appropriations of *Die Meistersinger* by the Nazis are
worth examining in greater detail. First, from 1935 on, it was performed at
the end of the first day of the annual Nazi Party rally in Nuremberg.[73] That
year marked the premiere of Benno von Arendt's famous production

in which the closing scene self-reflexively resembled the party rally itself, with masses of people in formation on stage and row after row of flags; Arendt worked closely with Hitler on the production and followed many of his suggestions.[74] The conflation of *Meistersinger* with the *Reichsparteitage* leaves a trace in Leni Riefenstahl's use of the meditative Act 3 prelude (the "Wach auf!" theme in particular) for the shots of Nuremberg at daybreak in her propaganda film of the 1935 rally, *Triumph des Willens*.[75] It was also memorialized in book form by Richard Wilhelm Stock, whose lavishly illustrated and beautifully produced *Richard Wagner und die Stadt der Meistersinger* was given as a present to guests at the 1938 *Reichsparteitage* performance.[76] In it, Stock mentions no less than seven times that *Meistersinger* was the "official opera" of the rally. For example:

> With the elevation of *Die Meistersinger von Nürnberg* to the festival of the *Reichsparteitage*, the *political* genius *Adolf Hitler* established an eternal memorial to the *artistic* genius *Richard Wagner* in the city of the Meistersinger. The annual *Reichsparteitage* in Nuremberg, which embraces the greatest national holiday of the German people, will be opened in perpetuity by this ingenious German work.[77]

Stock's book is a poisonous and hate-filled piece of Nazi propaganda, belying the attractiveness of the publication and the beauty of the opera itself.

Die Meistersinger also had a significant role in the wartime Bayreuth festivals (the *Kriegesfestspiele*), run under the auspices of the National Socialist (Nazi) organization Kraft durch Freude (Strength through Joy), which aimed to "bring culture to the masses to strengthen the popular commitment to the racial community."[78] Annually, 20,000–30,000 "guests of the Führer" attended these performances; these guests were primarily front soldiers and armament workers, although there were also numerous special guests from the Reich and its allies. The 1943 festival was also commemorated in book form by Stock, in a reissue of most of his 1938 work, along with a new introduction and a curious sort of postlude consisting of comments from attendees purporting to show how their love for the German fatherland and the treasures of the German spirit were fanned by Wagner's genius – which was, in fact, the moral aim of the wartime festivals.[79]

In short, *Meistersinger* became, in Hans Rudolf Vaget's words, "the exemplary stay-the-course opera [*Durchhalte-Oper*], the musical equivalent of *Kolberg*."[80] I would argue that these uses of *Meistersinger* represent the creation of collective, cultural memory constitutive of nation (as discussed above) through performances of the work in its entirety or in excerpt, and through its evocation, allusion, or even quotation in speeches and newspapers.

Interestingly, however, despite every incentive to do so, the Nazis did not promote the purported anti-Semitic elements of *Die Meistersinger* (even if they did foment anti-Semitism in articles and statements about *Meistersinger* and other Wagner works). Indeed, David Dennis has noted that there is "no evidence that Nazi cultural politicians, or their volkish [*sic*] forebears and associates, referred in public discourse to ... Beckmesser as Jewish, or to his fate in *Die Meistersinger* as foreshadowing National Socialist policies against Jews."[81] Instead, the Nazis focused on Wagner's genius and on the idealistic and transcendental nature of his "holy, German art."[82] Their reception of *Meistersinger* related more to its role as an icon of Germanness, tradition, and cultural conservatism. Dennis traces four primary themes here: first, an emphasis on the dual image of Nuremberg as a symbol of the timeless stability of German art and culture and Nuremberg as the "new epicenter of our German cultural will," saved from the Jews by linking it with the *Reichsparteitage* and Wagner's opera;[83] second, a focus on the character of Hans Sachs as a charismatic, genius-leader emerging from the *Volk* and leading it in its fight;[84] third, a lesson on the role of the *Volk* within the *Gemeinschaft* (whereby their artistic judgement is valorized over that of the [Jewish] professional critic);[85] and, fourth, a de-emphasis on Walther's symbolic role in the aesthetics of the future (as the agent of the new and modern).[86] To Dennis's four themes, I would add a fifth one that emerges regularly: the alleged role of the Jews in blocking performances of the opera and undermining its popularity.[87]

Characteristically, Thomas Mann resisted this appropriation – but his was a lone voice. In his 1933 "Sorrows and Grandeur of Richard Wagner," Mann wrote:

> It is thoroughly inadmissible to ascribe a contemporary meaning to Wagner's nationalist gestures and speeches – the meaning that they would have today. To do so is to falsify and abuse them, to sully their romantic purity ... It is nothing but demagogy when today the "German sword" lines – or indeed that key statement at the end of *Die Meistersinger*: "Zerging' in Dunst das Heil'ge Röm'sche Reich, uns bliebe gleich die heil'ge deutsche Kunst" ... – are thundered tendentiously into the auditorium by the basses, in order to achieve an added patriotic effect.[88]

Mann wanted to see the work as unsullied and apolitical – the same tendency behind the "Hier gilt's der Kunst" fig leaf used in 1924 and 1933 (and again in 1951; see below) – but it was too late: *Die Meistersinger* had long been highly politicized. Hans Vaget has suggested that the opera is more metapolitical than political, arguing that the "absence of any overt political agenda ... accounts for the extraordinary political import that Wagner's opera has had over time."[89] In my estimation, however, the distinction is a false one: metapolitics are just as political as real politics.

Sachs's final speech remained the locus of the nation-building aspects of the work – and was certainly understood as such. Goebbels quoted it as the culmination of his 1933 Bayreuth speech; it forms the closing peroration of Stock's *Meistersinger* books; and it was doubtless used similarly on myriad other occasions as well. Its message did not fall on deaf ears – there are numerous indications that it was heard and understood. For example, one of the regular summaries of the populace's mood and morale prepared by the Gestapo for the leadership from reports from its informants around the country commented that, after the 1943 Bayreuth festival performances of *Meistersinger*, "Listeners said that especially the 'national qualities' [*Töne*] at the end had never before moved them so deeply."[90] The postlude to the wartime edition of Stock's book (1943) includes many similar statements. The understanding was well established: even before the Nazis came to power, Alfred Lorenz, an early Nazi sympathizer, described the passage beginning with "Habt acht!" as a "primally forceful, splendid warning, which, up to the present day, two generations after its composition, ought to be cried again and again in the ears of us Germans – although now they are no princes who plant their foreign vanities in our land."[91] And it continued in this role until the very end: Fritz Kempfler, the Nazi mayor of Bayreuth, was present at the last Bayreuth wartime performance of *Die Meistersinger* on 9 August 1944 and later wrote that "at Hans Sachs's speech, 'Even should the Holy Roman Empire fall [*sic*] into mist, for us there would yet remain holy German art!' shivers went up my spine because I knew that in a few months we would be standing on top of the ruins of the Reich."[92]

Performing what?

Obviously, *Die Meistersinger von Nürnberg* would continue to be performed after the war. Indeed, according to Patrick Carnegy, the first postwar *Meistersinger* in Europe took place as early as 10 May 1945 by the La Scala company (in a temporary location); it was repeated when La Scala reopened in 1947.[93] It continues to be performed regularly around the world, particularly on special occasions to celebrate art itself. Not surprisingly, then, *Die Meistersinger* was chosen for the reopening of the Bayreuth festival in 1951 – and once again, a card was distributed with the depoliticizing fig leaf, "Hier gilt's der Kunst."[94] It continues to stand as an emblem of the German nation, although it is probably impossible to hear the final words the same way after the Third Reich.

In terms of staging, traditional productions were the rule much longer than for other works – and not just in Bayreuth. It was in Bayreuth, however, that Wieland Wagner staged his famous production of 1956 that came to be known as "The Mastersingers *without* Nuremberg." Gone were the half-timbered houses, the flags, and the traditional costumes. In their place was spare and symbolic production, devoid of German national elements. But such a visual depoliticization of the work is not the same thing as coming to terms with the past (*Vergangenheitsbewältigung*), but more like the mere avoidance of that past.[95] Such is the power of collective memory. Rudy Koshar has pointed out a similar reluctance to confront Germany's identification with Nazism openly and fully in the continued use of the Nazi Party rally grounds in Nuremberg by the city until well into the 1970s.[96] In many ways, a similar reluctance to remember lies behind the current performance tradition of rehabilitating Beckmesser in the final scene by bringing him back for the final chorus.[97] In recent years, traditional productions have been more the rule than the exception.

Yet, as a work of art, *Die Meistersinger von Nürnberg* is not necessarily any more compromised than Haydn's imperial theme (the theme of the German national anthem) or any other work appropriated by the Nazis, such as Beethoven's symphonies. In Thomas Grey's words, "to label the Nazi regime a '*Meistersinger* state' . . . is to capitulate to the Nazis' own flattening appropriation of Wagner."[98] We need to continue to engage with *Die Meistersinger* as both a work of art and a historical artefact. While critical theory has certainly popularized the idea that the meaning of a work is not frozen with the death of its creator, neither is it frozen after a particular moment in its reception history. While *Meistersinger* was used and understood by Wagner, his contemporaries, his successors, and the Nazis to construct a collective, cultural memory of the German nation, the nature of the nation continued to shift – and continues to do so today. Unquestionably, there are nationalistic elements embedded within the work (and clearly connected to Wagner's writings), but interpretations of *Die Meistersinger*, whether of a creative or a scholarly nature, that focus solely on these aspects ignore much else that is relevant in the work, such as the great humanity of Sachs's "Wahn" monologue at the opening of Act 3.

The ambiguous nature of *Die Meistersinger* and its reception is nicely expressed by the American critic Joseph Horowitz in an essay entitled "Wagner and the American Jew – a Personal Reflection." I will leave him with the final words:

I treasure Wagner's representation of the outsider. I feel myself drawn
particularly to his humor and his pain, which I feel as a connection to my
own Jewishness ... [Hans Sachs's final speech] seems to me less of a racist
attack than an aesthetic error. I can't see Beckmesser's putative Jewish
essence; he yearns for empathy ... Which is the "true" Wagner – the ironic
outsider or the hot-blooded nationalist? This freedom to decide makes him
alternately a relation or an enemy for Jews like me.[99]

9 *Parsifal*: redemption and *Kunstreligion*

GLENN STANLEY

The long road to *Parsifal*

The *Ring* complete, the Bayreuth festival a fragile reality, Wagner turned –
or more precisely returned, after a long hiatus – to work on *Parsifal* in
1877. He finished the poetic text in April and then labored for five years
on the music, fighting ill health and struggling to ensure the future of the
festival along the way. He composed act by act, drafting "compositional"
and "orchestral" sketches virtually simultaneously, sometimes making use
of material conceived earlier and occasionally revising the verbal text.[1]
After finishing the orchestral sketch in April 1879, Wagner needed almost
three years until he concluded work on the full score, in January 1882.
Further revisions and rehearsals fraught with diverse problems preceded
the first performances in the summer of 1882, when the aging master
celebrated himself and his achievement by conducting the last act of the
final performance – a true *Schwanengesang*.

The opera *Parsifal* is a "summation and consummation,"[2] a late work and
Wagner's self-described "last card."[3] He drew it from a very mixed deck that
he had begun to assemble already in the 1840s. In the intervening decades he
completed an intellectual and artistic journey whose course was defined by
the many twists and turns, detours and reversals, through which the opera
accrued a rich assortment of philosophical ideas and poetic-dramatic and
musical elements. If Wagner had composed a "Parzifal"[4] on Wolfram von
Eschenbach's medieval epic in 1845, when he first read the poem, it would
have joined *Tannhäuser* and *Lohengrin* to form a trilogy of Romantic
operas on medieval Christian legends. (As late as 1868, Wagner wrote that
Parzifal, as he still spelled the title, was "in the genre of *Lohengrin*.")[5] It
would have shared their pre-music drama forms and styles, and lacked
essential elements of plot and character of the eventual, mature *Parsifal* that
are, at most, only adumbrated in the medieval poem, from which the earlier
prose sketches depart in important ways. (Eschenbach's Parsifal is married,
and his Grail community consists of men and women who live celibately
together.) Many of the most important features of the drama as we know it
were only developed in the prose drafts from 1865 to 1877, and in the
libretto: the penetrating psychological characterizations, the themes of
Schopenhauerian pessimism and compassion (*Mitleid*),[6] Buddhist notions

of reincarnation (Kundry's former lives) and respect for all forms of life (the swan episode), nature as holy and healing, and the seductive role of the Flower maidens. A very crucial change came earlier, during work on *Tristan und Isolde* in 1859: the spear wound that leads to Tristan's death reminded Wagner of Amfortas, who in *Parsifal* is wounded by Klingsor with the holy spear Amfortas himself had once wielded. (Wagner even briefly considered the possibility that Parsifal, in search of the Grail, should stumble on Tristan in the third act.) Thereupon Wagner transformed the Grail from Eschenbach's "magic stone without specifically Christian significance"[7] into a sacred relic associated with the blood of Christ in the form of transubstantiated wine. The acquisition of mystical redemptive (and life-sustaining) properties by the Grail had momentous implications. The culminating scenes of Acts 1 and 3, revolving around the Grail ceremony (see Table 9.1), establish the basis for the large-scale symmetrical design of the entire opera and also set up the dramatic teleology established by Amfortas's failure to reveal the Grail in Act 1 and resolved by Parsifal's intervention in Act 3. These scenes also emphasize Wagner's preoccupation with the symbolic role of (pure) blood in the Christian liturgy, which he relates to the wound and blood of Amfortas and the healing work of Parsifal, who restores Amfortas's spear to the Grail community which he will lead.

Blood and spear are instruments and symbols of redemption, and redemption is generally acknowledged to be the central idea of the opera. Titurel dies between Acts 2 and 3, and Klingsor is liquidated along with the Flower maidens; otherwise, all who remain are redeemed through Parsifal's compassion and wisdom (although, contrary to the medieval sources, Kundry's salvation comes at the price of her death). The Grail knights and squires are also redeemed and, significantly, at the end of the opera they have the last word, proclaiming the "redemption of the redeemer." Earlier it is this group that urgently articulates its need for the Grail's sustenance; the communal voice applies great pressure on Amfortas in both acts. Moreover, in the finales to these acts, an offstage chorus also includes women's voices. These voices help create a grand sonority appropriate for these climactic moments, but their presence can also be interpreted symbolically, to the effect that a metacommunity, more ideal and abstract than the men and boys of the Grail community, seeks and receives redemption. In this light, we can perceive a strongly articulated presence of a social collectivity, despite the fact that this element of the opera has been neglected in the reception history, which has focused on individual characters. This pattern of reception ignores ideas central to the genesis of *Parsifal*: Wagner's critiques of modern society, his calls for its regeneration, and his proposals for accomplishing this task. The question whether the metacommunity symbolizes all of humanity, just

Table 9.1 Parsifal *"scenes" and dramatic episodes*

Act I	Act II	Act III
Prelude (mm. 1–110) **I. Domain of the Grail (Outdoors) mm. 111–1073** **A. Gurnemanz, Squires, Kundry, Amfortas mm. 115–742** 115 Gurnemanz, Squires (until 924) 196 Kundry (until 1072), brings balsam 239–383 Amfortas (song to nature, 264–88) 383–741 Gurnemanz: narration: Titurel, Amfortas, Klingsor, spear, wound, "reiner Tor" **B. Parsifal, Gurnemanz, Kundry mm. 742–1073** 742–98 Swan 799–938 Gurnemanz rebukes Parsifal (song 805–48) 938–1073 Parsifal: narration **Transition to Grail castle 1073–1205** "Verwandlung" music (orchestral "Prelude" to "Scene" II, 1105–56) **II. Grail castle 1205–1666** (Parsifal present but silent) 1205–45 Knights, etc., procession and ritual 1246–1405 (Titurel) Amfortas "passion" 1405–1666 Knights, etc, Grail revealed, procession, Parsifal's incomprehension	**Prelude (mm. 1–61)** **I. Klingsor's Castle mm. 61–426** 61 Klingsor 132 Kundry (dialog with Klingsor) 299 Klingsor's narration: Parsifal storms the castle **II. Magic garden ("Second Act" in score) mm. 427–1539** **A. Flower maidens 427–738** 427–85 Flower maidens' narration: Parsifal storms castle 485–560 Parsifal, Flower maidens: dialog 561–738 Song to Parsifal ("Komm holder Knaben") **B. Kundry and Parsifal 739–1539** 739–81 Kundry as seductress, dismisses maidens 781–956 Kundry: narration: Parsifal and Herzeleide (Parsifal reacts at beginning and end) 956–90 Kiss 991–1044 Parsifal: epiphany ("Amfortas!") 1045–94 Parsifal: yearning for faith and redemption 1095–1126 Parsifal narration: Kundry seduction of Amfortas; Amfortas (Kundry caresses Parsifal); Parsifal renounces Kundry (1120–25) 1126–1275 Kundry narration: Christ mocked, yearns for redemption 1275–1340 Parsifal renounces Kundry: plea for redemption 1341–1438 Parsifal and Kundry: dialog: seduction/redemption/renunciation 1439–86 Kundry curses Parsifal 1486–1539 Klingsor, Parsifal, Kundry: spear, destruction of garden and castle, Parsifal leaves Kundry	**Prelude (mm. 1–45)** **I. Domain of the Grail mm. 46–795** 46 Amfortas, Kundry 82–118 Orchestral, Kundry's awakening 175–229 Parsifal, unrecognizable in helmet and armor 230–49 Orchestral, bidden by Amfortas, Parsifal removes helmet 250–332 Parsifal recognized, Parsifal narration: wandering, search for Grail 333–420 Gurnemanz: narration: desolation, Titurel's death 421–59 Parsifal: paroxysms of guilt 460–600 Gurnemanz: Parsifal free from guilt, blessed, baptized, proclaimed (future) king 601–22 Parsifal baptizes Kundry 623–795 Parsifal, Gurnemanz: Good Friday music **Transition to Grail castle 796–857** **II. Grail castle 858–1141** 858–928 Knights, procession, and ritual 929–1029 Amfortas "passion" ("Titurel's corpse") 1030–87 Parsifal intervenes 1088–1141 Grail revealed, closing chorus and orchestral music

Christians, or only Christian-Aryans has proved to be a litmus test for interpretations of the "*Parsifal* ideology."[8]

The context in which Wagner addressed these issues developed in the late eighteenth century, when the notion of art as a potential savior of religion arose in response to the perception that German society was yielding its national identity to foreign, secular–Enlightened influences and the belief that religion must play a crucial role in Germany's national redemption. "More than anything else, the sight of a great and sublime work of art can accomplish ... the miracle of religious conversion," averred Friedrich Schleiermacher in 1799. His essay *On Religion: Addresses to Its Cultured Despisers* inaugurated the German-Romantic intellectual movement now known as *Kunstreligion* (the "religion of art," a Hegelian formulation first applied to Hellenic art and its social functions). Schleiermacher linked his call for religious revival to *Volksgeist* theories of national culture (Herder), and this combination proved potent in the early nineteenth century, when the Erweckungsbewegung, a proto-nationalist religious revival movement, gained force in the wake of the collapse of the Holy Roman Empire and the French occupation of Prussia and other German states. *Kunstreligion* has often been advanced as the aesthetic foundation of *Parsifal*; the emphasis thereby has been on content, that is, how it embodies religious ideas, rather than on agency, how it propagates ideology and galvanizes opinion.[9] Yet the latter issue relates more closely to the theory of *Kunstreligion* than does the former, and Wagner's conception of *Parsifal* was framed substantially from this latter perspective.

But not from this perspective alone. By the 1880s Wagner's thought comprised an intellectual synthesis that fused a Christian-based idea of *Kunstreligion* and a contemporary understanding of the functions of the theater in the culture and society of ancient Greece with the modern cause of German nationalism. As we shall see, *circa* 1850 Wagner framed his original festival concept on the antique model, but he was well aware of the popular appeal of contemporary German music festivals before 1848 and, although he sometimes commented on them derisively, they provided a more immediate and successful example of *Kunstreligion* in practice than did the model of ancient Greece. Flourishing within a broader festival culture in Germany, these festivals provided a prominent forum for the exercise of cultural nationalism and religious aesthetics for more than three decades until the revolutions of 1848.[10] Some of the first festivals celebrated the defeat of France (earlier ones perforce celebrated Napoleon triumphant in Thuringia); others were planned in conjunction with anniversaries of major figures and events in German history. Oratorios by Handel, Haydn, and contemporary composers (Mendelssohn, Louis Spohr, Friedrich Schneider) were the featured works.[11] The occasional oratorio on a national theme (e.g., Carl Loewe's *Gutenberg*, composed in 1837 for a festival celebrating the dedication of a monument in Mainz) invariably emphasized religion, in the case of *Gutenberg* the printing of the Bible. The emphasis on oratorios perfectly accommodated *Kunstreligion* theory with respect to subject matter and, crucially, to performance ensemble. Choral societies, the driving force behind the music festivals, embodied *Kunstreligion* like no other group could. Individuals participated in collective activities that supported religious-national agendas, as well as the survival of church music itself, in crisis since the late eighteenth century. (This was the cultural environment in which Wagner composed *Das Liebesmahl der Apostel* in 1843, a short oratorio for male chorus and orchestra).

Music festivals acquired further cultural meaning through their association with the festivals of the ancient Greek republic – the model of an ideal society, especially for liberal Germans, among whom Wagner at this time must be reckoned. Greek art was interpreted in Herderian terms as a unifying national and religious force.[12] In August Wilhelm Schlegel's theory of classical tragedy (*Vorlesungen über dramatische Kunst und Literatur*, 1801–04), the chorus represents "the national common will," and symbolizes the participation of the people in the public life of their country. This idea was applied to choral societies as institutions and also to the function of the chorus in the oratorios they performed. In oratorio the chorus is identified as Christian, and sometimes German, yet festivals of various kinds synthesized Hellenic and German-Christian ideals and symbols.

The German revolutions of 1848–49 interrupted festivals of all kinds for several years and also undermined the idealistic notion that the arts could exert a strong and positive force in public life. But just then, as his long exile was beginning, Wagner set about articulating his vision of a festival in which antique Greek festivals and drama provided an aesthetic and institutional model for an "artwork of the future" entrusted with the "mission of redemption" in a "religion of the future" (*Art and Revolution*, *The Artwork of the Future*). As in the earlier German choral festivals, the *Volk* is crucial as both active agent in and beneficiary of Wagner's envisioned reform of German culture and national redemption. But contrary to the Christian orientation of these festivals, Wagner, under the influence of Ludwig Feuerbach, accuses Christianity (in *Art and Revolution*) of undermining classic art and its social functions (see, for example, *PW* I:41–44). Christianity is not, however, entirely abandoned. The prose sketch of an opera, *Jesus von Nazareth* (1849), expresses his interest in Christ as a historical figure, and the last sentence of *Art and Revolution* reveals some vestige of the Hellenic–Christian orientation typical of the time: "Let us therefore erect the altar of the future, in life as in the living art, to the two most sublime teachers of mankind – Jesus, who suffered for all men; and Apollo, who raised them to their joyous dignity" (*PW* I:65).

As his Parisian writings from 1840–41 show, Wagner had harbored nationalistic sentiments since his early intellectual maturity, and these feelings emerged in full force during the Franco-Prussian war (1870–71) and the early years of the Wilhelminian empire. The nationalism so resonant in *Die Meistersinger* also sets the tone of numerous contemporary essays on musical, cultural, and political topics. Wagner's passing enthusiasm for the war against France and the new German Empire contributed to the nationalistic turn in his thought. And fundraising efforts for the Festspielhaus in Bayreuth were also pitched in a patriotic key. Peter Cornelius, minor composer and ardent Wagnerian, proclaimed that Wagner's operas were the "artistic objectification of the newly awakened German spirit" ("Deutsche Kunst und Richard Wagner" / "German Art and Richard Wagner," in the *Deutsche Zeitung*, 1871) and Nietzsche declared (and later must have regretted declaring) that Bayreuth was a matter for the "entire nation, not just a group with specific musical interests" ("Mahnruf an die Deutschen" / "An Appeal to the Germans," 1873).[13]

Finally, in the late 1870s, a strong Christian orientation emerged to join the Greek and German-nationalist mix, a development that required the rewriting of some recent Wagnerian history. The *Ring* and the festival idea were now Christianized: Heinrich von Wolzogen, editor of the *Bayreuther Blätter*, transformed Brünnhilde into a Christian embodiment of the "Religion of Compassion" (the association with *Parsifal* is pronounced and conscious).[14] Heinrich Porges, best known for his detailed reports about rehearsals and productions at Bayreuth, identified three essential components of Wagner's theory of cultural reform as the culture of classical Greece, German nationalism, and Christianity.[15] Wagner himself, in the essay "Religion und Kunst" (1880), formulated one of the most precise definitions of *Kunstreligion* and identified music as the most Christian and ideal (i.e., German) of all the arts: "Where religion becomes artificial it is reserved for art to save the spirit of religion by recognizing the figurative value of the mythic symbols … and revealing their deep and hidden truth through an ideal presentation" (*PW* VI:213, 223–24). Mediated by art, "the great regeneration can spring from nothing but the deep soil of a true religion" (*PW* VI:243) and, in the context of this essay by Wagner, that true religion can only be Christianity. In Wagner's later writings and those of the new "Wagnerians" on religious, cultural, and philosophical topics, the voices of Schleiermacher and his allies can be heard clearly, and Wagner's debts to early nineteenth-century thinkers should caution us not to overstate the nature and extent of Wagner's modernity. Their concerns provided the intellectual framework and impetus for Wagner's conception of the Bayreuth festival and for *Parsifal*, the "sacred festival drama" (*Bühnenweihfestspiel*) and the highest and purest artistic embodiment of the festival idea. With respect to *Parsifal*, at least, do the advanced, even "modernist" artistic means that imprint themselves on large portions of the score serve deeply conservative intellectual and social ends? There is ample evidence to support this view.[16]

Dramatic forms and music styles in *Parsifal*

Two distinct operatic genres coalesce in *Parsifal*. Wagner's own "music drama" informs the monologues, dialogues, and narrations of Acts 1 and 3, and of Act 2, apart from the Flower maiden episode.[17] French grand opera and Wagner's own earlier brand of "grand Romantic opera" are revisited (as they had been in *Die Meistersinger*) in the processions and choruses of the Grail scenes of Acts 1 and 3. These two approaches are merged in Act 3, when stylistic elements of music drama, including dissonant presentations of the Grail and other originally diatonic motives, accompany the knights as they bear Titurel's corpse onstage and later insist that Amfortas fulfill his responsibilities as king ("Enthüllet den Gral, Walte des Amtes").

Otherwise, the religious pageantry and the music of these scenes recall similar moments in *Tannhäuser* and *Lohengrin*, reminding us of their thematic commonalities. The chorus sings in a largely diatonic, "historicist" Romantic language that contrasts sharply with the prevailing chromaticism of the music drama and integrates the contrapuntal and homophonic textures of nineteenth-century "motet style."[18] This retrospective music does, however, share important features with the late-style elements of *Parsifal* – lyrical orchestral and vocal writing, common leitmotifs, and continual "symphonic" unfolding – to create a masterful synthesis of styles. Wagner's recourse to tradition is bound up with his conception of the Grail, in particular with the social component of religious ritual that required extensive use of the chorus. Accordingly, the scenes with chorus possess significantly more dramatic and "ideational" weight than they claim in most conventional nineteenth-century opera. The chorus no longer functions primarily as a stage-filling sonorous backdrop for the leading characters (as it mostly does in *Tannhäuser* and *Lohengrin*), but rather, as in *Die Meistersinger*, it acts as a collective protagonist, whose condition and fate are fused with those of the individuals. The role of the chorus in classical Greek theater informs this great dramaturgical achievement.[19] The chorus as protagonist was central to the conception of the opera from the outset. Wagner began the intensive work on the score with the Grail scene of Act 1: in the summer of 1877 Cosima recorded his excitement upon finding the melody to "Nehmet hin mein Blut" (which necessitated minor changes to the text) and his realization that "this

Ex. 9.1a

Ex. 9.1b

Ex. 9.1c

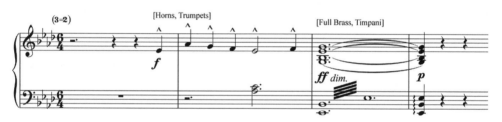

Ex. 9.1d

communion scene will be the main scene, the core of the whole."[20] This melody (Example 9.1a) became the first of three important themes in the Prelude to Act 1, all of which feature prominently in the Grail scenes in both acts. (The Prelude was completed in October, meaning that the basis for the Grail music had been established well before the first act was completed in

January 1878.) In the first Grail scene the opening musical gesture of "Nehmet hin" is refashioned into a close paraphrase of the Lydian reciting tone in the tradition of Latin liturgical chant (Example 9.1d): "Wein und Brot des letzten Mahles" / "Wine and bread of the last meal." The only other explicit allusion to traditional sacred music in *Parsifal* is the so-called Dresden Amen (Example 9.1b), a liturgical formula in use since the later eighteenth century that had already been cited by Mendelssohn in his Symphony No. 5 ("Reformation"). The second principal theme of the Prelude (Example 9.1c), immediately following, also evokes chant by framing and then filling in a rising fourth; the majesty and instrumental brilliance of its initial homophonic sequential presentations conjure up the Wagnerian world of the 1840s and present a short-lived image of a powerful and triumphant Christianity – the Grail knights in their ideal state.

Through frequent citation and development of these ideas, the mystical-religious character of the Prelude and the Grail scenes informs the greater part of the opera, even Kundry's attempted seduction of Parsifal in Act 2, where Kundry's erotic longings compete with, but also come to resemble, her passion for redemption. The Grail knights' urgent yearning for corporeal and spiritual nourishment through the Grail also possesses an erotic character that is sublimated, as their experience of the Grail provides a kind of religious ecstasy. The *sensual* nature of their religious music links the knights with Kundry, and for good reason: they all crave redemption, and this association provides a good example of the relationship between individuals and the group discussed above. The conflation of the erotic with the mystical-religious (which itself has a long cultural history) emerges most clearly in the occasional chromatic relationship between the tonalities of successive statements of the diatonic Grail themes (e.g., the Prelude to Act 1, mm. 44–54, and intermittently in the Grail scenes) or in temporary chromatic deviations within a through-composed, largely diatonic passage. Two of the latter occur at the very end of Act 3: the enharmonic shift on the pitch A♭ (V^7 of D♭) to G♯ ($\hat{3}$ of V/A) on the text "Höchstens Heiles Wunder" ("the miracle of the highest salvation") and, somewhat later, the unmediated, purely orchestral shift from a D♭ chord to an A-minor chord, as Kundry dies and Parsifal blesses the knights while holding the Grail aloft, which articulates the sensual nature of the longing for redemption as well as the occult character of religious ritual and the mystery of belief.

The sense of otherworldliness and timelessness established in the Prelude and first scene of Act 1 prevails throughout *Parsifal*. These qualities are conveyed through the predominantly slow tempos, slow harmonic and melodic rhythms, long arching phrases, and the lack of strongly defined, regular meter and rhythmic activity. The languor of the Flower maidens'

Ex. 9.2

Ex. 9.3

music in Act 2 even recalls the lassitude of most of Act 1 until the Grail scene; their appeals to Parsifal lack vigor, complementing the knights' own weariness. Even the most agitated sections of Amfortas's monologues and the mostly slow-moving dialogue between Kundry and Parsifal are but brief intensifications of the prevailing lethargy or exhaustion. Klingsor, too, is trapped in this musical-psychological environment. Despite his "outsider" status, he is not a villain in the style of the *Ring*; the rhythms and the phonemes of his texts lack in the main the emphatic cadences and guttural harshness of a Hunding or a Hagen. And his primary motive (Example 9.2), first stated during Gurnemanz's Act 1 narration of the events leading to Amfortas's injury, presents an eerie, chromaticized dialectical equivalent to the Grail motives – he is, after all, a failed, would-be Knight of the Grail.

The strongest early contrasts to the prevailing lassitude occur in the music that accompanies the first appearances of the two other characters who are not members of the Grail community. Early in Act 1 Kundry is swept onstage in a violent eruption that disturbs the placid melancholy of the early morning in the forests of the Grail realm. Her motive (Example 9.3) becomes one of the most important and highly developed ideas in the opera. One of its functions is to foreshadow Parsifal's similarly disruptive entrance later in the act, which commingles the violence of his killing of the swan and his own characterization as a young, rash heroic hunter (fanfare gestures in the brass) – the "Siegfried" of medieval Spain, as it were. This music (Example 9.4b) follows the first complete statement of the motive of sympathy or compassion (*Mitleid*), setting the prophetic text "Durch Mitleid wissend, der reine Tor" (Example 9.4a). This Prophecy motive is a modulating phrase, harmonically open, comparable to Erda's sibylline utterances in the *Ring*. The juxtaposition of these two ideas distills

Ex. 9.4a

Ex. 9.4b

the contrast between the young Parsifal of Act 1 and the wise and holy figure
he will become. The pause before his entrance dramatizes this contrast, but
it seems a forced, and even trivial, departure from Wagner's more typical
procedure of seamless transitions.

The music of *Parsifal* owes debts not only to its familial predecessors
of the 1840s, but also to the recent music dramas. Explicit reminiscences of
the style of *Tristan und Isolde* figure prominently in the first mention
of Kundry's ointment for Amfortas (Act 1, m. 178) and in the kiss in Act 2
(m. 983). Siegmund's celebration of nature's rebirth in spring in Act 1 of
Die Walküre ("Winterstürme wichen dem Wonnemond") echoes forth in
Amfortas's own invocation of spring ("Nach wilder Schmerzensnacht
nun Waldes Morgenpracht!"). Precedents for the "Transformation" music
leading to the Grail scene of Act 1 ("Hier wird Raum zur Zeit") and its
analogue in Act 3 were established in the *Ring* (e.g., Siegfried's "Rhine
Journey" and Hagen's "Watch" in *Götterdämmerung*). In view of all these
derivations, the question arises: is *Parsifal* principally a retrospective work?
There are no fundamental innovations in the poetic forms or musical-dramatic
structure, but it has often been argued that its most thoroughly chromatic
music (including most of Amfortas's part, the interaction of Kundry and
Parsifal in Act 2, and the Prelude to Act 3) moves beyond *Tristan* and
foreshadows early twentieth-century developments in the music of
Debussy (*Pelléas et Mélisande*, 1903), Schoenberg (String Quartet op. 10,
1908), or Mahler.[21] However, despite occasional moments of pushing
tonality to its outer limits, *Parsifal* is not, in its essence, an avant-garde
work, but rather much more a synthesis and distillation of a half-century

of compositional practice. Dictated by the contingencies of *Kunstreligion*, the Grail scenes counterbalance the musical-dramatic elements of the opera unlike in *Tristan und Isolde*, a more thoroughly progressive work. On the whole *Parsifal* may be considered a locus classicus of late nineteenth-century Romanticism. If it were truly modern and truly radical, like the expressionistic operas of Strauss and Berg, could it have achieved the widespread canonic status that it soon received when the Bayreuth performance monopoly expired in 1912 and that it still enjoys today?

The music of Amfortas: suffering and redemption

Parsifal is full of memorable, powerfully expressive leitmotifs. Yet the music that accompanies the first mention of Amfortas is very understated. A primary motive and two derivatives (henceforth A1, A2, and A3, or the "motivic complex" in combination) are first heard early in Act 1 (Example 9.5), when Gurnemanz tells the squires to assist the king while he bathes in the lake. Gurnemanz speaks laconically; after the reminder, he mentions neither Amfortas's wound nor his suffering, only the litter upon which he is carried. This justifies the tepid music, which proves to be a brilliant dramatic stroke, because it provides a neutral basis from which substantial, sometimes overwhelming, intensifications trace a great arc of suffering throughout the opera, culminating in the Grail scene of Act 3. Its trajectory is rivaled only by the arching development of the highly expressive Pain motive embedded in the first theme of the Act 1 Prelude[22] (see Example 9.1a), and it is the process, not the original material itself, that justifies its designation as the "motive of Suffering" by Hans von Wolzogen.[23]

The motivic complex unfolds in the middle of Gurnemanz's admonitions and produces no significant turn of musical-dramatic events. The primary form (A1) completes a conventional perfect cadence in its own tonic B major: this unusual, "formalizing," conclusion for a Wagnerian motive helps to establish the matter-of-fact expressive-dramatic character. Moreover, because Gurnemanz sings the melody in unison with the cellos, it lacks distinct leitmotivic identity and supplies no additional information. The music is not completely lacking in tension: A1 and A2 begin with an off-beat, accented G♮ that forms a weird, chromatically altered melodic major third with the preceding B. The resulting augmented triad contrasts with the prevailing diatonic harmonies of the beginning of the act; and the pair of major thirds foreshadows the chromatic altered major and minor thirds that figure prominently in the music associated with Klingsor and Kundry-as-seductress. A3 retains these elements in a C-minor context. The slow-moving syncopations in the melody of A1 (half-note G on the

Ex. 9.5

second beat) are extended and combined with more animated rhythmic disturbances in the upper strings in A2 and A3; they combine with the dissonant harmonies to create the first faint sense of unease in the act. The triplets in the accompaniment become an important independent sub-motive; they carry over into the recitative-like period directly following and help to sustain tension leading up to the first mention of Amfortas's pain, and they often return thereafter.

The derivatives A2 and A3 are freed from the vocal part and become full-fledged instrumental motives. In this guise they introduce modest but portentous intensifications. A2 begins like A1 but quickly deviates: the

Ex. 9.6

initial descending third and linear triplets do not lead to a cadence; instead the B-G leap is repeated (stretto effect) and is followed by a modulating rising line that culminates in a G-F natural descending whole-step whose rhythms are very close to the melodic thirds stated in A1 and earlier in A2 (more stretto). The G-F begins a new longer descending line that introduces the chromatic pitch Db, then leaps a diminished seventh to yet another chromatic pitch, Ab (G# in the piano-reduction example), and fails to complete a regular cadence. (The upper-voice accompaniment adds a further chromaticism and half-step descent, A-G#.) A3 restores the melodic contours of A1; the quasi-deceptive cadence on V⁶/A minor rounds off this brief "poetic-musical period" but does not close it harmonically, thus paving the way for its further development.

Over the course of the opera this material is developed in two ways. First, elements of the original forms melt into a general language of suffering that their chromaticism and contours have helped prepare. This music is especially prominent in Amfortas's two Grail monologues and in the second part of the Act 2 Kundry–Parsifal scene, when the shock of her kiss begins the process of his enlightenment. In these contexts A2 is particularly important: the whole-step G-F paraphrase (m. 155) of the original third B-G (mm. 151, 154) and the even more forceful variant of a descending half-step introduced later in Act 1 are the basis for highly chromaticized lines that extend the descending figures within the original motivic complex. They are sometimes combined with or juxtaposed against other motives or motivic fragments (Pain, Compassion, Klingsor, and Kundry) and they often blend together in a way that obscures their motivic origin. A good example of this occurs during the Act 1 Grail scene, when a fragment of A1 initiates the climactic stages of Amfortas's monologue (Example 9.6). It is stated just twice ("des eig'nen sündigen Blutes Gewell" etc., mm. 1356–60), and, with the *piano* dynamic and thin texture, lacks any particular musical emphasis. Yet it still stands out and triggers more intense music. As Amfortas passionately discusses his sin and suffering, the Klingsor motive predominates, and the

Pain motive is also heard; these distinct ideas emerge from a web of numerous chromatic descending lines that are derived from A2. On the words "der Göttliche weinet" (m. 1372), the descending third of A1 and the descending half-step derived from the whole step in A2 are presented simultaneously at the beginnings of chromatic descents.

Second, the original forms and variants retain their identity but gain rhetorical weight, as in the beginning of the passage given in Example 9.6. This occurs with some frequency through the opening scene of Act 1, and is later reserved for several extremely dramatic situations. The dual association of the first motivic statements with Amfortas and the litter motivates the first recurrences, when Amfortas is being carried to and from the lake (directly after Kundry's lines "ich bin müde," "fort, fort ins Bad," and Gurnemanz's "Die Wunde ist's die nie sich schliessen will," mm. 239–41, 366–83, and 546–59). It is also heard when, in a meaningful symbolic gesture, the swan Parsifal has killed is borne away on the very same litter (Gurnemanz: "Versäumt den König im Bade nicht! Helft!," mm. 916–24).[24] These passages are intensifications of the original motives with respect to dynamics, register, and orchestration. They tell the listener much more about the nature of Amfortas's pain (which has been explained by Gurnemanz but without great expressive weight) than had been previously revealed. And their formal function is as important as their expressive one. They effect transitions between episodes in the first scene of Act 1 (see Table 9.1) and, by maintaining their place in the symphonic web of motives, they stay alive in the listener's ear.

The passage after Kundry's "Ich bin müde" (Example 9.7, mm. 264–76) begins a lengthy period that contains Amfortas's majestic F-major/B-flat major hymn to nature (mm. 264–88); it is introduced and concluded by motivic statements that combine the opening of A1 (third and triplet descent) and the extended interior of A2; a fragment of A1 supports his first line about a "wilde Schmerzensnacht" ("wild night of pain"). The primary orchestral melodic idea (first statement mm. 272–76) is interwoven into this motivic context: the C-B♭ of m. 273 reinterprets the whole-step of the original A2 in the orchestra to produce a tranquil, pastoral expression of Amfortas's (and Wagner's) trust in the power of nature to comfort. In tone and meaning this passage prefigures the "Good Friday" music, which, however, does not make use of ideas from the motivic complex.

The passage shown in Example 9.6 directly follows iterations of the Pain motive on the text "Durchzückt von seligsten Genusses Schmerz, des heiligsten Blutes Quell, fühl' ich sich gießen in mein Herz" ("Transfixed by rapturous and joyful pain, the fount of that holy blood, I feel it flowing in my heart"). The direct succession of this text and the A1 statements lay the groundwork for a crucial passage in the Act 2 seduction, when, after Kundry's kiss, Parsifal exclaims "Sie brennt in meinem Herzen" ("It burns in my

Ex. 9.7

heart"), with reference to Amfortas's wound (Example 9.8). Here the A1 motive resounds *fortissimo*, in orchestral unisons in nearly all the wind parts, thus forming an effective climax to Parsifal's foregoing cries, "Amfortas! Die Wunde! Die Wunde!" Mediated by presentations of the Kundry motive, these statements reinforce the nexus Parsifal-Kundry-Amfortas. The sparing use of the motive in both of these passages actually strengthens its effect; the succession of motives in each effectively depicts the process of the characters' thoughts and feelings.

In the Act 3 Grail scene, when Amfortas refuses to reveal the Grail and pleads for death (Example 9.9), the motive of Suffering becomes, for the first and only time, the basis for an extended passage. This period falls into two parts: (1) Amfortas's lines "Nein! Nicht mehr!" to the point at which he

Ex. 9.8

Ex. 9.9

tears open his robe (mm. 1000–11), where variants and fragments of the motivic complex permeate the entire orchestral-vocal texture and the falling third of the motives' opening gesture powers his refusal ("Nicht mehr!") to fulfill his obligation to his subjects; and (2) the subsequent eight measures (mm. 1011–18), a sequence in the winds (each statement with fuller orchestration) on an extension of A1 rising over the syncopated accompaniments of the original statements, with a variant of A3 in the

Ex. 9.10

basses and cellos; the strings in octaves complete the sequence, emphasizing A3, on the word "blood." Like its Act 1 counterpart, this passage gives way to Klingsor music, as the episode reaches its shattering climax.

Soon thereafter, the very last appearances of this complex of motives (Example 9.10, m. 1035) provide an apotheosis and a yielding, as Amfortas relinquishes authority to Parsifal and envisions redemption. The first one (directly following Parsifal's text "Nur eine Waffe taugt," etc.) begins softly in A major and emphasizes a diatonic descending third leap in the basses (instead of the original chromatic third) and then, when his anguish changes to sublimated ecstasy (as given in the verbal instructions in the score), continues in the ethereal upper winds. As Parsifal continues to speak, F major, G major, and finally B major are implied as background tonalities, but formal closure is always avoided. The last statement ("Gesegnet sei Dein Leiden" / "O blessed be thy suffering") settles strongly on the dominant of

B major. A perfect cadence in B major would have closed the tonal circle begun with the first statement of A1, but the tortuous history of Amfortas's suffering and his reign concludes in transition, leading first to a harmonically unstable version of the *Mitleid* motive and then to the final triumphant statement of his fanfares (G major). Parsifal's succession to power is synthesized with these final representations of his character in an extremely refined way, which convincingly prepares the mystical religious conclusion of the opera.

"What does *Parsifal* preach?"

The initial response to *Parsifal* was mixed and heated, along fault-lines familiar from the reception of Wagner's other operas.[25] Attempts to decipher meaning and message focused on the text and the story rather than on the music.[26] Members of Wagner's inner circle spearheaded successful efforts to make Christian-German regeneration the predominant theme of the early reception, as exemplified by Hans von Wolzogen's essay "Die Religion des Mitleidens" ("The Religion of Compassion," 1883), which designated Parsifal as the preacher of a new religion of compassion, in answer to the question "What does *Parsifal* preach?"[27] (Wolzogen also acknowledged the presence of Kantian, Schopenhauerian, and Buddhist elements in the opera, and the latter two, along with the questions of morality, sexual longing, and renunciation, became prominent aspects of its critical reception.) Elsewhere, he discussed the strong contrasts between Christianity and "pagan" religions that Wagner, in his view, had drawn in the opera and in the "regeneration" essays (from 1878 to 1882).[28] Writers representing the organized churches in Germany and Austria endorsed the opera from a *Kunstreligion* perspective, but the presentation of Eucharistic rituals on stage was sometimes criticized.[29] *Parsifal* was the last straw for Nietzsche, who publicized his disgust that Wagner "suddenly sank down, helpless and broken, before the Christian cross,"[30] while privately admitting his admiration for some of the music. Interest in the symbolic and psychological aspects of the opera was strong from the beginning and became, in the twentieth century, the second main stream of reception, largely independent of religious and cultural redemption.

In the 1880s the critics Paul Lindau and Max Kalbeck pointed to anti-Semitic tendencies they perceived in *Parsifal*, while Anton Seidel, the Viennese conductor and close associate of Wagner, celebrated the opera's Aryan-blood symbolism.[31] This was an idea that Wagner had pursued in several of the regeneration essays, notably "Christentum und Heldentum" ("Christianity and Heroism," 1881), in which he advocates the ideas of an Aryan master race, a Christ of Aryan descent, and challenges Aryan-Christians to defend themselves against the encroachments of

Judaism in order to redeem themselves, Germany, and all of humankind. Conservative-nationalistic critics emphasized these themes up through the era of the Third Reich, when, however, the more conventionally Christian aspects of the drama were deemed problematic or ideologically suspect (see also chapter 14). On the whole, anti-Semitism remained only an undercurrent in early *Parsifal* reception, and this is not surprising in view of the lack of clearly identified Jewish characters (but see the discussion of Kundry below) and of explicit anti-Semitic utterances in the opera. Moreover, anti-Semitism, already strong and on the rise in the 1880s and 1890s, was still less virulent than it would become after World War I. In the more heated ideological context of Weimar Germany in the mid-1920s, Paul Bekker asked – rhetorically – how *Parsifal* could share themes of decay and redemptive regeneration with the late essays and yet lack any trace of the anti-Semitic ideology articulated in these texts.[32] Bekker's trenchant association of the opera and the regeneration essays anticipated fierce debates of the late twentieth century, but critiques such as his were, of course, suppressed during the Third Reich and largely avoided in the immediate postwar years.

No strikingly new patterns in the reception history of *Parsifal* emerged while the Wagner family retained monopoly performance rights until 1912, although some non-Bayreuth productions introduced modernizing elements of stage design and action immediately thereafter. Thomas Mann's essay "The Sorrows and Grandeur of Richard Wagner" (1933) is both a milestone in *Parsifal* reception and, in many respects, a departure from the mainstream of earlier interpretations. Mann attached no importance to the idea of collective redemption, but rather stressed individual suffering which Wagner portrayed from the perspective of a "Christian-ascetic" ethos that makes *Parsifal* an "oratorio of redemption." Mann did not comment on anti-Semitism or racism in the opera and in general dismissed the relevance of Wagner's social theories, thereby anticipating an important stream of post-World War II Wagner reception that interpreted his art primarily in "purely" aesthetic categories. For Wagner (and every artist), writes Mann,

> new experiences of "truth" mean new stimuli to play, new expressive possibilities – nothing more. [The artist] believes in them – takes them seriously – only to the degree that is necessary in order to bring them to the highest pitch of expression and make the deepest possible impression with them. Consequently he is very much in earnest about them, earnest to the point of tears – but then again, not totally, and therefore not *at all*.[33]

The ironic tone of the last sentence and the anti-heroic, non-ideological take on *Parsifal* and on Wagner per se were intolerable to cultural authorities and political officials in the newly ascendant Third Reich. The immediate outcome was fateful for Mann and his family, who were forced into exile. During the 1930s, some party ideologues, e.g., Alfred Rosenberg, viewed *Parsifal* as too Christian and pacifist (Parsifal breaking his bow in Act 1 and removing his armor in Act 3) and called for its removal from the repertory. But the anti-Semitic and Aryan streams of *Parsifal* reception were generally recognized as being congenial to propaganda efforts. As John Deathridge has shown, Hitler opposed only overtly Christian productions (as noted in a diary entry by Joseph Goebbels from November 1941) and, contrary to frequent assertions, *Parsifal* was often performed in Germany into the early 1940s.[34]

After the war, in an intellectual atmosphere largely defined by the wish to break with the past and to ignore recent catastrophes, Wieland and Wolfgang Wagner sought to escape from tradition and minimize nationalistic elements of Wagner's operas with their modernist abstract productions in Bayreuth.[35] Traditional religious elements in *Parsifal* were de-emphasized despite the fact that they would have caused little offense in the conservative value system of the Federal Republic in the 1950s. Productions outside Bayreuth often followed these leads, while critical writing on the opera tended to focus on formal and psychological-symbolic aesthetic issues. In the immediate aftermath of the Holocaust, all but the most unscrupulous apologists felt obliged to acknowledge and condemn Wagner's anti-Semitism, but, well into the 1970s, most German writers on Wagner treated this as an unfortunate aberration that had no real bearing on his art. Hence Theodor Adorno, who had returned to Germany after his exile in the United States, was virtually alone, when, in his *Versuch über Wagner* and several independent essays also published in the 1950s, he exposed aspects of Wagner's thought and art that recent history had made "unbearable." But even Adorno pleaded, in his essay "Wagner und Bayreuth" (1952), for a postwar "de-ideologization" (*Entideologisierung*) of the operas, which alone would permit access to their aesthetic truths.[36] Adorno's several writings on *Parsifal* reflect this perspective; he is primarily interested in the music, less so in the drama; he offers no detailed analysis of nationalistic and racial content in the opera (but see n. 55), and there is nothing about the opera in the chapter "Social Character" in *In Search of Wagner*. Adorno supported the postwar Bayreuth productions.

And so things stood by and large until the late 1970s, when, in the wake of the political and cultural upheavals symbolized by the year 1968, an ever-growing number of West Germans systematically began to confront Nazism and the historical processes that led to it. In this context, the Germanist and cultural historian Hartmut Zelinsky identified in *Parsifal* the propagation of a "new religion of redemption through destruction."[37] His essay appeared in a 1978 volume of the often provocative monograph series *Musik-Konzepte*, entitled *Richard Wagner: Wie antisemitisch darf ein Künstler sein?* (*Richard*

Wagner: How Anti-Semitic May an Artist Be?). In the *Parsifal* centenary summer of 1982 and in the several years thereafter, Zelinsky published essays attacking the apologetics of mainstream German Wagner interpretation and declaring the presence in *Parsifal* of a coded but clear anti-Semitism based on an "ideology of blood."[38] Kundry is "the representative of everything associated by Wagner with Judaism." Her baptism and death are the artistic realization of ideas advanced in *Das Judentum in der Musik* and the "regeneration" essays.[39] Zelinsky drew on the work of the American author Robert Gutman, who in 1968 had revived Bekker's association of the opera with the "regeneration" essays, identifying the role of blood as the dramatic embodiment of anti-Semitic and racist ideas, and characterizing the Grail knights as Aryan-Christian warriors.[40]

Joachim Kaiser, the chief music critic of the liberal Munich newspaper *Süddeutsche Zeitung*, and Carl Dahlhaus, West Germany's leading musicologist of the postwar era, led the angry responses in the press. Their most fundamental criticism was the lack of a serious engagement with the music of the opera by both Zelinsky and Gutman.[41] In a monograph published in Germany in 1982, another prominent Wagner critic, the Germanist Dieter Borchmeyer, defended *Parsifal* as a "poem about peace" and "a [Christian] religion of love and compassion" unsullied by the racist and anti-Semitic thinking of the regeneration essays, despite its implicit critique of Judaism and pagan religion.[42] In the 1990s the American scholar Marc Weiner made the first substantial response to the German critics of Gutman and Zelinsky, vigorously pursuing anti-Semitic content throughout Wagner's music and dramaturgy. In *Parsifal*, in addition to Klingsor as castrated Jew, Weiner "hears" the scent of Jews musically represented in the flower-garden scene of Act 2; in Act 3, the converted Kundry relinquishes her impaired Jewish gait and walks like a Christian.[43]

Much of this polemic has an all-or-nothing character, and it is no coincidence that musicologists and music critics, who often de-emphasize the importance of the ideological content of Wagner's operas, led the defense against attacks that were largely advanced by literary critics and social theorists. More differentiated positions have emerged in recent work that call to mind Adorno's ambivalence. Laurence Dreyfus and Deathridge agree that *Parsifal* is a complex artistic masterpiece in which the words and music must be taken equally seriously. Some of the ideas expressed in the text may be reprehensible, but these alone do not determine the whole content of the opera. Nevertheless, some important differences divide them. Dreyfus accuses Paul Lawrence Rose (who developed Gutman's ideas while adding little about the music) of a reductive "essentialism" that disregards aesthetic qualities.[44] Yet he accepts Rose's assertions about the role of anti-Semitism and Aryan supremacy in *Parsifal*. In a highly personal statement with troubling connotations, Dreyfus contends: "The deeply touching musical insights into the experience of remorse, memory, feminine pain and forgiveness are *more than adequate compensation* for the fact of knowing even that one might personally have been excluded from just such a moment of Wagnerian compassion" (emphasis added).[45] Deathridge, whom Dreyfus also criticizes for reducing the general problem of the ideological content of Wagner's operas to one of malevolent ideas vs. great art, is much more disturbed than Dreyfus about the noxious elements in Wagner's vision of German regeneration, which he sees as the defining ideological thrust of the opera. With the clever irony expressed in the title of his recent essay, "Strange Love, Or, How We Learned To Stop Worrying and Love Wagner's *Parsifal*,"[46] Deathridge does not indulge in aestheticism and does not dismiss the problems Wagner's ideas have caused for admirers of this great and beautiful work of art.

Deathridge has been joined by numerous contemporary writers (notably Dahlhaus)[47] who have dismissed the significance of a Christian ideology in the opera; he cites Wagner in a letter to von Wolzogen to the effect that, "although we mercilessly relinquish the Church, Christianity, and even the whole phenomenon of Christianity in history, our friends must always know that we do it for the sake of that very same Christ ... whom we want to protect in His pristine purity."[48] Documentary evidence (letters, diaries, etc.) leaves little doubt that Wagner had ambivalent feelings about Christianity,[49] but it is useful to distinguish between his attitude toward church institutions and dogma (he was a vehement anti-Catholic, which caused tension with Liszt) and his views about the symbolic and ideological meaning of Christianity in contemporary life. Wagner does this, however subtly, in these comments. Why should Christ matter so much to him, if a "pristine" Christianity has no meaning for the present and future? Numerous other contemporary writers, among them the great-granddaughter Nike Wagner, stress precisely Christianity as the central ideology of *Parsifal* and the basis for redemption in the Wagnerian mode.[50] I believe that Wagner made use of *Parsifal* to advance a number of interrelated aims: Christianity provides the traditional framework of faith in which the moral and ethical issues of the opera are discussed; it functions as a galvanizing idea for personal and group salvation; and it is the basis for personal and social and cultural identity and a bulwark against the foreign Other. This last concern is even articulated in the setting of the action in the libretto, which specifies the location of Montsalvat on the "northern mountains of Gothic Spain"; Klingsor's realm on the "southern slope of the same mountains, facing Arabic Spain." We may at the very least conclude that Wagner appropriated the powerful status of Christianity for his regeneration agenda because he felt that it was strategically expedient to do so. From this perspective, the nature of his "true" personal beliefs becomes irrelevant.

Because the questions of race and anti-Semitism have so much dominated the recent reception history, other troubling ideological aspects of *Parsifal* have been largely neglected. Paul Robinson's remark about *Parsifal*'s "misogyny" is one of very few in this vein.[51] Kundry must die – not only because she is Jewish-identified, but because she is a woman. (Catherine Clément's study of women in opera touches on *Parsifal* but does not pursue the case of Kundry, even though the idea that women in opera must die "because they are women" is a general premise of the book.)[52] Peter Wapnewski denounces *Parsifal* as a "profoundly inhuman spectacle, glorifying a barren masculine world whose ideals are a combination of militarism and monasticism."[53] In my view, Wapnewski describes the Grail community very accurately, although Wagner composed moments of tender, non-sexual bonds of friendship and fraternity, e.g., the opening of Act 1, Gurnemanz and the boys. I would argue that the crisis in Montsalvat is principally one of leadership: Amfortas refuses to act on behalf of his *Volk*, and Parsifal intervenes. He is able to exercise power and authority and to save the suffering Grail knights and initiates. Moreover, Parsifal is ambitious – in the first scene of Act 3, he informs Gurnemanz that he will be the next Grail king; he is a foreign, albeit welcome, usurper. In the end, despite his hard-won knowledge and compassion, his renunciation of sexuality, and his religious conversion, the persona of the young warrior hero lives on, as we hear in the final and most magnificent statement of his fanfare motive, when he accepts his role as the new leader of the Grail community. The sharp contrast of this music with the rest of the final scene (indeed with much of Parsifal's music in the opera) emphasizes and celebrates his power and authority, not his wisdom or compassion. The spear he wields is not only a Christian "symbol of peace"[54] derived from the crucifixion; it is also an archetype of strength and authority (with phallic connotations) – Parsifal here calls it a "weapon." The knights prostrate themselves before a Christian warrior, an absolute leader, the object of a cult of personality, a savior. They demonstrate their subservience and loyalty to a leader who has come from afar to save a *Volk* in need. Not withstanding the Christian orientation, some of the most important social configurations in *Parsifal* uncannily anticipate the mythos of the *Führerprinzip* in Nazi Germany.[55]

An uninformed visitor to a performance of *Parsifal* may well fail to discern any ideological suggestions beyond surface trappings of medieval Christianity in the Grail rites. Yet after learning of Wagner's personal ideological and social views in the *Parsifal* period (and their exegesis by recent critics) this listener may well experience the opera in a fundamentally different way. In such a case the distinctions emphasized by Wagner's defenders between ideas internal or external to the work become specious. Such distinctions, which have been rendered increasingly suspect by new critical methodologies, also fail to respect Wagner's own concept of *Gesamtkunstwerk*, particularly when they emphasize music as the "inner" and therefore true drama that redeems the suspect external or contextual implications. Despite occasional laments to the contrary, Wagner attached great importance to and worked hard on the symbolic-ideological meanings of his *mise en scène*. Sets, costumes, symbolic objects, and the positioning and movements of individuals and groups create impressions perhaps less powerful than the music as such, but stronger and more enduring than words alone. Modernizing productions that suppress the "embarrassing" relics of tradition run the risk of suppressing or distorting authorial meaning, if they do not do so deliberately. A strong case can be made for an occasional traditional production based on the Bayreuth original. This would be neither an act of veneration, nor an exercise in would-be authenticity, nor an appeasement of a conservative public, but rather serve as a deconstructive essay in "critical-historicism" that would peel away layers of cultural interpretation and expose the artifact as originally imagined by Wagner himself. This might not be as much fun as Christoph Schlingenschief's 2004 production of *Parsifal* in Bayreuth, in which light shows, rabbits, an obese naked woman, and *Doppelgänger* of Jesus and Osama bin Laden all failed to create the hoped-for scandal predicted on the basis of disputes between the *enfant terrible* director and the Bayreuth establishment in the weeks prior to the premiere. But it would serve a valuable hermeneutic function in allowing as much as possible of Wagner's original vision to emerge in full force.

To viewers titillated and edified by the violence, suffering, and religiosity that made Mel Gibson's film, *The Passion of Christ*, a huge success in 2004, *Parsifal* has everything to offer and more, such as a healthy dose of eroticism. And it is an incomparably more complex and far greater work of art. For many, *Parsifal* itself has become the Holy Grail of Bayreuth, enjoying a privileged status among Wagner's music dramas. It is the traditional Good Friday opera in New York, Salzburg, and elsewhere around the globe. Its seductive power inspires and infuriates; its controversial nature enhances its allure. Wagner would be gratified and probably amused to witness all that he hath wrought with *Parsifal*, his last card and trump.

PART III

Ideas and ideology in the *Gesamtkunstwerk*

10 The urge to communicate: the prose writings as theory and practice

JAMES TREADWELL

Wagner had just turned twenty-one when his first published essay appeared, and he was busy with his last on the day he died. Writing for publication was a perpetual accompaniment to his working life. One has only to browse through a catalogue of his titles, and the image of an artist brooding with immense concentration over vast and intricate music dramas, each of them years in the making, gives way to a very different picture: a Wagner who dashed off anything from anecdotal squibs to solemn tracts whenever the impulse struck. This body of work is substantial enough that it cannot be left out of any account of the composer; and, since most of it bears on questions of operatic theory and practice, and much of it refers directly to Wagner's own operas, it virtually demands that we refer to it whenever we are thinking about the more familiar productions of Wagner's genius. Since an essay of this length cannot hope to introduce the themes and propositions of even a few of the major writings, my purpose instead will be to consider the question of their relation to the operas. What can we do with them? How should we read Wagner's published prose to help understand him as a composer and dramatist?

Much of his published writing sets out to answer this very question. In the characteristically melodramatic words of *A Communication to My Friends*, a semi-autobiographical essay of 1851, "I was burning to write Something that should take the message of my tortured brain, and speak it in a fashion to be understood by present life" (*PW* I:378; *GS* IV:331; the remark mediates, in this context, an apologetic reference to the "tortured" style of his recent theoretical essays and an exposition of the unrealized dramatic project *Jesus of Nazareth*). The urge to be understood, to transmit his ideas to the public, is fundamental to Wagner. In this respect, his writing exploits a distinctive feature of nineteenth-century musical culture. It was an age when the art of music finally became inseparable from its critical discourse. Musical journals proliferated, especially in France and Germany; creative schools were identified and placed in opposition to each other; musical critics became influential figures in their own right (some, like Eduard Hanslick, virtual celebrities); partisans took up one side or another of a theoretical debate and fought acrimoniously with each other in print. Wagner's contributions to this noisy welter of writing about music frequently seem intended to explain and justify his own position in the contested territory of nineteenth-century musical culture. Acting as his own critic, his own partisan, he seems to be telling us what his operas are for, and what they are about.

As a result, readers after Wagner's death and well into the twentieth century often approached his writings as if listening to oracular wisdom. Working with the assumption that anything he wrote about his own works must be the final key to their meaning, they tried to extract coherent theoretical and philosophical "systems" from his published writings, and then interpret the operas as expressions of those systems. But the notion that prose works and music dramas speak with the same voice, that they are complementary aspects of the same conception in Wagner's mind, is full of dangers. If Wagner's writings simply tell us what to think, our understanding and appreciation of his operas are reduced, not enlarged. There is no reason to assume that the "message" of his "brain" (as *A Communication* puts it) comes across clearly and unambiguously in the published theoretical essays, any more than the richness and depth of the operas are overwritten and effaced by the same "message" beaming visibly from the stage during a performance. In the past four decades or so, more nuanced and subtle critical readings of Wagner's prose works have shown that they cannot be reduced to a coherent system. I will not therefore be assuming that their main function is to decode or explain the operas. We need to see Wagner's writing as an aspect of his creative personality, not a technical handbook to his more important stage-works. What they tell us about his genius can then be used as a way of thinking about the habits and characteristics of his music dramas.

Wagner's character as a writer

The best-known and most influential of Wagner's prose works are the sequence of increasingly lengthy essays produced at impressive speed in the immediate aftermath of his flight from the Dresden uprising of 1849, collectively known as the "reform essays" or the "Zurich" writings: *Art and Revolution* (1849), *The Artwork of the Future* (1849), and *Opera and Drama* (1850–51). Because they coincide with the turn toward Wagner's mature musico-dramatic style, and also because they explicitly propose the idea of the *Gesamtkunstwerk* as a radically new version of opera's internal construction and external relationships, they give the misleading impression that Wagner's prose is primarily a theoretical exercise – that is, a way of defining and accounting for the principles of his art. In fact, all three of these works are distinguished by their energetic efforts to coerce many different fields of enquiry into the service of a unified theory of art, rather than by the kind of things we associate with theoretical writing: careful distinctions, precision of argument, clarity of overall purpose. Wagner is not a naturally reflective writer. What marks out his work most of all is its excitability, the intensity of its response to whatever stimulus has provoked it. Moreover, the stimulus is never far off; Wagner writes on a subject when that subject is directly in front of him, not when he has meditated on it. His publications are distinctively occasional (in the sense of responding to occasions). This is what gives his prose its rhetorical fervor, its preference for rhapsody over rumination. It is very easily, and very often, overwhelmed by powerful literary influences, depending on what Wagner has been reading at the time: the spirits of Heinrich Heine, Ludwig Feuerbach, Arthur Schopenhauer, or Joseph-Arthur Gobineau (among others) frequently seem to be using his pages as a medium.

If one wants a general picture of Wagner's writing habits, it would be better to think of him as a journalist than a theoretician. Treating ideas for their own sake does not come naturally to him. Addressing readers as urgently and powerfully as possible, on the other hand, seems to have been a habit he was born with. He draws a similar distinction himself in the course of *A Communication to My Friends*, while trying to explain why "thought and criticism" – theoretical writing about art – are required of an artist: "This attribute is necessarily developed in him through the survey of his position towards our public life, which he cannot look on with the cold indifference of a sheer critical experimentalist, but with the warm desire to address himself intelligibly thereto" (*PW* I:281; *GS* IV:241). The adjectives are apt: Wagner's words are characteristically "warm," not to say heated, rather than cool-headed. Theory, accordingly, is not an end in itself but an aspect of a polemical act of publication. If one reads across the whole spectrum of the prose works, from the contributions to the Paris *Revue et Gazette Musicale* and the Dresden *Abend-Zeitung* of the early 1840s to the essays distributed in Wagner's own late mouthpiece, the *Bayreuther Blätter*, one gets the impression of a continuum linking eager, opinionated journalism to outright propaganda. The "theoretical" writings are best seen as a phase of that continuum, informed by the same attitudes and conducted in a similar manner, rather than an entirely different kind of activity.

This can lead to some incongruities between the material Wagner writes about and the purposes he wants it to serve. At its weakest, his writing suffers the problems of poor journalism: a tendency to speak vociferously on subjects of which he has only an amateur grasp, and a faith at crucial moments that impassioned eloquence can take the place of argument. On home ground, though, Wagner is an excellent reporter and investigator. His writing about the professional business of opera – stage management, acting, singing, audiences, repertoire, and so on – is enlivened and strengthened, not distracted, by its "warmth." For the purposes of this essay, though, attention needs to be paid to the works that propose generalized ideas about his art.

The Zurich writings and the idea of music drama

Wagner's publications of 1849–51 – the three "reform" essays on music and drama named above, along with a number of related works such as "Art and Climate," "Judaism in Music," "A Theater in Zürich," and *A Communication to My Friends* – represent the closest his prose work ever comes to being an end in itself. This is because, uniquely, he wrote virtually no music during that period. With *Lohengrin* behind him and the gigantic Nibelung project lying in wait, writing for once has the appearance of a necessary stage in his creative career, rather than an incidental outgrowth of other circumstances. For once, also, writing here accurately describes compositional principles and procedures that would later show themselves to be fundamental to the mature Wagnerian music drama. In his career as a whole, Wagner writes surprisingly little about his own operas, and what he does say tends to be confined to relatively utilitarian details; but in the Zurich "reform" writings there is no doubt that the *Ring* project, as it was conceived in those early stages, is the point of reference for everything he has to say. This is, then, the most plausible place to experiment with reading Wagner's writing in the light of his operas, and in turn to think about his operas in the light of those readings.

When Wagner found himself in Zurich in July 1849, a proscribed exile with no obvious prospects for pursuing his career as a composer, and sat down to write instead, theoretical questions about how to construct the music of the future were not uppermost in his mind. Not surprisingly, given recent events, the first essay – *Art and Revolution* – proposes "to discover the meaning of Art as a factor in the life of the State, and to make ourselves acquainted with it as a social product" (*PW* I:31; *GS* III:9). This is a more systematic approach to an issue that Wagner had addressed regularly (and perceptively) in his Paris journalism of the early 1840s, well before his radical rethinking of opera had begun. He had always been sensitive to the collusion between art and its audiences. Very few of his reports on musical matters in Paris consist of formal or analytic criticism, or even broad commentary on operatic schools and tendencies. His interest is primarily in opera's social situation, often construed politically (the contrast between France and Germany is an organizing theme throughout). In the distinctive ironic fictions of those years – "A Pilgrimage to Beethoven," "An End in Paris," "A Happy Evening" – music is imagined essentially as a matter of who hears it, when, and how. *Art and Revolution*, then, begins as a continuation of a familiar and unresolved debate, though now (under the influence of Feuerbach as well as the upheavals of 1848–49) in a mood of earnest historical enquiry rather than the mordant irony (derived from Heine) of the Paris essays. Only gradually does the *Ring* project exert its gigantic gravitational pull on the trajectory of the essay.

The earliest written versions of a Nibelung drama date from late 1848. Its progress toward the four completed *Ring* libretti of 1852 is thus exactly contemporary with the succession of essays from *Art and Revolution* and *The Artwork of the Future* to *Opera and Drama* (1850–51) and *A Communication to My Friends* (1851). Inevitably, then, Wagner's meditations on the social and historical development of opera toward an idealized "artwork of the future" came to be aligned with the specific musico-dramatic forms imagined in his own future artwork. However, these remain two distinct purposes (even in *Opera and Drama*, which is certainly the closest Wagner comes to writing a theoretical prescription for his own mature compositional style). In *Art and Revolution*, Wagner concentrates on exposing how "[o]ur modern stage materialises the ruling spirit of our social life" (*PW* I:43; *GS* III:19–20). Only toward the end does the (unnamed) figure of Siegfried appear as the icon of a revolutionary cure for an art diseased by its bourgeois commercialism and egoism. The "free, strong, and beauteous man" (*PW* I:58; *GS* III:35), whose love and death are to form the subject of the revolutionary drama, and who is to be to the new society what Aeschylus's Orestes was to Periclean Athens, is certainly imported from Wagner's libretto for *Siegfrieds Tod* (*Siegfried's Death*; the precursor to *Götterdämmerung*). The essay also ends with some intimations of the idea of an independent theater dedicated exclusively to the full realization of music drama, the idea that became the Bayreuth festival; and this is at least as important an aspect of Wagner's reflections on his art in the Zurich essays as are the details of compositional and dramaturgical practice worked out in *Opera and Drama*. But at this stage there is no direct effort to describe the utopian future artwork by imagining the form of his own music drama.

The first sign of a significant attempt to think through social and political problems by theorizing musico-dramatic issues comes in a few marginal jottings made on the manuscript of *Art and Revolution*. After some notes on the barrenness of modern commercialized sensibility appears a parenthetical remark on the revolution in the history of music prophesied by Beethoven's choral symphony: "(the word stands higher than the tone)" (*PW* VIII:362; *SSD* XII:252). In its most simplified, germinal form, this is the single idea which links the Zurich writings with Wagner's mature style. Here he begins to imagine a genuinely new way of organizing an operatic work. But it is also an idea that can be derived historically (the credo of "prima le parole" that extends back to the origins of opera) and explored in sociopolitical terms. The next of the Zurich essays, *The Artwork of the Future*, takes as its theme the individual arts (dance, music, poetry, architecture, sculpture, painting) and their interrelation within the drama. Using a comparative framework to treat the relations between the arts allows Wagner to talk about aesthetics in exactly the same terminology that he uses to talk about politics: egoism versus collectivity, gradual historical disintegration, the inevitability of a revolutionary reordering of hierarchies, and so on. In fact, the central sociopolitical concept in *The Artwork of the Future* – the "folk" (*das Volk*) as an idealized notion of communal Germanic identity – gradually becomes indistinguishable from the central aesthetic concept, the union of all the arts in "the collective artwork . . . the *Drama*" (*PW* I:193; *GS* III:159). "Who, then," Wagner asks, "will be the *Artist of the Future?* . . . Let us say it in one word: the *Folk*" (*PW* I:204–05; *GS* III:169). The Zurich writings here discover an enormously powerful and flexible metaphor. Art and politics can stand in for each other, each seeking a revolutionary reorganization of its principles. So Wagner can turn his concern with art as a "social product" into a theorization of art's purely internal relationships: he can map the interrelations of poetry, music, and dance exactly as if he were still discussing the reordering of society which the revolutions of 1848–49 seemed to herald.

The effects of this metaphorical mode of argument on Wagner's political thought are, predictably, uninspiring. If any support were needed for the argument that even in Dresden in 1849 Wagner was a profoundly bourgeois revolutionary, this would confirm it. He cannot help thinking that the solution to the "hideous oppressor, modern Civilisation" (*PW* I:208; *GS* III:173) lies somewhere in the field of aesthetics: the "folk" is not a proletariat but a composer-in-waiting. In "Judaism in Music," written between *The Artwork of the Future* and *Opera and Drama*, the double-edged aspect of Wagner's metaphorical technique becomes all too clear: if social questions are aesthetic questions, then judgements about bad music can be blithely rewritten as judgements about bad people, and what Wagner sees as the merely cosmopolitan, populist brilliance of Meyerbeer or the superficial, derivative polish of Mendelssohn is turned into a specifically Jewish problem, a sign of "the Jew's prime essence" (*PW* III:82; *GS* V:67). Such an argument fits easily into the general pattern of Wagner's writing about art in the Zurich essays: another strong reason for not reading them simply as theoretical accounts of how music drama is to be made.

With *Opera and Drama*, the focus of Wagner's writing tilts over, changing from a vision of social revolution (as it certainly is in *The*

Artwork of the Future) to a remaking of art. In *The Artwork of the Future*, the intuition that poetry needs to regain at least a position of equality with music is given a specifically political weight. "Absolute Music," by which Wagner means instrumental music presented as an end in itself with no determinate object or content, "can now and never ... bring the physical and ethical Man to distinct and plainly recognisable presentment" (*PW* I:122–23; *GS* III:93). It "lacks the *Moral Will*" (*ibid.*); it can't do anything to bring about the artwork or the society of the future. In *Opera and Drama*, the question becomes an aesthetic one. In Wagner's uncharacteristically clear and pithy words, the problem is "*that a Means of expression (Music) has been made the end, while the End of expression (the Drama) has been made a means*" (*PW* III:17; *GS* III:231).

Here finally is an identifiably theoretical proposition about opera. Accordingly, it is in *Opera and Drama* that we find the Zurich writings' most direct anticipations of the nature of Wagnerian music drama. At the general level, the single most important theoretical principle – and this is a thread running through all the published work of 1849–51 – is the conception of opera as a coherent dramatic event, the product of a kind of *auteurisme* which directs every aspect of the work toward the achievement of a dramatic aim. With this idea, Wagner excluded some of the fundamental assumptions of opera in the middle of the nineteenth century. Theatrical brilliance of the sort for which Parisian grand opera was particularly celebrated could no longer distract from the dramatic goal: no more pandering to audiences' sensationalist cravings, no aesthetics of excess. More significantly, musical brilliance could also no longer be an end in itself: this militates against the construction of opera as a series of more or less self-contained "numbers" (aria, duet, finale, and so on) and forbids the mangling or masking of the libretto to fit the sung melody, or indeed any ornamental approach to setting words to music. In fact, the whole decorative aspect of music comes under suspicion, including (as Wagner's opponents were quick to point out) melody itself. This genuinely radical idea anticipates the most striking formal difference between Wagner's mature operas and everything that had come before. The open, continuous musical structure achieved in all the works after *Das Rheingold*, and the conception of each of their acts (from *Die Walküre* onwards) as a single progressive musical sequence flowing smoothly through the changes required by the motion of the plot, is clearly related to the idea of music as an integral aspect of the drama itself rather than a way of producing separate aesthetic effects (such as beauty, grandeur, pathos, or whatever any individual moment in the plot calls for). In theory at least, Wagner will not allow music to detach the ear from the audience's other senses and thoughts.

Opera and Drama pursues this basic premise very thoroughly. As well as deducing the historical causes of the error into which opera has fallen, Wagner considers (rather more convincingly) the barriers between audience and artist that have become institutionalized as a result of its mistake. The essential question then becomes: what form can the artist use to communicate his inward dramatic aim to an audience, in such a way that the audience immediately feels and understands it? In other words: in what form can a proper work of art, a fully expressive and expressed drama, actually exist? Without attempting to summarize the very congested routes this argument travels, we can at least see that the question allows for some detailed and specific writing about the drama's nuts and bolts.

The third and last part of *Opera and Drama* offers precise formulae for such details as rhyme, prosody, word-setting, harmony, orchestration, tonality, and "Melodic Moments" or what have come to be called "leitmotifs" (*PW* II:346; *GS* IV:200) as elements of large-scale musical structures, correct articulation of the sung line, *dramatis personae* (no choruses or superfluous "extras"), and other components of the artwork of the future. Here, that artwork can straightforwardly be named as the *Ring*, full prose sketches for which were completed in the months after *Opera and Drama* was finished. Many of these detailed prescriptions correspond to Wagner's eventual compositional practice in the tetralogy. The most interesting (by some distance – Wagner's comments on the proper function of consonants, for example, are, to say the least, belabored) are those relating to "the poetic-musical '*period*'" (*PW* II:294; *GS* IV:154), and to leitmotif. Here again are two of the most distinctive and radical features of Wagner's mature style being outlined and justified in print before being put to work in the scores.

Both discussions are of great interest in their own right. Still, the temptation to read them as instructions for understanding the compositional techniques of Wagner's music dramas needs to be resisted. The relatively brief but enormously suggestive section on the "period" as a harmonic unit tells us a great deal about Wagner's unprecedentedly expressive and adventurous use of expanded tonality; but to take these few pages of *Opera and Drama* and try to make all his subsequent operas obey their prescriptions, as Alfred Lorenz did in his exhaustive *Geheimnis der Form bei Richard Wagner* (1924–33), is deeply quixotic. The purpose of the passage is to include tonality in an overall theory of drama's idealized intelligibility. Wagner writes that a series of "periods" should together display to the audience "the nature of Man ... in the surest and most seizable [*begreiflichste*] of fashions" (*PW* II:294; *GS* IV:154). This is transparently not to do with music theory, but with the revolutionary ideology of the artwork of the future and its relationship to its audience. It may (and indeed surely does) tell us a lot about the powerful originality of Wagner's tonal conceptions: but (as critics of Lorenz's work have long known) it does not tell us what Wagnerian tonality is, or how it necessarily functions.

The longer section on "prophetic or reminiscent melodic moments" or, more familiarly, leitmotifs (*PW* II:346; *GS* IV:200), should be read the same way. It is, undoubtedly, remarkable to see the practice of leitmotif set out as a theoretical aim in a prose work of 1851, given that Wagner was to make this rather abstract idea the basic structural principle of infinitely subtle musical architecture on the largest scale. However, *Opera and Drama* does not say much about that process. Here is what it says leitmotifs do:

> These Melodic Moments, in themselves adapted to maintain our Feeling at an even height, will be made by the orchestra into a kind of guides-to-Feeling (*Gefühlswegweisern*) throughout the whole labyrinthine ... building of the drama. At their hand we become the constant fellow-knowers of the profoundest secret of the poet's Aim, the immediate partners in its realisement. (*PW* II:346; *GS* IV:200)

Again, Wagner's real subject is the utopian relationship between the new kind of art he is imagining and its audience: the idea that the artwork of the future literally makes itself understood. Accordingly, he argues in *Opera and Drama* that not only can motives recall an emotion and situation from an earlier moment in the score, but that they can actually make one know (or at any rate intuit) what is going to happen later – hence "prophetic" as well as "reminiscent." This is ideology, not music theory. It tells us much more about how the *Ring* was imagined than how it was put together.

I say "the *Ring*" because beyond the tetralogy the relation between the Zurich writings and Wagner's music dramas is stretched even looser. Many of the detailed technical prescriptions outlined in part 3 of *Opera and Drama* were forgotten even by the time of *Tristan und Isolde* (1857–59), especially those relating to poetic style and word-setting. (The essay published in 1861 as "*Zukunftsmusik*," a sort of postscript to the Zurich writings, tries as best as it can to account for the distance between *Tristan* and the earlier essays.) Indeed, insofar as the original conception of *Tristan* had a theoretical basis at all, it was as a project that would have been anathema to the Zurich writings: a popular work ready to make an easy and immediate impact on contemporary audiences. It turned out to be Wagner's most revolutionary score, but, needless to say, not because he suddenly reminded himself of the demands he had made on his own work in print at the beginning of the decade. His intuitions about the expressive and dramatic potential of sung

drama were as essential a part of his creative genius at the time of *Tristan* as
they were at the beginning of his period of exile, and indeed as they remained
throughout his life. It would be more than a little perverse to privilege the
particular form those intuitions took in the years 1849 and 1850 over all the
other ways they found expression, just because during those months they
happened to have found their way into print.

Interpreting the Zurich writings

For all their insights into Wagner's thinking at the period when his mature
style was coming into its own, then, these essays certainly do not add up to
a blueprint for Wagnerian music drama. Nor are we safe with a broader
interpretation of their content as the "theoretical" foundation of his later
scores. The problem with this approach is its implication that "theory" is
antecedent to, and operates at a higher level than, "practice." A simple
cautionary tale illustrates the consequent dangers. In *A Communication
to My Friends*, written immediately after the libretto of *Der junge Siegfried*
(*Young Siegfried*; the precursor of the *Ring*'s third opera, *Siegfried*),
Wagner claims that his hero appeared to him as "the Human Being in
the most natural and blithest fulness of his physical life":

> [H]is movements . . . so bore themselves in [the] face of all encounter, that
> error and bewilderment . . . might heap themselves around until they
> threatened to destroy him, without the hero . . . ever holding anything the
> rightful master of himself and his own movements, [except for] the natural
> outstreaming of his restless fount of Life [*die notwendige Ausströmung des
> rastlos quellenden inneren Lebensbrunnens*].   (PW I:375; GS IV:328)

Is this, then, how the Siegfried of the *Ring* should appear? The idea of a
heroically unfettered bodily self-expression is certainly a theoretical proposition, and it describes the character's behavior in the eponymous opera rather
well. Yet Wagner's fairly purple prose is agitated by a fervor that belongs
specifically to the political turmoil of northern Europe in the middle of
the nineteenth century. This interpretation of Siegfried would have significantly different implications in 1876, when the opera was first performed, or
(to take a perhaps too obvious example) in 1933. It cannot possibly endure
now as a principle for determining the meaning of *Siegfried* – at least not
without a self-imposed blindness so willful as to render the whole matter of
interpretation completely pointless. Very much the same blindness would
afflict anyone who tried to identify all the "prophetic" motives (i.e., anticipatory leitmotifs) in Wagner's post-*Lohengrin* operas, or tell us which "unfail-
ingly intelligible" feeling is the "dominant Emotion" of each of their

"periods" (*PW* II:294; *GS* IV:154). As I have already suggested, it seems better not to think of the Zurich writings – or Wagner's other published pronouncements on his own art – as theoretical documents at all, in any strict sense.

Another approach that has sometimes been popular is what one might call the symptomatic interpretation. The suggestion here is that Wagner's writings generally, and especially the Zurich essays, are symptoms of a creative practice, and a fundamentally musical one, despite the pre-eminence of "drama" in these writings. Their profuse and scattershot energy, their frequent irritability, result in this reading from the fact that they are side effects of a creative effort that is in truth working in an entirely different medium. Even the book-length *Opera and Drama* might be seen as something Wagner had to get out of his system while his genius grappled inwardly with the musico-dramatic challenges of the Nibelung project. This approach has the virtue of recognizing Wagner's limitations as a prose writer, and as a theorist. It observes that his publications are often interesting and full of thought, but very rarely cogent or persuasive. It believes that the operas are more likely to tell us about the prose works than vice versa: in other words, that Wagner's scores were always developed in musico-dramatic contexts, and that writings like the Zurich essays are relatively clumsy approximations of those artistic intuitions in the foreign medium of print.

This aptly accounts for the incongruity one inevitably feels when one puts Wagner's scores side by side with his published writings about them. The danger of the approach, however, is that one ends up throwing the critical baby out with the musicological bathwater. Accepting that Wagner's tortuous struggle to describe his radical compositional techniques in print is a half-success at best, we should still retain an interest in what is left over in the prose writings: not just the rhetorical and ideological stances which prop up his writing about music, but the content of all those other essays where he comments (sometimes very acutely) on issues other than the nature of his own art. The "symptomatic" interpretation comes a little too close to being a license not to bother thinking about Wagner's prose at all. There is now a substantial body of critical literature in English alone demonstrating that his writings reward subtle and attentive readings. Treated as literary documents, rather than as verbatim accounts of what Wagner thought, they appear to have much to offer.

An introductory essay does not lend itself to exemplifying this sort of interpretation, which works best at a much more detailed level. We can however outline a generalized reading of the Zurich writings, which might in turn point still more broadly toward a viable way of reading Wagner's prose in relation to his stage-works.

Early in 1852, not long after finishing *A Communication to My Friends*, Wagner wrote a letter to the *Neue Zeitschrift für Musik*, a leading German musical periodical, published under the title "On Music Criticism." It resumes some of the broad arguments of *The Artwork of the Future* about art's relation to the public, but adds some interesting comments about the function of writing about music in particular. In accord with the utopian idea of a self-evident art propounded throughout the writings of 1849–52, Wagner says that the very fact that music requires "a literary-journalistic intervention" (*PW* III:67; *GS* V:58) itself illustrates the current defects in the art of music. The artwork of the future will speak on its own behalf, in unmediated and fully expressive communication with its public: "And then, my honoured friend, you may close your Journal for Music: it dies, because the Artwork lives!" (*PW* III:73; *GS* V:64). Correspondingly, Wagner's own writing might be understood as an effort to give his (as yet unwritten) drama the voice that it does not yet itself possess. Throughout the Zurich writings, he emphasizes that his new ideas about opera relate fundamentally to its power to communicate itself meaningfully and unmistakably. Above all he wants his music drama to be *explicit*. We might read the prose works not as ("theoretical") descriptions of how this aim is to be achieved, but as manifestations of this explicitness in action: polemical addresses to an audience which themselves adopt the kind of stance toward the public the subsequent drama will be supposed to achieve. Further, and perhaps more tellingly, we might then say that the Zurich essays demonstrate and enact a self-consciousness about being explicit: an attitude fundamentally oriented by its desire to make itself heard. Over and above the technical details and theoretical propositions they contain, they articulate a commitment to art's expressiveness and meaningfulness. They are themselves signs of this idea: as published polemics, they make the new art speak, or rather foreshadow its voice. In this reading, their significance would ultimately lie not so much in what they say about the music drama but in how they open up the whole field of speaking and hearing as an essential aspect of Wagner's art: how they make communication, interpretation, and meaning central to the whole project of the artwork of the future. Their subject, one might say, is less "opera and drama" than "a communication to my friends."

Speaking music

Wagner's post-*Lohengrin* operas certainly present themselves as if they have a message the world needs to hear. No other major composer has poured so much energy into controlling the circumstances of his or her work's performance. There is something entirely and characteristically Wagnerian about the episode of the 1861 Paris *Tannhäuser* production (with its exhausting rehearsal schedule and its attendant propaganda war), or the manipulations of Ludwig II's patronage, or the Bayreuth festival. His enthusiasm for publication is allied to this side of his creative personality. The writings themselves seem above all an effort to imagine music having the very thing it most conspicuously lacks, the power of speech. From the earliest essays to the last, variations on the theme of giving music a speaking voice recur: Beethoven's musings on his choral symphony in "A Pilgrimage to Beethoven," the idea of leitmotif in *Opera and Drama*, the justification of program music in the 1857 essay "On Franz Liszt's Symphonic Poems," the interpretation of melody as (quasi-sung) *melos* in *On Conducting* (1870), the Schopenhauerian "sounding message" that music communicates in *Beethoven* (1870; *PW* V:70; *GS* IX:71), the "ghostly voice" of a dramatic idea that becomes a musical idea in "On Opera Poetry and Composition in Particular" (1879; *PW* VI:170; *GS* X:173), and so on. Reading Wagner's writings reveals the self-consciousness, the calculated urgency of his attempts to make himself heard. It may help us hear that same urgency in his scores as well.

Some suggested reading

English readers interested in exploring Wagner's writings are severely handicapped by the shortage of alternatives to William Ashton Ellis's poor translations in the standard edition (*Richard Wagner's Prose Works*, 8 vols.). An already difficult work like *Opera and Drama* becomes all but unreadable in his rendering. He does better with Wagner's less earnest moods. Fortunately, the more informal pieces provide a better way into Wagner's body of writings anyway (and it might well be argued that they are in the end more significant and interesting than the deliberately analytical essays). A rewarding selection (I use Ellis's titles here) might be: "A Pilgrimage to Beethoven" (1841); "On the Overture" (1841); "Halévy's 'Reine de Chypre'" (1841); "Judaism in Music" (1850); *A Communication to My Friends* (1851); "On Franz Liszt's Symphonic Poems" (1857); "Ludwig Schnorr of Carolsfeld" (1868); *On Conducting* (1870); *The Destiny of Opera* (1871); *Actors and Singers* (1872); "A Glance at the German Operatic Stage of To-Day" (1873); "The Public in Time and Space" (1878); "On the Application of Music to the Drama" (1879); "'Parsifal' at Bayreuth, 1882" (1882). A thumbnail summary of most of Wagner's significant published works, with some commentary, can be found in Jürgen Kühnel, "The Prose Writings," in *The Wagner Handbook*, ed. Ulrich Müller and Peter Wapnewski, translation ed. John Deathridge (Cambridge, MA, 1992), 565–638. For a fuller account, see Alan David Aberbach, *The Ideas of Richard Wagner* (Lanham, MD, 1984; 2nd edn. 1988).

11 Critique as passion and polemic: Nietzsche and Wagner

DIETER BORCHMEYER

"I cannot say by what means I might ever enjoy the *purest* radiant happiness other than through Wagner's music: and that even though it by no means always speaks of happiness, but [also] of the terrible and uncanny subterranean powers of human activity, of the sorrow contained in all happiness and the transience of our happiness; the happiness that issues from this music must have to do rather with the way it speaks." Thus wrote Nietzsche in an unpublished fragment from the summer of 1875.[1]

"Happiness" (*Glück*): the word occurs no less than five times in this one sentence. This was written at a time when Nietzsche had already begun to distance himself from Wagner in many ways. All the same, that music – as Thomas Mann wrote in his 1933 essay "The Sorrows and Grandeur of Richard Wagner" – was the "great love and passion of Nietzsche's life."[2] Yet Nietzsche's love was not for the music alone; it was just as much for Richard Wagner the person, the "old magician" as he repeatedly called him. "I loved him, and none other." That comment, all the more remarkable for its lapidary formulation, was written in the spring of 1885, two years after Wagner's death.[3]

For more than a century a dense thicket of legends and rumors has continued to grow up around Nietzsche's relationship to Wagner. The many unpublished writings and fragments – which have only recently become available in a reliable, unexpurgated edition (that of Colli and Montinari) – indicate that the "break" with Wagner was hardly so rigorous as it has long been represented, based on an insufficient knowledge of the documentary sources. The younger Nietzsche's attitude toward Wagner intertwined passion with critique, just as passion is merged with polemics in the later writings. That is why Mann could perceive the late polemics as really "a panegyric in reverse, another form of eulogy."[4]

Nietzsche was twenty-four when he eventually made the personal acquaintance of Wagner at the house of the Orientalist scholar, and Wagner's brother-in-law, Hermann Brockhaus in Leipzig. His involvement with the composer's works and cultural agenda dates back to the early 1860s, however. The earliest statements betray an ambivalence toward the "music of the future," still beholden as he was to a classicist musical aesthetic from which he would only gradually free himself, and not without misgivings, in the course of the decade. The real "break-through" occurred in the months just prior to the personal meeting with Wagner in the Brockhaus home: "I cannot bring myself to remain criti-cally cool toward his music," he wrote to Erwin Rohde on 27 October 1868, following a concert that included the preludes to *Tristan und Isolde* and *Die Meistersinger*; "every nerve and fiber of my being is excited, and I can't think when I have experienced such a lasting sense of exaltation [*Entrücktheit*] as I did in listening to the latter overture."[5]

A slightly earlier letter to Rohde (8 October 1868) is the first significant appreciation of the Wagner phenomenon. Here Nietzsche intensively con-fronts the criticisms of his teacher from Bonn, the classical philologist and Mozart scholar, Otto Jahn. While he accuses him of listening to Wagner's music with his "ears half shut," he allows that Jahn is "right on a number of points, in particular his view that Wagner represents a modern brand of dilettantism that wants to consume and digest all varieties of artistic interest." The latter formulation was not new with Jahn, but had been leveled at Wagner's activities from the beginning, as it continued to be into the twen-tieth century, notably by Mann and Theodor Adorno, for example. Nietzsche, however, goes on to retract his teacher's pejorative expression "dilettantism" and reformulates it suggestively: "[It] is precisely this aspect, however, that must strike one with awe, how significantly each of these artistic abilities is present within his person, and what inexhaustible energy is coupled with this multifaceted artistic talent; whereas ordinarily, the more varied and compre-hensive the cultivation of 'culture' in an individual, the more it exhibits to us a faded countenance, weak legs, and enervated loins."[6] This, then, is an espe-cially powerful brand of dilettantism, as opposed to a feeble, "weak-loined" philistine culture.

"He was not constrained by a traditional family involvement in any individual art," Nietzsche writes in the fourth of his *Untimely Meditations*, "Richard Wagner in Bayreuth": "he might as easily have adopted painting, poetry, acting, or music for a career as academic scholarship; and the superficial view of him might suggest that he was a born dilettante."[7] And there follows the formulation about a "perilous pleasure in the superficial tasting of one thing after another [*gefährlichen Lust an geistigem Anschmecken*]," anticipating a fundamental idea of the 1883–85 *Essais de psychologie contemporaine* by the diagnostician of French *décadence*, Paul Bourget, that would become so important in Nietzsche's later thought. (Bourget would make this tendency to eclectic aesthetic sam-pling, the fluctuation between heterogeneous forms of existence and spirit, the fulcrum of a new conception of "dilettantism.")

Juxtaposed to this positive reformulation of the charge of dilettantism in the letter to Rohde of 8 October 1868 is a preview of the later diagnosis of decadence, as Nietzsche continues: "Furthermore Wagner commands an emotional sphere quite alien to the likes of O. Jahn; Jahn is one of those ordinary, healthy minds to whom the Tannhäuser legend or the Lohengrin atmosphere remain a closed book." And then comes the famous sentence that so fascinated Mann all his life, indeed one that summed up for him Nietzsche's entire nature prior to the personal apostasy leading to the doctrine of the "superman" and the "will to power": "I take pleasure in the same element in Wagner as in Schopenhauer: the ethical atmosphere, the Faustian scent, the cross, death, the grave, etc."[8] Precisely this ethical aura of the "cross" will be cited, paradoxically, as the deepest grounds for his later alienation from Wagner, with respect to *Parsifal*. At any rate, we can see from the few examples cited here that nearly all the great themes of Nietzsche's analysis and critique of Wagner over the subsequent two decades are already hinted at even before he became personally acquainted with the composer.

On Whit Monday of 1869, just appointed professor of classical philology at the University of Basel, Nietzsche first visited Richard Wagner and Cosima von Bülow at their house, Tribschen, near Lucerne. Subsequently he became a sort of adoptive grown son, a supplement to Wagner's own newborn son Siegfried ("Fidi"). "Strictly speaking, you are the only real gain that life has brought me, and second only to my wife in that respect," Wagner writes on 25 June 1872 (he had married Cosima in August 1870); "fortunately, of course, I now have Fidi, too; but I need a link between him and me, and only you can forge that link, much as the son is linked to the grandchild" (*SL* 809). Wagner adopts Nietzsche in the role of a son – shades of King Marke and Tristan.

The alliance concluded between Wagner and Nietzsche (according to the latter's letter to Erwin Rohde of 28 January 1878) has as its foundation Nietzsche's first major essay, *The Birth of Tragedy from the Spirit of Music*, along with its preliminary studies. Greek tragedy and Wagnerian music drama are continuously mirrored in these writings. The final sentence of the lecture "The Greek Musical Drama" ("Das griechische Musikdrama," 1870) is symptomatic: "That which we hope from the future was once a reality, from a past of more than two thousand years."[9] The "artwork of the future" is given witness and legitimacy through the proof that, in essence, it has already existed. If Nietzsche appears almost more Wagnerian than Wagner in this point (while the latter always emphasized the historical difference between Greek tragedy and modern music drama, apart from all their affinities), he also distances himself from the composer, in a manner at once careful and consequential, at the same time he was working on *The Birth of Tragedy* – though admittedly this occurred in unpublished fragments. In a note from the spring of 1871 Nietzsche speaks of the "incredible aesthetic superstition" he sees in the claim that "Beethoven in the fourth movement of the Ninth gave a solemn testimony concerning the limits of absolute music and thus unlocked the portals to a new art in which music is said to be able to represent even images and concepts."[10] This had been a central thesis of Wagner's. Its symbolic ratification was the performance of the Ninth Symphony in conjunction with laying the foundation stone of the Bayreuth festival theater in May 1872: the Ninth as the cornerstone of the musical drama.

The concept of "absolute music" (or, at any rate, the term) goes back to Wagner himself, who used it in his Zurich reform writings of 1849–51, but in an exclusively negative sense. Of course, Nietzsche knew that Wagner's reading of Schopenhauer had led to a significant shift in the tendencies of his musical-aesthetic thought. In a fragment dating from 1874 he explicitly distinguishes Wagner's "older aesthetics," according to which music is the "means" and drama the "end" of artistic expression (*Opera and Drama*), from a "new" (Schopenhauerian) doctrine that sees the relation of music to drama as that of a "general concept" to a specific "example."[11] In the polemical context of *On the Genealogy of Morals* (1887) Nietzsche would recall this alleged "theoretical contradiction between his earlier and later aesthetic creed," with a sarcastic comment on how the latter, under Schopenhauer's influence, makes the musician into "a kind of mouthpiece of the 'in itself' of things, a telephone from the beyond."[12]

If this Schopenhauerian "new doctrine" is true, Nietzsche writes in 1874, "then the general concept should in no way be dependent on the individual example; that is, absolute music is vindicated and even music for the drama must be absolute music."[13] This is already his conviction at the time of *The Birth of Tragedy*. In the posthumous fragments dating from 1870–71 he maintains that even the value of an opera "will be all the higher, the more freely, unconstrainedly, and dionysically the music is able to unfold and the more it is allowed to ignore all so-called dramatic demands."[14] The concept of "dramatic music" is placed by Nietzsche in quotation marks up through his latest writings in order to emphasize its illusory character, and its distance from what counts as music per se – "pure" music.

After "freeing himself" from Wagner, Nietzsche posed the skeptical question as to whether the "old" doctrine did not in fact remain more constitutive for the works than the "new"; in other words, he accused Wagner of continuing to compose music for the sake or purposes of drama, despite the conversion to Schopenhauer's views. Wagner was simply not capable of writing absolute music, but relied always on a scenic stimulus. His true "end" was, from start to finish, really to establish an "attitude," while music in fact remained a "means": Nietzsche doggedly reiterates this notion throughout his writings and stray jottings of the 1880s (for example, section 368 of *The Gay Science*). Whether as Wagnerian or as anti-Wagnerian, Nietzsche proves himself an unconditional advocate of absolute music.

Nietzsche visited Bayreuth in May 1872 to attend the foundation-laying ceremonies for the festival theater. These festive days were among the happiest of his life. Then at the end of May there appeared Ulrich von Wilamowitz-Moellendorf's pamphlet against *The Birth of Tragedy*, entitled *The Philology of the Future* (*Zukunftsphilologie*), aiming to show how, from a strictly philological point of view, Nietzsche's advocacy of the "music of the future" was absurd. Wagner wrote an open letter in defense of Nietzsche, though he was in no position to repair the young man's professional reputation. Even his teacher Friedrich Ritschl distanced himself, admonishing him in serious tones: "[A] rigorous scholarly riposte to the Wilamowitz pamphlet would be the only worthy thing; but this ought not to assume, in addressing R[ichard] W[agner], an antagonistic character with regard to philology." "If you and your friends," Ritschl continues, "seek salvation along another path, I will always retain a strictly non-partisan regard for the seriousness and ideality of your striving; but I can never agree that art and philosophy are the *only* means of instructing humanity."[15]

Unlike the Tribschen visits, those to Bayreuth repeatedly showed up differences between Nietzsche and Wagner, the fallout from which appears in a series of critical aphorisms from 1874–75. These represent preliminary studies to the fourth of the "Untimely Meditations," the essay "Richard Wagner in Bayreuth" (1876). The notes from 1874 are an attempt to portray Wagner's character in a faithful chiaroscuro. Here he is already described as a musical rhetorician and a "displaced actor." Again we read of Wagner the "dilettante," alongside the assertion that "[n]one of our great composers was still such a bad composer as [Wagner] when he was 28 years old."[16] Nearly all of the character failings Wagner would later be charged with are hinted at here, albeit in a conciliatory light: that he cannot abide "any other individuality" beside his own (e.g., Brahms), his "penchant for pomp and luxury," his "tyrant's love for the colossal," his "intemperance and lack of restraint" in everyday manners (in distinct contrast to his discipline as an artist), the questionable character of his supporters, and, not least, his hatred of the Jews.[17] In the published essay ("Richard Wagner in Bayreuth") these observations are largely suppressed. This fourth "meditation" retains a purely epideictic, eulogistic character, an "honorary speech" (*Festrede*), as Nietzsche himself puts it more than once. As often as possible he seeks to reconcile his own views with Wagner's, to continue thinking as a Wagnerian, to some extent. Among the core ideas of this substantial essay is the depiction of

Wagner as an "anti-Alexander" who ties up again the unloosed Gordian knot of culture, binding anew the dissipative tendencies of the day by virtue of the "astringent power" of his art, corresponding to the "condensational" and "simplifying" qualities of myth described in part 2 of *Opera and Drama*.[18] He repeatedly invokes the idea of Wagner as a sort of Aeschylus *redivivus*, still trying to dismiss the historical gulf separating Greek tragedy from modern music drama. This affinity, like that of Kant and the Eleatics, or Schopenhauer and Empedocles, is obscured but not effaced by the historical distance; "time is only a cloud which makes it hard for our eyes to perceive the fact" and the "pendulum of history has swung back to the point from which it started its swing into enigmatic and distant lost horizons."[19]

The Bayreuth festival of 1876, to which "Richard Wagner in Bayreuth" meant to pay homage, was later interpreted as the peripeteia in Nietzsche's relationship to Wagner. "*What had happened?* Wagner had been translated into [a] German! The Wagnerian was now master over Wagner; *German* art! the *German* master, *German* beer!" Thus we read of that moment in *Ecce homo*.[20] The satirical tone should be met with some skepticism, considering Nietzsche's catastrophic state of health; the searing migraines he was experiencing played at least some part in his quick flight from Bayreuth. "I must summon all my strength," he wrote to his sister on 6 August 1876, "in order to bear the boundless disappointments of this summer."[21] Clearly the phrasing admits of ambiguity. Behind the desperation of enduring the long performances in his poor state of health there also lurks a disillusion with the nature of the festival itself, with all its trappings of a grand social gala; to his migraine-smitten eyes, it had departed all too far from the ideal that had so inspired him back at the time of the foundation-laying ceremonies.

The definitive split with Wagner can be dated, at the latest, at the end of April 1878, when the first part of *Human, All Too Human* arrived in Bayreuth. Hardly four months earlier Wagner had sent Nietzsche the private printing of the *Parsifal* libretto, with a dedication in which he added to his name the mock honorific "Ober-Kirchenrat" (high church-counselor), in a playful allusion to the work's religious content. In *Ecce homo* Nietzsche spoke of an ill-fated crossing of paths of these two publications: "I felt as if I heard an ominous sound – as if two swords had crossed."[22] But that is another deliberate stylization of the facts, for in truth the text of *Parsifal* had lain on Nietzsche's desk for more than a quarter of a year. Furthermore, as long ago as Christmas 1869 he had read together with Cosima (as her diaries attest) the detailed 1865 prose sketch for *Parsifal*, and felt genuinely moved by it. And as late as 10 October 1877 he wrote to Cosima: "The glorious promise of Parcival [*sic*] may console us for many things for which we want consolation."[23] Before long, though, he would no longer feel the need for that particular consolation. The impression of his first reading of the libretto is reflected in a letter to Reinhardt von Seydlitz of 4 January 1878: "More Liszt than Wagner, spirit of the Counter-Reformation; for me, all too accustomed as I am to Greek things, to what is human in a generally valid way, it is all too Christian, time-bound, limited." He allows that "the situations and their sequence" are "the highest poetry" and constitute "an ultimate challenge to music." He allows that "the situations and their organization" are "poetic in the extreme" and constitute "one of the greatest challenges for music."[24]

If Nietzsche's judgement of the *Parsifal* libretto, despite all his reservations, nonetheless included a modicum of praise, Wagner's opinion of *Human, All Too Human* four months later turned out to be completely damning. His essay "Public and Popularity," published in the August 1878 issue of the new *Bayreuther Blätter*, contained in its third section a disguised polemic against the new book and its author. He mocks the unnamed representatives of "science" who "look down upon us artists, poets, and musicians as the belated progeny of a corrupt style of *Weltanschauung*, while setting up natural-scientific or historical modes of epistemology over all 'metaphysical skylarking,' such that a purely cognitive subject remains the sole valid authority, ruling *ex cathedra*. A worthy figure to conclude the world tragedy!" (GS X:84–85).

And indeed, in *Human, All Too Human* the metaphysical-aesthetic speculations of the earlier writings cede to a new authority in the "spirit of scientific inquiry." In this way the author arrogates the view earlier expressed by his teacher Ritschl in criticizing *The Birth of Tragedy* for the way it demoted "cognition" (*Erkenntnis*) and allowed only the arts a "transformative, redemptive, and liberating power."[25] In part 1 of *Human, All Too Human* Wagner is not directly named. But it was no secret to him (as his allusion to Nietzsche's new critique in "Public and Popularity" suggests) that, for Nietzsche, he was now the chief representative of a declining ("metaphysical") culture. The aim of his music, it is now suggested, is to make manifest to contemporary and future audiences the principles and sensibility of that culture: its only role is that of a cultural "swan-song." But how could Wagner, of all people, accept a purely retrospective role, he whose sense of artistic mission was always so future-oriented, and whose work had so long been derided by the catchphrase "music of the future"? He saw matters quite differently: Nietzsche had succumbed to a modern bourgeois-philistine doctrine of "progress" in declaring his separation from a deeper, genuine view of culture.

The second Bayreuth festival (1882), featuring the premiere of *Parsifal*, once again put Nietzsche into a state of the greatest critical agitation. He could not bring himself to attend the festival, but he did faithfully study the score of the new work. His opinion was thoroughly negative: "musical

Hegelianism" ("Hegelei in Musik"), he dubbed this last work of Wagner's in a letter to Malwida von Meysenbug of 13 July 1882.[26] But when he first heard a performance of the Prelude, toward the beginning of 1887 in Monte Carlo, he reversed his earlier opinion, at least as regards the music. A remark recorded at this time speaks of "the greatest consolation granted to me in a long time. The power and emotional stringency are indescribable; I can think of nothing else that draws such depths from Christianity and elicits such sharply drawn sympathy." More emphatic still is the letter to Heinrich Köselitz (also known as Peter Gast) of 21 January 1887: "Has Wagner ever done anything *better*?" And there follows a panegyric account of Wagner's late style, praising exactly what he had elsewhere condemned: the deep conception of Christianity and in particular the Christian-Schopenhauerian cardinal virtue of "sympathy."[27]

Wagner's death on 13 February 1883 represented a deep breach in Nietzsche's emotional world. Upon receiving news of it he was literally thrown from his sickbed, and the sorrow over the irreplaceable human loss he had suffered at the time of their original estrangement was now felt just as keenly as the definitive sense of emancipation, the decisive step toward self-realization this event made possible. He was even moved to write a letter of condolence to Cosima – the letter is unfortunately not preserved, and we do not know if Cosima actually read it. Three drafts do exist, however, and they read like a last, desperate, and painful attempt to re-establish contact with this former friend. In all three Cosima is hailed as "the woman best revered in my heart." "You have lived for a goal and sacrificed everything for its sake; you felt the ideal over and above the man, and to that undying part you and your name now belong forever."[28]

And was it not this same ideal to which Nietzsche wished to ally his own name, that "undying part," the legacy in view of which all the dubious elements of the mortal Wagner become immaterial? Three years later he expresses in a letter to Friedrich Overbeck (27 October 1886) the hope that the "cultured" among Wagner's disciples will recognize "that I believe every bit as much today as I once did in the ideal to which Wagner subscribed – what does it matter if I stumbled on all the human, all-too-human obstacles that R[ichard] W[agner] himself put in the way of that ideal?"[29] In the letter to Peter Gast six days after Wagner's death Nietzsche distinguishes again between the aging Wagner, "against whom I had to defend myself," and "the real Wagner." Regarding the latter, he hoped to become "in good measure his heir."[30] That is one of the most significant formulations of Nietzsche's posthumous relation to Wagner. The king is dead; Nietzsche declares himself the heir to the throne.

The most decisively anti-Wagnerian work, prior to the last polemics of *The Case of Wagner* and *Nietzsche contra Wagner*, is the philosophical-poetic opus, *Thus Spake Zarathustra* (1883–85), even if it never mentions Wagner by name, in keeping with its fictional conception. With his penchant for finding symbolic significance in external events Nietzsche later saw an "ominous connection" in the chronological coincidence of his finishing the first part of *Zarathustra* at the time of Wagner's death: "the *finale* . . . was finished exactly in that sacred hour in which Richard Wagner died in Venice," he noted in *Ecce homo*. Wagner's death became styled in a sense as the end of a cultural regime, from whose ashes the phoenix of a new culture was to arise, the "high man" to be born. His death reflected the death of the old gods, from which (according to the teachings of Zarathustra) the "super-man" would emerge. *Zarathustra* is the radical counterthrust to the world of the late Wagner – Nietzsche's "anti-*Parsifal*."

In the chapter "Of the Priests" in part 2 of the book there is a direct allusion to the closing formula of *Parsifal*: "redemption for the redeemer [*Erlösung dem Erlöser*]." "I am moved to compassion for these priests. I also find them repulsive," Zarathustra says to his disciples; "prisoners they are to me, and marked men. He whom they call Redeemer has put them in fetters: in fetters of false values and delusive words. Would that someone would yet redeem them from their redeemer!"[31] In *Parsifal* it is rather the Grail, the mystical embodiment of the savior that has been profaned by the guilt of Amfortas, that stands in need of redemption from "guilt-stained hands [*aus Schuldbefleckten Händen*]," according to the "divine lament" perceived by Parsifal in Act 2 following Kundry's kiss. This will be effected through Parsifal's rescue: "redemption for the redeemer," or "salvation to the savior." In *Zarathustra* it is not the redeemer who lies in fetters, but in some sense the "priests" Amfortas and Parsifal himself who have been cast in the chains of "false values" by the redeemer and his morals inimical to life. The real priest here is the creator, the Ober-Kirchenrat Richard Wagner himself. Whoever lives near the priests, warns Zarathustra, "lives near black ponds out of which an ominous frog sings its song with sweet melancholy [*Tiefsinn*]."[32] And is that not in fact the music of Richard Wagner, whom Nietzsche dubs in *The Case of Wagner* (section 7) "our greatest melancholiac in music, full of glances, tendernesses, and comforting words . . . the master in tones of a heavy-hearted and drowsy happiness."[33]

One of the most important themes in Nietzsche's negotiation of Wagner's intellectual legacy after 1883 is the composer's affinity with the Romantically rooted aesthetic trends in France, culminating in modern *décadence*. "The more French music learns to form itself in accordance with the actual needs of the *âme moderne*, the more it will 'Wagnerize' – that one can predict – and it is doing enough of that even now" – thus the aphorism 254 from *Beyond Good and Evil*.[34] And, indeed, Wagner's immense influence on French music, literature, and art of the late nineteenth and early twentieth centuries has confirmed this intuition to a remarkable extent. Aphorism 256 of the same work summarizes these claims: "Let the German friends of Richard Wagner ponder whether there is in Wagner's art anything outright German, or whether it is not just its distinction that it derives from *supra-German* sources and impulses. Nor should it be underestimated to what extent Paris was indispensable for the development of his type, and at the decisive moment the depth of his instincts led him to Paris."[35] This affinity of Wagner with the spirit of the French is for Nietzsche an important sign of hope, in fact, for the possibility of overcoming the great malaise of the century, nationalism. "Owing to the pathological estrangement which the insanity of national[ism] has induced, and still induces, among the peoples of Europe; owing to all this and much else that today simply cannot be said, the most unequivocal portents are now being overlooked, or arbitrarily and mendaciously rein-terpreted – that *Europe wants to become one*."[36] Wagner's art with its metanational tendencies and his European-wide appeal are an important signal of that desire, despite the countertendency to suppress it of which Nietzsche complains.

At the end of September 1888 Nietzsche's most important anti-Wagnerian polemic appeared: *The Case of Wagner* became the laboratory for his "diagnosis of the modern soul," with the analysis of modern *décadence* at its center. *Décadence* suggests, to begin with, simply decay, decline. But with Baudelaire the idea experienced a positive "transvalua-tion" or *Umwertung* (to use a Nietzschean term). Now it was precisely from decay, the fading of vitality, declining life, and a sympathy with death that a new, higher aesthetic sensibility would be born. In a frequently irritating dialectic Nietzsche combines the traditionally negative view of decadence with its Baudelairean transvaluation, so that the selfsame phe-nomenon manifests now positive, now negative aspects. And that applies to Wagner as the artist of decadence, *par excellence*. One thing is clear for Nietzsche: whoever wants to overcome decadence must first have experi-enced it for himself and looked into its very depths. "I am, no less than Wagner, a child of this time, that is, a decadent: but I comprehended this, I resisted it," he writes in the foreword to *The Case of Wagner*.[37]

For all his proclamation of the values of newly ascendant life and the "will to power," Nietzsche retains an instinctive bond to Christianity, the art of Wagner, the virtues and weaknesses of "declining life." It is this Nietzsche, Mann wrote in the notes to a projected essay on "Mind and Art" ("Geist und Kunst," 1909), whom we want to identify as "our Nietzsche," as opposed to the prophet of the "will to power" and the amoral ascendancy of life: "From him we have learned psychological susceptibility, the experience of Christianity, of modernity – experiences from which we will never fully distance ourselves, no more than he himself ever did."[38] This claim of Mann's is confirmed once again in Nietzsche's passionate return to *Tristan* in the very last days of his fully conscious existence: "it is the central work and of a fascination which has no parallel, not only in music but in all the arts," he writes in a letter to Carl Fuchs on 27 December 1888.[39] And then on 31 December, to Peter Gast, just three days before his paralytic collapse: "You will find in *Ecce homo* an astonishing page about *Tristan*, about my whole relationship with Wagner. W[agner] is altogether the foremost name in *E. H.*"[40] This "astonishing page" is from the sixth section of the chapter "Why I Am So Clever." "But to this day," he writes here, "I am still looking for a work that equals the dangerous fascination and the gruesome [*schauerlich*] and sweet infinity of *Tristan* – and look in all the arts in vain. All the strangenesses of Leonardo da Vinci emerge from their spell at the first note of *Tristan* . . . I think I know better than anyone else of what tremendous things Wagner is capable, the fifty worlds of alien ecstasies for which no one besides him had wings; and given the way I am, strong enough to turn even what is most questionable and dangerous to my advantage and thus to become stronger, I call Wagner the great benefactor of my life. That in which we are related – that we have suffered more profoundly, even from each other, than men of this century are capable of suffering – will link our names again and again, eternally; and as certainly as Wagner is merely a misunderstanding among Germans, just as certainly I am and always shall be."[41] In regard to Wagner, that is truly Nietzsche's final spiritual testament!

For his thinking, Wagner was always the ultimate paradigm. Only thus can one explain the vacillation of critical temperature between glowing heat and icy coldness. The gulf between an incorruptible "ideal" and an all-too-corruptible reality was for Nietzsche the great scandal of the "Wagner case." All the same he tried to bridge this gulf in the few dream-like moments of happiness in his life and his aesthetic experiences, or in his vision of a "star friendship" (*Sternen-Freundschaft*; section 279 of *The Gay Science*), which remains the most moving formulation of his relationship to Wagner: "We were friends and have become estranged. But this was right, and we do not want to conceal and obscure it from ourselves as if we had reason to feel ashamed . . . That we have to become estranged is the law *above* us; by the same token we should also become more venerable for each other – and the memory of our former friendship more sacred. There is probably a tremendous but invisible stellar orbit in which our very different ways and goals may be *included* as small parts of this path – let us rise up to this thought! . . . Let us then *believe* in our star friendship, even if we should be compelled to be earth enemies."[42]

12 The Jewish question

THOMAS S. GREY

No question has exercised the Wagner literature of the last fifteen or twenty years like that of Wagner's anti-Semitism. From a strictly biographical point of view, of course, there is no question: Wagner's well-documented antagonism to the Jews as a presence in nineteenth-century Europe is a simple matter of record, although scholars can debate the exact origins, the shifting contours, or other "nuances" of his attitudes. The real question has to do with the consequences of these facts, either for our understanding of the operas or for any possible consensus regarding Wagner's implication in the murderous anti-Semitic policies of the Nazi regime that came to power in Germany fifty years after his death. These are almost certainly two separate questions. To argue that the extermination of European Jewry attempted in the later years of the Third Reich was a direct result of social messages encoded in Wagner's dramas and their music would be more than a little preposterous. But to argue that Wagner as a historical figure (which includes his writings and public persona, and indeed his artistic oeuvre) contributed in some significant way to the cultural climate in which Nazi ideologies could take root is by no means preposterous. It is the undeniable affinities between Wagner, "Wagnerism," Bayreuth, and Hitler (if not the entirety of the Nazi Party) that give the question of Wagner's anti-Semitism a moral urgency quite incommensurate with such other perennially popular topics as his adultery or his reckless borrowing and spending habits.[1] The great surge in attention to the theme of Wagner and the Jews in recent years might be attributed in part to a political and social turn in academic criticism at large, in reaction to the paradigms of aesthetic autonomy that dominated the earlier post-World War II generation. In the particular case of Wagner, the desire – even imperative – to rehabilitate him after 1945 was a major factor in discouraging scholarly attention to his notorious anti-Semitism.[2] However disturbing this component of the Wagner phenomenon remains today, we perhaps find the whole question ever more compelling as the notion of art's social significance, for better or worse, becomes ever more remote.

In the earlier nineteenth century the "Jewish question" referred to issues of Jewish emancipation: assimilation and enfranchisement in cultural as well as political terms. Depending on who posed it, the question asked either how this should be effected, or whether it should happen at all. For those, like Wagner, who grew to resent the effects of Jewish emancipation, the "question" became reformulated as a "problem," especially once the process of granting full political rights in Germany drew toward completion after 1869. As much as any anti-Semitic politician of the later nineteenth century, Wagner helped disseminate the view that, despite (or even because of) rapid assimilation, a Jewish presence in Germany and in Europe was a "problem" in need of a solution. What seems to have begun as personal animus with roots in his Parisian experiences between 1839 and 1850, in particular his early dealings with Giacomo Meyerbeer, became by the last years of Wagner's life a mania: an international "problem" with the broadest of cultural and historical implications, as he saw it.[3] Again, Wagner's contribution to the fully political anti-Semitism of the Nazi regime – which can never be precisely calculated, of course – is sooner to be sought in his contribution to the cultural and increasingly racialized discourse of "questions" and "problems" than in any subliminal messages conveyed (perhaps) by the characters, situations, and musical language of his dramas. Furthermore, the canonization of the once radical Richard Wagner as the guiding spirit of German culture by the end of the century made the domestication of his social views on the part of conservative nationalists all the more natural.

An inconvenient truth: the documentary record

The central text of Wagnerian anti-Semitism is of course the essay "Judaism in Music" ("Das Judentum in der Musik"), published pseudonymously in the *Neue Zeitschrift für Musik* in 1850. It was reprinted under the author's own name, with slight revisions and a long afterword, in 1869, and again in the fifth volume of the *Gesammelte Schriften* (first edition 1872). The apparently sudden, vehement eruption of this antagonism to the presence of "the Jews" in modern culture in the 1850 essay was for a long time regarded as a puzzling phenomenon, especially in light of Wagner's commitment to contemporary liberal, emancipatory causes. But as Paul Lawrence Rose has emphasized, the anti-capitalistic rhetoric of the social revolutionaries of 1848 – Karl Marx himself very much included – had fully absorbed several generations' worth of anti-Jewish feeling.[4] Wagner himself addressed the apparent conflict of principles quite succinctly toward the beginning of his essay, and in terms that immediately characterize the defamatory "straight-talking" tone that is meant to guide the whole enterprise. "In supporting their emancipation," he explains, we modern, liberal Germans "were supporting an abstract principle rather than a concrete example":

> All our liberalism was a somewhat confused intellectual game, in so
> far as we proposed freedom for the Jews with no knowledge of the race
> [*Volk*], indeed with a distaste for any contact with them. Consequently
> our desire to give the Jews their rights sprang much more from principle
> than from real sympathy, and all the writing and talking about Jewish
> emancipation failed to mask our unwillingness to have any actual dealings
> with them.[5]

As usual in Wagner's writing, "we" means both himself and the German
people, or even people in general. But it is difficult to say what he had
thought about Jews up to this point in his life, whether based on personal
experience, generalized observation, or inherited prejudice, and so the
question remains why he suddenly let loose with this now notorious blast
against them in September 1850.

Both Jacob Katz and Rose argue persuasively that the outburst of
"Judaism in Music" was the result of personal resentment, envy, and
suspicion toward the person of Giacomo Meyerbeer accumulating mainly
in the period from 1847 through 1850, but with roots in the unhappy,
unsuccessful years in Paris at the very beginning of the decade. Specific
events of this period include a frustrated attempt to make professional
headway in Berlin through a production of *Rienzi* in the fall of 1847 (the
first time Wagner became specifically convinced that Meyerbeer was
working against rather than for him); the visit to Paris in a profoundly
disaffected mood in June 1849, newly exiled from Saxony and looking
(at Liszt's behest) for operatic work in the French capital; and a longer,
still more alienating sojourn in Paris from February through June 1850.
During this first year of exile after the insurrection in Dresden Wagner's
antagonism toward the modern operatic, economic, and cultural establishment (as personified in Meyerbeer) grew to a fevered pitch, even as
he fought once more, without conviction and without success, to break
into it in Paris. The success of Meyerbeer's *Le prophète* during this same
period – his first major new opera since *Les Huguenots* of 1836 – increased
Wagner's bitterness, and it was in fact a discussion of Meyerbeer's latest
work in the pages of the *Neue Zeitschrift für Musik* that provided the
ostensibly proximate cause of the publication of "Judaism in Music."[6]

Without attempting a psychoanalytic investigation into the origins of
Wagner's (or anyone's) anti-Semitic mentality, it is telling to juxtapose
passages from one of Wagner's early letters soliciting Meyerbeer's
patronage with a letter to Liszt after the publication of the "Judaism"
essay.[7] In the first letter, written from Paris on 3 May 1840, Wagner
is updating Meyerbeer, momentarily in Berlin, on the state of his affairs in
Paris. He strikes a tone of amazing, almost parodic obsequiousness (as if
appealing to a "Jewish" way of thinking?), addressing Meyerbeer as his

"deeply revered lord and master." Hoping to leave behind journalism, arranging, and other piecework for Maurice Schlesinger's publishing firm, Wagner offers himself – for what purpose is obscure – to the all-powerful Meyerbeer:

> I have reached the point of having to sell myself . . . But my head & my heart are no longer mine to give away, – they are your property, my master; . . . I realize that I must become your slave, body & soul, in order to find food & strength for my work, which will one day tell you of my gratitude. I shall be a loyal & honest slave, – for I openly admit that I am a slave by nature; it gives me endless pleasure to be able to devote myself unconditionally to another person, recklessly, & in blind trust . . . Buy me, therefore, Sir, it is by no means a wholly worthless purchase! *(SL* 68; *SB* I:388–89)

And he returns to this rhetoric of human commodification in his closing salutation: "Your property: Richard Wagner." As with most classic cases (Caliban, Gollum, Uriah Heep), obsequious fawning masks or mutates into vicious resentment: Wagner projects his own hypocrisy back onto Meyerbeer, who is figured as the sly, slinking, envious *Unmensch*. Eleven years later, after two frustrating visits to Paris in the first year of his exile, he recalls to Franz Liszt the abjection of his early Parisian experience by way of explaining the publication of "Judaism in Music" and his "long suppressed resentment against this Jewish business":

> Meyerbeer is a special case, as far as I am concerned: it is not that I hate him, but that I find him infinitely repugnant. This perpetually kind and obliging man reminds me of the darkest – I might almost say the most wicked – period of my life, when he still made a show of protecting me; it was a period of connections and back-staircases, when we were treated like fools by patrons whom we inwardly deeply despised . . . I cannot [help] sensing in Meyerbeer my total antithesis, a contrast I am driven loudly to proclaim by the genuine despair that I feel whenever I encounter, even among many of my friends, the mistaken view that I have something in common with Meyerbeer. *(SL* 222; *SB* III:545–46)

Wagner goes on to congratulate himself for having publicly effected this dissociation from Meyerbeer "with such zeal." The impulse was indeed not new, for as far back as 1843, at the time of the first performances of *Der fliegende Holländer* (*The Flying Dutchman*), he had remonstrated with Robert Schumann for claiming to find "Meyerbeerian" elements in that opera. What could that possibly mean, he protested, "except perhaps a sophisticated striving after superficial popularity"; and how could he ever have drawn "inspiration from *that* particular source, the merest smell of which . . . is sufficient to turn my stomach" (25 February 1843: *SL* 105). It is not difficult to detect in this vehement disowning of a purported "protector" and mentor, now charged with cunning treachery, shades of young Siegfried's instinctive rebellion against his foster-father Mime.

As has often been pointed out, the array of anti-Jewish sentiments expressed in "Judaism in Music" was by no means new or unique to Wagner in 1850; but these sentiments had rarely been expressed in such a concentrated, vehement fashion in modern times. Indeed, Wagner prides himself on this very point. The great "service" he has to offer here is to articulate the "question" in all candor, pulling no punches, telling it like it is. The only way to deal with the question is to put all one's cards on the table, to acknowledge "people's instinctive dislike of Jewishness" ("What I refer to is simply what exists"), to "proclaim the natural revulsion aroused in us by Jewishness" rather than gloss over it politely ("Judaism in Music," 24–25; *GS* V:66–67). He makes it clear, too, that the issue is no longer one of religious difference – though by the time of *Parsifal* he would revive that as well – but one of cultural and ethnic difference: between one *Volk* and another. (Wagner is obviously feeling his way toward the as yet uncodified theory or "science" of race.) The most immediate issue remains the external, circumstantial one of economics: modern capitalism as a legacy of Jewish usury, and the destructive effect of the ("Jewish-controlled") market economy on the affairs of art. From circumstances, however, Wagner quickly turns toward appearances ("unpleasantly foreign") and essences: the Jewish nature (*Wesen*), the effect of "Jewish speech," and "Jewish influence on music" (see "Language and music," 211–15). The idea that a "people" so culturally and temperamentally alien, so fundamentally uncreative, should control the financial and institutional reins of art is naturally, to Wagner, intolerable. Where in his contemporary "reform" treatises on art and opera he had been at pains to establish the once and future bond between art and the *Volk*, here Wagner insists on the unbridgeable gulf between even assimilated, educated Jews and the people of the German nation. Distinctions between the common or ordinary Jews and affluent, cultured Jews are effortlessly dissolved in the broader essentializing discourse of "the Jew." While in other contexts Wagner has no trouble damning the artistic sterility of perfectly German composers such as Heinrich Marschner, Franz Lachner, or Joseph Rheinberger (not to mention Brahms!), or inveighing against the pedantry of eminently *völkisch* musical writers such as W.H. Riehl, in the heat of his anti-Jewish tirade all creative flaws identified in Jews are wholly and essentially Jewish. Necessarily he finds different faults in Mendelssohn than in Meyerbeer (the recently deceased Mendelssohn provides a foil, of sorts, for the real target in Meyerbeer). But these differences are likewise dissolved in the all-encompassing condition of Jewishness.

The insistence on cultural, ethnic, and proto-racial "essences" in the essay points directly to the problem of its much cited and much debated ending. Having compared bad and worse in Mendelssohn and Meyerbeer, Wagner compares bad and better in the figures of the writers Heinrich Heine and Ludwig Börne. If religious conversion and baptism are not the answer to the Jewish "question," is cultural assimilation? (Full legal enfranchisement or gradual ethnic assimilation by intermarriage are not issues raised in the essay.) The answer Wagner calls for is the complete repudiation of "Jewishness," as achieved by Börne, an early radical journalist who had died in 1837.[8] Invoking the legendary figure of the Wandering Jew (Ahasuerus), prototype for his own Flying Dutchman, Wagner prescribes "redemption through self-denial" as the answer to the "curse" of Jewishness. But this "can be achieved by only one thing, and that is the redemption of Ahasuerus – decline and fall!" ("Judaism in Music," 39; GS V:85). Whether this call for an end to Jewishness by means of its willed "decline" (*Untergang*) – Wagner also speaks of "self-annihilation" in the preceding sentence – is strictly figurative, or whether it anticipates at some level the ruthlessly physical annihilation prescribed by the Nazi "final solution" is the continuing point of debate. (The fate of Kundry in *Parsifal* resonates with the question without clearly answering it.) The answer will have to depend ultimately on personal convictions regarding the character of Richard Wagner, which is to say that there can be no single, definitive answer.

Having thus "unburdened" himself on the subject in the 1850 essay, Wagner continued to air freely his views on the "Jewish question" for the rest of his life. At first this was just among individual friends and acquaintances; it would be some time before he put his own name to these views in print. Only a small circle – including the *Neue Zeitschrift* editor Franz Brendel, Liszt, Theodor Uhlig, and the other young disciples Karl Ritter and Hans von Bülow – knew for a fact that Wagner was the author of the essay first published under the name "K. Freigedank." (The pseudonym, meaning roughly "free-thinker," did at least clearly announce itself as such.) Not until 1869 did Wagner, rather unexpectedly, decide to reissue the essay as an independent brochure under his own name, lightly revised and extended by a sizeable afterword addressed to a Parisian friend and patron Marie Muchanoff (previously Kalergis, née Countess Nesselrode). Some years before this, anti-Jewish murmurings were coupled with the traditional critique of French political and artistic hegemony in Europe in a series of articles published in the *Süddeutsche Presse* (1867; reprinted as *Deutsche Kunst und deutsche Politik*, 1868), when Wagner thought to use his newfound influence with Ludwig II of Bavaria as a means of influencing, in turn, public opinion on matters cultural and broadly political.

The more concrete denunciations of the "Judaism" essay regarding the corrosive effects of Jews and the "Jewish spirit" on the Germans were revived in a series of journal entries written for Ludwig in the fall of 1865, though published only later (1878) in the *Bayreuther Blätter* as "Was ist Deutsch?" ("What Is German?").

It was, in any case, the reissue of the 1850 essay as an independent publication by the now famous "Richard Wagner" that first brought his vehement anti-Semitism to the attention of a wide public in 1869. In this year, on the eve of German unification, the North German federation of states, headed by Prussia, granted full civil rights to Jewish citizens. However much Wagner may have been opposed to such legislation, it does not seem to have been the immediate cause behind the republication, since he had arrived at the decision already before the beginning of the year. In a letter to his part-Jewish disciple Karl Tausig in April 1869 he claimed rather that it had been the "unprecedented insolence of the Viennese press" upon the appearance of *Die Meistersinger*, the "continual, brazen lie-mongering about me, and its truly destructive effects" that induced him to take the reckless "step" of going public with the essay (*SL* 749). And, indeed, the new afterword is preoccupied not with the politics of Jewish emancipation, but with the wholly personal *idée fixe* that an out-and-out conspiracy of the "Jewish press" is working to undermine the cause of Wagner and his artwork of the future. His nemesis of the past decade, Eduard Hanslick, is implicated as the ringleader of this movement, given his increasing prominence as the voice of the Viennese musical establishment. Yet the conspiracy Wagner imputes to him and his fellow critics is not predicated on vengeance for the parody of anti-Wagnerian critics in Beckmesser, but on a (wholly undocumented, wholly conjectural) resentment against the original, pseudonymous "Judaism" essay.[9]

Beginning in 1869, the diaries kept by Cosima von Bülow (soon to be Cosima Wagner) until 1883 offer an intimate portrait of the role of anti-Jewish sentiment in Wagner's everyday conversation. The correspondence after 1850 (before then Wagner had kept largely mute on the subject, even in his letters) offers ample documentation as well, though less consistent in tone and frequency; some of Wagner's most impassioned attacks on the Jewish "threat" are to be found in the letters to King Ludwig, whom Wagner persistently attempted to convert to his views on the matter, always in vain. The enterprise of the Bayreuth festival consumed most of Wagner's attention (also as writer and publicist) for a time after 1870. But in the last five years of his life the *Bayreuther Blätter* provided a forum for further pronouncements on the issue of Jews and Judaism, now against the background of a public program of anti-Semitism – for the first time under that rubric – being carried out in Germany and Austria by the likes of Bruno Bauer, Wilhelm Marr, Julius Stöcker, and Bernhard Förster. Although Wagner famously declined, in 1880, to sign the anti-Semitic petition that Förster wanted to submit to the German Reichstag calling for a curb on the civic rights being granted to the Jews, there is no doubt that the newly racialized discourse of anti-Semitism played a large role in Wagner's late "regeneration" essays speculating – often wildly and almost incomprehensibly – on the means of shepherding the German people, and perhaps the rest of humanity, toward a utopian future founded upon the fairly fuzzy principles of an art-based Wagnerian faith.

Rose sees the essay on "German-ness" ("Was ist Deutsch?"), drafted in 1865, as inaugurating this late corpus of writings upon its publication in 1878. If "What Is German?" moves beyond the personal concerns of the 1869 afterword to issues of national culture and identity, the later essays chart a still broader, global territory. "Religion and Art" (*Bayreuther Blätter*, October 1880) speculates on the "fall of man" from a loosely post-Darwinian perspective, in terms of his degeneration into the carnivorous, warlike aggressor of modern Western civilizations. On the face of it, the essay seems to propose an innocuous, even distinctly virtuous Bayreuthian variant of the Salvation Army, committed to promoting pacifism, vegetarianism, kindness to animals, temperance, and of course spiritual elevation through art and music. The intellectual foundations of this vision owe something to Schopenhauer, including his broad philosophical-ideological critique of the Judeo-Christian ethical legacy. But particularly in the series of three "supplements" to this essay published between December 1880 and September 1881 ("What Avails This Knowledge?," "Know Thyself," and "Heroism and Christianity") Wagner's long-cultivated, visceral anti-Semitism repeatedly asserts itself, poisoning any lofty idealism with an all-too-human rancor. These are the only works of Wagner written under the influence of Count Arthur Gobineau and his (pre-Darwinian) *Essay on the Inequality of Human Races* (originally published 1853–55). Personally, however, Gobineau evinced no more than a casual, "aristocratic" brand of anti-Jewish prejudice, while as a theorist he promoted Semitic racial solidarity as a good example. It was his diagnosis of the ongoing "degeneration" of Germanic-Aryan stock in Europe that inspired Wagner's speculation on the possibilities of "regeneration" through a cooperation of racial, cultural, and aesthetic factors. These "regeneration" writings of the Bayreuth period are a complicated, contradictory brew. The ongoing fulminations against the Jews are ominous enough in the context of a renewed and newly racial anti-Semitism in Germany of the 1870s and 1880s. The speculative, utopian strain, for all that it might suggest strategies for Wagner's ethical redemption in the eyes of posterity, must also give us serious pause considering the consequences of such radical utopian agendas in the course of the following century.

Language and music: anti-Semitism in the operas?

The foregoing recital of evidence serves only to remind us of an established fact: that Richard Wagner was a vocal anti-Semite throughout the second half of his life. Of this there has never been any question. For us today, the actual "Jewish question" in the case of Wagner is that regarding the possible relation of his anti-Semitism to his creative oeuvre. (The historical impact of this element in the works constitutes a related, more imponderable question, if we agree that such an element exists.) This is often identified as the only aspect of his anti-Semitism that might matter, since Wagner only matters any more as the author of his operas or music dramas, while the opinionated ideologist faded from cultural relevance along with the phenomenon of "Wagnerism" nearly a century ago.[10]

The question of anti-Semitism in the works begins and ends, probably, with *Parsifal*. And, more broadly, it is safe to say that the question really applies only to the operas written after 1850, that is, the mature "music dramas" fully executed only after *Lohengrin* (1848), the experience of the 1849 revolutions, and the "Judaism" essay. (The role of a messianic *Führerprinzip* in *Rienzi* or *Lohengrin*, or of the Wandering Jew legend in the character of the Flying Dutchman would have at most an indirect bearing on the question; reading any of the pre-1850 operas as anti-Semitic allegory would require much special pleading.) Although the essay "Religion and Art" and its three supplements were all written after both the libretto and score of *Parsifal* had been completed, they are plainly conceived in large part as commentaries on themes at work in the drama: spiritual and physical decline and regeneration (the Grail knights, Amfortas), a new theology of compassion for living things (Amfortas, the swan, even Kundry and nature at large – *was all da blüht und bald erstirbt*), and a vaguely mystical reinterpretation of Christian motifs such as Christ's blood, the Eucharist, and redemption. The agency of art in effecting "redemption" is no less important than that of moral and spiritual factors, as suggested by *Parsifal* as well as the late writings. And race, or "blood"? Robert Gutman was one of the first to draw attention to the explicitly anti-Semitic implications of these commentaries for a reading of the opera, its symbols, and its music.[11] Since then, Hartmut Zelinsky, Paul Lawrence Rose, and Marc Weiner have reiterated and developed the case for reading *Parsifal* as implicitly, but still deeply, anti-Semitic in conception.[12] Even apart from the "regeneration" essays, the centrality of Christian imagery and ritual in *Parsifal* and the fairly explicit Orientalizing and feminizing of the enemy agents, Klingsor and Kundry, and their environments make such a reading easily available. Arguments against this approach might identify it as narrowing or lowering the range of otherwise available meanings, as capitulating to obsolete, "essentializing" habits of thought better ignored (if they really were Wagner's), or as privileging surface representations over profounder meanings and experiences provided by the music.[13] Yet the case "against" *Parsifal*, if one accepts it, differs from hypotheses about anti-Semitic elements in the other works in concerning precisely the fundamental themes and textures of the drama, not merely isolated caricatures or allusions to ethnic-cultural stereotypes.

The most common objection to charges that the operas reflect the composer's deep-seated anti-Semitism is the obvious absence of overtly Jewish characters. That absence should hardly surprise us. Jewish characters and caricatures could find a place in realistic novels or in the spoken theater, especially contemporary farces or comedies of manners, but hardly in grandly idealistic music dramas based on German mythology, legend, or medieval romances.[14] The incorporation of explicit Jewish caricatures into the operas would have jeopardized their claim to being serious, timeless works of art. Fromenthal Halévy and Eugène Scribe might portray the plight of medieval Jewry from a modern, liberal-enlightened perspective in their highly successful grand opera of 1835, *La Juive* (a work early admired by Wagner and never renounced), but it is impossible to imagine where Wagner might have found plausible source material for some sort of anti-*Juive* without resorting to subliterary medieval propaganda. Scurrilous pamphleteering and high art were, for him, quite separate spheres. (Kundry, as a female manifestation of the Wandering Jew of medieval legend, is a possible, partial exception, suggested by Klingsor's reference to one of her past lives in the person of Herodias. But the issue is left ambiguous – deliberately, one assumes – and at any rate, she is no caricature.)

Hence the importance of his own scurrilous pamphlet *Judaism in Music* (in its independent reincarnation of 1869) in mediating between personal ideology and public art. If Wagner could not plausibly represent "real" Jews in his operas, he might construct characters who could be perceived as acting, sounding, and behaving "like Jews," and this might involve various levels of his synthetic *Gesamtkunstwerk*: language, singing, gesture, and orchestral music.[15] Wagner's decision to identify himself as the author of *Judaism in Music* is important here, since it could then be regarded as a key to such potential readings for anyone with a desire to use it so. Nearly all modern interpretations of anti-Semitic content in the operas refer to this key, although we still have very little evidence of whether or not Wagner's contemporaries chose to avail themselves of it.

The arguments about Jewish "difference" in *Judaism* all stem from the fundamental issue of language. The stereotype, in no way original to Wagner, is presumably as old as the diaspora, and is neatly summed up by the "easily assimilated" Old Lady from Rovnogobernia in Bernstein's

Candide ("I never lerrrned zuh hu-mann leng-vege ..."). As traditionally adhering to their own distinct ethnic enclaves, in this view, Jews have not absorbed the native languages of Europe as true mother tongues. (Bernstein's Old Lady identifies hers, tongue in cheek, as "a high-middle Polish.") Thus, Wagner argues, they remain cultural outsiders in every other regard, as well. The Central European Jewish lingua franca of Yiddish – what Wagner and his contemporaries referred to as Jewish-German *Jargon* or *Mauscheln* – is read as emblematic of a tendency to appropriate and distort all genuine cultural forms, from speech to writing to philosophical or political thought to singing, acting, and musical composition. Mendelssohn's adept but "soulless, formalistic" emulation of the German tradition from Bach to Beethoven and Meyerbeer's grotesque extremes of descriptive and "characteristic" music are but separate, distant points on a spectrum of uncreative, distortional adaptation of European musical idioms. Beckmesser's sorry efforts at an original love song in Act 2 of *Die Meistersinger* are surpassed in ineptitude only by his attempt to purloin Walther's prize-song in Act 3. Beckmesser's is a paradigmatic case in the way it involves language (poetry) and music at once, inextricably confounded in Wagner's representation. Upon his first appearance in the *Ring* cycle, in the opening scene of *Das Rheingold*, Alberich is a similarly awkward, unskilled suitor for the hand of native and natural beauty. His entrance is immediately marked as an intrusion on the natural order; the tone (even tonality) of his music, of his text, and of his physical behavior underlines this alien, intrusive, destructive status. Any anti-Jewish allegory here, it is true, must take account of the fact that the original sin of the myth – the theft of the Rhine-gold and the cursing of love – results from Alberich's rejection by the fair Rhine maidens. But then (the allegory could have it), he should never have shown up where he was not wanted. Indeed, as Theodor Adorno famously put it, "all the rejects of Wagner's works are caricatures of Jews": "The gold-grubbing, invisible, anonymous, exploitative Alberich, the shoulder-shrugging, loquacious Mime, overflowing with self-praise and spite, the impotent intellectual critic Hanslick-Beckmesser."[16]

If Wagner believed himself to have been a victim of a "Jewish conspiracy" in the press, as he insisted in 1869, there would also seem to have been something of a conspiracy of silence about the implicit "Jewishness" of the characters so readily recognized by Adorno. Apart from the case of *Parsifal*, where the prominence of religious motifs sometimes forced issues of Christianity vs. Judaism into the foreground, earlier productions of and critical reactions to the *Ring* and *Die Meistersinger* seem almost never to have articulated such insights into Wagner's "Jewish" characterizations, even up through the Nazi period in Germany.[17] And, yet, the preponderance of negative evidence is not enough to prove what individuals did or did not perceive in Wagner, especially in light of some very telling remarks attributed to Gustav Mahler in the memoirs of Natalie Bauer-Lechner. Rehearsing a complete *Ring* cycle in Vienna for the 1898–99 season, Mahler complained about the excessively "Jewish" characterization given to the role of Mime by the tenor Julius Spielmann ("The worst thing about it is the *Mauscheln*"). Not that Mahler disagreed with this interpretation: "Although I am convinced that this figure is the true embodiment of a Jew, intended by Wagner in the spirit of persiflage (in every trait with which he has imbued him: the petty cleverness, the greed, the whole *Jargon* so perfectly suggested by both music and text), this should – for God's sake – not be exaggerated and laid on so heavily, as Spielmann does – and in Vienna, at the 'Royal-Imperial Court Opera,' of all places, it would be pure lunacy, an all-too-welcome scandal for the Viennese!" To this he added that he knew of only one perfect interpreter of the role, "and that is *me!*"[18] Mahler's observation has been noted often enough, but not sufficiently contextualized. The element of caricature is clear to *him*, as it was apparently to Julius Spielmann, but he assumes that it is *not* common knowledge to the Viennese audience at large, or at any rate, that it would be highly impolitic to make a point of it in performance. A "conspiracy of silence" might in fact be an apt way of summing up the whole question of how the anti-Semitic portraiture of Wagner's "villains" was received prior to Adorno.[19]

Significantly, Mahler's remarks concerned the interpretation of Mime's role in *Siegfried* rather than *Das Rheingold*. In the prologue to the *Ring*, Mime is the chief representative of the Nibelungs as an oppressed, exploited proletariat. By scene 3 of the opera, after forging the ring, Alberich may well become the avatar of the modern industrial plutocrat, as George Bernard Shaw described him, and such plutocrats may have been quintessential Jews in Wagner's mind. But, even though Mime develops some of his characteristic vocal and gestural tics in his *Rheingold* scenes, there is no way of distinguishing him, dramatically, from the Shavian or Marxian working class. Throughout the first two acts of *Siegfried* the situation is quite otherwise. Freed from the invisible whip of Alberich, Mime now employs all his cleverness and guile to exploit the young Siegfried, in turn, while the rest of the Nibelungs are nowhere to be seen. Moreover, the whole process of Siegfried's self-discovery in these two acts constantly turns on his observations of Mime's difference. (Here music, even more than language, plays the vital role: in addition to his characteristic wheedling, keening, and kvetching, Mime's musical-gestural persona distinctly embodies the fidgety "Jewish restlessness" of which Wagner complained both in public and in private.)[20] The more he observes this, the more Siegfried registers an instinctive loathing for his foster father, "false" in every respect. By the time he is given the opportunity to murder Mime, in honest self-defense, there seems to be really no other viable solution to the Mime "problem." Even if we were to forget Wagner's characterization of his own relationship to Meyerbeer in the letter to Liszt of 18 April 1851 – and there is every reason *not* to forget it, since Wagner was drafting the text of *Siegfried* only a few weeks later – one would have to be culturally tone-deaf not to see how Siegfried's attitude toward Mime reflects a great deal of Wagner's attitude toward the Jews, whether in the guise of friends or enemies.

Sympathy for the devil

"R. tells me he once felt every sympathy for Alberich," Cosima notes of an evening discussion with her husband on 2 March 1878, after reading some Walter Scott. Dieter Borchmeyer has cited this observation as proof that Wagner could not have imagined Alberich or the other Nibelungs as "Jews."[21] The observation as well as Borchmeyer's interpretation of it raise a number of issues regarding the composer's personal life and private communications as evidence in the matter of the Wagnerian "Jewish question." Wagner's numerous friendships with Jews have long served as Exhibit A in the case for his defense. Of course, these "friendships" run a whole psychological gamut. At the beginning of 1847 he could still maintain to Eduard Hanslick (!) that "Meyerbeer is a very close personal friend of mine," whom he has "every reason to value ... as a kind & sympathetic man," before going on to explain in the next breath how he represents everything "offensive about ... the opera industry today" (letter of 1 January 1847: *SL* 135). He several times expressed his sympathy, of a sort, for the "tragic" case of Mendelssohn, as he called it. Even in the case of Jews who really could be counted as personal friends, such as Tausig, Levi, Heinrich Porges, or Joseph Rubinstein, Wagner's sympathies were an ambivalent affair. Any of them might be treated with sublime condescension (granted, perhaps no more than any friends of Wagner could expect), and the friendship with Hermann Levi is often characterized as an unstable mix of genuine affection, admiration, impatience, and downright sadism.

But to return to the case of Alberich. Richard and Cosima were comparing Alberich with the new villain, Klingsor. "R. tells me that he once felt every sympathy for Alberich, who represents the ugly person's longing for beauty" – thus the complete remark from the diaries. This feeling accords well enough with Alberich's dilemma at the opening of *Rheingold*, though it begins to sound less friendly. "In Alberich the naïveté of the non-Christian world, " he goes on, "in Klingsor the peculiar quality which Christianity brought into the world; just like the Jesuits, he does not believe in goodness, and this is his strength but at the same time his downfall, for through the ages *one* good man does occasionally emerge!" "Non-Christian" might seem to imply Jewish, but "naïveté" was hardly a trait Wagner associated with Jews, and one has to assume he is merely alluding to the pagan mythological world of the *Ring*. Klingsor – one of the weaker candidates for crypto-Judaism in the canon of Wagner villains – is likened to a Jesuit, another object-class of Wagnerian animus, but not at any rate Jewish by creed or (presumably) race. The larger point here, which has been made by Borchmeyer among others, is that throughout the volumes of candid remarks on his works recorded by Cosima, Wagner seems never once to have commented on the "Jewish" qualities of any of his dramatic characters or their music. The same applies to the more voluminous (if not always equally frank) evidence of Wagner's private correspondence. If Wagner had really intended subtexts of anti-Semitic caricature and allegory in the music dramas, it is indeed difficult to explain the absence of any references to such subtexts in the extensive private record of his thoughts and opinions, a record not otherwise lacking in candor. Could it be that the "conspiracy of silence" started at home?

Intentions do matter here, whatever the status of hard evidence. It makes little sense to speak of an anti-Semitic content filtering into the fabric of the works unconsciously, to suppose that Wagner's anti-Semitism was such an ingrained part of his psychology that, all unawares, he painted his villains with "Jewish" traits simply because this is how he felt and imagined evil. (Such pagan archvillains as Ortrud or Hagen have very little about them we can identify with Wagner's ideas of Jewishness, however labile those ideas often seem.)[22] Moreover, Wagner – a voracious interpreter of the most varied phenomena who assiduously recorded his own dreams – was far too self-conscious an artist to remain oblivious of such a dimension of his own work, even if we could suppose it to have evolved "unconsciously," at first. If we are to take seriously the possibility of an anti-Semitic layer in some parts of Wagner's oeuvre, we must believe that he was aware of it, whether or not this awareness was communicated aloud or committed to writing.[23] Hans R. Vaget articulates a plausible reading of the situation when he suggests that, on the whole, Wagner strove to keep his "anti-Jewish obsession" out of his creative work in view of the "broad, universal acceptance" he sought for it, and yet in a few cases (Beckmesser's role and Mime's in *Siegfried*) he finally couldn't quite help himself.[24] Wagner, in writing his operas, no less than the Nazis in staging them, Vaget argues, wanted to preserve a pure, "auratic" quality in them that would have been compromised by instrumentalizing them as "crude propaganda."[25]

One more component of the Wagnerian "Jewish question," if we accept the idea that his creative work might not have remained uninfluenced by his anti-Semitism, is how we ought to respond to it, as readers, listeners, critics, performers, producers, and so forth. This question, too, has been subject to considerable debate, most publicly in the long-running informal ban on performances of Wagner in Israel. Scholarly and critical discussion, so often preoccupied with proving or disproving the relevance of anti-Semitism to the works, less often gets to the point of outlining a practical response, apart from those who, like Michael Tanner or Bryan Magee, deny the relevance and hence the need for a response.[26] David Levin has argued that critics as well as producers might draw attention to an "aesthetics" of anti-Semitism (or, Wagnerian anti-Semitism as an "aesthetic practice") in works such as *Die Meistersinger* or *Siegfried* without necessarily trying to dignify the alleged elements of caricature with straightforward, "realistic" representation.[27] It might seem surprising that modern opera directors still deeply committed to an ethos of radical provocation (and none more so than directors of Wagner) have so rarely wanted to touch this theme; they might reasonably worry that to make Wagner's anti-Semitism manifest on stage might confuse critique with simple complicity, or at any rate, that pointing up implicit caricature would more likely offend than provoke.[28] Slavoj Zizek engages some of these issues in his introduction to a recent reissue of Adorno's *In Search of Wagner* under the title "Why Is Wagner Worth Saving?" but offers only ambiguous answers. He condemns the hypocrisy of those who would defend and preserve the "beautiful music" while denouncing, if not simply denying, proto-Fascist and racist elements in the dramas. But it is unclear how neo-Freudian, neo-Marxist, and Lacanian interpretations solve the problem any differently than picturesque, Romantic-nostalgic productions would – by looking away.[29]

One way or another, we are left with the problem of making our peace with Wagner – revolutionary, intellectual, artist, and bigot – and justifying our sympathy with this complicated devil, at least as the author of his works. If nothing more, we can always rely on the fact that he did not make his anti-Semitism an *explicit* element of his operas (for that much is a fact), while much that *is* explicit remains liberal, generous, psychologically perceptive, touching, and, indeed, beautiful, if also sometimes long-winded and obscure. Still, despite current tendencies to argue otherwise, the question, or problem, of Wagner's anti-Semitism should not and cannot finally be limited to arguments about its relevance to the dramas and their music. It was Wagner's great aim to be much more than a musician, more than a composer of operas. The writer Berthold Auerbach, another of his Jewish friends and one whom he much admired during the years they both lived in Dresden, later reflected with dismay on the rise of public anti-Semitism in the new German Reich and its growing public acceptance. "Richard Wagner also had his effect in this. For he was the first to acknowledge himself as a Jew-hater, and he proclaimed Jew-hatred to be quite compatible with culture."[30] If Wagner influenced the tragic course of German anti-Semitism in the generations to follow, it was through his prominence as a public figure, indeed *as* a famous artist and composer, but not through the music he composed.

PART IV

After Wagner: influence and interpretation

13 "Wagnerism": responses to Wagner in music and the arts

ANNEGRET FAUSER

Wagner's impact on Western culture can hardly be overestimated. When Howard Shore describes his use of leitmotifs in the Oscar-winning score for the blockbuster trilogy *The Lord of the Rings* (2001–03), for example, he reveals himself as but one recent musician in a long line of creative artists affected by Wagner the composer.[1] Wagner's theories about musical theater can be felt even in contemporary discussions of Broadway musicals, such as *Oklahoma!* (1943) and *Rent* (1996).[2] As for modern opera, Olivier Messiaen's *Saint François d'Assise* (1983), Luciano Berio's *Un re in ascolto* (1984), and Karlheinz Stockhausen's cycle *Licht* (1977–2004) are among the more recent responses to the challenges posed by Wagner almost 150 years ago. In fact, artists from all disciplines over the last century and a half have likewise relied on aesthetic concepts shaped prominently by Wagnerian ideas about the nature of art, whether Symbolist poets such as Charles Baudelaire, Paul Verlaine, and Stéphane Mallarmé; *avant-garde* painters such as Wassily Kandinsky, Pablo Picasso, Joseph Beuys, and Anselm Kiefer; the sculptors Hans Arp and Auguste Rodin; or the architects of the Bauhaus. Media technology itself, when related to art, has drawn its aesthetic justification from Wagner's thoughts.[3] And his political and social views influenced the Zionist Theodor Herzl as well as the anti-Semitic fascist Adolph Hitler, with repercussions still powerfully felt in concert life today – in Israel, above all, but worldwide as well. This expansive and often cult-like reception phenomenon is usually designated by the term "Wagnerism" – one of the few *isms* associated with the name of an individual composer. Indeed the term became quickly associated with an ideologically tinted reception of Wagner's music and writings as an all-encompassing theoretical system, whose partisan followers invoked the perceived teachings of the master rather as Marxists invoke those of that famous German contemporary.

Any discussion of Wagnerism, however, needs to distinguish between specifically compositional and musical-aesthetic responses to Wagner's oeuvre, on the one hand, and more general literary, artistic, and political reactions to his music and writings, on the other. In contrast to writers and painters, of course, composers had to engage with Wagner in his primary medium – that of sound. This created very different anxieties, challenges, and opportunities, and it demanded strategies for the engagement with Wagner other than those adopted by non-musicians. As musical Wagnerism spread through Europe and the United States, composers and critics tried to make use of (or resist) Wagnerian approaches while avoiding direct imitation. Writers, painters, sculptors, and architects, however, had the freedom to use Wagnerian ideas without threatening their originality. But both groups were fascinated by Wagner's new emphasis on the materiality of art, by his analysis of its constituent elements, and by his demand for their synthesis in some newly integrated, "total" artwork. Wagner thus opened the way to modernism with its ever increasing focus on the manipulation and meaning of the artistic medium itself.

Musical responses to Wagner

For composers, Wagner offered both challenges and promises. His theoretical writings claimed a new role for the musician-poet as a possible redeemer of modern society, while his music employed textural and sonic means that would influence compositional techniques not only in opera but also in symphony, symphonic poem, and song. Intertwined with these musical and aesthetic frameworks was the strong element of musical nationalism in Wagner's works and writings as well as in their musical and critical reception. Eventually, the very phenomenon of musical Wagnerism called forth a whole new pattern of negative responses, mainly in the earlier twentieth century, in an effort to get out from under the composer's suffocating influence.

Wagner's musical language was perceived as offering two important new pathways for composers. On the one hand, it contained such fascinating musical elements as expanded chromatic harmony, quasi-polyphonic voice leading, the dramaturgical use of orchestral timbre, and idiosyncratic combinations of instruments. On the other, Wagner offered fresh approaches to musical organization with his leitmotifs, his endless melody (related to Arnold Schoenberg's concept of "musical prose"), and his rebalancing of musical texture, especially in the relation of voice and orchestra. While many of these elements, even the so-called *Tristan* chord (F–B–D♯-G♯; perhaps his most famous harmonic signature), can also be traced to predecessors and contemporaries of Wagner, it was his use of them within a cohesive compositional and aesthetic framework that led to a near-universal Wagnerian influence on European music at the end of the nineteenth century.

The musical reception of Wagner might best be viewed in different lights depending on whether one is considering specific works (teasing out the separate strands defining the reception of, say, *Tannhäuser* and *Lohengrin*, on the one hand, or the *Ring* and the remaining music dramas, on the other), his musical output as a whole, or even just his theories of music drama. Broadly speaking, however, composers engaged with Wagner's musical language essentially in two different ways. Musicians such as Camille Saint-Saëns, Giacomo Puccini, or Nikolai Rimsky-Korsakov mined this language for those elements that could be incorporated into their own musical fabric just as they would appropriate elements of Beethoven, Verdi, or Gounod. Others, like Ernest Chausson, Henri Duparc, Augusta Holmès, Hugo Wolf, or Anton Bruckner tried to engage with the totality of Wagner's work and theories either to follow in his footsteps as composers of a new kind of opera ("music drama"), or to develop these Wagnerian impulses in other genres (the art song or the symphony).

Given Wagner's own compositional output and aesthetic hierarchies, music drama became the prime genre for composers to engage with Wagnerian models. Particularly in France, where opera had been regarded as a reflection of the "nation's image" since the founding of the Académie Royale de Musique under Louis XIV, the musical and dramatic challenges posed by Wagner became central to his reception as both a threat to, and potential savior of, this central genre.[4] In the first half of the nineteenth century, Paris had become not only the "capital of the nineteenth century," as Walter Benjamin famously put it but, more particularly, the center of European opera: French grand opera set the international standard for the genre, and the most important European venue even for Italian opera – especially between the 1820s and 1850s – was arguably the Parisian Théâtre Italien. Moreover, Franco-German relations were famously problematic throughout the nineteenth century, and Wagner's own love–hate relationship with Paris was fully reciprocated in both directions. Hence the irony that the first wave of musical Wagnerism was located within French opera. After discussions of Wagner's so-called system of composition from 1852 onward in journals such as the *Revue et Gazette Musicale de Paris*, and especially following the *Tannhäuser* scandal of 1861, Wagner became an unavoidable and controversial figure of reference, whether in critical discourse or compositional appropriation.[5]

We might identify three forms of Wagner reception in French musical theater: literary references, musical appropriations, and the notion of the "musician-poet." At first, Wagner's influence prompted a shift of opera plots from the traditional historical subjects of *grands opéras* such as Rossini's *Guillaume Tell* (1829), Meyerbeer's *Les Huguenots* (1836), or Verdi's *Vêpres siciliennes* (1855) – denounced by Wagner as distracting the audience through *faits divers* (assorted historical "headlines," so to speak) – to the realm of medieval legends, more apt for the presentation of eternal truths, in Wagner's view. Ernest Reyer's *Sigurd* (1884) – first conceived in the 1860s and based on a French translation of the *Nibelungenlied* – and Hector

Berlioz's *Les Troyens* (1863), which set the Latin (and by extension thus French) legend of the *Aeneid*, counted as Wagnerian operas, even though their musical organization was strongly rooted in the forms of *grand opéra*. French medieval legends became the literary sources of self-conscious choice in Wagnerian works of the 1880s and 1890s, as, for example, in Edouard Lalo's *Le roi d'Ys* (1888), Vincent d'Indy's *Fervaal* (1897), Claude Debussy's *Pelléas et Mélisande* (1902), and Ernest Chausson's *Le Roi Arthus* (1903). In this way, Wagner's influence could be melded with more inherently nationalist concerns, especially important after the French defeat in the Franco-Prussian war of 1870–71. The Wagnerian traits of Jules Massenet's *Esclarmonde* – premiered in May 1889 during the World's Fair as the Parisian opera to showcase French achievement on the musical stage – were avidly discussed by the Parisian press.[6] Journalists tried to show their philological erudition by exploring the medieval literary sources in great detail, assessing the literary pedigree of this French opera in contrast to Wagner's own uses of medieval literature.[7] Once Wagnerian rhetoric had established legendary epic as a source for operatic subjects, the trend could be emblematic even as it mutated. Thus, Gustave Charpentier's use of an urban "legend" – that of Montmartre – for his opera *Louise* (1900) might be viewed as much in the spirit of Wagnerism as the continued recourse to medievalism in works such as Lili Boulanger's unfinished *La Princesse Maleine* (1916–18).

Wagnerian influence extended far beyond mere subject matter. Massenet, Reyer, and Saint-Saëns tried to find a path that would integrate the self-consciously "French" compositional style of earlier *grand opéra* with Wagnerian elements of orchestration, motivic organization, and chromatic harmony. How self-conscious composers were about these choices can be seen in the score of *Esclarmonde*, where Massenet cites the *Tristan* chord when Esclarmonde's sister asks about her love interest in the hero Roland ("But you think of him?").[8] The musical pun – itself very Wagnerian, if one recalls that composer's self-quotation of *Tristan und Isolde* in the last act of *Die Meistersinger* – shows a high degree of self-reflexivity on the part of Massenet and his contemporaries when engaging with the sound-world of Wagner.

While these composers seem to have striven for the "happy medium" so characteristic of French aesthetics of the nineteenth century, others chose a far more difficult route of engagement. Taking on the entire "system" of music drama, Chabrier, Chausson, d'Indy, Holmès, and Debussy all tried to find their voices in the shadow of the German giant. Their letters reveal how difficult this was. Chausson wrote to Raymond Bonheur in the course of working on his Arthurian music drama, *Le Roi Arthus*: "Wagner, whom I no longer feel weighing on me when I write symphonic music, now haunts me terribly. I flee him as much as I can, but flee all I want, he is always here, near me, waiting for me very spitefully and making me write piles of things that I erase. I am very annoyed about this. I have to escape this devil of a man, however. It is a question of life or death."[9] Some months later, Debussy announced to Chausson that he had destroyed a scene from *Pelléas* because he discovered "the ghost of old Klingsor, alias R. Wagner," in some of its newly composed music.[10] At stake for these composers was success or failure in the nationalist enterprise of creating the modern French master-work, building on Wagner yet transcending him at the same time.[11] While Massenet could quote the *Tristan* chord as a kind of musical joke in *Esclarmonde*, Chausson and Debussy had to fight for artistic survival because their musical grammar and vocabulary was initially so dangerously close to Wagner's. And while later music historians have often tried to show the differences between those French composers and their model, the musicians themselves – who sought to achieve musico-dramatic organi-cism through Wagnerian uses of leitmotif, orchestration, and form – were deeply aware of the anxieties created by so strong an influence. Debussy's own quotations of *Tristan* in his *Prélude à l'après-midi d'un faune*, *Pelléas et Mélisande*, and even the satirical *Golliwogg's Cakewalk* are far more anxious, it seems, than Massenet's.

Wagner's impact on French opera was also evident in attitudes toward the libretto. No longer satisfied by the formal and stylized language of an Eugène Scribe or Michel Carré, many musicians looked for a different literary quality in playwrights such as Maurice Maeterlinck or Auguste Villiers de l'Isle Adam – a trend that would lead to the twentieth-century phenomenon of *Literaturoper*, that is, the setting of prose plays as operas. (Debussy's *Pelléas et Mélisande*, Richard Strauss's *Salome*, and Alban Berg's *Wozzeck* are prime examples.) Another trend adopted particularly in France was the notion of the musician-poet: Charpentier, Chausson, d'Indy, and Albéric Magnard all wrote their own librettos, as did, notably, a significant number of women composers. While this was originally born of necessity (access to professional librettists was scarce), female opera composers Célanie Carissan, Marie Clémence Vicomtesse de Grandval, Holmès, Marguerite Olagnier, Rita Strohl, and Pauline Thys could now point to the example of Wagner and his male disciples for validation of a practice that might otherwise be perceived as amateurish.[12] Indeed, in a review of Holmès's 1889 *Ode triomphale*, the critic praised her as the one French musician-poet worthy of Homer and Wagner, showing how widely this concept had penetrated French critical discourse.[13]

The French preoccupation with Wagner as the colossus looming over the operatic production of the later nineteenth and early twentieth centuries was increasingly shared by other European musical cultures. Especially in

Italy – a nation proud of its native operatic tradition – Wagner became an irritant. The *Lohengrin* craze in Bologna in the 1870s (following the first production of a Wagner opera in Italy) was something of an exception, and it stood in stark contrast with the wariness other leading operatic centers, such as Milan or Turin, exhibited toward the German composer.[14] But like French composers – and mediated through them – Italian composers started to engage with Wagnerian music and aesthetics. In the wake of efforts of the progressive poetic faction known as the Scapigliatura (including Verdi's later collaborator, Arrigo Boito) to forge a modern Italian literature, writers such as Ferdinando Fontana, with his tract *In teatro* (1884), found in Wagner a guiding spirit in the search for a renewed and modern musical theater. Composers responded to the challenge with alacrity. Like Massenet, Giacomo Puccini appropriated Wagnerian techniques, such as the use of leitmotifs, the dramaturgical use of orchestration, and declamatory musical prose, while retaining some of the formal structures of older opera. Prime examples for this approach are his *La Bohème* (1896) and *Tosca* (1900).[15] Indeed, both are through-composed and tightly organized through leitmotifs and timbral dramaturgy, while incorporating at least vestiges of traditional Italian arias and ensembles, as in Tosca's "Vissi d'arte" or Rodolfo's "Che gelida manina." Conceived as an Italian counter-cycle to Wagner's *Ring*, the musician-poet Ruggero Leoncavallo's project of a "Poema epico in forma di Trilogia Storica" was meant to bring the glory of Italy's past on the *fin de siècle* stage. Only the first opera of the trilogy, *I Medici* (1893), was ever finished – and Leoncavallo made his musical engagement with Wagner audible from the first moment with a quotation of the well-known Venusberg scene from *Tannhäuser*.[16]

Both Italy and France had faced in Wagner a powerful foreign figure who had publicly slandered their proud operatic traditions in print. In Germany itself, Wagner was a central participant in the musical development of the slowly forming nation, chastising fellow German musicians for their lack of vision. He became involved in controversies (the New German School, for example) whose focus was not necessarily opera, but instrumental music. Nevertheless, composers sympathetic to Wagnerian ideals – such as Peter Cornelius and Engelbert Humperdinck – found it almost impossible to escape the shadow of Wagner, as, for example, in Cornelius's *Der Cid* (1865) or Humperdinck's *Hänsel und Gretel* (1893).[17] But for them, and even for Hugo Wolf, comic opera provided a space relatively unthreatened by Wagnerism. They followed instead the successful traditions of Albert Lortzing and Friedrich von Flotow, whereas Wagner's *Die Meistersinger von Nürnberg* was, in any case, rarely viewed as a comic opera in the traditional sense. A later German attempt at a Wagnerian operatic cycle in August Bungert's *Homerische Welt* (1898–1903) remained marginal to

German music history.[18] It was not until Richard Strauss that a major German composer successfully confronted the Wagnerian challenges to music drama head-on. After the failure of the overtly Wagnerian music drama *Guntram* (1894) and the *succès de scandale* of the ribald one-act comedy *Feuersnot* (1901), Strauss found his voice as a post-Wagnerian opera composer in *Salome* (1905) and *Elektra* (1909). Both works count as key examples of *Literaturoper*, and Strauss's setting pushed the envelope of Wagnerian music in terms of through-composed prose setting, chromatic harmony, and orchestration.

Wagner reception in opera elsewhere in Europe and in the United States can be traced mainly through the recourse to medieval legends or other patriotic subjects associated with specific nation-building. Thus, in Finland, for example, Jean Sibelius began work on an opera based on legends from the national epic *Kalevala*, while in Russia Rimsky-Korsakov composed *Mlada* (1892), a music drama whose plot stemmed from the mythology of the Baltic Slavs, with overtones of the Norse mythology of Wagner's *Ring*.[19] Composers in other countries looked at medieval plots – for example, the Hungarian Ferenc Erkel in *Bánk bán* (1861) – folk legends, and fairy tales. In musical terms, the influence of Wagnerian music drama often remained limited to the use of leitmotifs, orchestral effects, and Wagnerian musical allusions within more traditional operatic forms, these remaining in the vein of either French *grand opéra*, middle Verdi, or the Wagner of *Rienzi* and the "Romantic" operas through *Lohengrin*.

While the operatic stage formed the center of musical Wagner reception, instrumental music became nevertheless an important locus of engagement with the composer. The symphony stood in need of a new legitimization in post-Wagnerian aesthetics after the infamous declaration in *Das Kunstwerk der Zukunft* (*The Artwork of the Future*; 1849) that the genre had died with Beethoven's Ninth Symphony. Wagner's attack needs to be seen in the context of the aesthetic debates in Germany in the middle of the nineteenth century, where symphonic music was celebrated as the acme of national musical accomplishment in a highly competitive European environment, whereas France and Italy maintained primacy in opera.[20] In order to wrest the claim to superiority from his operatic European neighbors as well as his German symphonic colleagues, Wagner identified music drama as the genre that not only fulfilled the potential of opera in its widest definition but also superseded the symphony in representing the highest of human aspirations in idealized form.[21] In response to these challenges, symphonic composers such as Anton Bruckner and Gustav Mahler in Austria tried to reconcile the ideologies of post-Wagnerian modernism as a cult of rupture, progress, sonic expansion, and the "artwork of ideas" with the aesthetic and formal demands of the post-Beethovenian symphony.[22] When Mahler wrote that symphony meant to him "constructing a world with all the resources of the available techniques," he transformed the rhetoric of the Wagnerian *Gesamtkunstwerk* into the realm of symphonic music.[23] The full spectrum of sonorities – from the apparently trivial sounds of pastoral cowbells in his sixth symphony to the massed choir and orchestra of the "Symphony of a Thousand" (No. 8) – was thus available to the composer to convey his *Weltanschauung* through the hallowed genre of the symphony, in which "in fact the whole world is mirrored."[24] The cyclic thematic structure associated with Beethoven was reinterpreted through the lens of Wagnerian leitmotivic organization in this reinvented symphonic genre of the *fin de siècle*; the chromatic harmony and rich orchestration associated, especially, with the sonic world of *Tristan* and *Parsifal*, could be employed as signifiers of musical modernity in works whose ever increasing length and scope created an ideological and musical mirror to Wagnerian music drama in the increasingly sacralized ritual of bourgeois concert life.

In France, this trend started with César Franck, whose D-minor Symphony (1888) not only paid homage to Beethoven's Ninth but explored Wagnerian (and Lisztian) techniques in its musical organization and language. Franck's pupils, especially Chausson and d'Indy, pushed this trend further, while simultaneously engaging in a nationalist rhetoric that pitted the French modernist development of the symphony against the alleged weaknesses of Johannes Brahms or the likes of Joachim Raff. Edouard Lalo's criticism of Brahms as symphonic composer is typical for this polemic, wherein he described the Second Symphony as a badly orchestrated piece of chamber music.[25] This ideological view of the symphony as an alternative to music drama, embodying messages of eternal truth, became seductive given that, with the shift from opera to instrumental music, it was less fraught with anxieties of influence. Hybrid works such as Mahler's *Das Lied von der Erde* (1909) and Schoenberg's *Gurrelieder* (1911) would push the boundaries of the Wagnerian symphony even further, as did the opulent synesthesia of Alexander Scriabin's *Poème de l'extase* (1905–08).

Musical Wagnerism also found its way into chamber music. Best known among these works is Schoenberg's string sextet *Verklärte Nacht*, op. 4 (1899), which might almost be read as an early modernist "cover" of Wagner's *Parsifal*, reversing the redemptive self-sacrifice of Kundry in life-affirming celebration of sexual ecstasy and human worldliness.[26] Schoenberg's chamber-musical *Gesamtkunstwerk* relies on a sophisticated listener's memory of the world of *Parsifal* (still only performed in Bayreuth at this time, but available as a score) and on her experience with nineteenth-century program music to decode the musical narrative.[27] Schoenberg's use of leitmotif, his expansion of Wagnerian chromaticism by pushing quasi-polyphonic voice-leading to extremes, and his references to *Parsifal* (in particular the quotation of "Kundry's laughter" in mm. 137–40 and the optimistic D-major ending of the work) create an intertextual engagement with Wagner that surely was not lost on his Viennese audience.

Not only instrumental music but also song provided a field for composers to engage with Wagner. Especially in France, song – whether accompanied by piano, ensemble, or orchestra – played with chromatic harmony and voice-leading in Wagnerian ways. Characteristic examples are such exquisite miniatures as Henri Duparc's *Phidylé* and *Invitation au voyage*, Gabriel Fauré's settings of Paul Verlaine, especially *La bonne chanson*, and Boulanger's *Clairières dans le ciel*. Indeed, the sixth song in Boulanger's cycle, "Dans l'immense tristesse," is built entirely on an ostinato motive drawn from the opening of *Tristan*. In Germany, Hugo Wolf's oeuvre reflects a new Wagnerian aesthetics of song composition, as do the song cycles by Mahler and Richard Strauss, while in Britain such composers as Amelia Woodeforde-Finden – especially in her "Kashmiri Song" from the *Four Indian Love Lyrics from "The Garden of Kama"* (1903) – draw on Wagner's chromatic harmony to infuse the Orientalist settings with sensuously modern sonorities. The song-cycle, however, that pushed the post-Wagnerian emancipation of dissonance and musical prose, as expressive means, to their limits was Schoenberg's *Buch der hängenden Gärten* (1908). When Richard Strauss, in his *Four Last Songs* (1948), had late recourse to Wagnerian sounds and textures, those formerly modernist sonorities had turned into self-conscious signifiers of musical nostalgia for that epoch of "Wagnerism" that was now long past.

Extra-musical Wagnerism

Fascinated by Wagnerian reflections on the materiality and interdependence of the arts in his theoretical writings, writers and visual artists also used Wagnerian notions of the *Gesamtkunstwerk* as a catalyst to explore their own methods of artistic production. Thus, the artistic medium (whether language or painting) was no longer transparent in the act of representation, but became itself an object of creative exploration. But if the self-conscious reflection on artistic materiality was one aspect of Wagnerism in the arts, a second strain can be found in more specific subject matters associated with Wagner: not only operas, but also plays inspired by Wagner delved into the abstraction of legends, pushing them further toward the investigation of the human psyche in all its facets, whether in the theater of the decadent movement (Oscar Wilde's *Salome* or Villiers de l'Isle-Adam's *Axel*) or in symbolist paintings (Odilon Redon, Gustave Moreau, or the English pre-Raphaelites).

Again, France acted as a prism for the development of Wagnerism in its broader sense, with poetry and literary criticism leading the avant-garde. From the late 1850s onwards, poets and writers picked up on the strange sonorities of Wagner's librettos, which Charles Nuitter, Alfred Ernst, and Victor Wilder had tried to render in French in such a way that the translations reflected the idiosyncrasies of Wagner's alliterative *Stabreim*.[28] In contrast to earlier conventions of libretto translation, where the foreign language was rendered in idiomatic French, these translations tried to capture what was specifically Wagnerian in the original German even to the detriment of comprehension in French. The syntax, sonorities, and often hermetic structure of Symbolist poetry by Baudelaire, Verlaine, and Mallarmé can thus be traced back to the order and choice of words in these translations. Prepared by reading the libretti and Wagner's theories about art (in particular his "Lettre sur la musique," published in Paris in 1860 and subsequently in German as *"Zukunftsmusik"*), poets such as Baudelaire opened themselves up to the experience of the performance of Wagner's music as a sonic revelation of artistic truth. Baudelaire's famous *Tannhäuser* essay and, later on, Mallarmé's equally influential "Richard Wagner: rêverie d'un poète français" (1885) became signal texts in the aesthetic foundation of French Symbolism. Wagnerian concepts such as the leitmotif and "word-tone melody" found their equivalent in the Symbolist poetics of "correspondence" – explored lyrically in Baudelaire's poem "Correspondances" from *Les Fleurs du mal* (1857), and in a more explicit form in Arthur Rimbaud's famous "Délires II" from *Une saison en Enfer* (1873), where he assigned specific colors (red, blue, green) to corresponding vowels:

> I have invented the color of vowels! – *A* black, *E* white, *I* red, *O* blue, *U* green. – I have decided upon the form and the movement of each consonant and, with instinctive rhythms, I have flattered myself to have invented a poetic word accessible, one day, to all senses. I reserved the translation for myself.[29]

Other poets took up the system of correspondence, in particular René Ghil who related instrumental timbres, colors, emotions, and letters in his *Traité du verbe* (1885), while Mallarmé claimed that his poetry was, in fact, music.[30]

By exploring the medium of poetic language and its "sonic" materiality, its ability to become expressive merely as sound, conflating signifier and signified, poets tried to forge an artistic tool that could express what was beyond the one-dimensional prose of words and reach what was deemed to be the "inexpressible." This poetic Wagnerism of the French Symbolists and Decadents was picked up in the 1880s and 1890s by the literary avant-garde of Europe and became melded with Freudian psychology (which itself had strong Wagnerist undertones, for example, in its reference to figures and archetypes of myth). This is reflected in the works of such diverse authors, and of diverse nationalities, as Richard Dehmel, Peter Altenberg, Stefan George, August Strindberg, Henrik Ibsen, Oscar Wilde, Gabriele d'Annunzio, and Hugo von Hofmannsthal. Even after World War I, neither Gertrude Stein's famous challenge to Symbolist complexity ("A rose is a rose is a rose") nor James Joyce's literary *Gesamtkunstwerk*, *Ulysses*, could have been written without the influence of European Wagnerism. Indeed, during the later nineteenth century and in the early decades of the twentieth, both the question of art's purpose in society and the continuous debate about language and meaning were shaped either in response to or rejection of Wagnerian concepts, whether openly or latently.

Painters were quick to latch on to these debates and to the possibilities they suggested to the creators of so representational an art-form as painting and engraving. Painting as taught at art schools all over Europe had rendered the medium itself invisible in the service of painterly perfection. The well-known portraits by Franz Xavier Winterhalter and Jean-Auguste-Dominique Ingres offer a good example of this academic approach to visual representation that had become normative by the middle of the century. But with the advent of photography as a mechanical rival to this form of painting, the medium and meaning of painting as the art so highly placed in the canon of artistic disciplines since the Renaissance – when painting and poetry were famously related in the claim that the visual in art should be expressive in a similar manner to the verbal (*ut pictura poesis*) – took on an urgent need of aesthetic justification. While already a point of discussion in the Romantic aesthetics of an Eugène Delacroix, Caspar David Friedrich, or William Turner, the self-conscious exploration of the painterly medium to convey emotion and significance that lay below the surface of the represented object received a new, avant-garde validation in the guise of Wagnerian aesthetics.

Just as the physical constituents of language were foregrounded by poets, the painterly elements of line, color, and form were explored as visible means of expression in themselves. Painters such as Pierre Bonnard, Paul Cézanne, and Paul Gauguin relied on Wagnerian ideas of leitmotif and tone-color when working toward an equivalent to rhythmic structure and musical organization in their use of specific colors and lines throughout the painting.[31] The tendency to outline an object – instead of aiming for a representation so perfect that it no longer seemed painted but real – became a means of alienation from the simple object character of the representation in order to create a more abstract composition of color, line, and form. This emotive and synesthesic use of painterly materiality found its full potential in the abstract compositions and experiments of, for example, the artists associated with the groups Der blaue Reiter and Die Brücke, and especially with works that themselves carried explicitly musical titles, such as Kandinsky's *Improvisations* of the 1910s, or Franz Marc's *Sonatine for violin and piano* (1913).[32] The well-known association of musicians with these circles (for example, Schoenberg with Der blaue Reiter or Mahler with the Vienna Secession) acted as a source of mutual influence, pushing a Wagnerist agenda well into the fields of modernism.

While on the one hand a new emphasis on the materiality of painting evolved as one aspect of visual Wagnerism, an issue more commonly associated with Wagnerian aesthetics is that of representation versus transcendence. In order to escape the realism and perceived banality of journalistic etchings and photographs that were too close to everyday life, painters tried to grasp in the grand subjects they associated with Wagner the deeper truths of the soul. The inclusion of symbolic objects, colors, and subjects – for example in Moreau's *Salome* paintings – reinterpreted a centuries-old tradition of painterly symbolism (found, for example, in Renaissance depictions of the Virgin and Child) within a rejuvenated vocabulary of Wagnerism. Furthermore, as in Wagnerian music drama, the subjects themselves were often influenced by the German composer. Some painters (Henri Fantin-Latour, for example) were famous for their renderings of scenes from Wagner's operas, while others – in particular the pre-Raphaelites, such as Edward Burne-Jones with his Percival cycle – found inspiration in Wagner's operas for their own explorations of medieval legends.

These trends were similarly influential in other art forms. Novels like Thomas Mann's *Buddenbrooks*, Leon Tolstoy's *War and Peace*, and Marcel Proust's *À la recherche du temps perdu* present self-conscious literary equivalents to Wagner's *Ring des Nibelungen* in constructing a complete, self-contained artistic world. D'Annunzio's Decadent novel *Il trionfo della morte* (1894) is but one literary reworking of the world of *Tristan*, full of references to the opera and to Wagner's own person and biography, and culminating in a forced love-death.

Yet it was in the context of the theater that the ideas of Wagner became most pervasive. As a dedicated space of theatrical cult based on Wagner's theories of the *Gesamtkunstwerk* and its staging, Bayreuth provided a model that galvanized producers and directors in all branches of theater. Influenced by Friedrich Nietzsche's reflections on the Wagnerian revival and ancient Greek drama in *The Birth of Tragedy* (1871) and by graphic artist and architect Peter Behrens, who hailed the modern theater as "celebrations of life" (*Feste des Lebens*), reformers such as Adolphe Appia and Edward Gordon Craig searched for a new, expressive drama that replaced Victorian realism with Symbolist and abstract stages that left behind the *fait divers* character to direct audiences' perception onto the deeper messages of the piece represented onstage.[33] One of Wagner's central notions – removing the separation of stage and audience – influenced in particular architects such as Erich Mendelsohn, Bruno Taut, and Henry van de Velde who dreamed of theaters that would break the traditional, box-like structure with its proscenium-framed stages by incorporating the structure of antique arenas or the spatial interaction of Japanese theater.[34] A key building in this movement was the Große Schauspielhaus in Berlin by the young architect Hans Poelzig, who redesigned the former Zirkus Schumann in 1919 as a monumental arena theater for the director Max Reinhardt. Greek tragedy, Shakespeare, and avant-garde were presented in a new "theater for the people" that had its ideological roots in Wagner's theories of a non-bourgeois and non-capitalist theater developed in his post-revolutionary Zurich writings of 1849–51 and further mediated through Nietzsche and others. Theatrical festivals, theoretically for the masses, were legitimized through these Wagnerian dramatic theories and the model of Bayreuth, either in antique arenas such as Béziers and later Verona, or in newly constructed buildings, like those of the Salzburg festival.

Indeed, during the high point of European Wagnerism across the turn of the nineteenth and twentieth centuries, musical Wagner reception and artistic Wagnerism could come together in theatrical festivals of this kind, as for instance when Déodat de Séverac's open-air spectacle *Héliogabale* was performed in the arena of Béziers, in Provence, before 15,000 spectators as an occasion to "educate the masses" through the "noble teachings of history and legend."[35] In this case, the Wagnerian claim to reviving Greek theater was countered with a nationalist French music drama, performed in a space whose link to antiquity was far more tangible than that of Bayreuth could ever claim. How strongly these French festivals of the *fin de siècle* were indebted to Wagnerian rhetoric is obvious from an earlier performance, which took place in the Orange amphitheater in 1894. Saint-Saëns, in the role of Wagnerian "musician-poet," wrote an *Hymne à Pallas Athénée* performed here by Lucienne Bréval. The singer, dressed in Greek costume, "sang the magnificent Greek liturgy under a large fig tree ... and with the sky forming the only ceiling of the theater, the beautiful pagan prayer rose freely to the caressing stars."[36] Saint-Saëns's hymn celebrated the rebirth of Greek drama, culture, and politics in its new Mediterranean successor (France), and thereby presented a barely disguised challenge to the German composer – once his hero, but by now an aesthetic and musical opponent.

By the turn of the twentieth century, Wagner had become a key figure in European culture, and by its middle his ideas had so permeated artistic and aesthetic discourses that their acceptance (or rejection) was less a statement of Wagnerism than the upholding or denying of presumed universal truths. As a writer who forged a theoretical system that placed art at the center of existence, in a position previously occupied by religion (or, in the case of G. W. F. Hegel, philosophy), Wagner had shifted the role of art from its traditional marginality in terms of politics, history, and economics. To this theoretical paradigm shift, Wagner's music added a seductive sound-world that swept away audiences and fellow musicians across Europe, challenging composers and inspiring painters, sculptors, and poets. But his theoretical and musical offerings contained a darker side that would become more and more obvious in the twentieth century. In the world of *Realpolitik*, the Wagnerian systems of a total work of art (*Gesamtkunstwerk*) translated easily into all-encompassing political total-itarianism, in which Hitler's "empire of a thousand years" could become a demagogue's artwork of the future. While this late and abusive stage of ideological Wagnerism delivered a belated *coup de grâce* to the phenom-enon, musical and aesthetic responses to Wagner still continue: the open-ing example of Shore's score for *The Lord of the Rings* will obviously not be the last.

14 Wagner and the Third Reich: myths and realities

PAMELA M. POTTER

The subject of music in Nazi Germany invariably elicits the name Wagner, whether as a reference to Hitler's legendary adulation of the composer, to the notorious admiration for Hitler on the part of the composer's (post-humous) daughter-in-law and Bayreuth festival director, Winifred Wagner, to the presumed prominence of Wagner's music in the Third Reich, or to Wagner's anti-Semitism as a harbinger of the extermination of European Jewry. Yet the multiple roles of "Wagner" – the man, the family, the works, and the cultural-ideological legacy – in the Third Reich cannot be understood without peeling away several layers of myth. While some of these myths arose in Hitler's Germany, most were inspired by German expatriates and developed from postwar debates resulting from the desperate attempts to explain how a highly cultured people could carry out such atrocities. Scholars have only recently begun to sort the myth from the reality in assessing the functions of Wagner and Bayreuth in Nazi culture, politics, and musical life. The following exploration will examine the many roles of the phenomenon of "Wagner" in the Nazi state, considering Nazi-era realities as well as their postwar historical interpretations and, sometimes, distortions.

"Wagner's Hitler" and "Hitler's Bayreuth"

Almost since the founding of the festival, Bayreuth had become a watering hole for right-wing pan-Germanists and the *Bayreuther Blätter* a forum for rabid nationalism and anti-Semitic dialogue, especially after World War I. As the fiftieth anniversary of Wagner's death, on 13 February 1933, occurred a mere fortnight after Hitler's assumption of power, *völkisch* Wagnerites seized the opportunity to promote the Wagner cause in the new political order. Reacting to Thomas Mann's sincere yet ambivalent tribute to Wagner ("The Sorrows and Grandeur of Richard Wagner"),[1] Munich's cultural luminaries lodged a formal protest accusing Mann of linking the master to Jewish–Marxist-inspired psychoanalysis and of degrading the works as amateurish. This led not only to Mann's exile but also galvanized Wagner's right-wing advocates to renew the composer's own notions of himself as a victim of Jewish intrigue and to see him as the inspiration for a new social and cultural order – in this case Hitler's. These events unleashed a series of attempts to seek connections between the two towering figures of Hitler and Wagner and to recklessly position the composer as a prophet of the Third Reich. Revisionist biographers repackaged Wagner as sowing the seeds of Nazi ideology in his writings; as a political opponent of France, liberalism, and the parliamentary system; and as a consistently racist anti-Semite, a prototypical German, and a proponent of subjugating art to the service of the nation. Each reinvention of Wagner conveniently ignored any aspects of his life and work that would clash with the Nazi worldview.[2]

The language that was used to link Wagner to Hitler was strong and emotional: designating Wagner as spiritual Führer,[3] alluding allegorically to the march from Bayreuth to Munich (where the Nazi Party had its beginnings),[4] representing the Third Reich as a fulfillment of Wagner's political goals,[5] and even asserting that Wagner would without a doubt have been a National Socialist and could be inducted into the party posthumously.[6] Wagner's essay "Judaism in Music" was cited as one of the first German attempts to come to terms with the "problem" of the Jewish race in Europe,[7] and musicologists were implored to continue Wagner's mission of getting to the bottom of the "Jewish question" (although only a small number actually heeded the call).[8] Instead they focused on analysis and critical editions of the works, biographical and genealogical studies, and documentary projects, many of which were to be carried out under the auspices of the incipient Richard Wagner Research Center at Bayreuth, a one-man operation founded by Otto Strobel in 1939 with Hitler's blessing.[9]

It was more the simultaneous musings of Germans in exile, however, that planted the seeds that would flower after the war into theories about Wagner's influence over Hitler, the Germans, and the extermination policies of the Nazi government. In 1937–38, exiled philosopher Theodor W. Adorno wrote an extensive musical and sociological analysis of Wagner's oeuvre and its impact on Germany, proposing that Wagner's *Ring* served the important function of providing the Germans with a much needed mythology and claiming to read anti-Semitism not only in Wagner's prose but also in several of his musical works.[10] In 1938, Thomas Mann's essay "Brother Hitler" placed the dictator as well as the author himself within an artistic lineage that could be traced back to Wagner,[11] and in 1941 Emil Ludwig cited Wagner as one of the most dangerous figures in German history.[12] The connection was further strengthened when, in November 1938, the Palestine Symphony Orchestra decided to refrain from performing the overture to *Meistersinger* after learning of the *Kristallnacht* pogrom, a decision that later sparked a hotly disputed ban on Wagner's music that has lasted to the present day.[13]

The ongoing controversy in Israel, combined with the suggestions that Wagner's writings established the roots of racial theory and that the operas contained anti-Semitic caricatures, have inspired a wealth of analyses and raised ethical questions about performing Wagner's music. Despite a prolonged period of silence in Germany on music in the Third Reich after the war, Hartmut Zelinsky came forward in 1976 (the centenary of the Bayreuth festival) with a daring attempt to trace "Bayreuth idealism" as an unbroken tradition from Wagner down to Hitler and a rich source of inspiration for Hitler's worldview.[14] That same year witnessed the shocking revelations of Winifred Wagner, whose ingenuous testimony to her undying loyalty to Hitler was cunningly caught on film by director Hans Jürgen Syberberg.[15] Shortly thereafter an issue of *Musik-Konzepte* dedicated to Wagner appeared with the subtitle "How Anti-Semitic May an Artist Be?"[16]

Over the years, the complex web of allegations linking Wagner and Hitler have drawn not only on nationalism, anti-Semitism, and an ideal of racial purity, but also on Hitler's attraction to Wagnerian heroes (including the supposition that the "Führer" designation was inspired by the conclusion to *Lohengrin*), his modeling the title of *Mein Kampf* on that of Wagner's autobiography *Mein Leben*, the similarity of his formulation in *Mein Kampf* of his decision to enter politics with a parallel statement by Wagner, and their common ability to turn politics into mythology and mythology into history.[17] There have even been references to shared behavioral traits such as self-praise, theatricality, pomposity, reckless determination, belief that all had to be destroyed in order to build anew, and even vegetarianism and love of dogs.[18] More recently, Joachim Köhler's provocatively titled *Wagner's Hitler* fully explores the possibility of Hitler's fulfillment of Wagner's prophecies, citing Wagner as the chief source for Hitler's anti-Semitism and program of genocide. A recent conference on Wagner and the Third Reich shows how, if somewhat qualified by conflicting evidence, these affinities are still being explored and analyzed.[19]

Yet while there may indeed exist a larger framework of intellectual traditions and political ideologies embracing both Wagner and Hitler, clear evidence of direct connections between the two is difficult to pin down. Any attempt to isolate Wagner's and Hitler's political and ideological similarities forces both figures into two-dimensional portrayals, crediting both of them with an unrealistic degree of consistency and single-mindedness throughout their careers. Furthermore, there is no clear evidence that Hitler's familiarity with Wagner extended beyond an enthusiasm for the music.[20] Casting aside the large accumulation of rumor, Dina Porat has painstakingly exposed the futility of finding concrete connections between Wagner and Hitler, insisting that any of Hitler's inspirations drawn from Wagner were highly personal, limited to his admiration for Wagner's music, and without explicit reference to any of Wagner's published anti-Semitic statements.[21]

Yet even if Hitler's obsession with Wagner may not have driven him to comb Wagner's writings for political inspiration, his youthful infatuation with Wagner's music did drive him to make the pilgrimage to Bayreuth in 1923, shortly before the festival reopened after a ten-year hiatus in the wake of World War I. As a young man Hitler had been thoroughly enchanted by Wagner's music and was also attracted to the anti-Semitic writings of Wagner's son-in-law, Houston Stewart Chamberlain, author of the most respected racially based anti-Semitic treatise of the time, *The Foundations of the Nineteenth Century* (which, incidentally, mentions Wagner only sparingly and makes no reference to his anti-Semitic writings[22]). In 1923, while holding a rally in Bayreuth, Hitler had an opportunity to meet with and deeply impress the ailing Chamberlain as well as to forge friendships with Siegfried and Winifred, the latter of whom not only idolized Hitler but also gained him access to Munich's social elite. Following the *Putsch* that led to Hitler's imprisonment in Landsberg, Winifred publicly defended Hitler while sending him food and paper during his incarceration (contrary to the widespread myth, this was probably not the paper used to write *Mein Kampf*).[23] Although Hitler had to distance himself from Bayreuth, at least publicly, in the late 1920s to keep politics out of the establishment, he surreptitiously kept up his relationship with the Wagner family. Within two weeks of becoming chancellor, he openly renewed his ties by ceremoniously celebrating the fiftieth anniversary of Wagner's death in Leipzig along with Winifred, Wolfgang, and other political and cultural leaders.[24]

As chancellor, Hitler was not only a frequent and honored guest at Bayreuth and paternal figure to the Wagner children (their father Siegfried having died in 1930), he was also a benefactor. Each year he purchased tens of thousands of marks worth of tickets, he provided over 50,000 marks for each new production, he arranged for the festival to be held every year starting in 1938, and in 1940 he provided for half a million marks to keep the festival running.[25] From 1934 onward, the festival also benefited from its association with the "Strength through Joy" program (Kraft durch Freude), the cultural and recreational branch of the massive Nazi labor organization (Deutsche Arbeitsfront, or DAF), which offered discounted prices and tour packages to workers.[26] Winifred wanted to suspend the festival when the war broke out, but Hitler averted its closure by designating it an official wartime festival, opening it up to soldiers and workers and thereby facilitating government subsidies.[27] Hitler's move was not merely a gesture of goodwill toward the culture-starved: the Bayreuth festival was actually suffering, and the Nazi government could boost attendance by bringing in workers and soldiers. Hitler's support of Bayreuth also had foreign-policy benefits: the international significance of the festival was something he could not easily ignore, and his visible patronage lent cultural prestige to a regime otherwise regarded as barbarian by the outside world.[28] Hitler even used Bayreuth and its personnel to conduct foreign policy, carrying on diplomacy at the festival complex, offering productions as gifts to foreign leaders, and sending festival stars abroad as artistic ambassadors.[29]

It is undeniable that Bayreuth became a showpiece for the Third Reich as well as one of Hitler's pet projects, but mythology further embellished the associations both during and after the Third Reich. Rumors of an impending marriage of Hitler and Winifred proliferated during the years he was in power, and Winifred's undying devotion to Hitler long after the end of the war was the unsettling centerpiece of Syberberg's 1976 film.[30] The next generation of Wagners (specifically Winifred's sons) initially shunned or downplayed that relationship, but their children felt the need to exorcise any remaining demons, publicly denouncing the family's ties with Hitler and, in the process, possibly exaggerating the extent of its infamous complicity. Inspired by their aunt Friedelind's rejection of the family's cozy relationship with Hitler,[31] Richard's great-grandchildren Gottfried and Nike have further emphasized the family's dark side. Nike critiques the Wagner and Bayreuth legacies in the context of German cultural history and scrutinizes her grandmother Winifred's testimonies for lies and inaccuracies, and Gottfried in his autobiography traces his lifelong preoccupation with uncovering the truth about the Nazis and breaking his family's enduring silence on their political past.[32]

The music and the dramas

Perhaps the most contentious question is the extent to which Wagner's stage-works reinforced or even inspired the National Socialists' aggressively imperialist and murderous aims. Much disagreement has arisen regarding allegations of the musical works' inherently nationalistic and anti-Semitic content, their prominence on the opera stages of Hitler's Germany, and their use in the concentration camps to accompany inmates to their deaths. *Die Meistersinger* and *Parsifal* have generated the most debate, owing both to their potential ideological messages and to their specific performance history in the Third Reich: *Meistersinger* for its nostalgic and nationalistic implications as well as its pride of place in official Nazi Party events, and *Parsifal* for its allusions to Aryan racial purity and Hitler's personal intervention to honor Wagner's wishes to restrict its performance to Bayreuth. *Lohengrin*, the *Ring*, and *Rienzi* have posed different challenges to those seeking to assess Wagner's impact on Nazi musical life and Hitler's personal connections to these works. In the end, however, presumptions about Wagner's potential ideological significance for the Nazis inevitably weaken when one considers the documented decline of Wagner productions on German stages and, with a few notable exceptions, minimal evidence of Nazi exploitation of those productions for political or ideological purposes.

The ongoing scrutiny of Wagner's potential influence on Hitler and of Hitler's conspicuous presence in Bayreuth has tended to overshadow the facts about the performance of Wagner's works during the Third Reich. Although Hitler took a serious interest in the further existence of the Bayreuth festival, Wagner's music suffered in the general repertoire throughout the rest of Germany. The Wagner cult, which had been so prominent in the late nineteenth century, was a thing of the past. The youth movement and its successor, the Hitler Youth, shunned Wagner as well as all other individualist excesses of Romanticism in favor of communal music-making and folk song, while young composers of the 1920s and 1930s saw no purpose in continuing along Wagner's path.[33] Productions of Wagner operas fell off dramatically after 1926, lagging far behind those of Verdi, Puccini, Mozart, and Lortzing; by 1942–43 the most popular operas on the German stages were *Madama Butterfly*, *Tosca*, and *La Bohème*.[34]

The feeble attempts during the Third Reich to repopularize Wagner's music had only limited success. Although Richard Eichenauer in his study on music and race identified Wagner's harmony as a manifestation of his Germanic racial lineage and praised it for its "simplicity" and "clarity,"[35] Wagner's music had in fact become too inaccessible for the general audiences of an emergent mass culture. Attempts to integrate his music into the school curriculum resulted only in awkward simplifications of the music in the form of marches to make it playable for young students.[36] Certain Wagner "hits" were cut up and used as background music for the propaganda films of Leni Riefenstahl, newsreels, and radio announcements. But these were only token gestures and made no progress in getting a broad band of listeners interested in Wagner's music; and, in any case, the music of Beethoven and Bruckner was just as widely exploited for such purposes.[37]

That being said, certain Wagner works undoubtedly enjoyed special status at state and party events, with *Die Meistersinger* earning a particular pride of place. In the early years of the new party, the Nazi press called special attention to *Meistersinger* performances and, from 1933 on, the work rose in prominence as the centerpiece of official ceremonies. The Leipzig commemoration of Wagner's death which Hitler attended featured the Prelude, and a full production at the Berlin State Opera concluded the Day of Potsdam in March 1933, the event staged to mark the beginning of a new era in Germany and accompanied by a dramatic torchlight parade on Unter den Linden.[38] Opening the 1933 Bayreuth festival, *Meistersinger* was not only broadcast on German radio but was also accompanied by a radio address by propaganda minister Joseph Goebbels. Hitler reportedly added an air of respectability to the festivities by requesting that the audience refrain from singing the national anthem or "Horst Wessel" song at the end of the production, as had become the custom since 1924, and Goebbels's lengthy radio address used the opportunity to designate the opera as the most appropriate work in all of German literature and art for expressing the present spiritual struggles of the German nation. He dwelled on the timeliness of the final "Wach auf!" ("Awake!") chorus as a call for the German nation to rouse from its deep political and spiritual narcotic state that persisted throughout the years of the Weimar Republic. He maintained that only in present conditions could Wagner ever be fully appreciated, crediting Hitler with giving Bayreuth the importance it deserved by honoring it with his presence. He then declared the work "the incarnation of our nationhood [*Volkstum*]" and ended his speech with a misquotation of the final chorus of *Meistersinger* (Goebbels omitted the words in square brackets: "Therefore I say to you: honor your German masters! [Then you will conjure up good spirits; and if you should favor their endeavors,] even should the Holy Roman Empire dissolve in mist, for us there would still remain holy German art!").[39] When Goebbels presided over the official opening of the Reich Culture Chamber in November of the same year, the "Wach auf!" chorus followed his inaugural speech.[40]

The work gained even more political currency when Hitler declared that its full production should become a regular feature of the Nuremberg party rallies beginning in 1935. Observers seized on the symbolic significance of this coupling, seeing it as final retribution for the "Jewish" attempts to thwart its premiere in Nuremberg during Wagner's lifetime and crediting Hitler for preserving the integrity of the work by linking it with the party festivities.[41] *Meistersinger* also held special significance during the war. In 1943, the Bayreuth festival averted closure but was scaled down to stage only one work, *Meistersinger*, to which Hitler invited 30,000 soldiers and workers to attend sixteen special performances. Robert Ley, head of the DAF, addressed the invited audience and reminded them that they were about to see the finest example of the German culture they were struggling to preserve. Ley, emulating Goebbels's radio broadcast, also ended his speech with the lines from the final chorus glorifying "holy German art."[42]

The political exploitation of *Meistersinger* during the Third Reich has caused postwar interpreters to jump to conclusions about the work's larger ideological relevance for the Nazi regime and its policies. Yet it is important to consider that the festive and ceremonial nature of the work, rather than implications of xenophobia, may have led to this exploitation, especially given that such uses of *Meistersinger* were not limited to the Nazi years in Germany.[43] More important, however, is the way in which the political prominence of the work has been distorted into a rationale for the Holocaust, as postwar debates have focused not so much on its ceremonial exploitation but rather on the presumed anti-Semitism in the characterization of Beckmesser. Recent exposés by Barry Millington and Marc Weiner have found the Beckmesser character to provide some of the most convincing evidence of Wagner's anti-Semitism and its enduring legacy in the Third Reich.[44] Yet the close examinations of David Dennis and Thomas Grey have uncovered not one shred of evidence that Nazi-era audiences or music critics ever picked up on any Jewish traits in the character of Beckmesser. Surely, had there been any anti-Semitic stereotypes, Nazi stage directors would have exploited them and critics would have noticed them.[45]

The prominence of *Lohengrin*, *Parsifal*, and *Rienzi* came nowhere near that of *Meistersinger* in the Third Reich but nevertheless was noteworthy. In 1936, *Lohengrin*, no longer in the repertoire, was revived to celebrate the one thousand years since the death of Henry the Fowler (commemorated in the opera). Hitler orchestrated a revival and financed a lavish new production, which was broadcast on international radio.[46] In the case of *Parsifal*, Hitler was intent on honoring Wagner's wish that Bayreuth have exclusive performance rights within Germany, and, when that did not succeed, he played a significant role in mounting a new Bayreuth production with designer Alfred Roller in 1934.[47] Zelinsky and others, however, have interpreted Hitler's attentiveness to the opera as evidence of *Parsifal*'s potential meaning for the Nazis' goals to preserve racial purity and eliminate the Jews. Zelinsky interpreted the work as consistent with the National Socialist aims to privilege a German-Aryan form of Christianity over such "Judaized" incarnations as Catholicism and to promote an ideology of blood and race. He further regarded Kundry as representing the Jews and her baptism and redemption through death as an omen for the Final Solution.[48] It seems, however, that Hitler actually harbored misgivings about the work and especially during the war contemplated secularizing it as much as possible, while Goebbels, Rosenberg, and Himmler deemed it "ideologically unacceptable" and were even determined to terminate any further productions of this overly "pious" and "emotional" display.[49]

Rienzi, in spite of its overt debt to the grand operas of Meyerbeer, gained prominence in the Third Reich as the work that got Hitler "hooked" during a 1905 performance, and thereafter its overture was featured at the opening of the party rallies. On his fiftieth birthday, Hitler received the autograph full score of *Rienzi* as a gift and presumably took it with him to the bunker where it was most likely destroyed. Saul Friedländer regards *Rienzi* as even more central to Hitler's anti-Semitic motives than *Parsifal*, dismissing the latter as too mild in its implied solution to the Jewish problem. Despite its presentation of a leader who ultimately causes his own downfall, *Rienzi*, Friedländer maintains, inspired Hitler by justifying political and ideological fanaticism.[50] In the case of both works, the earliest and latest of the canonic Wagner operas, Friedländer's assertions become problematic when one considers, first, that Hitler never expressed any of the connections attributed to him, either publicly or privately, and that the production of these operas in the Third Reich was so infrequent that the ideological messages they allegedly bore would not have had much opportunity to be broadcast. In Hamburg, for example, the number of *Parsifal* productions fell dramatically in the 1930s, and the opera was banned throughout the Reich midway through the war on the order of Goebbels, while *Rienzi* was the only opera not to have been treated to a new production in the Nazi years.[51]

There are, to be sure, various allusions to the propagandistic value of the operas in the observations of music critics, individual Wagner fans, and Nazi ideologues. Critics praised productions that highlighted the "heroic" and "populist" aspects of the works, and they might take it upon themselves to cite ideologically pertinent audience responses (for instance, one woman's remark about Lohengrin as the quintessential, pure-blooded Aryan male, whose noble character could only belong to members of the white race in its purest form).[52] The leading Nazi ideologue, Alfred Rosenberg, recognized the Nordic beauty-ideal in the characters of Lohengrin and Siegfried, and Nordic perseverance in the characters Tristan and Isolde, even though in other contexts he did not hesitate to expound upon the problems he had with Wagner's works in general.[53] The imagery of the sword-wielding, dragon-slaying Siegfried was exploited in war propaganda, and the *Ring* as a whole was cited by Nazi critics for glorifying the preservation of a pure and noble Germanic race.[54] But it was actually Adorno, as mentioned above, who more systematically theorized the *Ring*'s importance in providing the Germans with a much needed mythology. As Adorno points out, its themes of honor, duty, violence, and revenge fulfilled the requirements of mythology by displaying onstage actions that were proscribed by civil codes of conduct, attributing all such acts ultimately to the rule of Fate.[55] Later scholars have elaborated upon Adorno's insights into potentially anti-Semitic components in the characterizations of Alberich and Mime.[56] But even if anti-Semitic connotations in the character of Mime might have been obvious to nineteenth-century audiences,[57] there is no more evidence here than in the case of Beckmesser in *Die Meistersinger* that any such interpretation was actually exploited during the Third Reich.[58] Indeed, with regard to Nazi-era productions in general, Jens Malte Fischer has argued that even in Bayreuth artistic freedom continued to reign, as "Jewish" singers were retained for their talent, and luminaries of the Weimar years with modernist and even Marxist backgrounds (e.g., Heinz Tietjen and Emil Preetorius) launched productions that were just as controversial as the postwar experiments under Wieland Wagner.[59]

Was Wagner's music, then, in any way actively applied to the promulgation of anti-Semitism during the years of the Third Reich? Despite the gruesome allegations of its use to accompany the murder of inmates of the death camps, any anti-Semitic policies linked to Wagner's music were generally limited to assuring that it not be "tainted" by Jewish hands. For example, with the founding of the Jewish Culture League (a joint effort by the Jewish community and the Nazi government to forestall the economic side effects of throwing Jews out of work, while still isolating them from German cultural life), Nazi officials overseeing the music programs were so vague in outlining their prohibitions on Jews performing "German" works that Jewish leaders took it upon themselves to advise against playing Wagner, Weber, or Lortzing in an act of self-censorship.[60] The idea of Jews "defiling" Wagner was reinforced in the 1938 "Degenerate Music" exhibit, which cited Otto Klemperer's controversial *Fliegende Holländer* (*Flying Dutchman*) production at the Kroll Opera in 1929 (whose provocative element was really Ewald Dülberg's modernistic stage designs) and his *Tannhäuser* at the Berlin State Opera as incidents of "Jews against Wagner."[61] We also know from testimonies that concentration camp orchestras played music from operettas, symphonic classics, popular tunes, and even Yiddish folk melodies but that Wagner was explicitly off-limits.[62] However, after the war, unsubstantiated claims that Wagner's music accompanied Jews to their death took on momentum, probably as a response to a new, broader public awareness of Wagner's anti-Semitic writings, of the Wagner family's relationship to Hitler, and of the exploitation of Wagner's legacy in the Third Reich. The disintegration of German–Israeli relations in the 1970s contributed to a raging controversy from the 1980s on about whether or not to play Wagner's music in Israel.[63]

This particular association illustrates most graphically the moral conundrum posed by mentioning Wagner and the Nazis in the same breath and the ethical implications for continuing to stage Wagner's work. The controversy in essence has much less to do with the man or the music than with the psychological associations invoked by his image. The question of performing Wagner in Israel has less to do with Wagner's own attitudes toward the Jews, the content or quality of the music, or even its putative uses and abuses in the hands of the Nazis, and more to do with the horrible memories it conjures up in the minds of Holocaust survivors, who still form a vocal, if no longer numerous, part of the concert-going public in Israel. The dilemma reaches far beyond this small group of concert-goers, however, as the atrocities carried out in the name of German culture have projected a distasteful image onto Wagner as a symbol of German arrogance, paranoia, and xenophobia, despite the irony that the potential anti-Semitic and nationalist implications in his work, so diligently identified and analyzed since the Holocaust, may have been largely misunderstood, even ignored, in Nazi Germany. The revelation of German atrocities after the war forced all thinking individuals in the Western world to reconcile the irreconcilable: that the nation that produced Goethe, Beethoven, and, indeed, Wagner could also be the nation drawn to Hitler, Nazism, and genocide.

15 Wagner on stage: aesthetic, dramaturgical, and social considerations

MIKE ASHMAN

> There is no living style in the theater other than that of its time, whether it strikes future generations as unbearable *kitsch* or as greatness worthy of imitation. WIELAND WAGNER

Did Richard Wagner invent the modern opera stage director?[1] Or, at least, did the scenic and dramaturgical requirements of his stage-works establish the function of stage direction as a necessary and integral part of modern opera production? The answers to these questions – a qualified and a definite "yes," respectively – have been frequently confirmed during the last half-century, a time when Wagner stagings have been perceived increasingly as a touchstone for major trends and styles of opera production worldwide. The main focus of the present chapter will be on Wagner stagings since the first postwar Bayreuth festival of 1951; but it is necessary first to consider some aspects of the first hundred years of Wagner onstage.

Wagner directs Wagner

Richard Wagner grew up, worked, and died in an age where there were no specialist opera directors. Stage productions were realized by a haphazard combination of stage manager, ballet master, composer, librettist, conductor, principal male singer, and (occasionally) a dramaturg.[2] This tradition – or rather lack of one – died hard. As late as 1855 so theatrical a composer as Verdi could write with naïve delight about a newly published pamphlet prescribing the *mise-en-scène* of *Les vêpres siciliennes* that now "any child could do the staging."[3] Wagner himself had to be involved twice with compromised stagings of *Der fliegende Holländer* (*The Flying Dutchman*; the Dresden premiere in 1843 and his improvised Zurich "festival" of 1852) before confessing to Liszt that he had finally learned "with much trouble and toil, how important to this opera the décor is" (2 May 1852; *SB* IV:484–85).

What he termed "the vulgar stage career" of his work began for Wagner with his "shouting drastic directions concerning the necessary movement" at the hastily assembled Magdeburg premiere of *Das Liebesverbot* (*The Ban on Love*) in 1836. Struggling to achieve adequate first productions of *Rienzi*, *Der fliegende Holländer*, and *Tannhäuser* in Dresden encouraged

15.1. *Götterdämmerung*, Act 3 (conclusion): stage design by Josef Hoffmann for the first Bayreuth festival, 1876.

him to begin a lifelong campaign for detailed musico-dramatic preparation of opera for the stage, in a fine detail that no composer would approach until the collaboration between Puccini and the Ricordi house in the 1900s. After two production *débâcles* at supposed centers of operatic excellence (the *Tannhäuser* scandal in Paris in 1860–61 and the aborted attempt at a premiere of *Tristan und Isolde* in Vienna, 1862–63) Wagner called for a continuous working collaboration between chief musical coach, conductor, and stage director. The latter, who must be appointed with "a care entirely unknown as yet," was to be "an official of equal standing with the two other collaborators." By the time of his work on the Munich premiere of *Die Meistersinger* (June 1868) – the third and dramatically best realized of his "model" productions for King Ludwig II – Wagner had invented for himself the idea of a production "team," comprised of an arbiter and supreme demonstrator (here the composer himself), a "stage manager" to look after the details of business, props, and characters' exits and entrances, and an adventurously used choreographer.[4] At the first Bayreuth festivals he refined this plan: he himself became the stage director of the first complete *Ring* (1876) and of *Parsifal* (1882), supported by a choreographer-cum-assistant director and a number of music staff, some of whom fulfilled the present-day function of stage management.

Hagiographic accounts of Wagner's passion and skill for demonstrating movement and atmosphere in rehearsal – and for impersonating characters, especially his "villains" – are as legion as they are imprecise.[5] The least reverential (and best) comes from Richard Fricke, the Dessau ballet master who was the choreographer and assistant stage director for the 1876 Bayreuth *Ring* (and the 1882 Bayreuth *Parsifal*). His summary of the composer/director's work noted that "he just has to sweat out all over again what he has been through in composing the piece . . . in this frame of mind he is compelled to block a scene and then do it differently another day."[6] These much-remarked changes of mind suggest less the excitable, absent-minded genius than the improvisatory stage director-as-*auteur*, more interested in the psychological *Gestalt* of a scene than the blocking of ordinary exits and entrances.

The purely technical demands of Wagner's operas (especially the scenic transformations required in *Tannhäuser*, the *Ring*, and *Parsifal*) are as great – and have always been as much discussed – as their dramatic and musical ones.[7] But while the composer's passion for fine detail and a naturalism in operatic acting (then rarely experienced) made important new demands on his singing actors, the visionary mobility of his stage directions frequently outstripped the imaginative faculties of the nineteenth-century court theater painters and the technical facilities at their disposal. Even though Wagner's design teams for Bayreuth were novel – a mix of artists and even academics working in tandem with studio designers, all in closely supervised collaboration with himself as stage director – their achievements (in comparison with, say, the Saxe-Meiningen theater company toward the end of the century) still appeared bound to a dated historical realism. Only in staging *Parsifal* did Wagner begin to escape from a naturalistic (or historical) basis for his scene settings and properties, bullying the painter Paul von Joukowsky to design flowers for Klingsor's magic garden so enormous "that the maidens might seem to grow out of them" and (recalling hints from Fricke during the *Ring* rehearsals) reducing and stylizing the movement in the ground production.[8]

Wagner without Wagner

The famous comment made to Fricke regarding the planned (but unrealized) 1877 revival of the *Ring* cycle at Bayreuth following the 1876 premiere – "next year we'll do everything differently" – suggests that Wagner had no belief at all that he was handing down a tradition of production for his works. Notwithstanding, his widow Cosima – jumping into a breach for which she (and other members of the family) had little professional training – maintained that "the creator of dramas from the spirit of music has left us with everything for the performance of his works in the most precise detail. Even the lighting of individual figures or groups at various dramatic moments is quite fixed."[9] When she extended the repertoire of the Bayreuth festival beyond the *Ring* and *Parsifal*, she based her work on earlier productions with which her husband had in some way been involved, turning (as her grandson Wieland was to observe) "the virtue of fidelity into the sin of fossilization."[10]

Cosima's curatorial attitude made it increasingly clear to outside observers of Bayreuth (and of imitation productions in other leading opera houses) that the attempt to confine the music dramas to the pictorial world of nineteenth-century grand opera meant imprisoning them.[11] Heralded by the writings of the Swiss scenographer Adolphe Appia (1862–1928), the first new staging theories concerned the performing space and the possibility of establishing dramas of the mind, rather than dramas of specific location.[12] Following the composer's own recorded thoughts, Appia believed that Wagner's "vision" issued "from the womb of music," that "the means to achieve a fusion between actor and scenic environment did not exist before the advent of Wagnerian drama," and that the music contained "the drama's *original* life."[13] He proposed a greatly enhanced role for lighting, a reduction of scenery to symbols of the physical and psychological action, a simplification and stylization of costume, and a manner of acting based more on dance than on conventional theatrical style. Although the fullest realization of these aims had to wait, at least on the Wagnerian stage, until the work of Wieland Wagner in the 1950s, Appia's writings and drawings rapidly began to influence stage designers in the years leading up to World War I.[14] In Vienna in 1905 Alfred Roller (with conductor Gustav Mahler as his close collaborator, and as stage director in all but name) cleared the relics of 1876 Bayreuth clutter out of the company's new *Rheingold*; Valhalla became "a jumbled, unreal heap of Cyclopean blocks" and a huge color range was implemented in the lighting plan.[15] With the operatic debut of theater director Vsevolod Meyerhold in St. Petersburg (1909), Alexander Chervachidze reduced the sets for *Tristan* to just a single sail, castle walls, rocks, and a cyclorama. In Freiburg (1913) Ludwig Sievert took up directly Appia's suggestion of envisioning the Grail temple in *Parsifal* as a kind of petrified forest, thus making for a symbolic (and smooth) transformation from the exterior domain of the Grail into the temple in Act 1.

15.2. *Der fliegende Holländer*: design for the Dutchman's ship by Ewald Dülberg for the Kroll Opera, Berlin, 1929.

The intentionally provocative productions on the European continent in the post-1918 period – an age that, from a cultural viewpoint, seemed, in Otto Klemperer's apposite phrase, "in opposition to Wagner" – helped prove the composer's dramaturgy in new fires. A classic example was the *succès de scandale* of the Berlin Kroll Opera's production of *Der fliegende Holländer* of 1929, directed by Jürgen Fehling, designed by Ewald Dülberg, and conducted by Klemperer (using the original Dresden "blunt ending" version of the score). The production was staged in modern dress on a luridly colored, Bauhaus-influenced set shorn of any architectural reality; the cast acted in the expressionist style of contemporary art films like Fritz Lang's *Metropolis*. A supporting publicity essay by Ernst Bloch was entitled *Rettung Wagners durch surrealistische Kolportage* (*Surrealist Intervention as Wagner's Salvation*). The conservative, increasingly Nazi-dominated press accused the Kroll of "cultural Bolshevism," perhaps the first of many times that experimental Wagner directors have been branded as left-wing crazies. Other productions of the time that took a new look at Wagner's dramaturgy and scenography were created in Darmstadt by Arthur Maria Rabenalt, in Berlin by the team of Franz Ludwig Hoerth/Emil Pirchan, and in Duisburg by Saladin Schmitt/ Johannes Schroeder[16] – their Appia-influenced *Ring* especially annoying

Siegfried Wagner, who dismissed it as "Expressionist colored light music" (almost exactly the words used by his wife Winifred to describe the 1950s productions of their son Wieland).

Further radicalism in German Wagner staging was soon halted by the imposition of the new Nazi government's ultraconservative and reductive artistic policies. An exemplar of this style was shown at Nuremberg in 1935 when the Reichsbühnenbildner Benno von Arendt was instructed to provide *Die Meistersinger* with a flag-lined festival meadow for Act 3, reminiscent of the Parteigelände staging field for Hitler rallies just down the road. Ironically, Bayreuth itself – protected by Chancellor Hitler's close personal interest – entered a period of cautious experimentation following the deaths of Cosima and Siegfried Wagner in 1930. With designers such as Emil Preetorius and Alfred Roller, the stage shapes at least – if not the ground productions – revealed a constructive awareness of both Appia's geometry and more recent expressionist ideas.[17]

Postwar revolutions

Apart from those few, largely exceptional developments in Bayreuth, the war years put experimentation with staging Wagner into the deep freeze. In the occupied European areas, this was due to Nazi ideology, while the ideas of Appia and the expressionists had still not traveled abroad to the Americas by that time, at least in the realm of opera. The era since World War II, however, has witnessed a series of revolutions in the staging of Wagner and of opera in general, at least in Western Europe. The first major new trend was embodied in the stripped-down or denaturalized settings of shapes and light created by Wieland Wagner at Bayreuth and other German houses in the years 1951–66 for his own ground productions with stylized but intense psychological confrontation between characters. Wieland's work and influence put the theories of Appia, and the ambitions of prewar intellectual iconoclasts, onto German opera stages and soon onto stages around the world.

A second trend evolved from the realistic "music theater" style of opera staging developed by Walter Felsenstein at Berlin's Komische Oper between 1947 and his death in 1965. It was continued and expanded by his disciples Joachim Herz (mainly in Leipzig) and Götz Friedrich.[18] Herz chose to remain in communist East Germany (the DDR), and his first group of Wagner productions did not receive their due attention elsewhere. Friedrich's first Wagner productions were in the West in the 1970s: a Bayreuth *Tannhäuser* and a London *Ring*. An offshoot of the "music theater" approach married Herz's quest for realism to the super-naturalism (and visual sumptuousness) of Italian-influenced theater of the 1970s.[19] This was best seen in the Bayreuth centenary *Ring* production of Patrice Chéreau/Richard Peduzzi/Jacques Schmidt – the first *Ring* to be fully televised. The influence of the "music theater" style was still to be felt in stagings of the *Ring* in Bayreuth and Berlin from the late 1980s to the 1990s by the production team of Harry Kupfer/Hans Schavernoch/Reinhard Heinrich. Grounded in essentially naturalistic character interpretation and acting, these productions were placed in abstract settings, though items of scenery and props could be precisely "realistic."

A third overall production trend rediscovered the methodology of the constructivist directors and designers of the post-Revolutionary Soviet theater. This took a non-narrative approach to staging: the naturalistic sequence of a work's story and/or settings was often deliberately questioned or subverted, the better to examine other aspects or tensions latent within the piece. Such a style had already reached West European spoken theater in the 1920s – for example, in the stagings (as in the plays themselves) of Bertolt Brecht – and even in opera productions like those of Berlin's Kroll Opera. This style was notably further developed half a century later in the *Ring* cycles mounted by Ruth Berghaus/Axel Manthey in Frankfurt (1985–87), by Richard Jones/Nigel Lowery in London (1994–95), by four autonomous production teams in Stuttgart (1999–2000), and by David Alden/Gideon Davey in Munich (2002–03).

Wieland Wagner

Wieland's favored tactic of *Entrümpelung* (cleaning up, stripping away) can be literally observed in the development of his Bayreuth designs for *Die Walküre*. The production began in 1951 as a highly simplified version of the prewar Heinz Tietjen/Emil Preetorius staging. Already by 1953, the naturalistic tree, doorway, and other bric-a-brac in Act 1 had vanished in favor of a back-lit rectangle and a rootless central pillar. By 1957 just that pillar, plus a triangular beam construction, remained in a lit circle, the whole placed on a *Scheibe* – a circular (and thus "ring-shaped") disc that Wieland invented as a unifying device for the whole cycle. Likewise, in 1951 the Valkyries' rock of Act 3 comprised an Appia-styled platform (indicating a cliff) and an abstract tree; from 1953 on it became simply a domed empty space at the top of the world, fronting an apparently endless cyclorama sky.

The *Parsifal* that reopened the postwar Bayreuth festival in 1951 was a comprehensive spiritual confrontation with the work, with scenery motivated entirely by the "expression of Parsifal's changing spiritual states."[20]

Bayreuther Festspiele 2001 (www.bayreuther-festspiele.de)
Die Walküre, 3. Akt, Inszenierung und Bühnenbild: Wolfgang Wagner, 1960
(c) Bildarchiv Bayreuther Festspiele

15.3. *Die Walküre*, Act 3: directed and designed by Wolfgang Wagner; Bayreuth festival, 1960.

Bayreuther Festspiele 2001 (www.bayreuther-festspiele.de)
Siegfried, 3. Akt, Inszenierung und Bühnenbild: Wieland Wagner, 1951
(c) Bildarchiv Bayreuther Festspiele

15.4. *Siegfried*, Act 3 (final scene): directed and designed by Wieland Wagner; Bayreuth festival, 1951.

The Grail domain of the opening scene was a lit empty space with cyclorama and projections; the Grail temple was a bare raised plinth with the knights grouped around it in an almost complete circle, its architecture suggested by the red-gold outline of four pillars. Within this framework the singers' movement was often slow or non-existent, with the space between people used to striking effect: Wieland's dramatic confrontations took place either a long way apart or nose-to-nose. There is a certain irony in the fact that his handling of the chorus gave it that very function of "a scenic machine made to walk and sing"[21] to which his grandfather Richard had so strenuously objected. But few choruses in earlier, more conventional operatic productions can have contributed to the drama to the extent that Wieland Wagner managed in such moments as the arrival of the knights in the Grail temple, the entry of the guests from *Tannhäuser*, or the celebration of the Norwegian sailors on the quayside in *Der fliegende Holländer*.

Live recordings (and singers' accounts) show clearly Wieland Wagner's detailed work on text and meaning, still exceptional for its time: clarity of enunciation, dramatic shading of phrases (the actor's quest for a telling "reading" of lines), and dynamic use of pauses or added expressive sounds. Notable examples of the latter include the terror of the Rhine maidens as Alberich nears the gold (*Rheingold*, scene 1), Sieglinde's orgasmic scream as Siegmund draws the sword from the tree (*Walküre*, end of Act 1), or the knights' cry of pain and protest as Titurel's coffin is opened in Act 3 of *Parsifal*.[22]

In 1961, while imitations of his work were starting to spring up in many leading European opera houses,[23] Wieland began a major rethink of his Wagner interpretations. "There can of course be no talk of anything being completed," he remarked. In letters to his collaborators and in interviews he sought to widen the net of dramaturgical and visual influences on his productions, citing Brecht (for a 1963 *Meistersinger*), Picasso and Jackson Pollock (for the ever-developing *Parsifal* begun in 1951), Henry Moore (for the symbolic, sculpted shapes in the 1962 *Tristan*), and "primitive" artists like the Australian painter Sidney Nolan (for the 1965 *Ring*). While his new *Ring, Tristan*, and restudied *Tannhäuser* became more hieratic and abstract in their settings and more statuesque in their movement and blocking, much of *Die Meistersinger* was played as Elizabethan theater with broadly comic characterization and comic-strip stylizations of Renaissance costumes.

Of Wieland's work preserved on film little has made it into the public domain.[24] A poor quality black-and-white video of his *Tristan* (we can only imagine the rich blues and reds of the lighting) shows us clearly, as no extant contemporary report remarks, how every character onstage is

15.5. *Tristan und Isolde*, Act 3: directed and designed by Wieland Wagner; Bayreuth festival, 1962.

15.6. *Götterdämmerung*, Act 2: directed and designed by Wieland Wagner; Bayreuth festival, 1965.

possessed to distraction by longing and desire. This Act 2 love duet has little visible movement, yet it reaches the hottest of emotional temperatures. Similarly, in Wieland's *Holländer* staging it is the sheer humor of the production that stays in the mind, be it broad quasi-farce (the characterization of Daland) or black comedy (the relentless, drunken walking on the spot of the Act 3 chorus of Norwegian sailors).[25]

After Wieland

If Wieland's tactics were often those of reduction, the next generation of Wagner directors redressed the balance. "Once I didn't want to do Wagner, but now I have to produce him all the time, and I start immediately when the music does," commented Friedrich on his decision to show action in moments like all the *Ring* preludes, and even Siegfried's Rhine Journey, where stage directions presume the front curtain is closed.[26] Already in 1940, in his one-off Moscow staging of *Die Walküre*, Sergei Eisenstein had used a large mime group in Sieglinde's Act 1 narration to act out on the forestage the events she describes. Later in Germany both Ulrich Melchinger (Kassel, 1970–74) and Herz (Leipzig, 1973–76) led the way in using more locations and scenes in their *Ring* productions than literally prescribed by Wagner's stage directions. Act 2 of *Die Walküre* began either inside Valhalla, or in some interior distinct from the "wild rocky pass" of the stage directions (this became an almost universally repeated norm for stagings outside the USA from the 1970s on); Act 3 of *Siegfried* had at least three settings (the opening Erda scene often different from where the Wanderer next encountered Siegfried); and Siegfried's "Rhine Journey" (linking the Prologue and Act 1 of *Götterdämmerung*) and funeral procession (linking the two final scenes of Act 3) were shown on stage – the latter most poignantly in Herz's production, which showed Wotan grieving for the slain Siegfried, an image later reworked by Kupfer in Bayreuth. This trend would be sharply reversed in the 1990s and 2000s, when productions once more enjoyed the dynamic of playing as much of the action as possible in a single space.

Under the influence of his training with Walter Felsenstein, Herz made significant use of dramaturgical research in his productions of Wagner, reflecting aspects of the time and place in history in which the works were written, the major cultural influences on their creation, and events in Wagner's own life. This approach – commonplace in spoken theater and opera in East Germany, but regarded as suspiciously "political" by the first wave of West European music critics to assess its impact – fed into many Wagner stagings of the 1970s and 1980s. Herz's and Rudolf Heinrich's

15.7. *Götterdämmerung*, Act 3 (Wotan grieves during the funeral music for the slain Siegfried): directed by Joachim Herz, designed by Rudolf Heinrich; Leipzig, 1975.

1960 Leipzig *Meistersinger*, with its deliberate references in design and acting style to the comedies of the real-life Hans Sachs's near-contemporary Shakespeare, was a profound (and at first unacknowledged) influence on Wieland Wagner's 1963 Bayreuth production. Similarly, Herz's *Holländer* (stage version 1962, filmed 1964) anticipated three 1970s stagings in which events took place in one of the character's dreams – notably Harry Kupfer's at Bayreuth in 1978 (where Senta was his dreamer).[27] Lastly, Herz's and Rudolf Heinrich's *Ring* (Leipzig, 1973–76) opened up areas of interpretation and imagery which would resonate in European Wagner stagings for the next twenty-five years. Leaving behind Wieland's wide-open spaces and abstract symbols, their production returned to definite built settings, with many deliberately quoted epic but anachronistic nineteenth-century elements. It brought into clear focus the "contemporary" (that is, nineteenth-century) social and political motors of the story, alluded to the growing evils of fascism and capitalism, and steered the appearance of the costumes away from overliteral readings of their character descriptions as dwarf, god, or giant. Herz also made use of discarded moments from Wagner's early sketches and drafts, such as the presence of all the Nibelungs gathered outside Fafner's cave, or a whole gang of giants assembled to build

15.8. *Die Meistersinger*, Act 3 (the festival meadow): directed by Joachim Herz, designed by Rudolf Heinrich; Leipzig, 1960.

Bayreuther Festspiele 2001 (www.bayreuther-festspiele.de)
Die Meistersinger von Nürnberg, 3. Akt, Inszenierung und Bühnenbild: Wieland Wagner, 1964
(c) Bildarchiv Bayreuther Festspiele

15.9. *Die Meistersinger*, Act 3 (the festival meadow): directed and designed by Wieland Wagner; Bayreuth festival, 1964.

Valhalla. In the widest sense of the term, this was a "political" *Ring*, and one conceived and completed before the productions of Chéreau and Kupfer.[28]

Götz Friedrich, Felsenstein's other main disciple, described himself as "a radically inclined conservative." His first Wagner stagings shared some of Herz's broad political awareness, although the punchy detail of Friedrich's character direction, and his fondness for a measure of Wieland-type stylization in stage design, pulled in other, more purely theatrical directions. His 1972 *Tannhäuser* brought back the experimental fire lacking in Bayreuth since Wieland Wagner's 1965 *Ring*. Friedrich's starting point was similar to a famous radical Berlin staging by Jürgen Fehling in 1933, presenting the opera (somewhat like a romantic novel) as a battle between the Apollonian and the Dionysian, represented onstage by large symbolic props of a harp and a leopard skin. The Venusberg was a place of terror and death for Tannhäuser, and there was clear demonstration of the violence latent in the supposedly noble minstrel knights when Tannhäuser performed his hymn to Venus during the song contest. Friedrich emphasized Tannhäuser's status as the artist-outsider in a predominantly hostile and militaristic society. He had the roles of Venus and Elisabeth played by the same soprano, and had intended to end the opera with just Wolfram and the dying Tannhäuser onstage. A last-minute change to this plan sent the chorus on for the final scene in hurriedly found costumes which were (incorrectly) perceived to be red, and therefore a sign of Communist sympathies. As such, the ending of the premiere evening was loudly protested by conservative politicians and the press, the most divided and loudest audience reaction at Bayreuth since Wieland had done away with a literal representation of Nuremberg in his 1956 *Meistersinger*. As in many of his subsequent Wagner productions, Friedrich made use here of an essentially simple, and abstract, performing area as the basic set unit – surely influenced by the famous *Scheibe* Wieland had devised for his Bayreuth *Ring*s. His direction of the singers, however, had a modern, brutal, and often expressionistic energy – Tannhäuser and Wolfram torturing their harps like rock stars squeezing riffs out of electric guitars, Venus appearing topless, and the heartbroken Elisabeth, at the beginning of Act 3, literally crawling off stage. The production called a halt to two decades of worldwide Wieland Wagner imitation and opened the way for different production styles in "New" Bayreuth.[29]

After his work for Bayreuth, Friedrich staged a new *Ring* at the Royal Opera House, Covent Garden, in 1974. London in the 1970s was the home of the high-tech Broadway/West End musical, and its engineers were able to accommodate the mobile hydraulic platform – spectacularly simple in appearance, but technically challenging – designed by the Czech theater innovator Josef Svoboda as a *theatrum mundi* unit set for Friedrich's

15.10. *Götterdämmerung*, Act 1: Siegfried (Jean Cox) drinks the potion of forgetfulness, watched by Gutrune (Hanna Lisowska) and the reflection of Hagen (Bengt Rundgren); directed by Götz Friedrich, designed by Josef Svoboda; Royal Opera House, Covent Garden, 1976.

15.11. *Die Walküre*: Gwyneth Jones as Brünnhilde; directed by Götz Friedrich, designed by Josef Svoboda, costumes by Ingrid Rosell; Royal Opera House, Covent Garden, 1977.

production. With the addition of further abstract elements – a standing line of one-dimensional metal panels as a New York skyline look for Valhalla, green tagliatelle strips for the forest in *Siegfried*, hanging (and distorting) lenses for the plotting in the Gibichung Hall – the set gave a powerful, hitherto underexplored representation of the *Ring*'s physical geography, easily accomplishing in full view all the work's demanding scene transformations. In the graphically acted depictions of Alberich's adventures with the ring, Wotan's rage and despair in the tricky (and often statically realized) monologue in Act 2 of *Walküre*, and the running duel between Siegfried and Mime, Friedrich's work with his singers took the physicality of *Tannhäuser* even further. This combination of heightened realistic acting and dynamic scenic space in this *Ring* re-established the credibility of a heroic, dramatic approach to Wagner's theater, lost or forgotten in Europe since the war. Its impact on contemporary well-mannered British production styles proved considerable, not least in terms of lighting and design; major American houses, however, continued to take little notice of the new European experiments in opera staging.

The end of Romantic mythical staging

Ingrid Rosell's costumes for the 1974 Covent Garden *Ring*, although still reflecting the hierarchies or "races" of the story, leaned on mythic models that were newer than the Nordic sagas: Marilyn Monroe for Freia in *Rheingold*, astronauts for the giants, primitive chiefs for the gods, Wotan in a World War II general's greatcoat as Walvater, the god of battles in *Die Walküre*. In the Bayreuth centenary production of 1976, however, the French team of director Patrice Chéreau and costume designer Jacques Schmidt, who had worked together since high school (mostly in the spoken theater), went the whole hog by placing the entire *Ring* cast in human clothes of recognizable historical cut, for the first time in the work's performing history.

At Covent Garden, Rosell and Friedrich had encased the Nibelung brothers Alberich and Mime in black, but they were still the "dwarves" of folklore, and their Siegfried was still a young hero in a rationalized version of the libretto's "rough forest dress." For Bayreuth, however, the Alberich and Mime of Schmidt and Chéreau were real nineteenth- or early twentieth-century workmen, and Siegfried's torn and stained pullover and cord trousers were exactly what a rough-living teenage apprentice would live and sleep in. For Chéreau's production Richard Peduzzi introduced deliberate anachronism into the Italian neo-Romantic design world of Ezio Frigerio. His settings kept their extreme visual beauty even in the industrial

15.12. *Siegfried*, Act 1: René Kollo as Siegfried and Heinz Zednik as Mime; directed by Patrice Chéreau, designed by Richard Peduzzi; Bayreuth festival, 1976.

15.13. *Siegfried*, Act 1 (forging scene): directed by Patrice Chéreau, designed by Richard Peduzzi; Bayreuth festival, 1976.

age references of the hydroelectric dam where the Rhine maidens lived and the miniature blast furnace that Wotan-as-Wanderer wheeled on to do all the forging work for Siegfried.[30] The first three operas were presented in a basically nineteenth-century world (although some of the gods in *Rheingold* were stuck in time as obsolete eighteenth-century aristocrats), shifting into the early part of the twentieth for *Götterdämmerung*.

Chéreau's ground production brought filmically realistic acting (even in the late 1970s it set new standards for operatic production and the relation of action to music), a major exploration of subtext to point up dramatic motivation, and an unswervingly clear delineation of personal relationships. These last were marked by moments of exceptional tenderness (the growing mutual attraction of the Volsung twins, Wotan's embracing of the dead Siegmund) or of great violence (the deaths of both Siegmund and Siegfried by repeated spear thrusts which provoked audience protests of "Enough!" or the maltreatment of Alberich by both Rhine maidens and gods). Chéreau also went further with the radical (re)interpretation of character begun by Herz and Friedrich: the handling of Wotan as a consistently scheming bad loser; the strong paralleling of Wotan and Alberich in *Siegfried* (as with Herz they appeared in virtually identical costumes for their Act 2 colloquy, looking, *chez* Chéreau, like old, battered highwaymen); and the highly ambivalent treatment of the "innocence" of the Rhine maidens, portrayed as Victorian streetwalkers. By 2000 most of these character critiques had become irreplaceably embedded in the psyche of European Wagner production.

Chéreau's 1976–77 *Ring* production shocked and amazed as much as Wieland Wagner's first productions of the Bayreuth canon had done in the 1950s.[31] The sheer standard of stagecraft on display would have surprised no one, however, who knew the work of his team at the Théâtre National Populaire in Lyons and Paris, where much of the *Ring*'s scenography and dramaturgy was anticipated in (and at least once literally borrowed from) their earlier productions of Marivaux's *La dispute* and Edward Bond's play *Lear*. The wide diffusion of the filmed production has lent it a status that not even Wieland Wagner's work achieved (and Herz's never had a chance to).[32] Chéreau's *Ring* set alarm bells ringing in every German opera house. A mold was truly broken: the French director's definitive removal of the cycle's characters and settings from heroic, folkloristic mythology, as well as his challenging standards of acting and stagecraft, had raised the bar for interpretive Wagner staging.

Where the nineteenth-century history of labor and capital influenced Herz's 1970s *Ring* production, the theme of man destroying nature through misuse of mechanical-industrial energy was a recurring image in Chéreau's *Ring* – even down to the detail of the Woodbird in a cage (an image borrowed by Chéreau from Bond's *Lear*). Ecological catastrophe now became the mainspring image behind Friedrich's second *Ring* production (Berlin, 1984–85) and those of Kupfer in Bayreuth (1988–92) and Berlin (1993–96). Friedrich and his designer Peter Sykora set the action in

15.14. *Der fliegende Holländer*, Act 1: directed by Harry Kupfer, designed by Peter Sykora; Bayreuth festival, 1978.

a massive "time-tunnel," a last-resort shelter where survivors of a nuclear Armageddon re-enact the play of the *Nibelung's Ring* in an attempt to understand man's downfall. Despite his much-publicized respect for Chéreau's Bayreuth achievement, Friedrich pulled back from a complete humanizing of the characters, retaining the modernized mythical feel that he had essayed in London. His new direction of the character of Wotan (weaker and more ambivalent), of Siegfried's appearance and relationship with Mime, and of the general acting style (less realistic, more cartoonish) showed his awareness of the work not just of Chéreau but of contemporary German directors like Ruth Berghaus and Hans Neuenfels. Although characteristically strong and lucid, the end result of this second Friedrich *Ring* exemplified the difficulties of the search for new narrative staging options of the cycle in Europe after Chéreau.[33]

One further variation on the historically modernized narrative approach was placed on the Bayreuth stage by Kupfer in 1988. Kupfer had been staging Wagner operas in the DDR since the early 1960s and had made a strong Bayreuth debut in 1978 with a *Fliegende Holländer*, distinctly *après* Herz and the strongest realization to date of a contemporary fascination with telling the opera's story from one character's viewpoint. Set in an oppressive 1840s society (the period both of the opera's composition and of the first major writings of Marx and Engels), the Kupfer/Peter Sykora interpretation had Senta onstage from the rise of the curtain up to her suicide by defenestration at the end of the evening, dreaming of freeing a chained slave of a Dutchman from a ship's hold (in the image of a vagina). This vision returned in the scene of Daland's homecoming, blotting out the intentionally faceless silhouette of the unspecified, all-purpose suitor that her father had provided, and liberating the "dream" lover with whom Senta sang the love duet.[34]

Kupfer's late 1980s Bayreuth *Ring* seemed, like Friedrich's second staging of the cycle, to take place after some world-wasting catastrophe. It played on designer Hans Schavernoch's "road of history," a stage so bare that it made Wieland Wagner's abstractions of the 1950s look crowded. To it was added a necessary epic minimum of realistic, industrial scenery: a gantry for Alberich's new industrialized Nibelheim, a bombed-out boiler for Mime's smithy. Kupfer and Schavernoch also brought modern technology (and its social conditioning) into Wagnerian scenography: lasers made the Rhine and the fire surrounding Brünnhilde, televisions were provided for bored, cocktail-sipping onstage spectators to watch the end of the world. From his singers Kupfer secured performances of unremitting physical and emotional energy, high on the kind of close-contact acting that opera, and Wagner in particular, had avoided for many years. Like Wagner's beloved Feuerbach, Kupfer believed that the gods were created by humans in their own image. His *Rheingold* set the tone: the gods have rarely been so athletic, coming on wrapped in flowers and laurels to celebrate their move into Valhalla, looking part-rock star, part-biker chief, part-Albert Herring as May King. Wotan had boundless energy, ranging from the jokey chauvinism of his opening cajoling of Fricka to a terrifying descent into lust for power when he has Alberich's ring on his hand. A wholly camp, wholly cynical Loge outdid even Wotan in athleticism; Alberich managed both to be gross in his corruption and danger and to elicit a generous measure of sympathy. Later on in the cycle Kupfer traced the fate of the Volsungs (all red-haired) with huge, physically expressed emotion. The musical interpretation of the cycle under Daniel Barenboim closely seconded the line taken by the production: the "Entry of the Gods into Valhalla" (often just a vacant *fortissimo* purple passage for orchestra) was intentionally artificial and bombastic, the sweeping phrases of Wotan's "Farewell" to Brünnhilde broken up and self-questioning.[35]

An end to narrative staging?

By 1980 some demythologization of Wagner's dramas was becoming commonplace, most frequently by relocating characters and settings to other time periods. But his narrative and musical symbols remained essentially undisturbed by post-1945 stage productions until, in 1982,

15.15. *Parsifal*, Act 1: Kundry (Gail Gilmore) lying with Amfortas (John Bröcheler), as narrated by Gurnemanz; directed by Ruth Berghaus, designed by Axel Manthey; Frankfurt, 1982.

another revolution began. Choreographer and director Ruth Berghaus, trained in East Germany, mounted a centenary production of *Parsifal* in Frankfurt[36] and followed this up three years later with a *Ring* cycle; these stagings were as novel and radical as Wieland Wagner's, Herz's, and Chéreau's had been in the preceding decades. Berghaus and her frequent collaborator, the designer Axel Manthey, essayed a non-naturalistic, non-narrative approach to opera production – a Roland Barthes-ian "writing degree zero" which offered "signs" in set and costumes to delineate the essential points of the drama.[37] Their stage geography was emotional and "signed" rather than indicative of any particular time and place. Although conventional melodramatic tension was almost banished, and facts or suggestions about the work were often presented in isolation from naturalistic action, Berghaus had not come from a dance background for nothing. Her productions certainly built up a gripping narrative tension, even if that "narrative" was far from a Romantic, naturalistic illustration of plotline. Psychological states were often shown physically: in *Parsifal*, Gurnemanz was a blind Tiresias of a schoolteacher lecturing the squires on a blackboard about the coming of the "savior"-fool; Parsifal himself played with toy crown and sword in a red romper suit; the gods in

Das Rheingold were hampered in their dealings with others by walking on small, square platforms; all the unfree descendants of an equally unfree Wotan – Volsungs, Valkyries, and Siegfried, as well as the Woodbird – identified themselves with a hand over one eye gesture. In the Frankfurt pit, Michael Gielen's factual, unemotional handling of the music mirrored the production's anti-illusionist quest.

This tactic of calling into question the whole premise of conveying narrative-dramatic information in the staging of a work (or "deconstruction," as it is often called, in a term borrowed loosely from the writings of Jacques Derrida) figured large in European Wagner staging from the late 1980s on. In Brussels (1991) Herbert Wernicke placed the *Ring* in a single unit setting which retained geographical elements from all four works during the cycle. Costumes were part-modern, part-folkloric. Many of the ground production's ideas – including an omnipresent grand piano with Erda seated at it, and an actor impersonating Brünnhilde's long-banished horse Grane (also to be seen in Munich in 2003) – were purely theatrical rather than subtextually interpretive.

Richard Jones and Nigel Lowery were interrupted in a first, rather Berghausian *Ring* for the Scottish Opera after completing only the first two operas of the cycle (1989 and 1991). London's Royal Opera House picked up their intentions (if not the productions per se) with a new cycle in 1994–95. Denuded of naturalistic scenery and filled with references to pop art, twentieth-century theater, and fairy tale, the production invented a new vocabulary of shock and wonder for key points in the action. When Alberich, in flippers and snorkel, stole the gold (slipper) from the Rhine maidens in all-over nude fat-lady prosthetics, the entire cast from the rest of the evening, Erda included, rushed onstage as if they had just missed the most important moment in their lives. The "Valhalla" reached by a mock-civic ceremony of forging the (unseen) rainbow bridge was a star swinging in the sky, toward which the gods groped up like so many lost wise men. Dancers in blue represented the river Rhine, and the tree in Hunding's hut was similarly a "live" actor who collapsed and died when the sword was pulled from him. The riddle scene of Act 1, scene 2, of *Siegfried* was played on the move, with Mime attempting to escort the apparently blind, stick-carrying Wanderer out of his dwelling (shades of Beckett's *Waiting for Godot*). The sword was forged on a domestic cooking stove using the pots and pans with which Mime was also preparing the poisoned drink – the whole involving much to-ing and fro-ing through swinging doors reminiscent of Goldoni's *Servant of Two Masters*. In *Götterdämmerung*, Brünnhilde entered the Gibichung Hall as Gunther's intended with a paper bag over her head and, at the moment in his story just before his murder, Siegfried actually refused the draught of remembrance offered

15.16. *Das Rheingold*, scene 2: directed by Richard Jones, designed by Nigel Lowery; Royal Opera House, Covent Garden, 1994.

15.17. *Siegfried*, Act 3 (final scene): directed by Richard Jones, designed by Nigel Lowery; Royal Opera House, Covent Garden, 1996.

15.18. *Götterdämmerung*, Act 3: directed by Richard Jones, designed by Nigel Lowery; Royal Opera House, Covent Garden, 1996.

him by Hagen because, in this reading, he clearly did not need it. As a final *coup de théâtre* a colossal wall of cardboard boxes was pushed over at the cathartic moment when, according to the stage directions, the dead Siegfried is supposed to lift his finger with the ring on to prevent Hagen stealing it (in the course of the production, this effect was repositioned several times).[38] The acting achieved in these performances was as distinctive in its pantomimic theatricality as that in Chéreau's Bayreuth production had been for its realism.[39]

The explicit ("deconstructionist") reordering of narrative and naturalistic stage directions in the interest of alternative interpretive insights has been taken further in recent German productions. In her Weimar *Ring* of 2001–02 Christine Mielitz interrupted Brünnhilde's "Immolation" scene to have read out one of the later, alternative passages of text (culminating in the line "I saw the world end") that Wagner did not actually set. In a *Meistersinger* production for Hamburg in 2003 Peter Konwitschny actually staged his (and many others') objections to the pan-Germanic tone of Hans Sachs's final address by having members of the company interrupt the interpreter of the role each evening with questions about the meaning of Wagner's text. Only when some resolution to the debate had been reached did the performance proceed.[40] The Stuttgart

Opera decided to mark the millennium with a *Ring* in which a certain amount of deconstruction had taken place before concepts for the production were submitted: the project was assigned to four different, modernist production teams, one opera apiece. All the productions played in versions of contemporary dress, all sought solutions to Wagner's narrative in contemporary images (while Christoph Nel's *Walküre* often deliberately distanced the narrative by splitting action between two stages), all eschewed (or, in Peter Konwitschny's handling of the scenes at Brünnhilde's rock in *Götterdämmerung*, parodied) nineteenth-century Romantic grand opera props or gestures. Joachim Schlömer's *Rheingold* played on a unit interior setting, a courtyard with balconies, lifts, and a large water fountain. The movement of the Rhine maidens and Loge bear witness to the director's choreographic background. The Jossi Wieler/Sergio Morabito *Siegfried* – with Anne Viebrock's shabby modernized interiors for Acts 1 and 3 – reinvents Siegfried, his friends, and his enemies, including a latently gay and psychotic Mime to Siegfried's teenage brat. Fight scenes often ducked in modern stagings (Siegfried vs. Fafner, Siegfried's breaking of the Wanderer's spear) are given prominence in a ground production that restores the violence and fear of the opera's mythic sources. The multi-level scenes of Nel's *Walküre* (Acts 2 and 3) and the final part of Brünnhilde's "Immolation" scene under Konwitschny (house lights up, "dead" cast members walking into the wings, and the final stage directions projected on the closed house curtain) are further classic alienatory examples typical of contemporary European Wagner staging.[41]

To open their *Ring* production in Munich in 2002–03 the American director David Alden and his British designer Gideon Davey started with a *Siegfried* informed by postwar American mythologies.[42] The "hero" was a fast food-quaffing, gadget-laden overgrown teenager with a flashy chrome car whose battery he used to power the forging of his sword. (Later he listened to the Woodbird on a ghetto-blaster.) Mime's dangerous and acquisitive character was represented by his tatty suburban apartment and lethal weapon collection, a small-town "redneck" stockpiling for an inevitable battle with gods and heroes. At the same time he attempted to play the "perfect hostess" to young Siegfried. The Wanderer was a Schigolch-like drop-out tramp (with Schigolch-like secrets about his family relationships). Act 2 portrayed the "forest" as a space for Siegfried's further emotional journey, with various eggs placed there by Wotan: from out of them came a toy dinosaur, some dancing legs (a first hint of sex), the Woodbird, and, eventually, the "dragon" as a huge blow-up female figure, part mother-figure and part representation of sexual fear. Also brought into play was a small upper area of foliage, modeled after an Henri Rousseau painting. The Woodbird was a smiling Barbie airhead of a young woman

15.19. *Götterdämmerung*, Act 3: directed by David Alden, designed by Gideon Davey; Munich, Bavarian State Opera, 2003. Photograph © Wilfried Hoesl

who became intoxicated by the party drinks Mime laid out to celebrate Siegfried's slaying of Fafner. In Act 3 Erda appeared on a sofa thrust into the Wanderer's space, like a whore visiting a traveling salesman. The fire around the "rock" was presented by an actor literally in flames, and Siegfried awoke Brünnhilde from the terminally crashed, up-ended sports car in which Wotan had sent her off at the end of *Die Walküre* (a deliberately short ride in a fast machine). *Götterdämmerung* played almost exclusively in a large white room with a brutally clinical rape scene (Siegfried as Gunther taking the ring from Brünnhilde), an inserted depiction of Alberich's ravishing of Grimhild, a parody beer-hall chorus of Gibichung vassals (horned helmets included), a shrewd examination of the Rhine maidens' many roles (whores, prophetesses), and the presence at the end of huge rats as an image of the decay of civilization. In a Brechtian manner, the staging continuously interrupts and questions the narrative, allowing space for the music to live and comment on the action in its own way, and providing spectators with (as Wagner surely intended) at least two simultaneous lines of narrative to absorb. A frequent tactic is to upfront immediately a scene's main dramatic thrust (e.g., Siegfried disguised as Gunther wears a rapist's mask); giving away the narrative game thus directly allows for greater concentration on other aspects of the scene in question.

The American writer, director, and designer Robert Wilson has turned to *Lohengrin*, *Parsifal*, and the *Ring* among his opera stagings of the past ten years. His work sits somewhere between the schools of narrative abandoned and narrative maintained. Shapes, space, light, and movement are all. Plot lines, scenes, even vital stage props are reassessed in the light of these four performance imperatives. In *Lohengrin*, for example, Ortrud and Elsa have mirroring movements to suggest that they represent different aspects of one character. The soprano Anja Silja, muse to Wieland Wagner and frequent creator of leading roles in his new productions (and later Ortrud in Wilson's Brussels *Lohengrin*), has hailed Wilson as Wieland's only true successor in terms of use of space and movement for dramatic purposes.

Narrative maintained: modern and conservative approaches

In the 2000s both Keith Warner (in Tokyo and London) and Robert Carsen (in Cologne) found ways of stoking the old fires of narrative tension and psychological character study in their *Ring* productions while working in a modernistic manner. Set and costume designer David Fielding brought to Warner's Tokyo production (the first *Ring* cycle mounted by a Japanese company) the wide palette of colors and shapes he inherited from German models in the 1970s, notably a distinctive use of dramatically perspectived interiors. To this was added film and slide projection (for water, fire, and the final catastrophe at the end of *Götterdämmerung*) which extended and challenged the dynamics of the constructed scenery and lighting. For London, Warner collaborated with designer Stefanos Lazaridis to realize (in similar fashion to their 1999 Bayreuth *Lohengrin*) a jigsaw-like design of interlocking symbolic images, a playing space of possibilities and hints for the story and its actors rather than a merely descriptive scenic backing. With his singers Warner concentrates on an intense plotting of the characters' emotional lives and histories, clearly informed (especially in the case of Wotan) by his reading of Wagner's favorite philosophers on the subjects of divinity, love, and sacrifice. This approach leads Warner to present quite openly in his staging Wotan's making love to Erda, and to suggest an almost incestuous relationship between the god and his daughter Brünnhilde when their farewell embrace in *Walküre* became a passionate kiss.

Carsen, with his designer and "coproducer" Patrick Kinmouth, created in his *Walküre* and *Siegfried* an aesthetic beauty in the spirit of Patrice Chéreau/Richard Peduzzi, including realistically based modern settings (and costumes) of often epic grandeur: the battlefields of *Die Walküre* with a big stage full of the dead, or a forest of fire-scorched trees in front of Fafner's unseen cave. This is matched by some cunningly realized modern parallels to difficult character appearances (the dragon Fafner is a mechanical digger, Erda the cleaning lady in the stateroom of a Valhalla now in mothballs).[43] Nikolaus Lehnhoff, once an assistant to Wieland Wagner, has continued to stage Wagner in major houses using contemporary designers such as Erich Wonder and Raimund Bauer. His productions encompass a sparse, realistic acting style from principal roles, emotional and text-oriented, contrasting with a greater abstraction in both chorus work and scenery.[44]

"The operas were wrested back from visual abstraction or political commentary, and given in a version which employed the latest stage technology to depict as accurately as possible the mythical vision that Wagner had intended." This statement was issued by the press office of the New York Metropolitan Opera after completing the intentionally backward-looking *Ring* cycle that conductor and artistic director James Levine had commissioned from the German team of Otto Schenk and Jürgen Rose in 1987–89. Their "version" of Wagner's "mythical vision" was realized by re-creating in three dimensions assorted Romantic German stage solutions vintage 1876–1940. The ground production consisted of largely static tableaux that came to life only when individual cast members paraded their own natural acting instincts or individual interpretation. Expensively cast with a mix of European stalwarts and contemporary American leading lights accompanied by the polished quality of James Levine's orchestra, this *Ring* remained (as was surely intended) largely a musical experience.[45] Less conservative, but essentially under the same banner, were the *Ring* cycles mounted in Seattle by François Rochaix/Robert Israel (1986) and Stephen Wadsworth/Thomas Lynch (2001), notable for their spectacular special effects: flying Valkyries on horseback, airborne "swimming" Rhine maidens, the fire around Brünnhilde. (Artistic director Speight Jenkins similarly cited the use of present-day technology "to create scenes as described by Wagner.")

Politics and racism

The embracing of the Bayreuth festival and the traditional arsenal of Wagnerian iconography by extreme right-wing politics in the Nazi era,[46] not to mention Wagner's own publicly displayed anti-Semitism, has exerted a subtle but significant effect on postwar European Wagner production and its quest for new staging strategies. It may be oversimplistic to state that the timeless, mythical direction Wieland Wagner took in his post-1951 productions was governed by what one commentator has termed "a throwing into deep shadow" of now politically tainted elements (such as the pan-Germanic iconography and production aesthetic of "old" Bayreuth). But Wieland's mission statement regarding *Die Meistersinger* in 1956 ("recently the work seems to have become an awkward cross between Lortzing and the *Reichsparteitag*") should at least be taken as an indicator of the pressures and responsibilities of that moment. An adjunct to this political backdrop – and one not without irony – has been the initial hostile reaction (in the years up until 1989) by American and West European press and audiences to aspects of productions by directors "from the East" which appeared to stress the socialist aspect of Wagner's work.[47]

The question of whether the composer's anti-Semitism influenced his stage-works as much as it did his writings and personal relationships has also not been ignored onstage (we can trace it back as far as Mahler in the 1890s, at least in the form of a remark made in rehearsal).[48] In more recent times, Kupfer's *Die Meistersinger* (Amsterdam, 1995) dealt especially with the cruel treatment of Beckmesser (often believed, like Alberich and Mime, to be a Semitic caricature whose fate is modeled on the unfortunate central figure of the Grimms' tale "The Jew in the Thorn Bush").[49] The view of *Parsifal* promulgated by Berghaus and others has pointed up the (Aryan-)Christian exclusionist/racist nature of the Grail brotherhood, and the Mime and Alberich of Chéreau's and Kupfer's productions exhibited stereotypically Jewish features.

Conclusions

The first move toward a dramaturgical concept of Wagner staging was made before the end of the nineteenth century: that is, the suggestion that the relationships between characters, and what they discussed, could function in different times and spaces (as was being proved already in the 1880s in productions of Wagner's adored Greek dramatists, Shakespeare, and Goethe). The more interventionist and radical approaches of the 1920s and 1930s in Europe, when they had barely reached Britain and the United States, were halted in their tracks by the rise of totalitarian state intervention. Between 1951 and the present day the director's interpretative involvement with music, text, and scenography has increased by leaps and bounds. Productions over the past half-century have called upon images and dress from many ages, both real and imaginary, and increasingly deploy alternative narrative techniques to make their points. Stage directors, like conductors and singers before them, have come out from behind the works, starting to interpret them selectively. Often, this has come to mean the abandoning of the attempt to present a work "straight" – a narrative-dominated ground production with scenery that represents in a naturalistic, pictorial manner the literal word of a libretto's stage directions – in favor of making a firm statement (or statements) about aspects of a work which strike its current interpreters with especial contemporary resonance. No one production has to carry the cross of being definitive or all-embracing. Since the 1980s the challenge has become to find a visual imagery and a methodology of ground production that go beyond a simple illustrative mechanism for the music and narrative in the operas. In a fast-moving technological age in which substantial information about new productions can be disseminated rapidly (and awareness of a multitude of options presents its own challenges), the entire method of telling a story on the operatic stage is now open to question and reappraisal.

16 Criticism and analysis: current perspectives

ARNOLD WHITTALL

Wagner's prominence on the present-day musical scene is due primarily to the continued commitment of performers, and of the promoters and producers of opera who employ them. As the second centenary of his birth approaches, stagings of Wagner's works show no signs of failing to attract large audiences; the demand for tickets for Bayreuth is currently as great if not greater than at any time in the festival's history. Wagner the cultural phenomenon also remains a subject of immense interest to writers and scholars of all kinds.[1] Alongside the definitive edition of his compositions which commenced publication in 1970 (*Richard Wagner: Sämtliche Werke*), there is an ongoing edition of his complete correspondence (*Sämtliche Briefe*), a magisterial catalogue of works (*Wagner Werk-Verzeichnis*), and a multitude of commentaries for specialists and non-specialists alike. Such commentaries are especially valuable in helping to illuminate the increasingly distant world in which Wagner lived and worked. With such reliably authentic texts established or in progress, specialized research on Wagner continues to probe those texts for meaning and significance. The emphasis may be on essentially musical or more broadly cultural matters, but the primary objective is to explain the continued importance of Wagner and his works to the contemporary world.

In the interests of economy and contemporaneity, this chapter emphasizes relatively recent English-language texts, both critical and analytical. The earlier history of Wagner reception is a large subject in itself,[2] and only a few of its more essential aspects can be touched on here. But it is clear that even the earliest commentators found themselves caught up in a critical environment defined by strongly polarized opinions about the value as well as the content of his works. The impulse to justify Wagner's huge ambition and originality through elucidation was therefore especially strong, and no writer was more industrious, or more influential, in this regard than Hans von Wolzogen, whose introductory glosses on the *Ring* (1876), *Tristan und Isolde* (1880), and *Parsifal* (1882) emphasized Wagner's thematic ideas (the "leitmotifs") and their connections with the poetic as well as musical texts as a whole.[3]

Among early commentators who approached Wagner and his work more broadly, and more critically, none was more important than Friedrich Nietzsche. Later commentators have sometimes accused him of irrelevance.

Bryan Magee, for example, claims that the "decisive flaw" of his writings "lies in the fact that he never addresses himself to Wagner's works as works of art. He engages with them ... in a way that is impervious to artistic considerations, as if his works were first and foremost vehicles for ideas."[4] Nevertheless, Nietzsche's ideas about the relation of Dionysian and Apollonian characteristics in ancient vs. modern art and culture resonate down the decades in many later accounts of how Wagner's works reflect an essentially modernist aesthetic, involving both interaction and conflict between stability and instability, continuity and discontinuity.[5] The grand historical sweep and intricate cultural perspectives of such critical writing – often characterized as hermeneutic – have long been complemented by the kind of analysis that gives close technical attention to textual and musical matters, and whose terminology often derives from clues provided in Wagner's own writings.

Voluminous and contradictory in some respects though these writings are, there is clear evidence – especially in the late essay "On the Application of Music to the Drama" (1879; *PW* VI:173–91; *GS* X:176–93) – of how the composer understood the special technical and formal qualities of his own work. This essay is not the only piece of Wagner's writing which commentators have used to provide basic tools for the interpretation of his compositions: for example, the concept of the "poetic-musical period" found in *Opera and Drama* (1851) features prominently in many discussions. As Thomas Grey has noted, however, the *Opera and Drama* description "amounts to little more than a theoretical – and rather unlikely – correlation of alliterative verse (*Stabreim*) with patterns of harmonic progression within a musical phrase of unspecified proportions."[6] In the 1879 essay, by contrast, Wagner is more specific, looking back on and quoting from actual work (*Lohengrin* and the *Ring*), not theorizing in advance about what that work should be like.

For present-day musicological commentators, the essence of Wagner is found in the move away from separate operatic numbers to musico-dramatic through-composition, with all the consequent issues about how integrated or diversified (centripetal or centrifugal) the resulting forms might be. In "On the Application of Music to the Drama," Wagner noted that, while his "new form of dramatic music" was as thematically unified – and therefore coherent – as the movements of a symphony, it was not restricted to the kind of harmonic progressions and modulations appropriate for symphonic music as traditionally conceived. And there is no more strongly characterized or consistently developed topic in Wagnerian critical analysis down to the present than the issue of how the twin processes of thematic integration and harmonic innovation serve the purposes of the (mainly mythic) dramatic subject matter which

Wagner chose to explore through them. In 1879 Wagner also commented that because true "dramatic pathos" is excluded from the symphonies of Haydn and Beethoven, symphonic music has no need of the "rhetorical dialectics" that musical drama requires (*PW* VI:176). As will be noted below, later writers have seized on this apparent declaration of faith in conflict and discontinuity, while noting that it must be set against Wagner's no less pertinent belief in a balancing "art of transition" or seamless transformation.[7] Consequently, as many writers aim to show, Wagner's dramatic subject matter comes to life not just through its powerfully expressive dialogues between voices and orchestra, but through fluctuations between continuity (stability) and discontinuity (instability) in formal design, as well as through fluctuations between the confirmation and undermining of those basic tonalities by means of which his motivically saturated music unfolds.

From harmony to form

The task of explaining and justifying Wagner's harmonic innovations has been a particular concern of writers interested in the theory and practice of tonality. Cyrill Kistler's pioneering harmonic analysis of Wagner's music appeared as early as 1879, the same year as the composer's essay "On the Application of Music to the Drama."[8] Robert W. Wason describes Kistler as "the author of the first practical harmony book which assumes the Wagnerian style as a norm," and claims that by the early 1880s "*Tristan* had become the touchstone for any system of harmony aspiring to legitimacy."[9] Analyses of the *Tristan* chord like those by Kistler or Karl Mayrberger[10] sought to ascribe its special qualities both to its unusual intervallic construction and to its ambiguous tonal function. But in the 1880s it was not generally envisaged that the tonal system itself might actually disintegrate, rather than continuing to be constructively enriched by chromaticism.

It is understandable that the *Tristan* chord, even when removed from its context in a particular musical phrase or formal structure, should be endlessly fascinating to theorists of harmony; Wagner's use of other "half-diminished" seventh chords to promote tonal ambiguity at moments of great dramatic tension and instability similarly remained of absorbing interest into the twentieth century, as the writings of Arnold Schoenberg,[11] Ernst Kurth, and many others confirm. Kurth, for example, made the important general point that, "everywhere, Romanticism exploits the ability to hear one and the same phenomenon in two or more ways; it is fond of this coexistence and its indefiniteness."[12]

Indeed, the very "indefiniteness" of the *Tristan* chord has made it possible for theorists to regard it as a post-tonal or even atonal entity, thereby promoting that very breakdown of tonality of which Wagner's own practice stopped short.[13] The theory which enables the chord to be described as a pitch-class set emerged only after 1950. But the tonally disruptive potential of the chord, and of Wagner's use of it, was well understood by those early twentieth-century theorists who were experiencing the consequences for composition of the breakdown of tonal order and, as they saw it, of the formal coherence that went with that order. For Heinrich Schenker, Wagner was directly to blame for the excesses of Schoenberg and his school, since it was he who had decided "in the service of drama, to make expressiveness, indeed overexpressiveness, the guiding principle of music."[14]

At the opposite extreme to Schenker's rejection of the structural viability of music drama comes Alfred Lorenz's defense of Wagner's works as coherent, consistent formal structures, nominally based on those ideas about the "poetic-musical period" outlined in *Opera and Drama*.[15] While Schenker's blinkered approach to vocal music of all kinds remains a problem for those who believe that he understood the essence of tonality better than any earlier theorist, Lorenz's bold but naïve claims about Wagner's reliance on a small nexus of form-schemes – primarily based on the ABA (*Bogen* or arch) and AAB (bar) forms – have fueled endless debates between those who prize Wagner as the enemy of everything systematic and those who see him as a progressive but not destructively radical composer, more significant for his transformation of existing compositional conventions than for his rejection of them.[16]

Methods and meanings

In response to this kind of broad interpretation of Wagner's musico-dramatic achievement, critical and analytical commentary tends to broaden its own focus to include the cultural function and significance of his works, not only as works or documents of their time, but as "events" which are constantly being reinterpreted through performance and analysis. As noted earlier, Nietzsche's importance for later Wagner commentary derives from his deeply ambivalent responses, highlighting the inherent and profound ambiguities of the works themselves. Thomas Mann was well aware of this, and there is a quasi-Nietzschean intensity in declarations such as the following: "Wagner's healthy brand of sickness, his diseased brand of heroism, are just one instance of the contradictions and convolutions inherent in his nature, its ambiguity and equivocality."[17]

Mann had a shrewd understanding of Wagner as an individual in history: "He went the way of the German middle classes: from evolution to disillusion, and finally to pessimism and a resigned turning-inwards under the protection of a powerful state."[18] Such comments, linking life to work, also abound in the writings of the leading English Wagnerian of the first half of the twentieth century, Ernest Newman, whose four-volume biography remains a formidable achievement, acknowledged even by those later scholars who find aspects of it (mainly the tendency toward hero worship) unsympathetic.[19] Mann was no more inclined than Newman to allow awareness of Wagner's weaknesses to dilute his appreciation of the rich ambiguity of a creative genius whose music "is not wholly and entirely music, any more than the dramatic text that it turns into poetry is wholly and entirely 'literature.' It is psychology, symbolism, mythology, emphasis – all of these things; but it is not music in the purest and fullest sense" – or at least in the sense understood by critics and musicians of an earlier era.[20] Mann was therefore well placed to respond to Theodor W. Adorno, a musically trained philosopher who, through political conviction and personal experience, was much more disposed to implicate the composer in later atrocities: "The form of nationalism that he embodied, especially in his work, exploded into National Socialism, which could draw on him, via [Houston Stewart] Chamberlain and [Alfred] Rosenberg, for its rationalization."[21]

Mann noted that Adorno's monograph *In Search of Wagner* (*Versuch über Wagner*) "never becomes wholly negative,"[22] though what Gyorgy Markus terms its "overheated and at times disturbingly exaggerated polemics" – however understandable, given the time when it was written (1937–38, but published only in 1952) – makes it hard to accept as even-handed critical commentary. For Markus, "the task of the *Versuch* is not merely that of interpretation and criticism ... it is to perform an act of *exorcism*."[23] It was not Adorno's last word, however, and the later essay, "Wagner's Relevance for Today" (1963), confirms his unexorcizable fascination, partly admiring, partly deploring, with a music-dramatist whose essential modernism inheres in the way he creates "the feeling of leaving solid ground behind, of drifting into uncertainty." This feeling "is precisely what is exciting and also compelling about the experience of Wagnerian music. Its innermost composition, the thing one might, by analogy to painting, call its *peinture*, can in fact be apprehended only by an ear that is willing to cast itself, as the music does, into uncertainty."[24] As always with Adorno, this essay is much stronger on the general than the particular. But his essential critical observation, "that ... what is magnificent in his work cannot be cleanly divided from what is questionable"[25] reinforces a basic, binary way of thinking that has guided many critics and musicologists more concerned than Adorno himself was to discuss Wagner's texts and techniques in detail.

From Dahlhaus to Darcy

The twentieth-century growth of musicology as a serious academic discipline had a particularly strong impact in the United States, even though it took some time for any authoritative work on Wagner to appear. The skillful blending of critical and technical topics in Joseph Kerman's early essay on *Tristan*, "Opera as Symphonic Poem,"[26] proved immensely influential. So too were Robert Bailey's close studies of the sketches and drafts for *Siegfrieds Tod* and *Tristan und Isolde*, which led on to his no less penetrating analytical work on the large-scale structural role of tonality in the music dramas.[27] But neither Kerman nor Bailey was as productive or as provocative in his contribution to Wagner studies after the 1960s as the German scholar Carl Dahlhaus, and the English translations of many of his books ensured that his impact was as great, if not greater, in North America and the United Kingdom as it was in Germany itself.

The first of Dahlhaus's Wagner essays was published in 1969, the year of Adorno's death, and Dahlhaus is generally regarded as the scholar most directly responsible for developing Adorno-like perspectives in Wagner interpretation, bringing those perspectives closer to the musicological mainstream.[28] Given the context of his early life in Germany, Dahlhaus was as prone as Adorno himself was to view the Wagner phenomenon with skepticism. Nevertheless, in Dahlhaus's case that skepticism is stronger with respect to what he saw as the blinkered and deluded attempts of the Nazi sympathizer Lorenz to impose strict hierarchic discipline on Wagner's forms than it was with respect to the possibility of implicating Wagner himself in responsibility for later political developments. The result, Stephen McClatchie has claimed, is that "if Lorenz may be criticized for inflexibly insisting that all of Wagner's music is perfectly structured tonally and formally, Dahlhaus too may be censured for his own inflexible insistence on the opposite."[29] As detailed study reveals, however, there is more to Lorenz than the rigid insistence on a single mode of interpretation, just as there is more to Dahlhaus than a rigid refutation of that model. Just as Lorenz's formal schemes, or periods, for all the arbitrariness with which he imposes boundaries on them, are able to embody considerable degrees of variation within their borders, so Dahlhaus's "insistence on concentrating on only short sections of the works at a time" is not a prescription for ignoring all larger-scale aspects, and it is in any case compensated for by the brilliantly cogent thinking that is provocatively hermeneutic rather than prescriptively formalist in tone. McClatchie's suggestion that "Dahlhaus obscures or minimizes the large-scale structural techniques and symmetries in Wagner's music" risks too ready a reimposition of idealistic conceptions about quasi-classical symphonic coherence and integrity in which the subtleties and ambiguities of the modernist dimension in Wagner's work – highlighted by Dahlhaus – are in danger of being swept aside.[30]

An alternative to Lorenz in the demonstration of "large-scale structural techniques" appeared when Felix Salzer defied his teacher Schenker's condemnation of Wagner's work. In *Structural Hearing: Tonal Coherence in Music* (1952), Salzer sought to apply his version of voice-leading technique to music which ranged far more widely than the Bach to Brahms canon, and he included a group of linear reductions of a 78-bar span from Act 1 of *Parsifal* which aimed to show how a deep "background" motion from A to C is "composed out" in six stages of increasing elaboration.[31] Subsequent attempts to analyze Wagner in ways which adopt or adapt Schenkerian principles have tended to follow Salzer's practice of dealing with well-defined sections from larger structures rather than with those larger structures complete. William Mitchell's graphing of the Prelude to Act 1 of *Tristan* (1967) is such a pioneering enterprise, concerned solely with the linear elements that constitute the musical fabric.[32] But later engagements with Wagnerian voice-leading, such as Christopher Wintle's account of Siegfried's Funeral Music and Gutrune's Monologue from Act 3 of *Götterdämmerung* (1988), Matthew Brown's study of Isolde's Act 1 Narrative, and Patrick McCreless's "Schenker and the Norns" (both 1989), as well as William M. Marvin's much more recent work on *Die Meistersinger* (2003), aim to explore the parallels between musical procedures and dramatic, textual elements.[33] The most ambitious and comprehensive attempt to analyze an entire work according to voice-leading principles is probably Warren Darcy's book-length treatment of *Das Rheingold* (1993), which embodies many of the most salient topics of concern to present-day Wagner analysts.

As an alert and well-trained musicologist, Darcy understands the importance of sketch study, and of the dangers of the kind of positivistic formalism that downplays issues of dramatic content, textual meaning, and cultural context. But his work is in essence a defense of what he terms the "highly architectural" aspect of Wagner's forms[34] – something he believes that Dahlhaus denied – and an attempt to complement the post-Schoenbergian concept of "extended tonality" (as reflected in Bailey's notion of "directional" or "expressive" tonality) with a demonstration of the continued significance of diatonic fundamentals.[35] Darcy also recontextualizes

Bailey's alternative notion of "associative tonality" – the idea that musico-dramatic forms on the largest scale are governed by tonal (not just motivic) recurrences in which "every step of the chromatic scale is imbued with semantic meaning" – making the claim that "each key, at whatever level it appears, simultaneously serves a linear and/or harmonic purpose, and is never invoked as a mere tonal 'calling card.'"[36]

Fusion, diffusion

What might be regarded as the present-day mainstream of Wagner analysis endorses Darcy's initiative in part: for example, Anthony Newcomb claims that "we misrepresent Wagner if we fail to discuss him as a composer in the tonal tradition, and we ignore his greatest virtue if we fail to discuss his ability to give powerful and coherent shape to vast stretches of musical time."[37] This is not, however, to declare the music dramas "symphonic": Carolyn Abbate's view of this putative quality of the scores as a "myth"[38] is also generally endorsed. Newcomb's prescription is therefore to balance those large-scale shapings against the kind of smaller-scale detailing which observes the modernist principle "that the essence of Wagnerian form lies in its ambiguity and incompleteness,"[39] and therefore mediates to a degree between Lorenz and Dahlhaus. Such a balance would require complementing Darcy's hyperorganic reading of *Das Rheingold* with a view of the work as a sequence, or network, of interacting, interrelated, but not "classically" unified formal units – a matter of musical "prose."[40] This reinstates, up to a point, Lorenz's Wagner-derived idea of the relatively small-scale poetic-musical period as the principal formal unit, but gives new emphasis to the differences between periods linked by music exemplifying "the art of transition" and those embodying the juxtapositions and disjunctions that obtain when "rhetorical dialectics" is in play.

This mode of interpretation was brought into focus in a book published just after Darcy's: *Nineteenth-Century Music and the German Romantic Ideology* by John Daverio (1993). This includes some analysis of sections from *Parsifal* which, on the one hand, "marks the culmination of Wagner's technique of spinning out large-scale continuities through the 'art of transition.'" On the other, the *Parsifal* material "invites interpretation as a concatenation of musical fragments according to what Wagner called the principle of 'rhetorical dialectics'" leading to a "new organicism": "rhetorical dialectics is saved from degenerating into mere disconnectedness through the application of mediating procedures," while "the art of transition ... not only allows for elements of disruption, it feeds on them."[41] In this way Daverio provides a useful template for the explication of Wagner's stage-works along the lines of Adorno's perception of a kind of music in which "integration and disintegration are entwined."[42]

Daverio's thesis – that the Romantic artwork's "almost obsessive striving for organic interconnectedness" is countered by "a skeptical attitude toward the realization of an ideal organic unity in the modern era"[43] – came at a time when a "new" musicology was seeking to bring social, cultural, and psychological contexts to bear on artefacts whose very status as "works" (implying something permanently fixed as a printed text) was also open to question. In an early contribution that remains one of the most detailed and challenging, Carolyn Abbate was so disturbed by what she termed the "comfortable values" of the kind of analysis that emphasized formal models and tonal fundamentals in Wagner that she provided an extended interpretation of Wotan's monologue from Act 2 of *Die Walküre* which involved the argument that "unstructured harmonic improvisation" was of the essence, and that the various cadential progressions contained within it were detached from rather than integral to the overall design.[44] This analysis provides many new insights into both music and drama, though in underlining the "unstructured" ambiguities with little if any allowance for a balancing integration, it risks providing too extreme a response to those excessively unified interpretations which Abbate rightly deplores. Similarly, a discussion of *Tristan* such as Abbate might advocate, dealing only with "fissures" and "ruptures" and implying that no significant engagement with the organic and the orderly can be found, seems to miss some of the most characteristic tensions in Wagner's mature style.[45]

In another early and no less stimulating application of "new musicological" perspectives to Wagner, Lawrence Kramer considered aspects of *Tristan* from within a broader discussion of "Musical Form and Fin-de-Siècle Sexuality," contending that, just as Freud's *Three Essays on the Theory of Sexuality* "(re)articulate certain radical changes in the concept of sexuality that emerge in late-nineteenth-century culture," so Wagner's opera along with Hugo Wolf's Goethe setting "Ganymed" "do the same thing."[46] Kramer does not exclude formal, technical features from his analysis, and his observation that, "as a general technique, the overlap of closure and continuation is basic to Wagner's mature style" acknowledges the formal significance of the "art of transition," though he carries the interpretation into psychological and erotic realms in which "what counts as a fulfillment [i.e., closure] is actually a rapturous occasion of unfulfillment [i.e., continuation]."[47] Kramer also attaches as much importance to the discussion of ambiguity in Wagner as any harmonic or tonal analyst. Indeed, he calls on the relatively formalistic work of Bailey and Allen Forte to demonstrate a "lack of definite structural boundaries" which, "like the achievement of closure through intensification, conforms to the rhythm of libidinal desire."[48] He therefore moves critical perspectives back from the purely musical into the orbit of Freudian psychology, concluding that "*Tristan und Isolde* . . . is a radical work not only in its musical procedures but also in its sexual ideology."[49]

Perhaps the first Wagner monograph to conform more consistently to the prescriptions of new musicology is Jean-Jacques Nattiez's *Wagner Androgyne* (1993), a "study in interpretation" whose governing interpretive concept is given in its title. For Nattiez, the myth of the androgynous has particular interpretive power because it transcends the limitations of other strategies – structuralism, Marxism, and feminism – by conforming to an essentially modernist criterion: it "allows us a brief glimpse of the perfect image of unity while at the same time telling us that this unity does not exist."[50] Nattiez may not be wholly successful in convincing his readers that androgyny is more than a synonym for ambiguity. Yet the final stages of the book (292–97) – which answer "Yes" to the question, "Is the *Tristan* Chord an Androgynous Chord?," on the grounds that the chord is not merely a technically multivalent construct, but is also implicated profoundly in the work's meaning in ways to which all other analytical "plots" fail to do justice – are particularly persuasive, penetrating much more deeply than the more limited and conventional kinds of hermeneutic criticism.

Like *Wagner Androgyne*, another monograph from the mid-1990s, Thomas Grey's *Wagner's Musical Prose: Texts and Contexts* (1995), takes the interaction between Wagner's prose writings and his compositions as an interpretive starting point. Grey homes in on such crucial yet problematic technical concepts as the poetic-musical period, the process of *Entwicklung* or evolution, "endless melody," and leitmotif, never losing sight of the all-important matter of how small-scale and large-scale elements interconnect. He also places Wagner in a multiplicity of contexts that cast well-varied light on the fundamental relations between words and music, diagnosing a "kind of hermeneutic double counterpoint of questions and answers in which the musical and dramatic strata continually shift positions."[51] Such considerations come fairly close to John Daverio's, with its perspectives derived from "On the Application of Music to the Drama," and Grey's final chapter includes a particularly valuable analysis of Tristan's "Delirium" (Act 3). Here he argues that "while the 'symphonic' logic of the passage (Tristan's peroration and its aftermath) is purely developmental, divorced from clearly articulated tonal goals, this development is driven, finally, by dramatic motives of delirium and collapse – by extremes of 'pathos' that Wagner would have considered unwarranted as affective or psychological motives to merely instrumental form. But the extremes are tempered, as Wagner claimed, by transition. And the transition . . . seems to have been motivated by a psychology as much musical as dramatic. At the same time, while there is an audible logic, even compulsion, to this musical process, an awareness of the 'poetic motive' or psychology supplements what might still be understood as music's 'need' or 'lack.'"[52]

Present polarities

A very different modernist interpretative strategy appears in Marc A. Weiner's 1997 Postscript to *Richard Wagner and the Anti-Semitic Imagination* (originally published in 1995), which makes bold claims about Wagner's own objectives: "Wagner intentionally crafted his music dramas as multi-layered, enigmatic works which, he hoped, would appeal not to the intellect but to the 'feeling' of his contemporary and future German audience."[53] For Weiner this multivalence determines that "the works are both mimetic and they are not; they contain racist corporeal icons (of the voice, smell, gait, and sexuality, to name but a few), but these icons function both mimetically and metaphorically." On this basis, Weiner asserts that "to maintain . . . that anti-Semitism is either completely absent from or irrelevant to an appreciation of Wagner's aesthetic accomplishments is to misunderstand this subtle interplay of mimetic sign and polyvalent signification. It is to rob the works of their inherent tensions and ambiguities, to diminish their subtlety as well as their importance as cultural and historical documents."[54]

By polarizing the argument in this way, Weiner is able to avoid engagement with the majority of recent commentators who, while accepting that anti-Semitism is neither absent from, nor irrelevant to, the interpretation of Wagner's works, believe that the topic itself needs to be contextualized, rather than polarized, by aspects which are held to transcend mundane, corporeal considerations – in Wagner's compositions, if not in his prose writings.[55] But it is not possible to reconcile the views of commentators who honestly believe that the greatness of Wagner's works involves their transcendence of their own time and its "cultural practice" with Weiner's claims, or with Gary Tomlinson's Adorno-inspired assertion that "Wagner's music dramas, like other gestures of late modernism that would follow them, were captured in the gravitational field of the commodity form" whose "effect was a false, overcompensating objectification of the noumenal."[56]

Tomlinson employs a dense weave of musical and philosophical perspectives to further his claim that "*Parsifal* represents Wagner's last, most radical striking of the unique balance that is basic to his mature aesthetic: the balance between a putatively autonomous musical continuity and a musical articulation determined by extramusical forces." Tomlinson develops his initial insight with the argument that *"Parsifal* directs our attention to magical objects at the same time as it undermines their magical capacities," and he concludes that *"Parsifal* poses the predicament of all sacred noumena, and finally all magic *tout court,* in the late modern West. It brings to light an objectification that broaches the spiritual only as it evanesces in exchange and simultaneously claims not to do so."[57] The point, as Tomlinson seeks to clarify in a protracted footnote, is that *Parsifal* fails to embody Wagner's intention to "exalt" the sublime, Christian aspects of the work's materials and to erase the story's involvement with sinister, pagan magic. It remains conflicted, ambiguous in ways which those whose responses resolve out into submission to a sense of harmonious beauty and aspiring spirituality have difficulty in accepting.[58]

Other writers who have begun to engage with Adorno's sociocultural critique of Wagner include John Deathridge and Lydia Goehr. British musicologist Deathridge has traversed a broad spectrum of Wagner scholarship, from studies of the compositional sources of *Rienzi* and *Lohengrin* to re-evaluation of biography and its sources to essays in Wagnerian cultural criticism, often informed, in turn, by close readings of compositional and biographical source material.[59] Goehr's *The Quest for Voice: On Music, Politics, and the Limits of Philosophy* looks especially to Wagner and his oeuvre in addressing traditional themes of German Romantic criticism, questions of musical "formalism" and autonomy, and other issues in performance and reception. The relation of music drama to the concept of aesthetic autonomy, as theorized by Adorno and others, is also taken up in a more recent essay comparing the cases of two monuments of operatic-musical culture, *Don Giovanni* and *Tristan.*[60]

The philosopher Roger Scruton has also attempted to deal with a Wagnerian drama in terms of an essential relationship, or tension, not between sacred and profane magic, as in *Parsifal,* but between "sex and the sacred" in *Tristan und Isolde.* Like Tomlinson, Scruton devises concrete technical observations to support his argument, but his starting point is very different: whereas Tomlinson moves from a consideration of Kant's philosophy to an elaboration of Adornian skepticism (in which Wagner is just one of an extensive cast of characters), Scruton is an open worshipper at the shrine of Wagner's special greatness, and his move from Kant to Schopenhauer lays the foundations for an interpretation in which Tomlinson's keyword, "failure," is not to be found.

For Scruton, Wagner was "one of the great humanists of modern times," and *Tristan* embodies a religious idea – "that sacrifice is the price of redemption."[61] Nevertheless – and controversially, at least for those

Wagnerians who refuse to detach the composer from specifically Christian beliefs and practices – this is "a redemption that needs no God to accomplish it." Scruton concludes that "through their sacrifice" Tristan and Isolde "restore belief in our human potential and renew in us the will to live. Hence the redemption of the lovers in death is also a renewal of the community in life."[62]

Although Scruton seems to endorse Schopenhauer's view that "music is not a form of representation," he does not reject the determination of meanings which can and must be verbalized. Nevertheless, as Scruton (like almost all commentators on Wagner) demonstrates, it is not so much that what he describes in the music dramas "defies translation into words or gestures"; rather, the power of the thing described cannot be matched by words or gestures, despite the fact that it can only be analyzed and interpreted by those means. So, when Scruton boldly seeks his own way of technically explaining the "magic" and "mystery" of the *Tristan* chord, his interpretation, projecting complex cultural perspectives back onto musical materials, seems forced. While he willingly acknowledges the importance of *Tristan* for the emergence of musical modernism, his own account of it remains idealistically organicist, his belief in its "formal perfection" preventing the risky intrusion of any sense of those "rhetorical dialectics" advocated by Daverio and others.[63] The seductions of synthesis prove too much for the critic and analyst concerned more with Wagner's greatness than with his modernism.

But, after Scruton, *Tristan* continues to provoke diverse interpretations. In one of the most challenging, what David Lewin dramatizes as the radical absence of synthesis "between the traditional teleology of tonality . . . and the propensity of abstract intervallic structuring ('atonality')" results in the conclusion that "not even . . . the most explicit 'final' B major" succeeds "in laying the Tristan Chord to rest. The chord asserts itself, as itself, through and despite all such attempts to rationalize it in the goal-driven world of functional tonality."[64] By contrast, Eric Chafe's more extended and also more conservative analysis finds not unmediated opposition, but a "double perspective," a "compound of romantic and anti-romantic, tonal and atonal elements."[65] In that compound it is the organically interconnected art of transition that has the dominant function over more incidental discontinuities.

The circle of Wagner criticism and analysis traced in this chapter can be closed, if only provisionally, by a return to the kind of theoretical work on basic musical materials that has by no means been eclipsed by the proliferation of hermeneutic commentaries. David Kopp has provided a fairly comprehensive summary, and although – as the title of Lewin's 1984 article indicates[66] – possible relationships between technical functions and dramatic, poetic meanings need not be excluded from this type of discourse, it is the nature and validity of those technical functions which tend to be placed at its heart. Kopp demonstrates what he describes as "a very familiar instance of a complete ascending circle of minor thirds" from Act 2 of *Tristan*, and he provides three analyses "which highlight different aspects of the chord relations in the passage."[67] The different qualities of each neatly confirm how strongly perceptions about multivalence in harmonic and tonal analysis can complement those literary, philosophical explorations of ambiguity considered earlier in this chapter. The former might be relatively Apollonian, the latter rather more Dionysian: the former are certainly much more specialized, far less of an "easy read" than the latter. Nevertheless, it seems probable that the issues raised by the two approaches, both separately and in combination, will keep Wagner criticism and analysis fully occupied for many years to come.

Notes

1 Wagner lives: issues in autobiography

1. For a summary of Wagner in film, see Ulrich Müller, "Wagner in Literature and Film," in *Wagner Handbook*, ed. Müller and Peter Wapnewski, translation ed. John Deathridge (Cambridge, MA, and London, 1992), 373–93.

2. See *Gesammelte Schriften und Dichtungen* in ten volumes (*GS*), posthumously expanded as *Sämtliche Schriften und Dichtungen* (*SSD*) in sixteen. The notorious, though not entirely misleading, English translation in *PW* is based on *GS* and has been modified throughout.

3. First published privately in four volumes in 1870, 1872, 1874, and 1880; and publicly, with minor cuts, in 1911. All references are to the English translation by Andrew Gray, edited by Mary Whittall and published without an index in 1983 (*ML*), based on the complete, fully annotated 1976 German edition by Martin Gregor-Dellin. The detailed index of the first (anonymous) English translation, incidentally, first published in two volumes in London in 1911 by Constable and Company Ltd., is superior to any in the various German editions.

4. The most interesting are the so-called Red Pocket-Book (*Die rote Brieftasche*, reproduced in *SB* I:81–92), the Brown Book (*Das braune Buch*, ed. Joachim Bergfeld [Zurich, 1975; trans. George Bird, London, 1980]), and the diary written for the eyes of King Ludwig II in 1865 (in Otto Strobel, ed., *König Ludwig II. und Richard Wagner: Briefwechsel*, 5 vols. [Karlsruhe, 1936, 1939], IV:5–34, hereafter *Ludwig–Wagner*).

5. See Martin Geck, *Die Bildnisse Richard Wagners* (Munich, 1970).

6. See *SB* and *Wagner Brief-Verzeichnis*, ed. Werner Breig, Martin Dürrer, and Andreas Melke (Wiesbaden, 1998).

7. See Stewart Spencer, *Wagner Remembered* (London, 2000).

8. John Deathridge, "A Brief History of Wagner Research," in *Wagner Handbook*, 202–23. The only major biography to be published since is Joachim Köhler's, *Der letzte der Titanen: Richard Wagners Leben und Werk* (Munich, 2001), trans. Stewart Spencer as *Richard Wagner: The Last of the Titans* (New Haven and London, 2004). Despite some welcome critical moments, its wearying length and naïve fusion of art and life ("Like the composer, the young hero [Siegfried] grows up in straitened circumstances," p. 363) turn it ultimately into yet another low-grade *biographie romanesque*, of which, as I suggest in my earlier essay, there are already more than enough. Despite all attempts at critical distance, its journalistic hyperbole is a crude mirror image of Wagner's own methods, and does scant justice to his importance as a formidable bellwether of German ideology.

9. The definitive account is Samuel Schoenbaum, *Shakespeare's Lives* (Oxford, 1970). An abridged and updated edition was published in 1991. A notable and actually well-grounded attempt is Stephen Greenblatt, *Will in the World: How Shakespeare Became Shakespeare* (New York and London, 2004), which derives many suppositional details from reading the dramatic texts against the record of politics and daily life in London during the years Shakespeare was active there.

10. Unfortunately none of the key texts concerning this important issue has been translated. See Winfried Schüler, *Der Bayreuther Kreis von seiner Entstehung bis zum Ausgang der wilhelminischen Ära: Wagnerkult und Kulturreform im Geiste völkischer Weltanschauung* (Münster, 1971); Michael Karbaum, *Studien zur Geschichte der Bayreuther Festspiele (1876–1976)* (Regensburg, 1976); Hartmut Zelinsky, *Richard Wagner: Ein deutsches Thema – Eine Dokumentation zur Wirkungsgeschichte Richard Wagners, 1876–1976* (Frankfurt, 1976).

11. Lytton Strachey, *Eminent Victorians* (London, 1974; first published 1918), 7.

12. Carl Friedrich Glasenapp, *Richard Wagners Leben und Wirken*, 2 vols. (Cassel and Leipzig, 1876–77); *Das Leben Richard Wagners in sechs Büchern dargestellt*, 6 vols., 3rd–5th edns. (Leipzig, 1908–23).

13. *CWD*. I use the published translation (by Geoffrey Skelton), modified where noted. Extracts are cited by the date of the relevant entry and hence easily located in either the English or the German edition.

14. Theodor W. Adorno, "Wagner, Nietzsche, Hitler," in *Gesammelte Schriften*, vol. XIX, ed. Rolf Tiedemann and Klaus Schultz (Frankfurt, 1984), 405.

15. From a letter dated 25 January 1880 in *Ludwig–Wagner*, III, 169.

16. From the Neuchâtel preface to Rousseau's *Confessions* cited in Laura Marcus, *Auto/biographical Discourses: Theory, Criticism, Practice* (Manchester, 1994), 23.

17. See, for example, Trev Lynn Broughton, *Men of Letters, Writing Lives: Masculinity and Literary Auto/Biography in the Late Victorian Period* (London and New York, 1999), in particular chap. 3 on the famous Froude–Carlyle debate and "Married Life as a Literary Problem" (83–112).

18. Cited in Marcus, *Auto/biographical Discourses*, 46.

19. From a letter of 12 November 1864, in *Ludwig-Wagner*, I, 36–37.

20. First published complete in *Das braune Buch*, 111–47.

21. Otto Strobel, "Foreword" to *Ludwig-Wagner*, I, ix. In this and all subsequent chapters, all emphasis in quoted texts is original unless otherwise noted.

22. Georges Gusdorf, "Conditions and Limits of Autobiography," in James Olney, ed., *Autobiography: Essays Theoretical and Critical* (Princeton, 1980), 38. See also the discussion of Gusdorf's seminal essay in Marcus, *Auto/biographical Discourses*, 154–62.

23. Gusdorf, "Autobiography," 43.

24. John Deathridge and Carl Dahlhaus, *The New Grove Wagner* (London, 1984), 7. See also Klaus Kropfinger, *Wagner and Beethoven: Richard Wagner's Reception of Beethoven*, trans. Peter Palmer (Cambridge, 1991), 32–33. After coming up empty-handed, Kropfinger, whose innate conservatism in any case makes it difficult for him to challenge Wagner's authority, asks a bit desperately: "was there … ever any need for such a falsification? Does Wagner's extraordinary – and well-documented – early commitment to Beethoven's Ninth not speak for itself?" Well, yes and no: from a psychoanalytical perspective alone, not to mention its ideological ramifications, Wagner clearly needed to invent an autobiographical myth in which a powerful female (mother) figure is fused with a dominant (paternal) male authority. That would have been much harder to do with the Ninth Symphony, given the absence in it of famous solo arias, and hence the lack of an iconic woman singer with whom it could be unmistakably identified.

25. See the brilliant re-reading of it in Tamara S. Evans, "'Am Mythenstein': Richard Wagner and Swiss Society," in Reinhold Grimm and Jost Hermand, eds., *Re-Reading Wagner* (Madison, 1993), 3–22.

26. See Egon Voss, "Die Wesendoncks und Richard Wagner," in Axel Langer and Chris Walton, eds., *Minne, Muse und Mäzen: Otto und Mathilde Wesendonck und ihr Zürcher Künstlerzirkel* (Zurich, 2002), 117.

27. Cited in Evans, "'Am Mythenstein,'" 17.

28. Max Fehr, *Richard Wagners Schweizer Zeit*, 2 vols. (Aarau and Leipzig, 1934, 1954), II, 21.

29. Richard Wagner, *Eine Mitteilung an meine Freunde*, GS IV:239, 244; PW I:278–79, 283.

30. GS IV:240; PW I:280.

31. Laura Marcus, "The Newness of the 'New Biography,'" in Peter France and William St. Clair, eds., *Mapping Lives: The Uses of Biography* (Oxford, 2002), 194.

32. Wagner was an admirer of Thomas Carlyle's biography of Frederick the Great, but as one example among many chastised the author for the "completely unphilosophical cultivation of his mind" (*CWD*: 21 March 1873; trans. modified).

33. At the end of the score of *Die Meistersinger*, for instance, is the entry: "Thursday, 24 October 1867/ Evening 8 o' clock." See WWV, 478.

34. Compare the original text of the passage in the *Autobiographical Sketch* (*SB* I:100) with the "official" 1871 version (*GS* I:9).

35. Compare the text in GS and SSD with the French original, titled *De la musique allemande*, in *Revue et Gazette Musicale*, Paris, 12 July 1840, in Robert Jacobs and Geoffrey Skelton, trans. and eds., *Wagner Writes from Paris …: Stories, Essays, and Articles by the Young Composer* (London, 1973), 45, 50. The passage cut from the collected writings begins here on p. 50 – "Handel and Gluck abundantly proved this, and in our time another German, Meyerbeer, has provided a fresh example" – and continues until the end of the paragraph.

36. For evidence that Wagner was still working on the essay during 1849, see WWV, 329–30. In a letter of 16 September 1849 to Theodor Uhlig, he states explicitly that he is expanding and re-editing the piece "in a whole variety of new ways [*mannigfach neu*]" (*SB* III:122).

37. Richard Wagner, *Mein Leben*, ed. Martin Gregor-Dellin (Munich, 1976), 786. The phrase is not in the English edition, which excludes the "Annals."

38. See, for example, Ernest Newman's entirely convincing exposure of Wagner's and Cosima's ruthless behavior toward Malvina Schnorr von Carolsfeld (the first Isolde), who threatened to expose their illicit relationship to King Ludwig II. The official Bayreuth legend had it that Wagner was human kindness itself in his treatment of the singer. See Ernest Newman, *The Life of Richard Wagner*, 4 vols., (repr. Cambridge, 1976), IV, 3–37.

39. Friedrich Nietzsche, *The Will to Power*, trans. Walter Kaufmann and R. J. Hollingdale,

ed. Walter Kaufmann (New York and London, 1968), 272.

40. Roger Hollinrake, "The Title-Page of Wagner's 'Mein Leben,'" *Music and Letters* 54 (1970), 416.

41. Letter of 15 August 1888 from Köselitz to Nietzsche, *Nietzsche Briefwechsel*, ed. Giorgio Colli and Mazzino Montinari, III/6 (Berlin and New York, 1984), 270.

42. Friedrich Nietzsche, *The Birth of Tragedy and The Case of Wagner*, trans. Walter Kaufmann (New York, 1967), 182.

43. Letter of November 1872 to Rohde, *Nietzsche Briefwechsel*, II/3 (Berlin and New York, 1978), 86.

44. Nietzsche, *The Birth of Tragedy and The Case of Wagner*, 166.

45. Cited in Broughton, *Masculinity and Literary Auto/Biography*, 141.

46. Isolde Vetter, "Wagner in the History of Psychology," in *Wagner Handbook*, 118–55. On the critical tradition of such Wagnerian pathologies, neuroses, and deviant conditions, see also Thomas Grey, "Wagner the Degenerate: Fin-de-Siècle Cultural 'Pathology' and the Anxiety of Modernism," *19th-Century Studies* 16 (2002), 73–92; Mitchell Morris, "Tristan's Wounds: On Homosexual Wagnerians at the Fin-de-Siècle," in Sophie Fuller and Lloyd Whitesell, eds., *Queer Episodes in Music and Modern Identity* (Urbana, IL, 2002), 271–91.

47. Letter of 5 December 1866 in Cosima Wagner and Ludwig II of Bavaria, *Briefe*, ed. Martha Schad (Bergisch Gladbach, 1996), 301.

48. Cited in Newman, *The Life of Richard Wagner*, I, 80.

49. Cited in Gregor-Dellin's afterword to *Mein Leben* (*ML* 751–52). Sulzer was among a small group to receive this early printed excerpt at Christmas 1870. "But a few days later," he recalls to Mathilde Wesendonck, "I received a note – which I attributed at the time to his wife's intervention – asking me to send the *mysterium* back" (*ML* 750).

50. Gusdorf, "Autobiography," 39.

51. Cited in Vetter, "Wagner in the History of Psychology," 125.

2 *Meister* Richard's apprenticeship: the early operas (1833–1840)

1. Many details of Wagner's earliest musical, literary, and dramatic impressions as recounted in *My Life* (for example, *ML* 22–37) are corroborated in his "Autobiographical Sketch" published in 1843; allowing for a certain degree of deliberate self-fashioning (even at that date) in the context of his first rise to public visibility, these correspondences

probably vouch for a basic level of accuracy. The earlier (1843) résumé of his encounter with Logier's harmony treatise is suggestive regarding the psychology of this crucial if somewhat random turn in his artistic education: "[T]his study did not bear such rapid fruit as I had expected: its difficulties both provoked and fascinated me; I resolved to become a musician" (*PW* I:5). Regarding the role of music imagined for *Leubald*, he remarked in the later memoirs that "the various categories of ghosts belonging to my spirit world would first receive their distinctive coloring from the corresponding musical accompaniment" (*ML* 31).

2. In a set of "Observations on the Italian Opera in Comparison with the German" written around 1837, the Italian-trained north German composer Otto Nicolai noted the problem of stylistic choices – high and low, native and foreign – that plagued German composers, especially of opera, at this juncture; "When a nation's taste is so dispersed as this, the artist does not know in which direction to turn." Nicolai's essay is excerpted and translated by Ernest Newman, *The Life of Richard Wagner*, 4 vols. (New York, 1937–46; reprint, Cambridge, 1976), I, 117.

3. The most comprehensive study of Wagner's early musical training remains Otto Daube's *"Ich schreibe keine Symphonien mehr": Richard Wagners Lehrjahre nach den erhaltenen Dokumenten* (Cologne, 1960).

4. That is not to say he took the rejection of *Die Feen* by the Leipzig theater administration sitting down, or in silent resignation – which would have been most uncharacteristic. An impassioned apologia for his first operatic effort, emphasizing the soundness of his musical education (in contrast to the tenor of his later accounts) and his practical experience with opera, was sent to the singer and stage director in Leipzig Franz Hauser, in March 1834 (*SB* I:149–55).

5. The same views are elaborated in an essay on Meyerbeer and *Les Huguenots* unpublished during Wagner's lifetime but apparently written sometime between 1837 and 1840 (*SSD* XII:22–30); similar views about the genre of French grand opera as an ideal synthesis of modern styles figure in discussions of Fromental Halévy from Wagner's time in Paris (1840–42), particularly a series on Halévy and *La reine de Chypre* published in the *Revue et Gazette Musicale* between February and May 1842 (*SSD* XII:131–48, 406–13; see *PW* VIII:175–200).

6. On the turn from grand opera "back" toward a new conception of German Romantic opera, as well as the biographical context of this turn,

see Thomas Grey, ed., *Richard Wagner: Der fliegende Holländer* (Cambridge, 2000), chaps. 1 and 4.

7. Interestingly, the only such union that is explicitly consummated – the union of Alberich and the Gibichung woman Grimhild, behind the scenes of the *Ring*, so to speak – issues in villainy (Hagen).

8. Most commentaries on *Die Feen* claim that Wagner reversed the fate of Gozzi's pair, Cherestanì and Farruscad, by conferring immortality on Arindal rather than making Ada a mortal. The epilogue to *La donna serpente*, however, as spoken by Cherestanì, announces the happy couple's intent to "dwell in Eldorado," that is, the immortal realm from whence she hails.

9. Looking over copies of some of his early writings ("Bellini: Ein Wort zu seiner Zeit," 1837, and "Die deutsche Oper," 1834), in which he had criticized Weber's style, Wagner remarked to Cosima that he knew *Euryanthe* at that time "only from one bad performance" (*CWD*: 27 May 1878). However, a vocal score had been published in 1824, and it seems unlikely Wagner would not have made some attempt to familiarize himself with the most ambitious opera of the master he so revered.

10. "Young Germany" was not an organized literary or political movement, but more a perceived nexus of affinities among a disparate group of liberally inclined (mainly Prussian) writers inspired by the events of 1830 in France and united against the political oppressions of the Metternich era. Romanticism, Hegelian metaphysics, and the broader hegemony of philosophical idealism in German intellectual life were all targets of Young German opposition. The name derives from the dedication ("to thee, young Germany") of a collection of lectures by Ludolf Wienbarg (*Ästhethische Feldzüge*, 1834) and from the novel by Wagner's youthful associate Heinrich Laube entitled *Das junge Europa* (5 vols., 1833–37), although Heinrich Heine was in a sense the spiritual mentor. Among many studies see, for example, the documentary collection by Jost Hermand, ed., *Das junge Deutschland: Texte und Dokumente* (Stuttgart, 1998).

11. Katharine Eisaman Maus, introduction to *Measure for Measure*, in Stephen Greenblatt et al., eds., *The Norton Shakespeare* (New York, 1997), 2023.

12. Luzio in fact proposes to her already in Act 1, rather suddenly, in between strophes of the cabaletta of their duet, otherwise given over to expressing their mutual resolve to rescue Claudio. The various marriages proposed at the end of *Measure for Measure* are all highly problematic, unlikely ones, as if deliberately undermining this convention of comic closure. Wagner's pairing off of Isabella and Luzio trumps any of Shakespeare's couplings for sheer absurdity, though he mitigates this in reforming Shakespeare's Lucio as best as he can.

13. Whatever the influence of modern French–Italian opera and "Young German" literary enthusiasms on Wagner's revision of *Measure for Measure*, the theme of carnivalesque subversion in *Das Liebesverbot* externalizes elements already present in Shakespeare. On the relevance of "carnival" as ritualized subversion (in the Rabelaisian sense theorized by Mikhail Bakhtin), see Anthony Gash, "Shakespeare, Carnival and the Sacred: *The Winter's Tale* and *Measure for Measure*," in Ronald Knowles, ed., *Shakespeare and Carnival: After Bakhtin* (New York and London, 1998), 177–210. "In fact no play could illustrate Bakhtin's serio-comic conception of carnival more fully than *Measure for Measure*," Gash suggests, where the "festive topic of the world upside down provides a unifying motif" (*ibid.*, 202). Shakespeare's Duke explicitly invokes the topic in describing the libertine condition of his realm that he sets out to correct at the beginning of the play: "And liberty plucks justice by the nose; / The baby beats the nurse and quite athwart / Goes all decorum" (*Measure for Measure*, Act 1, scene 3, lines 29–31).

14. Friedrich Lippmann offers a systematic analysis of Italian influences on structures of melody, phrase, and "number" in early Wagner, in "*Die Feen* und *Das Liebesverbot*, oder die Wagnerisierung diverser Vorbilder," in Carl Dahlhaus and Egon Voss, eds., *Wagnerliteratur-Wagnerforschung* (Mainz, 1985), 14–46. See also the contributions of Egon Voss and Klaus Hortschansky to the conference proceedings, *Richard Wagner und seine "Lehrmeister,"* ed. Christoph-Hellmut Mahling and Kristina Pfarr (Mainz, 1999).

15. The sadomasochistic overtones of Friedrich's aria, especially in this cabaletta phase, do have some point of reference in Shakespeare's Angelo, whose desire appears to be enflamed by Isabella's psychic torment. Angelo feeds both sides of this psychological equation with threats of drawn-out punishment for her brother Claudio (*Measure for Measure*, Act 2, scene 4).

16. Wagner does manage, at any rate, a rather close simulacrum of the "market chorus" from Act 3 of Auber's *La muette* ("Au marché qui vient de s'ouvrir, venez, hâtez-vous

d'accourir") in the carnival scene that opens his Act 2 finale ("So jubelt in das Fest hinein, zur Lust begeist're uns der Wein"), likewise in D major.

17. Without the mediating (or meddling) role of Shakespeare's Duke, it falls to Wagner's Isabella to devise this tactic on her own. However out of keeping this might be for the original Isabella, it fits perfectly well with Wagner's more modern, free-thinking version of the character. On the other hand, Isabella's scheme in *Das Liebesverbot* requires only that Friedrich be caught in a masked assignation, and thus skirts the actual "bed trick" altogether.

18. *The Last Days of Pompeii* (1834) actually postdates Giovanni Pacini's successful proto-grand opera, *L'ultimo giorno di Pompei* (1825, with famously spectacular sets by Alessandro Sanquirico), but resonates distinctly with the newly popular musical-theatrical genre, as it does with the "sublime" catastrophic panoramas of John Martin – noted, for example, in the *Oxford Companion to English Literature*, ed. Margaret Drabble (Oxford, 1985), 144.

19. For a more detailed account of the impact of Spontini and *Fernand Cortez* on Wagner, see Anno Mungen, "Wagner, Spontini und die Grand Opéra," in *Wagner und seine "Lehrmeister,"* 129–43. For the next few years, as Mungen notes, Berlin was kept in mind as a perhaps more likely alternative to Paris for the staging of the German grand opera Wagner was intent on producing. Wagner gives a detailed account of the aging Spontini's visit to direct *La vestale* in Dresden (while Wagner was Royal Kapellmeister there in the mid-1840s) in *My Life* (*ML* 278–90), derived in part from his "memoirs" of Spontini (*GS* V:86–104; *PW* III:123–52); these, in turn, started from a short obituary Wagner published in the Zurich *Eidgenössische Zeitung* on 25 January 1851.

20. On the historical figure of Cola di Rienzo in relation to Wagner's operatic hero, see Dieter Borchmeyer, *Drama and the World of Richard Wagner*, trans. Daphne Ellis (Princeton, 2003), chap. 2, esp. 46–64.

21. There seems to be no firm evidence as to when Wagner encountered *Les Huguenots*, whether as text, as score, or in performance. Helmuth Weinland proposes a number of dramaturgical and compositional parallels between *Les Huguenots* and *Rienzi*, but does not address the biographical question of when or in what manner Wagner may have become acquainted with the work: "Wagner und Meyerbeer," in Helmuth Weinland, *Richard Wagner zwischen Beethoven und Schönberg* (*Musik-Konzepte* 59; Munich, 1988), 31–72.

22. Rosalie died suddenly in 1837, a year after her marriage to Oswald Marbach, just as Wagner was beginning *Rienzi*. Wagner's passionate attachment to Rosalie is a central psychobiographical thread in Joachim Köhler's *Richard Wagner: The Last of the Titans*, trans. Stewart Spencer (New Haven and London, 2004).

23. August Kubizek, *Adolf Hitler, mein Jugendfreund* (Graz, 1966), 135.

24. "Die Stunde naht, mich ruft mein hohes Amt . . . Bald seht ihr mich, das Werk naht der Vollendung!" The historical Rienzi, Irene Erfen notes, styled himself in explicitly Christ-like terms, although politically he was closer to a dictator than an elected representative of the people: Erfen, "Volk! Volk! Tod dem Tribunen!" in Peter Csobádi et al., eds., *"Weine, weine, du armes Volk": Das verführte und betrogene Volk auf der Bühne*, 2 vols. (Anif-Salzburg, 1995), II, 610.

25. And, in fact, the same tendency applied to the imitation of poetic pathos even earlier in *Leubald und Adelaïde*, where, as Wagner himself admitted, he "had taken the most extravagant forms of speech to be found in *King Lear* and *Götz von Berlichingen* and used them with the most incredible exaggeration" (*ML* 27).

26. Wagner did not expect that this "divertissement" would be performed in its entirety, despite his efforts to integrate it thematically with the drama. Somewhat grudgingly, he allowed the elaborate pantomime to be omitted from later versions of the score.

27. He related these Hoffmannesque impressions to other spectral and visionary tendencies of his childhood, for example, that of fixing on inanimate objects – such as pictures or furniture – until "bursting into a loud shriek, because they seemed . . . to come alive" (*ML* 13). His early enthusiasm for Beethoven's Ninth Symphony is likewise connected to this audio-visionary temperament, if with perhaps more than a touch of retrospective stylization.

28. On the role of leitmotif in *Der Ring des Nibelungen*, see also chap. 6.

29. One wonders, too, if Wagner noticed, at least in retrospect, the Duke/Friar's sermon to Claudio, "Be absolute for death" (Act 3, scene 1) – a veritably Schopenhauerian lecture on the nature of the "Will" to life and the reasons to renounce it.

30. Speaking to the poet Ferdinand about what worlds are appropriate to operatic representation, Hoffmann's composer, Ludwig, explains how it is the poet's job to invent a realm unlike our own where music

and singing seem to be naturally at home. "Then, dazzled by [its] brilliant colors, we willingly believe ourselves as in a blissful dream to be transported from our meager everyday existence to the flowery avenues of that romantic land, and to comprehend only its language, words sounding forth in music": Hoffmann, "The Poet and the Composer," in *E. T. A. Hoffmann's Musical Writings*, trans. Martyn Clarke, ed. David Charlton (Cambridge, 1989), 196.
31. Friedrich Schiller, *Geschichte der merkwürdigsten Rebellionen und Verschwörungen aus den mittlern und neuern Zeiten* (Leipzig, 1788), 107.

3 To the Dresden barricades: the genesis of Wagner's political ideas

My thanks to the Nationalarchiv der Richard-Wagner-Stiftung Bayreuth and the Bibliothèque de l'Opéra Paris, where research was done to prepare this article. My thanks also to PSC-CUNY for a grant facilitating my research.
1. For more on the Young Germans, see chap. 2, n.10.
2. Richard Wagner, "The Revolution," in *Jesus of Nazareth and Other Writings*, PW VIII:232–38. The relation between Ellis's translations and English is famously vague, and I have modified them on occasion.
3. Wagner to Minna Wagner, 14 May 1849: *SL* 145.
4. Wagner to Minna Wagner, 14 May 1849: *SL* 146.
5. Wagner to Theodor Uhlig, 27 December 1849: *SL* 184.
6. Richard Wagner, *Opera and Drama*, PW II:157; see *GS* IV:34.
7. Richard Wagner, "What Is the Relation Between Republican Aims and the Monarchy?" (the "Vaterlandsverein" speech): *PW* IV:137–39 (*SSD* XII:220–29).
8. Joachim Bergfeld, ed., *The Diary of Richard Wagner, 1865–1882: The Brown Book*, trans. George Bird (London, 1980), 96.
9. Mikhail Bakunin, "The Reaction in Germany," in J. M. Edie, J. P. Scanlan, and M. B. Zeldin, eds., *Russian Philosophy*, vol. I (Knoxville, TN, 1976), 406.
10. Barry Millington, *Wagner* (Princeton, 1992), 26.
11. Ludwig Feuerbach, "Principles of the Philosophy of the Future," in *The Fiery Brook: Selected Writings of Ludwig Feuerbach* (Garden City and New York, 1972), 175.
12. Wagner to Samuel Lehrs, 7 April 1843: *SL* 107, 108.
13. "Wonders from Abroad," in Robert L. Jacobs and Geoffrey Skelton, trans. and

eds., *Wagner Writes from Paris* (London, 1973), 156.
14. On the Rhine as a national symbol in German Romantic musical culture generally, see Cecelia Hopkins Porter, *The Rhine as Musical Metaphor: Cultural Identity in German Romantic Music* (Boston, 1996).
15. Herbert Marcuse, *Reason and Revolution* (Boston, 1960), 179–80.
16. G. W. F. Hegel, *The Philosophy of Right*, trans. T. M. Knox (Oxford, 1973), 5–6.
17. "What Is German?" in Charles Osborne, ed. and trans., *Richard Wagner: Stories and Essays* (La Salle, IL, 1973), 53.
18. As Jacob Katz has noted, there is evidence that Wagner had drafted some form of "Judaism in Music" during his later years in Dresden. Minna Wagner referred in 1850 to "that essay in which you defame an entire race," which, she says, Richard had had her read two years earlier. See Jacob Katz, *The Darker Side of Genius: Richard Wagner's Anti-Semitism* (Hanover, NH, and London, 1986), 52.
19. For some of the arguments, see Theodor Adorno, *In Search of Wagner* (London, 2nd edn., 2005), 12–17; Barry Millington, "Nuremberg Trial: Is There Anti-Semitism in *Die Meistersinger*?," *Cambridge Opera Journal* 3 (1991), 247–60; Paul Lawrence Rose, *Wagner: Race and Revolution* (New Haven and London, 1992); Marc A. Weiner, *Richard Wagner and the Anti-Semitic Imagination* (Lincoln, NE, and London, 1995); Michael Tanner, *Wagner* (Princeton, 1996), 26–30. For an evaluation of some of their implications, see Mitchell Cohen, "Wagner as a Problem," *German Politics and Society* 16:2 (Summer 1998), 94–130.
20. Wagner to Franz Liszt, 18 April 1851: *SL* 222.
21. Wagner to Robert Schumann, 5 [February] 1842: *SL* 88.
22. See Simone Lässig, "Emancipation and Embourgeoisement: The Jews, the State, and the Middle Classes in Saxony and Anhalt-Dessau," in James Retallack, ed., *Saxony in German History: Culture, Society, and Politics, 1830–1933* (Ann Arbor, MI, 2000), 99–118. My account of Saxon Jewry draws from this article.
23. K. Freigedank (Richard Wagner), "Das Judentum in der Musik," *Neue Zeitschrift für Musik* 33 (3, 6 September 1850), 112; reproduced in facsimile in Manfred Eger, *Wagner und die Juden* (Bayreuth, 1985), 19. "Untergang" is translated by Charles Osborne as "decline and fall" in Osborne, *Richard Wagner: Stories and Essays*, 39. My references are to this translation with modifications based on the original.

24. See the appendix, Ludwig Feuerbach, *The Essence of Christianity*, trans. George Eliot (New York and Evanston, 1957), 298. On Feuerbach's anti-Jewish views, see Marx W. Wartofsky, *Feuerbach* (Cambridge, 1982), 319–21.

25. Arthur Schopenhauer, *Essays and Aphorisms*, ed. and trans. R. J. Hollingdale (London, 1970), 155.

26. Bruno Bauer, "The Jewish Question," in L. S. Stepelevich, ed., *The Young Hegelians: An Anthology* (Cambridge, 1983), 197.

27. Karl Marx, "Bruno Bauer, *Die Judenfrage*," in Marx, *Early Writings*, ed. and trans. T. B. Bottomore (New York, 1964), 21.

28. Karl Marx and Friedrich Engels, "The Holy Family or Critique of Critical Criticism: Against Bruno Bauer and Company," in Marx and Engels, *Collected Works*, vol. IV trans. Richard Dixon et al. (New York, 1975), 110.

29. Marx, "Bruno Bauer, *Die Judenfrage*," 11.

30. See Karl Marx, "Bruno Bauer, 'Die Fähigkeit der heutigen Juden und Christen frei zu werden,'" in Marx, *Early Writings*, 32–40.

31. Wagner, "Judaism in Music," in Osborne, *Richard Wagner: Stories and Essays*, 25.

32. *Ibid.*, 27.

33. *Ibid.*, 28.

34. *Ibid.*, 29.

35. *Ibid.*, 32–33.

36. *Ibid.*, 34.

37. Karl Kautsky, *Are the Jews a Race?* (originally *Rasse und Judentum* [Stuttgart, 1914]; English trans. of 2nd [1921] edn. [New York, 1926]), 105–06.

38. Richard Wagner, "Artisthood of the Future" ("Künstlertum der Zukunft"): *PW* VIII:348–49 (translation emended).

39. See Richard Wagner, "Know Thyself" ("Erkenne dich selbst"): *GS* X:268; see *PW* VI:268.

40. "Evidence against the sometime Kapellmeister Wagner concerning his participation here in the May insurrection in the year 1849," in *Wagner: A Documentary History*, ed. H. Barth, D. Mack, and E. Voss (New York, 1975), 174.

41. Wagner to August Röckel, 2 May 1849: *SL* 145.

42. Hans von Bülow to his mother, May 1849, in *Wagner: A Documentary History*, 174.

43. *The Confession of Mikhail Bakunin: With the Marginal Notes of Tsar Nicolas II*, trans. Robert C. Howes (Ithaca and London, 1977), 147–48.

44. Wagner to Liszt, [16? December 1854]: *SL* 323.

45. Arthur Schopenhauer, *The World as Will and Representation*, vol. I, trans. E. F. J. Payne (New York, 1969), 411.

46. Richard Wagner, "On the Name 'Musikdrama'": *PW* V:304.

4 The "Romantic operas" and the turn to myth

1. *Der fliegende Holländer* was designated a "Romantische Oper in 3 Aufzügen" (*WWV* 63, Drucke XV), *Tannhäuser* initially a "große romantische Oper in 3 Acten" (*WWV* 70, Drucke XX), and *Lohengrin* a "Romantische Oper in drei Akten" (*WWV* 75, Drucke XII). In 1859–60, Wagner's attempts to Tristanize *Tannhäuser* persuaded him to rename it a "Handlung in 3 Aufzügen" (*WWV* 70, Drucke XXIV).

2. August Wilhelm Schlegel, *Vorlesungen über dramatische Kunst und Litteratur*, ed. Eduard Böcking, 3rd edn., 2 vols. (Leipzig, 1846), I, 16.

3. Adolf Wagner's influence on the young Wagner is well charted by Joachim Köhler, *Richard Wagner: The Last of the Titans*, trans. Stewart Spencer (New Haven and London, 2004).

4. See "The Poet and the Composer," in David Charlton, ed., *E. T. A. Hoffmann's Musical Writings*, trans. Martyn Clarke (Cambridge, 1989), 169–209.

5. Heinrich Heine, *Werke* IV, ed. Helmut Schanze (Frankfurt, 1968) 290. As Egon Voss has demonstrated, Wagner's work on *Die Feen* was probably motivated by a misguided and untimely attempt to curry favor with his family; see "*Die Feen*: Eine Oper für Wagners Familie," in "*Wagner und kein Ende*": *Betrachtungen und Studien* (Zurich, 1996), 15–30.

6. For more on the Young Germans, see chap. 2, n. 10.

7. Novalis, *Hymnen an die Nacht / Heinrich von Ofterdingen*, ed. Paul Kluckhohn and Richard Samuel (Munich, 1985), 131 and 55.

8. Their common identity was suggested to Wagner by C. T. L. Lucas, *Ueber den Krieg von Wartburg* (Königsberg, 1838), 271–73.

9. It is significant that in discussing the genesis of *Das Liebesverbot*, Wagner specifically refers to Heine as a member of the anti-Romantic, Young German movement (*GS* IV:253).

10. The narrative had appeared in the first volume of *Der Salon* in December 1833; see Heinrich Heine, *Sämtliche Werke*, ed. Manfred Windfuhr (Berlin, 1973–), vol. V, 769–77 and 806; see also Barry Millington, "The Sources and Genesis of the Text," in Thomas Grey, ed., *Richard Wagner*: Der fliegende Holländer (Cambridge, 2000), 25–35. The relevant passage in his "Autobiographical Sketch" of early 1843 (*SB* I:109) seems to imply that Wagner did not read the text until after his sea

journey from Riga to London in 1839 and that it was Heine himself who added it to his reading list following their acquaintance in Paris in the autumn of 1839. By contrast, Wagner's letter to Ferdinand Heine of August 1843 (*SB* II:314–15) and *A Communication to My Friends* (*GS* IV:258) both state that the composer was already familiar with Heine's account of the legend when he left Riga.

11. At this point it is customary for writers to mention Edward Fitzball's "nautical burletta" *The Flying Dutchman; or, The Phantom Ship*, which opened at the Adelphi Theatre, London, on 4 December 1826. This play, it is claimed, was Heine's model. In the latest contribution to this vexed question, Barry Millington ("Sources and Genesis of the Text") argues that Heine arrived in London in time to see the final performance of the 1826–27 season, on Saturday, 7 April. Unfortunately, this date is ruled out by the fact that Heine was still in Hamburg on the 12th; see Heinrich Heine, *Briefe*, ed. Friedrich Hirth (Mainz, 1950), vol. I, 307. Enquiries made of the Rothschild Archive in London have failed to find any evidence to support the claim that Heine was in London by the 6th. In any case, the literary conceit of the play-within-a-play is so widespread in Romantic literature that Heine had no need to attend the theater in order to find the inspiration there: among well-known examples of the device are three works by Ludwig Tieck, *Der gestiefelte Kater* (1797), *Die verkehrte Welt* (1798), and *Prinz Zerbino* (1799), to say nothing of Friedrich Schlegel's *Lucinde* (1799), and Clemens Brentano's *Godwi* (1801).

12. A translation of the complete text may be found in Grey, *Richard Wagner*: Der fliegende Holländer, 166–69.

13. For fuller coverage of this topic, see George G. Anderson, *The Legend of the Wandering Jew* (Providence, RI, 1965); Mona Körte and Robert Stockhammer, eds., *Ahasvers Spur: Dichtungen und Dokumente vom "Ewigen Juden"* (Leipzig, 1995); and Dieter Borchmeyer, "The Transformations of Ahasuerus: *Der fliegende Holländer* and His Metamorphoses," in his *Richard Wagner: Theory and Theatre*, trans. Stewart Spencer (Oxford and New York, 1991), 190–215.

14. See Friedrich Sengle, *Biedermeierzeit* (Stuttgart, 1971), and Borchmeyer, "The Transformations of Ahasuerus," 194–200.

15. In Act 2, immediately before Erik recounts his dream, Senta "sinks into a magnetic sleep so that it seems as though she, too, is dreaming the dream that he relates" (*GS* I:276).

16. Other examples of such a love-death may be found in Tieck's *Franz Sternbalds*

Wanderungen (1798) and *Der getreue Eckart und der Tannenhäuser* (1799), Novalis's *Hymnen an die Nacht* (1799), Zacharias Werner's *Wanda, Königin der Sarmaten* (1810), and E. T. A. Hoffmann's *Die Elixiere des Teufels* (1815–16) and his opera *Undine* (1816).

17. Novalis, *Hymnen an die Nacht*, 17: "Ich fühle des Todes / Verjüngende Flut, / Zu Balsam und Aether / Verwandelt mein Blut – / Ich lebe bey Tage / Voll Glauben und Muth / Und sterbe die Nächte / In heiliger Glut" ("I feel in my veins / Death's youth-giving flood: / To ether and balm / It changes my blood – / By day I am filled / With faith and desire, / And nightly I die / In heaven's hallowed fire").

18. In his "Autobiographical Sketch" of 1843, Wagner had spoken of "the genuinely dramatic treatment of the redemption of this Ahasuerus of the oceans, which Heine himself had invented" (*SB* I:109), but when he included this text in his collected writings in 1871, he changed this to "the treatment of the redemption of this Ahasuerus of the oceans, which Heine had taken over from a Dutch play of the same name" (*GS* I:17). In much the same spirit, Wagner had already downplayed Heine's originality both in 1851 in *A Communication to My Friends* (*GS* IV:258), and *My Life* (*ML* 162), where Heine is not mentioned at all. (This passage was dictated during the winter of 1866–67.)

19. For a more detailed account of Wagner's debt to Heine, see Hans-Jürgen Schrader, "Schnabelewopskis und Wagners 'Fliegender Holländer,'" in Markus Winkler, ed., *Heinrich Heine und die Romantik / Heinrich Heine and Romanticism: Erträge eines Symposiums an der Pennsylvania State University (21.-23. September 1995)* (Tübingen, 1997), 191–224.

20. Achim von Arnim and Clemens Brentano, *Des Knaben Wunderhorn: Alte deutsche Lieder*, 3 vols. (Heidelberg, 1806–08), I, 86–90.

21. Ludwig Bechstein, *Der Sagenschatz und die Sagenkreise des Thüringerlandes* (Hildburghausen, 1835), 13.

22. For a discussion of the importance of the role of the Wartburg in German nationalist thinking, see Timothy McFarland, "Wagner's Most Medieval Opera," in *Richard Wagner*: Tannhäuser (English National Opera Guide no. 39), ed. Nicholas John (London, 1988), 25–32.

23. "Fraüw venus vnd das wil ich nit / Ich mag nit lenger bleyben / Maria mutter reyne magdt / Nun hilff mir von den weyben / Herr danheüser jr solt vrlaüb han / Meyn lob das solt jr preysen / Wo jr do in dem landt vmbfart / Nempt vrlaüb von dem greysen" (143). It may

also be significant that Bechstein, unlike Hoffmann, spells the Landgrave's name Herrmann, an unusual form taken over by Wagner.

24. Bechstein (*Der Sagenschatz*, 137) had already associated Tanhäuser (*sic*) with the early thirteenth-century Wartburg court of Herrmann of Thuringia and thus with the song contest of 1206–07. For a speculative life of the shadowy figure of Tannhäuser, see Stewart Spencer, "Tannhäuser und der Tanhusaere," in Ursula and Ulrich Müller, eds., *Opern und Opernfiguren: Festschrift für Joachim Herz* (Anif-Salzburg, 1989), 241–47; J. W. Thomas, *Tannhäuser: Poet and Legend* (Chapel Hill, 1974); and Mary A. Cicora, *From History to Myth: Wagner's* Tannhäuser *and Its Literary Sources* (Bern, 1992).

25. In spite of Wagner's claims to the contrary (*ML* 213), Lucas's volume does not contain the *Wartburgkrieg* but only a detailed commentary on Docen's incomplete 1807 edition. As with his letter to Franz Müller of 9 January 1856, listing the sources of the *Ring* (*SB* VII:334–37), Wagner sought to plume himself with academic feathers. Alfred Meissner commented on Wagner's "professorial air" in the mid-1840s; see Meissner, *Geschichte meines Lebens*, 2 vols. (Vienna, 1884), I, 169.

26. Friedrich Heinrich von der Hagen, *Minnesinger: Deutsche Liederdichter des zwölften, dreizehnten und vierzehnten Jahrhunderts, aus allen bekannten Handschriften und früheren Drucken gesammelt und berichtigt*, 5 vols. (Leipzig, 1838), IV, 160–90 (Walther von der Vogelweide), 192–230 (Wolfram von Eschenbach), 421–34 (Der Tanhuser), 463–68 (Der tugendhafte Schreiber), 487–510 (Reinmar von Zweter), and 745–53 (Der Krieg auf Wartburg). (None of Biterolf's works has survived.)

27. From von der Hagen's edition (*Minnesinger*, vol. II, 3–19), Wagner appears to have taken over the motifs of the Landgrave's hostility to the Welfs (strophe 6) and Biterolf's belligerence (strophes 12–14).

28. For a fuller treatment of this subject, see Stewart Spencer, "*Tannhäuser*: mediävistische Handlung in drei Aufzügen," in Spencer, ed., *Wagner 1976* (London, 1976), 40–53.

29. The contents of Wagner's library in Dresden are listed by Curt von Westernhagen, *Richard Wagners Dresdener Bibliothek 1842–1849* (Wiesbaden, 1966), 84–113. Among the medieval themes picked up and developed by Wagner are the ineluctability of fate, the perversity of women, and the destructive nature of love.

30. The seven-year truce referred to by Heinrich – the historical Henry the Fowler (c. 876–936) – occurred between 926 and 933.

31. Wagner continued to insist on this specific historical setting long after he claims to have abandoned history as a basis for opera: see his letter to Ferdinand Heine of 31 October 1853 (*SB* V:457–58). Perhaps the very historicity of *Lohengrin* was one of the reasons why he felt a repeated need to distance himself from it: see his letters to Adolf Stahr of 31 May 1851 (*SB* IV:57), Franz Liszt of 8 September 1852 and 8 May 1857 (*SB* IV:458 and VIII:320), Robert Franz of 28 October 1852 (*SB* V:87), and Julie Ritter of 29 December 1852 (*SB* V:143).

32. Friedrich Schlegel, *Gespräch über die Poesie*, ed. Hans Eichner (Stuttgart, 1968), 312.

33. Anton Wilhelm Florentin von Zuccalmaglio, "Die deutsche Oper," *Neue Zeitschrift für Musik* (hereafter *NZfM*) 6 (1837), 191; Louise Otto, "Die Nibelungen als Oper," *NZfM* 23 (1845), 49–52, 129–30, 171–72, 175–76, and 181–83; and Franz Brendel, "Vergangenheit, Gegenwart und Zukunft der Oper," *NZfM* 23 (1845), 33–35, 37–39, 41–43, 105–08, 109–12, 121–24, 149–52, and *NZfM* 24 (1846), 57–60 and 61–64. Elsewhere, Friedrich Theodor Vischer struck a similarly nationalistic note in his *Kritische Gänge*, 2 vols. (Tübingen, 1844), I, 399–410, where he promotes the idea of using the *Nibelungenlied* as the source of a "national" epic opera.

34. See, for example, K. W. Göttling, *Ueber das Geschichtliche im Nibelungenliede* (Rudolstadt, 1814); and Franz Joseph Mone, *Untersuchungen zur Geschichte der teutschen Heldensage* (Quedlinburg, 1836).

35. For a note on the dating of *The Wibelungs*, see Barry Millington's chapter (5) in this volume.

36. Richard Wagner, *Das braune Buch*, ed. Joachim Bergfeld (Zurich, 1975), 112 and 113; trans. George Bird as *The Diary of Richard Wagner: The Brown Book 1865–1882* (London, 1980), 95 (translation emended).

37. Particularly important were Franz Joseph Mone, *Einleitung in das Nibelungen-Lied* (Heidelberg, 1818); Karl Lachmann, *Zu den Nibelungen und zur Klage* (Berlin, 1836), 333–49; and Jacob Grimm, *Deutsche Mythologie*, 2nd edn. (Göttingen, 1844), esp. 345. (Here the verbal parallel with *GS* II:131 is too obvious to be overlooked: like Grimm, Wagner draws an analogy between Siegfried and Fafner on the one hand and Apollo and Python on the other.) Joachim Köhler (*Richard Wagner*, 293–99) argues that Wagner may also have been familiar with Schelling's

speculations on myth in *The Essence of Human Freedom* (1809).

38. Georg Wilhelm Friedrich Hegel, *The Philosophy of History*, trans. J. Sibree (New York, 1956), 231–32 and 250–74. Wagner owned the second edition of 1840 and read it in 1847.

39. *Des Aischylos Werke*, trans. Johann Gustav Droysen, 2 vols. (Berlin, 1832), I, 161. In his "Annals," Wagner writes of the "awesome impression" left by his reading of Droysen's translation in 1847; see Wagner, *Das braune Buch*, 111.

40. See Theodore M. Andersson, "The Doctrine of Oral Tradition in the Chanson de Geste and Saga," *Scandinavian Studies* 34 (1962), 219–36; and Petra-Hildegard Wilberg, *Richard Wagners mythische Welt: Versuche wider den Historismus* (Freiburg im Breisgau, 1996).

41. See George L. Mosse, *Germans and Jews* (Detroit, 1987), 34–115.

5 *Der Ring des Nibelungen*: conception and interpretation

1. The *Entwurf* (sketch) was originally headed "Die Nibelungensage (Mythus)." Wagner renamed it when including it in his collected writings in 1871.

2. For discussion of significant parallels between the *Ring* and the *Prometheus* trilogy of Aeschylus, as reconstructed by its German translator, J. G. Droysen, see Hugh Lloyd-Jones, "Wagner and the Greeks," in *The Wagner Compendium*, ed. Barry Millington (London and New York, 1992), 158–61.

3. The only works composed during these years were the Polka, *WWV* 84, and *Eine Sonate für das Album von Frau M[athilde] W[esendonck]*, *WWV* 85, both written for Mathilde Wesendonck.

4. See *WWV*, 328–30. See also *Wagner* 4 (1983), 87–89, for English translation.

5. The dating is from Petra-Hildegard Wilberg, *Richard Wagners mythische Welt: Versuche wider den Historismus* (Freiburg im Breisgau, 1996), 79–85. *WWV* gives February 1849.

6. This peroration was suppressed by Wagner when he prepared the text for his collected writings in 1871. For the centrality of *The Wibelungs* and the Barbarossa legend to Wagner's creative impulse, see Joachim Köhler, *Richard Wagner: The Last of the Titans*, trans. Stewart Spencer (New Haven and London, 2004), 245–55. See the published ending of the essay in *GS* II:155; *PW* VII:298.

7. The project was taken up again, with a view to completing it, by Adolf Hitler, no less. He designed sets and costumes, but his compositional skills fell short of the task. See Joachim Köhler, *Wagner's Hitler: The Prophet and His Disciple*, trans. Ronald Taylor (Cambridge, 2000), 91–92.

8. What eventually became the fourth *Ring* drama, *Götterdämmerung*, and at this point all that existed of the *Ring* project.

9. Fifty copies of the *Ring* poem had been printed privately by Wagner in 1853.

10. It is probably no coincidence that the Stadttheater in Riga, where Wagner had been music director from 1837 to 1839, boasted an amphitheater-like auditorium and a sunken pit. For a plan of the theater, see Oswald Bauer, *Richard Wagner geht ins Theater* (Bayreuth, 1996), 77.

11. First published in 1899, the *Grundlagen* achieved bestseller status: by 1915 over 100,000 copies had been sold; by 1938 a quarter of a million.

12. See Köhler, *Wagner's Hitler*, 120–32, for Chamberlain's own role as spiritual mentor to first Wilhelm II and later Hitler.

13. Richard Voss, *Aus einem phantastischen Leben* (Stuttgart, 1923), 366–67.

14. See Udo Bermbach, "Richard Wagner as Prophet of the World War," *Wagner* 21/2 (July 2000), 87–109.

15. See *ibid.*, 105–09.

16. See Köhler, *Richard Wagner: The Last of the Titans*, 162–77.

17. Walter Benjamin, *Reflections* (New York, 1978), 158.

18. Theodor Adorno, *Versuch über Wagner* (Frankfurt, 1952; trans. Rodney Livingstone, *In Search of Wagner*, London, 1981; 2nd edn. 2005). The essay was written, however, in the years immediately prior to World War II (1937/38).

19. Adorno, *In Search of Wagner* (2005), 4–5, 143.

20. *Ibid.*, 122.

21. Geoffrey Skelton, *Wieland Wagner: The Positive Sceptic* (London, 1971), 178.

22. Robert Donington, *Wagner's* Ring *and Its Symbols: The Music and the Myth* (London, 1963).

23. Deryck Cooke, *I Saw the World End: A Study of Wagner's* Ring (Oxford, 1979).

24. *Ibid.*, 27. Cooke is also critical of Shaw's interpretation, which he dismisses as "brilliant Shavian invective" rather than a fully rounded exegesis.

25. Jean-Jacques Nattiez, *Wagner Androgyne: A Study in Interpretation*, trans. Stewart Spencer (Princeton, 1993).

26. *Ibid.*, xiv.

27. *Ibid.*, 76.

28. See chap. 15; Barry Millington, "What Shall We Do for a Ring," in Stewart Spencer and

Barry Millington, eds., *Wagner's* Ring of the Nibelung: *A Companion* (London, 1993), 25–28; Mike Ashman, "Producing Wagner," in Barry Millington and Stewart Spencer, eds., *Wagner in Performance* (New Haven and London, 1992), 29–47; Patrick Carnegy, "Designing Wagner: Deeds of Music made Visible?," *ibid.*, 48–74; Patrick Carnegy, *Wagner and the Art of the Theatre: The Operas in Stage Performance* (New Haven and London, 2006).

29. See Roger Hutton, "The 1988 Bayreuth *Ring* as Theory and as Theatre," *Wagner* 10/2 (1989), 66–80.

30. See Simon Williams, *Wagner and the Romantic Hero* (Cambridge, 2004), 142–69.

31. See in particular Marc A. Weiner, *Richard Wagner and the Anti-Semitic Imagination* (Lincoln, NE, and London, 1995).

6 Leitmotif, temporality, and musical design in the *Ring*

1. In the 1871 "Report in the Form of an Epilogue" to the publication of the *Ring* poem (*GS* VI:266; *PW* III:266). See also n. 8 below.

2. The idea of using the *Nibelungenlied* as the source of a distinctively German grand opera had been in the air for some time (see chap. 4). Wagner's quondam colleague and nemesis from the Riga years, Heinrich Dorn, anticipated him with a "grand Romantic opera" in five acts, *Die Nibelungen*, produced by Franz Liszt (no less) in Weimar, 1854. See Adelyn Peck Leverett, "Liszt, Wagner, and Heinrich Dorn's *Die Nibelungen*," *Cambridge Opera Journal* 2 (1990), 121–44. On the revolutionary context of Wagner's first ideas for his *Ring of the Nibelung* cycle, see also chaps. 3 and 4.

3. The original verse drafts of the first two dramas (the last two of the cycle) were slightly revised before Wagner had the whole text privately printed the next year; only with the first public printing of the texts (Leipzig, 1863) did they acquire their definitive titles of *Siegfried* and *Götterdämmerung*.

4. We should keep in mind, though, that at least since the decline of old-style *opera seria*, opera had offered a freer scope for modulation, abrupt contrasts, and loosely concatenated approaches to form than had traditional instrumental genres.

5. Wolzogen's guides were the model for many more published across the later nineteenth century and beyond. Christian Thorau examines the larger critical context of leitmotif before and after Wolzogen, as well as related hermeneutic and analytical issues, in his monograph *Semantisierte Sinnlichkeit: Studien zur Rezeption und Zeichenstruktur des*

Leitmotivtechnik Richard Wagners (Stuttgart, 2003). On the origins of the term itself ("leitmotif," German *Leitmotiv*) in relation to the metaphor of the *Leitfaden*, see also Thomas Grey, ". . . *wie ein rother Faden*: On the Origins of 'Leitmotif' as Critical Concept and Musical Practice," in Ian Bent, ed., *Music Theory in the Age of Romanticism* (Cambridge, 1996), 187–210.

6. The theory of associative motives or leitmotifs is developed, very gradually, across sections 5 and 6 of part 3 of *Opera and Drama* (*GS* IV:173–204; *PW* II:316–50), starting from an analysis of the expressive or "linguistic" capacities of modern instrumental music and the complementary relationship between musical (emotional) and verbal (rational) modes of "speech." The more specific ideas about how musical themes or motives will establish a network of "anticipations" and "recollections" of concrete dramatic utterances or gestures is developed in section 6, and especially toward the end of it. Wagner is most consistent in speaking of leitmotifs as *melodische Momente* (melodic moments or elements) while reserving the term "motive" (*Motiv, Grundmotiv, Hauptmotiv*) for the dramatic motifs, the elements with which the musical ideas are to be associated, or which inspire them. See also Thomas Grey, *Wagner's Musical Prose: Texts and Contexts* (Cambridge, 1995), 319–26.

7. Wolzogen's original *Leitfaden* for the *Ring* gave ninety leitmotifs. Ernest Newman's commentaries on the *Ring* dramas (*The Wagner Operas* [New York, 1949; repr. 1981], vol. II) supply nearly 200 examples, a figure that includes transformations and combinations of leitmotifs, as well as some musical figures or gestures for which he does not claim leitmotivic status. J. K. Holman's more recent guide to the *Ring* gives as many as 145: *Wagner's* Ring: *A Listener's Companion and Concordance* (Portland, OR, 1996).

8. Cooke's most comprehensive presentation of this "genealogical" approach to leitmotif in the *Ring* is the audio commentary he provided to accompany the first high-fidelity recording of the cycle under Georg Solti (London Records), still available as a supplement to the CD reissue of that groundbreaking recording. Cooke took his cue from Wagner's own reference to the "malleable nature-motives" (*plastischen Naturmotive*) that were his starting point for the "new path" of *Das Rheingold*, "which I had then to evolve in ever more individualized forms to undergird the emotional tendencies of the broadly ramified action and its characters" (*GS* VI:266; see *PW* III:266); see also n. 1 in this chapter.

9. On this concept from part 3 of *Opera and Drama*, see Grey, *Wagner's Musical Prose*, 181–211; see 375–77 for the translation of the relevant portion of *Opera and Drama* (*GS* IV:152–55).

10. Carolyn Abbate (following Adorno) suggests the same with regard to Kundry, whose soul has "transmigrated" between different bodies over many centuries, and who returns as the same "person," but inwardly and outwardly transformed, in each act of *Parsifal*: "Metempsychotic Wagner," in her *In Search of Opera* (Princeton, 2001), 108.

11. Skepticism toward the omniscience of leitmotivic orchestral discourse in the *Ring* is a leitmotif of Carolyn Abbate's writing on Wagner. See for example *Unsung Voices: Music and Narrative in Nineteenth-Century Opera* (Princeton, 1991), and "Wagner, 'On Modulation,' and *Tristan*," *Cambridge Opera Journal* 1 (1989), 33–58.

12. On the "Annunciation of Death" scene as musical dialogue, and an evolving series of "poetic-musical periods," see Grey, *Wagner's Musical Prose*, 228–41.

13. The only obstacle facing Sigurd in the *Volsunga Saga* at this juncture is that he has so overloaded his horse with treasure from the newly won dragon's horde that it refuses to move. See *The Saga of the Volsungs*, trans. Jesse L. Byock (Berkeley and Los Angeles, 1990), 66 (episode 20).

14. Wagner himself, in his famous explanatory gloss on the *Ring of the Nibelung* dramas written to August Röckel early in 1854, provides a more immediate psychological explanation of Wotan's behavior: "Faced with the prospect of his own annihilation, he finally becomes so instinctively human that – in spite of his supreme resolve – his ancient pride is once more stirred, provoked moreover (mark this well!) by his jealousy of Brünnhilde . . . He refuses . . . to be thrust aside, but prefers to fall – to be conquered" (letter of 25/26 January 1854: *SL* 308). As Wagner further notes, Wotan's anger at the climax of the confrontation is genuine, and unpremeditated. That is, if he begins by putting Siegfried to a ritualistic test, he ends by taking Siegfried's resistance personally, however much it may be necessary and expected.

15. While the C-major horn-call, a motive associated with the previous wedding scene, is afterwards identified explicitly with the Gibichung hunting party (as they call for Siegfried), Hagen's steer-horn has no clear dramatic justification as an offstage effect here. Its presence is rather an uncanny echo from the past, and conceivably related to whatever has

just led Siegfried astray: "Some elf" (*Albe*; cf. Alberich), he says, as he wanders on to the scene where he will encounter the Rhine maidens. The C-major horn-call, incidentally, relates by virtue of its initial, accented descending leap (here a fifth) to a whole complex and cannily developed family of motives associated with the Gibichung clan throughout the opera: Hagen (involving a tritone), Gunter (with dignified dotted march-rhythms), and Gutrune (a legato variant of the "wedding" call, including the rising steps that follow here the initial fifth descent).

16. Thus, Siegfried's narrative revisits the "double-tonic complex" of E and C that figured prominently throughout the final act of *Siegfried*. On Robert Bailey's concept of such "double-tonic complexes" in Wagner (especially typical of *Tristan, Meistersinger*, and this last act of *Siegfried*, all composed across the extended decade 1857–69), see Robert Bailey, ed., *Wagner: Prelude and Transfiguration from* Tristan und Isolde (New York, 1985), 121–22. The idea has been taken up since then in many studies of Wagner's music, above all of *Tristan und Isolde*.

17. John Deathridge has called attention to Wagner's own private identification of this motive (in a letter of 6 September 1875) as the "Glorification of Brünnhilde" in several contexts, originally in a review of Wagner literature in *19th-Century Music* 5 (1981), 84. Earlier, when completing his first draft of the score, Wagner referred to it as "Sieglinde's praise for Brünnhilde" and noted "I am glad I kept [it] back . . . to become as it were a hymn to heroes" (*CWD*: 23 July 1872). See also Grey, *Wagner's Musical Prose*, 367–73.

7 *Tristan und Isolde*: essence and appearance

1. Thomas Mann, *Buddenbrooks: The Decline of a Family*, trans. T. J. Reed (New York, 1993), 448, 720–21.

2. [Editor's note:] These polarities in the drama, music, and experience of *Tristan und Isolde* are explored at length in the recent monograph by Roger Scruton, *Death-Devoted Heart: Sex and the Sacred in Wagner's* Tristan and Isolde (New York, 2004). On the association of Wagner, and above all *Tristan*, with illness and decay at the end of the century, see also Thomas Grey, "Wagner the Degenerate: Fin-de-Siècle Cultural 'Pathology' and the Anxiety of Modernism," *19th-Century Studies* 16 (2002), 73–92.

3. Thomas Mann, "Wagner and the Present Age" (1931), in Mann, *Pro and Contra Wagner*, trans. Allan Blunden (Chicago and London, 1985), 88–89. Nietzsche speaks, for example, of

"the dangerous fascination and the gruesome sweet infinity of *Tristan*" in *Ecce Homo* (1888), ed. and trans. Walter Kaufmann (New York, 1969), 250.

4. Frank Kermode, foreword to Mario Praz, *The Romantic Agony*, trans. Angus Davidson, 2nd edn. (Cleveland and New York, 1968), v.

5. See Raymond Furness, *Wagner and Literature* (Manchester, UK, 1982), 44; and Praz, *The Romantic Agony*, 296, 413 (n. 60). Peter Gay catalogues responses to *Tristan* by more ordinary audience members that nonetheless resemble those of the literary decadents in *The Bourgeois Experience: Victoria to Freud*, vol. II, *The Tender Passion* (Oxford and New York, 1986), 264–66.

6. Quoted in Robert Bailey, ed., *Richard Wagner: Prelude and Transfiguration from* Tristan und Isolde (New York, 1985), 19.

7. Friedrich Nietzsche, "Richard Wagner in Bayreuth," from *Unfashionable Observations* (*Unzeitgemäße Betrachtungen*), trans. Richard T. Gray, *The Complete Works of Friedrich Nietzsche*, ed. Ernst Behler, vol. II (Stanford, 1995), 303.

8. [Ed.] The last of these is a "love scene" only in a paradoxical, if dramatically apt, sense, considering that it consists of two solo "visions" experienced by the characters in isolation, and linked only by the briefest (and yet overwhelmingly intense) moment of reunion just before Tristan's death. The first "love scene" is rather an extended standoff that ends, fatefully, in a rapturous declaration of love.

9. On the concept (and Wagner's practice) of tonal pairing, see Bailey, *Richard Wagner: Prelude and Transfiguration from* Tristan und Isolde, 121–39. Bailey's ideas have served as a point of departure for numerous other analytical studies. See for example William Kinderman, "Dramatic Recapitulation and Tonal Pairing in Wagner's *Tristan und Isolde*," in Kinderman and Harold Krebs, eds., *The Second Practice of Nineteenth-Century Tonality* (Lincoln, NE, and London, 1996), 180–95. Lawrence Kramer relates the role of these stepwise and half-stepwise tonal shifts to ideas about the Freudian construction of desire (the libido) as possibly embodied in the music of *Tristan*; see Kramer, *Music as Cultural Practice 1800–1900* (Berkeley and Los Angeles, 1990), 154–56.

10. Hölderlin developed this argument in the essay "Über die Verfahrungsweise des poetischen Geistes" ("On the Operations of the Poetic Spirit," 1800) and "Über den Unterschied der Dichtarten" ("On the Difference of Poetic Modes," also 1800). Both essays are translated in Friedrich Hölderlin, *Essays and Letters on Theory*, ed. and trans.

Thomas Pfau (Albany, NY, 1988), 62–82, 83–88.

11. The relevant passage from this letter is translated (and discussed), along with a transcription of the December 1856 sketches, by Robert Bailey in "The Method of Composition," in *The Wagner Companion*, ed. Peter Burbidge and Richard Sutton (New York, 1979), 308–15.

12. [Ed.] And, for that matter, Wagner sketched the famous Prelude in its entirety before setting any of the libretto, as such. Bailey's detailed studies of the musical genesis of Act 1 of *Tristan* have been supplemented in the meantime by Ulrich Bartels: *Studien zu Wagners* Tristan und Isolde *anhand der Kompositionsskizze des zweiten und dritten Aktes*, 3 vols. (Cologne, 1995).

13. Carolyn Abbate, "Wagner, 'On Modulation,' and *Tristan*," *Cambridge Opera Journal* 1 (1989), 33–58.

14. Thomas Grey has taken this approach to Tristan's "Delirium" scene, where the dense leitmotivic texture answers to a poetic theme (the return of Tristan's memory), while the monologue also exhibits a more fundamentally musical design of intensification, climax, and dissolution: *Wagner's Musical Prose: Texts and Contexts* (Cambridge, 1995), 342–47.

15. Nattiez mounts a similar argument regarding the figures of Siegfried and Brünnhilde in *Wagner Androgyne: A Study in Interpretation*, trans. Stewart Spencer (Princeton, 1993), 76–84, an idea further developed by Grey with regard to details of the prose writings and the music (as well as text) of *Siegfried*, Act 3, scene 3, in *Wagner's Musical Prose*, 153–72.

16. Abbate, "On Modulation," 48–49; Nattiez, *Wagner Androgyne*, 153–54. James McGlathery also sees Tristan as the "leading" figure in that he introduces Isolde to the "mysterious connection between erotic desire and mystical longing for death." See McGlathery, *Wagner's Operas and Desire* (New York, 1998), 178. Lawrence Kramer argues more or less the reverse, finding Tristan to be the passive role (and tendentially masochistic), with Isolde as the more active, dominant one (Kramer, *Music as Cultural Practice*, 165).

17. Charles Baudelaire, "Richard Wagner and *Tannhäuser* in Paris," in Baudelaire, *The Painter of Modern Life and Other Essays*, ed. and trans. Jonathan Mayne (London, 1964), 120.

18. Nietzsche, "Richard Wagner in Bayreuth," 303.

19. A cadence effected, notably, through the definitive, long-deferred resolution of the

Tristan chord introduced in the first measures of the Prelude. [Ed.] For an extended discussion of Schopenhauer's significance for Wagner (*Tristan* and beyond), see Bryan Magee, *The Tristan Chord: Wagner and Philosophy* (London and New York, 2000).

20. Mann, "Sorrows and Grandeur of Richard Wagner," in Mann, *Pro and Contra Wagner*, 124–25.

21. Schlegel, *Friedrich Schlegel's Lucinde and the Fragments*, ed. and trans. Peter Firchow (Minneapolis, 1971), 127 (trans. emended).

22. Tristan becomes "night-sighted" (*nachtsichtig*) in the course of the Act 2 love scene. See Novalis, *Hymns to the Night*, trans. Dick Higgins, 3rd edn. (Kingston, 1988), 13; see also Schlegel's description of Lucinde as "consecrated to the night" ("der Nacht geweiht") in *Friedrich Schlegel's Lucinde*, 126. Novalis's reference to "Night's initiates" ("Nacht Geweihte") also occurs in *Hymns to the Night* (nos. 14–15), echoed verbatim in Act 2 of *Tristan* (Tristan: "O nun waren wir Nacht-Geweihte!"), beginning Tristan's speech immediately prior to the central lyrical episode, "O sink hernieder, Nacht der Liebe."

23. Carl Dahlhaus, *Richard Wagner's Music Dramas*, trans. Mary Whittall (Cambridge, 1979), 51. For similar views, see Ernst Bloch, *Essays on the Philosophy of Music*, trans. Peter Palmer (Cambridge, 1985), 53; Dieter Borchmeyer, *Richard Wagner: Theory and Theatre*, trans. Stewart Spencer (Oxford and New York, 1991), 338; and, even more emphatically expressed, McGlathery, *Wagner's Operas and Desire*, 177, 185, 187.

24. [Ed.] On these various deployments of the opening "motive complex," see also Joseph Kerman, "*Tristan und Isolde*: The Prelude and the Play," in Kerman, *Write All These Down* (Berkeley and Los Angeles, 1994), 335–50.

25. The term "endless melody" was coined in response to his critical detractors in the essay "*Music of the Future*" ("*Zukunftsmusik*") of 1860, with an emphasis on the continuous presence of motivically significant material, continuously developed and continuously eloquent in expressive effect or "meaning." The broader identification of "endless melody" with seamless continuity is also relevant: see Grey, *Wagner's Musical Prose*, 252–55.

26. The theorist Ernst Kurth singled out harmonic disturbances of this sort for their "sensuous" or "absolute" harmonic effect, i.e., their tendency to detach themselves from their immediate (functional) tonal surroundings. As an example of such an "absolute" harmonic effect or progressions (*absolute Fortschreitungswirkung*) he cited the

juxtaposition of A♭ and A♮ triads in the "Death-Devoted Head" motive ("Todgeweihtes Haupt"). His primary example of this category was, not surprisingly, the *Tristan* chord itself. See Kurth, *Romantische Harmonik und ihre Krise in Wagners* Tristan, 2nd edn. (Berlin, 1923), 262–67; and Lee A. Rothfarb, *Ernst Kurth as Theorist and Analyst* (Philadelphia, 1988), 158–60.

27. *CWD*: 16 January 1871. On the relationship of Wagner's libretto to Gottfried, see Arthur Groos, "Appropriation in Wagner's *Tristan* Libretto," in Groos and Roger Parker, eds., *Reading Opera* (Princeton, 1989), 13–25.

28. Borchmeyer, *Richard Wagner: Theory and Theatre*, 146.

29. Friedrich Nietzsche, *The Birth of Tragedy and The Case of Wagner*, trans. Walter Kaufmann (New York, 1967), 175.

30. Mann, "An Essay on the Theater" (1908), in Mann, *Pro and Contra Wagner*, 25. Mann reiterated this theme time and again. See also, for example, "Coming to Terms with Richard Wagner" (1911), *Reflections of a Non-Political Man* (1915–18), "Ibsen and Wagner" (1928), "Sufferings and Grandeur of Richard Wagner" (1933), and "Richard Wagner and *Der Ring des Nibelungen*" (1937) as translated in Mann, *Pro and Contra Wagner*, 46, 55, 84, 102, 187–92.

31. See also the discussion of leitmotif technique as it emerged in the *Ring* cycle, chapter 6 in this book.

32. Kerman, "Opera as Symphonic Poem," in Kerman, *Opera as Drama*, 2nd edn. (Berkeley and Los Angeles, 1988), 165.

33. Wagner's account of the deaths of Tristan's parents departs radically from the medieval sources. In Gottfried's poem, Tristan's mother Blanchefleur dies of grief after her husband, Riwalin, falls in battle.

34. Around the time he was setting to work on *Tristan und Isolde* Wagner planned to address this same theme in a project entitled *Die Sieger* (*The Victors*), a dramatization of a Buddhist legend. As he explained in his autobiography, the significance of this tale of a Tschantala girl and her love for Ananda, chief disciple of the Buddha, lay in its showing how "the past life of the suffering principal characters was entwined with the new phases of their lives" (*ML* 528).

8 Performing Germany in Wagner's *Die Meistersinger von Nürnberg*

1. Friedrich Nietzsche, *Beyond Good and Evil* (part 8: Peoples and Fatherlands), §240, trans. Walter Kaufmann, *Basic Writings of Nietzsche* (New York, 1968), 364.

2. Karl Storck, *Das Opernbuch* (Stuttgart, 1899), cited in Gerhard Bott, ed., Die

Meistersinger *und Richard Wagner: Die
Rezeptionsgeschichte einer Oper von 1868 bis
heute. Eine Ausstellung des Germanischen
Nationalmuseums in Nürnberg, 10. Juli bis 11.
Oktober 1981* (Nuremberg, 1981), 155. This
and all other translations are my own, unless
otherwise indicated.

3. Joseph Goebbels, "Richard Wagner und das
Kunstempfinden unserer Zeit," in *Signale der
neuen Zeit: 25 ausgewählte Reden* (Munich,
1934), 191–96 (first published at the time as
"Richard Wagner und das Kunstempfinden
unserer Zeit: Rundfunkrede von
Reichsminister Dr. Goebbels," *Völkischer
Beobachter*, 8 August 1933; "Reichsminister
Dr. Goebbels huldigt Richard Wagner," *Der
Angriff*, 7 August 1933).

4. Hofmannsthal to Richard Strauss, 1 July
1927, quoted in Hans Rudolf Vaget, "The
'Metapolitics' of *Die Meistersinger*: Wagner's
Nuremberg as Imagined Community," in
Vaget, ed., *Searching for Common Ground:
Diskurse zur deutschen Identität 1750–1871*
(Cologne, 2000), 275.

5. Theodor Adorno, "Bilderwelt des
Freischütz," in *Gesammelte Schriften* XVII
(Frankfurt, 1982), 36.

6. Theodor W. Adorno, "Wagner's Relevance
for Today," in Adorno, *Essays on Music*, ed.
Richard Leppert, trans. Susan H. Gillespie
(Berkeley and Los Angeles, 2002), 585.

7. Thomas Mann to Richard Braungart, 14
April 1950, in Hans Rudolf Vaget, ed., *Im
Schatten Wagners. Thomas Mann über Richard
Wagner: Texte und Zeugnisse, 1895–1955*
(Frankfurt, 1999), 206. It was *Die Meistersinger*
that provoked Mann's well-known comment
that "certainly, there is a lot of 'Hitler' in
Wagner," in "Richard Wagner und kein Ende"
(1950): *Im Schatten Wagners*, 203–04.

8. Thomas Mann, "The Sorrows and Grandeur
of Richard Wagner" ("Leiden und Größe
Richard Wagners," 1933), in Mann, *Pro and
Contra Wagner*, trans. Allan Blunden
(Chicago, 1985), 145.

9. Rudy Koshar, *Germany's Transient Pasts:
Preservation and National Memory in the
Twentieth Century* (Chapel Hill and London,
1998), 151. Goebbels defined *Leistung* in the
cultural realm in his speech at the opening of the
Reichskulturkammer on 15 November 1933; see
ibid., 153–54. The "Wach auf!" chorus from
Meistersinger was also performed at this event.

10. This latter type of nation Meinecke termed
a *Staatsnation*.

11. Benedict Anderson, *Imagined
Communities: Reflections on the Origin and
Spread of Nationalism*, rev. edn. (London,
1991; orig. edn. 1983).

12. The discussion of nation and nationalism
in this paragraph is taken largely from the
introduction to Abigail Green, *Fatherlands:
State-Building and Nationhood in Nineteenth-
Century Germany* (Cambridge, 2001); see also
Eric Hobsbawm, "Introduction" to Hobsbawm
and Terence Ranger, eds., *The Invention of
Tradition* (Cambridge, 1983), 1–14; George
L. Mosse, *The Nationalization of the Masses:
Political Symbolism and Mass Movements in
Germany from the Napoleonic Wars Through
the Third Reich* (Ithaca, 1991); and Konrad H.
Jarausch and Michael Geyer, *Shattered Past:
Reconstructing German Histories* (Princeton,
2003), in particular chap. 8, "A Struggle for
Unity: Redefining National Identities,"
221–44.

13. Green, *Fatherlands*, 6–7, and Alon
Confino, *The Nation as Local Metaphor:
Württemberg, Imperial Germany, and
National Memory, 1871–1918* (Chapel Hill and
London, 1997), 4.

14. John Gillis, "Memory and Identity: The
History of a Relationship," introduction to
Gillis, ed., *Commemorations: The Politics of
National Identity* (Princeton, 1994), 3, 5. See
also Koshar, *Germany's Transient Pasts*; Mieke
Bal, Jonathan Crewe, and Leo Spitzer, eds.,
Acts of Memory: Cultural Recall in the Present
(Hanover, NH, and London, 1999); and
Confino, *Nation as Local Metaphor*.

15. Bal, introduction to Bal, Crewe, and
Spitzer, *Acts of Memory*, vii.

16. Koshar, *Germany's Transient Pasts*, 10.

17. *Ibid.*, 9.

18. Gillis, "Memory and Identity," 4.

19. Confino, *Nation as Local Metaphor*, 8.

20. The three examples in the parenthesis are
as follows: Celia Applegate, *A Nation of
Provincials: The German Idea of Heimat*
(Berkeley and Los Angeles, 1990); Koshar,
Germany's Transient Pasts; and Green,
Fatherlands.

21. Historian Wolfgang J. Mommsen has
argued that the development of a rich cultural
life was a means for the bourgeoisie to create its
political ideal: "Kultur als Instrument der
Legitimation bürgerlicher Hegemonie im
Nationalstaat," in Hermann Danuser and
Herfried Münkler, eds., *Deutsche Meister –
böse Geister? Nationale Selbstfindung in der
Musik* (Schliengen, 2001), 61–74.

22. See Manfred Hettling and Paul Nolte,
"Bürgerliche Feste als symbolische Politik im
19. Jahrhundert," in Hettling and Nolte, eds.,
*Bürgerliche Feste: Symbolische Formen
politischen Handelns im 19. Jahrhundert*
(Göttingen, 1993), 7–36; and the very useful
review essay by Michael Maurer, "Feste

und Feiern als historischer Forschungsgegenstand," *Historische Zeitschrift* 253 (1991), 101–30. For a very general overview, in English, see Max L. Baeumer, "Imperial Germany as Reflected in Its Mass Festivals," in Volker Dürr, Kathy Harms, and Peter Hayes, eds., *Imperial Germany* (Madison, WI, 1985), 62–74.

23. Hettling and Nolte, "Bürgerliche Feste als symbolische Politik," 18.

24. *Ibid.*, 30.

25. Gillis, "Memory and Identity," 9. Prussia expended considerable effort to establish a national festival after 1870–71, but its attempts to institutionalize its 1870 defeat of France at the battle of Sedan, the Kaiser's birthday, or anniversary of the founding of the Reich all came to naught. Instead, it was the Nazis' pantheon of events and celebrations that finally succeeded in establishing a national festival culture.

26. Theodor Adorno, *In Search of Wagner*, trans. Rodney Livingstone (London, 1981), 120–21.

27. Hannu Salmi, *Imagined Germany: Richard Wagner's National Utopia* (New York, 1999). This work is a condensed and rewritten version of his dissertation, "'Die Herrlichkeit des deutschen Namens . . .': die schriftstellerische und politische Tätigkeit Richard Wagners als Gestalter nationaler Identität während der staatlichen Vereinigung Deutschlands" (Turku, 1993).

28. Letter of 19 March 1866, *SL* 345. He also once commented "I am the most German being. I am the German spirit" (from Joachim Bergfeld, ed., *The Diary of Richard Wagner, 1865–1882: The Brown Book* [London, 1980], cited in Salmi, *Imagined Germany*, 55).

29. In *Eine Mitteilung an meine Freunde* (1851) he called Sachs the "final manifestation of the artistically creative spirit of the *Volk*" and contrasted him with petty bourgeois Meistersingers and their pedantry (*GS* IV: 284–85).

30. Salmi cites a letter from Wagner to Gabriel Monod, 25 October 1876, that seems to imply that Wagner's strategy was a conscious one, that his polemics against the French were a "means to make the Germans themselves create authentic culture" (*Imagined Germany*, 14).

31. *Ibid.*, 33.

32. *Ibid.*, 50.

33. *Ibid.*, 41.

34. *Ibid.*, 79. "Was ist Deutsch?," a shortened and revised version of the 1865 diary entries, was first published in the *Bayreuther Blätter* in 1878. The diary entries themselves were not published in their original form until 1936: see volume IV of Otto Strobel, ed., *König Ludwig II. und Richard Wagner: Briefwechsel*, 5 vols. (Karlsruhe, 1936, 1939).

35. Salmi, *Imagined Germany*, 49; see also 124–25, and, for an assessment of Wagner's relationship with Bismarck vis-à-vis Ludwig II, 159–65.

36. *Deutsche Kunst und deutsche Politik* (*GS* VIII:49); trans. in Salmi, *Imagined Germany*, 56.

37. Letter of 27 March 1866, cited in Reinhold Brinkmann, "Lohengrin, Sachs und Mime oder Nationales Pathos und die Pervertierung der Kunst bei Richard Wagner," in Danuser and Münkler, *Deutsche Meister – böse Geister? Nationale Selbstfindung in der Musik*, 213.

38. This idea, of course, is not new; see Salmi, *Imagined Germany*, 134–38. Vaget describes *Meistersinger* as "Wagner's most complete and resounding answer to the question of 'Was ist deutsch'"; "the most complete articulation of his aesthetic and political beliefs" ("'Metapolitics,'" 273). But Thomas S. Grey has argued that "Wagner's cultural chauvinism – his antagonism toward the French and the Jews, grounded in a paranoid persecution complex – leaves only a faint imprint on the work, though it can easily be traced to [his] contemporaneous essays" ("Wagner's *Die Meistersinger* as National Opera [1868–1945]," in Celia Applegate and Pamela Potter, eds., *Music and German National Identity* [Chicago and London, 2002], 100).

39. "Nachgelassene Fragmente," in Friedrich Nietzsche, *Sämtliche Werke: Kritische Studienausgabe in 15 Bänden*, ed. Giorgio Colli and Mazzino Montinari (Berlin, 1980), VIII, 266. This aphorism was often cited by Thomas Mann.

40. See Peter Uwe Hohendahl, "Reworking History: Wagner's German Myth of Nuremberg," in Reinhold Grimm and Jost Hermand, eds., *Re-Reading Wagner* (Madison, WI, 1993), 43. In writing the text of *Die Meistersinger*, Wagner drew on Gervinus's chapter on Hans Sachs.

41. *SL* 749. On the nexus of *Die Meistersinger*, Hanslick, Beckmesser, and the Jews, see Thomas Grey, "Masters and Their Critics: Wagner, Hanslick, Beckmesser, and *Die Meistersinger*," in Nicholas Vazsonyi, ed., *Wagner's* Meistersinger: *Performance, History, Representation* (Rochester, NY, 2003), 165–89.

42. "Richard Wagner und das Judentum: Ein Beitrag zur Kulturgeschichte unserer Zeit, von einem Unparteiischen" (Elberfeld, 1869); reprinted in Jens Malte Fischer, *Richard Wagners "Das Judentum in der Musik": Eine*

kritische Dokumentation als Beitrag zur Geschichte des Antisemitismus (Frankfurt am Main and Leipzig, 2000), 314.

43. Wagner himself noted this phenomenon in "Wollen wir hoffen?" (1879): "[*Meistersinger*] was difficult to perform, rarely met with even a tolerable degree of success and was lumped together with ordinary 'operas,' shouted down by the Jews and treated by German audiences as a curiosity to be greeted with a shake of the head" (*GS* X:120; translation from Stewart Spencer, "Wagner's Nuremberg," *Cambridge Opera Journal* 4 [1992], 39).

44. Adorno, *In Search of Wagner*, 21.

45. For an excellent summary, see Hans Rudolf Vaget, "'Du warst mein Feind von je': The Beckmesser Controversy Revisited," in Vazsonyi, *Wagner's* Meistersinger, 190–208.

46. Marc A. Weiner, "Reading the Ideal," *New German Critique* 69 (1996), 69.

47. David J. Levin, *Richard Wagner, Fritz Lang, and the Nibelungen: The Dramaturgy of Disavowal* (Princeton, 1998), 149–50.

48. David J. Levin, "Reading Beckmesser Reading: Antisemitism and Aesthetic Practice in *The Mastersingers of Nuremberg*," *New German Critique* 69 (Fall 1996), 129; see also Levin, "Reading a Staging/Staging a Reading," *Cambridge Opera Journal* 9 (1997), 47–71.

49. David Dennis, "'The Most German of All German Operas': *Die Meistersinger* Through the Lens of the Third Reich," in Vazsonyi, *Wagner's* Meistersinger, 98–119.

50. The use of the bar form was later elevated to a "secret" of Wagnerian form by Alfred Lorenz, who regarded the entirety of *Die Meistersinger* as a gigantic bar form. See Alfred Lorenz, *Das Geheimnis der Form bei Richard Wagner*, vol. III, *Der Musikalische Aufbau von Richard Wagners "Die Meistersinger von Nürnberg"* (Berlin, 1930; repr., Tutzing, 1966), 9–14.

51. Arthur Groos seems to have been the first to point out the connections between *Meistersinger* and nineteenth-century festival culture, but notes that it would be overstating the case to see the *Festwiese* as the same thing as "increasingly nationalized mass celebrations of the 1860s": Groos, "Constructing Nuremberg: Typological and Proleptic Communities in *Die Meistersinger*," *19th-Century Music* 16 (1992), 18–34.

52. Although a version of this speech is found in all extant drafts of the text, when composing the music in 1867, Wagner considered ending the opera with the Prize Song. He was dissuaded from this, however, by Cosima and ultimately replaced twenty-three lines with eight chauvinistic new lines – precisely those quoted above. For a discussion of the evolution of Sachs's final speech, see Grey, "Wagner's *Die Meistersinger* as National Opera." In this article, Grey explores the question of whether *Meistersinger* was a national opera by design and demonstrates that many aspects of the 1845 sketch are in fact more overtly nationalistic than the final version. Cosima's role in preserving these lines is oddly anticipatory of her later role as the center of the Bayreuth Circle; see Winfried Schüler, *Der Bayreuther Kreis von seiner Entstehung bis zum Ausgang der wilhelminischen Ära: Wagnerkult und Kulturreform im Geiste völkischer Weltanschauung* (Münster, 1971).

53. Spencer, "Wagner's Nuremberg," 33. See also Koshar, *Germany's Transient Pasts*.

54. Letter to Ludwig II, 24 July 1866: *SL* 701. See also *SL* 708, where Wagner calls Nuremberg "the abode of the 'artwork of the future'" and argues that the nation would also be such an art work – an aesthetic state. In "Wollen wir hoffen?" Wagner recalls his initial desire to have the premiere of the work in Nuremberg (*GS* X:119).

55. Hohendahl, "Wagner's German Myth of Nuremberg"; Groos, "Constructing Nuremberg"; Spencer, "Wagner's Nuremberg." Spencer's article also discusses the eight visits to Nuremberg made by Wagner during his lifetime. See also Dieter Borchmeyer, "Nuremberg as an Aesthetic State," in Borchmeyer, *Drama and the World of Richard Wagner*, trans. Daphne Ellis (Princeton, 2003), 180–211, and Nicholas Vazsonyi's introduction to *Wagner's* Meistersinger, 1–20. Nineteenth-century constructions of the myth of Nuremberg largely stem from Ludwig Tieck and Wilhelm Heinrich Wackenroder: *Herzensergießungen eines kunstliebenden Klosterbruders* (c. 1796).

56. Michael P. Steinberg, *Listening to Reason: Culture, Subjectivity, and Nineteenth-Century Music* (Princeton, 2004), 169. In this regard, Hohendahl ("Wagner's German Myth of Nuremberg," 57) refers to *Die Meistersinger* as a "phantasmagoria" and points out contradictions in the work.

57. Salmi, *Imagined Germany*, 181.

58. Bott, Die Meistersinger *und Richard Wagner*. This source also surveys images (largely from the nineteenth century) of Nuremberg, Sachs, and folk festivals. See also Hohendahl, "Wagner's German Myth of Nuremberg"; Grey, "*Die Meistersinger* as National Opera"; and Grey, "Selbstbehauptung oder Fremdmißbrauch? Zur Rezeptionsgeschichte der *Meistersinger*," in Hermann Danuser and Herfried Münkler, *Deutsche Meister – Böse Geister: Nationale*

Selbstfindung in der Musik (Argus, 2001), 305–20.

59. Grey, "*Die Meistersinger* as National Opera," 87–91.

60. See, for example, Frederic Spotts, *Bayreuth: A History of the Wagner Festival* (New Haven, 1994); Brigitte Hamann, *Winifred Wagner oder Hitlers Bayreuth* (Munich, 2002; also published as *Winifred Wagner: A Life at the Heart of Hitler's Bayreuth*, trans. Alan Bance [London, 2005]); Berndt W. Wessling, ed., *Bayreuth im Dritten Reich. Richard Wagners politische Erben: Eine Dokumentation* (Weinheim and Basel, 1983).

61. Hamann, *Winifred Wagner*, 130. The quoted words, "Hier gilt's der Kunst" come from Eva's dialogue with Sachs in Act 2 of *Die Meistersinger*.

62. Thomas Mann, *Reflections of a Nonpolitical Man*, trans. Walter D. Morris (New York, 1983), 18. Nietzsche's aphorism is also used as the epigram to Mann's fifth chapter, "Burgherly Nature," 71.

63. *Ibid.*, 71.

64. *Ibid.*, 311. In *Palestrina*, *Meistersinger*'s "Ehrt eure deutschen Meister!" is given theatrical form in the vision of the nine historical composers in the final tableau of Act 1; see Stephen McClatchie, "Hans Pfitzner's *Palestrina* and the Impotence of Early Lateness," *University of Toronto Quarterly* 67 (1998), 812–27.

65. For a discussion, see Modris Eksteins, *Rites of Spring: The Great War and the Birth of the Modern Age* (Toronto, 1989), 325.

66. Peter Raabe, "Wagners Meistersinger in unserer Zeit," in Raabe, *Die Musik im Dritten Reich: Kulturpolitische Reden und Aufsätze* (Regensburg, 1935), 71–72; translation from Dennis, "*Die Meistersinger* Through the Lens of the Third Reich," 113.

67. Michael Karbaum, *Studien zur Geschichte der Bayreuther Festspiele (1876–1976)* (Regensburg, 1976), 86. After the performance of *Meistersinger* that concluded the Day of Potsdam, Goebbels wrote contentedly in his diary (22 March 1933) that "the Wacht-Auf [*sic*] chorus finally acquired again its true meaning [*Sinn*]" (*ibid.*).

68. Goebbels, "Richard Wagner und das Kunstempfinden unserer Zeit," 191; translation from Dennis, "*Die Meistersinger* Through the Lens of the Third Reich," 109.

69. David Dennis offers a comprehensive survey and analysis of *Meistersinger* productions under the Nazis in "*Die Meistersinger* Through the Lens of the Third Reich."

70. Vaget, "Beckmesser Controversy," 207. According to her biographer, Winifred

Wagner was among the honorary guests for the entire day (Hamann, *Winifred Wagner*, 236).

71. The card is reproduced in Hamann, *Winifred Wagner*, 256. Vazsonyi has pointed that Hitler forbade singing of *Deutschlandlied* after *Meistersinger*, "almost as if the *Deutschlandlied* were no longer necessary since the opera *in toto* had itself become part of Germany's national music" (Vazsonyi, "Introduction. *Die Meistersinger*: Performance, History, Representation," in *Wagner's* Meistersinger, 14).

72. Spotts, *Bayreuth Festival*, 193.

73. For a discussion of the location, program, and structure of the *Reichsparteitage*, see Peter Reichel, *Der schöne Schein des Dritten Reiches: Faszination und Gewalt des Faschismus* (Munich and Vienna, 1991); Hans-Ulrich Thamer, "Faszination und Manipulation: Die Nürnberger Reichsparteitage der NSDAP," in Uwe Schultz, ed., *Das Fest: Eine Kulturgeschichte von der Antike bis zur Gegenwart* (Munich, 1988), 352–68. The rally continues the instrumentalization of Nuremberg discussed in Koshar, *Germany's Transient Pasts*, 140–41, 180–81. Many commentators have noted the lack of enthusiasm toward Wagner felt by many party members. For example, Heinz Tietjen, "Die Wahrheit über Bayreuth" (1945), states that the Nuremberg performances played to half-empty houses and that most leaders in the party disliked Wagner and were "ordered" to Bayreuth: document XX-3 in Karbaum, *Studien zur Geschichte der Bayreuther Festspiele*, 112–13.

74. Hamann, *Winifred Wagner*, 305.

75. Of course, the choice may actually have been that of composer Herbert Windt, who was responsible for scoring the film.

76. According to Hamann, *Winifred Wagner*, 667, n. 75.

77. Richard Wilhelm Stock, *Richard Wagner und die Stadt der Meistersinger: Den Großen von Bayreuth Richard und Cosima Wagner zum Gedächtnis in ihrem 125. und 100. Geburtsjahr* (Nuremberg, 1938), 28; see also 7, 8, 9, 23, 38, and 126.

78. Shelley Baranowski, *Strength Through Joy: Consumerism and Mass Tourism in the Third Reich* (Cambridge, 2004), 214. Baranowski notes that in 1942 the KdF became the seventh office of the Reichskulturkammer; as the "purveyor of culture to the masses" (*ibid.*, 213), the KdF organized performances of Goethe, Lessing, Kleist, Schilling, Bach, Brahms, Schubert, Beethoven, Mozart, and Wagner (as well as of popular culture). Verena Wagner's husband, Bodo Lafferentz, was the leader of the

KdF Office for Travel, Hiking, and Vacation and was also involved in cultural programming for the KdF.

79. Richard Wilhelm Stock, *Richard Wagner und seine* Meistersinger: *Eine Erinnerungsgabe zu den Bayreuther Kriegsfestspielen 1943* (Nuremberg, 1943).

80. Vaget, "Metapolitics," 272. *Kolberg* was a 1945 film by Veit Harlan, sponsored by Goebbels, which depicted Prussia's perseverance against Napoleon.

81. Dennis, "*Die Meistersinger* Through the Lens of the Third Reich," 103. See also Dina Porat, "'Zum Raum wird hier die Zeit': Richard Wagners Bedeutung für Adolf Hitler und die nationalsozialistische Führung," in *Richard Wagner und die Juden*, ed. Dieter Borchmeyer, Ami Maayani, and Susanne Vill (Stuttgart and Weimar, 2000), 207–20.

82. Hubert Kolland, "Wagner-Rezeption im deutschen Faschismus," in Christoph-Hellmut Mahling and Sigrid Wiesmann, eds., *Bericht über den Internationalen Musikwissenschaftlichen Kongreß Bayreuth* (Kassel, 1981), 494–503; Vaget, "Hitler's Wagner"; and Vaget, "Beckmesser Controversy."

83. Stock, *Richard Wagner und die Stadt der Meistersinger*, 8–9.

84. Dennis cautions against overstating parallels between Nazi views of Sachs and *Führerprinzip*, but notes they are "undeniable" ("*Die Meistersinger* Through the Lens of the Third Reich," 117). He also reminds us (112) that Alfred Rosenberg referred to Sachs as a model for the Nordic soul in *Der Mythus des 20. Jahrhunderts: Eine Wertung der seelisch-geistigen Gestaltenkämpfe unserer Zeit* (Munich, 1940).

85. There is a clear parallel here between *Meistersinger* and Goebbels's 1936 call for *Kunstbetrachtung* instead of cultural criticism (which he banned); see Vaget, "Hitler's Wagner," 23–24. Stock makes explicit identification between *Festwiese* and the public: "The people on the Nuremberg festival meadow, with their uneducated taste and true instinct for the true, noble, and beautiful, as well as their recognition of Walther von Stolzing's genuine artistry, are also Richard Wagner's public" (Stock, *Richard Wagner und die Stadt der Meistersinger*, 191).

86. See Dennis, "*Die Meistersinger* Through the Lens of the Third Reich," 119.

87. Wagner claimed that the Jews prevented it from being first performed in Nuremberg instead of Munich. See Stock, *Richard Wagner und die Stadt der Meistersinger*, 7.

88. Mann, "Sorrows and Grandeur of Richard Wagner," 140–41.

89. Vaget, "Metapolitics," 278. Vaget sees a number of elements comprising the metapolitical content of *Meistersinger*: Nuremberg presented as a *Volksgemeinschaft*; Sachs's charismatic leadership; a celebration of the subordination of the will of the individual to that of the community; the thematicization of precursorship; and the canonization of German art and artists (as well as the valorization of this canon).

90. 27 September 1943, in *Meldungen aus dem Reich*, XV, ed. Heinz Boberach (Herrsching, 1983), 5810–11.

91. Lorenz, *Geheimnis der Form*, III, 168–69. Lorenz analyzed the final speech as a potentiated bar form (for him, a particularly Germanic form), with "Habt acht!" marking the beginning of the Abgesang (which Lorenz understood as an intensification of feeling); see Stephen McClatchie, *Analyzing Wagner's Operas: Alfred Lorenz and German National Ideology* (Rochester, NY, 1998), 129–35.

92. Fritz Kempfler, "Lebenserinnerungen" (unpublished typescript), cited in Hamann, *Winifred Wagner*, 478. Kempfler misquotes the first word of the speech, writing "Zerfiel" instead of "Zerging."

93. Patrick Carnegy, "Stage History," in John Warrack, ed., *Richard Wagner:* Die Meistersinger von Nürnberg (Cambridge, 1994), 143. He notes that cuts were often made in "politically sensitive passages" after the war – one assumes that Sachs's final speech was one of these.

94. Hamann, *Winifred Wagner*, 574.

95. See Jeffrey Herf, *Divided Memory: The Nazi Past in the Two Germanys* (Cambridge and London, 1997). The production, which, in its reminder of the vanished prewar Nuremberg, was seen as a political mortification by conservatives, is discussed in Spotts, *Bayreuth Festival*, 218–21. It was restaged in four subsequent years (1957, 1958, 1959, 1961) before being replaced by a slightly more traditional production.

96. Koshar, *Germany's Transient Pasts*, 209.

97. Vaget, "Beckmesser Controversy," 204.

98. Grey, "*Die Meistersinger* as National Opera," 101. Grey is alluding to a chapter entitled "Der Meistersinger-Staat" in Joachim Köhler's *Wagners Hitler: Der Prophet und sein Vollstrecker* (Munich, 1997; also published as *Wagner's Hitler: The Prophet and His Disciple*, trans. Ronald Taylor [Cambridge, 2000]), 347–81.

99. Joseph Horowitz, "Wagner und der amerikanische Jude – eine persönliche Betrachtung," in *Richard Wagner und die Juden*, 248.

9 *Parsifal*: redemption and *Kunstreligion*

1. William Kinderman has written several essays on the compositional genesis of *Parsifal*; the most recent and most comprehensive is "The Genesis of the Music," in William Kinderman and Katherine R. Syer, eds., *A Companion to Wagner's* Parsifal (Rochester, NY, 2005), 133–77.

2. The phrase serves as the title of Dieter Borchmeyer's important essay on *Parsifal* in *Richard Wagner: Theory and Theatre*, trans. Stewart Spencer (Oxford and New York, 1991), 368–403. On the "lateness" of *Parsifal*, see Anthony E. Barone, "Richard Wagner's *Parsifal* and the Theory of Late Style," *Cambridge Opera Journal* 7 (1995), 37–54 (from his Ph.D. dissertation [Columbia, 1996]). I would like to thank Anthony Barone for his helpful commentary on portions of this text.

3. "Parsifal is my last card," said Wagner to Cosima, in connection with a reference to the racial theories of Gobineau and his remark that "The Germans were the last card that nature played" (*CWD*: 28 March 1881).

4. Wagner retained Eschenbach's spelling until the 1870s, when he mistakenly came to believe that the Arabic "fal Parsi" meant "reiner Tor" ("pure fool"), and thus changed the "z" to "s."

5. See the letter of 24 April 1868 to the publisher Franz Schott, in *Dokumente zur Entstehung und ersten Aufführung des Bühnenweihfestspiels*, ed. Martin Geck and Egon Voss (Richard Wagner Gesamtausgabe 30) (Mainz, 1970), 20 (document 27). Two years earlier (5 September 1866) Wagner had told King Ludwig II of Bavaria that the "tone color" of "Parzifal" is present in *Lohengrin* and *Tristan und Isolde* (*ibid.*, document 26). In 1877 he clearly distinguished *Parsifal* from *Lohengrin*, "with which it has not the least to do" (*ibid.*, 23, document 49, from a letter to Carl Friedrich Glasenapp, 25 June 1877); but in Cosima's diary for 12 March 1878, he says, "Certainly [*Parsifal*] should be like *Lohengrin*, but with the help of a few 'swannishnesses,' even more beautiful." The volume of documents in the Gesamtausgabe is an invaluable collection that contains the two prose drafts, the first version of the libretto, documents pertaining to the first performance and its preparation as well as all of Wagner's notes, drafts, comments about the opera in letters, and remarks by family and associates. Cosima's diary entries are especially informative, as are Wagner's letters to Mathilde Wesendonck in the 1850s and to King Ludwig II of Bavaria from the late 1860s up to the first performance.

6. Wagner did not need Schopenhauer to discover the themes of sexual longing, renunciation, and redemption, which already form the core of *Tannhäuser*; but he treats them with much more psychological depth and understanding in both the words and the music of *Tristan* and *Parsifal*.

7. See Lucy Beckett's illuminating discussion of Wagner's debts to and departures from Eschenbach in the first chapter of her handbook on the opera, *Richard Wagner*: Parsifal (Cambridge, 1981), 1–24; on text sources, see also Mary A. Cicora, "Medievalism and Metaphysics: The Literary Background of *Parsifal*," in Kinderman and Syer, *A Companion to Wagner's* Parsifal, 29–55.

8. Based on his reading of the opera and the regeneration essays of the late 1870s, Borchmeyer argues that Wagner hoped that "humanity might yet be regenerated" (*Richard Wagner: Theory and Theatre*, 402); for Borchmeyer, this is seen as an inclusive vision.

9. See Glenn Stanley, "The Oratorio in Prussia and Protestant Germany: 1812–1848," Ph.D. diss., Columbia University, 1988 (chap. 2, "Nationalism, Religion, and Music in Early Nineteenth-Century Germany"), 16–42. See also Beckett, *Richard Wagner*: Parsifal, 103–49. With respect to *Parsifal*, the most extensive discussion of the slippery term – variously used to describe art in the service of religion, replacing religion as an outlet for devotion and contemplation, or simply appropriating religious themes – is that by Adolf Nowak, "Wagners *Parsifal* und die Idee der Kunstreligion," in Carl Dahlhaus, ed., *Richard Wagner: Werk und Wirkung* (Regensburg, 1971), 161–75. On the earlier context of the idea in Germany, see also Celia Applegate, *Bach in Berlin: Nation and Culture in Mendelssohn's Revival of the* St. Matthew Passion (Ithaca, NY, and London, 2005).

10. The invaluable although somewhat deterministic study by George Mosse, *The Nationalization of the Masses: Political Symbolism and Mass Movements in Germany from the Napoleonic Wars Through the Third Reich* (New York, 1975), discusses political aspects of the entire festival movement in nineteenth-century Germany.

11. Most of the oratorios are on biblical themes from both testaments; the smaller number of oratorios on historical national themes also often have strong religious overtones. See Stanley, "The Oratorio in Prussia and Protestant Germany" (chap. 3, "Music Festivals"), 43–79.

12. In the eighteenth century, Jean-Jacques Rousseau had advanced the idea of the festival

in antique Greece as the model for contemporary events (Mosse, *Nationalization*, 73–74), and many German admirers of classic Greek art embraced this idea, which became an important element in Wagner's concept of the Bayreuth festival (see also 78–80 in this book).

13. Friedrich Nietzsche, *Sämtliche Werke: Kritische Studienausgabe*, ed. Giorgio Colli and Mazzino Montinari, 15 vols. (Berlin, 1980), I, 896.

14. See Heinrich von Wolzogen, "Nibelungen und Christenthum," *Neue Zeitschrift für Musik* 73 (1877), 505–08, 515–17, 525–28, 540–42.

15. Heinrich Porges, "Richard Wagner und das deutsche Volk," *Neue Zeitschrift für Musik* 73 (1877), 187–89, 199–201, 207–09.

16. Edward Lippman writes that "the identification of music and religion which we have with equal clearness both in *Parsifal* and in the essay on 'Religion and Art' of 1880 is only a final transformation of early Romantic aesthetics": "The Aesthetic Theories of Richard Wagner," in Lippman, *The Philosophy and Aesthetics of Music* (Lincoln, NE, and London, 1999), 190.

17. The musical style and the dramatic function of the Flower maidens is not easy to determine. The scene has analogs and precedents in the Venusberg scene in *Tannhäuser* and the Rhine maidens in the *Ring*. I find the scene superfluous; the only plausible dramaturgical argument in its favor is that it demonstrates how well Parsifal can resist ordinary feminine charms and just how dangerously seductive Kundry is. The women's chorus offers some relief from the predominating maleness of the opera; it also provides some warm-up "soft-core" titillation before the serious eroticism of the Kundry–Parsifal scene begins. Eduard Hanslick and Paul Bekker liked this scene more than anything else in *Parsifal*; this is understandable when we consider that neither admired Wagner's would-be weighty philosophical ideas, which here are noticeably lacking. Bekker even calls it "the most important scene in the work!" (*Richard Wagner: His Life in His Work*, trans. M. M. Bozman [New York, 1931; repr., Westport, CT, 1971], 501).

18. Leon Botstein finds the music of the Grail ritual "decidedly Mendelssohnian in both thematic material and orchestration." See his "The Aesthetics of Assimilation and Affirmation: Reconstructing the Career of Felix Mendelssohn," in R. Larry Todd, ed., *Mendelssohn and His World* (Princeton, 1991), 15.

19. In both *Parsifal* and *Lohengrin*, according to Borchmeyer, "The chorus plays a role influenced partly by Aeschylean tragedy, partly by the Christian liturgy. In *Parsifal* it no longer has the character of a mass comprised of many individuals, who, as it were, enter together by chance and sing with a single voice . . . Once again it becomes the 'ideal collective.'" In the final scene of Act 3 the entreaties of the Grail are "emotionally the most powerful choral scene to be found in any piece of world theatre since the time of Aeschylus" (Borchmeyer, *Richard Wagner: Theory and Theatre*, 384).

20. Geck and Voss, *Dokumente*, 24, document no. 54. According to Glasenapp (*ibid.*, document 52), the Grail themes had been sketched during work on the poetic text.

21. One of the first to argue for progressive elements in *Parsifal* was Ernest Newman, *The Wagner Operas* (New York, 1949; repr. 1981), 706 (with reference to the Act 3 Prelude). For more recent literature, see Constantin Floros, "Studien zur *Parsifal*-Rezeption," in Heinz-Klaus Metzger and Rainer Riehn, eds., *Richard Wagner*: Parsifal (*Musik-Konzepte* 25) (Munich, 1982), 43, who writes that the Prelude to Act 3 "anticipates the style of Arnold Schoenberg by twenty years" in relation to the slow movement of Schoenberg's String Quartet op. 10 of 1908, and compares the music of the Flower maidens to the women's chorus of Debussy's *Sirènes*. It has often been suggested that the orchestral technique in *Parsifal* departs from Wagner's other late works, in part as a result of Wagner's experience of the acoustics in the theater in Bayreuth. I would argue that Wagner selected from a rich orchestral palette that he had been developing for decades. The refined colors and textures that permeate the music effectively render the quietude and sublimation of most of the dramatic action.

22. William Kinderman discusses this motive in "Wagner's *Parsifal*: Musical Form and the Drama of Redemption," *Journal of Musicology* 4 (1985), 432–33, 439–42.

23. See von Wolzogen, *"Parsifal": ein thematischer Leitfaden durch Dichtung und Musik* (Leipzig, 1882), trans. Ian Bent in Bent, ed., *Music Analysis in the Nineteenth Century*, vol. II, *Hermeneutic Approaches* (Cambridge, 1994), 97.

24. This is the last statement of the motive in the act. An allusion to it, consisting of descending lines, chromaticism (in contrast to the diatonic ritual music), and occasional triplets, occurs when Amfortas is borne away on the litter after the Grail is unveiled (m. 1589). This is a wonderful passage in which this music of suffering begins as a subsidiary idea to the second theme of the Prelude, which is used for the ritual, but gains strength, finally

overcoming the ritual music, as the attention shifts back to Amfortas until he exits.

25. The best overview in English of the early reception of *Parsifal* is provided by Mary A. Cicora, Parsifal *Reception in the* Bayreuther Blätter (New York, 1987).

26. Floros notes that *Parsifal* is one of "the least criticized scores" in Wagner's oeuvre: "Studien zur *Parsifal*-Rezeption," 43.

27. Hans von Wolzogen, "Die Religion des Mitleidens," *Bayreuther Blätter* 5 (1883), 96–146.

28. See Wolzogen, "*Parsifal*": *ein thematischer Leitfaden*, 88–105.

29. Susanna Grossman-Vendrey, *Bayreuth in der deutschen Presse*, 3 vols., vol. II (Regensburg, 1977), 52–57.

30. Friedrich Nietzsche, *Nietzsche contra Wagner*, in *The Portable Nietzsche*, trans. Walter Kaufmann (New York and London, 1959), 676.

31. Lindau, who admired some elements of the score, wrote for the *Kölnische Zeitung*; his essays on *Parsifal* were reprinted in *Bayreuther Briefe vom reinen Thoren:* Parsifal *von Richard Wagner* (Breslau, 1886); Seidel's "R. Wagner's *Parsifal* und Schopenhauer's Nirwana" appeared in the *Bayreuther Blätter* 11 (1888), 277–306. See Paul Lawrence Rose, *Wagner: Race and Revolution* (New Haven and London, 1992), 168–69.

32. Bekker, *Richard Wagner: His Life in His Work*, 467–77. Without pursuing a detailed analytical argument, he did offer some musical interpretation for his thesis: "the Jew . . . must stand for dissonance, for the element which breaks up harmony" (473–74).

33. Thomas Mann, *Pro and Contra Wagner*, trans. Allan Blunden (Chicago, 1985), 120.

34. John Deathridge, "Strange Love, Or, How We Learned to Stop Worrying and Love Wagner's *Parsifal*," in Julie Brown, ed., *Western Music and Race* (Cambridge, 2007), 65–83. I thank Professor Deathridge for making his text available to me before publication. [Editor's note:] On the question of a ban, official or unofficial, on performances of *Parsifal* at Bayreuth and throughout the Reich during the later years of the Nazi regime, see also Katherine R. Syer, "*Parsifal* on Stage," in Kinderman and Syer, *A Companion to Wagner's* Parsifal, 304–05.

35. See Syer's illuminating study (with many wonderful images) of the production history, "*Parsifal* on Stage," 277–338.

36. The essay, which originated as a lecture given in Bayreuth, is printed in Rolf Tiedemann and Klaus Schultz, eds., *Musikalische Schriften*, 6 vols., vol. III (Frankfurt, 1984), 210–25.

37. The phrase figures in the title of Zelinsky's essay, "Die Feuerkur des Richard Wagner oder die neue Religion der Erlösung durch Vernichtung," in Heinz-Klaus Metzger and Rainer Riehn, eds., *Richard Wagner: Wie antisemitisch darf ein Künstler sein?* (*Musik-Konzepte* 5) (Munich, 1978), 79–112.

38. To support his arguments Zelinsky drew profusely on Cosima's diaries, which had then only recently been edited by Martin Gregor-Dellin. Zelinsky vigorously attacked Gregor-Dellin for supposed misreadings and falsifications of the diaries in the essay "Rettung ins Ungenaue: Zu Martin Gregor-Dellins Wagner-Biographie," in Metzger and Riehn, *Richard Wagner*: Parsifal, 74–115. See also by Zelinsky "Der verschwiegene Gehalt des *Parsifal*," published in the same volume and reprinted along with "Richard Wagners letzte Karte: Der verschwiegene Gehalt des *Parsifal*," in Attila Csampai and Dietmar Holland, eds., *Richard Wagner*, Parsifal: *Texte, Materialien, Kommentare* (Reinbek, 1984), 244–56.

39. Zelinsky relates that Wagner (as reported by Cosima) called the entrance of the timpani in the original orchestration of the baptism scene in Act 3 "a sonority of destruction" (*Vernichtungsklang*): "Richard Wagners letzte Karte," 27. Deathridge (in "Strange Love") attacks this interpretation as a tendentious misreading of the term *Vernichtungsklang*, which Deathridge thinks Wagner meant in a strictly musical sense.

40. Robert W. Gutman, *Richard Wagner: The Man, His Mind, and His Music* (New York and London, 1968), chaps. 15 and 16. Gutman's work became a primary source for those critics who agree that *Parsifal* presents an "optimistic" (i.e., non-Schopenhauerian) view of the human race as redeemable by Christ's pure (i.e., Aryan, non-Jewish) blood.

41. The responses by Dahlhaus and Kaiser as well as Zelinsky's reply are printed in Csampai and Holland, Parsifal: *Texte, Materialien, Kommentar*, 257–69. Dahlhaus published his methodological critique in an article, "Erlösung dem Erlöser," in the *Süddeutsche Zeitung*, 27 August 1982, 21–22.

42. Borchmeyer acknowledges Wagner's explicit identification of Kundry with the Wandering Jew (in the prose draft of 1865), but argues that she really "embodies heathen nature, as yet unredeemed" rather than personifying specifically Jewish characteristics: *Richard Wagner: Theory and Theatre*, 368–403 (quote on 393); see also 391–95. (The translation appeared in 1991; the German original was published in 1982.)

43. Marc A. Weiner, *Richard Wagner and the Anti-Semitic Imagination* (Lincoln, NE, and London, 1995), 228–30.

44. Rose, *Wagner: Race and Revolution*, 135–69. I find Rose's discussion of Aryan Christianity in *Parsifal* very convincing.

45. Laurence Dreyfus, "Hermann Levi's Shame and *Parsifal*'s Guilt: A Critique of Essentialism in Biography and Criticism," *Cambridge Opera Journal* 6 (1992), 142.

46. See n. 34.

47. Dahlhaus repeatedly argues that Christianity provides at most a historical backdrop without confessional-dogmatic or ideological substance. See, for example, the chapter on *Parsifal* in his *Richard Wagner's Music Dramas*, trans. Mary Whittall (Cambridge, 1979), 142–44. In this vein, compare also Edward Rothstein, "When Ritual Strangles *Parsifal*," *New York Times*, 29 March 1992, 31.

48. Letter of 17 January 1880 to Hans von Wolzogen, from Wagner, *Richard Wagner: Ausgewählte Schriften und Briefe 2*, ed. Alfred Lorenz (Berlin, 1938), 376–77.

49. Borchmeyer depicts Wagner as a true and highly informed Christian and provides significant biographical and documentary evidence to support this view (*Richard Wagner: Theory and Theatre*, 368–403).

50. Nike Wagner views *Parsifal* as an "ideological crusade," in which everything "is ultimately forced into the unequivocal unity of Christian redemption": *The Wagners: The Dramas of a Musical Dynasty*, trans. Ewald Osers and Michael Downes (Princeton, 1998), 134. See also the final chapter in Beckett, *Richard Wagner: Parsifal*, 129–49.

51. Paul Robinson, *Opera, Sex, and Other Vital Matters* (Chicago, 2002), 136–37: "Wagner's own contribution to asceticism in *Parsifal* is more genuinely Schopenhauerian [than *Tristan und Isolde*], not least in its misogyny, but *Parsifal*'s obsessive concern with redemption fits badly with Schopenhauer's pessimism and hatred of Christianity."

52. Catherine Clément, *Opera, or the Undoing of Women*, trans. Betsey Wing (Minneapolis, 1988).

53. Peter Wapnewski, "The Operas as Literary Works," in *Wagner Handbook*, ed. Ulrich Müller and Peter Wapnewski, translation ed. John Deathridge (Cambridge, MA, 1992), 91.

54. Borchmeyer, *Richard Wagner: Theory and Theatre*, 399.

55. In the chapter "God and Beggar" from his *Versuch über Wagner*, Adorno remarks in passing: "the glorified blood-brotherhood of *Parsifal* is the prototype of the sworn confraternities of the secret societies and Führer-orders of later years" (Adorno, *In Search of Wagner*, trans. Rodney Livingstone [New York, 1981, 140]). I thank Anthony Barone for calling my attention to this passage.

11 Critique as passion and polemic: Nietzsche and Wagner

Translation by Thomas S. Grey.

1. Friedrich Nietzsche, *Sämtliche Werke: Kritische Gesamtausgabe*, ed. Giorgio Colli and Mazzino Montinari (Berlin and New York, 1967–), IV/1, 311. Where this edition is cited (hereafter *Werke*), translations are by the editor; other published translations are cited individually. An English translation of the Colli/Montinari series is being published by Stanford University Press; published to date are *Unfashionable Observations* (1995), *Human, All Too Human I* (1997), and *Unpublished Writings from the Period* of Unfashionable Observations (1999).

2. Thomas Mann, *Pro and Contra Wagner*, trans. Allan Blunden (Chicago and London, 1985), 101.

3. "Ich habe ihn geliebt und Niemanden sonst" (*Werke*, VII/3, 226).

4. Thomas Mann, "Sorrows and Grandeur of Richard Wagner," in Mann, *Pro and Contra Wagner*, 101. Mann's original speaks of "einen Panegyrikus mit umgekehrten Vorzeichen," a phrase whose literal connotation is either the alteration (inversion) of mathematical signs or of a musical key signature.

5. Friedrich Nietzsche to Erwin Rohde (Hamburg), 27 October 1868, in Nietzsche, *Briefwechsel*, ed. Giorgio Colli and Mazzino Montinari (Berlin and New York, 1975), I/2, 332 (hereafter *Briefwechsel*).

6. *Briefwechsel*, I/2, 322; see also *Selected Letters of Friedrich Nietzsche*, ed. and trans. Christopher Middleton (Chicago and London, 1969), 33.

7. Friedrich Nietzsche, "Richard Wagner in Bayreuth," in *Untimely Meditations*, ed. Daniel Breazeale and trans. R. J. Hollingdale (Cambridge, 1997), 200 (translation emended).

8. *Briefwechsel*, I/2, 322. [Ed.] Nietzsche's original involves a faintly ironic sequence of rhymes: "die ethische Luft, der faustische Duft, Kreuz, Tod und Gruft etc."

9. *Werke*, III/2, 22.

10. Nietzsche, "On Music and Words," in Carl Dahlhaus, *Between Romanticism and Modernism*, trans. Mary Whittall (Cambridge, 1980), 113.

11. *Ibid.*, 106–07 (quoting Schopenhauer, *Parerga and Paralipomena*, vol. II, section 224).

12. Friedrich Nietzsche, *On the Genealogy of Morals*, trans. Walter Kaufmann and R. J. Hollingdale (New York, 1969), 103.

13. *Werke*, III/4; see also Nietzsche, *Unpublished Writings from the Period of Unfashionable Observations*, trans. Richard T. Gray (Stanford, 1999), 328.

14. *Werke*, III/3, 195.

15. Letter from Friedrich Ritschl to Nietzsche, 2 July 1872 (*Briefwechsel*, II/4, 33). Ritschl had struck a similar note in defense of textual and empirical scholarship already upon his first acquaintance with *The Birth of Tragedy*, writing on 14 February 1872: "You can hardly presume that the 'Alexandrian,' scholarly person ought to reject rational *cognition* [*Erkenntniss*] and look to art alone for some transformative, redeeming, and liberating power" (*Briefwechsel*, II/2, 541).

16. *Werke*, III/4, 370, 373; translation from Nietzsche, *Unpublished Writings*, 346 (see also 318).

17. *Werke*, III/4, 379, 406; IV/1, 267; Nietzsche, *Unpublished Writings*, 323, 346.

18. See Nietzsche, "Richard Wagner in Bayreuth," section 4, 209 (Hollingdale renders *Gegen-Alexander* as "counter-Alexander"). On the propensity of myth toward condensation (*Verdichten*) and simplification of plot, see, for example, *Opera and Drama*, part 2, section 2 (*GS* IV:30–34; *PW* II:152–56). [Ed.] The ideal of a maximally "condensed" dramatic material recurs throughout *Opera and Drama*.

19. Nietzsche, "Richard Wagner in Bayreuth," section 4, 208–09.

20. Nietzsche, *Basic Writings of Nietzsche*, ed. and trans. Walter Kaufmann (New York, 1968), 740.

21. *Briefwechsel*, II/5, 182.

22. Nietzsche, *Basic Writings*, 744.

23. *Briefwechsel*, II/5, 288.

24. *Ibid.*, 300; translation from Nietzsche, *Selected Letters*, 166.

25. See n. 16.

26. *Briefwechsel*, III/1, 224.

27. *Ibid.*, 330; see also Nietzsche, *Selected Letters*, 260.

28. *Briefwechsel*, III/1, 330.

29. *Ibid.*, III/3, 273.

30. *Ibid.*, III/1, 333–34; translation from Nietzsche, *Selected Letters*, 208.

31. Nietzsche, *Thus Spake Zarathustra*, trans. Walter Kaufmann, in *The Portable Nietzsche* (New York and London, 1959), 203. Kaufmann renders the ambiguity of the opening line quoted here ("Es jammert mich dieser Priester") by dividing it in two: "I am moved by . . ." and "I find them repulsive."

32. Nietzsche, *Thus Spake Zarathustra*, 204.

33. Nietzsche, *The Case of Wagner*, trans. Walter Kaufmann, in *The Birth of Tragedy and the Case of Wagner* (New York, 1967), 171 (also in *Basic Writings*, 627).

34. Nietzsche, *Basic Writings*, 383.

35. *Ibid.*, 387.

36. *Ibid.*, 386.

37. Nietzsche, *The Case of Wagner*, 155 (*Basic Writings*, 611).

38. Paul Scherrer and Hans Wysling, *Quellenkritische Studien zum Werk Thomas Manns* (Bern and Munich, 1967), 144. See also the excerpts from these notes printed in Mann, *Pro and Contra Wagner*, 37–44.

39. *Briefwechsel*, III/5, 554.

40. *Ibid.*, 567; translation from Nietzsche, *Selected Letters*, 344.

41. *Ecce homo*, trans. Walter Kaufmann (New York, 1969), 250–51 (also in *Basic Writings*, 706–07).

42. Nietzsche, *The Gay Science*, trans. Walter Kaufmann (New York, 1974), 225–26.

12 The Jewish question

1. Michael Tanner may have a point that traditional harping on certain of Wagner's personal failings is exaggerated, and disproportionate either to the facts of the case (his supposedly rampant adultery) or to the larger biographical and historical picture (his consumption of borrowed funds). But to include his anti-Semitism in this same category, as Tanner does, is hardly justified; the facts are of a different order from the one (adultery) and the consequences surely incommensurate with the other (borrowing). See Tanner, *Wagner* (Princeton, 1996), chap. 2, "Prejudices and Banalities," 14–30.

2. Early exceptions were Leon Stein's monograph on *The Racial Thinking of Richard Wagner* (New York, 1950), focusing on the biography and writings, and Adorno's subsequently influential discussion of anti-Semitic psychology and caricature in Wagner's creative oeuvre in *In Search of Wagner*, trans. Rodney Livingstone (London, 1981; 2nd edn. 2005). Adorno first drafted his "essay" (originally, *Versuch über Wagner*) in 1937–38 while in exile in London and New York, and it was first published in Germany (Frankfurt) in 1952. The most recent overview of the subject is Milton E. Brener, *Richard Wagner and the Jews* (Jefferson, NC, and London, 2006), essentially a short biography highlighting the theme of Wagner's relations with individual Jews.

3. There is scant evidence of Wagner's experiences of or reactions to Jews in the period of his childhood or youth in Germany, before the Parisian sojourn of 1839–42. Jacob Katz reviews such evidence as there is in chapter 3 ("Wagner's 'Philo-Semitism'") of *The Darker Side of Genius: Richard Wagner's Anti-Semitism* (Hanover, NH, and London, 1986), 20–32. Katz interprets the earlier record as suggesting that, whatever anti-Jewish prejudices Wagner might have been absorbing from childhood through his thirties, his attitude toward individual Jews of his acquaintance was not yet colored by a categorical antipathy to the group, or "race," which only began to coalesce during the year or two before the essay "Judaism in Music" (1850). The limited information we have in the case of Wagner's earliest documented Jewish friend, the impecunious student-scholar Samuel Lehrs whom he befriended in Paris, suggests a sincere and untroubled relationship.

4. Paul Lawrence Rose, *Wagner: Race and Revolution* (New Haven and London, 1992), especially chaps. 1–4. Rose cites above all J. G. Fichte (1762–1814) as the progenitor of a revolutionary discourse steeped in anti-Jewish rhetoric (in chap. 1, 6–22). The currency of "the Jewish question" as a locution derives in part from Karl Marx's 1844 essay of that title, responding to an earlier essay under the same title by Bruno Bauer (see Rose, *Wagner: Race and Revolution*, 20–22, as well as Mitchell Cohen's chapter [4] in this volume).

5. *GS* V:67; translation from Charles Osborne, *Richard Wagner: Stories and Essays* (New York and London, 1973), 24. Further references are to this translation, as well as the original in *GS* V, both of which incorporate the few changes and additions made to the text in 1869.

6. The most comprehensive presentation of this immediate journalistic context is by Jens Malte Fischer in his edition of the essay with commentary and documentation of its reception: *Richard Wagners "Das Judentum in der Musik": Eine kritische Dokumentation als Beitrag zur Geschichte des Antisemitismus* (Frankfurt am Main and Leipzig, 2000), 18–32, 208–13. Paul Lawrence Rose believes that the essay had already been drafted by 1848, based on a remark in a letter from Minna Wagner to Richard (8 May 1850) complaining bitterly about the turn to "miserable politics" resulting in his current exile. Minna also refers here to an "essay in which you slander whole races which have been fundamentally helpful to you," which he had pressed her to read "two years ago." She cites this incident as one principal source of their subsequent

differences. See Rose, *Wagner: Race and Revolution*, 49–50. Whatever may have prompted this possible first draft (Mendelssohn's death or, as Rose argues, frustration with the Berlin production of *Rienzi* and a polemical anti-Jewish preface to Heinrich Laube's play *Struensee*, all in 1847), the Parisian experiences during the first year of his political exile (1849–50) seem to be the crucial factor in Wagner's decision to publish it.

7. Starting from the premise of Wagner's tendency to paranoia or persecution mania, Bryan Magee offers a convincing summary of three key factors in the psychology of his anti-Semitism, building on some of the texts and biographical details mentioned here. These are: (1) the troubled years in Paris, including his abasement before Meyerbeer, (2) his habitual need to borrow, in conjunction with the role (individual and institutional) of Jews as creditors, and (3) his revolutionary-political convictions (the whole nexus analyzed by Rose, that is), especially an abiding belief in the fundamental evils of property and the conventional, unjust mechanisms of its distribution. See the appendix, "Wagner's Anti-Semitism," to Magee, *The Tristan Chord: Wagner and Philosophy* (London and New York, 2000), 344–48.

8. On the example of Börne, see Katz, *The Darker Side of Genius*, 44–45, and Rose, *Wagner: Race and Revolution*, 80, 83–86 (also on Börne vs. Heine).

9. On this context of the 1869 reissue of the essay, see Thomas Grey, "Masters and Their Critics: Wagner, Hanslick, Beckmesser, and *Die Meistersinger*," in Nicholas Vazsonyi, ed., *Wagner's* Meistersinger: *Performance, History, Representation* (Rochester, NY, 2003), 165–89.

10. Such a view, of course, sidesteps the question of Wagner's relevance to the evolution of Nazi ideology and its historical consequences, touched on in chapter 14. This subject has also been newly addressed in a recent essay by Paul Lawrence Rose, "Anti-Semitism in Music: Wagner and the Origins of the Holocaust," in Matthew Bribitzer-Stull, Alex Lubet, and Gottfried Wagner, eds., *Richard Wagner for the New Millennium: Essays in Music and Culture* (New York and London, 2007).

11. Robert Gutman, *Richard Wagner: The Man, His Mind, and His Music* (New York, 1968), chap. 15 ("*Parsifal* and Polemics: Eroticism, Vegetarianism, Racism, and Redemption"), 389–420, and chap. 16 ("Moral Collapse: 'Heldentum' and *Parsifal*"), 421–40.

12. For Zelinsky, see especially his contributions to Attila Csampai and Dietmar

Holland, eds., *Richard Wagner, Parsifal: Texte, Materialien, Kommentare* (Reinbek, 1984), and Heinz-Klaus Metzger and Rainer Riehn, eds., *Richard Wagner: Wie anti-semitisch darf ein Künstler sein?* (*Musik-Konzepte* 5; Munich, 1978). Rose discusses *Parsifal* in light of the last phase of Wagner's prose writings in chapter 9 ("Regeneration and Redemption: 1876–1883") of *Wagner: Race and Revolution*. Marc Weiner analyzes the implications of Klingsor's self-castration and especially the figure of Kundry under the somewhat unlikely rubric of odor or smell (e.g., the notion of a *foetor judaicus* going back to Tacitus, though reinterpreted here in terms of perfumed Arabian *Düfte*); see Weiner, *Richard Wagner and the Anti-Semitic Imagination* (Lincoln, NE, and London, 1995), 183–93 and 228–59.

13. Laurence Dreyfus develops some of these objections in conjunction with a rereading of the Hermann Levi affair (the problems arising from the Jewish background of the conductor assigned to conduct the first performance at Bayreuth) in "Hermann Levi's Shame and *Parsifal*'s Guilt: A Critique of Essentialism in Biography and Criticism," *Cambridge Opera Journal* 6 (1994), 125–45.

14. The rather wide repertoire of Jewish representations in nineteenth-century German drama (even before 1850) is the subject of a study by Hans-Joachim Neubauer, *Judenfiguren: Drama und Theater im frühen 19. Jahrhundert* (Frankfurt and New York, 1994). Neubauer discusses such topics relevant to the "Wagner question" as theatrical representations of Yiddish ("Jewish *Jargon*"), perceptions of Jewish voice types, accentual patterns, and perceptions of all these as distortions of standard German. On the novel, see Martin Gubser, *Literarischer Antisemitismus: Untersuchungen zu Gustav Freytag und anderen bürgerlichen Schriftstellern des 19. Jahrhunderts* (Göttingen, 1998).

15. Thus the premise of Weiner's *Richard Wagner and the Anti-Semitic Imagination*, Barry Millington's "Nuremberg Trial: Is There Anti-Semitism in *Die Meistersinger?*," *Cambridge Opera Journal* 3 (1991), 247–60, and his response to critics of this line of reasoning ("Wagner Washes Whiter") in the *Musical Times* 137 (December 1996), 5–8. Millington's 1991 essay was especially influential as one of the first attempts to apply Adorno's insinuations about such subtexts in a more detailed critical analysis (beyond the more generalized assertions of Rose, for instance, in *Wagner: Race and Revolution*).

16. Adorno, *In Search of Wagner* (2005), 12–13. Adorno's account of anti-Semitic traces in the operas in the chapter "Social Character" is the earliest attempt to define these as broadly characteristic of the oeuvre, and remains the most influential.

17. David Dennis, for example, claims to have found "no evidence that Nazi cultural politicians, or their *völkisch* forebears and associates, referred in public discourse to the character of Sixtus Beckmesser as Jewish" in his extensive examination of productions and writings during the Third Reich ("*Die Meistersinger* Through the Lens of the Third Reich," in Vazsonyi, *Wagner's* Meistersinger, 103).

18. *Gustav Mahler in den Erinnerungen von Natalie Bauer-Lechner*, ed. Knud Martner, rev. ed. Herbert Killian (Hamburg, 1984), 122.

19. Cosima (*CWD*: 3 May 1881) noted this interesting yet casual and non-committal reaction to a rehearsal of *Siegfried*, Act 1, for the *Ring* productions overseen by Angelo Neumann in Berlin: "Mime 'a Jewish dwarf,' R. says, but excellent." Milton E. Brener, who notes that the singer was Julius Lieban, the son of a Jewish cantor, interprets the qualification ("but") as proof that Wagner himself could not have intended Mime as a crypto-Jewish figure (*Richard Wagner and the Jews*, 290). It is not entirely clear whether Wagner was responding to the interpretation, or at any rate the effect, of the performance, or simply to the fact of Lieban's own Jewishness and his (possibly?) short stature. Either way, the remark is no smoking gun. But if indeed Lieban chose to bring out an aspect of the role as he understood it, as Spielmann did later for Mahler in Vienna, it is another small piece of evidence that certain people (in these cases, Jewish singers charged with studying the part of Mime) did in fact perceive such implications.

20. In "Judaism in Music" he complains of "that prickling unrest which is to be found in Jewish music from beginning to end, except where it is replaced by ... soulless, unfeeling inertia," presumably with the aim of hitting Meyerbeer and Mendelssohn in one swipe ("Judaism in Music," 34; *GS* V:78). Some weeks after the Russian-Jewish pianist Joseph Rubinstein presented himself to the Wagners as a volunteer amanuensis in Bayreuth, Cosima reported: "In the evening . . . R. comes to meet us, bringing with him J. Rubinstein, whom he had called for out of pity, though he finds his restless Jewish character very unsympathetic; during the recent reading he could not stay still for a moment, and R. says, 'Though the rustling of a beloved woman's dress might entrance one [. . .] this masculine deportment

is not exactly encouraging'" (*CWD*: 31 August 1872).

21. Dieter Borchmeyer, "The Question of Anti-Semitism," in *Wagner Handbook*, ed. Ulrich Müller and Peter Wapnewski, translation ed. John Deathridge (Cambridge, MA, and London, 1992), 183.

22. In the final chapter of *Richard Wagner and the Anti-Semitic Imagination* (307–47), Weiner argues at some length that Hagen exhibits symptoms attributed in the nineteenth century to the effects of masturbation (enervation, eye trouble, social isolationism), but has some trouble establishing a clear connection with Hagen's "mixed" racial identity as the offspring of a German mother (Grimhild) either raped or bought by a Jewish-identified Alberich. Wagner's notorious concern for Friedrich Nietzsche on this count had nothing to do with Nietzsche's genealogy, after all. Hagen, it is true, broods over his ignoble lineage and alienation in Acts 1 and 2 of *Götterdämmerung*, but then he is supposed to be singing in his (troubled) sleep at the opening of Act 2. Summoning the Gibich vassals later in the same act, he evinces as much musical-vocal stamina as anyone in the whole cycle. And whether brooding or brutal, Hagen's musical persona could hardly be more different from Mime's.

23. There is some evidence that Wagner did indeed maintain a personal code of silence on some meanings he himself understood in his works. For instance, discussing *Parsifal* with Cosima one day (*CWD*: 5 January 1882), he alluded to his own (private) understanding of the famous, enigmatic final words, "Erlösung dem Erlöser." "I know what I know and what is in it [*Parsifal*]," he told her; "and the new school, Wolz[ogen] and others, can take their lead from it. He then hints at, rather than expresses, the content of this work, 'salvation to the savior' – and we are silent after he has added, 'Good that we are alone.'" The closing lines of *Parsifal* have been interpreted as alluding to the redemption or cleansing of a true, Aryan Jesus from the Hebraic/Semitic version established by the gospels and St. Paul. Hartmut Zelinsky cites this passage from the diaries as "decisive proof" that the "redemption of an Aryan Jesus from Judaism" was the true if secret agenda of the opera, whose dissemination was left to the "Bayreuth school" of Wolzogen and later ideologues such as Houston Stewart Chamberlain ("Die 'Feuerkur' des Richard Wagner, oder die 'neue Religion' der 'Erlösung' durch 'Vernichtung,'" in Metzger and Riehn, *Wie antisemitisch darf ein Künstler sein?*, 99; see also 103–12).

24. Hans R. Vaget, "'Du warst mein Feind von je': The Beckmesser Controversy Revisited," in Vazsonyi, *Wagner's* Meistersinger, 203. Vaget reconsiders here, among other issues relating to alleged anti-Semitic undertones in the opera, the often-cited idea that Beckmesser's role involves textual and situational allusions to the Grimms' fairy tale, "The Jew in the Thorn Bush." Vaget finds the allusions palpable, but he does hold out the possibility that they might not be fully conscious or intended on Wagner's part. It is worth remembering, in any event, that *Die Meistersinger* in no way restages the action of the Grimms' tale (unless we consider Beckmesser's failure and public derision in the song contest as a symbolic form of public execution). When Theodor Adorno first cited the tale of the "Jew in the Thorn Bush" in connection with the "social character" of Wagner's works, he only meant to highlight a characteristically malicious glee on Wagner's part in the dramatic and musical manipulation of his "villains" generally (Adorno, *In Search of Wagner*, 10–11), though he, too, may have been prompted by noticing traces of the tale in the text.

25. Vaget, "Beckmesser Controversy," 206.

26. Magee's appendix on "Wagner's Anti-Semitism" (see n. 7), following a largely clear-sighted analysis of the biographical and historical dimensions, concludes with a vehement, not a little petulant, denunciation of the trend to identify anti-Semitism in the operas (*Wagner and Philosophy*, 371–80), despite a rhetorical claim that he does "not regard the allegation as impossible" (371). The contentiousness of the subject presses many writers to adopt an absolute stance pro or con. One could, however, use some of Magee's own observations in arguing that anti-Semitic traces in the operas are at once "real" but peripheral; or that their presence, however faint, might be legitimately, interestingly problematic in artistic and social terms, as in his own example of *The Merchant of Venice* (371–72). It is not clear that "Judaism in Music" (27; *GS* V:69–70) expressly refutes the very idea of "representing" Jews in the theater, as Magee claims (375) in arguing that Wagner would never have done so; Wagner's original text and his later (1869) footnote cited here are explicitly concerned only with the (non-)viability of Jewish actors. Even so, Magee's reading might simply serve to fuel the argument he so adamantly rejects: that Wagner was constrained to resorting to allegory or cryptograms in smuggling his anti-Jewish agenda onto the stage.

27. David J. Levin, "Reading Beckmesser Reading: Antisemitism and Aesthetic Practice in *The Mastersingers of Nuremberg*," *New German Critique* 69 (Fall 1996), 127–46; Levin, "Reading a Staging / Staging a Reading," *Cambridge Opera Journal* 9 (1997), 47–71; Levin, *Richard Wagner, Fritz Lang, and the Nibelungen: The Dramaturgy of Disavowal* (Princeton, 1998), *passim*, but especially 3–12, 73–95, 123–29.

28. Mike Ashman (see chap. 15) notes some partial exceptions to this general rule of avoidance in productions of *Meistersinger* directed by Harry Kupfer, *Parsifal* by Ruth Berghaus, and Patrice Chéreau's 1976–80 Bayreuth *Ring*, which changed the face of postwar Wagner productions in so many ways.

29. After proposing a reinscription of "the tradition of radical revolutionary parties" in place of "proto-Fascist elements" and a highlighting of "the conflict between Oedipal dynamics and the post-Oedipal universe," Zizek asserts: "[I]t is only through such a betrayal of the explicit theses of Adorno's Wagner study [i.e., his analysis of 'Fascist' and anti-Semitic tendencies] that, today, one can remain faithful to its emancipatory impulse." See Slavoj Zizek, foreword to Adorno, *In Search of Wagner* (2005), xxvi–xxvii. Citing earlier three particularly egregious examples of Siegfried's "unconstrained 'innocent' aggressivity" in his behavior toward Mime, Zizek's response is to generalize ("the repulsion felt by the ego when confronted with the intruding foreign body") and update ("One can easily imagine a neo-Nazi skinhead uttering just the same words in the face of a worn-out Turkish *Gastarbeiter*," xvii). In view of the extreme consequences of post-Wagnerian anti-Semitism in Germany, this way of deflecting or redefining the "relevance" of the issue seems questionable, and recalls to some extent Daniel Mendelssohn's recent objections to the promotion and reception of *Brokeback Mountain* as concerned primarily with "universal" themes of love, sorrow, loss, etc., rather than with the experience of homosexuality (*New York Review of Books*, 23 February 2006 and 6 April 2006).

30. From a letter of 6 December 1880 responding to a debate in the Reichstag over the Anti-Semitic Petition then circulating; quoted in Rose, *Wagner: Race and Revolution*, 127.

13 "Wagnerism": responses to Wagner in music and the arts

I am grateful to the graduate students in my seminar on "Wagner and Wagnerism: Critical

and Compositional Reception" for their stimulating discussions and interesting questions, and to Tim Carter for critical comments on an earlier version of this text.

1. Interview with Howard Shore, in *The Lord of the Rings: The Fellowship of the Ring*, Special Extended DVD Edition, disc 3, New Line Home Entertainment (N5559), 2002. I am grateful to Joseph Singleton for sharing this information with me.

2. On *Oklahoma!*, see Tim Carter, *Oklahoma! (1943): The Making of an "American" Musical* (New Haven and London, 2007).

3. See Friedrich Kittler, "Wagners wildes Heer," in Wolfgang Storch, ed., *Les Symbolistes et Richard Wagner – Die Symbolisten und Richard Wagner* (Berlin, 1991), 37–43.

4. For the concept of *grand opéra* as the nation's image, see Jane F. Fulcher, *The Nation's Image: French Grand Opéra as Politics and Politicized Art* (Cambridge, 1987).

5. For Fétis's criticism in 1852 and its impact on Wagner reception, see Katharine Ellis, "Wagnerism and Anti-Wagnerism in the Paris Periodical Press," in Annegret Fauser and Manuela Schwartz, eds., *Von Wagner zum Wagnérisme: Musik, Literatur, Kunst, Politik* (Leipzig, 1999), 51–83.

6. On Massenet's *Esclarmonde*, see Annegret Fauser, *Musical Encounters at the 1889 Paris World's Fair* (Rochester, NY, 2005), 59–78; Steven Huebner, *French Opera at the Fin de Siècle: Wagnerism, Nationalism, and Style* (Oxford, 1999), 82–101.

7. A selection of these reviews is published in Annegret Fauser, ed., *Dossier de presse parisienne: Jules Massenet, "Esclarmonde" (1889)* (Heilbronn, 2001).

8. "Mais vous songez à lui?" See Huebner, *French Opera at the Fin de Siècle*, 90.

9. "Wagner, que je ne sens plus peser sur moi, quand j'écris de la musique symphonique, me hante maintenant terriblement. Je le fuis tant que je peux, mais j'ai beau fuir, il est toujours là, près de moi, me guettant très méchamment et me faisant écrire des tas de choses que j'efface. J'en suis sérieusement ennuyé. Il faut pourtant y échapper, à ce diable d'homme. C'est une question de vie ou de mort" (Ernest Chausson to Raymond Bonheur, 13 May 1893, cited in Chausson, *Ernest Chausson: Ecrits inédits*, ed. Jean Gallois [Paris, 1999], 341).

10. Claude Debussy, *Lettres: 1884–1918*, ed. François Lesure (Paris, 1980), 58. See also Carolyn Abbate, "*Tristan* in the Composition of *Pelléas*," *19th-Century Music* 5 (1981), 117–41.

11. How thoroughly nationalist this quest for the new French masterwork was has been shown in James Ross, "Crisis and

Transformation: French Opera, Politics and the Press, 1897–1903" (D.Phil. diss., Oxford University, 1998).

12. See Florence Launay, "Les compositrices françaises de 1789 à 1914" (Ph.D. diss., Université Rennes 2, 2004), 599–600.

13. See quotation in Fauser, *Musical Encounters*, 133.

14. Ute Jung, *Die Rezeption der Kunst Richard Wagners in Italien* (Regensburg, 1974). On the impact of *Lohengrin* in Bologna, which culminated in the conferral on Wagner of honorary citizenship in October 1872, see especially 15–33.

15. On Puccini's Wagnerism, see Jürgen Maehder, "Erscheinungsformen des Wagnérisme in der italienischen Musik des fin de siècle," in Fauser and Schwartz, *Von Wagner zum Wagnérisme*, 575–621.

16. *Ibid.*, 604.

17. Barry Millington, "The Nineteenth Century: Germany," in *The Oxford Illustrated History of Opera*, ed. Roger Parker (Oxford, 1994), 231.

18. Sieghart Döhring and Sabine Henze-Döhring, *Oper und Musikdrama im 19. Jahrhundert* (Laaber, 1997), 293.

19. *Ibid.*, 296.

20. See Siegfried Oechsle, "Nationalidee und große Symphonie: Mit einem Exkurs zum 'Ton,'" in Hermann Danuser and Herfried Münkler, eds., *Deutsche Meister – Böse Geister: Nationale Selbstfindung in der Musik* (Schliengen, 2001), 166–84.

21. On Wagner's aesthetics, see chap. 10 of the present volume. For an excellent introduction into the aesthetics of nineteenth-century symphony, see Mark Evan Bonds, "Symphony: The Nineteenth Century," in *New Grove Dictionary of Music and Musicians*, 2nd edn., ed. Stanley Sadie and John Tyrrell, 29 vols. (London, 2001), XXIV, 833–41.

22. The "artwork of ideas" is the rubric under which Carl Dahlhaus discusses the rapprochement of post-Wagnerian symphonic music (including the symphonic poem) with the Schopenhauerian tenets of Wagner's later aesthetics. See Dahlhaus, *Nineteenth-Century Music*, trans. J. Bradford Robinson (Berkeley and Los Angeles, 1989).

23. Natalie Bauer-Lechner, *Recollections of Gustav Mahler*, ed. Peter Franklin, trans. Dika Newlin (Cambridge, 1980), 40 (translation emended by the author).

24. Mahler's 1896 comment is given in Peter Franklin, *Mahler: Symphony No. 3* (Cambridge, 1991), 12.

25. Edouard Lalo, *Correspondance*, ed. Joël-Marie Fauquet (Paris, 1989), 123–24.

26. I owe this idea to a paper by Irina Iliescu, "Liquidating *Parsifal:* A Reading of *Verklärte Nacht,*" written for my graduate seminar "Wagner and Wagnerism: Critical and Compositional Reception" (University of North Carolina, Fall Semester 2004).

27. *Parsifal* was still under copyright and would be free only on 1 January 1914, when musical stages around the globe vied to be the first to bring out the opera. For a different interpretation of *Verklärte Nacht* as reflecting the ending of *Tristan und Isolde*, see Camilla Bork, "'Tod und Verklärung': Isoldes Liebestod als Modell künstlerischer Schlußgestaltung," in Hermann Danuser and Herfried Münkler, eds., *Richard Wagners Revolution und ihre Folgen in Kunst und Politik* (Schliengen, 2002), 161–78, esp. 171–74.

28. See Jean Louis Jam and Gérard Loubinoux, "D'une Walkyrie à l'autre . . . Querelles de traductions," in Fauser and Schwartz, *Von Wagner zum Wagnérisme*, 401–30.

29. "J'inventai la couleur des voyelles! – *A* noir, *E* blanc, *I* rouge, *O* bleu, *U* vert. – Je réglai la forme et le mouvement de chaque consonne, et, avec des rythmes instinctifs, je me flattai d'inventer un verbe poétique accessible, un jour ou l'autre, à tous les sens. Je réservais la traduction" (cited in Annegret Fauser, *Der Orchestergesang in Frankreich zwischen 1870 und 1920* [Laaber, 1994], 65).

30. *Ibid.*, 66.

31. Matthias Waschek, "Zum Wagnérisme in den bildenden Künsten," in Fauser and Schwartz, *Von Wagner zum Wagnérisme*, 535–46.

32. For a richly illustrated introduction into these movements, see the exhibition catalogue *Vom Klang der Bilder: Die Musik in der Kunst des 20. Jahrhunderts (Staatsgalerie Stuttgart, 1985)*, ed. Karin von Maur (Munich, 1985).

33. Jens Malte Fischer, "Das 'Kunstwerk der Zukunft' und seine theatralischen Folgen," in Danuser and Münkler, *Richard Wagners Revolution und ihre Folgen*, 217.

34. See, for example, Bruno Taut, "Zum neuen Theaterbau," *Das Hohe Ufer* 1/8 (1919), 204–08.

35. Cited in Andrea Musk, "Regionalism, *Latinité*, and the French Musical Tradition: Déodat de Séverac's *Héliogabale,*" in Jim Samson and Bennett Zon, eds., *Nineteenth-Century Music Studies* (London and Aldershot, 2002), 239.

36. "[C]hanta la magnifique liturgie grecque sous un grand figuier . . . et, comme la voûte du ciel forme le seul plafond de ce théâtre, la belle prière païenne montait librement vers les

caressantes étoiles" (Santillanne, "Lucienne Bréval," *Gil Blas*, 25 September 1895).

14 Wagner and the Third Reich: myths and realities

1. Thomas Mann, "The Sorrows and Grandeur of Richard Wagner," in Mann, *Pro and Contra Wagner*, trans. Allan Blunden (Chicago, 1985), 91–148.
2. Hubert Kolland, "Wagner und der deutsche Faschismus," in Hanns-Werner Heister and Hans-Günter Klein, eds., *Musik und Musikpolitik im faschistischen Deutschland* (Frankfurt, 1984), 129–30; Kolland, "Wagner-Rezeption im deutschen Faschismus," in Christoph-Hellmut Mahling and Sigrid Wiesmann, eds., *Bericht über den Internationalen Musikwissenschaftlichen Kongreß Bayreuth 1981* (Kassel, 1984), 495ff.; Reinhold Brinkmann, "Wagners Aktualität für den Nationalsozialismus: Fragmente einer Bestandaufnahme," in Saul Friedländer and Jörn Rüsen, eds., *Richard Wagner im Dritten Reich* (Munich, 2000), 127–30.
3. Walter Engelsmann, "Kunstwerk und Führertum," *Die Musik*, 1933, quoted in Joseph Wulf, *Musik im Dritten Reich: Eine Dokumentation* (1966; repr. Berlin, 1983), 313; Siegmund von Hausegger, "Richard Wagner als Führer in die Zukunft," *Deutsches Wesen*, July 1933, 3, quoted in Hartmut Zelinsky, *Richard Wagner: Ein deutsches Thema – Eine Dokumentation zur Wirkungsgeschichte Richard Wagners 1876–1976* (Frankfurt, 1976), 279.
4. Franz Rühlmann, "Richard Wagners deutsche Sendung," *Deutsche Musikkultur* 1941, quoted in Wulf, *Musik im Dritten Reich*, 318; Kolland, "Wagner-Rezeption," 497.
5. Alfred Lorenz, introduction to *Richard Wagner: Ausgewählte Schriften und Briefe*, vol. I (Berlin, 1938), 3.
6. Karl Richard Ganzer, *Richard Wagner, der Revolutionär gegen das 19. Jahrhundert* (1934), quoted in Wulf, *Musik im Dritten Reich*, 313–14.
7. Kurt Engelbrecht, *Deutsche Kunst in Italien* (1933), quoted in Wulf, *Musik im Dritten Reich*, 312.
8. Alfred Lorenz, "Musikwissenschaft und Judenfrage," *Die Musik* 31 (1938), 177–79. The most thorough attempt was that of Karl Blessinger, who wrote *Judentum und Musik* (note the similarity to Wagner's title) in which he attacked the destructive influence of nineteenth-century Jews exclusively, focusing on Mendelssohn, Meyerbeer, Offenbach, and Mahler. His focus solely on Jewish composers of the nineteenth century takes its cue from Wagner's dismay with his contemporaries, and his vindictive tone, far surpassing that of Wagner, exploits colorful biological metaphors in the spirit of current rhetoric in race studies. See Karl Blessinger, *Judentum und Musik* (Berlin, 1944), first published as *Mendelssohn, Meyerbeer, Mahler: Drei Kapitel Judentum in der Musik als Schlüssel zur Musikgeschichte des 19. Jahrhunderts* (Berlin, 1938).
9. Stephen McClatchie, "Wagner Research as 'Service to the People': The Richard-Wagner-Forschungsstätte, 1938–1945," in Michael Kater and Albrecht Riethmüller, eds., *Music and Nazism: Art Under Tyranny, 1933–1945* (Laaber, 2002), 150–69.
10. Theodor Adorno, *In Search of Wagner*, trans. Rodney Livingstone (London and New York, 1981), 114–29.
11. Hans Rudolf Vaget, "'Du warst mein Feind von je': The Beckmesser Controversy Revisited," in Nicholas Vazsonyi, ed., *Wagner's Meistersinger: Performance, History, Representation* (Rochester, NY, 2002), 190–91.
12. Horst Weber, "Das Fremde im Eigenen: Zum Wandel des Wagnerbildes im Exil," in Friedländer and Rüsen, *Wagner im Dritten Reich*, 215; Frederic Spotts, *Hitler and the Power of Aesthetics* (London, 2002), 240–44.
13. Na'ama Sheffi, *The Ring of Myths: The Israelis, Wagner, and the Nazis*, trans. Martha Grenzeback (Brighton, 2001), 46–49.
14. Zelinsky, *Richard Wagner*, 278–80.
15. Hans Jürgen Syberberg, dir., *Winifred Wagner und die Geschichte des Hauses Wahnfried 1914–1975* (1976).
16. Heinz-Klaus Metzger and Rainer Riehn, eds., *Richard Wagner: wie antisemitisch darf ein Künstler sein? (Musik-Konzepte 5)* (Munich, 1978).
17. Hitler's resolve in *Mein Kampf* to become a politician ("Ich aber beschloss, Politiker zu werden") is purportedly based on Wagner's similarly worded resolve to become a composer ("Ich beschloß, Musiker zu werden"); see Joachim Fest, "Richard Wagner – Das Werk neben dem Werk: Zur ausstehenden Wirkungsgeschichte eines Großideologen," in Friedländer and Rüsen, *Wagner im Dritten Reich*, 33; and Joachim Köhler, *Wagner's Hitler: The Prophet and His Disciple*, trans. Ronald Taylor (Cambridge, 2000), 206.
18. Vaget, "Beckmesser Controversy," 191; Fest, "Richard Wagner – Das Werk neben dem Werk," 32–35; Frederic Spotts, *Bayreuth: A History of the Wagner Festival* (New Haven, 1994), 141.
19. In *Richard Wagner im Dritten Reich* (edited by Friedländer and Rüsen), Joachim Fest asserts that Hitler carried out Wagner's ideas but misunderstood and exaggerated them; Udo

Bermbach proposes that Hitler appropriated but inverted Wagner's belief that artists should dictate politics; David Levin looks to Wagner's writings and music dramas to find similarities in Hitler's and Wagner's characterizations of enemies and villains; Reinhold Brinkmann sees a more indirect connection between a Nazi aesthetic of monumental art and Wagner's theatrical vision; and Saul Friedländer acknowledges the absence of direct evidence that Wagner inspired Hitler, though he nevertheless highlights more subtle connections between *Parsifal* and racial purity, *Rienzi* and fanaticism, and the anti-Semitic Bayreuth circle and Hitler.

20. Spotts, *Hitler*, 234–37.

21. Dina Porat, "'Zum Raum wird hier die Zeit': Richard Wagners Bedeutung für Adolf Hitler und die nationalsozialistische Führung," in *Richard Wagner und die Juden*, ed. Dieter Borchmeyer, Ami Maayani, and Susanne Vill (Stuttgart and Weimar, 2000), 207–20. See also Dieter Borchmeyer, "Renaissance und Instrumentalisierung des Mythos: Richard Wagner und die Folgen," in Friedländer and Rüsen, *Wagner im Dritten Reich*, 66–91.

22. See David Clay Large, "Ein Spiegelbild des Meisters? Die Rassenlehre von Houston Stewart Chamberlain," in *Wagner und die Juden*, 150ff. Even Köhler must admit the absence of references to Wagner, both in Chamberlain's work and in Hitler's *Mein Kampf* (Köhler, *Wagner's Hitler*, 116).

23. David Clay Large, "Wagners Bayreuth und Hitlers München," in Friedländer and Rüsen, *Wagner im Dritten Reich*, 202–06.

24. Brigitte Hamann, *Winifred Wagner: A Life at the Heart of Hitler's Bayreuth*, trans. Alan Bance (London, 2005), 122–32; Spotts, *Bayreuth*, 141–43, 164.

25. Fred K. Prieberg, *Musik im NS-Staat* (Frankfurt, 1982), 307.

26. Hamann, *Winifred Wagner*, 229–30, 322–26.

27. Michael Karbaum, *Studien zur Geschichte der Bayreuther Festspiele (1876–1976)* (Regensburg, 1976), 91–93.

28. Brinkmann, "Wagners Aktualität," 125–26.

29. Hamann, *Winifred Wagner*, 254–57.

30. David C. Large, "Wagner's Bayreuth Disciples," in Large and William Weber, eds., *Wagnerism in European Culture and Politics* (Ithaca, 1984), 131–32; Syberberg, *Winifred Wagner und die Geschichte des Hauses Wahnfried 1914–1975*.

31. Friedelind Wagner and Page Cooper, *Heritage of Fire: The Story of Richard Wagner's Granddaughter* (New York, [1945]); also published as *The Royal Family of Bayreuth* (London, [1948]).

32. Nike Wagner, *The Wagners: The Dramas of a Musical Dynasty*, trans. Ewald Osers and Michael Downes (Princeton, 1998); and Gottfried Wagner, *The Twilight of the Wagners: The Unveiling of a Family's Legacy*, trans. Della Couling (New York, 1997).

33. Brinkmann, "Wagners Aktualität," 112–14, 121–22.

34 Kolland, "Wagner-Rezeption," 501–02; Jens Malte Fischer, "Wagner-Interpretation im Dritten Reich: Musik und Szene zwischen Politisierung und Kunstanspruch," in Friedländer and Rüsen, *Wagner im Dritten Reich*, 143–45.

35. Richard Eichenauer, *Musik und Rasse*, 2nd edn. (1937), quoted in Wulf, *Musik im Dritten Reich*, 312.

36. Kolland, "Wagner-Rezeption," 501.

37. *Ibid.*, 498–99; Fischer, "Wagner-Interpretation," 146.

38. David Dennis, "'The Most German of All Operas': *Die Meistersinger* through the Lens of the Third Reich," in Vazsonyi, *Wagner's Meistersinger*, 107.

39. Joseph Goebbels, "Richard Wagner und das Kunstempfinden unserer Zeit," reprinted in Attila Csampai and Dietmar Holland, eds., Die Meistersinger von Nürnberg: *Texte-Materialien-Kommentare* (Munich, 1981), 194–97. Kolland ("Wagner und der deutsche Faschismus," 132) analyzes the significance of Goebbels's specific alterations of Wagner's text, discussing as well the corruption of the meter and the change from "Drum sag ich Euch" to the more emphatic "Drum sag ich's Euch."

40. Dennis, "'Most German of All Operas,'" 110.

41. Richard Wilhelm Stock, Preface to *Richard Wagner und die Stadt der Meistersinger* (1938), quoted in Csampai and Holland, Die Meistersinger von Nürnberg, 200–01.

42. In Richard Wilhelm Stock, *Richard Wagner und seine* Meistersinger: *Eine Erinnerungsgabe zu den Bayreuther Kriegsfestspielen 1943* (Nuremberg, 1938 [rev. 1943]); Dennis, "'Most German of All Operas,'" 107–12; Fischer, "Wagner-Interpretation," 146.

43. Fischer, "Wagner-Interpretation," 145.

44. Barry Millington, "Nuremberg Trial: Is There Anti-Semitism in *Die Meistersinger?*," *Cambridge Opera Journal* 3 (1991), 247–60; Marc A. Weiner, *Richard Wagner and the Anti-Semitic Imagination* (Lincoln, NE, and London, 1995).

45. Dennis, "'Most German of All Operas,'" 100–06; Thomas Grey, "Bodies of Evidence," *Cambridge Opera Journal* 8 (1996), 191n; Grey, "Wagner's *Die Meistersinger* as National Opera

(1868–1945)," in Celia Applegate and Pamela Potter, eds., *Music and German National Identity* (Chicago, 2002), 97–99.

46. Hamann, *Winifred Wagner*, 251–54.

47. *Ibid.*, 212–19, 225–26; Spotts, *Bayreuth*, 184–85; on Hitler's longstanding admiration for Roller, see Spotts, *Hitler*, 223–24, 236.

48. Hartmut Zelinsky, "Verfall, Vernichtung, Weltentrückung: Richard Wagners antisemitische Werk-Idee als Kunstreligion und Zivilisationskritik und ihre Verbreitung bis 1933," in Friedländer and Rüsen, *Wagner im Dritten Reich*, 309–41.

49. Spotts, *Hitler*, 235–36; Hamann, *Winifred Wagner*, 348–49.

50. Saul Friedländer, "Hitler und Wagner," in Friedländer and Rüsen, *Wagner im Dritten Reich*, 171–75.

51. Hamann, *Winifred Wagner*, 348–49; Kolland, "Wagner-Rezeption," 502. [Editor's note] On the question of a ban, official or unofficial, on performances of *Parsifal* at Bayreuth and throughout the *Reich* during the later years of the Nazi regime, see also Katherine R. Syer, "*Parsifal* on Stage," in William Kinderman and Syer, eds., *A Companion to Wagner's* Parsifal (Rochester, NY, 2005), 304–05.

52. Brinkmann, "Wagners Aktualität," 130–32; Friedrich Baser, "Richard Wagner als Künder der arischen Welt," *Die Musik*, 1933, quoted in Wulf, *Musik im Dritten Reich*, 311.

53. Alfred Rosenberg, *Der Mythus des 20. Jahrhunderts* (1933), quoted in Wulf, *Musik im Dritten Reich*, 318; Brinkmann, "Wagners Aktualität," 123–24.

54. Rainer Schlösser, *Das Volk und die deutsche Bühne* (1935), quoted in Wulf, *Musik im Dritten Reich*, 319.

55. Adorno, *In Search of Wagner*, 114–29.

56. Weiner, *Wagner and the Anti-Semitic Imagination*.

57. Gustav Mahler reacted to the *Ring* with the observation: "No doubt with Mime, Wagner intended to ridicule the Jews (with all their characteristic traits – petty intelligence and greed – the jargon is textually and musically so cleverly suggested)" (Henry-Louis de la Grange, *Mahler*, vol. I [New York, 1973], 482).

58. Fischer, "Wagner-Interpretation," 148.

59. *Ibid.*, 148–56.

60. Bernd Sponheuer, "Musik auf einer 'kulturellen und physischen Insel': Musik als Überlebensmittel im Jüdischen Kulturbund 1933–1941," in Horst Weber, ed., *Musik in der Emigration 1933–1945: Verfolgung – Vertreibung – Rückwirkung* (Stuttgart, 1994), 115–16.

61. Hans Severus Ziegler, *Entartete Musik: Eine Abrechnung*, 2nd edn. (Düsseldorf, 1939), 25.

62. Joza Karas, *Music in Terezín 1941–1945* (New York, 1985), 61; Sheffi, *Ring of Myths*, 51.

63. Sheffi, *Ring of Myths*, chaps. 7 and 8.

15 Wagner on stage: aesthetic, dramaturgical, and social considerations

1. The term used throughout this chapter for the person who conceives and rehearses the staging of an opera is "director" (German *Regisseur*); in the UK this role used to be known as the "producer."

2. A "dramaturg," in contemporary spoken and music theater, is responsible for literary and backup research to a production concept. This may include work in actual rehearsal and on program material. (Although many directors make use of such research, the post is only just beginning to establish itself outside the German-speaking countries.) In Wagner's years as Kapellmeister at the Dresden court theater, there was a Literator ("the literary manager") or Oberregisseur für Schauspiel und Oper ("chief director of plays and opera") who participated in the actual staging of the operas performed. For an account of Wagner's active role in the production process, see his description of a last-minute coaching session with Ludwig Schnorr von Carolsfeld for a performance of *Tannhäuser* in Munich (1865) in his "Recollections of Ludwig Schnorr von Carolsfeld" (*GS* VIII:180–82; *PW* IV:230–32).

3. The first of eight or nine production books issued in conjunction with the premieres of Verdi's later operas, this one for *Les vêpres siciliennes* was thirty-eight pages long and fairly generalized, especially as regards chorus movement. This publication derived from a tradition some decades old of issuing such *livrets de mise-en-scène* for the more important operatic productions at the Paris Opéra and Opéra Comique. Verdi himself exported the practice to Italy in a series of *disposizioni sceniche* for his later works. By 1887 the *disposizione scenica* for *Otello* had 111 pages, including 270 blocking diagrams showing positions and moves for the cast. Since 1993 Ricordi has republished the original production books for *Simon Boccanegra*, *Otello*, and *Un ballo in maschera*.

4. His *Meistersinger* team, the Stuttgart stage manager Reinhard Hallwachs and the choreographer Lucile Grahn, were able to manage an effective staging of the complex riot scene at the conclusion of Act 2. On Wagner's recommendation, both were engaged subsequently for the Munich *Rheingold*

premiere in 1869 (before the composer himself opposed this unofficial premiere of the opera before the completion of the cycle).

5. See Angelo Neumann's account of Wagner at the Vienna *Tannhäuser* production of 1875 in his *Erinnerungen an Richard Wagner*, 2nd edn. (Leipzig, 1907), 9–10; see the English version, *Personal Recollections of Wagner*, trans. Edith Livermore (London, 1909), 9–10: "how he dominated, moved and inspired his company – assigning places, prescribing gestures, and arranging expressions." Regrettably, Neumann has nothing to say in detail about what Wagner actually did to achieve all this.

6. Richard Fricke, *Bayreuth vor dreissig Jahren* (Dresden, 1906), 113 (entry of 1 July 1876). This diary was reissued in Germany only in 1983, with a foreword by Joachim Herz; trans. Stewart Spencer as "Bayreuth in 1876," *Wagner* 11 (1990), 93–109, 134–50, and 12 (1991), 25–44. (A more recent translation by George R. Fricke, the composer's grandson, *Wagner in Rehearsal 1875–1876*, ed. James Deaville with Evan Baker, *Franz Liszt Studies* 7 [Stuyvesant, NY, 1998], is wholly inadequate.) This is the only realistic, close-quarters account of Wagner at work in staging rehearsals. Fricke described other "contemporary" accounts and notes by Wagner's disciple Heinrich Porges and by J. Zimmermann (editor of the *Bayreuther Tagblatt*) as "inaccurate and superficial." Fricke's diary accounts of rehearsing *Parsifal* seem to have been lost or suppressed.

7. Although Wagner regularly attacked the Paris Opera and all its works and composers (especially Giacomo Meyerbeer), that did not stop him from secretly admiring – and not so secretly borrowing from – the technical achievements and effects of those stagings. The majority of the *Ring*'s transformations (both of stage and people) have clear antecedents in stage-works first created in that theater. Later, in his review of the Munich *Rheingold* premiere, Eduard Hanslick complained that the talk of the town after this production was all of "swimming nixies, colored steam, the castle of the gods, and the rainbow," but "only rarely about the music"; quoted in Oswald Georg Bauer, *Richard Wagner: The Stage Designs and Productions from the Premieres to the Present*, trans. Stewart Spencer (New York, 1983), 222.

8. "Ground production" is the motivation and positioning of the actor-singers achieved through work with the director in a given production.

9. Cosima Wagner to Count Hermann Keyserling, quoted in Dietrich Mack, ed.,

Cosima Wagner. Das zweite Leben: Briefe und Aufzeichnungen, 1883–1930 (Munich and Zurich, 1980), 630.

10. *Tristan* and *Die Meistersinger* were first staged at Bayreuth in productions based on their Munich premieres. The first Bayreuth *Tannhäuser* was based on the famous Paris revival of 1861 and the first *Lohengrin* on the "model" production of Vienna in 1875 overseen by the composer. For *Holländer* in 1901 Cosima commissioned "original" on-site research (but in Sweden). Against Cosima's conservative staging policy must be set her establishment of the Bayreuth festival as a regular event and her opening up of the casts to international singers.

11. Bernard Shaw's rants against Bayreuth productions encouraged his writing of *The Perfect Wagnerite* (1898) whose parallels between the *Ring* and its contemporary social history would so interest later twentieth-century stage directors.

12. "Scenography" refers to the whole process of visualizing a production for the stage through set, costume, and lighting design.

13. Adolphe Appia, *La mise en scène du drame wagnérien* (Paris, 1895); trans. Peter Loeffler, *Staging Wagnerian Drama* (Basel and Boston, 1982), 48–50.

14. Contrary to what is often believed (and was actually stated by Wieland Wagner), Cosima Wagner did *not* fully shut the door on the possibility of Adolphe Appia working in Bayreuth. After looking at costume sketches that he submitted for *Tannhäuser* (which she did not like), she did suggest to Houston Stewart Chamberlain that Appia might become "costume designer and lighting consultant for Bayreuth" (letter of 23 October 1888, quoted from Mack, *Cosima Wagner: Das zweite Leben*, 14.

15. Henry-Louis de la Grange, *Gustav Mahler*, vol. II, *Vienna: Triumph and Disillusion (1904–1907)* (London, 1999), 77–95.

16. The production team responsible for a staging is cited in the order director/set designer/costume designer. When only two names are listed, the same designer was responsible for both set and costumes. The designer in opera pre-dates the presence of the director by several centuries; the idea that the designer's contribution should go beyond providing appropriate but emotionally neutral backdrops to the action was new to the nineteenth century, encouraged in Germany by the work of Weber in Dresden and Goethe in Weimar. By the 1900s close collaboration of designer and director in a staging concept of a work was becoming the norm.

17. Film excerpts from rehearsals for the 1938 *Götterdämmerung* (Martha Fuchs and Max Lorenz in Heinz Tietjen's production) reveal stiff, hieratic minimal acting.

18. Although the term "music theater" has become virtually synonymous with the postwar productions of Walter Felsenstein, it was not a term that he himself used or approved. Felsenstein himself did not stage any Wagner in this post-1945 part of his career, whereas Joachim Herz directed all the mature works in Germany, the Soviet Union, and Britain.

19. As exemplified by the theater productions of Giorgio Strehler/Ezio Frigerio in Milan from the mid-1950s onward.

20. Wieland Wagner to Hans Knappertsbusch, letter of May 1951, quoted in Dietrich Mack, *Der Bayreuther Inszenierungsstil* (Munich, 1976), 104. For further explanation of Wieland's production, see his (and Kurt Overhoff's) psychological schema "Parsifal's Cross," first published in the 1951 Bayreuth festival program book.

21. *GS* III:270; *PW* II:63. Many sources think that Wieland's wife, the choreographer Gertrud Reissinger, made a huge contribution to such scenes.

22. See, for example, the 1958 *Rheingold* conducted by Hans Knappertsbusch (various labels, including Hunt 34041–53), Karl Boehm's *Walküre* (Philips 412 478-2PH4, recorded 1967) and any of the thirteen Knappertsbusch *Parsifals* that have so far emerged on disc from his Bayreuth performances of 1951–64 (the best sound is on Philips 464 756-2PM4, recorded 1962).

23. For example, *Ring* productions of the Royal Opera House, Covent Garden, from 1961–64, directed by Hans Hotter and designed by Günther Schneider-Siemssen.

24. Known to exist are Bavarian Radio filmings of Act 1 of the first *Meistersinger* in 1959, and Act 3, scene 1, of the second *Meistersinger* in 1963 (this last is occasionally on offer from American pirate sources; both were rejected for public screening on technical and artistic grounds by Wieland); and brief excerpts from Act 2 of the *Götterdämmerung* performances from the second *Ring* cycle (Hagen's summoning of the vassals and the vengeance-oath trio sung by Gunther, Hagen, and Brünnhilde). In 1968 Japanese TV filmed the Osaka festival performances of the second *Tristan* and *Walküre* productions that toured there by a representative Bayreuth ensemble under Pierre Boulez (it has been issued unofficially on video, most recently by the Bel Canto Society 8998404623) and Thomas Schippers (on unofficial DVD from Premiere Opera).

25. In 1961 Wieland Wagner directed what was effectively a revival of his 1959 Bayreuth production for the Royal Danish Opera, Copenhagen. This production, revived by the original assistant director Peter Petersen, was still being performed in Copenhagen in 1999.

26. Personal communication with author, London, September 1976.

27. Staged in Berlin (Komische Oper), Leipzig, and Moscow (1963), and then filmed for DEFA (the East German state film company). The film – the first ever of a "complete" Wagner opera – used actors miming to a cut (97-minute) version of the score, prerecorded using an early version of four-channel stereo sound. A DVD release is mandatory.

28. *Wagner* 19/1 (January 1998) contains representative photos of Joachim Herz's major Wagner productions, together with an English translation of his lecture "Wagner and Theatrical Realism, 1960–1976."

29. The production was filmed for video (and later put on laserdisc in Japan) in 1978, Philips 070 412-3PH2 (and 070 412-1); and released on DVD in 2008. Like all productions from the Festspielhaus, it was recorded specially outside the main festival season. This first project undertaken by Unitel in the venue has problems finding a compromise between the production's original lighting and what was necessary for the cameras, and doesn't quite capture the production at its freshest.

30. This was one of several ideas in the production anticipated by Herz/Heinrich in Leipzig. Another was the composite design of Valhalla, made up from recognizable strands of great buildings from European history.

31. Crucial changes were made after the first year of performances to the sets for *Rheingold*, scenes 2 and 4, and the various appearances of the Valkyries' rock.

32. Filmed in 1979–80 for television in a coproduction between Unitel, the Bayreuth festival, and Bavarian Radio. A recording (vinyl and later CDs) was issued in 1981 from the filmed material (Philips 434 421-24-2). After extensive broadcasting (sometimes, as in the UK, in a soap-opera format of one act at a time), the filming was issued by Philips on video (070 401-3, 070 402-3, 070 403-3, 070 404-3), laserdisc (same numbers with suffix-1) and finally DVD (suffix-9). Made in collaboration with Chéreau, the filming gets in close, capturing the visceral impact of the acting, if (inevitably) not always the beauty and spaciousness of Peduzzi's sets. In 2005 the DVDs were reissued (Deutsche Grammophon).

33. Before his death in 2001 Friedrich completed a third *Ring* production for Finnish Opera, Helsinki, 1996–99. With the Austrian designer Gottfried Pilz he mixed the bright primary colors and cartoon-sharp acting of contemporary deconstructionist stagings into a synthesis of his own London and Berlin productions.

34. The production was filmed at the time of a 1985 revival; it is a technical success, but the result is not as sharp as the premiere run of performances. It was released on Philips video (070 406-3), laserdisc (suffix-1), and finally, in 2005, DVD (Deutsche Grammophon 00440 073 4041). In Kupfer's 2001 Berlin production of the work the central symbol of the prison ship holding the imaginary Dutchman changed sex to become a phallus.

35. The production was filmed in 1991–92 and released on Teldec video (4509-91122-233, 4509-94193-94 -3) and laserdisc (suffix-1). This was the first really successful attempt to capture a Bayreuth stage production on film, maintaining a fine balance between close-up detail and the scale of the overall stage picture. DVD release commenced in 2005, especially successful in capturing the laser work. The "soundtrack" of these films (i.e., from the same assemblage of performance material) was released simultaneously on CD. Kupfer went on to become the first director in history to have his productions of all the mature Wagner operas put on at a single festival (Berlin, Deutsche Staatsoper, April 2003). A DVD release of his Berlin *Ring*, filmed at inconsistent revivals at the Teatro Liceu, Barcelona, in 2004, was made in 2005 (Opus Arte OA 0910-13D).

36. The Frankfurt Opera at this time was noted for a radical staging policy that actively rejected production concepts it considered too traditional. Other major Berghaus/Gielen productions included *Die Zauberflöte*, *Die Entführung aus dem Serail*, *The Makropoulos Case*, and *Les Troyens*. None of these productions were filmed for official release but the house's one-camera videos of the *Ring* production may be viewed by appointment.

37. Interviewed in Cardiff while staging *Don Giovanni* there in 1984, Berghaus commented that, whereas "symbols" can mean all things to all men, "signs" are unambiguously clear. As is the case with Wieland Wagner, the sheer humor of Berghaus's work has been insufficiently commented upon.

38. This production was not officially preserved on film. In contrast to the Gielen/Berghaus 1985–87 Frankfurt *Ring* or the Barenboim/Kupfer 1988 Bayreuth *Ring*, Bernard Haitink's handling of the music was in no way related to the psychology or pacing of what happened onstage.

39. When the cycle was presented complete in 1996–97, Siegfried got his drink – one of many detail changes made at that time.

40. Similarly in Konwitschny's 2005 *Fliegende Holländer*, the performance of the final scene, the Dutchman's "salvation," is played on tape instead of being sung and played by the actual performers.

41. DVD releases of the Stuttgart *Ring* were filmed at performances in 2002–03 (arte edition 2052068-98).

42. The Alden/Davey team succeeded Herbert Wernicke, who died after the opening of *Das Rheingold*.

43. A DVD of the Warner/Fielding *Siegfried* has been released in Japan; the Warner/Lazaridis London cycle awaits release on DVD; there is no official filming of the Carsen cycle.

44. A 1987-originated *Ring* from Munich is available on video (EMI MVB 99 1276-87 3) and laserdisc (LDE 99 1276-87 1); *Parsifal* (recorded in Baden-Baden 2004) is on DVD (Opus Arte 0915D); and *Lohengrin* on DVD (Opus Arte 09640).

45. Recorded at revivals during the 1990s, the Met *Ring* is on DVD (Deutsche Grammophon 073 043-9). That a Romantic, historically inclined Wagner staging can have dramaturgical validity and life was demonstrated by Jean-Pierre Ponnelle's Bayreuth *Tristan und Isolde* of 1981 (available on Philips video VHS 070 409-3, laserdisc-1, DVD DG 0730449).

46. Winifred Wagner's close friendship with Hitler – and his strong endorsement by other family members, notably Houston Stewart Chamberlain – resulted in Hitler giving Bayreuth his close personal and financial patronage from 1924 to 1940, acting also as surrogate father and counsellor to the young Wieland Wagner. However, his frequent advice on purely artistic matters was not often accepted. See Brigitte Hamann, *Winifred Wagner: A Life at the Heart of Hitler's Bayreuth*, trans. Alan Bance (London, 2005) – an unnecessary abridgement of the original German text (Munich, 2002), although made with the author's consent.

47. A reaction which reached a sort of apogee in early 1981, when the London *Daily Telegraph* devoted one of its leader columns to a piece entitled "Marx Brothers at the Opera."

48. "I am convinced that this character was intended by Wagner as the living parody of a Jew," Mahler remarked while rehearsing a new Mime for a *Siegfried* revival in Vienna in 1898; "It's clear from all the aspects he's given to Mime – his petty obsessions, his covetousness, the whole clever kit of musical and verbal

tics": quoted in Herbert Killian, *Gustav Mahler in den Erinnerungen von Natalie Bauer-Lechner* (Hamburg, 1984), 122.
49. Wagner was fond of this motif. He alludes to it obliquely in a private parody of the words of Senta's Ballad, which he made up for himself in Paris in the early 1840s (see *Richard Wagner: Sämtliche Werke*, vol. XXIV, *Dokumente und Texte zu* Der fliegende Holländer, ed. Egon Voss (Mainz, 2004), 176; see also John Deathridge, "Wagner's 'Pale' Senta," *Opera Quarterly* 21/3 (2005), and at several points in Act 1 of *Siegfried*. A more direct allusion occurs at the beginning of Act 3 of *Parsifal*, when Gurnemanz discovers Kundry in a thorn bush.

16 Criticism and analysis: current perspectives
1. For example, Nicholas Vazsonyi's recent edited collection *Wagner's* Meistersinger: *Performance, History, Representation* (Rochester, NY, 2003) contains contributions from a singer (Dietrich Fischer-Dieskau), a conductor (Peter Schneider), a producer (Harry Kupfer), and a philosopher (Lydia Goehr), as well as from historians and musicologists.
2. For a succinct but stimulating introduction to the vast subject of Wagner reception and writing in all its phases up through the 1980s, see John Deathridge, "A Brief History of Wagner Research," in *Wagner Handbook*, ed. Ulrich Müller and Peter Wapnewski, translation ed. John Deathridge (Cambridge, MA, 1992), 202–23.
3. See H. von Wolzogen: "Prelude," "Act 1 [scene 1]," from *Parsifal: A Thematic Guide Through the Poetry and the Music* (1882), in Ian Bent, ed., *Music Analysis in the Nineteenth Century,* vol. II, *Hermeneutic Approaches* (Cambridge, 1994), 88–105. A recent study of the leitmotif phenomenon and its critical dissemination is Christian Thorau's monograph *Semantisierte Sinnlichkeit: Studien zur Rezeption und Zeichenstruktur der Leitmotivtechnik Richard Wagners* (Stuttgart, 2003).
4. Bryan Magee, *The Tristan Chord: Wagner and Philosophy* (London and New York, 2000), 325. See also Dieter Borchmeyer's essay in this volume (chap. 11).
5. "Modernist" as used here refers to art of the past 150 years or so that is uneasy with organicism and that questions the emphasis on unity which so much technical and critical analysis involves.
6. Thomas Grey, *Wagner's Musical Prose: Texts and Contexts* (Cambridge, 1995), 182.
7. Wagner referred to "my most delicate and profound . . . art of transition" in a letter to

Mathilde Wesendonck of 29 October 1859 (*SL* 475; *SB* XI:329).
8. Cyrill Kistler, *Harmonielehre für Lehrer und Lernende* (Munich, 1879).
9. Robert W. Wason, *Viennese Harmonic Theory from Albrechtsberger to Schenker and Schoenberg* (Ann Arbor, MI, 1985), 90. For other accounts of the history of *Tristan* chord analysis, see Jean-Jacques Nattiez, *Music and Discourse: Towards a Semiology of Music*, trans. Carolyn Abbate (Princeton, 1990), 216–38; David W. Bernstein, "Nineteenth-Century Harmonic Theory: The Austro-German Legacy," in *The Cambridge History of Western Music Theory*, ed. Thomas Christensen (Cambridge, 2002), 791–94; and Thomas Grey, "Magnificent Obsession: *Tristan* as the Object of Musical Analysis," in Nikolaus Bacht, ed., *Music, Theatre and Politics in Germany, 1850–1950* (London and Burlington, VT, 2006), 51–78.
10. For translated extracts from Karl Mayrberger's *Die Harmonik Richard Wagner's an den Leitmotiv aus "Tristan und Isolde" erläutert* (1882), see Ian Bent, *Music Analysis in the Nineteenth Century*, vol. I, *Fugue, Form and Style*, (Cambridge, 1994), 221–52. On the differences between analytical approaches, like Mayrberger's, and hermeneutic ones, like Wolzogen's, see the discussion in Bent, *Hermeneutic Approaches*, 88–105.
11. See Arnold Schoenberg, *Structural Functions of Harmony*, ed. Leonard Stein, 2nd edn. (London, 1969), 76–77.
12. Ernst Kurth, *Selected Writings*, ed. and trans. Lee A. Rothfarb (Cambridge, 1991), 134 (from Kurth, *Romantische Harmonik und ihre Krise in Wagners "Tristan"* [Berlin, 1920; 2nd edn. 1923]).
13. See for example Allen Forte, "New Approaches to the Linear Analysis of Music," *Journal of the American Musicological Society* 51 (1988), 315–48.
14. Heinrich Schenker, *Free Composition*, ed. and trans. Ernst Oster (New York and London, 1979), 106 (original title, *Der freie Satz* [Vienna, 1935]).
15. The four volumes of Lorenz's *Das Geheimnis der Form bei Richard Wagner* were published in 1924–33 (Berlin; repr. Tutzing, 1966).
16. For a full account of Lorenz's work and its cultural-political contexts, see Stephen McClatchie, *Analyzing Wagner's Operas: Alfred Lorenz and German Nationalist Ideology* (Rochester, NY, 1998).
17. Thomas Mann, "The Sorrows and Grandeur of Richard Wagner" (1933), in Mann, *Pro and Contra Wagner*, trans. Allan Blunden (London, 1985), 128.

18. *Ibid.*, 141.

19. Ernest Newman, *The Life of Richard Wagner*, 4 vols. (New York, 1937–46; reprint, Cambridge, 1976). See the discussion in Deathridge, "A Brief History of Wagner Research."

20. Mann, "Sorrows and Grandeur," 107.

21. Theodor W. Adorno, "Wagner's Relevance for Today" (1963), in his *Essays on Music*, ed. Richard Leppert, trans. Susan H. Gillespie (Berkeley and Los Angeles, 2002), 585.

22. Mann, "Sorrows and Grandeur," 206.

23. Gyorgy Markus, "Adorno's Wagner," *Thesis Eleven* 56 (1999), 49.

24. Adorno, "Wagner's Relevance for Today," 591.

25. *Ibid.*, 596.

26. In Joseph Kerman, *Opera as Drama* (New York, 1956; 2nd edn., Berkeley and Los Angeles, 1988), 158–77.

27. Robert Bailey, "Wagner's Musical Sketches for *Siegfrieds Tod*," in H. S. Powers, ed., *Studies in Music History: Essays for Oliver Strunk* (Princeton, 1968), 459–94; Bailey "The Genesis of *Tristan und Isolde* and a Study of Wagner's Sketches and Draft for the First Act" (Ph.D. diss., Princeton University, 1969). (See also nn. 32 and 35 below.)

28. The most widely cited works by Dahlhaus are *Richard Wagner's Music Dramas*, trans. Mary Whittall (Cambridge, 1979; originally published as *Wagners Konzeption des Musikdramas* [Regensburg, 1971]); *Between Romanticism and Modernism: Four Studies in the Music of the Later Nineteenth Century* (1974), trans. Mary Whittall (Berkeley and Los Angeles, 1980); and *Nineteenth-Century Music* (1980), trans. J. Bradford Robinson (Berkeley and Los Angeles, 1989). For an extended bibliography, see J. Bradford Robinson, "Dahlhaus, Carl," in *The New Grove Dictionary of Music and Musicians*, 2nd edn., ed. Stanley Sadie and John Tyrrell, 29 vols. (London, 2001), VI, 836–39.

29. McClatchie, *Analyzing Wagner's Operas*, 184.

30. *Ibid.*, 184 and n. 48.

31. Felix Salzer, *Structural Hearing: Tonal Coherence in Music*, 2 vols. (New York, 1952), I, 216–18; II, 232–33.

32. William J. Mitchell, "The *Tristan* Prelude: Techniques and Structure," in William J. Mitchell and Felix Salzer, eds., *The Music Forum*, vol. I (New York, 1967), 163–203; repr. in Robert Bailey, ed., *Richard Wagner: Prelude and Transfiguration from* Tristan and Isolde (New York, 1985), 242–67.

33. Christopher Wintle, "The Numinous in *Götterdämmerung*," in Arthur Groos and Roger Parker, eds., *Reading Opera* (Princeton, 1988), 200–34; Matthew Brown, "Isolde's Narrative: From *Hauptmotiv* to Tonal Model," and Patrick McCreless, "Schenker and the Norns," in Carolyn Abbate and Roger Parker, eds., *Analyzing Opera: Verdi and Wagner* (Berkeley and Los Angeles, 1989), 180–201 and 276–97; William M. Marvin, "The Function of 'Rules' in *Die Meistersinger von Nürnberg*," *Journal of Musicology* 20 (2003), 414–60.

34. Warren Darcy, *Wagner's Das Rheingold* (Oxford, 1993), 215.

35. See Robert Bailey, "The Structure of the *Ring* and Its Evolution," *19th-Century Music* 1 (1977), 48–61; and Bailey, "The Method of Composition," in *The Wagner Companion*, ed. Peter Burbidge and Richard Sutton (New York, 1979), 269–338.

36. Darcy, *Wagner's Das Rheingold*, 218.

37. Anthony Newcomb, "The Birth of Music out of the Spirit of Drama: An Essay in Wagnerian Formal Analysis," *19th-Century Music* 5 (1981–82), 64.

38. Carolyn Abbate, "Opera as Symphony, a Wagnerian Myth," in Abbate and Parker, *Analyzing Opera: Verdi and Wagner*, 92–124.

39. Newcomb, "The Birth of Music," 64.

40. For the origins and significance of this usage, see Grey, *Wagner's Musical Prose*, esp. 283–87.

41. John Daverio, *Nineteenth-Century Music and the German Romantic Ideology* (New York, 1993), 17, 189.

42. See Max Paddison, *Adorno's Aesthetics of Music* (Cambridge, 1993), 158 (citing Adorno's 1966 essay "Form in der neuen Musik").

43. Daverio, *Nineteenth-Century Music*, 16–17.

44. Carolyn Abbate, *Unsung Voices: Opera and Musical Narrative in the Nineteenth Century* (Princeton, 1991), 176, 192.

45. Carolyn Abbate, "Wagner, 'On Modulation,' and *Tristan*," *Cambridge Opera Journal* 1 (1989), 33–58; see also the discussion in Grey, *Wagner's Musical Prose*, 339–41.

46. Lawrence Kramer, *Music as Cultural Practice, 1800–1900* (Berkeley and Los Angeles, 1990), 135.

47. *Ibid.*, 148, 149.

48. *Ibid.*, 157.

49. *Ibid.*, 165. See also Kramer's "The Waters of Prometheus: Nationalism and Sexuality in Wagner's *Ring*," in Richard Dellamora and Daniel Fischlin, eds., *The Work of Opera: Genre, Nationhood, and Sexual Difference* (New York, 1997), 131–59.

50. Jean-Jacques Nattiez, *Wagner Androgyne: A Study in Interpretation*, trans. Stewart Spencer (Princeton, 1993), 300.

51. Grey, *Wagner's Musical Prose*, 107.

52. *Ibid.*, 348.

53. Marc A. Weiner, *Richard Wagner and the Anti-Semitic Imagination* (Lincoln, NE, and London, 1995), 358.

54. *Ibid.*, 359.

55. For recent commentaries, see Hans Rudolf Vaget, "'Du warst mein Feind von je': The Beckmesser Controversy Revisited," in Nicholas Vazsonyi, ed., *Wagner's* Meistersinger: *Performance, History, Representation* (Rochester, NY, 2003); Dieter Borchmeyer, *Drama and the World of Richard Wagner*, trans. Daphne Ellis (Princeton, 2003), 196–211; and Simon Williams, *Wagner and the Romantic Hero* (Cambridge, 2004), 142–46.

56. Gary Tomlinson, *Metaphysical Song: An Essay on Opera* (Princeton, 1999), 131.

57. *Ibid.*, 135, 142.

58. For further discussion of these issues with reference to *Parsifal*, see Arnold Whittall, "Wagner and Real Life," *Musical Times* 137 (1996), 5–11.

59. The latter category of Deathridge's writing on Wagner is represented in the newly published collection of his essays *Wagner Beyond Good and Evil* (Berkeley and Los Angeles, 2008).

60. Lydia Goehr, *The Quest for Voice: On Music, Politics, and the Limits of Philosophy* (Berkeley and Los Angeles, 1998), and Goehr, "The Curse and Promise of the Absolutely Musical: *Tristan and Isolde* and *Don Giovanni*," in Goehr and Daniel Herwitz, eds., *The Don Giovanni Moment* (New York, 2006), 137–60.

61. Roger Scruton, *Death-Devoted Heart: Sex and the Sacred in Wagner's* Tristan and Isolde (New York, 2004), 3, 159.

62. *Ibid.*, 3, 194.

63. *Ibid.*, 75, 115, 197.

64. David Lewin, "Amfortas's Prayer to Titurel and the Role of D in *Parsifal*: The Tonal Spaces and the Drama of the Enharmonic C♭/ B," *19th-Century Music* 7 (1984), 336–49; repr. in *Studies in Music with Text* (Oxford, 2006), 214, 218.

65. Eric Chafe, *The Tragic and the Ecstatic: The Musical Revolution of Wagner's* Tristan und Isolde (New York, 2005), 8.

66. Lewin, "Amfortas's Prayer to Titurel and the Role of D in *Parsifal*."

67. David Kopp, *Chromatic Transformations in Nineteenth-Century Music* (Cambridge, 2002), 223.

Select bibliography

Primary sources

Wagner's music, writings, and correspondence

Bergfeld, Joachim, ed., *The Diary of Richard Wagner, 1865–1882: The Brown Book*, trans. George Bird (London, 1980); orig. *Das braune Buch* (Zurich, 1975).

Burke, J. N., ed., *Letters of Richard Wagner: The Burrell Collection* (New York, 1950).

Deathridge, John, Martin Geck, and Egon Voss, eds., *Wagner Werk-Verzeichnis: Verzeichnis der musikalischen Werke Richard Wagners und ihrer Quellen* (Mainz and New York, 1986) [*WWV*].

Jacobs, Robert L., and Geoffrey Skelton, trans. and eds., *Wagner Writes from Paris …: Stories, Essays, and Articles by the Young Composer* (London, 1973).

Kesting, Hanjo, *Franz Liszt–Richard Wagner: Briefwechsel* (Frankfurt, 1988).

Spencer, Stewart, and Barry Millington, eds., *Selected Letters of Richard Wagner* (London and New York, 1988) [*SL*].

Strobel, Otto, ed., *König Ludwig II. und Richard Wagner: Briefwechsel*, 5 vols. (Karlsruhe, 1936, 1939).

Wagner, Richard, *Gesammelte Schriften und Dichtungen*, 10 vols. (Leipzig, 1887–1911) [*GS*].

  Mein Leben, ed. Martin Gregor-Dellin (Munich, 1976).

  My Life, trans. Andrew Gray (Cambridge, 1983) [*ML*].

  Richard Wagner: Stories and Essays, trans. Charles Osborne (La Salle, IL, 1973).

  Richard Wagner's Prose Works, trans. William Ashton Ellis, 8 vols. (New York, 1966; orig. edn., 1895–1912) [*PW*].

  Sämtliche Briefe, ed. Gertrud Strobel, Werner Wolf, et al. (Leipzig, 1967–2000; Wiesbaden, 1999–) [*SB*].

  Sämtliche Schriften und Dichtungen, 16 vols. (1911–16) [*SSD*].

  Sämtliche Werke, ed. Carl Dahlhaus (Mainz, 1970–) [*SW*].

  Three Wagner Essays, trans. Robert L. Jacobs (London, 1979).

  Wagner Brief-Verzeichnis, ed. Werner Breig, Martin Dürrer, and Andreas Melke (Wiesbaden, 1998).

Other diaries, memoirs, documents, chronologies

Fricke, Richard, *Bayreuth vor dreissig Jahren* (Dresden, 1906), trans. George R. Fricke as *Wagner in Rehearsal 1875–1876*, ed. James Deaville with Evan Baker, *Franz Liszt Studies* 7 (Stuyvesant, NY, 1998); also "Bayreuth in 1876," trans. Stewart Spencer, *Wagner* 11 (1990), 93–109, 134–50, and 12 (1991), 25–44.

Gautier, Judith, *Le collier des jours: souvenirs de ma vie* (Paris, 1909; Eng. trans. 1910).

Gregor-Dellin, Martin, *Wagner-Chronik: Daten zu Leben und Werk* (Munich and Kassel, 1983).

Hartford, Robert, ed., *Bayreuth: The Early Years (An Account of the Wagner Festival 1876–1914, as Seen by the Celebrated Visitors and Participants)* (Cambridge, 1980).

Heckel, Karl, *Die Bühnenfestspiele in Bayreuth* (Leipzig, 1891).

Kietz, M., *Richard Wagner in den Jahren 1842–1849 und 1873–1875: Erinnerungen von Gustav Adolph Kietz* (Dresden, 1905).

Mack, Dietrich, ed., *Cosima Wagner. Das zweite Leben: Briefe und Aufzeichnungen 1883–1930* (Munich and Zurich, 1980).

Neumann, Angelo, *Erinnerungen an Richard Wagner*, 2nd edn. (Leipzig, 1907), trans. Edith Livermore, *Personal Recollections of Wagner* (London, 1909).

Porges, Heinrich, *Wagner Rehearsing the* Ring: *An Eye-Witness Account of the Stage Rehearsals of the First Bayreuth Festival*, trans. Robert L. Jacobs (Cambridge, 1983).

Schemann, Ludwig, *Meine Erinnerungen an Richard Wagner* (Stuttgart, 1902).

Spencer, Stewart, *Wagner Remembered* (London, 2000).

Strobel, Otto, *Richard Wagner, Leben und Schaffen: Eine Zeittafel* (Bayreuth, 1952).

Wagner: A Documentary Study, ed. Herbert Barth, Dietrich Mack, and Egon Voss (New York, 1975).

Wagner, Cosima, *Cosima Wagner's Diaries*, ed. Martin Gregor-Dellin and Dietrich Mack, trans. Geoffrey Skelton, 2 vols. (New York and London, 1978–80) [*CWD*]; orig. *Cosima Wagner: Die Tagebücher*, 2 vols. (Munich, 1976–77).

Wagner, Siegfried, *Erinnerungen* (Stuttgart, 1923; 2nd edn. 1935).

Weissheimer, Wendelin, *Erlebnisse mit Wagner, Liszt und vielen anderen Zeitgenossen nebst deren Briefe* (Stuttgart, 1898).

Wolzogen, Heinrich von, *Erinnerungen an Richard Wagner* (Vienna, 1883, 2nd edn. 1891).

Secondary sources

Abbate, Carolyn, *In Search of Opera* (Princeton, 2001).

"The Parisian 'Venus' and the 'Paris' *Tannhäuser*," *Journal of the American Musicological Society* 36 (1983), 73–123.

Unsung Voices: Music and Narrative in Nineteenth-Century Opera (Princeton, 1991).

Abbate, Carolyn, and Roger Parker, eds., *Analyzing Opera: Verdi and Wagner* (Berkeley and Los Angeles, 1989), 92–124.

Aberbach, Alan David, *The Ideas of Richard Wagner* (Lanham, MD, 1984; 2nd edn. 1988).

Richard Wagner's Religious Ideas: A Spiritual Journey (Lewiston, NY, 1996).

Adorno, Theodor, *Versuch über Wagner* (Frankfurt, 1952), trans. Rodney Livingstone, *In Search of Wagner* (London, 1981; 2nd edn. 2005).

"Wagner's Relevance for Today," in Adorno, *Essays on Music*, ed. Richard Leppert, trans. Susan H. Gillespie (Berkeley and Los Angeles, 2002), 584–601.

Appia, Adolphe, *La mise en scène du drame wagnérien* (Paris, 1895); trans. Peter Loeffler, *Staging Wagnerian Drama* (Basel and Boston, 1982).

Bailey, Robert, ed., *Richard Wagner: Prelude and Transfiguration from* Tristan und Isolde (New York, 1985).

"The Structure of the *Ring* and Its Evolution," *19th-Century Music* 1 (1977), 48–61.

"Wagner's Musical Sketches for *Siegfrieds Tod*," in H. S. Powers, ed., *Studies in Music History: Essays for Oliver Strunk* (Princeton, 1968), 459–94.

Barone, Anthony, "Richard Wagner's *Parsifal* and the Theory of Late Style," *Cambridge Opera Journal* 7 (1995), 37–54.

Bartels, Ulrich, *Studien zu Wagners* Tristan und Isolde *anhand der Kompositionsskizze des zweiten und dritten Aktes*, 3 vols. (Cologne, 1995).

Bartlett, Rosamund, *Wagner and Russia* (Cambridge, 1995).

Barzun, Jacques, *Darwin, Marx, Wagner: Critique of a Heritage* (Boston, 1941; 2nd edn. 1958).

Baudelaire, Charles, "Richard Wagner and *Tannhäuser* in Paris," in Baudelaire, *The Painter of Modern Life and Other Essays*, ed. and trans. Jonathan Mayne (London, 1964).

Bauer, Oswald, *Richard Wagner geht ins Theater* (Bayreuth, 1996).
  Richard Wagner: The Stage Designs and Productions from the Premieres to the Present, trans. Stewart Spencer (New York, 1983).

Beckett, Lucy, *Richard Wagner*: Parsifal (Cambridge, 1981).

Bekker, Paul, *Richard Wagner: His Life in His Work*, trans. M. M. Bozman ([New York, 1931]; repr., Westport, CT, 1971).

Bermbach, Udo, *Richard Wagner: Stationen eines unruhigen Lebens* (Hamburg, 2006).
  Der Wahn des Gesamtkunstwerks: Richard Wagners politisch-ästhetische Utopie (Stuttgart, 2004).

Berry, Mark, *Treacherous Bonds and Laughing Fire: Politics and Religion in Wagner's* Ring (Aldershot, UK, and Burlington, VT, 2006).

Borchmeyer, Dieter, *Drama and the World of Richard Wagner*, trans. Daphne Ellis (Princeton, 2003).
  Richard Wagner: Theory and Theatre, trans. Stewart Spencer (Oxford and New York, 1991).
  Richard Wagner und die Juden, ed. Dieter Borchmeyer, Ami Maayani, and Susanne Vill (Stuttgart and Weimar, 2000).

Bott, Gerhard, ed., Die Meistersinger *und Richard Wagner: Die Rezeptionsgeschichte einer Oper von 1868 bis heute. Eine Ausstellung des Germanischen Nationalmuseums in Nürnberg, 10. Juli bis 11. Oktober 1981* (Nuremberg, 1981).

Brener, Milton E., *Richard Wagner and the Jews* (Jefferson, NC, and London, 2006).

Carnegy, Patrick, *Wagner and the Art of the Theatre: The Operas in Stage Performance* (New Haven and London, 2006).

Chafe, Eric, *The Tragic and the Ecstatic: The Musical Revolution of Wagner's* Tristan und Isolde (New York, 2005).

Cicora, Mary A., *From History to Myth: Wagner's* Tannhäuser *and Its Literary Sources* (Bern, 1992).
  Parsifal *Reception in the* Bayreuther Blätter (New York, 1987).
  Wagner's Ring *and German Drama* (Westport, CT, 1999).

Cohen, Mitchell, "Wagner as a Problem," *German Politics and Society* 16/2 (Summer 1998), 94–130.

Cooke, Deryck, *I Saw the World End: A Study of Wagner's* Ring (Oxford, 1979).

Csampai, Attila, and Dietmar Holland, eds., Die Meistersinger von Nürnberg: *Texte-Materialien-Kommentare* (Munich, 1981).

eds., *Richard Wagner,* Parsifal: *Texte, Materialien, Kommentare* (Reinbek, 1984).

Dahlhaus, Carl, ed., *Richard Wagner: Werk und Wirkung* (Regensburg, 1971).

Dahlhaus, Carl, *Richard Wagner's Music Dramas,* trans. Mary Whittall (Cambridge, 1979); orig. *Wagners Konzeption des Musikdramas* (Regensburg, 1971).

Danuser, Hermann, and Herfried Münkler, eds., *Richard Wagners Revolution und ihre Folgen in Kunst und Politik* (Schliengen, 2002).

Darcy, Warren, *Wagner's Das Rheingold* (Oxford, 1993).

Deathridge, John, *Wagner Beyond Good and Evil* (Berkeley and Los Angeles, 2008).
Wagner's Rienzi: *A Reappraisal Based on a Study of the Sketches and Drafts* (Oxford, 1977).

Deathridge, John, and Carl Dahlhaus, *The New Grove Wagner* (London, 1984).

Donington, Robert, *Wagner's* Ring *and Its Symbols: The Music and the Myth* (London, 1963).

Dreyfus, Laurence, "Hermann Levi's Shame and *Parsifal*'s Guilt: A Critique of Essentialism in Biography and Criticism," *Cambridge Opera Journal* 6 (1994), 125–45.

Eger, Manfred, *Wagner und die Juden* (Bayreuth, 1985).

Ewans, Michael, *Wagner and Aeschylus: The* Ring *and the* Oresteia (London, 1982; Cambridge and New York, 1983).

Fauser, Annegret, and Manuela Schwartz, eds., *Von Wagner zum Wagnérisme: Musik, Literatur, Kunst, Politik* (Leipzig, 1999).

Fehr, Max, *Richard Wagners Schweizer Zeit,* 2 vols. (Aarau and Leipzig, 1934, 1954).

Finck, Henry T., *Wagner and His Works,* 2 vols. (New York, 1893).

Fischer, Jens Malte, *Richard Wagners "Das Judentum in der Musik": Eine kritische Dokumentation als Beitrag zur Geschichte des Antisemitismus* (Frankfurt am Main and Leipzig, 2000).

Friedländer, Saul, and Jörn Rüsen, eds., *Richard Wagner im Dritten Reich* (Munich, 2000).

Friedrich, Sven, *Richard Wagner: Deutung und Wirkung* (Würzburg, 2004).

Furness, Raymond, *Wagner and Literature* (Manchester, UK, 1982).

Geck, Martin, *Die Bildnisse Richard Wagners* (Munich, 1970).

Glasenapp, Carl Friedrich, *Das Leben Richard Wagners,* 3rd edn. (Kassel, 1894–1911), trans. and enlarged by William Ashton Ellis, *Life of Richard Wagner,* 6 vols. (London, 1900–08).

Gregor-Dellin, Martin, *Richard Wagner: Sein Leben, sein Werk, sein Jahrhundert* (Munich, 1980).

Grey, Thomas, "Magnificent Obsession: *Tristan* as the Object of Musical Analysis," in Nikolaus Bacht, ed., *Music, Theatre, and Politics in Germany, 1850–1950* (London and Burlington, VT, 2006), 51–78.

ed., *Richard Wagner*: Der fliegende Holländer (Cambridge, 2000).

"Wagner the Degenerate: Fin-de-Siècle Cultural 'Pathology' and the Anxiety of Modernism," *19th-Century Studies* 16 (2002), 73–92.

"Wagner's *Die Meistersinger* as National Opera (1868–1945)," in Celia Applegate and Pamela Potter, eds., *Music and German National Identity* (Chicago and London, 2002), 78–104.

Wagner's Musical Prose: Texts and Contexts (Cambridge, 1995).

". . . *wie ein rother Faden*: On the Origins of 'Leitmotif' as Critical Concept and Musical Practice," in Ian Bent, ed., *Music Theory in the Age of Romanticism* (Cambridge, 1996), 187–210.

Grimm, Reinhold, and Jost Hermand, eds., *Re-Reading Wagner* (Madison, WI, 1993).

Groos, Arthur, "Appropriation in Wagner's *Tristan* Libretto," Groos and Roger Parker, eds., *Reading Opera* (Princeton, 1989), 13–25.

"Constructing Nuremberg: Typological and Proleptic Communities in *Die Meistersinger*," *19th-Century Music* 16 (1992), 18–34.

Grunsky, Karl, "Reim und musikalische Form in den Meistersingern," *Richard Wagner-Jahrbuch* 5 (1913), 138–87.

"Wagner als Symphoniker," *Richard Wagner-Jahrbuch* 1 (1906), 227–44.

Gutman, Robert, *Richard Wagner: The Man, His Mind, and His Music* (New York, 1968).

Hamann, Brigitte, *Die Familie Wagner* (Reinbek, 2005).

Winifred Wagner oder Hitlers Bayreuth (Munich, 2002); trans. Alan Bance, *Winifred Wagner: A Life at the Heart of Hitler's Bayreuth* (London, 2005).

Hollinrake, Roger, *Nietzsche, Wagner, and the Philosophy of Pessimism* (London, 1982).

Holman, J. K., *Wagner's Ring: A Listener's Companion and Concordance* (Portland, OR, 1996).

Horowitz, Joseph, *Wagner Nights: An American History* (Berkeley and Los Angeles, 1994).

Huebner, Steven, *French Opera at the Fin de Siècle: Wagnerism, Nationalism, and Style* (Oxford, 1999).

Janz, Tobias, *Klangdramaturgie: Studien zur orchestralen Theaterkomposition in Wagners Ring des Nibelungen* (Würzburg, 2006).

Kahane, Martine, and Nicole Wilde, *Wagner et la France* (Paris, 1983).

Karbaum, Michael, *Studien zur Geschichte der Bayreuther Festspiele (1876–1976)* (Regensburg, 1976).

Katz, Jacob, *The Darker Side of Genius: Richard Wagner's Anti-Semitism* (Hanover, NH, and London, 1986).

Kerman, Joseph, "Opera as Symphonic Poem (*Tristan und Isolde*)," in Kerman, *Opera as Drama*, 2nd edn. (Berkeley and Los Angeles, 1988), 158–77.

"*Tristan und Isolde*: The Prelude and the Play," in Kerman, *Write All These Down* (Berkeley and Los Angeles, 1994), 335–50.

Kienzele, Ulrike, ". . . *daß wissend würde die Welt!*" *Religion und Philosophie in Richard Wagners Musikdramen* (Würzburg, 2005).

Kinderman, William, "Dramatic Recapitulation and Tonal Pairing in Wagner's *Tristan und Isolde*," in Kinderman and Harold Krebs, eds., *The Second Practice of Nineteenth-Century Tonality* (Lincoln, NE, and London, 1996), 180–95.

"Wagner's *Parsifal*: Musical Form and the Drama of Redemption," *Journal of Musicology* 4 (1985), 431–46.

Kinderman, William, and Katherine R. Syer, eds., *A Companion to Wagner's* Parsifal (Rochester, NY, 2005).

Kirchmeyer, Helmut, *Das zeitgenössische Wagner-Bild*, 7 vols. (Regensburg, 1967–90).

Kitcher, Philip, and Richard Schacht, *Finding an Ending: Reflections on Wagner's* Ring (New York, 2004).

Köhler, Joachim, *Der letzte der Titanen: Richard Wagners Leben und Werk* (Munich, 2001); trans. Stewart Spencer as *Richard Wagner: The Last of the Titans* (New Haven and London, 2004).

Wagner's Hitler: The Prophet and His Disciple, trans. Ronald Taylor (Cambridge, 2000).

Kolland, Hubert, "Wagner-Rezeption im deutschen Faschismus," in Christoph-Hellmut Mahling and Sigrid Wiesmann, eds., *Bericht über den Internationalen Musikwissenschaftlichen Kongreß Bayreuth* (Kassel, 1981), 494–503.

Koppen, Erwin, *Dekadenter Wagnerismus: Studien zur europäischen Literatur des fin de siècle* (Berlin and New York, 1973).

Kramer, Lawrence, *Music as Cultural Practice, 1800–1900* (Berkeley and Los Angeles, 1990).

"The Waters of Prometheus: Nationalism and Sexuality in Wagner's *Ring*," in Richard Dellamora and Daniel Fischlin, eds., *The Work of Opera: Genre, Nationhood, and Sexual Difference* (New York, 1997), 131–59.

Krehbiel, Henry E., *Studies in the Wagnerian Drama* (New York, 1891; 2nd edn. 1893).

Kropfinger, Klaus, *Wagner and Beethoven: Richard Wagner's Reception of Beethoven*, trans. Peter Palmer (Cambridge, 1991).

Kunze, Stefan, *Der Kunstbegriff Richard Wagners* (Regensburg, 1983).

Kurth, Ernst, *Romantische Harmonik und ihre Krise in Wagners* Tristan (Berlin, 1920; 2nd edn. 1923); selections trans. Lee A. Rothfarb in Kurth, *Selected Writings* (Cambridge, 1991).

Large, David C., and William Weber, eds., *Wagnerism in European Culture and Politics* (Ithaca, 1984).

Lavignac, Albert, *The Music Dramas of Richard Wagner and His Festival Theatre in Bayreuth*, trans. Esther Singleton (New York, 1901); orig. *Le voyage artistique à Bayreuth*, 1897.

Leverett, Adelyn Peck, "Liszt, Wagner, and Heinrich Dorn's *Die Nibelungen*," *Cambridge Opera Journal* 2 (1990), 121–44.

Levin, David J., "Reading Beckmesser Reading: Antisemitism and Aesthetic Practice in *The Mastersingers of Nuremberg*," *New German Critique* 69 (Fall 1996), 127–46.

Richard Wagner, Fritz Lang, and the Nibelungen: The Dramaturgy of Disavowal (Princeton, 1998).

Lippman, Edward, "The Aesthetic Theories of Richard Wagner," in Lippman, *The Philosophy and Aesthetics of Music* (Lincoln, NE, and London, 1999), 179–91.

Lorenz, Alfred, *Das Geheimnis der Form bei Richard Wagner*, 4 vols. (Berlin, 1924–33; repr., Tutzing, 1966).

"Parsifal als Übermensch," *Die Musik* 1 (1901–02) 1876–82.

Mack, Dietrich, *Der Bayreuther Inszenierungsstil* (Munich, 1976).

Magee, Bryan, *Aspects of Wagner* (London, 1968; 3rd edn. 1988).

   The Tristan Chord: Wagner and Philosophy (London and New York, 2000).

Magee, Elizabeth, *Richard Wagner and the Nibelungs* (Oxford, 1990).

Mahnkopf, Claus-Steffen, ed., *Richard Wagner – Konstrukteur der Moderne* (Stuttgart, 1999).

Mann, Thomas, *Pro and Contra Wagner*, trans. Allan Blunden (Chicago [also, London and Boston], 1985).

Marvin, William M., "The Function of 'Rules' in *Die Meistersinger von Nürnberg*," *Journal of Musicology* 20 (2003), 414–60.

May, Thomas, *Decoding Wagner: Invitation to His World of Music Drama* (Pompton Plains, NJ, and Cambridge, 2004).

Mayer, Hans, *Richard Wagner in Bayreuth: 1876–1976* (Stuttgart, 1976).

   Richard Wagner: Mitwelt und Nachwelt (Stuttgart, 1978).

   Richard Wagners geistige Entwicklung (Düsseldorf, 1954).

McClatchie, Stephen, *Analyzing Wagner's Operas: Alfred Lorenz and German Nationalist Ideology* (Rochester, NY, 1998).

   "Wagner Research as 'Service to the People': The Richard-Wagner-Forschungsstätte, 1938–1945," in Michaal Kater and Albrecht Riethmüller eds., *Music and Nazism: Art Under Tyranny, 1933–1945* (Laaber, 2002), 150–69.

McCreless, Patrick, *Wagner's* Siegfried: *Its Drama, History, and Music* (Ann Arbor, MI, 1982).

McGlathery, James M., *Wagner's Operas and Desire* (New York, 1998).

Metzger, Heinz-Klaus, and Rainer Riehn, eds., *Richard Wagner*: Parsifal (Munich, 1982).

   eds., *Richard Wagner: Wie anti-semitisch darf ein Künstler sein?* (Munich, 1978).

Millington, Barry, "Nuremberg Trial: Is There Anti-Semitism in *Die Meistersinger*?," *Cambridge Opera Journal* 3 (1991), 247–60.

   Wagner (Princeton, 1992).

Millington, Barry, and Stewart Spencer, eds., *Wagner in Performance* (New Haven and London, 1992).

Morris, Mitchell, "Tristan's Wounds: On Homosexual Wagnerians at the Fin-de-Siècle," in Sophie Fuller and Lloyd Whitesell, eds., *Queer Episodes in Music and Modern Identity* (Urbana, IL, 2002), 271–91.

Nattiez, Jean-Jacques, *Wagner Androgyne: A Study in Interpretation*, trans. Stewart Spencer (Princeton, 1993).

Newcomb, Anthony, "The Birth of Music out of the Spirit of Drama: An Essay in Wagnerian Formal Analysis," *19th-Century Music* 5 (1981–82), 38–66.

Newman, Ernest, *The Life of Richard Wagner*, 4 vols. (New York, 1933–46; repr., Cambridge, 1976).

   Wagner as Man and Artist (London, 1914; 2nd edn. 1924).

   The Wagner Operas (orig. title *Wagner Nights*), (New York, 1949; repr. 1981).

Nietzsche, Friedrich, *The Birth of Tragedy and The Case of Wagner*, trans. with commentary Walter Kaufmann (New York, 1967).

   Nietzsche contra Wagner, in *The Portable Nietzsche*, trans. Walter Kaufmann (New York and London, 1959), 661–83.

"Richard Wagner in Bayreuth," in *Untimely Meditations*, ed. Daniel Breazeale and trans. R. J. Hollingdale (Cambridge, 1997); also in *Unfashionable Observations* (*Unzeitgemäße Betrachtungen*), trans. Richard T. Gray (*The Complete Works of Friedrich Nietzsche*, ed. Ernst Behler, vol. II, Stanford, 1995).

Peterson-Berger, Olof Wilhelm, *Richard Wagner als Kulturerscheinung* (Leipzig, 1917; orig. in Swedish, Stockholm, 1913).

Petzet, Detta, and Michael Petzet, *Die Richard Wagner-Bühne König Ludwigs II.* (Munich, 1970).

Preetorius, Emil, *Richard Wagner: Bild und Vision* (Berlin, 1942).

Rather, L. J., *The Dream of Self-Destruction: Wagner's* Ring *and the Modern World* (Baton Rouge, LA, 1979).

Reiger, Eva, *Minna und Richard Wagner: Stationen einer Liebe* (Düsseldorf and Zurich, 2003).

Rose, Paul Lawrence, *Wagner: Race and Revolution* (New Haven and London, 1992).

Salmi, Hannu, *Imagined Germany: Richard Wagner's National Utopia* (New York, 1999).

Wagner and Wagnerism in Nineteenth-Century Sweden, Finland, and the Baltic Provinces: Reception, Enthusiasm, Cult (Rochester, NY, 2005).

Schüler, Winfried, *Der Bayreuther Kreis von seiner Entstehung bis zum Ausgang der wilhelminischen Ära: Wagnerkult und Kulturreform im Geiste völkischer Weltanschauung* (Münster, 1971).

Scruton, Roger, *Death-Devoted Heart: Sex and the Sacred in Wagner's* Tristan and Isolde (New York, 2004).

Sessa, Anne Dzamba, *Richard Wagner and the English* (London and Cranbury, NJ, 1978).

Shaw, Bernard, *The Perfect Wagnerite: A Commentary on the Niblung's Ring* (New York, 1967).

Sheffi, Na'ama, *The Ring of Myths: The Israelis, Wagner, and the Nazis*, trans. Martha Grenzeback (Brighton, 2001).

Smart, Mary Ann, *Mimomania: Music and Gesture in Nineteenth-Century Opera* (Berkeley and Los Angeles, 2004).

Spencer, Stewart, ed., *Wagner 1976* (London, 1976).

Wagner Remembered (London, 2000).

"Wagner's Nuremberg," *Cambridge Opera Journal* 4 (1992), 21–41.

Spencer, Stewart, and Barry Millington, eds., *Wagner's* Ring of the Nibelung: *A Companion* (London, 1993).

Spotts, Frederic, *Bayreuth: A History of the Wagner Festival* (New Haven, 1994).

Stein, Jack M., *Richard Wagner and the Synthesis of the Arts* (Detroit, 1960; rpt. 1973).

Stein, Leon, *The Racial Thinking of Richard Wagner* (New York, 1950).

Storch, Wolfgang, ed., *Les Symbolistes et Richard Wagner – Die Symbolisten und Richard Wagner* (Berlin, 1991).

Tanner, Michael, *Wagner* (Princeton, 1996).

Taylor, Ronald, *Richard Wagner: His Life, Art and Thought* (London, 1979).

Thorau, Christian, *Semantisierte Sinnlichkeit: Studien zur Rezeption und Zeichenstruktur der Leitmotivtechnik Richard Wagners* (Stuttgart, 2003).

Truscott, Harold, "Wagner's *Tristan* and the Twentieth Century," *Music Review* 24 (1963), 75–85.

Vaget, Hans Rudolf, ed., *Im Schatten Wagners. Thomas Mann über Richard Wagner: Texte und Zeugnisse, 1895–1955* (Frankfurt, 1999).

Vazsonyi, Nicholas, ed., *Wagner's* Meistersinger: *Performance, History, Representation* (Rochester, NY, 2003).

Voss, Egon, *Richard Wagner und die Instrumentalmusik: Wagners symphonischer Ehrgeiz* (Wilhelmshaven, 1977).

  "Wagner und kein Ende": Betrachtungen und Studien (Zurich, 1996).

Wagner, Friedelind, and Page Cooper, *Heritage of Fire: The Story of Richard Wagner's Granddaughter* (New York, [1945]); also pub. as *The Royal Family of Bayreuth* (London, [1948]).

Wagner, Gottfried, *The Twilight of the Wagners: The Unveiling of a Family's Legacy*, trans. Della Couling (New York, 1997).

Wagner, Nike, *The Wagners: The Dramas of a Musical Dynasty*, trans. Ewald Osers and Michael Downes (Princeton, 1998).

The Wagner Companion, ed. Peter Burbidge and Richard Sutton (New York, 1979).

The Wagner Compendium, ed. Barry Millington (London and New York, 1992).

Wagner Handbook, ed. Ulrich Müller and Peter Wapnewski, translation ed. John Deathridge (Cambridge, MA, and London, 1992).

Wapnewski, Peter, *Der traurige Gott: Richard Wagner in seinen Helden* (Berlin, 1981; 2nd edn. 2001).

Warrack, John, ed., *Richard Wagner*: Die Meistersinger von Nürnberg (Cambridge, 1994).

Watson, Derek, *Richard Wagner: A Biography* (London, 1979).

Weiner, Marc A., *Richard Wagner and the Anti-Semitic Imagination* (Lincoln, NE, and London, 1995).

Weismüller, Christoph, *Musik, Traum, Medien: Philosophie des musikdramatischen Gesamtkunstwerks* (Würzburg, 2001).

Wessling, Berndt W., ed., *Bayreuth im Dritten Reich. Richard Wagners politische Erben: Eine Dokumentation* (Weinheim and Basel, 1983).

Westernhagen, Curt von, *Richard Wagners Dresdener Bibliothek 1842–1849* (Wiesbaden, 1966).

Weston, Jessie L., *The Legends of the Wagner Drama: Studies in Mythology and Romance* (London, 1896).

Whittall, Arnold, "Wagner's Great Transition? From *Lohengrin* to *Das Rheingold*," *Music Analysis* 2 (1983), 269–80.

  "Wagner's Later Stage Works," in *New Oxford History of Music*, vol. IX (Oxford, 1990), 257–321.

Wilberg, Petra-Hildegard, *Richard Wagners mythische Welt: Versuche wider den Historismus* (Freiburg im Breisgau, 1996).

Williams, Simon, *Richard Wagner and Festival Theatre* (Westport, CT, 1994).

  Wagner and the Romantic Hero (Cambridge, 2004).

Wintle, Christopher, "The Numinous in *Götterdämmerung*," in Arthur Groos and Roger Parker, eds., *Reading Opera* (Princeton, 1988), 200–34.

Wolzogen, Hans von, *Thematischer Leitfaden durch die Musik zu R. Wagners Festspiel Der Ring des Nibelungen* (Leipzig, 1876).

Wagneriana: Gesammelte Aufsätze über Richard Wagners Werk vom Ring *bis zum* Gral (Leipzig, 1888).

Zelinsky, Hartmut, *Richard Wagner: Ein deutsches Thema – Eine Dokumentation zur Wirkungsgeschichte Richard Wagners, 1876–1976* (Frankfurt, 1976).

Ziino, Agostino, *Antologia della critica wagneriana in Italia* (Messina, 1970).

Zuckerman, Elliott, *The First Hundred Years of Wagner's* Tristan (New York, 1964).

Index

Abbate, Carolyn 120–21, 283, 301
Aberbach, Alan David 191
Adorno, Theodor W. 81, 82, 135, 137–38, 141,
    171, 172, 193, 213–14, 217, 236, 243–44,
    280–81, 284, 286, 287, 299, 301, 312, 313,
    315, 316, 317
Aeschylus 74, 75, 183, 197, 299, 310
Alden, David 252, 270, 324
Altenberg, Peter 231
Anderson, Benedict 136
Apel, Theodor 22, 28, 69
Appia, Adolphe 232, 249, 250, 251, 252, 322
Arendt, Benno von 145–46, 251
Ariosto, Ludovico 25, 130
Arp, Hans 221
Ashman, Mike 317
Auber, Daniel-François-Esprit 20, 21, 28,
    31, 35
    La muette de Portici 12, 19, 27, 28, 32,
    34, 293
Auerbach, Berthold 57, 217

Bach, Johann Sebastian 55, 142, 213, 282, 307
Bailey, Robert 116, 281, 282–83, 284, 301, 302
Bakhtin, Mikhail 293
Bakunin, Mikhail ("Dr. Schwartz") 51, 52–53, 57,
    58, 61–62
Bal, Mieke 136
Balzac, Honoré de 130
Baranowski, Shelley 307
Barbarossa, Friedrich 12, 72, 75–77, 78, 299
Barenboim, Daniel 265, 324
Bartels, Ulrich 302
Barthes, Roland 266
Baudelaire, Charles 121, 201, 221, 230
Bauer, Bruno 58, 77, 210, 314
Bauer, Raimund 273
Bauer-Lechner, Natalie 214
Bayreuth 6, 15, 20, 196, 210, 291, 316
Bayreuth festival 6, 9, 52, 62–63, 79–81, 82, 83, 87,
    103, 134, 143–44, 145, 146, 148–49, 151,
    156, 157, 162, 171, 175, 183, 191, 193, 195,
    196, 197, 198, 203, 209, 228, 232, 233,
    235–45, 246, 247–49, 251–52, 256, 257,
    259, 261, 263–65, 269, 272, 273, 274,
    276, 306, 307, 310, 311, 315, 317, 322,
    323, 324
Bechstein, Ludwig 70, 298
Becker, Nikolas 54
Beckett, Lucy 309
Beckett, Samuel 267

Beethoven, Ludwig van 18, 23, 28, 54, 62, 85,
    149, 183, 191, 213, 223, 228, 240, 245,
    278, 307
    Egmont 18
    Fidelio 8, 19, 20, 25, 26, 32
    Ninth Symphony 18, 19, 52, 183, 191, 195, 227,
    228, 291, 294
Behrens, Peter 232
Bekker, Paul 170, 172, 310, 311
Bellini, Vincenzo 19, 21, 22, 28, 37, 293
    I Capuleti e i Montecchi 19, 20, 27
Benjamin, Walter 81, 223
Bent, Ian 325
Berg, Alban 162, 225
Berghaus, Ruth 84, 252, 264, 266–67, 274,
    317, 324
Berio, Luciano 221
Berlioz, Hector 223
Bermbach, Udo 319
Bernstein, Leonard 212–13
Beuys, Joseph 221
bin Laden, Osama 175
Bismarck, Otto von 134, 305
Blanqui, Auguste 54
Blessinger, Karl 319
Bloch, Ernst 82, 250, 303
Blum, Robert 50
Boccaccio, Giovanni 27
Boehm, Karl 323
Boieldieu, François-Adrien 28
Boito, Arrigo 226
Bond, Edward 263
Bonheur, Raymond 224, 317
Bonnard, Pierre 231
Borchmeyer, Dieter 172, 215, 294, 309, 310,
    311, 312
Börne, Ludwig 208, 314
Botstein, Leon 310
Boulanger, Lili 224, 229
Boulez, Pierre 323
Bourget, Paul 193
Bradford, Gamaliel 10
Brahms, Johannes 85, 196, 207, 228,
    282, 307
Brecht, Bertolt 82, 252, 254, 271
Brendel, Franz 85, 208
Brener, Milton E. 313, 315
Brentano, Clemens 297
Bréval, Lucienne 233
Brinkmann, Reinhold 320
Brockhaus, Hermann 192–93

Brown, Matthew 282
Bruckner, Anton 223, 227, 240
Bülow, Hans von 61, 208
Bulwer-Lytton, Edward 34
Bungert, August 226
Burne-Jones, Edward 232
Burrell, Willoughby (Mrs.) 15

Carissan, Célanie 225
Carlyle, Thomas 291
Carnegy, Patrick 148
Carolsfeld, Ludwig Schnorr von 191, 321
Carolsfeld, Malvina Schnorr von 291
Carré, Michel 225
Carsen, Robert 84, 272, 324
Cézanne, Paul 231
Chabrier, Emmanuel 224
Chafe, Eric 288
Chamberlain, Houston Stewart 80, 81, 238, 280,
    299, 316, 320, 322, 324
Charpentier, Gustave 224, 225
Chausson, Ernest 223, 224–25, 228, 317
Chéreau, Patrice 83, 84, 252, 259, 261, 264, 266,
    269, 272, 274, 317, 323
Chervachidze, Alexander 249
Cicora, Mary A. 311
Clarke, Norma 14
Clément, Catherine 174
Colli, Giorgio 192
Cooke, Deryck 82, 88, 299, 300
Cornelius, Peter 156, 226
Craig, Edward Gordon 232

d'Annunzio, Gabriele 116, 231, 232
D'Indy, Vincent 224, 225, 228
Dahlhaus, Carl 123, 172, 173, 281–82, 283, 311,
    312, 318
Darcy, Warren 283
Daube, Otto 292
Daverio, John 283–84, 285, 288
Davey, Gideon 252, 270, 324
Deathridge, John 8–9, 171, 172–73, 287, 301, 311,
    325, 327
Debussy, Claude 161, 224–25, 310
Dehmel, Richard 231
Delacroix, Eugène 231
Dennis, David 141, 147, 242, 307, 308, 315
Derrida, Jacques 139, 267
Devrient, Eduard 79
Devrient, Karl 19
Docen, Bernhard Joseph 298
Donington, Robert 82–83
Dorn, Heinrich 300
Dreyfus, Laurence 172–73, 315
Droysen, Johann Gustav 72, 74, 299
Dülberg, Ewald 244, 250
Duparc, Henri 223, 229
Dürer, Albrecht 142

Eichenauer, Richard 240
Eisenstein, Sergei 256
Ellis, William Ashton 191, 295
Empedocles 197
Engels, Friedrich 76, 264
Erfen, Irene 294
Erkel, Ferenc 227
Ernst, Alfred 230
Eschenbach, Wolfram von 71, 151–52, 309
Ettmüller, Ludwig 71
Euripides 74
Evans, Tamara S. 291

Fantin-Latour, Henri 232
Fauré, Gabriel 229
Fehling, Jürgen 250, 259
Fehr, Max 9
Felsenstein, Walter 251, 256, 259, 323
Fest, Joachim 319
Fétis, François-Joseph 317
Feuerbach, Ludwig 52–53, 57, 73, 75, 77, 155, 181,
    183, 265
Fichte, Johann Gottlieb 67, 314
Fielding, David 272, 324
Fischer, Jens Malte 244, 314
Fischer-Dieskau, Dietrich 325
Fitzball, Edward 297
Floros, Constantin 310, 311
Flotow, Friedrich von 226
Fontana, Ferdinando 226
Förster, Bernhard 210
Forte, Allen 284
Franck, César 228
Frantz, Constantin 52, 138, 140
Franz, Robert 298
Frederick II (the Great), King of Prussia 291
Freud, Sigmund 16, 104, 231, 284, 285, 302
Fricke, George R. 322
Fricke, Richard 248, 322
Friedländer, Saul 243, 319, 320
Friedrich, Caspar David 231
Friedrich, Götz 84, 251, 256, 259–61,
    263–65, 324
Friedrich August II, King of Saxony 61
Friedrich Wilhelm IV, King of Prussia 58, 60
Fries, Jakob 55
Frigerio, Ezio 261, 323
Fuchs, Carl 202
Fuchs, Hanns 15
Fuchs, Martha 323
Furtwängler, Wilhelm 145

Gash, Anthony 293
Gast, Peter ("Köselitz") 14, 199, 202
Gauguin, Paul 231
Gay, Peter 302
George, Stefan 231
Gervinus, Georg Gottfried 140, 305

Geyer, Ludwig 14, 18
Ghil, René 230
Gibson, Mel 175
Gielen, Michael 267, 324
Gillis, John 136, 137
Glasenapp, Carl Friedrich 4, 309, 310
Gloekle, Ferdinand 71
Gluck, Christoph Willibald 22, 126, 291
Gobineau, Joseph-Arthur 181, 210, 309
Goebbels, Joseph 134, 144–45, 148,
    171, 241, 242, 243, 304, 307,
    308, 320
Goehr, Lydia 287, 325
Goethe, Johann Wolfgang von 18, 22, 245, 274,
    284, 307, 322
Goldoni, Carlo 267
Görres, Joseph von 71
Gottfried von Strassburg 130, 303
Gounod, Charles 223
Gozzi, Carlo 20, 24–26, 45, 67, 293
Grahn, Lucile 321
Grandval, Marie Clémence Vicomtesse de 225
Greenblatt, Stephen 290
Gregor-Dellin, Martin 15, 311
Grey, Thomas S. 143, 149, 242, 277, 285–86, 300,
    301, 302, 305, 306, 326
Grimm, Jacob 71, 72, 274, 298, 316
Grimm, Wilhelm 71, 274, 316
Groos, Arthur 306
Gusdorf, Georges 7–8, 16, 291
Gutman, Robert 172, 211, 311
Gutzkow, Karl 57, 68

Hagen, Friedrich Heinrich von der 70–71, 298
Haitink, Bernard 324
Halévy, Fromental 34, 191, 212, 292
Hallwachs, Reinhard 321
Handel, George Frideric 22, 126, 154, 291
Hanfstaengl, Ernst "Putzi" 144
Hanslick, Eduard 141, 143, 179, 209, 213, 215,
    310, 322
Hasse, Johann Adolph 22
Hauser, Franz 292
Haydn, Franz Joseph 149, 154, 278
Hegel, Georg Wilhelm Friedrich 55, 72, 73, 198,
    234, 293, 299
Heine, Ferdinand 297, 298
Heine, Heinrich 59, 67, 69–70, 181, 183, 208,
    293, 296–97
Heinrich, Reinhard 252
Heinrich, Rudolf 256, 257, 323
Heinse, Wilhelm 22
Henry I (the Fowler), King of Germany 242, 298
Henry III (the Lion), Duke of Saxony and
    Bavaria 76
Herder, Johann Gottfried von 139, 154, 155
Hérold, Ferdinand 20, 27, 29
Herwegh, Georg 9, 58, 122

Herz, Joachim 83, 251, 256–59, 263, 266,
    322, 323
Herzl, Theodor 221
Himmler, Heinrich 242
Hirschfeld, Magnus 15
Hitler, Adolf 36, 81, 135, 143, 144, 145, 146, 171,
    203, 221, 234, 235–45, 249, 251, 299, 304,
    307, 324
Hoerth, Franz Ludwig 250
Hoffmann, Ernst Theodor Amadeus 18, 23–24,
    46, 67, 70, 294, 297, 298
Hofmannsthal, Hugo von 134–35, 231
Hohendahl, Peter Uwe 306
Hölderlin, Friedrich 118, 121, 133, 302
Hollingdale, R. J. 313
Holman, J. K. 300
Holmès, Augusta 223, 224, 225
Homer 18, 225
Horowitz, Joseph 149
Hotter, Hans 323
Humperdinck, Engelbert 226
Hutchinson, Lucy 6
Huysmans, Joris-Karl 116, 302

Ibsen, Henrik 231
Ingres, Jean-Auguste-Dominique 231
Israel, Robert 273

Jahn, Otto 193, 194
Jenkins, Speight 273
Jesus of Nazareth (Christ) 77, 78, 156, 173,
    175, 316
Jones, Richard 84, 252, 267
Joukowsky, Paul von 248
Joyce, James 231
Jung, Carl Gustav 82

Kaiser, Joachim 172, 311
Kalbeck, Max 169
Kandinsky, Wassily 221, 232
Kant, Immanuel 67, 169, 197, 287
Katz, Jacob 205, 295, 314
Kaufmann, Walter 313
Kautsky, Karl 59–60
Kempfler, Fritz 148, 308
Kerman, Joseph 132, 281, 303
Kermode, Frank 115
Kiefer, Anselm 221
Kietz, Ernst Benedikt 78
Kinderman, William 302, 309, 310
Kinmouth, Patrick 272
Kistler, Cyrill 278
Kleist, Heinrich von 307
Klemperer, Otto 244, 250
Knappertsbusch, Hans 323
Köhler, Joachim 237, 290, 294, 298, 320
Kolland, Hubert 320
König, Heinrich 34

Konwitschny, Peter 84, 269–70, 324
Kopp, David 288–89
Köselitz, Heinrich (see Gast, Peter)
Koshar, Rudy 135, 136–37, 149
Kramer, Lawrence 284–85, 302
Kropfinger, Klaus 291
Krumpholz, Wenzel 85
Kubizek, August 36
Kühnel, Jürgen 191
Kupfer, Harry 83, 84, 252, 256, 257, 259, 263,
    264–65, 274, 317, 324, 325
Kurth, Ernst 278, 303

Lachmann, Karl 71, 72, 298
Lachner, Franz 207
Lafferentz, Bodo 307
Lalo, Edouard 224, 228
Lamartine, Alphonse de 54
Lang, Fritz 250
Laube, Heinrich 22, 68, 293, 314
Lazaridis, Stefanos 272, 324
Lehnhoff, Nikolaus 84, 273
Lehrs, Samuel 70, 314
Leoncavallo, Ruggero 226
Lessing, Gotthold Ephraim 307
Levi, Hermann 215, 315
Levin, David 141, 217, 320
Levine, James 273
Lewin, David 288
Ley, Robert 241–42
Lieban, Julius 315
Lindau, Paul 169, 311
Lippman, Edward 310
Lippmann, Friedrich 293
Liszt, Franz 8, 47, 56, 83, 116, 121, 173, 191, 198,
    205, 206, 208, 215, 228, 246, 298, 300
Loewe, Carl 155
Logier, Johann Bernhard 18, 292
Lorenz, Alfred 148, 186–87, 279, 281–82, 283,
    306, 308, 325
Lorenz, Max 323
Lortzing, Albert 226, 240, 244, 274
Louis XIV, King of France 223
Louis-Philippe I, King of France 85
Lowery, Nigel 252, 267
Lucas, C. T. L. 70, 296, 298
Ludwig II, King of Bavaria 4, 5, 7, 8, 15, 63,
    79, 139, 140, 142, 191, 209, 247, 290,
    291, 305, 309
Ludwig, Emil 236
Luther, Martin 55, 142
Lynch, Thomas 273

Maeterlinck, Maurice 225
Magee, Bryan 217, 276, 314, 316
Magnard, Albéric 225
Mahler, Gustav 161, 214, 227–28, 229, 232, 249,
    274, 315, 318, 319, 321, 324

Mallarmé, Stéphane 221, 230
Mann, Thomas 115, 122, 131, 135, 144, 147,
    170–71, 192, 193, 194, 201–02, 232, 235,
    236, 279–80, 303, 304, 305, 307, 312
Manthey, Axel 252, 266
Marbach, Oswald 294
Marc, Franz 232
Marcuse, Herbert 55
Marivaux, Pierre 263
Markus, Gyorgy 280
Marr, Wilhelm 210
Marschner, Heinrich 19, 25, 207
Martin, John 294
Marvin, William M. 282
Marx, Karl 58, 76, 204, 221, 264, 314
Massenet, Jules 224, 225, 226
Maus, Katharine Eisaman 27
Mayer, Hans 82
Mayrberger, Karl 278, 325
McClatchie, Stephen 281–82, 325
McCreless, Patrick 282
McFarland, Timothy 297
McGlathery, James 302
Meinecke, Friedrich 136, 304
Meissner, Alfred 298
Melchinger, Ulrich 84, 256
Mendelsohn, Erich 233
Mendelssohn, Daniel 317
Mendelssohn, Felix 59, 140, 154, 184, 207–08,
    213, 215, 310, 314, 315, 319
    A Midsummer Night's Dream 40
    Symphony in D major ("Reformation") 159
Messiaen, Olivier 221
Metternich, Klemens Wenzel von 55
Meyerbeer, Giacomo 22, 140, 204, 243,
    291, 319
    Les Huguenots 21, 35, 37, 56, 205, 223,
    292, 294
    Le prophète 12, 205
    Robert le diable 19, 27
    Wagner's attitude to 11–12, 21, 22, 23, 37–38,
    56–57, 59, 184, 205–08, 213, 215, 314,
    315, 322
Meyerhold, Vsevolod 249
Meysenbug, Malwida von 199
Mielitz, Christine 269
Millington, Barry 242, 297, 298, 315
Mitchell, William 282
Mommsen, Wolfgang, J. 304
Mone, Franz Joseph 71, 72, 298
Monod, Gabriel 305
Monroe, Marilyn 261
Montinari, Mazzino 192
Moore, George 116
Moore, Henry 254
Morabito, Sergio 270
Moreau, Gustave 230, 232
Mosse, George 309

Motte Fouqué, Baron de la 24
Mozart, Wolfgang Amadeus 19, 22, 25, 45, 126, 193, 240, 307
Muchanoff, Marie (Kalergis) 208
Müller, Franz 298
Mungen, Anno 294
Musset, Alfred de 54

Napoleon (Bonaparte) 23, 55, 142, 154
Nattiez, Jean-Jacques 83, 121, 285, 302, 325
Nel, Christoph 270
Neubauer, Hans-Joachim 315
Neuenfels, Hans 264
Neumann, Angelo 315, 322
Newcomb, Anthony 283
Newman, Ernest 280, 291, 300, 310
Nicolai, Otto 22, 292
Nietzsche, Friedrich 13–14, 16, 115, 116, 117, 121, 134, 136, 139, 140, 144, 156, 169, 192–202, 232, 233, 276–77, 279, 301, 307, 316
    The Case of Wagner 131, 199, 200, 201
    Nietzsche contra Wagner 199
    "Richard Wagner in Bayreuth" 193, 196, 197
Nolan, Sidney 254
Novalis (Friedrich Leopold von Hardenberg) 68, 69, 122–23, 297, 303
Nowak, Adolf 309
Nuitter, Charles 230

Offenbach, Jacques 319
Olagnier, Marguerite 225
Oliphant, Margaret (Mrs.) 6
Osborne, Charles 295
Overbeck, Friedrich 199
Overhoff, Kurt 323

Pacini, Giovanni 294
Peduzzi, Richard 252, 261, 272, 323
Péladan, Joséphin 116
Petersen, Peter 323
Pfitzner, Hans Erich 144
Picasso, Pablo 221, 254
Pilz, Gottfried 324
Pirchan, Emil 250
Planer, Minna (see Wagner, Minna)
Poelzig, Hans 233
Pohl, Richard 116
Pollock, Jackson 254
Ponnelle, Jean-Pierre 324
Porat, Dina 237
Porges, Heinrich 156, 215, 322
Preetorius, Emil 244, 251, 252
Proudhon, Pierre-Joseph 51–52, 57, 77
Proust, Marcel 232
Puccini, Giacomo 223, 226, 240, 247, 318
Puschmann, Theodor 14

Quinet, Edgar 54

Raabe, Peter 144
Rabenalt, Arthur Maria 250
Raff, Joachim 228
Redon, Odilon 230
Reinhardt, Max 233
Reissinger, Gertrud 323
Reyer, Ernest 223, 224
Rheinberger, Joseph 207
Riefenstahl, Leni 146, 240
Riehl, Wilhelm Heinrich 207
Rienzo, Cola di 35, 46, 294
Rimbaud, Arthur 230
Rimsky-Korsakov, Nikolai 223, 227
Ritschl, Friedrich 196, 198, 313
Ritter, Julie 298
Ritter, Karl 208
Robinson, Paul 174, 312
Rochaix, François 273
Röckel, August 47, 51, 52, 61, 83, 301
Rodin, Auguste 221
Rohde, Erwin 14, 193, 194
Roller, Alfred 242, 249–51, 321
Rose, Jürgen 273
Rose, Paul Lawrence 172, 204–05, 210, 211, 312, 314, 315
Rosell, Ingrid 261
Rosenberg, Alfred 171, 242, 243, 280, 308
Rossini, Gioachino 11, 12, 19, 26, 28, 223
Rousseau, Henri 270
Rousseau, Jean-Jacques 5, 309
Rubinstein, Joseph 215, 315–16
Ruge, Arnold 52, 58

Saint-Saëns, Camille 223, 224, 233
Salmi, Hannu 138–39, 140, 305
Salzer, Felix 282
San Marte (Albert Schulz) 71
Sanquirico, Alessandro 294
Sayn-Wittgenstein, Marie Princess of 8, 119
Schavernoch, Hans 252, 265
Schelling, Friedrich Wilhelm Joseph von 298
Schenk, Otto 273
Schenker, Heinrich 279, 282
Schiller, Friedrich 18, 46, 82
Schippers, Thomas 323
Schlegel, August Wilhelm 67, 155
Schlegel, Friedrich 71, 122–23, 126, 297, 303
Schleiermacher, Friedrich 154, 156
Schlesinger, Maurice 206
Schlingenschief, Christoph 175
Schlömer, Joachim 270
Schmidt, Jacques 252, 261
Schmitt, Saladin 250
Schneider, Friedrich 154
Schneider, Peter 325
Schneider-Siemssen, Günther 323
Schoenbaum, Samuel 290

Schoenberg, Arnold 97, 161, 222, 228–29, 232, 278, 279, 282, 310
Schopenhauer, Arthur 57–58, 62–63, 80, 82, 119, 121–22, 123, 151, 169, 181, 191, 194, 195, 197, 199, 210, 287–88, 294, 303, 309, 311, 312, 318
Schott, Franz 309
Schrader, Hans-Jürgen 297
Schröder-Devrient, Wilhelmine 8, 19, 20, 27, 28, 32, 33, 35, 61
Schroeder, Johannes 250
Schubert, Franz Peter 307
Schumann, Robert 85, 206
Scott, Walter 130, 215
Scriabin, Alexander Nikolayevich 228
Scribe, Eugène 23, 34, 37, 212, 225
Scruton, Roger 287–88, 301
Seidel, Anton 169
Semper, Gottfried 56–57, 79
Séverac, Déodat de 233
Seydlitz, Reinhardt von 198
Shakespeare, William 3, 18, 31, 32, 45, 130, 233, 257, 274, 290, 294
    Measure for Measure 21, 22, 27, 28, 29, 31, 33–34, 46, 50, 68, 293
Shaw, George Bernard 12, 80, 81, 214, 299, 322
Shore, Howard 221, 234
Sibelius, Jean 227
Sievert, Ludwig 249
Silja, Anja 272
Simrock, Karl 71
Smith, Anthony 136
Solti, Georg 300
Spencer, Stewart 298, 306
Spielmann, Julius 214, 315
Spitzer, Daniel 14, 16
Spohr, Louis 19, 25, 154
Spontini, Gaspare 26, 34–35, 294
Spotts, Frederic 145
Spyri, Bernhard 8
Stahr, Adolf 298
Stein, Gertrude 231
Stein, Leon 313
Stendhal (Marie-Henri Beyle) 114
Stock, Richard Wilhelm 146, 148, 308
Stöcker, Julius 210
Stockhausen, Karlheinz 221
Stolzing, Walther von 308
Strachey, Lytton 3–4
Strauss, David Friedrich 77
Strauss, Richard 162, 225, 227, 229
Strehler, Giorgio 323
Strindberg, August 231
Strobel, Otto 7, 236
Strohl, Rita 225
Sulzer, Jakob 15–16, 292
Svoboda, Josef 259
Syberberg, Hans Jürgen 237, 239

Syer, Katherine R. 311
Sykora, Peter 263, 264

Tanner, Michael 217, 313
Tasso, Torquato 25, 130
Tausig, Carl 140, 209, 215
Taut, Bruno 233
Thiers, Adolphe 54
Thomas of Brittany 130
Thorau, Christian 300, 325
Thys, Pauline 225
Tichatschek, Josef 35
Tieck, Ludwig 18, 70, 135, 297, 306
Tietjen, Heinz 244, 252, 307, 323
Tolstoy, Leon 232
Tomlinson, Gary 286–87
Turner, William 231

Uhlig, Theodor 78, 79, 208, 291

Vaget, Hans Rudolf 146, 147, 216, 305, 308, 316
Vazsonyi, Nicholas 307
Velde, Henry van de 233
Verdi, Giuseppe 223, 226, 227, 240, 246, 321
Verlaine, Paul 221, 229, 230
Vetter, Isolde 15
Viebrock, Anne 270
Villiers de l'Isle-Adam, Auguste, Comte de 225, 230
Vinci, Leonardo da 202
Vischer, Friedrich Theodor 298
Voss, Egon 296

Wackenroder, Wilhelm Heinrich 135, 306
Wadsworth, Stephen 273
Wagenseil, Johann Christoph 141
Wagner, Adolf (uncle) 18, 24, 67, 296
Wagner, Albert (brother) 20
Wagner, Carl Friedrich (father) 14, 18
Wagner, Cosima (second wife) 3, 4–5, 15, 130, 143, 157, 194, 197, 199, 209, 249, 251, 291, 293, 306, 311, 322
    diaries of 4, 6, 13, 116, 118, 122, 197, 209, 215–16, 309, 311, 315, 316
Wagner, Eva (daughter) 80
Wagner, Friedelind (granddaughter) 239
Wagner, Gottfried (great-grandson) 239
Wagner, Klara (sister) 18
Wagner, Minna (first wife) 21, 22, 23, 48–49, 295, 314
Wagner, Nike (great-granddaughter) 173, 239, 312
Wagner, Richard
    anti-Semitism, and 140–41, 169–70, 171–72, 196, 203–18, 235, 236–37, 244, 273–74, 286
        Jews, attitudes to 56–60, 184, 204–11, 215
    autobiography, attitudes to 4–6, 7–11
    background, family 18
        intellectual 18–19

Wagner, Richard (cont.)
  Bayreuth, and (*see* Bayreuth)
  Christianity, and 156, 173, 211, 288
  Dresden 218, 246
    Royal Kapellmeister in 47, 48, 52, 57,
      296, 321
    uprising, participation in 12, 49, 51, 60–62,
      180, 184, 205
  "endless melody" 222, 285, 303
  "Freigedank, K." (pseudonym) 56, 208
  "Freudenfeuer, W." (pseudonym) 52
  Gesamtkunstwerk 74, 180, 212, 222, 228, 229,
      232, 234
  Greek drama, and 74–75, 154, 155, 157, 183,
      194, 197, 233, 274
  harmonic language 124–26, 127–30, 278
    Tristan chord 124–26, 128, 222, 224, 225,
      278–79, 285, 288, 302, 303, 325
  Italian opera, changing attitude to 11
  leitmotifs, use of 87–114, 162–69, 186–87, 222,
      227, 228, 230, 231, 276, 285, 325
  modernism, and 222
  musical language 222
  mythology, and (medieval) 69–73
  nationalism 53–56, 156
  Paris, life in 54, 182–83, 204, 205–06, 223, 247,
      314, 325
  political ideas 49
    anarchy (*see* Bakunin, Mikhail; Proudhon,
      Pierre-Joseph)
    federalism, proponent of 51
    law, obsession with 50
    monarchy 51
  reception and influence 203, 221–34
    criticism 276–89
    France, in 223–25
    Germany, in 226–27
    Italy, in 225–26
    musical 222–29
    Nazism, and 144–48, 235–45, 251, 273,
      280, 314
    painting, influence on 231–32
    poetry and literature, in 230–31, 232
    theater, influence on 232–33
  Riga, in 299
  Romanticism, and 67–69
  stage director, as 246–49
  Switzerland, life in
    Zurich 182, 246
  Vaterlandsverein (Fatherland Society), and 48,
      50, 51, 61
  writings (*see also* WRITINGS)
      179–91, 277
    as autobiography 10–13
    reception of 180
    "Zurich" 180–90, 195, 233
  "Young Germany" movement, and 21, 22, 27,
      47, 68, 69, 71, 293, 296

WORKS (musical and dramatic)
Achilles 77
Die Feen (The Fairies) 20, 21, 22, 24–27, 34, 35,
      39–42, 45–46, 47, 67–68, 78, 292, 293, 296
*Der fliegende Holländer (The Flying
      Dutchman)* 11, 20, 23, 34, 35, 41, 45, 48,
      61, 67, 68, 69, 89, 121, 206, 244, 246, 250,
      254–56, 257, 264, 296, 322, 324
Friedrich I (Barbarossa) 49, 71, 75–77
Götterdämmerung 38, 50, 79, 80, 86, 95–97,
      104, 109–14, 161, 183, 256, 263, 267, 270,
      271, 272, 282, 299, 300, 301, 316, 323
    libretto 12
Die Hochzeit 24
Die hohe Braut (The High-Born Bride) 48, 50
Jesus von Nazareth 77, 155, 179
Der junge Siegfried (Young Siegfried) 79, 188
Leubald und Adelaïde 18, 69, 292, 294
Das Liebesmahl 155
Das Liebesverbot (The Ban on Love) 20, 21, 22,
      27–34, 35, 39, 42–45, 48, 50, 68, 97, 246,
      293, 294, 296
Lohengrin 24, 26, 36, 40, 45, 48, 67, 68, 71, 75,
      78, 85, 88, 121, 151, 157, 182, 211, 222,
      226, 227, 237, 240, 242, 272, 277, 296, 298,
      309, 310, 318, 322
Die Meistersinger von Nürnberg 45, 49, 62, 79,
      134–50, 156, 157, 209, 213, 224, 247, 254,
      257, 259, 269, 291, 301, 317, 321, 322, 323
    German nationalism, and 134–43
    reception 143–50, 193, 217, 226, 236,
      239–42, 244, 251, 274, 282
*Der Nibelungen-Mythus: Als Entwurf zu einem
      Drama* 74, 75, 299
Ninth Symphony, transcription of
      Beethoven's 19
Parsifal 42, 45, 63, 78, 143, 151–53, 248–49,
      252–54, 266, 272, 317, 322, 323,
      324, 325
    Amfortas's music 162–69
    intellectual context 151–57, 207, 208,
      211–12, 213, 287, 315, 316
    libretto 13, 197–98
    reception 169–75, 194, 198–99, 200, 228,
      239–40, 242–43, 274, 276, 282, 283–84,
      286–87, 318, 320, 321, 327
Polka (*WWV* 84) 299
Das Rheingold 54, 60, 75, 79, 85, 86–87, 89–93,
      94, 98–103, 104, 109, 185, 213, 214, 215,
      249, 254, 261, 262, 265, 267, 270, 282, 283,
      300, 321, 322, 323, 324
Rienzi 20, 21, 23, 26, 29, 34, 45–46, 48, 49, 50,
      52, 61, 68, 205, 211, 227, 240, 242, 243,
      246, 294, 314, 320
*Der Ring des Nibelungen (The Ring of the
      Nibelung)* 6, 9, 12, 39, 50, 52, 62, 72, 74,
      75, 78, 86–114, 115, 118, 131, 143, 151,
      156, 160, 161, 182, 186, 187, 188, 213, 214,

216, 222, 226, 227, 232, 240, 248–49, 250,
251–52, 254, 256, 257–64, 265, 266,
267–73, 277, 282, 293, 299, 300, 301, 310,
315, 317, 322, 323, 324
libretto 79, 86, 119, 183, 298, 300
interpretations 80–84, 236, 243, 276, 301,
321, 322
Die Sarazenin 71
Die Sieger 303
Siegfried 24, 50, 79, 80, 81, 83, 84, 103, 104–09,
112, 113, 119–20, 188, 214–15, 216, 217,
256, 261, 263, 267, 270, 272, 300, 301, 315,
324, 325
libretto 215
Siegfrieds Tod (*Siegfried's Death*) 12, 50,
78–79, 86, 109, 111, 183, 281
*Sonate für das Album von Frau M[athilde]
W[esendonck]* (*WWV* 85) 299
Tannhäuser 36, 42, 45, 47, 48, 54, 61, 67, 68, 69,
71, 121, 134, 151, 157, 190, 222, 223, 226,
244, 246, 247, 248, 251, 254, 259, 261, 296,
309, 310, 321, 322
Tristan und Isolde 31, 38, 62, 79, 143, 152, 161,
162, 187–88, 193, 202, 224, 225, 228, 229,
232, 247, 249, 254, 276, 278, 281, 282,
284–85, 287–88, 289, 301, 303, 309, 312,
318, 322, 323, 324
Tristan sketchbook 128
Die Walküre 14, 35, 38, 79, 93, 94–95, 104, 106,
109, 114, 161, 185, 252–54, 256, 261, 270,
271, 272–73, 284, 323
Wieland der Schmied 77–78
WRITINGS
Actors and Singers 191
"Annals" 7, 13, 291, 299
"Art and Climate" 182
Art and Revolution 74, 155, 180, 182–84
The Artwork of the Future (*Das Kunstwerk der
Zukunft*) 53, 74, 78, 155, 180, 183,
184–85, 190, 227
"Autobiographical Sketch" 11, 70, 292,
296, 297
Beethoven 138, 191
The Brown Book (*Das braune Buch*) 290,
291, 305
Collected Writings (*Gesammelte Schriften*) 204,
290
A Communication to My Friends 9–10, 36, 179,
180, 181, 182, 183, 188, 189, 191, 297
The Destiny of Opera 191
"An End in Paris" 183
German Art and German Politics (*Deutsche
Kunst und deutsche Politik*) 138, 139, 140,
208
"A Glance at the German Operatic Stage of
Today" 191
"Halévy's 'Reine de Chypre' " 191
"A Happy Evening" 183

"Heroism and Christianity" 210
Judaism in Music 56, 57, 58, 138, 140–41, 172,
182, 184, 191, 204–09, 211, 212, 236, 295,
314, 315, 316
"Know Thyself" 60, 210
"Ludwig Schnorr of Carolsfeld" 191
"*Music of the Future*" ("*Zukunftsmusik*") 187,
230, 303
My Life (*Mein Leben*) 3, 4–5, 7, 8, 9, 13–14, 15,
16, 19, 21, 69, 70, 237, 290, 292, 297
"Die Noth" 53, 60
On Conducting 191
"On Franz Liszt's Symphonic Poems" 191
"On German Music" 11–12
"On German Opera" 53
"On Music Criticism" 190
"On Opera Poetry and Composition in
Particular" 191
"On the Application of Music to the Drama"
128, 191, 277–78
"On the Name *Musikdrama*" 131
"On the Overture" 191
Opera and Drama 39, 43, 49, 52, 74, 75,
83, 86, 87, 98, 104, 130, 180,
183–87, 189, 191, 195, 277, 279,
300, 301, 313
"'Parsifal' at Bayreuth" 191
"A Pilgrimage to Beethoven" 183, 191
*Plan for the Organization of a German
National Theater for the Kingdom of
Saxony* 74
"Public and Popularity" 198
"The Public in Time and Space" 191
The Red Pocket-Book (*Die rote Brieftasche*)
7, 290
"Religion und Kunst" 156, 210, 211
"The Revolution" 53, 60
"Seamstress" letters 14–15, 16
"A Theater in Zürich" 182
"What Avails This Knowledge?" 210
"What Is German?" ("Was ist Deutsch?") 55,
138, 139, 209, 210, 305
Die Wibelungen 11, 12, 72, 76, 298, 299
"Wollen wir hoffen?" 306
Wagner, Rosalie (sister) 18, 21, 24, 35, 294
Wagner, Siegfried (son) 143–44, 145, 194, 238,
250–51
Wagner, Verena (granddaughter) 307
Wagner, Wieland (grandson) 81–82, 145,
149, 171, 244, 246, 249, 251, 252–56,
257–59, 263, 265, 266, 272, 273, 274,
322, 323, 324
Wagner, Winifred (daughter-in-law) 143, 235,
237, 238–39, 251, 307, 324
Wagner, Wolfgang (grandson) 171, 238
Wapnewski, Peter 174
Warner, Keith 84, 272, 324
Warnkönig, Leopold August 71

Wason, Robert W. 278
Weber, Carl Maria von 18, 23, 39, 244, 293, 322
   Euryanthe 18, 19, 25, 293
   Der Freischütz 18, 19, 54, 126
   Oberon 19, 25, 45
Weiner, Marc A. 141, 172, 211, 242, 286, 315, 316
Weinland, Helmuth 294
Weinlig, Theodor 20
Werner, Zacharias 297
Wernicke, Herbert 84, 267, 324
Wesendonck, Mathilde 9, 15, 116, 119, 122, 126–27, 128, 130, 292, 299, 309, 325
Wesendonck, Otto 8, 9
Westernhagen, Curt von 298
Whittall, Arnold 327
Wieck, Friedrich 18
Wieler, Jossi 270

Wienbarg, Ludolf 293
Wilamowitz-Moellendorf, Ulrich von 196
Wilde, Oscar 229, 231
Wilder, Victor 230
Wilhelm II, Emperor of Germany 81
Wilson, Robert 272
Windt, Herbert 307
Winterhalter, Franz Xavier 231
Wintle, Christopher 282
Wolf, Hugo 223, 226, 229, 284
Wolzogen, Hans von 81, 87, 88, 97, 107, 156, 162, 169, 173, 276, 300, 316, 325
Wonder, Erich 273
Woodeforde-Finden, Amelia 229

Zelinsky, Hartmut 171–72, 211, 237, 242, 311, 314, 316
Zimmermann, J. 322
Zizek, Slavoj 217, 317

Cambridge Companions to Music

Topics

The Cambridge Companion to Blues and Gospel
Music
Edited by Allan Moore

The Cambridge Companion to the Concerto
Edited by Simon P. Keefe

The Cambridge Companion to Conducting
Edited by José Antonio Bowen

The Cambridge Companion to Electronic Music
Edited by Nick Collins and Julio d'Escriván

The Cambridge Companion to Grand Opera
Edited by David Charlton

The Cambridge Companion to Jazz
Edited by Mervyn Cooke and David Horn

The Cambridge Companion to the Lied
Edited by James Parsons

The Cambridge Companion to the Musical
Edited by William Everett and Paul Laird

The Cambridge Companion to the Orchestra
Edited by Colin Lawson

The Cambridge Companion to Pop and Rock
Edited by Simon Frith, Will Straw, and John Street

The Cambridge Companion to the String Quartet
Edited by Robin Stowell

Composers

The Cambridge Companion to Bach
Edited by John Butt

The Cambridge Companion to Bartók
Edited by Amanda Bayley

The Cambridge Companion to Beethoven
Edited by Glenn Stanley

The Cambridge Companion to Berg
Edited by Anthony Pople

The Cambridge Companion to Berlioz
Edited by Peter Bloom

The Cambridge Companion to Brahms
Edited by Michael Musgrave

The Cambridge Companion to Benjamin Britten
Edited by Mervyn Cooke

The Cambridge Companion to Bruckner
Edited by John Williamson

The Cambridge Companion to John Cage
Edited by David Nicholls

The Cambridge Companion to Chopin
Edited by Jim Samson

The Cambridge Companion to Debussy
Edited by Simon Trezise

The Cambridge Companion to Elgar
Edited by Daniel Grimley and Julian Rushton

The Cambridge Companion to Handel
Edited by Donald Burrows

The Cambridge Companion to Haydn
Edited by Caryl Clark

The Cambridge Companion to Liszt
Edited by Kenneth Hamilton

The Cambridge Companion to Mahler
Edited by Jeremy Barham

The Cambridge Companion to Mendelssohn
Edited by Peter Mercer-Taylor

The Cambridge Companion to Mozart
Edited by Simon P. Keefe

The Cambridge Companion to Ravel
Edited by Deborah Mawer

The Cambridge Companion to Rossini
Edited by Emanuele Senici

The Cambridge Companion to Schubert
Edited by Christopher Gibbs

The Cambridge Companion to Sibelius
Edited by Daniel M. Grimley

The Cambridge Companion to Verdi
Edited by Scott L. Balthazar

The Cambridge Companion to Wagner
Edited by Thomas S. Grey

Instruments

The Cambridge Companion to Brass Instruments
Edited by Trevor Herbert and John Wallace

The Cambridge Companion to the Cello
Edited by Robin Stowell

The Cambridge Companion to the Clarinet
Edited by Colin Lawson

The Cambridge Companion to the Guitar
Edited by Victor Coelho

The Cambridge Companion to the Organ
Edited by Nicholas Thistlethwaite and Geoffrey
Webber

The Cambridge Companion to the Piano
Edited by David Rowland

The Cambridge Companion to the Recorder
Edited by John Mansfield Thomson

The Cambridge Companion to the Saxophone
Edited by Richard Ingham

The Cambridge Companion to Singing
Edited by John Potter

The Cambridge Companion to the Violin
Edited by Robin Stowell